JavaServer Faces:
The Complete Reference

Chris Schalk
Ed Burns
with James Holmes

New York   Chicago   San Francisco
Lisbon   London   Madrid   Mexico City
Milan   New Delhi   San Juan
Seoul   Singapore   Sydney   Toronto

The **McGraw·Hill** Companies

McGraw-Hill books are available at special quantity discounts to use as premiums and sales promotions, or for use in corporate training programs. For more information, please write to the Director of Special Sales, Professional Publishing, McGraw-Hill, Two Penn Plaza, New York, NY 10121-2298. Or contact your local bookstore.

JavaServer Faces: The Complete Reference

234567890 DOC DOC 01987

ISBN-13: 978-0-07-226240-7
ISBN-10:   0-07-226240-0

Sponsoring Editor Wendy Rinaldi	**Proofreader** Paul Tyler
Editorial Supervisor Patty Mon	**Production Supervisor** Jim Kussow
Project Editor Claire Splan	**Composition** Apollo Publishing Services
Acquisitions Coordinator Alex McDonald	**Illustration** Sue Albert
Technical Editor Adam Winer	**Series Design** Peter F. Hancik, Lyssa Wald
Copy Editor Mike McGee	**Cover Designer** Jeff Weeks

For my dad, Frank, the coolest
engineer/rocket scientist/cold warrior
there ever was!
As you used to say,
"If you're going to do something,
do it with *Audace!*"

—Chris Schalk

To Amy, my best friend, partner, and wife.
Thank you for helping me
achieve my dreams.

—Ed Burns

About the Authors

Chris Schalk is a Principal Product Manager and Java Evangelist for Oracle's application server and development tools division. Chris' primary expertise is Web application development and he works to define the overall set of Web development features for Oracle JDeveloper including JavaServer Faces and ADF Faces. Prior to product management, Chris held positions in both software development and technical marketing at Oracle and IBM. Chris holds a Bachelor's of Science in Applied Mathematics with a Specialization in Computer Science from the University of California at Los Angeles. Chris also maintains a popular blog on J2EE Web development at **http://www.jroller.com/page/cschalk**.

Ed Burns is a senior staff engineer at Sun Microsystems. Ed has worked on a wide variety of client and server-side Web technologies since 1994, including NCSA Mosaic, Mozilla, the Sun Java Plugin, Jakarta Tomcat, and most recently, JavaServer Faces. Ed is currently the co-spec lead for JavaServer Faces. Find Ed's blog and other goodies at **http://purl.ock.org/NET/edburns/**.

James Holmes is a leading Java Web development authority. He is a committer on the Struts project and author of *Struts: The Complete Reference*. Additionally, *Oracle Magazine* named him 2002 Java Developer of the Year. He maintains the most comprehensive list of JSF resources on his website at **http://www.jamesholmes.com/JavaServerFaces**. James is an independent consultant who develops applications for complex transactional environments, including ADP, Bank of America, IBM, SunTrust and UPS. For information on retaining James for Java development projects or training, contact him via email at james@jamesholmes.com. You can also visit his Web site at **http://www.JamesHolmes.com/**.

Contents at a Glance

Part I   The JavaServer Faces Framework

1   An Introduction to JavaServer Faces 3

2   Building a Simple JavaServer Faces Application 15

3   The JavaServer Faces Request Processing Lifecycle 35

4   Managed Beans and the JSF Expression Language 53

5   The Navigation Model 79

6   The User Interface Component Model 93

7   Converting and Validating Data 111

8   The JSF Event Model 145

Part II   Extending JavaServer Faces

9   Applying JSF: Introducing the Virtual Trainer Application 169

10   Building Custom UI Components 229

11   Building AJAX JSF Components 287

12   Building Non-UI Custom Components 321

13   Alternate View Description Technology and Facelets 359

Part III   Applying JavaServer Faces

14   Localization and Accessibility with JavaServer Faces 387

15   Securing JavaServer Faces Applications 403

16   Automated Testing and Debugging of JavaServer Faces Applications 445

Part IV   JavaServer Faces Tools and Libraries

17   Developing JSF Applications with Visual Development Environments 483

18   The JavaServer Faces Configuration File 531

19   The Standard JSF Component Library 613

20   The MyFaces Implementation and Component Library 683

Part V   Appendixes

A   Faces Console Quick Reference 765

B   Third-Party JSF Component Libraries 783

C   Migrating from Struts to Faces 805

D   JSF Futures: Apache Shale 813

Index 835

Contents

Foreword xix
Acknowledgments xxi
Introduction xxiii

Part I   The JavaServer Faces Framework

1   An Introduction to JavaServer Faces 3
What Is JavaServer Faces? 3
The History of JavaServer Faces 4
    The Common Gateway Interface 4
    The Servlet API 5
    JavaServer Pages 5
    Jakarta Struts 6
    The Birth of JavaServer Faces 7
The JavaServer Faces Design Goals 7
JSF—A Framework for Both "Corporate" Developers
    and "Systems" Developers 9
JSF Application Architecture 10
    The JSF Request Processing Lifecycle 12
    The JSF Navigation Model 13

2   Building a Simple JavaServer Faces Application 15
Application Overview 15
    The JSFReg Application Files 17
    Assembling the JSFReg Application 17
    The Configuration Files 18
    The JSP Pages 20
Setting Up Your JSF Development Environment 30
    Downloading the JSF Reference Implementation
        and Required Libraries 31
    Installing Tomcat or Any J2EE-Compliant Application Server ... 32
Compiling, Packaging, and Running the Application 32
    Compiling the Application 32
    Packaging the Application 33
    Deploying and Running the Application 34
Reviewing the Key Portions of the Application 34

3   The JavaServer Faces Request Processing Lifecycle 35
A High-Level Overview of the JSF Request Processing Lifecycle 35
    What Exactly Does the Request Processing Lifecycle Do? 36
    How Does It Differ from Other Web Technologies? 36
    Automatic Server-Side View Management and Synchronization ... 37
    What Are the Request Processing Lifecycle Phases? 38
Observing the Request Processing Lifecycle in Action 45
Advanced Topics Related to the Request Processing Lifecycle 48
    Using the immediate Attribute 49
    Processing Validations and Conversions Immediately 50
    Phase Listeners 51
Lifecycle Concepts to Remember 51

4   Managed Beans and the JSF Expression Language **53**
What Are Managed Beans?   53
    A Simple Managed Bean Example   54
    Initializing Managed Bean Properties   54
    Declaring Lists and Maps Directly as Managed Beans   61
    Managed Bean Interdependence   61
    Setting Managed Properties Using EL   62
Controlling Managed Bean Life Spans   63
The JSF Expression Language   65
    Important Expression Languages Changes Between JSF 1.1
        and JSF 1.2   65
    Unified EL Concepts   67
    Value Expressions   67
    Expression Operators   70
    Method Expressions   70
Web Application Development Details on Managed Beans   72
    How to Access Managed Beans Programmatically   72
    Using Managed Beans as Backing Beans for JSF Pages   75

5   The Navigation Model **79**
Overview of the Navigation Model   80
    Recalling MVC—The Controller   80
    The NavigationHandler—Behind the Scenes   81
    A Note on Faces Action Methods   83
Building Navigation Rules   83
    A Static Navigation Example   84
    A Dynamic Navigation Example   85
More Sophisticated Navigation Examples   89
    Using Wildcards   89
    Using Redirects   90
    Placing Navigation Rules Outside of faces-config.xml   91

6   The User Interface Component Model **93**
What Are UI Components?   93
    The Rise of Component-Based Web Development   94
    The Goal of JavaServer Faces UI Components   96
Introducing the JSF UI Component Architecture   99
    The UI Component Tree (View)   101
    The UI Component and Its Associated "Moving Parts"   103
UI Components and JSP   105
    Accessing UI Components Programmatically   105
    Helpful Advice for Binding UI Components in JSP   109

7   Converting and Validating Data **111**
Some Validation and Conversion Examples   112
Conversion and Validation Under the Covers   114
The Faces Converter System   117
    DateTimeConverter   119
    NumberConverter   119
    Associating a Converter with a UIComponent Instance   120
    The Lifetime of a Converter   125
    Custom Converters   126
The Faces Validation System   130
    LongRangeValidator   131
    DoubleRangeValidator   132

LengthValidator 132
The "required" Facility 132
How to Associate a Validator with a UIComponent Instance 133
Using JSP to Associate a Validator with a UIComponent Instance 133
Using JSP and the validator Attribute to Associate a Validator
    with a UIComponent Instance 134
Programmatically Associating a Validator with a UIComponent
    Instance 134
Custom Validators 136
Tie It All Together: Messages in a View 137
FacesMessage-Related Methods on FacesContext 137
The UIViewRoot and Its Locale Property 139
When and How FacesMessage Instances are Created and Added
    to the FacesContext 139
How FacesMessages Are Rendered 140

8   The JSF Event Model **145**
A High-Level Overview of the JSF Event Model 145
How JSF Events Work 146
The Faces Event Listener Interfaces and Event Classes 147
When Are Faces Events Processed? 148
The Anatomy of an Action Event 150
Handling an Action Event Earlier in the Faces Lifecycle 151
The Anatomy of a Value Change Event 152
Writing Custom Action and Value Change Listeners 153
Two Faces Event Examples 156
Using a Value Change Event to Auto-Fill Fields 156
Extending the Value Change Example 160
Working with Phase Events and Listeners 163
Using a PhaseListener to Observe the Faces Lifecycle in Action 163
Creating Custom Events and Listeners 166

Part II   Extending JavaServer Faces
9   Applying JSF: Introducing the Virtual Trainer Application **169**
A Quick Tour of the Virtual Trainer Application 169
Registering and Logging In to the Virtual Trainer Application 170
Creating a New Training Event Workout Plan 172
Selecting and Updating Training Events 172
Logging In as an Online Trainer and Updating Event
    Workout Comments 174
The Virtual Trainer Application Requirements 175
The Virtual Trainer Application Architecture 175
JSP Pages and Backing Beans 176
Building the Virtual Trainer Application 179
Basic Page Layout and Formatting 179
Creating a Simple Authentication System 181
Logging Out of the Virtual Trainer Application 185
Revisiting JSFReg—Building the Registration System 186
Building the Browse and Edit Pages of the Virtual Trainer
    Application 190
Using a Custom Scroller Component with a dataTable 195
Selecting and Editing a Single Row from a dataTable 197
Drilling Down to an Edit Form 198

        Deleting a Training Event 203
        Creating New Training Events 204
    Implementing Sortable Columns 209
        Implementing Data-Tier Sorting in Faces 210
        Implementing Web-Tier Sorting in Faces 212
    Taking the Next Step—Persisting Virtual Trainer Data 216
        How to Build a Persistence Layer 217
    Internationalizing the Virtual Trainer Application 225
        Final Comments on Virtual Trainer 227

10   Building Custom UI Components **229**
    Deciding When to Build a Custom UI Component 230
    What Are UI Components? 230
    The Moving Parts of a UI Component 230
    A Simple Hello World Example 232
        Building the HtmlHelloWorld Example 232
        A HelloWorld UI Component That Accepts Form Input 239
    A JSF Stock Quote Component 242
    An InputDate Component with Multiple Renderers 244
        Using the InputDate Component 245
        The Code Behind the InputDate Component 245
        The HtmlInputDateRenderer 246
        A WML InputDate Variation 253
    Dynamically Changing the Renderer at Runtime 256
    A Custom Chart Component 258
        Preparing the Chart Data Object 259
        Using the Chart Data Object 259
        Rendering an SVG Bar Chart 260
    Using JavaScript in a Custom JSF Component—A Slider Example 264
        The Challenge of Using Advanced JavaScript 265
        Using the JSF Slider Component 269
        Adding the Required JavaScript Library 270
    Advanced Custom JSF Component Development 270
        Updating the HtmlHelloInput UI Component
            to Use Method Binding 270
        Updating the HtmlHelloWorld and HtmlHelloInputMB
            Components for JSF 1.2 274
        Modifying the JSF 1.2 HtmlHelloWorldMB Component
            to Use Method Expressions 276
    Packaging JSF Components into a Self-Contained JAR 278
        Configuration Files 278
        Component Classes 280
        Associated Resources 280
    A JSF Components Package Example: components.jar 280
        Configuration Files 280
        Component Classes 284
        Associated Resources 285
    The Future of JSF Component Metadata 285

11   Building AJAX JSF Components **287**
    Introduction to AJAX 287
        Why All the Interest in AJAX? 288
        Why JSF and AJAX Are a Perfect Match 288
    AJAX Under the Hood 288
        How to Issue an XML HTTP Request 290
        Using XMLHttpRequest with HTML 291

DirectorySearch—A First AJAX Example Without JSF 292
  The Architecture of the AJAX(-Only) DirectorySearch 292
  What's Wrong with the AJAX-Only Version of DirectorySearch? 297
Building AJAX-Enabled JSF Components 297
  The High-Level Elements of an AJAX System in JSF 297
  An AJAX DirectorySearch JSF Component 299
  An AJAX SpellCheck JSF Component 303
AJAX Tips and Tricks 318
AJAX XMLHttpRequest Reference 319

12   Building Non-UI Custom Components **321**
Non-UI Custom Components and Decoration in JSF 321
Non-View Custom Components Explained 324
  PhaseListener 324
  Converter and Validator 326
  ViewHandler 326
  VariableResolver and PropertyResolver 327
  ELResolver (JSF 1.2) 330
  NavigationHandler 339
  ActionListener 340
  StateManager 341
  RenderKit 343
  Factories in JSF 351

13   Alternate View Description Technology and Facelets **359**
Motivation for Alternate View Description Technology 359
The Relationship of the ViewHandler to the Rest of the JSF System 360
  The Relationship Between ViewHandler, RenderKit, and
    the Act of View Construction 360
  The Relationship Between ViewHandler and
    the State Management System 362
How to Build and Install a Custom ViewHandler 362
  Using Decoration for the Custom ViewHandler 364
  General Considerations When Writing a Custom ViewHandler 367
The Facelets View Description Technology 368
  The Power of Templating in Faces 368
  Similarities and Differences Between JSP and Facelets 369
  Taglibs in Facelets 370
  Implementing a Facelets Taglib 370
  Using a Facelets Taglib 373
  Templating with Facelets 374
  Guide to Facelets Templating Tags 377
  Guide to Non-Templating Facelets Tags 380
The Design, Architecture, and Implementation of Facelets 380
  ViewHandler Methods Explained 383

Part III   **Applying JavaServer Faces**
14   Localization and Accessibility with JavaServer Faces **387**
Localization 387
  Some Benefits of the Localization Facilities Provided
    by JavaServer Faces 387
  A JSF Localization Example 389
  The Details Behind Faces Localization and Internationalization 393
  Internationalization Issues for Custom Components 398

Accessibility 399
    Why Accessibility Is Important 399
    Guidelines for Providing Accessibility in JSF Applications 399
    Give a Text Equivalent to Nontextual Content 400
    Use Markup and Stylesheets Properly 400
    Clarify Natural Language Usage 401
    Ensure That Pages Featuring New Technologies Transform
        Gracefully 401
    Ensure User Control of Time-Sensitive Content Changes 401
    Design for Device Independence 401
    Use the Label Element 402
    Context and Orientation Information 402

15   Securing JavaServer Faces Applications **403**
Aspects and Implementation of Web Application Security 403
Container-Managed Security 404
    Container-Managed Authentication 404
    Basic Authentication and the Concept of a "Realm" 405
    Form-Based Authentication 406
    Certificate Authentication 410
    Container-Managed Authorization and the Concept of Roles ... 412
    Container-Managed Data Security 412
    A Small Security Improvement in the Virtual Trainer 414
Application-Managed Security with JavaServer Faces 415
    Reviewing the Virtual Trainer 415
    Servlet Filters and Authorization 416
    PhaseListeners and Authorization 421
Implementing a "Remember Me" Feature 422
    RememberMeLoginComponent: Lifecycle and State Management ... 423
    RememberMeLoginComponent: Rendering Behavior 427
    RememberMeLoginComponent: Properties 431
    RememberMeLoginTag 432
    RememberMePhaseListener 434
Leveraging JAAS from a JSF Application 436
    Using JAAS Authentication in the Virtual Trainer 436
To Learn More about Security 444

16   Automated Testing and Debugging of JavaServer Faces Applications **445**
A Review of Software Testing Terminology 446
    Unit Testing 447
    Integration Testing 448
    System Testing 448
    Stress Testing 448
    Test Driven Development 448
Tools for the Automated Testing of Web Applications 449
    JUnit, the Most Popular Automated Testing Technology
        for the Java Platform 449
    Cactus, Server-Side Automated Unit Testing 453
    HTMLUnit: Testing the Virtual Trainer Application Flow 456
    Load Testing and Profiling a JSF Application 458
Debugging JSF Applications 467
    Debugging JSF Applications Without a Source-Level Debugger ... 467
    Logging Using the java.util.logging Facility 467
    Logging Using the Jakarta Commons Logging Facility 469
    Additional Non-Debugger Debugging Techniques
        for JSF Applications 472

Source-Level Debugging with Eclipse 473
Source-Level Debugging with NetBeans 475
JSF JSP Debugging with Oracle JDeveloper 478

Part IV   JavaServer Faces Tools and Libraries

17   Developing JSF Applications with Visual Development Environments **483**
The Application 484
Sun Java Studio Creator 485
   Getting Familiar with Java Studio Creator 485
   Building the Simple Virtual Trainer Application in Studio Creator 487
BEA Workshop Studio 492
   Getting Familiar with BEA Workshop Studio 492
   Building the Simple JSF Trainer Application 493
Oracle JDeveloper 10*g* 497
   Getting Familiar with JDeveloper 497
   Using Oracle's ADF Framework 508
IBM Rational Web Developer 513
   Getting Familiar with IBM Rational Web Developer 513
   Building the Simple JSF Trainer Application 514
Exadel Studio Pro 521
   Getting Familiar with Exadel Studio Pro 522
   Building the Simple JSF Trainer Application 522

18   The JavaServer Faces Configuration File **531**
Understanding XML DTDs 532
Understanding XML Schemas 533
Understanding How Configuration Files Are Processed 533
The Faces Configuration Elements 534
   The action-listener Element 541
   The application Element 542
   The application-factory Element 543
   The attribute Element 543
   The attribute-class Element 546
   The attribute-name Element 547
   The base-name Element 547
   The component Element 548
   The component-class Element 549
   The component-family Element 550
   The component-type Element 551
   The converter Element 551
   The converter-class Element 552
   The converter-for-class Element 553
   The converter-id Element 554
   The default-locale Element 554
   The default-render-kit-id Element 555
   The default-value Element 556
   The el-resolver Element 557
   The faces-config Element 558
   The faces-context-factory Element 559
   The facet Element 560
   The facet-name Element 561
   The factory Element 562
   The from-action Element 563
   The from-outcome Element 563

The from-view-id Element 564
The key Element 564
The key-class Element 565
The lifecycle Element 566
The lifecycle-factory Element 567
The list-entries Element 568
The locale-config Element 569
The managed-bean Element 570
The managed-bean-class Element 571
The managed-bean-name Element 572
The managed-bean-scope Element 572
The managed-property Element 573
The map-entries Element 574
The map-entry Element 576
The message-bundle Element 577
The navigation-case Element 578
The navigation-handler Element 578
The navigation-rule Element 579
The null-value Element 580
The phase-listener Element 582
The property Element 583
The property-class Element 584
The property-name Element 585
The property-resolver Element 586
The redirect Element 587
The referenced-bean Element 587
The referenced-bean-class Element 588
The referenced-bean-name Element 589
The render-kit Element 589
The render-kit-class Element 590
The render-kit-factory Element 591
The render-kit-id Element 592
The renderer Element 593
The renderer-class Element 594
The renderer-type Element 595
The resource-bundle Element 595
The state-manager Element 596
The suggested-value Element 597
The supported-locale Element 598
The to-view-id Element 599
The validator Element 600
The validator-class Element 601
The validator-id Element 601
The value Element 602
The value-class Element 604
The var Element 606
The variable-resolver Element 606
The view-handler Element 607
Extension Elements 608
Metadata Elements 609
Editing Configuration Files with Faces Console 611

19   The Standard JSF Component Library 613
A Brief Review of JSF and JSP Tag Nomenclature 613
Acquiring and Installing the Standard Libraries 614

What You Get (Binary) 614

What You Get (Source) 614

The Core and HTML Component Library Reference 614

The Standard Core Library 614

The actionListener Tag 616

The attribute Tag 617

The convertDateTime Tag 617

The convertNumber Tag 619

The converter Tag 620

The facet Tag 621

The loadBundle Tag 622

The param Component 622

The phaseListener Tag (1.2 Only) 623

The selectItem Component 624

The selectItems Component 624

The setPropertyActionListener Tag (1.2 Only) 625

The subview Component 626

The validateDoubleRange Tag 627

The validateLength Tag 628

The validateLongRange Tag 629

The validator Tag 630

The valueChangeListener Tag 630

The verbatim Component 631

The view Component 632

The Standard HTML Library 633

The column Component 635

The commandButton Component 636

The commandLink Component 638

The dataTable Component 640

The form Component 643

The graphicImage Component 645

The inputHidden Component 647

The inputSecret Component 648

The inputText Component 650

The inputTextarea Component 652

The message Component 654

The messages Component 656

The outputFormat Component 657

The outputLabel Component 658

The outputLink Component 660

The outputText Component 662

The panelGrid Component 663

The panelGroup Component 665

The selectBooleanCheckbox Component 666

The selectManyCheckbox Component 668

The selectManyListbox Component 671

The selectManyMenu Component 673

The selectOneListbox Component 675

The selectOneMenu Component 678

The selectOneRadio Component 680

20   The MyFaces Implementation and Component Library **683**

Acquiring MyFaces 684

What You Get (Binary) 684

What You Get (Source) 684

Using MyFaces 685
    Using the MyFaces JSF Implementation 685
    Using the MyFaces Tomahawk Library 685
The MyFaces Extended Components 687
    Common Extended Attributes 688
    The commandButton Component 688
    The commandLink Component 688
    The dataTable Component 690
    The graphicImage Component 692
    The inputHidden Component 692
    The inputSecret Component 692
    The inputText Component 693
    The inputTextarea Component 693
    The message Component 694
    The messages Component 695
    The outputLabel Component 696
    The outputText Component 697
    The panelGrid Component 697
    The panelGroup Component 698
    The selectBooleanCheckbox Component 698
    The selectManyCheckbox Component 699
    The selectManyListbox Component 699
    The selectManyMenu Component 700
    The selectOneListbox Component 700
    The selectOneMenu Component 701
    The selectOneRadio Component 701
The MyFaces Custom Components 702
    Common Attributes 704
    The aliasBean Component 706
    The aliasBeansScope Component 706
    The buffer Component 707
    The checkbox Component 707
    The collapsiblePanel Component 708
    The commandNavigation Component 709
    The commandNavigation2 Component 710
    The commandSortHeader Component 712
    The dataList Component 713
    The dataScroller Component 714
    The div Component 717
    The htmlTag Component 718
    The inputCalendar Component 718
    The inputDate Component 721
    The inputFileUpload Component 723
    The inputHTML Component 724
    The inputTextHelp Component 727
    The jscookMenu Component 728
    The jsValueChangeListener Component 730
    The jsValueSet Component 731
    The newspaperTable Component 731
    The panelNavigation Component 732
    The panelNavigation2 Component 734
    The panelStack Component 735
    The panelTab Component 736
    The panelTabbedPane Component 737
    The popup Component 738

The radio Component 740
The saveState Component 740
The selectOneCountry Component 741
The selectOneLanguage Component 742
The stylesheet Component 743
The tree Component 744
The tree2 Component 746
The treeColumn Component 748
The updateActionListener Tag 748
The MyFaces Custom Validators 749
The validateCreditCard Validator 750
The validateEmail Validator 752
The validateEqual Validator 752
The validateRegExpr Validator 753
The MyFaces Support for the Tiles Framework 754
Tiles Overview 755
Using the MyFaces Support for Tiles 756

Part V   Appendixes

A   Faces Console Quick Reference **765**
Supported Configuration Files 766
Acquiring and Installing Faces Console 767
Using Faces Console as a Stand-Alone Application 767
Using Faces Console Inside Borland JBuilder 768
Using Faces Console Inside Eclipse 770
Using Faces Console Inside IBM Rational Application Developer
    for WebSphere 773
Using Faces Console Inside IntelliJ IDEA 775
Using Faces Console Inside NetBeans and Sun ONE Studio (Forte) 777
Using Faces Console Inside Oracle JDeveloper 779
Configuring the Faces Console Output Options 781

B   Third-Party JSF Component Libraries **783**
Sun's Extended UI Component Library 783
JScape's WebGalileo Faces 784
Oracle's ADF Faces 784
Acquiring ADF Faces 784
ADF Faces Component Reference 784
ADF Faces Key Technologies 790
ADF Faces Partial Page Rendering Feature 790
The ADF Faces processScope 794
Using the ADF Faces Dialog Framework 796
ADF Faces Skinning Technology 800
Oracle JDeveloper's Visual Design Time Experience
    for ADF Faces 804
JSFCentral—A Reference for Third-Party Components 804

C   Migrating from Struts to Faces **805**
Similarities and Differences 805
Development Style 807
Migration Strategy: The Struts-Faces Integration Library 808
Satisfying Compile-Time and Runtime Dependencies 808
Declaring the FacesServlet 809
Mapping the FacesServlet 809

Replacing the Standard Struts Request Processor 809
Migrating the JSP Pages 810
Modifying the Action Forwards 811

D   JSF Futures: Apache Shale **813**
Shale, the Java Community Process, and Innovation 813
Migration Concerns: Should I Depend on Shale? 815
Getting and Running Shale 815
The Dialog Manager 816
The Application Manager 818
A Guide to Shale Features 818
ViewController (shale-core.jar) 818
Dialog Manager (shale-core.jar) 822
Application Manager (shale-core.jar) 825
Validation (shale-core.jar) 827
Remoting(shale-remoting.jar) 829
Accessing Static Resources 830
Invoking a MethodExpression 832
Conclusion and Resources 834

Index **835**

Foreword

What a difference a couple of years makes.

In March 2004, the Expert Group for the JavaServer Faces 1.0 specification (JSR-127) completed its work, and the Final Release was published. But it is interesting to go back a couple of years before that, to when the development process for JavaServer Faces was started.

At that time, there was a wide variety of framework choices for web application architects to choose from. The most popular framework (Apache Struts), as did most of the other frameworks available at the time, provided excellent support for the "Model 2" design pattern (encouraging a separation of presentation logic and business logic). However, Struts focused on the server-side logic, and provided only minimal assistance in creating sophisticated user interfaces. There was widespread tools support for Struts, but even here the primary focus was to assist the developer in managing Struts configuration artifacts, and defining page navigation flows. When it came down to designing the individual pages, the user was typically left staring at a blank page, and faced with the task of hand-entering all of the HTML and Struts custom tags necessary to develop a user interface.

In addition, the Java platform was seeing significant competition from other technologies—often supported by tools such as Microsoft Visual Studio—that supported a different style of development. A tool that could actually draw user interface components on the screen, rather than just showing the developer source code, could tremendously accelerate the development process. Coupled with a focus on simplified platform APIs, this sort of tool could dramatically broaden the population of developers who could leverage these capabilities to produce web applications with high-quality user interfaces.

For the Java platform to respond to this challenge, we needed to produce an API that filled the most obvious gap—a model for user interface components. Components allow complex behavior to be abstracted away from the concern of an application developer, allowing him or her to focus on the requirements of the application being developed. In addition, a component model would enable sophisticated pages to be composed dynamically. Components can be self-describing, enabling the development of tools that provide a visual development paradigm. Finally, the definition of this API as a standard, developed under the Java Community Process, would encourage the creation of a marketplace of third-party component libraries, all developed against this common API, that could be combined into a single application easily.

JavaServer Faces 1.0 was the initial answer to meeting these requirements. Immediately upon the final release, we saw the marketplace understand the reasoning, begin investigating the new technology, and start utilizing it to create applications. We observed a variety of component libraries begin to be developed (some open source, some commercial) that leveraged the new common standards. Even more exciting, the promise of an API that provided information to tools, as well as to application developers, led to the introduction of robust visual development tools based on JavaServer Faces, such as Sun Java Studio Creator and Oracle JDeveloper.

Of course, time does not suddenly stand still when you release a 1.0 version of a technology. Subsequent versions of JavaServer Faces have focused on improving the usability and functionality of the APIs. In particular, the most recent version (JavaServer Faces 1.2), the one discussed in this book, dramatically improves them—without requiring applications written to previous versions of the specification to be rewritten.

Today, we can still see a landscape of substantial choice in underlying frameworks for building web applications with Java. But we also see a community of vendors, framework developers, and users coalesce around this new standard. We see a wide variety of components become available, supporting everything from simple input fields to sophisticated AJAX-based behaviors. And we see a future that is bright.

But a technology by itself, no matter how powerful, cannot be fully utilized without examples and explanation. The book you hold in your hands is a comprehensive guide, providing everything you need to know in order to begin taking advantage of JavaServer Faces yourself. It is written by experts who have been directly involved in developing this technology and the tools around it. And it covers the latest available version, with all the most recent innovations. I commend it to you.

Finally, I want to personally thank Ed Burns, who shared Specification Lead responsibilities with me on JavaServer Faces 1.0, for his passion and dedication to excellence. His leadership, then and now, means that the continued development of JavaServer Faces is in good hands. Likewise, my thanks go out to the members of the Expert Group working on this standard, to the individuals and companies who have invested in supporting the technology, to Chris Schalk for co-authoring and helping to drive the production of this book, and to you, the developers who can leverage the fruits of all of our labors.

Enjoy your learning and use of JavaServer Faces!

Craig McClanahan
Portland, Oregon

Acknowledgments

Writing a book has always been one of those life-long goals; I had hoped that someday the stars would align and I would be in a position to have a go at it. Fortunately, the stars did align for me when I found that writing a book would actually be beneficial to both me and the company I work for. An initial thanks obviously goes to my Oracle co-workers Brian Fry, Rob Clevenger, Raghu Kodali, Lynn Munsinger, Blaise Ribet, and Roel Stalman for their initial encouragement and support. The subject matter for the book was a no-brainer for me as I was an early fan of the initial JSR that started JavaServer Faces. I just needed to find the time and hopefully some helpful allies to make it happen. Again, fortunately, this all fell into place as well.

I'm proud to now look back on the overall experience of writing my first book and have an overwhelming sense of pride and, of course, tons of appreciation to all who contributed to this effort. With these next few paragraphs I'll try to thank all of those who worked very hard on this project to bring it to completion.

First off I'd like to thank my co-author, Ed Burns, who joined our effort early on and contributed immensely to the project. It actually turns out that we have a lot in common outside of our professional lives in that we both have a passion for music and love to play the piano and trumpet. Having hit it off discussing music and taking turns jamming on the hotel piano at the ServerSide Symposium in Las Vegas last year, we found that co-authoring a book would serve as a great counterpart harmony! Speaking of music, our primary editor, Herb Schildt, is a music god in his own right. In fact, he was the keyboardist in the progressive rock band Starcastle long before he became a best-selling technical author and our primary editor. For this I would like to offer tremendous thanks to Herb. His extensive book writing experience and top notch prose expertise no doubt helped bump up the quality and establish credibility in the book authoring world.

I'd also like to especially thank Adam Winer for serving as our primary technical editor. Providing technical edits to over 20 chapters is no trivial task for a busy person as Adam, so I definitely thank him for his extremely helpful technical guidance on the project. His experience and association with the book also provides us with top-notch credibility in the enterprise Java world.

In addition to our primary authors and editors, I would like to thank our partners at McGraw-Hill/Osborne for believing in us and giving us the go ahead for this project. This includes our editorial director Wendy Rinaldi; Alex McDonald, who managed all of our content; and our project editor, Claire Splan. They really kept us on track and ensured that the book was another quality product from McGraw-Hill/Osborne.

There are also some special people who contributed in various ways to the project that I also have to thank. First off, I would like to thank Claire Dessaux for encouraging me early on and even helping me brainstorm some of the initial content for the book. With her help, we brainstormed the Virtual Trainer demo application featured in Chapter 9.

A big thank you definitely goes out to Matthias Wessendorf who served as a secondary technical reviewer for the MyFaces reference content in the book. Matthias is truly an asset to the MyFaces team and now Oracle as well. Thanks again.

I'd also like to thank Gavin King of JBoss and especially Steve Ebersole for helping out with some of the Hibernate content in Chapter 9. For handling persistence with Oracle TopLink, I'd also like to thank Doug Clarke and especially John Bracken of Oracle.

And finally I'd like to thank my extended family in the San Francisco bay area and Corvallis, Oregon, for their unwavering encouragement and support; this includes Mom, Frankie, Rudy, Vidya, Adrian, and Julian .A very special thank you also goes out to Claire again for allowing me to sit in front of the computer on many weekends instead of living it up in the bay area. We're way behind on our tennis, kayaking, and hiking schedule; hopefully, we can catch up this summer!

Chris Schalk
San Jose, CA

JavaServer Faces is a foundation technology that builds on top of many other layers of software technology. Like any foundation software product, it is the result of the hard work and dedication of many individuals and organizations. It's the same way with books that document such technologies, and I'd like to take the opportunity to thank some of the people who helped make this book, and JavaServer Faces itself, possible.

In a world where more and more information is available only online, and much of that information is coming from self-published individuals, I want to say that the publishing system is still the best way to deliver high-quality useful information in a portable and easily digestible way. A web reference is no substitute for a dog-eared, marked up, and well-worn book. After working with the publishing team at McGraw-Hill, Osborne, I know why this is so. Our editor, Herb Schildt, has been my mentor as well as providing sure guidance as I made my way through this large book. Thanks, Herb, for your veteran insights. Acquisitions coordinator Alexander McDonald did a great job keeping together all the disparate parts of the book, and the accompanying chapter re-numberings and edits. McGraw-Hill editorial director Wendy Rinaldi went through plenty of ups and downs on this project, but never lost confidence; I'm proud to deliver this book for her. Thanks to project editor Claire Splan. Rounding out the production team is our technical editor, Adam Winer, I can't think of a better person to technical edit a book on JSF. Your commitment to accuracy is legendary.

To my wonderful wife Amy. Thank you for your understanding and patience as I spent all this time on this book; you picked up the slack in our family big-time. I couldn't have done it without your help and commitment. Thanks also to my sons, Owen and Logan, for understanding why Daddy was away all that time.

I need to thank those that brought me to, worked on, and helped complete JSF. George Drapeau recommended I interview for the job of leading the implementation team back in 2001. Thanks, George! Amy Fowler, the original spec lead, profoundly influenced the success of JSF and was a joy to work with. Jim Driscoll, Mimi Hills and Tony Ng have been supportive managers throughout the development of JSF. To my original core JSF team of Jayashri Visvanathan and Roger Kitain, I give deepest thanks. You are the soul of this project and I've never worked with a better team. Ryan Lubke, Justyna Horwat, Jennifer Ball, Jennifer Douglas, Raj Premkumar, and Dennis MacNeil deserve thanks as the extended JSF implementation, quality, documentation, program management, and marketing team. Ryan, you also deserve special thanks for your unswerving commitment to quality and innovation in continuing to lead Sun's JSF implementation. I want to thank Jacob Hookom for his contribution to the JSF ecosystem in the form of Facelets, and his continuing creativity in establishing JSF as the best way to do AJAX. Thanks are also due to Bernhard Slominski, who came to the JCP as an individual contributor and introduced me to the W-JAX conference in Munich, Germany.

Special thanks goes out to Craig R. McClanahan. His contribution to the web and to JSF is tremendous. I learned a lot in working with him as co-spec lead for JSF 1.0.

I must give a special mention to Aaron L. Bartell <aaronbartell@gmail.com> (forced login PhaseListener) and Jürgen Höller (Spring DelegatingVariableResolver) for letting me use their code in this book. Thanks to Joe Ottinger and Hale Pringle for pedagogical advice (solicited and unsolicited ☺).

Of course, I have to thank Chris Schalk for bringing me in to this project and for being a great collaborator. I know I'm not the easiest person to work with at such close proximity, and I thank you for your patience and continued advocacy of the novice user and reader. Without you, there would be no book.

Finally, I want to thank the unswerving support team of Mom, Dad, Brendan Burns, Lisa Lane, Diana Dean, Jeff Beckberger, Joe McCabe, Vern Singleton, Papick Taboada, Mark Roth, and Pierre Delisle.

Ed Burns
Altamonte Springs, FL

Introduction

This book provides the reader with a comprehensive review of the entire set of technologies and programming methodologies associated with JavaServer Faces. It is intended for a wide audience with varied experience levels ranging from moderate levels of Web development experience to those who are advanced enterprise Java architects.

Each chapter is presented in a similar fashion where the concepts and simple examples are first explained with the latter part reserved for more advanced content. Also, as the book progresses through the chapters, progressively more advanced material is presented.

What Is in This Book?

This book provides in-depth content on the following topics:

- Tutorial content for using every aspect of JavaServer Faces technology.

- JSF 1.2 tips outlining the differences in the latest version of JSF and how best to use them.

- Expert Group Insights that offer the rationale behind the design of the technology, giving readers a better understanding of how to use JSF in their own work.

- Detailed coverage on custom UI component development with numerous examples.

- A comprehensive introduction to AJAX followed by instructions on how to build AJAX-enabled custom UI components.

- A complete guide to extending the entire JSF framework in areas such as security, non-JSP rendering, localization and accessibility, and Expression Language enhancements.

- Step-by-step coverage of how to use, debug, and test JSF inside of popular IDEs such as Sun Java Studio Creator, NetBeans, Oracle JDeveloper, and BEA Workshop Studio.

- Detailed coverage of the Jakarta Shale project, Craig McClanahan's vision for the future of JSF.

- A complete guide to the JSF config file by James Holmes, author of several popular books including Struts: The Complete Reference.

- Complete reference and tutorial information for the specification's Standard components, Apache MyFaces and Oracle ADF Faces component libraries.

Your Development Environment

While offering substantial coverage on a variety of Java- and JSF-enabled IDEs, this book does not require the reader to use any IDE at all. A simple base environment consisting of

- JDK 1.4 or 1.5,

- A JSP container such as Apache Tomcat 5.x, and

- The Apache Ant 1.5/1.6.x build tool

is all that a reader will need to try out the code samples from the book. For JSF 1.2 code, you will need a JSF 1.2–compliant environment such as provided by the Java EE 5 SDK.

Online Example Code Resources

Throughout the book there are references to online code, sometimes with a URL or simply referred to as the "online extension." All of the code examples in the book are available for download at McGraw-Hill/Osborne's Web site: **http://www.osborne.com**. In addition, the book's own Web site, **http://www.jsfcompref.com**, offers downloadable source code as well as live runnable demonstrations of the examples in the book.

Additional Online Resources

Both Chris and Ed maintain popular blogs on Java EE and Web development. Chris' blog is available at **www.jroller.com/page/cschalk**. Ed's blog can be reached at **purl.oclc.org/NET/edburns/**.

The JavaServer Faces Framework

CHAPTER 1
An Introduction to
JavaServer Faces

CHAPTER 2
Building a Simple JavaServer
Faces Application

CHAPTER 3
The JavaServer Faces Request
Processing Lifecycle

CHAPTER 4
Managed Beans and the JSF
Expression Language

CHAPTER 5
The Navigation Model

CHAPTER 6
The User Interface
Component Model

CHAPTER 7
Converting and
Validating Data

CHAPTER 8
The JSF Event Model

An Introduction
to JavaServer Faces

JavaServer Faces (JSF) is changing the way that Java-based Web applications are written. Designed to streamline the creation of user interfaces (UI) for high-performance Java Web applications, JSF also simplifies the development process. In short, JavaServer Faces offers an elegant solution to the key problems often associated with commercial-quality Web application development.

Before beginning an in-depth examination of JSF, it is important to understand in a general way what JavaServer Faces is and why it is important. Therefore, this chapter begins our discussion of JSF by describing its history, design goals, and lifecycle. It also explains how JavaServer Faces fits into the overall Web application development process.

What Is JavaServer Faces?

At its core, JavaServer Faces is a standard Java framework for building user interfaces for Web applications. Its key advantage is that it simplifies the development of the user interface, which is often one of the more difficult and tedious parts of Web application development. Although it is possible to build user interfaces by using foundational Java Web technologies (such as Java servlets and JavaServer Pages) without a comprehensive framework designed for enterprise Web application development, these core technologies can often lead to a variety of development and maintenance problems. JavaServer Faces avoids these problems by offering a robust, "best of breed" framework with well-established development patterns, built upon the experience of many pre-existing Java Web development frameworks.

JavaServer Faces was created through the Java Community Process (JCP) by a group of technology leaders including Sun Microsystems, Oracle, Borland, BEA, and IBM along with a collection of industry-known Java and Web experts. The original Java specification request (JSR 127) for JavaServer Faces was initiated in mid-2001 with Amy Fowler as the initial specification lead. In 2002, the role of specification lead was transferred to Ed Burns and Craig McClanahan, who became "co-spec leads." You may recognize Craig McClanahan as the originator of the popular Open Source Web application framework, Struts. After following the JCP's detailed review and balloting process, the JavaServer Faces Specification and Reference Implementation were formally released to the public in March of 2004.

JavaServer Faces is designed to simplify the development of user interfaces for Java Web applications in the following ways:

- Provides a component-centric, client-independent development approach to building Web user interfaces, thus improving developer productivity and ease of use.

- Simplifies the access and management of application data from the Web user interface.

- Automatically manages the user interface state between multiple requests and multiple clients in a simple and unobtrusive manner.

- Supplies a development framework that is friendly to a diverse developer audience with different skill sets.

Beyond these specifics, JSF offers another important benefit. It takes the best elements found through years of experience in Web application development and combines them into a single, comprehensive, and standard API for building Java Web application user interfaces. Furthermore, it brings unprecedented ease and productivity without sacrificing power and flexibility to J2EE Web application development.

The History of JavaServer Faces

Like most other important programming technologies, the creation of JSF was the result of an evolutionary process of refinement and adaptation in which new and better techniques replaced older ones. In the case of JavaServer Faces, the force that drove this evolution was the need for a simpler, more effective and efficient way to build dynamic Web user interfaces that are based on a well-designed and maintainable architecture. The story begins with CGI.

The Common Gateway Interface

In the mid-1990s, Web application development was still relatively new and the predominant technology for assembling Web applications used a simple method known as the Common Gateway Interface (CGI) for producing dynamic content. CGI was introduced by Rob and Mike McCool, who were originally from the HTTP server development team at the National Center for Supercomputering Applications (NCSA). Incidentally, NCSA was also responsible for the world's first graphical Web browser, Mosaic.

CGI is a technique that allows a Web page to invoke a server-side process to generate output dynamically, such as for a stock quote or reporting the number of Web site hits. The program that produced the dynamic output was usually an operating system (OS) shell script, a natively compiled program, or an interpreted language such as Perl. A CGI-enabled Web server allowed the CGI process to be invoked from an HTML page.

One of the major drawbacks to CGI is its inherent inefficiency. CGI is extremely resource-intensive for the Web server's host because each request to view a Web page with dynamic content results in a separate, new OS process, which is costly. Because of this, CGI does not offer an efficient scalable solution.

One early remedy to this problem was to create APIs that allowed developers to write dynamic modules that operated within the same memory space as the Web server. Each request would simply invoke a new thread as opposed to a new independent process, which was a lot less taxing on the server. The only downside to this approach was that it then required the developer to code Web applications to a specific Web server's API, such as Microsoft's ISAP or Netscape's NSAPI. Web developers basically had to choose between a proprietary API development approach or use the system-taxing CGI approach, with neither approach being entirely satisfactory.

The Servlet API

The next step forward in the evolution of Web application development was the introduction of the Java Servlet API in March of 1998. Prior to servlets, Java was not widely utilized as a server-side technology for Web applications. Instead Java was mainly used in Web pages in the form of Java Applets that would run on browser clients. Although Java Applets were relatively good at providing dynamic or animated content on Web pages, they were never really suited for broad Web application development. It wasn't until the Servlet API was created that Java became a valid server-side technology for Web development.

The Java Servlet API enabled Java developers to write server-side code for delivering dynamic Web content. Like other proprietary Web server APIs, the Java Servlet API offered improved performance over CGI; however, it had some key additional advantages. Because servlets were coded in Java, they provided an object-oriented (OO) design approach and more importantly were able to run on any platform. Thus, the same code was portable to any host that supported Java. Servlets greatly contributed to the popularity of Java, as it became a widely used technology for server-side Web application development.

Although an improvement, the Java Servlet API still had a problem: it only provided a low-level way to generate HTML, and was an often tedious and error-prone experience. Consider the awkward syntax of a servlet statement to print out an HTML table tag below:

```
out.println("<table width=\"75%\" border=\"0\" align=\"center\">");
```

Notice how the quote symbols (") have to be individually escaped using the backslash. Obviously, a better alternative for generating dynamic markup was needed.

JavaServer Pages

The next evolution in Java Web development came with the introduction of JavaServer Pages (JSP), as it provided a simpler page-based solution to generating large amounts of dynamic HTML-content for Web user interfaces. JavaServer Pages enabled Web developers and designers to simply edit HTML pages with special tags for the dynamic, Java portions. JavaServer Pages works by having a special servlet known as a *JSP container*, which is installed on a Web server and handles all JSP page view requests. The JSP container translates a requested JSP into servlet code that is then compiled and immediately executed. Subsequent requests to the same page simply invoke the runtime servlet for the page. If a change is made to the JSP on the server, a request to view it triggers another translation, compilation, and restart of the runtime servlet.

JSP provided an improvement, but was not a complete solution. As Web applications became more complex, JSP pages often tended to get cluttered with Java code, making them harder to manage and more error prone. What was needed was a better separation of Java application code from the presentation markup.

The first revision of JSP, version 1.1, provided a partial solution to this by offering an API for developers to build their own custom tag libraries where they could put their own code into custom tags, thus keeping it from cluttering a JSP page. Still, this was optional and inexperienced JSP developers would still tend to mix their presentation markup with their application code.

As the popularity of JSP grew, so did the development of custom tag libraries. Both vendors and open source developers began developing many different tag libraries, often to solve similar problems. In an effort to begin standardizing and consolidating these various tag libraries, the open source community developed the JSP Standard Tag Library (JSTL) through the auspices of the Jakarta Apache project. The JSTL tag library provided solutions to common Web development tasks, such as rendering data or iterating through collections of data. One of JSTL's key contributions to Java Web development was its introduction of a simple-to-use *Expression Language*, which greatly simplified how to interact with application data. As you'll see in later chapters, JavaServer Faces also uses an expression language similar to the one introduced by JSTL.

As JSTL's popularity grew, a proliferation of J2EE Web development frameworks from both vendors and the open source community also began to appear. These included Oracle's UIX, SiteMesh, WebWork, Tapestry, Turbine, Wicket, and Struts, to name a few. The goals for these frameworks were largely to simplify the UI development as well as provide a more manageable architecture for J2EE Web application development. As many readers will know, the open source framework Struts soon became one of most the popular technologies for enterprise J2EE Web application development. You will soon see how Struts has greatly influenced the design of JavaServer Faces.

Jakarta Struts

One of the most dominant J2EE frameworks to emerge in the last few years was the Jakarta Struts Web application development framework. Struts was created by Craig McClanahan and was offered to the open source community through Apache's Jakarta project. Struts proved to be a success because of its breadth and intelligent architecture.

One of the key reasons for Struts' popularity is that it elegantly solved the problem of separation of code between the user-interface and server-side code by embracing the Model-View-Controller (MVC) design paradigm. Recall that one of the primary problems with JSPs and servlets without a framework was that they tended to allow developers to fall into the bad habit of mixing their UI and server-side code, which led to predictable problems. Struts solved this problem by strictly following the MVC architecture design where the View is the user-interface code and the Model is the server-side code for processing application data. As you'll see shortly, JavaServer Faces also embraces the MVC approach and is similar to Struts in this regard.

In Struts, the Controller is simply a servlet that handles all incoming Web requests and dispatches them to the appropriate View components or pages. For accessing the Model or application data, Struts provides *Actions* that are Web-accessible execution points for Java. For the View, Struts provides a modest set of JSP tag libraries that are fairly low level. These tag libraries provide rendering for the common HTML elements, display messages, and support logic operations.

Although architecturally sound, Struts still often required a substantial amount of custom development for building user interfaces. Even when coupled with the usage of JSTL tags, user interface development could still be fairly complicated and was really not on par with what was available with other proprietary technologies such as Microsoft's ASP.Net where the user interface development experience is more component-based and usually less complex. With the widespread acceptance of Struts, the stage was set for the next advance: JavaServer Faces.

The Birth of JavaServer Faces

As Struts gained in popularity, the Java Community Process saw the benefits that Struts offered by explicitly following an MVC approach. However, Struts still lacked a robust user-interface-oriented framework similar to what is possible in other technologies, including traditional Java client technologies such as Swing. In short, a better way to handle the View tier was needed.

To address this need, several leading software vendors including Sun, Oracle, IBM, and BEA met through the Java Community Process in May of 2001 and voted to proceed with a comprehensive and detailed specification for building J2EE thin client Web applications whose primary goal was to provide a standard and much simpler way to build user interfaces for Java Web applications. This resulted in Java Specification Request (JSR) #127, and JavaServer Faces was born.

JavaServer Faces solves the problem of the View tier, without inventing new J2EE infrastructures. At its core, JSF combines an MVC design approach with a powerful, component-based UI development framework that greatly simplifies J2EE Web development while using existing JSP and servlet technologies. The way this was accomplished is spelled out in the original design goals specified by JSR #127.

The JavaServer Faces Design Goals

JSR #127 specified eight design requirements for JSF. They are shown here:

1. Create a standard UI component framework that can be leveraged by development tools to make it easier for tool users to both create high-quality UIs and manage the UI's connections to application behavior.

2. Define a set of simple, lightweight Java base classes for UI components, component state, and input events. These classes will address UI lifecycle issues, notably managing a component's persistent state for the lifetime of its page.

3. Provide a set of common UI components, including the standard HTML form input elements. These components will be derived from the simple set of base classes (outlined in #1) that can be used to define new components.

4. Provide a JavaBeans model for dispatching events from client-side UI controls to server-side application behavior.

5. Define APIs for input validation, including support for client-side validation.

6. Specify a model for internationalization and localization of the UI.

7. Automatic generation of appropriate output for the target client, taking into account all available client configuration data, such as browser version, etc.

8. Automatic generation of output containing required hooks for supporting accessibility, as defined by the Web Accessibility Initiative (WAI).

To accomplish goals 1 through 3, JavaServer Faces provides a component-centric API from which Web application user interfaces can easily be assembled. The JSF specification defines a set of base user interface components (referred to in the JSF specification as *UI components*) that can be used as is, or extended to achieve more specialized behaviors.

It's important to note that the term "UI component" is sometimes used, albeit slightly incorrectly, to actually mean the combination of three independent elements that make up a usable JSF component in a page. These are

1. The actual **UIComponent** class, which defines the behavior of the component, such as **UISelectOne,** which allows the user to "select one from many."

2. An optional **Renderer** class, which provides specific renderings of the component. For example, a **UISelectOne** component could be rendered in HTML as either a group of radio buttons or a "select" menu.

3. A **JSP tag,** which associates a **Renderer** with a **UIComponent** and makes them usable in a JSP as a single tag, **<h:selectOneMenu >**. It's also important to note that "pluggable" **Renderer** classes allow the UI component to not only be HTML tag-independent (radio or select), but client device–independent where the UI component can be rendered in any markup language, such as HTML, WML, and so on.

We'll cover the entire Faces UI component model in much greater detail in Chapter 6, but for now it is important to understand the key concepts of UI components.

The initial or "standard" UI components provided in the specification are accompanied with a set of "Core" and "HTML" JSP tag libraries. The Core component tag library enables common Web application operations such as assigning validations, converting input values, and loading resource bundles. The HTML component tag library creates and renders HTML components. These include components for displaying simple text labels, input fields, links and buttons as well as more complex container components for displaying tabular data or panels of child components.

To accomplish goal 4, which is to provide an event-based, JavaBean model way of interacting with application data, JavaServer Faces provides an easy-to-use mechanism by which Web-accessible user interface components are bound to server-side JavaBeans that are registered as "Managed Beans" in an XML file (**faces-config.xml**). Beans are bound to a user interface with a simple-to-use Expression Language, which is almost identical to JSTL's Expression Language syntax. Once bound, updating bean properties or invoking bean methods from a Web interface is handled automatically by the *JSF request processing lifecycle.*

JSF 1.2 TIP *JSF Version 1.2 will have a Unified Expression Language syntax with JSP 2.1 and JSTL. This is detailed in Chapter 4.*

The JSF request processing lifecycle also accomplishes goal 5 for handling input validation. In addition to providing a means to update server-side application data, the JSF request processing lifecycle and event model allows for the validation and/or data type conversion of data depending on certain events in the application, such as when a form is submitted or when UI components are accessed or manipulated. JSF provides built-in validation capabilities as well as the option to create custom validation. For data type conversion, such as when a date needs to be converted from a **String** data type supplied by an HTML input field to a **Date** type on the server, JSF has a set of pre-built converters that can convert **String** values to various data types. Both JSF validators and converters can be extended and customized in many ways. In Chapter 7 we'll step through how to use the built-in validators and converters as well as review the different ways of building custom validation and conversion.

JSF accomplishes goal 6, which is to allow for easy internationalization, by providing a simple way to handle multilingual message bundles and locales. Once a message bundle has been configured for a pre-defined set of supported locales, the JSF UI components can then automatically render themselves in the appropriate language based on the incoming request's locale setting. In Chapter 14 we'll review all the steps required for internationalizing a JSF application.

The seventh and eighth goals of the original JSF specification request, which is to have the ability to automatically generate the appropriate output (including output supporting accessibility) depending on the target client, is achieved by the JSF API's extremely flexible, *pluggable* rendering technology. This makes it possible to associate multiple renderers with a single UI component and have the appropriate renderer respond with the appropriate markup for the client. For example, it is possible to create a JSF UI component that can render itself in HTML when a browser makes a request or WML when a PDA or another WAP-enabled browser makes a request.

JSF—A Framework for Both "Corporate" Developers and "Systems" Developers

At the root of the JSF design goals was the desire to make J2EE Web applications development easier. Since J2EE Web development often required a substantial amount of extra effort to develop custom Web infrastructures, J2EE Web development was largely left to a smaller minority of "systems" developers who often have the technical aptitude to build their own Web infrastructures. Simplifying J2EE development was key to enabling larger and more diverse populations of developers to effectively take advantage of what J2EE technology has to offer. One such group, often referred to as "corporate" or "business" developers, make up a substantial portion of the overall software development population. Corporate developers are typically skilled in writing business logic or procedural code, but not always in lower-level or object-oriented development. In addition to traditionally fulfilling the needs of Java systems developers, JSF also addresses the needs of corporate developers, having been specifically designed with them in mind.

JSF simplifies Web development by providing a component-based way of developing Web user interfaces where one can simply insert several intelligent UI components onto a page, bind it to application data using a simple Expression Language, and be up and running. Corporate developers, which include "page authors" who are mostly focused on the construction of the UI, will find this simplified approach to Web user interface development very straightforward and easy to understand. Another benefit for corporate developers is that since JSF is a *standard*, development tools vendors are now supplying productive, visual development environments for JSF, yet further simplifying the development process and allowing corporate developers to focus more on fulfilling their business needs. In Chapter 17 we'll take a tour of the leading JSF development environments and experience what their environments have to offer.

While JSF simplifies Web application development, greatly empowering corporate developers in the world of J2EE Web development, the JSF API also provides enough flexibility and power to allow systems developers plenty of opportunity for advanced customizations and innovation. Thus, JSF satisfies both types of developers.

JSF Application Architecture

One of the most elegant design aspects of the JavaServer Faces specification is that it completely relies on existing J2EE Web technology at its foundation. This means that a JSF application is really just a standard J2EE Web application with a few specific configurations. These are

- An entry in the Web application's **web.xml** file, which enables the Faces Controller servlet when a certain URL pattern is specified, such as **/faces/***.

- A JSF configuration file, **faces-config.xml**, which allows for configuration of all elements of a JSF application. This file is treated as a peer of the **web.xml** file and is usually located in the Web application's **WEB-INF/** directory. The exact structure of this file and the elements contained within are detailed in later chapters.

- A **WEB-INF** directory with the following Java libraries:
  - The actual JSF libraries: **jsf-api.jar** and **jsf-impl.jar**.
  - Additional Apache "Commons" libraries: **commons-beanutils.jar**, **commons-collections.jar**, **commons-digester.jar**, and **commons-logging.jar**. Although not part of the core JSF technology, these libraries are relied upon by JSF and are thus required to be in the application's **WEB-INF/lib** directory.
  - JSTL jar files: **jstl.jar** and **standard.jar**.

NOTE *Some J2EE application servers may provide these jar files in the classpath as a default; so loading them into your WEB-INF may be optional. You may consult your J2EE application server's documentation to determine if the required jar files are pre-loaded.*

Once a J2EE Web application is properly configured for JSF, you can construct the View using, but not limited to, JavaServer Pages. Building JSF applications with JavaServer Pages is done by using JSF-enabled JSP tag libraries. For a JSP page to be JSF-enabled, it must first contain JSF JSP taglib directives provided by a JSF implementation. The following taglib directives are for the Core and HTML libraries from Sun's reference implementation:

```
<%@ taglib uri="http://java.sun.com/jsf/core" prefix="f"%>
<%@ taglib uri="http://java.sun.com/jsf/html" prefix="h"%>
```

In the body of the JSP, you must then add a **<f:view>** tag. This will become the base UI component of what will become a component tree in memory on the server when the page is requested for viewing. If the page processes form input, as opposed to just displaying output, you'll need to add a **<h:form>** tag as a child of the **<f:view>** tag. Subsequent children tags of the **<h:form>** tag will become the form elements such as **<h:inputText>**, which renders an input field, and **<h:commandButton>**, which renders a form submission button.

To understand how JavaServer Faces creates and manages a server-side tree of components in memory that directly corresponds to the components included in a page, consider the following JSF-enabled JSP page:

```
<%@ page contentType="text/html"%>
<%@ taglib uri="http://java.sun.com/jsf/core" prefix="f"%>
<%@ taglib uri="http://java.sun.com/jsf/html" prefix="h"%>
<f:view>
  <html>
    <body>
      <h:form >
        <h2>
          A Simple JSF Page
        </h2>
        <h:inputText value="#{modelBean.username}"/>
        <h:commandButton value="Click Here"/>
      </h:form>
    </body>
  </html>
</f:view>
```

As you can see in Figure 1-1, the JSF UI component tree instantiated on the server exactly matches the UI components in the page. Once the UI component tree is instantiated and in memory, it is possible to interact with the server-side UI components, and manipulate and change properties of these components on the server.

NOTE *JSF version 1.2 actually instantiates the surrounding markup or "template text" as JSF components as well. This improves rendering and provides programmatic access to the entire page.*

As you'll see in later chapters, knowing how to interact with the server-side UI component tree is often needed for more advanced JSF development. For basic JSF applications, one simply has to drop some UI components onto a page, set some attributes, and rely on the JSF built-in "plumbing" to take care of the job of processing input. Let's take a closer look at JSF's "plumbing," otherwise known as the JSF request processing lifecycle.

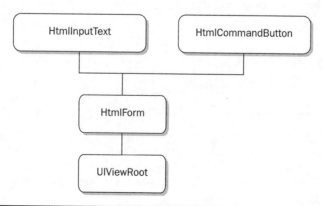

FIGURE 1-1 The JSF UI component tree

The JSF Request Processing Lifecycle

When a JSF-enabled JSP page is requested or when the user invokes an action on a UI component in a JSF-enabled JSP page, it is important to understand the exact sequence of events that occur on the server in order to fulfill the request to view or submit a JSF page. The sequence of events that are triggered during requests to JSF pages is known as the *JSF request processing lifecycle* or sometimes simply as the *JSF lifecycle*. This is shown in Figure 1-2.

We've already touched on what happens when a JSF page is requested for the first time where the JSF runtime creates a component tree in memory. In between requests when nothing is happening in the application, the component tree is often cached. Upon a subsequent request, the tree is quickly reconstituted and if form input values are sent in the request, they are processed and validations are executed. Upon successful validation, the server-side model values of the input fields are updated. What follows is continued event processing and any errors are reported. Once all event processing and model updates (if needed) have finished, a completed response is finally rendered back to the client.

A more detailed review of the JSF request processing lifecycle is presented in Chapter 3, but for now it is sufficient to know that the JSF lifecycle is simply the sequence of back-end "plumbing" events that automatically manage input data so the Web developer does not need to write code to process the request manually. This differs to a certain degree from most other Web technologies including CGI, PHP, and Struts, where the developer specifically writes code to handle the incoming requests and process the results. This is actually one of the advantages that JSF brings to Web application development. It removes the whole notion of having to process incoming Web requests. Instead, the Web developer can rely on the JSF lifecycle to handle back-end plumbing automatically and can use the JSF event model to jump in and do custom processing only when needed.

As a simple example where no custom events are handled, one simply has to bind a UI component such as an Input field to a managed bean's property and the lifecycle will automatically update the value of the managed bean's property with the value of the UI component. Recall the JSF JSP example where an **inputText** component is (value) bound to the "username" property of the managed bean "modelBean" using the JSF expression language (EL).

```
<h:inputText value="#{modelBean.username}" />
```

To allow the user to *submit* the form and initiate the JSF lifecycle, a **commandButton** UI component is added to the page using:

```
<h:commandButton value="Click Here"/>
```

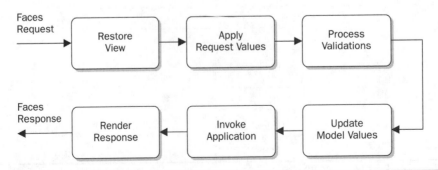

FIGURE 1-2   The JSF request processing lifecycle

Since the JSF lifecycle utilizes the JavaBeans event model, the user simply clicks on the rendered command button at runtime and the JSF lifecycle automatically updates the JavaBean's "username" property with the value provided in the input field!

More in-depth coverage of the JSF request processing lifecycle as well as JSF's expression language is detailed in later chapters.

The JSF Navigation Model

Like Struts, JSF follows a Model-View-Controller design paradigm. Recall that an MVC application is segmented into three distinct application components:

- The Model, which contains the business logic or non-UI code.
- The View, which is all the code necessary to present a UI to the user.
- The Controller, which is a front-end agent that directly handles the user's requests and dispatches the appropriate view.

These three elements, also depicted in Figure 1-3, combine to produce an architecture that yields distinct, separately maintainable code.

JavaServer Faces from the start was created to adhere precisely to the MVC design methodology. It does so by providing a clean way to separate presentation (View) code from the back-end business logic (Model) code. It also provides a front-end (Controller) servlet that handles all Faces requests and dispatches them, along with the necessary application data, to the appropriate View component (page). As you have seen, the View segment of a JSF application is created using JSF-enabled JSP pages with UI components. The Model is bound to methods and properties in "managed beans" specified in the **faces-config.xml**. Now, let's take a look at how the Faces Controller works in a JSF application.

As mentioned before, the Faces Controller is implemented as a servlet that responds to all requests conforming to a certain URL pattern, such as **/faces/***, as defined in the **web .xml**. A request that uses the appropriate Faces URL pattern can be considered a "Faces request" and when received by the Faces Controller, it processes the request by preparing an object known as the JSF context, which contains all accessible application data and routes the client to the appropriate View component (page). The rules that the controller uses for routing these requests are centrally managed in the **faces-config.xml** file and are known as the *JSF Navigation Model*.

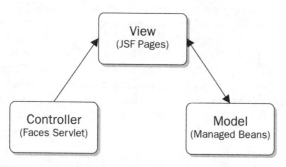

FIGURE 1-3 The Model-View-Controller design paradigm

The JSF Navigation Model is an elegant solution for keeping track of all navigations in the entire JSF application. This greatly improves the manageability of the application because it is easier to maintain a central navigation model rather than having to update multiple page links in multiple pages. The central location of the navigation model in an XML file is also very "tool friendly" in that vendor tools now offer visual ways to easily define JSF navigation models.

The navigation model is based on a set of "navigation rules," which define a "from" page (from-view-id) and one or many "to" navigation cases. Each navigation case has an associated "outcome" and "to" page (to-view-id). For example, to navigate from **page1** to **page2** when the outcome "success" is encountered, the following rule is specified in the **faces-config.xml**:

```
<navigation-rule>
  <from-view-id>/page1.jsp</from-view-id>
  <navigation-case>
    <from-outcome>success</from-outcome>
    <to-view-id>/page2.jsp</to-view-id>
  </navigation-case>
</navigation-rule>
```

As you can guess, a second navigation case can be defined for a "failure" outcome that will route the viewer to **page3.jsp**.

```
<navigation-rule>
  <from-view-id>/page1.jsp</from-view-id>
  <navigation-case>
    <from-outcome>success</from-outcome>
    <to-view-id>/page2.jsp</to-view-id>
  </navigation-case>
  <navigation-case>
    <from-outcome>failure</from-outcome>
    <to-view-id>/page3.jsp</to-view-id>
  </navigation-case>
</navigation-rule>
```

The next question you're wondering is, How is an "outcome" determined? This can either be hard-coded, or derived dynamically from the return value of a method that is triggered when a button is clicked. As you recall, UI components can be bound to both properties and methods so it is possible to associate a button click with a specific method in a managed bean, which can then return an "outcome" as a **String** value. The JSF event model then processes this "outcome" **String** value and follows any navigation case defined in the navigation model that corresponds to the outcome of the method.

Now that you know the history and theory behind JSF, and have seen a very simple example of a working JSF page, it's time to review a more detailed JSF example application. Chapter 2 develops a short, yet practical registration form example that exercises many of the key features of JavaServer Faces. It will also serve as one of several modules of a more intricate "Virtual Trainer" example application, which will be introduced in Part II of this book.

Building a Simple JavaServer Faces Application

One of the best ways to learn a new technology is to work through a simple, yet practical example. Towards this end, this chapter develops a typical Web registration application using JavaServer Faces (JSF) technology. A Web registration application provides just enough functionality to show how to use the core JSF technologies, such as User Interface (UI) components, managed beans, the Navigation Model, and basic data validation and conversion. In later chapters this registration application will be incorporated into a larger, more comprehensive "Virtual Trainer" example application that will be referenced throughout the book. For now, working through this registration example gives you an understanding of the key elements and architecture of a JSF application. It also provides an overview of the JSF development process.

In addition to showing how to build a simple JSF registration application, this chapter also explains how to set up your own JSF development environment, which will allow you to compile, package, and run the application. In the interest of ensuring a firm understanding of the core technology requirements of a JSF application, the application in this chapter will be built manually. In later chapters, you will see how to rapidly build JSF applications using several of the leading integrated visual development environments for JavaServer Faces.

Application Overview

This sample application is called JSFReg and it is a simple Web registration application similar to the ones that you've no doubt encountered numerous times while registering for numerous services on the Web today. The application is comprised of several JSP pages, each containing JSF UI components (more on those later), a Java class to temporarily store user information, and a set of configuration files and required runtime libraries.

The application's opening page includes a hyperlink to a page containing the registration form. The registration form allows users to enter their name, gender, and other basic personal information. A Register button is also included on the form, which, when clicked, invokes a validation on the data entered. If any validation errors occur, error messages are displayed next to the invalid input fields. The user can then revise the incorrect fields in order to pass validation. After the input data passes validation, the user can still revise any input data or proceed to confirm the registration. When the final confirmation button is clicked, a final page is displayed showing the actual "registered" data for the user. A registration Java method is also invoked at the same time. This Java method could actually be linked to a database or any service to perform an actual data record insertion. In this simple example, the Java registration method simply prints the message "Adding new user" to the standard output (or console) of the application server.

Figure 2-1 depicts all of the pages in the JSFReg application.

The somewhat detailed registration process with various options to go back and revise or proceed on to a confirmation page may seem a little excessive, but this was done intentionally to show how to handle different page navigation options depending on different cases. The registration page illustrates how to build a form using a collection of the various UI components provided in the JSF specification's standard HTML component library. These include input text fields, radio buttons, and a select menu, along with form submission buttons. The application's fairly robust validation requirements highlight both JSF's built-in validation and data type conversion technology as well as how to implement (very simple) custom validation logic. More thorough coverage of JSF validation and conversion is provided in Chapter 7.

Since JSF provides both a set of usable UI components along with a modest amount of built-in validation and data conversion capabilities, you'll see that a large portion of JSF application development is simply a matter of assembling user interfaces using ready-to-use UI components. As also highlighted in the example, these components can be configured with certain validations and then bound to existing Java bean properties and methods. The same components can also be bound to a set of page flow navigation rules known as the JSF *Navigation Model*, which provides navigation rules for the entire application. That in a nutshell is what JSF application development entails. Now let's take a closer look at how the example application is built.

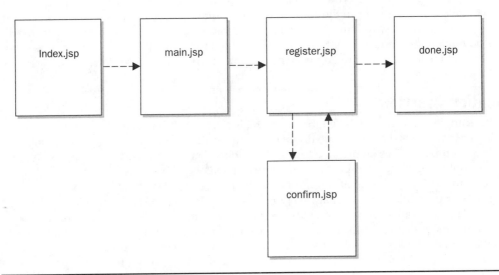

FIGURE 2-1 Diagram of JSFReg application

The JSFReg Application Files

All JSF applications are comprised of a specific set of required configuration files and Web content files. The key configuration files required are the **faces-config.xml**, and a standard J2EE Web application's configuration/deployment descriptor, **web.xml**. Web content files can be comprised of JSP and/or general HTML content such as HTML pages, images, and cascading style sheets (CSS).

The following table lists each file used in the JSFReg application and its purpose.

File	Description
faces-config.xml	The master configuration file required by all JSF applications. It contains a reference for all of the working parts of a Faces application.
web.xml	The J2EE Web deployment descriptor and master configuration file required by any J2EE Web application. A JSF application's **web.xml** file also has specific settings for JSF, such as the servlet mapping "/faces", which allows the JSF controller servlet to process this request separately from any other request.
index.jsp	A starter page with a JSP forward to the initial JSF-enabled JSP page: main.jsp: <jsp:forward page="/faces/main.jsp" /> Notice the path to **main.jsp** contains the "/faces/" mapping, which allows the Faces controller to prepare the JSF Context before routing to the **main.jsp** page.
main.jsp	The main Faces entry point of the application.
register.jsp	The application's JSP page that contains the registration form for the application. The registration form is comprised of the different JSF UI components that render the input fields, menus, and buttons.
confirm.jsp	A JSP page that displays the validated user-entered data with two buttons providing the options Edit or Confirm. Clicking the Edit button will send the user back to the registration form while clicking the Confirm button confirms the input and redirects to the final "done" page.
done.jsp	A JSP page that indicates that the user information was successfully submitted along with a final display of the confirmed user information.
Userbean.java	A Java class that is used as a "managed bean" by JSF to temporarily store the registration information supplied by the user. It contains the fields for the user's name, gender, e-mail, birth date, etc. It also contains a simple validation method for the e-mail address.

In addition to these core application files, additional Java libraries are also needed to compile and create a deployable packaged application. These details will be covered at the end of the chapter.

Assembling the JSFReg Application

Those of you already familiar with basic J2EE Web applications will notice that all JSF applications are simply standard J2EE applications, but with a few distinctions. These include a JSF setting in the Web application's **web.xml** file, a JSF configuration file (**faces-config.xml**), and the necessary runtime libraries. Let's review how to build the JSFReg application from scratch.

To start building JSFReg you'll need to create a development directory on your filesystem that will serve as the root directory for your J2EE Web application. This directory can actually reside anywhere on your filesystem, but to follow along with this example, use **C:\ JSReg**. This directory will contain all of the necessary elements for building the JSFReg Web application. This will include a Java source directory, **src**, as well as a J2EE Web module root directory, **web**, which will contain the final, deployable content. The **src** directory will contain the full path of the Java source files needed for this application. J2EE Web developers will recognize the **web** subdirectory as a standard J2EE Web module directory. It will contain the required **WEB-INF** sub-directory tree, which contains the Web module deployment descriptor, **web.xml**, along with the application's Web content, including JSP, HTML, images, CSS, and so on. The **WEB-INF** directory tree also includes the **lib** and **classes** subdirectories that will contain the application's runtime Java libraries and compiled classes. Later, when you compile the application, make sure to place the compiled Java class(es) into the **WEB-INF/lib/classes** directory before packing the application into a Web Archive (WAR) file. Your empty directory structure will look like what is shown in Figure 2-2.

Your complete directory structure will eventually contain the following files:

- C:\JSFReg\web\main.jsp
- C:\JSFReg\web\index.jsp
- C:\JSFReg\web\register.jsp
- C:\JSFReg\web\confirm.jsp
- C:\JSFReg\web\done.jsp
- C:\JSFReg\web\WEB-INF\web.xml
- C:\JSFReg\web\WEB-INF\faces-config.xml
- C:\JSFReg\web\WEB-INF\classes\   Contains the compiled Java classes
- C:\JSFReg\web\WEB-INF\lib\   Contains the required JSF runtime jar files
- C:\JSFReg\src\com\jsfcompref\jsfreg\Userbean.java

The Configuration Files

To begin building the application, first create a new Web module deployment descriptor (**web.xml**) and a Faces configuration file (**faces-config.xml**) file, both of which must reside in the **web/WEB-INF** directory. The **web.xml** file designates this directory structure as being a J2EE Web application. Once finished, this directory structure will be universally deployable to any standard J2EE Web container/application server.

FIGURE 2-2   JSFReg application directory structure

Here is the initial **web.xml** file:

```
<?xml version = '1.0' encoding = 'windows-1252'?>
<web-app xmlns:xsi="http://www.w3.org/2001/XMLSchema-instance"
xsi:schemaLocation="http://java.sun.com/xml/ns/j2ee
http://java.sun.com/xml/ns/j2ee/web-app_2_4.xsd" version="2.4"
xmlns="http://java.sun.com/xml/ns/j2ee">
  <description>Empty web.xml file for a Web Application</description>
  <servlet>
    <servlet-name>Faces Servlet</servlet-name>
    <servlet-class>javax.faces.webapp.FacesServlet</servlet-class>
    <load-on-startup>1</load-on-startup>
  </servlet>
  <servlet-mapping>
    <servlet-name>Faces Servlet</servlet-name>
    <url-pattern>/faces/*</url-pattern>
  </servlet-mapping>
</web-app>
```

The key thing to notice is that the **web.xml** file has a **Faces** servlet entry, **javax.faces .webapp.FacesServlet**, which serves as the Faces Controller servlet. The Faces Controller servlet is able to intercept all **Faces** requests, providing they have the **/faces/*** pattern that matches the servlet mapping's url-pattern. Actually the url-pattern can be set to anything, such as *****.faces** or ***.jsf**. It simply has to be a pattern that allows the application to distinguish Faces requests from non-Faces requests. All JSF-enabled pages must be accessed via a Faces request (using a suitable mapping pattern) so as to first invoke the Faces servlet Controller whose job is to prepare the JSF Context before routing to the requested page. More coverage on the JSF lifecycle and Context will be provided in later chapters.

Next, add a **faces-config.xml** file, which also resides in the **WEB-INF** subdirectory.

NOTE *The* **faces-config.xml** *file can actually be named anything and reside in any custom location (providing it's still accessible by the Web application). You can even have multiple faces configuration files. The default directory location is the* **WEB-INF** *directory. Non-default locations require an entry in the* **web.xml** *designating the name and location of the faces configuration file (or files). An initial empty* **faces-config.xml** *file will look like this:*

```
<?xml version="1.0"?>
<!DOCTYPE faces-config PUBLIC
  "-//Sun Microsystems, Inc.//DTD JavaServer Faces Config 1.1//EN"
  "http://java.sun.com/dtd/web-facesconfig_1_1.dtd">
<faces-config xmlns="http://java.sun.com/JSF/Configuration">
</faces-config>
```

JSF 1.2 TIP *If you're building an application for Faces version 1.2, the* **faces-config** *file must be specified using an XML schema, like this:*

```
<?xml version="1.0"?>
<faces-config xmlns=http://java.sun.com/xml/ns/j2ee
  xmlns:xsi=http://www.w3.org/2001/XMLSchema-instance
  xsi:schemaLocation="http://java.sun.com/xml/ns/j2ee
http://java.sun.com/xml/ns/j2ee/web-facesconfig_1_2.xsd"
    version="1.2">
</faces-config>
```

As you build the application, you'll be adding entries to the **faces-config.xml** file including navigation rules and managed bean(s).

The JSP Pages

Let's start with the **index.jsp** page. Typically, the **index.jsp** page is used as the starting page for JSP applications. So to follow this convention we'll simply provide a JSP forward to automatically forward the user to the first Faces-enabled page, **main.jsp**, using the **/faces/** url-pattern to initiate a Faces request:

```
<jsp:forward page="/faces/main.jsp" />
```

As the request is made, the Faces controller receives it and initiates the JSF lifecycle, which among other things will prepare the JSF Context and route the user to the JSF page, **main.jsp**. As we'll review in later chapters, the JSF Context provides a simple and consistent way to access application data from JSF pages.

The **main.jsp** page, shown in Figure 2-3, is the first JSF-enabled page in the application. It contains the single JSF UI component, **HtmlCommandLink**, which renders a simple HTML hyperlink linked to the registration page.

The purpose of this page is to show a very simple example of how to use the **HTMLCommandLink** component with a navigation rule. Let's examine the source code of the first JSF-enabled JSP page:

```
<%@ page contentType="text/html"%>
<%@ taglib uri="http://java.sun.com/jsf/core" prefix="f"%>
<%@ taglib uri="http://java.sun.com/jsf/html" prefix="h"%>
<f:view>
  <html>
    <head>
      <title>A Simple JavaServer Faces Registration Application</title>
    </head>
    <body>
      <h:form >
        <h2>
          JSF Registration App
        </h2>
        <h:commandLink action="register">
          <h:outputText value="Click here to register.."/>
        </h:commandLink>
      </h:form>
    </body>
  </html>
</f:view>
```

The first thing to notice is the two taglib directives at the top of the page:

```
<%@ taglib uri="http://java.sun.com/jsf/core" prefix="f"%>
<%@ taglib uri="http://java.sun.com/jsf/html" prefix="h"%>
```

These JSP directives allow the JSP page to use the JSF Core and HTML tag libraries that are provided in the JSF specification's Reference Implementation, which in turn allows the

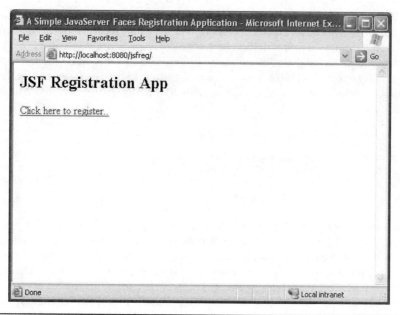

FIGURE 2-3   The JSFReg home page

JSP to use the underlying JSF UI components in the page. Keep in mind that JSF UI components are client-independent and can be used in different clients as long as there are corresponding renderers. The specifics on UI component rendering will be covered in later chapters but for now, the main thing to know is that JSF is designed to work not only with traditional HTML browsers as the client, but other types of clients as well, such as PDAs and other devices.

After the taglib directives, the next thing you'll notice is the **<f:view>** and **<h:form>** tags. These tags are the master parent tags of the entire page content. We'll cover this in more detail in later chapters but basically the thing to remember here is that as a JSF page is rendered for a client (such as a browser), an identical component tree is instantiated into memory on the server with the View component at its root.

Moving on to the first real, usable UI components, you see:

```
<h:commandLink action="register">
  <h:outputText value="Click here to register.."/>
</h:commandLink>
```

The **<h:commandLink >** is a JSP tag that invokes a JSF **HtmlCommandLink** UI component on the server, rendering an HTML hyperlink around any content in the body of the tag. An interesting thing to note about this component is that it renders as a link, but acts like a button, causing a form submit. In this case, the body of the tag is the child tag **<h:outputText>** that invokes an **HtmlOutputText** UI component, which simply renders the text from the **value** attribute to the client. The final and most important thing to notice is the **action** attribute of the **commandLink** tag. This is where the JSF event model comes in, as the **action** attribute of the tag actually describes how to process the event that gets fired when the link is clicked on. Since the **action** attribute is set to "register," an **ActionEvent** is passed to the JSF navigation model, where it will then look up a corresponding navigation case with the same **from-outcome** as "register" and follow its specified **to-view-id** navigation path. To understand this better, let's take a look at the navigation rule in the **faces-config.xml** that handles this "register" action. The navigation rule that handles this outcome is as follows:

```
<navigation-rule>
  <from-view-id>/main.jsp</from-view-id>
  <navigation-case>
    <from-outcome>register</from-outcome>
    <to-view-id>/register.jsp</to-view-id>
  </navigation-case>
</navigation-rule>
```

As you can see, this is a navigation rule that specifies a **from-view-id** or origin of **main.jsp** page and will navigate to the **register.jsp** page if a **from-outcome** event equals "register" as specified by the navigation case. When the rendered hyperlink in the page is clicked, the **action** attribute, "register," forces this **from-outcome** case to be "register," thus enabling the navigation to **register.jsp**.

Now let's have a look at the core of this example application, the **register.jsp** page, which is shown in Figure 2-4. When rendered in a browser, the page resembles any typical registration page.

Upon examination of the source of the page, you'll first notice the same taglib directives for the Core and HTML JSF tag libraries as well as the surrounding **<f:view>** and **<h:form>** tags followed by a series of input tags that render the different form fields in the page. You'll also notice that an HTML table is used to provide the layout structure of the form. As we'll

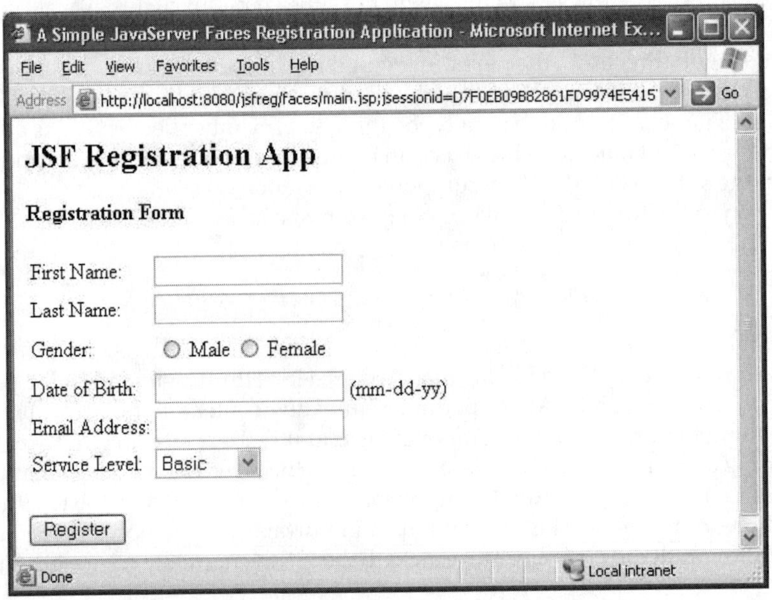

FIGURE 2-4   The JSFReg registration form page

cover later on, JSF also has components that provide layout structure as well such as the **<h: panelGrid>,** which provides a similar layout to an HTML table but without requiring row and cell tags. There is no requirement, however, to use one approach or the other.

```
<%@ page contentType="text/html"%>
<%@ taglib uri="http://java.sun.com/jsf/core" prefix="f"%>
<%@ taglib uri="http://java.sun.com/jsf/html" prefix="h"%>
<f:view>
 <html>
  <head><title>A Simple JavaServer Faces Registration Application</title></head>
    <body>
      <h:form>
        <h2>JSF Registration App</h2>
        <h4>Registration Form</h4>
        <table>
         <tr>
          <td>First Name:</td>
          <td>
           <h:inputText id="fname" value="#{UserBean.firstName}"
              required="true"/>
           <h:message for="fname"/>
          </td>
         </tr>
         <tr>
          <td>Last Name:</td>
          <td>
           <h:inputText id="lname" value="#{UserBean.lastName}"
              required="true" />
           <h:message for="lname"/>
          </td>
         </tr>
         <tr>
          <td>Gender:</td>
          <td>
      <h:selectOneRadio id="gender" value="#{UserBean.gender}"
        required="true"/>
       <f:selectItem itemLabel="Male" itemValue="male"/>
       <f:selectItem itemLabel="Female" itemValue="female"/>
      </h:selectOneRadio>
      <h:message for="gender"/>
          </td>
         </tr>
         <tr>
          <td>Date of Birth:</td>
          <td>
           <h:inputText value="#{UserBean.dob}" id="dob" required="true" >
            <f:convertDateTime pattern="MM-dd-yy"/>
           </h:inputText> (mm-dd-yy)
           <h:message for="dob"/>
          </td>
         </tr>
         <tr>
          <td>Email Address:</td>
          <td>
           <h:inputText id="email" value="#{UserBean.email}" required="true"
             validator="#{UserBean.validateEmail}"/>
           <h:message for="email"/>
```

```
        </td>
       </tr>
       <tr>
        <td>Service Level:</td>
        <td>
         <h:selectOneMenu value="#{UserBean.serviceLevel}">
          <f:selectItem itemLabel="Basic" itemValue="basic"/>
          <f:selectItem itemLabel="Medium" itemValue="medium"/>
          <f:selectItem itemLabel="Premium" itemValue="premium"/>
         </h:selectOneMenu>
        </td>
       </tr>
      </table>
      <p><h:commandButton value="Register" action="register" /></p>
    </h:form>
   </body>
  </html>
</f:view>
```

Let's examine the key aspects of this file, beginning with the first of two input field tags that accept input for the first and last name.

```
<h:inputText id="fname" value="#{UserBean.firstName}" required="true"/>
<h:message for="fname"/>
```

In order to require the user to enter a value, you'll notice the **required** attribute is set to "true." If the user attempts to leave the field blank while submitting the form, a built-in validation error message will appear exactly in the same location as the **<h:message>** tag. Notice that the message tag can actually reside anywhere in the page because it is linked to the **inputText** field by its ID "fname." This is an example of some of the built-in validation mechanisms provided by JSF. The next and most important thing to notice is the **value** attribute of the **inputText** tag: **#{UserBean.firstName}**. This is known as a JSF *value binding* expression and provides a direct linkage to the **firstName** property of the managed bean **UserBean**.

JSF 1.2 TIP *The syntax for JSF 1.1 value binding expressions is very similar to the JSP 2.0 Expression Language and serves an almost identical purpose. For JSF version 1.2 both JSF and JSP 2.1 use a Unified Expression Language. More information is provided on JSF 1.2 and the Unified Expression Language in later chapters.*

So what is a *managed bean*? You may have heard the terms "inversion of control" or "dependency injection." These are simply fancy terms for a way to hook together different parts of your application without introducing too much interdependence ("tight coupling"). Managed beans do just that. Basically, a managed bean is an officially registered Java class for a JSF application. It is a POJO (plain-old Java Object) that conforms to JavaBeans naming conventions. In order for a JSF application to refer to Java classes, and their methods and properties, it has to be available in the Java classpath and registered in the **faces-config.xml**. Here is the entry in the **faces-config.xml** for the **UserBean.java** class for this example application.

```
<managed-bean>
  <managed-bean-name>UserBean</managed-bean-name>
  <managed-bean-class>
```

```
      com.jsfcompref.register.UserBean
   </managed-bean-class>
   <managed-bean-scope>session</managed-bean-scope>
</managed-bean>
```

Once registered, a managed bean can be referred to in any UI component attribute using JSF value expressions. Finally, notice the managed-bean-scope; this is similar but not exactly identical to the scope setting of a standard JSP **useBean** directive that allows the developer to control the lifespan of the Java class by designating it with one of the following: *request, session, application,* or *none* settings.

NOTE *Further coverage of managed beans and scope settings is provided in Chapter 4.*

Now that we've shown how to register a Java class as a managed bean, let's take a look at the actual managed bean, **UserBean.java**, which is used in this example application:

```
package com.jsfcompref.register;
import java.util.Date;
import javax.faces.application.FacesMessage;
import javax.faces.component.UIComponent;
import javax.faces.component.UIInput;
import javax.faces.context.FacesContext;

public class UserBean {
   String firstName;
   String lastName;
   Date dob;
   String gender;
   String email;
   String serviceLevel;
   public UserBean() { }

   public String getFirstName() {
      return firstName;
   }

   public void setFirstName(String firstName) {
      this.firstName = firstName;
   }

   public String getLastName() {
      return lastName;
   }

   public void setLastName(String lastName) {
      this.lastName = lastName;
   }

   public Date getDob() {
      return dob;
   }

   public void setDob(Date dob) {
      this.dob = dob;
   }
```

```
public String getGender() {
  return gender;
}

public void setGender(String gender) {
  this.gender = gender;
}

public String getEmail() {
  return email;
}

public void setEmail(String email) {
  this.email = email;
}

public String getServiceLevel() {
  return serviceLevel;
}

public void setServiceLevel(String serviceLevel) {
  this.serviceLevel = serviceLevel;
}

public void validateEmail(FacesContext context, UIComponent toValidate,
                          Object value) throws ValidatorException {
  String eMail = (String) value;
  if(eMail.indexOf("@")<0) {
    FacesMessage message = new FacesMessage("Invalid email address");
    throw new ValidatorException(message);
  }
}

public String addConfirmedUser() {
  // This method would call a database or other service and add the
  // confirmed user information.
  System.out.println("Adding new user");
  return "success";
}
}
```

As you can see, the **UserBean** Java class is a straightforward Java bean with various fields—**firstName**, **lastName**, **gender**, **dob** (Date of Birth), and **serviceLevel**—all of which are of type **String** except **dob**, which is of type **Date**. Notice also the getters and setters for each field as well. Each of these fields is represented in the **register.jsp** registration form with corresponding JSF UI components, which are value bound to the bean properties. You'll also notice the extra methods: **validateEmail()** and **addConfirmedUser()**. These are custom methods that essentially do exactly what their name indicates. These methods are also bound to the UI components in the page. You will see how shortly.

Now that we've reviewed what managed beans are, as well as how to configure them and access their properties, let's get back to the **register.jsp** page. As you continue browsing the rest of the page, you see a radio button UI component that is actually made from a combination of tags:

```
<h:selectOneRadio id="gender" value="#{UserBean.gender}" required="true"/>
  <f:selectItem itemLabel="Male" itemValue="male"/>
  <f:selectItem itemLabel="Female" itemValue="female"/>
</h:selectOneRadio>
<h:message for="gender"/>
```

The main parent tag, **<h:selectOneRadio>**, is the one that is value bound to the **UserBean**'s gender property via the JavaBeans getter and setter. This means that whatever value is selected in the radio button control, it will be updated in the gender property of the managed bean when the form is submitted. For the individual select choices, the child tags **<f:selectItem >** provide both a displayed value or *itemLabel* along with an actual *itemValue*, which is the actual value used when a selection occurs. As before, a selection is required and if left blank, an error message will appear via the **<h:message >** tag.

Moving on to the next input field, you see the following code:

```
<h:inputText value="#{UserBean.dob}" id="dob" required="true" >
  <f:convertDateTime pattern="MM-dd-yy"/>
</h:inputText> (mm-dd-yy)
<h:message for="dob"/>
```

As before, this input field is required, but this time instead of being bound to a bean property that is a **String**, this **inputText** component is bound to the **UserBean.dob** property that is of type **java.util.Date**. In order to translate the incoming string value into the server-side **Date** type, a JSF converter is used with the tag **<f:convertDateTime>**. Notice the **pattern** attribute of the Converter tag also defines the expected date format pattern of "MM-dd-yy".

NOTE *To JSF, the uppercase "MM" actually means month and "mm" means minutes. However, most end users wouldn't necessarily know this so the date pattern prompt is left intentionally in lowercase (mm-dd-yy).*

When the user enters a date string following the specified format, the Converter will convert it to a **Date** object and assign it to the **UserBean.dob** property. However, if an incorrect date format pattern is used, a conversion error will be displayed.

To see what occurs when improper information is entered and submitted in the registration form, Figure 2-5 contains a screenshot of the registration page with various validation and converter error messages shown.

Notice the *Email Address* error message is shown when "foo" is entered? This is because the associated validation method **validateEmail()** in the **UserBean** managed bean is not accepting the "foo" string as a valid e-mail address:

```
<h:inputText id="email" value="#{UserBean.email}" required="true"
  validator="#{UserBean.validateEmail}"/>
<h:message for="email"/>
```

This is actually the simplest form of custom validation in JavaServer Faces. Another method for creating custom validation can be achieved by creating a separate **Validator** class and then registering it in the **faces-config.xml**. Also, an even more robust custom validation procedure involves creating a custom component with the validation built into it.

FIGURE 2-5   JSFReg with validation errors

Later chapters will examine many more validation examples. To understand how the simple e-mail validation works, let's examine the **validateEmail()** code again:

```
public void validateEmail(FacesContext context, UIComponent toValidate,
                          Object value) throws ValidatorException {
  String eMail = (String) value;
  if(eMail.indexOf("@")<0) {
    FacesMessage message = new FacesMessage("Invalid email address");
    throw new ValidatorException(message);
  }
}
```

The key thing to notice in the custom validation method is that the **value** of the field is checked to see if it contains an @ symbol and if it's not found, an appropriate "Invalid e-mail..." **FacesMessage** is created. A **ValidatorException** is then thrown, which halts further processing and causes the error message to appear next to the e-mail input field.

Moving on to the next input field in the **register.jsp** page, you see another input select menu. This time it is created with the **<h:selectOneMenu>** tag.

```
<h:selectOneMenu value="#{UserBean.serviceLevel}">
  <f:selectItem itemLabel="Basic" itemValue="basic"/>
  <f:selectItem itemLabel="Medium" itemValue="medium"/>
  <f:selectItem itemLabel="Premium" itemValue="premium"/>
</h:selectOneMenu>
```

This tag's usage is basically identical to the previous radio-button tag except that it renders a drop-down menu as opposed to a radio button. It has the same type of child **<f:selectItem>** tags as drop-down menu choices, but renders the different select choices.

Finally, at the bottom of the page is the **Register** button. When clicked it causes a form submission that triggers the JSF event model to perform a validation and update the Model or managed bean properties with the new input field values. To navigate to the confirmation page upon a successful validation of input data, the button has its **action** attribute set to the literal value "register."

```
<h:commandButton value="Register" action="register" />
```

Similar to the previous **commandLink** component in the **index.jsp** page, this **commandButton** uses the JSF **action** "register" to navigate to the **confirm.jsp** page by using the following navigation rule in the **faces-config.xml**:

```
<navigation-rule>
  <from-view-id>/register.jsp</from-view-id>
    <navigation-case>
      <from-outcome>register</from-outcome>
      <to-view-id>/confirm.jsp</to-view-id>
    </navigation-case>
</navigation-rule>
```

Upon a successful navigation to the **confirm.jsp** page, shown in Figure 2-6, the user sees the entered data along with buttons at the bottom of the page that provide the choice of either returning to the registration form (**register.jsp**) to revise any data entry, or proceeding on to the final **done.jsp** page to complete the registration process.

The values for the registration data displayed in the confirmation page use the standard **<h:outputText>** tags such as:

```
<h:outputText value="#{UserBean.firstName}"/>
...
<h:outputText value="#{UserBean.lastName}"/>
```

FIGURE 2-6   The JSFReg confirmation page

The two buttons at the bottom of the page are coded as:

```
<h:commandButton value="Edit" action="revise"/>
<h:commandButton value="Confirm" action="#{UserBean.addConfirmedUser}" />
```

The **Edit** button uses a hard-coded **action** value of "revise," which follows a corresponding navigation rule that returns the user to the **register.jsp** page. The **Confirm** button specifies an *action method*, **addConfirmedUser()**, that determines the outcome programmatically in the logic of the method. For this simple case, the action method simply prints the message "Adding new user" to standard output and always returns a "success" outcome.

```
public String addConfirmedUser(){
    // This method would call a database or other service to add the
    // confirmed user information. This version is not implemented.

    System.out.println("Adding new user");
    return "success";
}
```

NOTE *In a real world application, the method **addConfirmedUser()** would typically call an external data management method that could interface with a database or other type of data service.*

In order to handle the two navigation cases of returning to edit the data or continuing to the "done" page after successfully "adding" the user, both "revise" and "success" outcomes are specified in the final navigation rule in the **faces-config.xml**:

```
<navigation-rule>
  <from-view-id>/confirm.jsp</from-view-id>
    <navigation-case>
      <from-outcome>revise</from-outcome>
      <to-view-id>/register.jsp</to-view-id>
    </navigation-case>
    <navigation-case>
      <from-outcome>success</from-outcome>
      <to-view-id>/done.jsp</to-view-id>
    </navigation-case>
</navigation-rule>
```

After clicking on the Confirm button, the user is navigated to the final page of the application, **done.jsp**. This is shown in Figure 2-7.

The source code for this final page is similar to previous confirmation pages where the **outputText** UI components render the current values of the **UserBean** fields. However, this final page no longer needs the two Edit and Confirm buttons at the bottom of the page.

Setting Up Your JSF Development Environment

Now that we've reviewed the JSFReg sample application, let's walk through the steps needed to set up your computing environment for JavaServer Faces development so you can successfully compile and deploy it. As mentioned earlier, later chapters provide detailed information on using various integrated development environments (IDEs) to rapidly build JSF applications. This chapter provides instruction on how to set up a simple JSF development

FIGURE 2-7   JSFReg's confirmation complete page

environment without the aid of an IDE because it clearly shows each part of the process, and will work for all readers.

Downloading the JSF Reference Implementation and Required Libraries

Before downloading the JSF Reference Implementation (RI), make sure your environment has a Java Development Kit (JDK) to serve as the main compiler and runtime engine for your JSF development environment. If you do not have one installed on your system, you can download one from **http://java.sun.com**.

NOTE   *The JSFReg example in this chapter can be used with either JDK 1.4.2 or JDK 1.5 (5.0). This application is also built using Sun's JSF RI version 1.1.0, although it is possible to use Apache MyFaces implementation instead. More information on MyFaces is provided in Chapter 20.*

The next required downloadable component is the actual JSF RI package from Sun. The JSF RI includes documentation, samples, and the required runtime jar files for all JSF applications. The JSF RI can be downloaded from **http://java.sun.com/j2ee/javaserverfaces/download.html**. After downloading, you can save it in a distinct location such as **C:\JSF** so you can later easily refer to in your build processes. The key jar files that you'll need when building your JSF applications are **jsf-api.jar** and **jsf-impl.jar.** These files are located in your JSF distribution's lib directory (**C:\JSF\lib**).

In addition to the core JSF runtime jar files, JSF applications also require some key "commons" jar files. These include the libraries—**commons-beanutils.jar, commons-collections.jar, commons-digester.jar**, and **commons-logging.jar**—all of which are available at the Jakarta Apache Commons web page (**http://jakarta.apache.org/commons/**). But thankfully these libraries are also included in the JSF RI bundle in the same library directory (**C:\JSF\lib**) as well.

The other key jar files required for developing and deploying JSF applications are the JSTL 1.1 version of **jstl.jar** and **standard.jar**, both of which can be downloaded from **http://java.sun.com/products/jsp/jstl/downloads/index.html**.

NOTE *These libraries are provided in both the J2EE 1.4 JDK and the Java WSDP 1.4.*

Once you've downloaded your **jstl.jar** and **standard.jar**, you can place them in **C:\JSF\lib** as well for future use.

Installing Tomcat or Any J2EE-Compliant Application Server

In order to run and test your JSF applications a J2EE Web-tier server is also required. This book uses Tomcat version 5.5 for its core development environment, which can be freely downloaded from the Jakarta Apache Web site at **http://jakarta.apache.org**. As you install Tomcat or your J2EE-compliant application server, make a note of where it is located on your filesystem—for example, **C:\Tomcat**—because you'll need to refer to the **servlet-api.jar** file provided with Tomcat when you compile your application.

NOTE *An optional step is to download and install Apache Ant for simplified software builds. Apache Ant provides an easy-to-use open source technology for building and packaging your applications and can also be downloaded from Apache at **http://ant.apache.org**. Ant build scripts are provided in the free, downloadable files that contain the source code for the example applications in this book.*

Once your environment is set up correctly you should be able to install any of the JSF sample applications packaged in war files from the JSF RI into your Tomcat installation's **webapps** directory and they should auto-install and run as expected.

Compiling, Packaging, and Running the Application

Now that you have set up your JSF development environment and have reviewed the JSF application in detail, it's time to compile and package the application for deployment.

Compiling the Application

The JSFReg application is comprised of several files; however, only the Java source code files need to be compiled before you package and run the application. Because the Java source code files use the Servlet and JSF APIs, you need to add these libraries to your Java classpath. You could do this by updating your CLASSPATH environment variable. Alternatively, you can just specify the path when you compile the JSFReg application.

In preparation for building your application, you'll need to copy all of the runtime library **.jar** files that you downloaded earlier when setting up your JSF development environment to your JSFReg application's **WEB-INF\lib** directory.

Copy the following files to your JSFReg application's **C:\JSFReg\web\WEB-INF\lib** directory. These **.jar** files contain the JSF and associated library class files that are necessary for the JSFReg's application to run once it is packaged as a **.war** file.

- C:\JSF\lib\jsf-impl.jar
- C:\JSF\lib\jsf-api.jar

- C:\JSF\lib\commons-beanutils.jar
- C:\JSF\lib\commons-collections.jar
- C:\JSF\lib\commons-digester.jar
- C:\JSF\lib\commons-logging.jar

Assuming you placed the **jstl.jar** and **standard.jar** files in the same JSF lib directory, copy these files to your JSFReg's **WEB-INF\lib** directory as well:

- C:\JSF\lib\jstl.jar
- C:\JSF\lib\standard.jar

Assuming that you have installed Tomcat at **C:\Tomcat\jakarta-tomcat-5.5.7**, and placed the **JSFReg** application files at **C:\JSFReg,** open a command prompt session, and change directories to the JSFReg application's web directory **C:\JSFReg\web**. Next, enter the following command line to compile the JSFReg application:

```
C:\JSFReg\web>javac -classpath WEB-INF\lib\commons-beanutils.jar;
              WEB-INF\lib\commons-collections.jar;
              WEB-INF\lib\commons-digester.jar;
              WEB-INF\lib\commons-logging.jar;
              WEB-INF\lib\commons-validator.jar;
              WEB-INF\lib\jsf-api.jar;
              WEB-INF\lib\jsf-impl.jar;
              WEB-INF\lib\jstl.jar;
              WEB-INF\lib\standard.jar;
              C:\Tomcat\jakarta-tomcat-5.5.7\common\lib\servlet-api.jar
                 ..\src\com\jsfcompref\register\*.java
                 -d WEB-INF\classes
```

Notice that you must specify the path to each **.jar** file explicitly. Of course, if you update CLASSPATH, this explicit specification is not needed. You should also notice that the compiled code will be placed into the **WEB-INF\classes** directory, as specified by the

```
-d WEB-INF\classes
```

option of the command line.

Packaging the Application

Because JSF applications are standard J2EE Web applications, this application will be packaged using the standard J2EE Web Archive format. Packaging the application as a **.war** file allows the application to be easily deployed on any J2EE-compliant application server. Because you arranged the files for the JSFReg application in the standard J2EE Web directory structure, packaging them into a **.war** file is simply a matter of packaging the directory structure as is.

Now, change into the JSFReg application's web directory (**C:\JSFReg\web**) and issue the following command to package the entire JSFReg application into the J2EE Web archive **JSFReg.war**.

```
C:\JSFReg\web>jar cf JSFReg.war *
```

After you run the command, a **JSFReg.war** file will be created and be ready for deployment.

Deploying and Running the Application

Once you have packaged your application, running it is as simple as placing the Web Archive file into Tomcat's **webapps** directory and then starting up Tomcat. By default, Tomcat starts up on port 8080, thus the server can be accessed at **http://localhost:8080/**. To access the JSFReg application, point your browser to **http://localhost:8080/JSFReg/**. You'll notice that the name of your Web Archive file is used for the URL of your application. Because you packaged the application in a file called **JSFReg.war**, **/JSFReg/** is used in the application's URL.

When you first access the **http://localhost:8080/JSFReg/** URL, **index.jsp** will be run, and it will automatically forward to the JSF-enabled page at **/faces/main.jsp**. At this point you can click on the link to proceed to the registration page.

Reviewing the Key Portions of the Application

Before moving on to the more advanced features of JavaServer Faces technology, let's quickly review the core areas of JavaServer Faces discussed in the process of building the JSFReg application.

A JSF application is essentially a standard J2EE Web application but with the following specific aspects:

- A specific configuration in the **web.xml** that specifies the Faces Controller servlet and its url-pattern.
- A **faces-config.xml** configuration file for storing navigation rules, and references to managed beans and other JSF components.
- A set of required runtime libraries (jar files) that must be in the classpath upon compilation and placed in the Web application's **WEB-INF\lib** directory for deployment to J2EE application servers.

In building this example application you have seen that basic JSF development is a straightforward process, which typically involves:

- Building java classes and adding them as JSF managed beans
- Creating JSP pages to contain JSF UI component tags that are bound to the managed bean's properties and methods
- Defining a set of navigation rules

The JSFReg example used the Standard HTML UI components provided in the JSF Reference Implementation to build a registration form with different types of input fields, menus, and buttons that were bound to a managed bean's properties and methods. For JSFReg we specified both built-in validation and data conversion for the input fields. A custom validation method was also built and associated with an e-mail input field to validate an e-mail address. Finally, we devised a basic navigation model and bound the command buttons and links to these navigation cases.

Now that you have seen a complete, working example, you should have a solid understanding of the basic structure of a JSF application. It's now time to move on to more advanced aspects of JavaServer Faces.

The JavaServer Faces Request Processing Lifecycle

The preceding chapter presented a simple example of a JavaServer Faces application and introduced many of the practical aspects of JSF. However, there is one key aspect of JSF that will prove invaluable in progressing to more advanced JSF development: the *request processing lifecycle.* The request processing lifecycle serves as the "behind-the-scenes" engine that makes JavaServer Faces possible. This chapter examines the key concepts behind the JavaServer Faces request processing lifecycle and explains how it processes Web requests in a well-defined, event-based manner. A thorough understanding of the request processing lifecycle is important because its various phases will be referred to numerous times in later chapters where more advanced JSF development topics are covered.

A High-Level Overview of the JSF Request Processing Lifecycle

Historically, the bulk of the development required for a Web application has been devoted to processing HTTP requests from Web clients. As the Web transformed from a traditional, static document delivery model in which static Web pages were simply requested without parameters to a dynamic environment with Web applications processing numerous incoming parameters, the need to process increasingly complex requests has grown substantially. This has resulted in Web application development becoming rather tedious. For example, consider the following code used in either a Java servlet or a JSP scriptlet to process the incoming request parameters **firstname** and **lastname**:

```
String firstname = request.getParameter("firstname");
String lastname = request.getParameter("lastname");
// Do something with firstname and lastname
```

Now, consider that most advanced Web applications today process hundreds if not thousands of parameters and you'll see how this approach to processing parameters can easily become quite cumbersome.

As any experienced Web developer knows, writing code to process incoming request parameters usually involves the following:

- Writing code to perform validation and conversion to server-side data types on the incoming data as well as initiating error messages when validation/conversion fails.
- Writing code to update server-side data objects with the new data.
- Writing code to invoke any server-side applications that perform tasks such as issuing queries on a database.
- Writing code to render a response back to the client.

Fortunately, this is what the request processing lifecycle performs automatically in a consistent, event-based manner.

EXPERT GROUP INSIGHT *Of all the elements of JavaServer Faces that the Expert Group debated, the request processing lifecycle was the one that had the most input from the widest range of members and evolved the most over the development of the 1.0 specification. For example, initially, the view description was required to be in a separate XML file, in addition to the JSP page. This requirement was lifted with the invention of the* **ViewHandler** *class, which came about during discussions of the lifecycle.*

What Exactly Does the Request Processing Lifecycle Do?

In short, the request processing lifecycle performs all of the necessary back-end processing for which one would otherwise have to write his or her own code. In addition to processing incoming request parameters, it also manages a server-side set of UI components and synchronizes them to what the user sees in a client browser.

How Does It Differ from Other Web Technologies?

In contrast to other more traditional Web technologies, ranging from CGI and Java servlets to frameworks like Struts, the request processing lifecycle performs a majority of the common server-side Web development tasks automatically in a well-defined, event-based way.

With frameworks such as Jakarta Struts, where some of the request processing is more formalized in code with Form Beans and Struts Actions, the actual processing of the data is still done at a lower level compared to JSF. The Struts programming model provides less of an abstraction from the servlet API than that provided by JSF. For example, in Struts, you can define a Form Bean that represents the properties of your submitted form:

```
<form-bean name="loginbean" type="org.apache.struts.action.DynaActionForm">
  <form-property name="userid" type="java.lang.String"/>
  <form-property name="password" type="java.lang.String"/>
</form-bean>
```

Once defined, you can access the field values in your application, as shown here:

```
String userid = (String)((DynaActionForm)form).get("userid");
```

This is very similar to what you can do with JSF; however, with Struts you don't have the ability to *bind* the field properties directly to properties of Java classes and have their values synchronized automatically upon form submissions.

Automatic Server-Side View Management and Synchronization

As shown in Figure 3-1, the JSF request processing lifecycle's ability to automatically synchronize server-side Java Bean properties to a hierarchical set of components that are based on the UI presented to the client user is a major advantage over other Web technologies.

Since the Web is inherently stateless—that is, where one transaction between a client and server has no memory of the previous transaction—JavaServer Faces solves this problem by automatically maintaining a server-side *View* that exactly represents the current state of the client. This allows the JSF developer to focus on the server-side components, letting the request processing lifecycle, or "plumbing," take care of the synchronization of the server-side View, and what is presented in the client browser. The often-tedious job of writing code to handle each individual request value or change in state of the UI is handled automatically by the JavaServer Faces request processing lifecycle through a set of *phases* during which specific tasks are performed to process the data in a consistent manner.

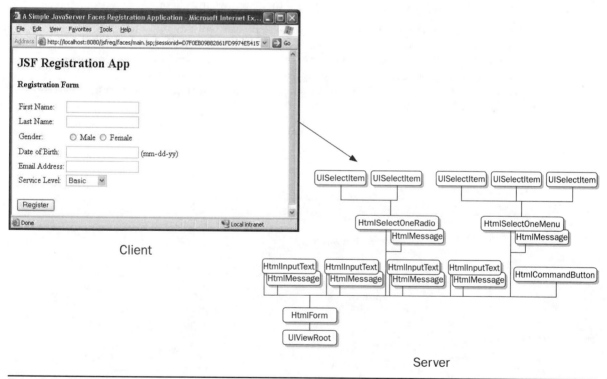

FIGURE 3-1 A server-side representation of the client's UI

What Are the Request Processing Lifecycle Phases?

The processing of incoming request data often requires different types of jobs, including: checking if the incoming data is valid, triggering server-side application logic to fulfill the request, and finally rendering the response to the client. The JSF request processing lifecycle performs these tasks in a consistent order and is governed by a set of well-defined phases. This approach allows each phase to clearly state the preconditions that exist before executing the phase, and the post conditions that exist after it is executed.

Here are the lifecycle phases:

- **Restore View**   Restores or creates a server-side component tree (View) in memory to represent the UI information from a client.

- **Apply Request Values**   Updates these server-side components with fresh data from the client.

- **Process Validations**   Performs validation and data type conversion on the new data.

- **Update Model Values**   Updates any server-side Model objects with new data.

- **Invoke Application**   Invokes any application logic needed to fulfill the request and navigate to a new page if needed.

- **Render Response**   Renders a response to the requesting client.

Figure 3-2 shows a high-level view of how these phases work together to form the request processing lifecycle. As you can see, it performs all the tasks for processing incoming data in a Web application. We'll be referring to the different events and phases in this figure throughout the rest of this chapter, and throughout the book.

Now, let's drill down and examine exactly what happens during the processing of each lifecycle phase.

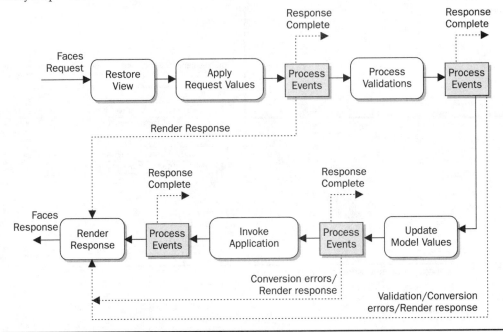

Figure 3-2   The JavaServer Faces request processing lifecycle

Restore View

As previously mentioned, the Faces View is a server-side tree of UI components that provides a mirror representation of the user interface presented in a client. (See Figure 3-3.) It is the job of the *Restore View* phase to either restore an existing View from a previous transaction or create a fresh View based on a new request. If the request is a new one ("non-postback"), a new View is created and will be stored in a parent container object known as the **FacesContext**. The **FacesContext** serves as storage for all of the data pertinent to the current request's run through the request processing lifecycle. Web developers needn't worry about application data in the **FacesContext** being accidentally mixed from multiple user requests because the servlet API guarantees that operations on a request are thread-safe—that is, all operations on the **FacesContext** are guaranteed to occur on a single thread, per user request.

Apply Request Values

After the View has been restored, the next phase, known as the *Apply Request Values* phase, performs the job of processing the incoming request values or name-value pairs of information. Each UI component node in the View hierarchy is now able to take on the updated values sent by the client as shown in Figure 3-4.

Behind the scenes, the JSF runtime applies request values to UI components by calling a high-level method (**processDecodes()**) on the View (or **UIViewRoot**) of the UI component tree. This causes all of the child components to call their **processDecodes**() methods recursively. As you will see in Chapter 10, the **processDecodes()** method, or more specifically the **decode()** method of UI components, is the method that allows the component to "decode" the incoming request name-value pairs and apply a matching new incoming value to the **value** attribute of the UI component.

It should be pointed out that only UI components that are capable of holding a value (such as an input field) can have new values applied to them. In general, there are two types of components: those that have values, such as text fields, checkboxes, and labels; and those that cause actions, such as buttons and links. All components that have a **value** attribute implement the **ValueHolder** interface. All form element type components that have values that are editable by the user implement the **EditableValueHolder** interface. All components that cause actions (buttons or links) implement the **ActionSource** interface.

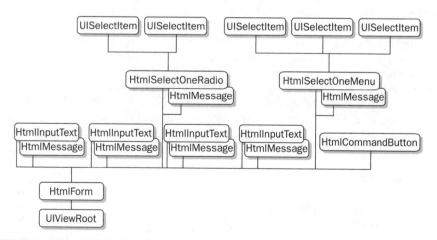

Figure 3-3 The server-side UI component tree, also known as the "View"

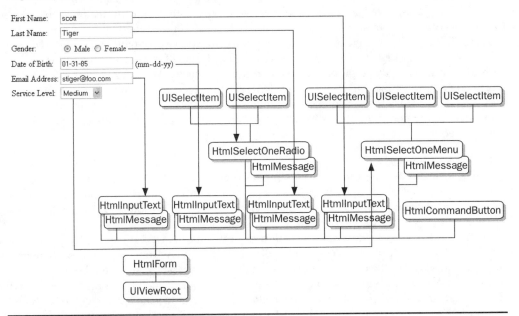

FIGURE 3-4 Applying the request values

JSF 1.2 TIP *For JSF 1.2, action components implement the ActionSource2 interface instead of ActionSource. ActionSource2 extends from JSF 1.1's ActionSource and allows for usage of 1.2's new Unified EL. Details on 1.2's Unified EL is provided in Chapter 4.*

For example, a button (**UICommand** or any component that implements **ActionSource**) doesn't get updated with a new value during form submission; it just needs to record whether or not it was clicked on. If clicked, this results in an event, called an action event (**ActionEvent**), being queued. Later you'll see exactly what an action event is and how it allows for execution of custom code that corresponds to a button or link click.

Although the request processing lifecycle processes the different phases in a consistent manner, the execution order of the phases can be altered for special cases. For example, you may want to add a Cancel button to a form. When clicked, it will skip all validation and simply navigate to another page without processing the values in a form. To alter the processing order of the request processing lifecycle, simply set the **immediate** attribute on a component. As described later in this chapter, setting the **immediate** attribute causes a different effect on different components.

Process Validations

Once the Apply Request Values phase is completed, the *Process Validations* phase, where conversion and validation of the incoming data occurs, is performed. (Data type conversion and validation is explained in detail in Chapter 7.) The JSF runtime initiates this phase by calling a master **processValidators()** method (on the **UIViewRoot** instance), which is similar to the **processDecodes()** method in that it recursively propagates down the component tree calling each component's **processValidators()** method. When each component's **processValidators()** method is called, any converter or validator associated with the component will be invoked.

NOTE *Data type conversion actually occurs before validation but is still initiated in the same Process Validations phase. This is needed because in order to perform a validation, the data must first be converted to its server-side data type.*

As you saw in the JSFReg example in Chapter 2, UI components can have validators and converters associated with them in several ways. In the example, a validation requirement was associated with some of the components either by setting an attribute of the component itself (such as setting the **required** attribute to "true" for an inputText component) or by registering custom validation code (such as when the e-mail validation method was attached to the component by setting its **validator** attribute). The example in Chapter 2 also had a converter associated with the "date of birth" (dob) **inputText (UIInput)** component by inserting a **convertDateTime** converter tag as a child of the input component.

Any component failing validation (or conversion) will have its valid property set to "false" and a **FacesMessage** will be queued onto the **FacesContext** as shown in Figure 3-5. Later, when the response is rendered back to the user (in the *Render Response* phase), the messages can be displayed using the Faces **Message** or **Messages** component so the user can correct and re-submit.

Update Model Values

Assuming the incoming data has passed validation and conversion it is now time for the data to be promoted and assigned to any Model objects that have been *value bound* to the UI component. Again, recall the example in Chapter 2. In it, we created a Java class, **UserBean**, which was registered as a managed bean, and bound its properties to the different UI components on the page using JSF Expression Language. It is during the *Update Model Values*

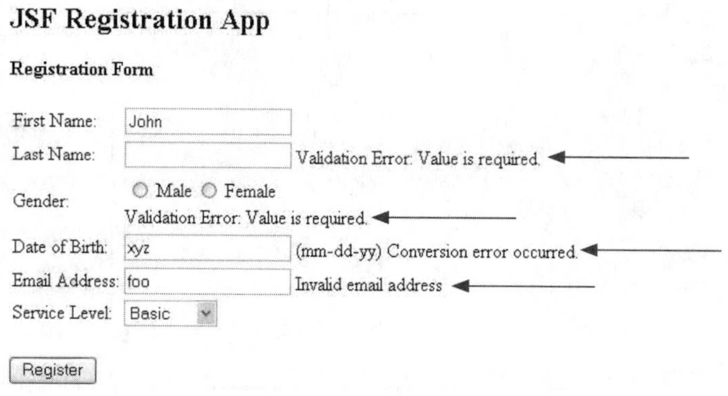

JSF Registration App

Registration Form

First Name:	John	
Last Name:		Validation Error: Value is required. ◄───────
Gender:	○ Male ○ Female	
	Validation Error: Value is required. ◄───────	
Date of Birth:	xyz	(mm-dd-yy) Conversion error occurred. ◄───────
Email Address:	foo	Invalid email address ◄───────
Service Level:	Basic ▾	

[Register]

FIGURE 3-5   Encountering validation and conversion errors in the Process Validations phase

phase when the actual managed bean or Model object's properties are updated with the new values of the UI components to which they were bound.

The actual mechanism behind this is similar to the other phases where a master **processUpdates()** method is called on the **UIViewRoot** instance and initiates a cascading set of **processUpdates()** component method calls, which in turn call individual **updateModel()** methods for each component of (or extend from) type **UIInput**. This is logical since **UIInput** type components (i.e., input fields, select menus) are the only type of components that can pass user input value on to a model property. As shown in Figure 3-6, at the end of this phase, any value-bound properties of any Model objects (managed beans) are updated with the new values from the components. This phase accounts for part of the magic of JavaServer Faces in that once you've bound your JavaBeans properties to a set of JSF UI components, they will be updated automatically without requiring any manual coding.

Invoke Application

So far you've seen how the JSF request processing lifecycle performs the job of taking incoming data from a Web request, validates and/or converts it to the appropriate server-side data type, and then assigns it to a model object. For Web developers this is only half of the job of writing Web applications. The other half consists of taking the incoming data and actually doing something with it, such as invoking an external method to process the data. This is where the *Invoke Application* phase comes in.

Recall earlier in this chapter that UI components can either hold values (implement **EditableValueHolder**) or they can be a source of an **ActionEvent** (implement **ActionSource**)

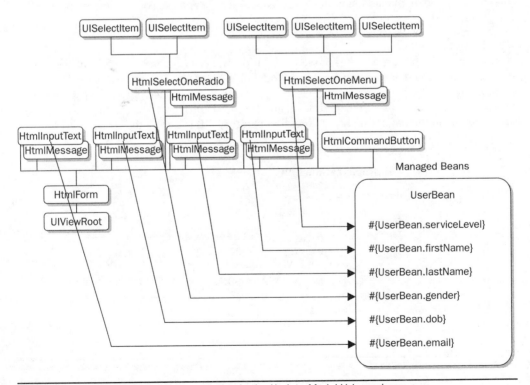

FIGURE 3-6   Updating Model object properties in the Update Model Values phase

such as a when a button (**UICommand**) is clicked. It is during the Invoke Application phase when any custom action code, also known as an *action method* or *action listener method,* is invoked.

Behind the scenes, it is in the Invoke Application phase that the **processApplication()** method of the **UIViewRoot** is called and it broadcasts any queued events for this phase to each **UIComponent** that implements **ActionSource** (or **ActionSource2** for JSF 1.2). This is achieved by calling each **UIComponent**'s **broadcast()** method, which essentially "fires" *action events,* and subsequently any action listeners will process these action events. Custom action methods or action listener methods can be written and bound to **UIComponents** (which implement **ActionSource**) to process action events using a *default action listener.* Writing custom action methods or action listener methods and binding them to **ActionSource** **UIComponents** provides the developer with a hook into the request processing lifecycle where a developer can then call any custom logic. This is illustrated in Figure 3-7.

Chapter 8 will revisit exactly how the JSF event model works and will provide more detail on the exact sequence of how Faces events are processed.

It should be noted that navigations to different pages also occur in the Invoke Application phase. Chapter 5 will review exactly how this occurs by describing a basic *login* application that uses a simple action method that is bound to a *login* (**UICommand**) button. When a user clicks on the button, it fires an action event, which in turn calls the custom action method during the Invoke Application phase to process the login credentials. Remember that this code will only execute if the incoming data has passed the earlier phases where conversion and validation was performed. When login is successful, a navigation to a new page occurs.

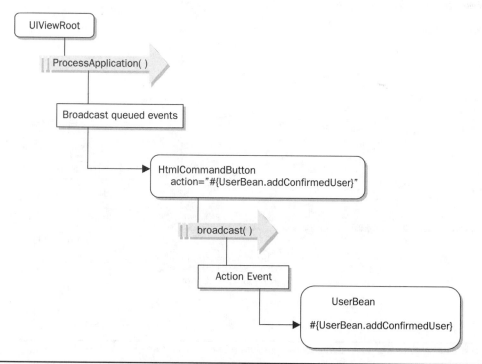

FIGURE 3-7   Invoking custom application logic in the Invoke Application phase

Render Response

Now we come to the final phase of the JSF request processing lifecycle where the response is rendered. To render the entire response back to the client, once again a cascading set of **encodeXX()** methods are called on each component. As you will learn in Chapter 10, encode methods are how UI components (or more specifically, their renderers) render the component to the client. The rendered markup language can be anything, such as HTML, WML, XML, and so on.

In addition to rendering the response to the client, the *Render Response* phase also saves the current state of the View in order to make it accessible and restorable upon subsequent Web requests. Figure 3-8 illustrates how the response has been rendered in a client markup. At this point the current state of the View is saved for future requests.

One other point: There are actually some more intricate, behind-the-scenes details associated with the Render Response phase that go beyond the scope of this chapter. These include: handling situations where static content, also referred to as "template" source, is interleaved with dynamic content from the components; dealing with a variety of dynamic output sources; and collating them together in a single viewable response while preserving the correct ordering. Normally, you won't need to deal with these details when using JSF.

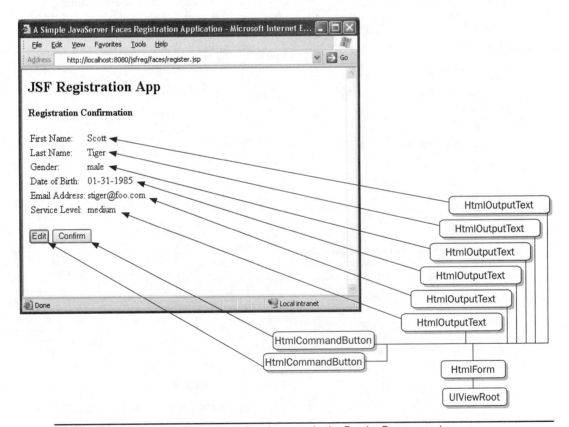

FIGURE 3-8   Rendering the response and saving state in the Render Response phase

JSF 1.2 TIP   *The Render Response phase was significantly redesigned in JSF 1.2 to solve some thorny problems arising from intermixing raw HTML, JSP custom tags, and JSF component tags together in one page. The primary cause for these problems was the requirement to execute the JSP page for rendering and build the component tree while doing so. This requires JSP and JSF to both write to the same output stream, which sometimes caused rendered output to appear in an unexpected ordering. The new approach in JSF 1.2 is to execute the page for the sole purpose of building the tree, not rendering it. Raw HTML/Markup in the page and JSP custom tag output are converted to transient* **UIOutput** *components that are not saved with the state of the page. Thus, after executing the page, the entire contents of the page are represented in the view hierarchy, which is then traversed recursively, just like many other lifecycle phases.*

Observing the Request Processing Lifecycle in Action

Now that you have seen the theory behind each request processing lifecycle phase, it's time to see the lifecycle in action. Recall the JSF Registration (JSFReg) application shown in Chapter 2 and again here in Figure 3-9. We will step through the lifecycle phases as a user interacts with the application and submits the registration form (**register.jsp**).

1. **Initial Request to View the register.jsp Page**   In order to view the registration form page in the first place, a user submits a request to the URL of the register page, which triggers a run through the request processing lifecycle in an abbreviated fashion. The request is processed first by the Faces Controller servlet, which creates a **FacesContext** instance for this request and initiates a call to the lifecycle. Since this is an initial request (also referred to as a "non-postback" request) to view the registration page, the Restore View phase creates an empty View (**UIViewRoot**) component tree and stores it in the **FacesContext** instance.

FIGURE 3-9   **register.jsp**: the registration page of the JSFReg application

After the View is created, the lifecycle immediately proceeds directly to the Render Response phase since there was no incoming field data in the request to validate or process (also referred to as a "non-postback" request). It is during this phase when the empty View component tree is populated with the components that are referenced in the source of the registration page and represent the input fields and submit button. Once the tree is populated, the components then render themselves to the client. At the same time, the state of the View component tree is saved for future requests. The user now sees the registration page rendered in a browser.

2. **User Enters Invalid Data in the Registration Page**   Let's say the user forgets to enter his last name and also enters the wrong format for the date, and then clicks Register (as illustrated in Figure 3-10).

As the JSF runtime receives the request, it enters the initial Restore/Create View phase and this time it restores the earlier View component tree that was saved after the user's previous request. This is commonly referred to as a "postback" because the HTTP method for this request is POST since it is "posting" new form data. The Apply Request Values phase is then entered and the components are updated with the incoming values from the request even though they may not be fully valid yet. No errors occur here because each UI component simply stores the *submitted values* as **String** values of the request parameter, not the actual converted (server-side data type) or validated value. The UI component stores this in a special pre-converted/validated **submittedValue** JavaBean property, which literally stores the **String** value of a request parameter.

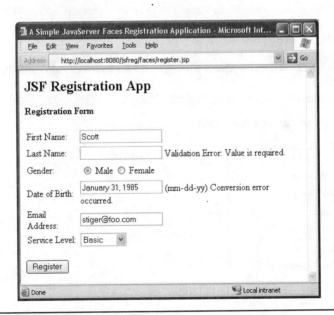

FIGURE 3-10   Entering invalid data in the registration page

As the Apply Request Values phase completes, the Process Validations phase is initiated. At this point a conversion error occurs when the incoming date value cannot be converted to a **java.util.Date** data type, which corresponds to the managed bean **UserBean**'s "dob" property, because of its invalid format. A message is queued, the component is marked invalid, and the processing continues. The remaining valid field values are applied to their respective UI components.

As each UI component has its validate method called, the component that is supposed to be holding the **lastName** value encounters a validation error because no value was supplied in the postback request. Recall that we set the "required" attribute of the Last Name input field to "true." As a result of the validation error, the lifecycle sets the state of the **lname** (last name) **UIInput** component to invalid and queues the appropriate Faces message indicating that the field requires a value. At this point the Process Validations phase is complete.

Because there were validation and conversion errors, the lifecycle jumps directly to the Render Response phase, which then renders the same registration page (**register.jsp**) with the appropriate error messages next to the last name field and the date field. Recall that individual Message components were assigned to each input field component by assigning their IDs, as shown here:

```
<h:inputText value="#{UserBean.lastName}" required="true" id="lname"/>
<h:message for="lname"/>
```

In addition to rendering a response to the client, the Render Response phase also saves the View component tree for future requests.

3. **User Corrects Validation Errors and Resubmits the Form**   Upon seeing the error messages in the response, the user corrects the form by supplying a last name and entering a properly formatted date value and re-submits. This time, as the request is processed, the Restore View phase restores the saved View tree and proceeds to the Apply Request Values phase where the new values are applied to the View component tree. The phase transitions to the Process Validations phase where this time no validation or conversion errors are encountered. The Update Model Values phase is then triggered. At this point, the managed bean's (**UserBean**) properties are now updated with the new values that were submitted in the form, as illustrated in Figure 3-11.

Once the Update Model Values phase completes, the next phase that is triggered is the Invoke Application phase. Recall that the Invoke Application phase provides a way for JSF developers to invoke any custom logic. For example, the application may need to execute code to query a database. The way this is performed is through action methods, which are invoked during the Invoke Application phase, but only if any action events are in the queue, such as when a button or link is clicked. With the JSFReg example, an action event is queued when the Register button is clicked, but since the **action** attribute of the Register button (**UICommand** component) is hard-coded to the literal value "register," no custom action method will be invoked and the Invoke Application phase completes. At this point the navigation handler processes the action event, and a navigation will occur. The result of the navigation event will then be displayed in the final Render Response phase.

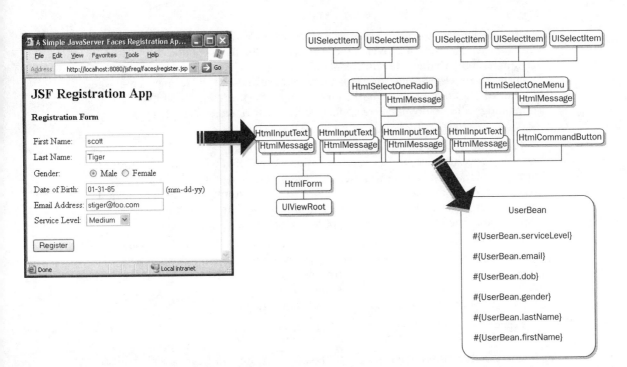

FIGURE 3-11   Updating the **UserBean** Model object with the validated values

Let's review that again. Once the registration page has successfully passed validation and the **UserBean** managed bean has been updated with the values submitted in the form, the lifecycle comes to the Render Response phase, where a formatted response needs to be sent back to the user. At this point, the response to be sent back to the client has to be determined. As we'll cover more extensively in Chapter 5, the navigation handler is responsible for determining whether to simply respond with the same page, or to *navigate* to a new page. Recall that the JSFReg example has an **action** attribute hardcoded to "register" and since this corresponds to a navigation rule (case) defined in the **faces-config.xml** file, a response will be rendered of the new page being navigated to (**confirm.jsp**). Remember that if either the registration button did not have its **action** attribute set or there was no corresponding navigation rule, the response rendered would simply be the same page and no navigation would occur. Figure 3-12 illustrates how the **NavigationHandler** uses the rules defined in the **faces-config.xml** to determine if a navigation is needed.

NOTE *A detailed description of the Faces Navigation Model is provided in Chapter 5.*

Advanced Topics Related to the Request Processing Lifecycle

Now that you've seen how the JSF request processing lifecycle works under default circumstances for a basic form, let's look at some of the slightly more complex examples.

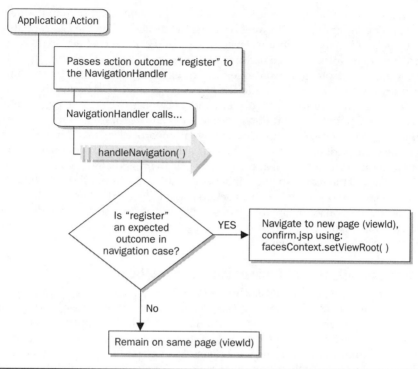

FIGURE 3-12   Rendering a response based on the outcome of an action in the Invoke Application phase

Using the immediate Attribute

This next section covers an extremely important feature of Faces known as the **immediate** attribute, which allows for more flexibility in how the lifecycle executes.

Processing Action Events Immediately

Suppose you want to add a Cancel button to the registration page so that clicking on the button would immediately route users back to the **main.jsp** page regardless of what was entered in the form. To implement this functionality, you have to add both a navigation rule that returns back to the main page and put a button or link component onto the page with an action set to the **from-outcome** of the navigation rule "cancel." Here is the new navigation rule in the **faces-config.xml**:

```
<navigation-rule>
  <from-view-id>/register.jsp</from-view-id>
    <navigation-case>
      <from-outcome>cancel</from-outcome>
      <to-view-id>/main.jsp</to-view-id>
    </navigation-case>
</navigation-rule>
```

Here is the new Cancel button added to the Register page with the hardcoded **action** set to "cancel":

```
<h:commandButton value="Cancel" action="cancel" />
```

However, if we stop here, we'll quickly run into a problem! As shown in Figure 3-13, if you tried running the application again but immediately clicked on the Cancel button, you would get stuck. This happens because even though you are just clicking on the Cancel button with an empty form, it is still handled as a "postback" request, meaning that the JSF lifecycle commences to process an assumed incoming set of name-value pairs from the form. But since the form is empty, validation errors are encountered before the navigation handler can process the "cancel" action event and a response of the same page is rendered back to the client. Obviously, a solution is needed that allows for exceptions to the normal flow of the lifecycle processing. This is exactly what JSF provides in its **immediate** attribute.

If an **immediate** attribute is added to the Cancel button (or any **UICommand** component) and its value is set to "true," it will allow the lifecycle to immediately bypass any validation and navigate back to the **main.jsp** page. In general, setting the **immediate** attribute to "true" on a **UICommand** component triggers an action event to be fired immediately during the Apply Request Values phase before the Process Validations phase so no validation errors are encountered. This has the effect of "short-circuiting" the lifecycle to avoid validation and cancel updating any values to the model.

Processing Validations and Conversions Immediately

Components that implement the **EditableValueHolder** interface (like an input field) have the option of having their validations and conversions performed immediately during the Apply Request Values phase or during the usual Process Validations phase, depending on the value of the **immediate** attribute supplied. If the value is "true," then validation and conversion occur immediately for that component. More importantly, having the **immediate** attribute set to "true" allows the component to be updated with a new validated value

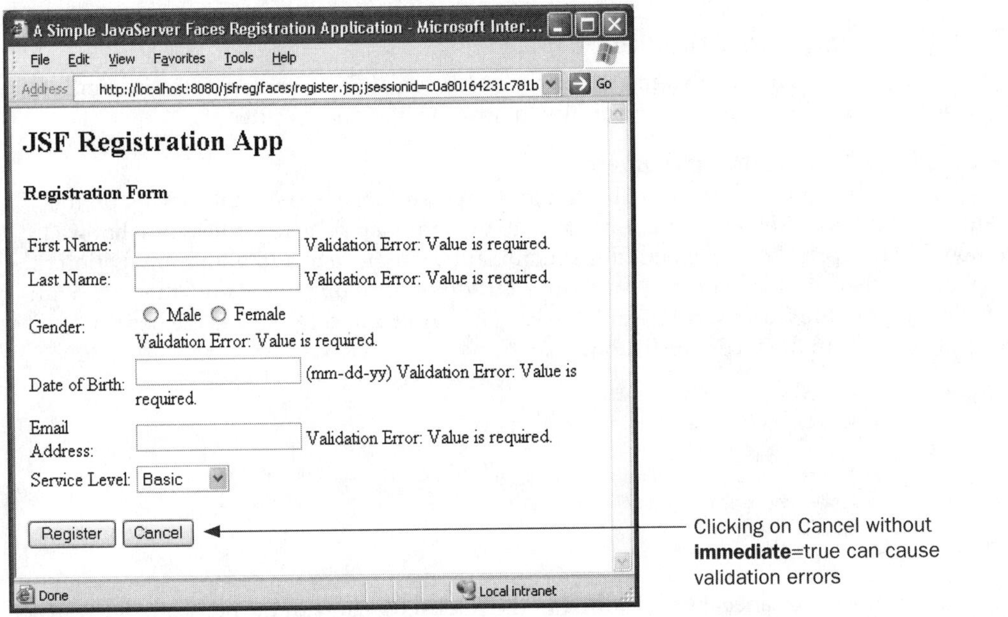

FIGURE 3-13   Getting stuck on a page because of validation errors

before entering the Process Validations phase where the rest of the validations will occur for non-**immediate** components. This is useful when performing UI-only modifications, such as enabling an input field to be editable without submitting and validating the entire data in a form.

In Chapter 8 you'll find more detailed coverage of how to modify UI properties without validating the contents in a form using the **immediate** property and *value change listeners*.

Expert Group Insight *The* **immediate** *attribute was initially present only on the* **ActionSource** *interface, but was added to the* **EditableValueHolder** *interface to enable the scenario where an input component is intended strictly to cause a change to happen in the UI, such as when a checkbox causes the UI to render differently if checked.*

Phase Listeners

There are times when you need code to execute at exact times within the request processing lifecycle. For example, you may want to double-check something within your View component tree before continuing on to the next phase. JavaServer Faces provides an easy way to do this by allowing for the development of custom Faces components known as phase listeners. In short, phase listeners provide a simple way to execute custom Java code at distinct points within the different phases of the lifecycle. For example, you may want to customize an error message based on a value supplied dynamically at runtime, or you may want to verify that a database connection has been established for this session ahead of processing the postback lifecycle.

Building a phase listener is simply a matter of writing a Java class that implements the **PhaseListener** interface. In the class you specify in which phase you want the code to execute along with the actual code you want to execute at this point in time. To add the phase listener to the JSF application it must be registered in **faces-config.xml**, or programmatically registered on the lifecycle instance.

Examples of building phase listeners are provided in both Chapter 8 and Chapter 11.

Lifecycle Concepts to Remember

This chapter has touched on a lot of areas in a fairly rapid way, but JSF developers needn't worry about having to understand every single item presented in this chapter before they can begin building JSF applications. Instead, new JSF developers can appreciate the JSF request processing lifecycle at a high level, understanding that it does most of the typically tedious (form processing) work for them. More advanced JSF developers and aspiring JSF component developers will find that the concepts covered in this chapter provide a solid foundation for moving on to the more advanced topics, including custom component development.

Before concluding this chapter, here are some key request processing lifecycle concepts to take into the rest of the book:

1. *The Faces request processing lifecycle does the "busy work" for you.*   In fact, that is why it was implemented—to take the tedious work of processing request parameter values out of Web application development and let the developer focus more on the application logic.

2. *New JSF developers needn't know every single detail of the lifecycle to build simple JSF applications.*   Thinking that you have to understand all of the details of the JSF lifecycle is kind of like thinking that in order to drive a car you must understand exactly how an engine works. For most drivers, simply knowing that your car occasionally needs gasoline is sufficient. However, having some understanding of how an engine works can often come in handy if a breakdown occurs or if you want to make modifications to improve engine performance.

3. *However, having a firm understanding of the request processing lifecycle provides a great foundation for advanced JSF development.*   As you progress from building JSF applications to building custom JSF components, you'll find that having a complete understanding of the entire request processing lifecycle is extremely helpful so that you will have a complete understanding of what is occurring behind the scenes at all times.

Managed Beans and the JSF Expression Language

Before server-side Java development was the norm, Java developers were fully responsible for instantiating and managing the properties of every single Java class or Java Bean in their application. This was perfectly logical because applications in the early days of Java were not multi-tiered, so all the logic for the entire application resided in the application developer's domain, often in a single virtual machine (VM).

As Java matured into more of a server-side oriented, distributed application technology, lightweight Java server containers have become prevalent because the actual plumbing needed to deliver a server-oriented application is beyond the scope of the application developer. This is what has led to the notion of *Inversion of Control* (IoC), where the container takes control of managing a portion of the application's Java Beans or Plain Old Java Objects (POJOs) so the application developer needn't write all the often-repetitive code to manage them. Inversion of control is sometimes referred to as *dependency injection* because one of the main benefits is the ability to have POJOs pre-populated with values through a declarative configuration syntax.

Because the JavaServer Faces framework runs entirely on a server in a servlet/JSP container, it is only natural that JSF comes equipped with a robust ability to offer Inversion of Control, where management of server-side Java Beans can be done in a highly efficient and mostly automated fashion. This is exactly what JSF provides with its Managed Beans Facility.

In the previous chapters we touched on the basics of how to register managed beans in simple applications. In this chapter we will examine in detail precisely how JSF provides an IoC-enabled container in its Managed Beans Facility, which enables you to fully leverage its strengths.

This chapter will also cover JSF's expression language (EL) in detail because the EL is the easiest way to access and manipulate managed beans and bind them to UI components in the View. The chapter concludes with important Web development information with regards to managed beans by showing how to access and work on managed beans programmatically and by introducing the *backing bean* concept as well as providing a few helpful hints on how to manage backing beans and pages.

What Are Managed Beans?

JavaServer Faces managed beans are essentially POJOs that store application data and are managed by the container. They are registered with the JSF runtime via an XML file and are lazily initialized at runtime when needed by the application. Any Java class (POJO) with a public, no-argument constructor that conforms to the Java Beans naming conventions for properties can be registered as a managed bean. Objects of type **java.util.List** and **java.util .Map** can also be registered as managed beans.

A Simple Managed Bean Example

Consider again from Chapter 2 the **UserBean** class, which holds the registration information of a new user. As you recall, **UserBean** was made available to a Faces application by registering it in the faces configuration file (**faces-config.xml**) using the following form:

```
<managed-bean>
   <managed-bean-name>userBean</managed-bean-name>
   <managed-bean-class>com.jsfcompref.register.UserBean</managed-bean-class>
   <managed-bean-scope>session</managed-bean-scope>
</managed-bean>
```

In this example, the class **com.jsfcompref.register.UserBean** is registered as a managed bean named "userBean" and has its scope set to **session**. The scope of a bean determines its lifetime. Scope settings are discussed later in this chapter. To access properties or methods of managed beans, you will use a compact, simple-to-use *expression language*, which will also be explained later in this chapter.

For example, to display the current value of the **firstName** property of **UserBean** in a JSF page, you can use an **<h:outputText>** tag (**UIOutput** component) and set its **value** attribute with the following JSF expression #{*userBean.firstName*}:

```
<h:outputText value="#{userBean.firstName}" />
```

At runtime, the JSF expression allows the value of the **firstName** property to be displayed in the page. As we'll review later in the chapter, the JSF expression language allows for a shorthand way to call the **getFirstName()** method of **UserBean** and display its value in the page using the **<h:outputText>** tag.

Recall that in addition to displaying the current properties of a managed bean, properties can also be updated if the managed bean has setter methods for those properties. To update properties of a managed bean, you can bind a property of the bean to a UI component that accepts an input value (implements **EditableValueHolder**) such as **UIInput**. Recall again the registration form used the **UIInput** component (with the JSP tag **<h:inputText>**) with its **value** attribute set with a JSF expression to accept the registrant's input values.

```
<h:inputText value="#{userBean.firstName}" />
```

In general, during a form submission (postback), the JSF request processing life cycle updates managed bean properties with new property values from **UIInput** components. In this example, it causes the **setFirstName()** method on **UserBean** to be called. More advanced uses of the JSF expression language will be provided later in the chapter.

Table 4-1 shows the basic elements used in a managed bean registration.

Initializing Managed Bean Properties

So far you have seen how to register a simple managed bean and relied on a JSF application to display or update bean properties. However, it is also possible to supply initial values to managed beans by providing additional information in the managed bean entry in the Faces configuration file. To do so, you will use the **<managed-property>** element.

Element	Description
<managed-bean>	Parent element of a managed bean in the Faces configuration file.
<description>	Description of the purpose of the managed bean. (Optional)
<display-name>	A display name of the managed bean. Intended for possible development tool usage. (Optional)
<icon>	Icon associated with this managed bean. Also intended for development tool usage. (Optional)
<managed-bean-name>	The published name of the managed bean. JSF expression language uses this name.
<managed-bean-class>	The fully qualified class name of the Java class being registered as a managed bean.
<managed-bean-scope>	The scope under which the newly instantiated bean will be registered. Can be: **none**, **request**, **session** or **application**.

TABLE 4-1   Elements Needed for a Basic Managed Bean Declaration

For example, to initialize the **firstName** and **lastName** properties of the **userBean** managed bean, you can add the following to the configuration:

```
<managed-bean>
  <managed-bean-name>userBean</managed-bean-name>
  <managed-bean-class>com.jsfcompref.register.UserBean</managed-bean-class>
  <managed-bean-scope>session</managed-bean-scope>
  <managed-property>
    <property-name>firstName</property-name>
    <value>Jane</value>
  </managed-property>
  <managed-property>
    <property-name>lastName</property-name>
    <value>Doe</value>
  </managed-property>
</managed-bean>
```

This has the effect of executing the setter methods for the **firstName** and **lastName** properties just after the bean is instantiated by the Faces life cycle. At runtime the registration form in the **register.jsp** page would no longer appear completely empty. As shown in Figure 4-1, the input fields bound to the pre-initialized properties will now appear with values upon an initial (non-postback) request.

Table 4-2 illustrates the elements required for initializing simple managed bean properties. A managed bean can have 0 to N sets of **<managed-property>** element trees.

In addition to initializing simple properties, managed beans containing **java.util.List** or **java.util.Map** properties can also be registered and initialized as managed properties. This is done by using either the **<list-entries>** or **<map-entries>** elements in a managed property definition.

FIGURE 4-1 An initial request of the registration page with pre-initialized **lastName** and **firstName**

Element	Description
<managed-property>	Parent element for managed property element tree. Is a child of a **<managed-bean>**.
<description>	A description of the managed property. (Optional)
<display-name>	A managed property display name. Intended for development tool usage. (Optional)
<property-name>	The case-sensitive name of the bean property to be initialized.
<property-class>	Used to specify the type of the property. The type specified can be either a primitive or a fully qualified class type. For example, the **String** class could have been specified with **<property-class>java.lang.String</property-class>** in the previous managed property example. However, in most cases this is not needed, as the Faces runtime is able to infer the correct data type. (Optional)
<value> or <null-value>	The **<value>** element provides the value with which to set the property. This value is taken as a **String** value and is converted to the corresponding data type of the property, prior to setting it to this value. When initializing a property to a **null** value, a **<null-value>** tag is used instead. Note: The **<null-value>** element cannot be used for primitive data types.

TABLE 4-2 The Managed Properties Elements

Initializing List Properties

For managed beans with a property of type **array** or of **java.util.List**, the <list-entries> element can initialize values for the list. Consider a slight augmentation to the registration example from Chapter 2 where **UserBean** now contains a **java.util.List** property named **sportsInterests**. In keeping with the overall sports theme presented in the Virtual Trainer example application in Chapter 9, the **sportsInterests** list could keep track of the different types of sports that this user may be interested in training for.

Here is how to initialize a set of sports for this user by using a managed property for a **List**.

```
<managed-bean>
...
  <managed-property>
    <property-name>sportsInterests</property-name>
    <list-entries>
      <value>Cycling</value>
      <value>Running</value>
      <value>Swimming</value>
      <value>Kayaking</value>
    </list-entries>
  </managed-property>
</managed-bean>
```

After initializing the **sportsInterests** property, the list values can be displayed in a JSF page using **<h:dataTable>** (**HtmlDataTable** UI component), as shown here.

```
<h:dataTable value="#{userBean.sportsInterests}" var="row" >
  <h:column>
    <h:outputText value="#{row}"/>
  </h:column>
</h:dataTable>
```

Individual items from the list can also be displayed by using an array style element reference in the JSF expression, like this:

```
<h:outputText value="#{userBean.sportsInterests[0]}"/>
```

The preceding code displays "Cycling" on a JSF page because this was the first value in the **<list-entries>** list.

The different list values shown in the previous example work fine since the default data type for **<list-entries>** is **java.lang.String**. However, if another data type is needed for the list then a **<value-class>** is added as a child to the **<list-entries>** element and is used to specify the data type of the list items.

Consider a new property to the **UserBean** called **racePlacement** where the finishing order is recorded for different racing events. In this example a **java.lang.Integer** type is specified with a **<value-class>** element.

```
<managed-bean>
...
  <managed-property>
    <property-name>racePlacement</property-name>
    <list-entries>
      <value-class>java.lang.Integer</value-class>
```

```
      <value>23</value>
      <value>12</value>
      <value>3</value>
      <value>1</value>
    </list-entries>
  </managed-property>
</managed-bean>
```

In a more generalized form, Table 4-3 shows the elements associated with defining a managed property with **List** entries.

As mentioned before, list entries can also support array type objects. For example, if the following **states** array (and the corresponding getter and setter methods) are added to a managed bean:

```
String states[] ={ "California", "Nevada", "Oregon" };
```

it is then possible to initialize further properties of the managed bean like this:

```
<managed-bean>
...
  <managed-property>
    <property-name>states</property-name>
    <list-entries>
      <value>New York</value>
      <value>Florida</value>
      <value>Texas</value>
    </list-entries>
  </managed-property>
</managed-bean>
```

This also illustrates the fact that although initial values may have been set in the original code, adding additional managed property list items simply adds to the existing list. At runtime the superset of list values will be available to the application.

Element	Description
<managed-property>	Same as before, the parent element for managed properties.
<property-name>	The name of the property, which must be of type **array** or **java.util.List**.
<property-class>	JSF uses the default type of **ArrayList** but any other list concrete class could be specified here.
<list-entries> (1 to N)	Parent element of the <**value-class**>, list values defined in multiple <**value**> or <**null-value**> elements.
<value-class>	When not using the default list type of **java.lang.String**, one must specify the list item data type here. (Optional)
<value> or <null-value>	The <**value**> element provides the value with which to set the property. When initializing a property to a **null** value, a <**null-value**> tag is used instead. Note: The <**null-value**> element cannot be used for primitive data types.

TABLE 4-3   Managed Property Elements for a **List**

Initializing Map Properties

In addition to offering the ability to initialize objects of type **array** and **java.util.List**, the JavaServer Faces Managed Bean Facility also offers a way to initialize managed beans with properties of type **java.util.Map**. Initializing **Map** values is very similar to initializing **List** values. Instead of **<list-entries>** the element **<map-entries>** is used as a parent element of a series of key and value pairs.

Consider an example that uses a **java.util.Map** instead of a **java.util.List** to define a set of **sportsInterests**. In this example, the key could be a short name of the sport such as "cycling," and the actual value could be a more verbose definition of the sport: "Any competitive athletic event where a bicycle is used."

So, for a **Map** version of the **sportsInterest** example, you could use the following to initialize the **Map** values:

```
<managed-bean>
...
  <managed-property>
    <property-name>sportsInterests</property-name>
    <map-entries>
      <map-entry>
        <key>Cycling</key>
        <value>Any competitive athletic event where a
bicycle is used.</value>
      </map-entry>
      <map-entry>
        <key>Running</key>
        <value>Any competitive athletic event where
the competitors are running or jogging.</value>
      </map-entry>
      <map-entry>
        <key>Swimming</key>
        <value>Any competitive athletic event where
the competitors are swimmming.</value>
      </map-entry>
      <map-entry>
        <key>Kayaking</key>
        <value>Any competitive athletic event where
the competitors use a kayak.</value>
      </map-entry>
    </map-entries>
  </managed-property>
</managed-bean>
```

To access the individual **Map** values at runtime, simply use a JSF expression with a key. For example, to access the value associated to the "swimming" key, the following expression can be used.

```
<h:outputText value="#{userBean.sportsInterests['Swimming']}"/>
```

Incidentally, it is possible to display all of the key/value pairs for a **Map** by simply referring to the **Map** in the expression: **#{userBean.sportInterests}**. This causes the entire map to be converted to a single string that contains all keys and values.

A more formalized listing of the elements needed for a managed **Map** property follows in Table 4-4.

Element	Description
<managed-property>	Same as before, the parent element for managed properties.
<property-name>	The name of the property.
<property-class>	JSF uses the default type of **HashMap** but any other **Map** concrete class could be specified here.
<map-entries>	Parent element of <**key-class**>, <**value-class**>, and **Map** entries.
<key-class>	Element specifying data type of the keys used in the map. When not specified, a **java.lang.String** is used as a default. (Optional)
<value-class>	Element specifying data type of the values used in the map. When not specified, a **java.lang.String** is also used as a default. (Optional)
<map-entry>(1 to N)	Parent element to a **Map** key/value element pair.
<key>	The **key** value used to look up an associated **value**.
<value> or <null-value>	The <**value**> element that is retrieved when the associated key is supplied. To initialize a **Map** property to a **null** value, a <**null-value**> tag is used. Note: The <**null-value**> element cannot be used for primitive data types.

TABLE 4-4   Managed Property Elements for a **Map**

In Table 4-4, notice that the type of the key and value are specified by <**key-class**> and <**value-class**>, respectively. However, both are optional, with both defaulting to **java.lang .String**. For this reason, the types of the key and value in the previous example were of the default **String** data type. The next example uses a key class of type **java.lang.Integer**. In this example, the key/value pairs consist of an integer zip code and the string name of the city in which that zip code is found.

```
<managed-bean>
...
  <managed-property>
    <property-name>cityRegistry</property-name>
    <map-entries>
      <key-class>java.lang.Integer</key-class>
      <map-entry>
        <key>94065</key>
        <value>Redwood City</value>
      </map-entry>
      <map-entry>
        <key>95118</key>
        <value>San Jose</value>
      </map-entry>
      <map-entry>
        <key>32801</key>
        <value>Orlando</value>
      </map-entry>
    </map-entries>
  </managed-property>
</managed-bean>
```

Declaring Lists and Maps Directly as Managed Beans

So far we have examined cases where existing beans had certain properties of type **List** or **Map** registered as managed properties. In fact, it is possible to declare brand new **List**s or **Map**s as managed beans entirely from the Faces configuration file. This is achieved by assigning the **<managed-bean-class>** directly as either a **List** or a **Map**.

NOTE *When declaring a managed bean directly as a **List** or a **Map**, you must use the concrete class types—**java.util.ArrayList** or **java.util.HashMap**—since it is impossible to call a constructor on an interface.*

The following example shows a **List** being declared entirely as a managed bean.

```
<managed-bean>
  <managed-bean-name>moreSports</managed-bean-name>
  <managed-bean-class>java.util.ArrayList</managed-bean-class>
  <managed-bean-scope>none</managed-bean-scope>
  <list-entries>
    <value>Skiing</value>
    <value>Tennis</value>
    <value>Rollerblading</value>
  </list-entries>
</managed-bean>
```

Notice that the **<managed-bean-scope>** is set to **none**. This simply means that this managed bean is not stored anywhere. Instead, it is instantiated on the fly whenever needed. The life cycles of managed beans are examined more closely a little later in the chapter, after you have seen how managed beans can be dependent on each other.

Managed Bean Interdependence

One of the most common criteria for IoC containers is that they be able to handle interdependencies between managed objects. The JavaServer Faces Managed Bean Facility does not fall short in this regard. Setting dependencies between managed beans can easily be done using the JSF expression language.

Consider the previous example where we declared a brand new **moreSports** managed bean from scratch that listed a new set of sports as **moreSports**. This list can now be referred in another bean through an expression. For example, you can add the values from the new list to the existing **sportsInterests** managed bean with the final result being a set of values from both lists.

```
<managed-bean>
...
  <managed-property>
    <property-name>sportsInterests</property-name>
    <list-entries>
      <value>Cycling</value>
      <value>Running</value>
      <value>Swimming</value>
      <value>Kayaking</value>
      <value>#{moreSports[0]}</value>
      <value>#{moreSports[1]}</value>
```

```
      <value>#{moreSports[2]}</value>
    </list-entries>
  </managed-property>
</managed-bean>
```

For a more general example of managed bean interdependency, consider a new custom class of type **com.jsfreg.register.Address** that contains **String** properties for **street**, **city** and **zipCode**. It can be registered as an independent managed bean using:

```
<managed-bean>
  <managed-bean-name>addressBean</managed-bean-name>
  <managed-bean-class>com.jsfreg.register.Address</managed-bean-class>
  <managed-bean-scope>none</managed-bean-scope>
</managed-bean>
```

Recall that a scope of **none** means that this bean is not initialized until requested by another managed bean.

Next, you could add two new properties **homeAddress** and **shippingAddress** of type **com.jsfreg.register.Address** to the original **UserBean**. You can then define these properties by using the following code:

```
<managed-bean>
  <managed-bean-name>userBean</managed-bean-name>
  <managed-bean-class>com.jsfreg.register.UserBean</managed-bean-class>
  <managed-bean-scope>session</managed-bean-scope>
  <managed-property>
    <property-name>homeAddress</property-name>
    <value>#{addressBean}</value>
  </managed-property>
  <managed-property>
    <property-name>shippingAddress</property-name>
    <value>#{addressBean}</value>
  </managed-property>
  <managed-property>
    <property-name>firstName</property-name>
  </managed-property>
</managed-bean>
```

As a request is made to a page with an expression of #{**userBean.homeAddress**}, a new instance of **UserBean** is created and stored in the **session** scope. Its properties **homeAddress** and **shippingAddress** will also be initialized as well. Subsequent postback operations could add values to the fields of the respective addresses of type **AddressBean** of the **UserBean**, using expressions that reference the address items:

```
<h:inputText value="#{userBean.homeAddress.street}"/>
```

The next question regarding managed bean interdependence is whether cyclical dependencies are possible with managed beans. Although some other IoC containers can handle cyclical dependencies, this is not the case for JSF managed beans. If two are made dependent on each other, a runtime error will occur.

Setting Managed Properties Using EL

An important point to note is that in addition to offering the ability to establish inter-bean dependencies using EL, it is also possible to set managed properties to any value accessible via EL. For example, the implicit object **param** can be used in an EL expression to set a property. This can be a handy trick that allows the application to assign a property based on an incoming **Request** parameter. As an example, consider if the previous **UserBean** had a property, **userid**, also of type **String**. It could be set as a managed property using a value from the implicit **param** object.

```
<managed-property>
  <property-name>userid</property-name>
  <value>#{param.userid}</value>
</managed-property>
```

In your JSP you could value-bind this property to a UI component:

```
Userid entered:<h:inputText value="#{UserBean.userid}"/>
```

To provide a value, of course, you would have to add the userid value as a request parameter:

```
http://host:port/yourapp/faces/yourpage.jsp?userid=cschalk
```

You can now see that it is possible to declare the entire initial state of your model tier using the managed bean facility. This makes for a very powerful and flexible system.

Controlling Managed Bean Life Spans

Similar to standard JSP, JavaServer Faces provides a way to define the scope of a managed bean instance by using a **scope** setting. A scope defines the lifetime of a bean, and is similar to the concept of scope in the Java language. In contrast to JSP, however, there is no "page" scope because managed beans have to exist and be accessible on postback, which is outside the scope of JSP. As you have seen in previous managed bean examples, the **<managed-bean-scope>** element of a managed bean defines how long the instance of the managed bean will survive. The different managed bean scopes are described in Table 4-5.

EXPERT GROUP INSIGHT   *Note the conspicuous absence of the* **page** *scope, which is present in JSP. This was intentional to avoid introducing any dependency on the JSP specification in the core JSF specification. The main reason for avoiding all such dependencies was to enable alternate page description technologies, aside from JSP, to be used with JSF. This topic is covered in detail in Chapter 12.*

When dealing with managed beans' different scopes, it is important to remember that managed beans can only reference other managed beans whose scope is either **none** or is greater than or equal to the calling bean's scope. This is described in Table 4-6.

A final word on scopes in general: It's best to put your beans in the narrowest scope possible, preferably **request**. Doing so helps prevent memory leaks by allowing the data to be garbage collected frequently, it encourages keeping your design lightweight because putting lots of data into the request each time is costly, and, most importantly, it cuts down on difficult to debug concurrency bugs that can happen when using session and application.

Scope	Description
none	Managed beans with a **none** scope are not instantiated nor stored in the **request**, **session**, or **application** objects. Instead, they are instantiated on demand by another managed bean. Once created, they will persist as long as the calling bean stays alive because their scope will match the calling bean's scope.
request	Managed beans registered with **request** scope will be instantiated and stay available throughout a single HTTP request. This means that the bean can survive a navigation to another page providing it was during the same HTTP request.
session	Managed beans registered with a **session** scope will be stored on the HTTP session. This means that the values in the managed bean will persist beyond a single HTTP request for a single user. This is ideal for a shopping cart type of usage where values must be stored and made available during multiple requests.
application	Managed beans registered with an **application** scope retain their values throughout the lifetime of the application and are available to all users.

TABLE 4-5   JSF Managed Bean Scopes

JSF 1.2 TIP Java EE 5 Annotations are for use in managed beans. There are two kinds of annotations you can use in a JSF managed bean: lifecycle annotations, and data access annotations. Let's discuss the former first.

Any scoped managed bean method annotated with @PostConstruct will be called after the managed bean is instantiated, but before the bean is placed in scope. Such a method must take no arguments, return void, and may not declare a checked exception to be thrown. The method may be public, protected, private, or package private. If the method throws an unchecked exception, the JSF implementation must not put the managed bean into service and no further methods on that managed bean instance will be called. Any scoped managed bean method annotated with @PreDestroy will be called before the bean is removed from the scope or before the scope in which the bean resides is destroyed, whichever comes first. The constraints placed on the method are the same as with @PostConstruct. If the method throws an unchecked exception, the implementation may log it, but the exception will not affect the execution in any way.

The data access annotations are: @Resource, @Resources, @EJB, @EJBs, @WebServiceRef, @WebServiceRefs, @PersistenceContext, @PersistenceContexts, @PersistenceUnit, and @PersistenceUnits. Usage of these annotations are beyond the scope of this book, but the @PersistenceContext annotation is particularly useful in gaining access to the Java Persistence API from your managed beans.

Managed Beans Defined with This Scope:	Can Only Reference Other Managed Beans of This Scope:
none	none
request	none, request, session application
session	none, session, application
application	none, application

TABLE 4-6   Scope Compatibility

The JSF Expression Language

In the preceding examples (and in earlier chapters) you saw how to access managed bean properties and invoke managed bean custom (action) methods using special expressions with delimiters #{ and }. These expressions follow syntactic rules defined by the Expression Language Specification. Let's now take a closer look at the expression language in JavaServer Faces.

One thing to understand at the outset is that there are differences between the expression language for JSF 1.1 and the expresssion language for JSF 1.2. In the following discussion, the key differences between the expression language for JSF 1.1 and JSF 1.2 are described.

Important Expression Languages Changes Between JSF 1.1 and JSF 1.2

The most fundamental difference between JavaServer Faces versions 1.1 and 1.2 is the introduction of the Unified EL Specification. With JSF 1.1, a JSF-specific implementation of EL was created and although very similar to other EL implementations, such as those used by JSP 2.0 and the JSP Standard Tag Library (JSTL), it still had significant differences. Because expression languages had become an increasingly popular and well-utilized technology across the Java Web tier, it was decided to generalize the EL concepts introduced specifically by JSF so that they could be used by a wider set of Java Web-tier technologies. This resulted in the creation of the *Unified EL*.

EXPERT GROUP INSIGHT *The Unified EL is now provided by the JSP 2.1 specification, though it is specified in a separate sub-document in that specification. This was done to facilitate eventually separating the Unified EL out into its own JCP specification for use by the entire Java platform. Also, separating the EL from the specific technology hosting it, such as the Java Web tier, means that several important concepts that were formerly in the domain of the EL, such as the notion of scope, are now outside of the EL proper and reside only in JSP or JSF. Even so, the rest of this discusson will treat these concepts as if they are a part of the core EL.*

JSF 1.1 developers needn't worry about having to change the syntax of their expressions to upgrade to 1.2, because the Unified EL accepts syntax compatible with JSF 1.1. For example, the following still holds true:

- JSF 1.2 expressions still use delimiters #{ and }.

- Expressions starting with #{ are still evaluated at runtime, which is referred to as *deferred evaluation*. Expressions starting with ${ are still evaluated at page compile time and are referred to as *immediate evaluation*.

JSF 1.2 TIP *The JSF 1.1 expression language is upwardly compatible with JSF 1.2.*

Examining the Evolution of the EL: Deferred vs. Immediate Expressions

The EL used in JSF 1.0 and 1.1 is an extension of the EL first used in the JSP Standard Tag Library (JSTL), and later in JSP versions 1.2 and 2.0. The main extension brought to the EL by JSF that is not present in previous versions is the concept of *deferred expressions*. In JSP, any ${} expression that appears in the page is evaluated immediately as the page is rendered. If an expression appears as the value of a JSP tag attribute, such as:

```
<c:set var="name" value="Falstaff" scope="page" />
<demo:customTag value='${pageScope.name}' />
```

then the JavaBeans property named **value** in the **CustomTag.java** tag handler class must have a type that matches the type to which the expression evaluates. Furthermore, the expression **${pageScope.name}** is evaluated immediately when the **demo:customTag** tag is encountered and the **setValue()** method of the **CustomTag.java** tag handler receives the evaluated value.

Immediate evaluation is perfectly adequate for JSP, but JSF needed something more. JSF introduced the request processing lifecycle (described in Chapter 3), which governs what happens when the form is submitted (postback). During a postback, the JSP page that rendered the markup that is being posted back is not known and not available to the JSF runtime, therefore any expressions in that page are not available since they were evaluated immediately when the page was rendered.

JSF introduced the deferred expression concept to allow expressions to be useful both during the rendering of the page, and during a postback. This concept allows a deferred expression, such as **#{user.name}**, to show a value to the user, and also to be the "target" of a value entered by the user. As described earlier, JSF reserves the #{} delimiter to mean "deferred expression" and allows JSP to claim ${} to mean "immediate expression." The #{} delimiter was chosen because it prevents the JSP runtime from evaluating the expression, allowing the JSF JSP Custom Tag handler to create the expression instance and store it in the component for later evaluation.

Figure 4-2 illustrates the evolution of the EL over time. The Unified EL used in JSF 1.2, JSP 2.1, and JSTL 1.2 adds the concept of deferred expression and allows JSP to be aware of deferred and immediate expressions.

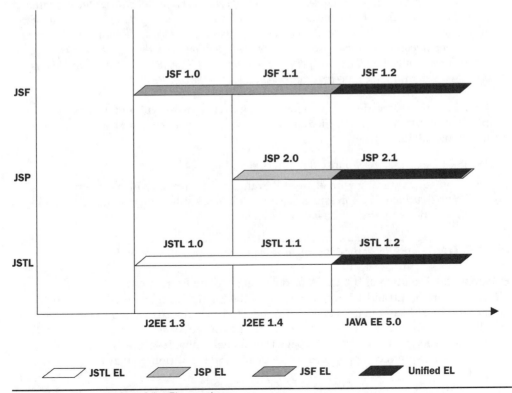

FIGURE 4-2 The evolution of the EL over time

EXPERT GROUP INSIGHT *In keeping with the design goal of being extremely extensible, it is possible to customize the semantics of the EL since the beginning of JSF. For more on how to do so, please see Chapter 12.*

Unified EL Concepts

The goal of having a Unified EL is to provide an easy and compact way to access application objects from any point in the application. A major force behind the need for a compact language to refer to objects was the increased usage of tag attributes in JSP or, in general, XML. Consider a tag with an attribute:

```
<MyTag attribute="value" />.
```

If *value* had to be derived dynamically at runtime, it could necessitate a long Java statement to obtain the value. Expression language provides a solution to this by:

1. Eliminating the need to always refer to container-managed parent objects (**request**, **session**, and **application**).

2. Shortening the expression by omitting **get** and **set** from object properties/methods.

3. Allowing navigation of an arbitrarily complex hierarchy of JavaBeans objects.

Value Expressions

Value expressions (referred to as *Value Binding Expressions* in JSF 1.1) are by far the most common usage of expressions in JSF applications. They allow for presenting (getting) dynamically evaluated results or setting bean properties at runtime using a compact expression. Value expressions can be used to evaluate a single value such as the value of a property of a managed bean or an expression that evaluates a final value from multiple sources including sources outside of Faces managed beans. Recall an expression used in previous examples:

```
<h:outputText value="#{userBean.firstName}"/>
```

The expression **#{userBean.firstName}** is a shorthand way to call the **getfirstName()** method of the **userBean** managed bean. In general, value expressions are evaluated behind the scenes by a **getValue()** method from a **ValueExpression** instance that is provided by the JSF runtime.

What Really Happens When an EL Expression Is Evaluated

As the expression **#{userBean.firstName}** is evaluated at runtime, the EL system breaks the expression down into two parts. The part before the first dot (or square bracket) is called the *base*. In this case, the base is **userBean**. The part after the first dot (or square bracket) is called a *property* and is recursively broken down into smaller parts; in this case it is just **firstName**. Generally, the base says *where to look for the bean instance* and the property parts are interpreted as *beans properties to get* from the base. The first thing the EL does is check if the value of the base is one of the implicit objects (described shortly). In this case, it is not, so the EL sets about looking for **userBean** in progressively wider scopes. It does this by first calling **getAttribute("userBean")** on the **ServletRequest**. Because the **userBean** managed bean was declared in the **session** scope, it is not found in the **ServletRequest**. The EL then calls **getAttribute("userBean")** on the **HttpSession**. In this case, the bean is found, so it is returned. (If the bean had not been found in the session, **getAttribute("userBean")** would have been called on the **ServletContext** for this application.) Once the EL has obtained the base it then proceeds to resolve properties against the base. With **firstName**, the **getFirstName()** method is called on the **UserBean** instance.

In addition to simply displaying dynamically derived values from value expressions, the output of a value expression can also be used to set an attribute of a UI component. A common usage is to set the **rendered** attribute to a value expression that evaluates to a **boolean** value. Consider the example:

```
<h:outputText rendered="#{userBean.manager}" value="#{Employee.salary}"/>
```

Notice the **rendered** attribute is defined with a value expression that derives a **boolean** value (assuming the **manager** field is of type **boolean**) by calling the method **isManager()**. This allows the **UIOutput** component to render conditionally based on whether or not the user is a manager.

Using Value Expressions to Update Model Data

Using expressions to display values in a Web page is nothing new. Indeed, the original EL in early versions of JSTL had this feature. The new feature introduced by JSF is the ability to use an expression to **set** a value when a form is submitted. This means value expressions can be used for updating Model objects. For example, if an input UI component (implements **EditableValueHolder**) is value bound to a managed bean property (Model object), upon postback the bean property will take on the updated value applied to the UI component. This occurs during the Update Model Values phase of the JSF request processing life cycle. Recall the input example from earlier in the chapter:

```
<h:inputText value="#{userBean.firstName}"/>
```

During a postback, if the value in the input field has changed, the new value will be applied to the managed bean (**UserBean**). This is handled behind the scenes by the **setValue()** method on the same **ValueExpression (ValueBinding)** instance calling userBean's **setFirstName()** method.

Other new features introduced by JSF include the ability to get a type of an EL expression as well as to find out if an EL expression is read-only or read-write.

Value Expression Syntax

So far you have seen only very basic examples of value expressions. Let's examine some more complex examples.

Recall the usage of a single dot (.) operator in previous examples. With EL it is also possible to use consecutive dot operators to traverse object hierarchies as shown in the expression:

```
<h:outputText value=="#{userBean.homeAddress.street}"/>
```

In this case the dot operator successively calls the getter methods, **getHomeAddress()** and **getStreet()**, as it traverses down the object hierarchy to retrieve a final value.

To access elements of an array or collection you can use brackets ([ ]) in the expression. Recall the expressions that were used in the managed property list for **sportsInterest**:

```
...
<value>#{moreSports[0]}</value>
<value>#{moreSports[1]}</value>
<value>#{moreSports[2]}</value>
```

This example also shows how JSF EL can be used outside of a JSP or a UI component. In this case, it was used in **faces-config.xml**.

In general square brackets can be used in both JavaBeans and Maps as well. Bracket syntax is really the core, primitive way to access properties and the dot syntax is provided as an easy-to-use alternative for simple property names.

In addition to user-created application objects, *implicit objects* are also accessible via value expressions. An *implicit object* is managed by the container. Table 4-7 lists the implicit objects along with a usage example.

Implicit Object	Type	Description
application (JSF 1.2 only)	ServletContext or PortletContext	The **ServletContext** or **PortletContext** depending on whether an application is running in a servlet or portlet context, respectively.
cookie	Map	A map view of values in the HTTP **Set-Cookie** header.
facesContext	FacesContext	The actual **FacesContext** instance.
header	Map	A map view of all the HTTP headers for this request.
headerValues	Map	A map view of all the HTTP headers for this request. Each value in the map is an array of strings containing all the values for that key.
param	Map	A map view of all the query parameters for this request.
paramValues	Map	A map view of all the HTTP headers for this request. Each value in the map is an array of strings containing all the values for that key.
request (JSF 1.2 only)	ServletRequest or PortletRequest	The **ServletRequest** or **PortletRequest** depending on whether the code is executing in a servlet or portlet environment, respectively.
session (JSF 1.2 only)	HttpSession or PortletSession	The **HttpSession** or **PortletSession** depending on whether code is executing in a servlet or portlet environment, respectively.
requestScope	Map	A map view of the request scoped attributes.
sessionScope	Map	A map view of the session scoped attributes.
applicationScope	Map	A map view of the application scoped attributes.
initParam	Map	A map view of the init parameters for this application.
view	UIViewRoot	The **UIViewRoot** for this **FacesContext**.

TABLE 4-7   Implicit Objects Available via EL

All of the above properties that are of type **Map** can be accessed using the #{**MapObject['key']**} expression form. For example, to display a request parameter, **userid**, in a JSF page, you can use

```
<h:outputText value="#{param['userid']}" />
```

or

```
<h:outputText value="#{param.userid}" />
```

Expression Operators

In addition to the [ ] and . operators used in some previous examples, the EL specification defines several other useful operators. These operators can be categorized into the following types: arithmetic, relational, logical, conditional, and empty. Table 4-8 shows these operators.

Here are some EL operator examples:

```
<h:outputText rendered=" #{userBean.serviceLevel == 'Premium'}"
value ="Congratulations, Premium members receive a
#{Discounts.basicDiscount * 10}% discount!" />
```

The discount example renders only for Premium members and provides them with a discount percentage ten times the basic discount value.

To show city temperatures in both Fahrenheit and Celsius, one can use:

```
<h:outputText value="Temperature for #{cityRegistry.city.name} is:
Fahrenheit: #{cityRegistry.city.fahrenheitTemp} Celsius:
#{(cityRegistry.city.fahrenheitTemp - 32) * 5 / 9}">
```

Method Expressions

Method expressions are similar to value expressions but instead of being used to retrieve and set managed bean (object) properties, method expressions are used to invoke public, non-static methods of managed beans. Recall the example in Chapter 2 where a method expression was bound to a **commandButton**:

```
<h:commandButton value="Confirm" action="#{userBean.addConfirmedUser}" />
```

Category	Operators
Arithmetic	**+, -, *, /** (or **div**), **%** (or **mod**)
Relational	**==** (or **eq**), **!=** (or **ne**), **<** (or **lt**), **>** (or **gt**), **<=** (or **le**), **>=** (or **ge**)
Logical	**&&** (or **and**), **‖** (or **or**), **!** (or **not**)
Conditional	**A ? B : C** (Evaluate **A** to Boolean. If true, evaluates and returns **B**. Otherwise evaluates and returns **C**.)
Empty	**= empty A** (If **A** is *null* or is an empty string, array, **Map**, or **Collection**, returns **true**. Otherwise returns **false**.)

TABLE 4-8   EL Operators

When clicked on, the method **addConfirmedUser()** is invoked as a result of the Confirm button being clicked.

Method expressions use a subset syntax of value expressions where only the dot operator or bracket operator([ ]) is used to traverse the object hierarchy to access a public non-static method. The other operators do not apply for method expressions.

Invocation of Methods via Method Expressions   Note that the EL does not include a way to pass arguments to methods. This is intentional to keep the EL as simple as possible.

EXPERT GROUP INSIGHT   *The Expert Group considered adding the ability to pass parameters to* **MethodExpressions** *in the EL but this was abandoned because it was felt this would encourage the bad coding practice of putting business logic directly into the page. The designers had learned their lesson from the abuse of Scriptlet technology, and didn't want to repeat their mistake.*

When used from a JSP page, the arguments to the **MethodExpression** depend on the context in which the expression is used. Table 4-9 provides the method expression details of the standard tags with the **ActionSource (ActionSource2)** behavioral interface. It lists the arguments and return type to which the method pointed to by the **MethodExpression** must conform. It also lists the tags and tag attributes for the **MethodExpression**.

Table 4-10 shows the standard tags/UI components with the **EditableValueHolder** behavioral interface and their method expression details. The single tag attribute, **valueChangeListener**, is bound to a value change listener method, which accepts a **ValueChangeEvent** argument and has a return type of **void**.

The standard tag **f:view** with its (JSF 1.2 only) attributes and method expression details are displayed in Table 4-11.

EXPERT GROUP INSIGHT   *To demonstrate the value of having a diverse community of experts developing the JSF specification, the entire concept of* **MethodExpressions** *and making them invokeable in response to a button press on a form came from Expert Group members who are part of the tool development community. This is one example of how the design of JSF is very tool friendly, but it is by no means designed exclusively for tools.*

Standard Tag Name	Tag Attribute	Return Type	Arguments	Description
h:commandLink, h:commandButton	action	String	none	Method to call when the **ActionSource** component is actuated. Returns a **String** for the **NavigationHandler** to determine where to navigate to.
	actionListener	void	ActionEvent	Method to call when the **ActionSource** component is actuated.

TABLE 4-9   **ActionSource (ActionSource2)** Standard Tags Method Expression Details

Standard Tag Name	Tag Attribute	Return Type	Argument	Description
h:inputHidden h:inputSecret h:inputText h:inputTextArea h:selectOneMenu h:selectOneListBox h:selectOneRadio h:selectManyMenu h:selectManyListBox h:selectManyRadio h:selectBooleanCheckbox	valueChangeListener	void	ValueChangeEvent	Called when the system detects that a component's value has changed.

TABLE 4-10   EditableValueHolder Standard Tags Method Expression Details

Note that the **action** attribute of tags that represent **ActionSource** components is special in that it can accept a literal string, or a **MethodExpression** as listed in the table. If given a literal string, the EL creates a special **MethodExpression** that simply returns the literal string. In this way, you can manually specify a navigation outcome. Navigation is covered in detail in Chapter 5.

Web Application Development Details on Managed Beans

Before concluding this chapter, it is necessary to examine two important higher-level application development concepts with managed beans. The first is how to access/update managed beans programmatically from Java directly. The second is the backing bean concept.

How to Access Managed Beans Programmatically

Although you have seen many examples that access and update managed bean properties, in both pages and in the faces configuration file, there is still one important thing to cover: how to access managed beans programmatically. To understand why this is important, consider the following scenario. Assume that a user has logged into an application. While that user is logged in, his or her personal information is stored in a managed bean with a

Standard Tag Name	Tag Attribute	Return Type	Arguments, In Order	Description
f:view	beforePhase (1.2 Only)	void	PhaseEvent	Method that will be called before every phase executes, except for the Restore View phase of the JSF request processing lifecycle.
	afterPhase (1.2 Only)	void	PhaseEvent	Method that will be called after every phase executes, except for the Restore View phase of the JSF request processing lifecycle.

TABLE 4-11   The Standard Tag **f:view** and Its Method Expression Details

scope setting of **session**, so it will remain alive during the life of the session. If a custom method needs to access any user-specific information, such as the user's **userid** or first name/last name, this can be done programmatically using the following Java code in JSF 1.1:

```
FacesContext context = FacesContext.getCurrentInstance();
ValueBinding currentBinding =
context.getApplication().createValueBinding("#{userBean.userid}");
String userid = (String) currentBinding.getValue(context);
```

To update this value, one can use the following:

```
currentBinding.setValue(context, "NewUserId");
```

Note that the entire **UserBean** instance can be retrieved by using the expression **#{userBean}** without any properties.

```
FacesContext context = FacesContext.getCurrentInstance();
ValueBinding currentBinding =
context.getApplication().createValueBinding(#{userBean});
UserBean myUserBean = (UserBean) currentBinding.getValue(context);
```

A slightly simpler variation is:

```
FacesContext context = FacesContext.getCurrentInstance();
UserBean myUserBean =
context.getApplication().getVariableResolver().resolveVariable(context, "userBean");
```

While the preceding Faces 1.1 code also works fine in a JSF 1.2 environment, you will see deprecated messages when you compile it. To avoid these messages, use the following (Faces 1.2) syntax for accessing managed beans programmatically in a 1.2 environment:

```
ELContext elContext = context.getELContext();
Application application = context.getApplication();
String userid = (String) application.evaluateValueExpressionGet(context,
"#{userBean.userid}",String.class);
```

To set the get or set the value, use:

```
ExpressionFactory expressionFactory = application.getExpressionFactory();
ValueExpression ve =.expressionFactory.createValueExpression(elContext,
"#{userBean.userid}",String.class);
userId = (String) ve.getValue(elContext);
ve.setValue(elContext, "newUserId");
```

Invoking a Method on a Managed Bean Programmatically

In addition to just accessing values of managed bean properties, JSF also provides a way to invoke a method of a managed bean. For example, if you want to execute the method **addConfirmedUser()**, which was introduced in the JSFReg application in Chapter 2, you would use the following:

```
Application application = FacesContext.getCurrentInstance().getApplication();
MethodBinding mb = application.createMethodBinding("#{UserBean.addConfirmedUser}",
null );

try
  {
```

```
     mb.invoke(context, null);
  }
catch (EvaluationException e)
  {
    Throwable wrapped = e.getCause();
  }
```

Notice in the previous code listing that the method **addConfirmedUser()** did not take any arguments so the second argument of the **invoke()** was null. However, if the **addConfirmedUser()** method accepted arguments that included a custom **UserInfo** object as well as an **Id** of type **String**, the Faces 1.1 method binding code would be as follows:

```
Object result = null;
MethodBinding mb = application.createMethodBinding(
    "#{UserBean.addConfirmedUser }",
    new Class [] { UserInfo.class, String.class} );

try
  {
    result = mb.invoke(context, new Object [] { UserInfo(),"joe.shmoe" });
  }
catch (EvaluationException e)
  {
    Throwable wrapped = e.getCause();
  }
```

Notice also that it is possible to retrieve the results of a method binding invocation shown here using **result** to store the return value. Here is how this method invocation is done in Faces 1.2:

```
...
elContext = context.getElContext();
MethodExpression me =
  expressionFactory.createMethodExpression(elContext,
    "#{UserBean.addConfirmedUser }", Void.TYPE,
    new Class [] { UserInfo.class, String.class});

try
  {
    result = me.invoke(elContext, new Object [] { UserInfo(), "joe.shmoe" });
  }
catch (ELException ele)
  {
    Throwable wrapped = ele.getCause();
  }
```

Note that any exception thrown by the invoked method is wrapped in an **EvaluationException** in Faces 1.1 and an **ELException** in the Faces 1.2 Unified EL. The **cause** must be extracted from these exceptions to see what really happened in the invoked method.

Further coverage of accessing managed beans programmatically is provided in Chapter 9 where the Virtual Trainer example application is reviewed in detail. Chapter 10 also shows how to create custom components that accept method expressions.

Using Managed Beans as Backing Beans for JSF Pages

Users of Microsoft Visual Basic or ASP.Net are familiar with the notion of having an associated source code file (or class) that provides the "back-end plumbing" that handles events, updates data, and so on for a specific page. This is known as the *backing bean* concept, and although not specifically required by the Faces specification, it is fully supported and recommended in most cases. In fact, several JSF-enabled integrated development environments (IDEs) enable or, in some cases, force this programming style on the developer. (You will see examples of this in Chapter 17 when we examine JSF development with several JSF-enabled IDEs.)

To implement a backing bean approach in JSF, you can create a Java class for each JSF page and register it as a managed bean. It is recommended that backing beans be declared to be in request scope. The most preferred usage is to have a single backing bean per page although this is not enforced by any specification. A common usage is also to name the class the same name as the page. For example, **login.jsp** would have an associated backing bean of **Login.java**. Placing the backing bean classes in a sub-package of ".backing" is also useful. Finally, the backing beans can also be registered in the **faces-config.xml** with "_Backing" added to their names so you always know which beans are backing beans.

In general the backing bean holds the following artifacts for a page:

- Properties corresponding to input fields on a page, such as string properties for **userid** and **password**.

- Action methods and action listeners that correspond to UI components that initiate action events, such as clicking on Register or Next Page buttons.

- Declarations of UI component instances that can be directly *bound* to the UI components used on the page. (We'll drill down on this usage in more detail in Chapter 6.)

In short, it is the responsibility of the backing bean to serve as a conduit from the page to server-side application logic. In other words, it serves as the "middle man" between the page and the back-end business logic. A typical set of pages and their corresponding backing beans that link to back-end business logic is shown in Figure 4-3.

To get a better idea of how the backing bean concept works, consider a typical login example. In this example you could have a page (**login.jsp**), which is built with a collection of **UIInput** components (input fields) to accept the login credentials. In this example, the backing bean can be a Java class, **Login.java,** which has a corresponding set of JavaBean properties (of type **String**) for temporarily storing the user's login credentials. To handle the user's button click on a Login button (**UICommand**), an action method, **checkUserCredentials()**, could be invoked. It could then call a back-end business method that performs a database or LDAP lookup of the user to determine whether the credentials are valid. Figure 4-4 illustrates this example.

Pages   Backing Beans

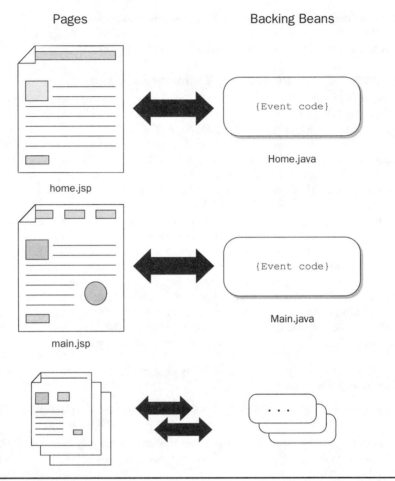

Figure 4-3   The backing bean concept illustrated

Here is a more advanced example of backing bean usage where a page, **employees_ table.jsp,** displays a scrollable table of employee information using a corresponding backing bean, **EmployeesTable.java**. In this example, the JSP page uses an **HtmlDataTable** (**<h:dataTable/>**) component to display a table of employee records. It also uses a custom **Scroller** UI component that works with methods in the backing bean to handle scrolling events such as next page, previous page, first, and last to navigate through the data being displayed by the table component. The JSP page could also have columns for row-level operations such as Edit and Delete. When the user clicks Edit, he or she would navigate to a different page to edit the row values in a form. Clicking on Delete would simply delete the selected record and remain on the same page. For this example, the backing bean (**EmployeesTable.java**) would most probably have the following:

- Any Java bean properties that are *value bound* to components in the page. In this example the **<h:dataTable> (HtmlDataTable)** component could be value bound to a Java bean property that returns either a **List**, **Result**, **ResultSet**, or an **Array**. For example:

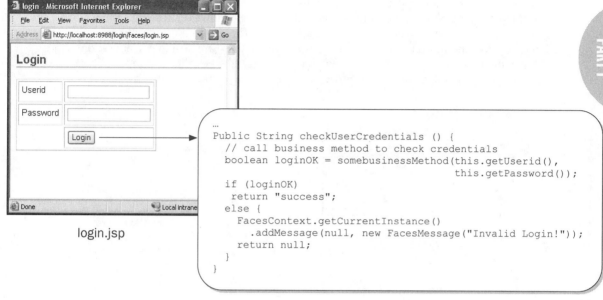

login.jsp

Login.java

FIGURE 4-4 The backing bean concept shown in a login example

<h:dataTable value="#{EmpTable_Backing.empList}" />
This is where the tabular data is initially retrieved; however, to manipulate the data, such as scrolling and so on, the **HtmlDataTable** component on the page can also be directly bound to a declared instance of **UIData** (or **HtmlDataTable**), which has the necessary methods to navigate through the tabular data.

- At least one instance of a **UIData** (or **HtmlDataTable**) component that is *directly bound* to the **DataTable** on the page such as:
<h:dataTable value="#{TrainingEventRegistry.eventlist}" binding="#{EmpTable_Backing.tableData}" />
In this example **EmpTable_Backing.tableData** is of type **UIData** and is used to perform data navigation operations on the tabular (**List**) data that was value bound to **HtmlDataTable**.

- An action listener method for handling table events such as scrolling through data.

Figure 4-5 illustrates our example where we have an **HtmlDataTable** component that is bound to both a **UIData** instance as well as value bound to a method that returns a **List**.

For more detailed **UIData** and **HtmlDataTable** examples, Chapter 9, which illustrates the Virtual Trainer example application, includes complete coverage of working with tabular data in Faces applications, including how to perform data navigation (scrolling) as well as inserting, updating, and deleting data associated with **HtmlDataTable** components.

Before concluding the chapter, here is a final thing to consider when using backing beans. It is possible to have more than one backing bean per page, or have multiple pages bound to properties of a single bean as there is no specified rule on this. This is left to the developer's discretion, but having numerous dependencies between multiple pages and multiple backing beans can become very hard to manage. However, it's still technically okay to have separate request-scoped managed beans for sub-sections of your page that get included and reused across multiple pages. Again, these are design considerations where the Faces application architect will have to weigh the benefits of standard OOP reuse mechanisms against raising the overall application architecture complexity.

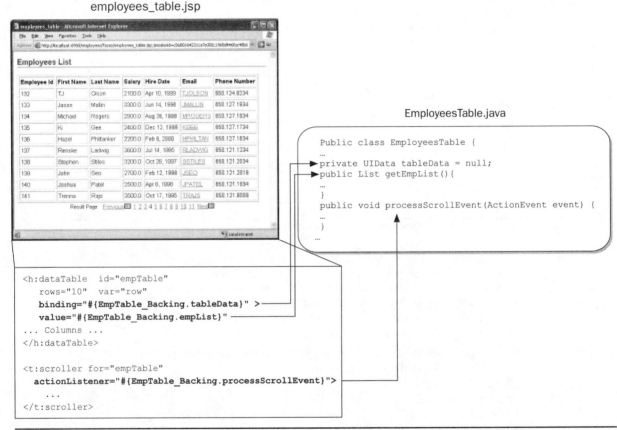

FIGURE 4-5   An **HtmlDataTable** bound to a **UIData** instance and a **List**

The Navigation Model

One of the most elegant design aspects of JavaServer Faces is its navigation model. The JSF Navigation Model allows for the definition of a JSF application's entire page flow, which is a collection of rules governing when and how page navigation should occur in an application. As you may recall, basic navigation was introduced in Chapter 2; however, this chapter goes further and examines the JSF Navigation Model in detail by describing both the architecture behind JSF navigation as well as the different types of navigation. The chapter concludes by presenting several examples of building navigation rules.

Since navigation page flow is easily portrayed visually, several JSF-enabled integrated development environments are now offering the ability to visually design the navigation page flow in a visual editor. Figure 5-1 shows Oracle JDeveloper's JSF navigation page flow designer.

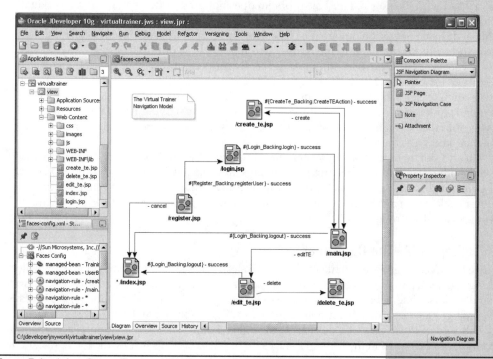

FIGURE 5-1 A JavaServer Faces navigation page flow in Oracle JDeveloper

Overview of the Navigation Model

Most developers will find the JSF Navigation Model very easy to work with. To build Faces navigation, one merely needs to understand how to create a set of Faces navigation rules and then bind them to the user interface. Behind the scenes, JSF navigation relies on the familiar Java event model for its underlying architecture. As you'll see in this chapter, the overall Faces Navigation Model and its event model–based architecture provide a streamlined solution to the overall task of creating and managing an enterprise application's many navigation scenarios.

Those familiar with Jakarta Struts will find JavaServer Faces Navigation Model somewhat similar in that all the navigation rules can be stored in a single XML configuration file. However, where Struts defines a series of navigable application nodes in the form of Actions and Forwards in its configuration file, JavaServer Faces builds navigation rules that link actual pages directly to each other using a series of rules.

A clear benefit of having all of the JSF navigation rules residing in a single XML file is that it makes navigation very "tool friendly." In addition to the previously shown JDeveloper, there are now a growing number of JSF development tools that offer visual navigation design. These tools allow developers to design all of the navigation in a JSF application by simply "drawing" or linking the pages together in a visual environment. In Chapter 17 we'll step through how to build navigation rules visually in JSF-enabled development tools.

Another benefit of centralized navigation rules is improved application management. Consider the classic problem when a page is renamed, such as changing **register.jsp** to **registration.jsp**, and all associated links in other pages referring to the old name need to be revised with the new name. This problem does not occur when using the JSF Navigation Model since all of the navigation rules with references to the old page name can easily be changed in one operation, in one file (**faces-config.xml**). This is obviously easier and less error-prone than editing all of the hard-coded references in multiple pages.

JavaServer Faces navigation is also tightly integrated into its event model. This approach enables it to handle both *static* and *dynamic* navigations. In contrast to a static navigation (case), which is hard-coded into your **faces-config.xml**, the navigation path for a dynamic link is determined at runtime. This is done by specifying navigation conditions (or cases) into the navigation rule for the different expected results of a special type of Java method known as an *action method*.

In addition to both static and dynamic navigation, the JSF Navigation Model can also handle other navigation types such as *wildcards* and *redirects*. These are examined later in the chapter, but first a little background on the exact sequence of events that occurs when a user clicks on a page to initiate a navigation event. To begin, it is useful to review the Model-View-Controller (MVC) theory.

Recalling MVC—The Controller

Since the JavaServer Faces architecture is intrinsically linked to the Model-View-Controller design pattern, any user interaction with a Faces application requires that the Faces Controller handle all user interactions, or requests. As you may recall from earlier chapters, the Faces controller is a Java servlet that is able to intercept all requests to any Faces-enabled pages. It does this by using its servlet mapping defined in **web.xml**. The most common Faces mapping conventions are URLs in the form of "/faces/*" or "*.faces". This is how the JSF application is able to differentiate the Web requests that are Faces-specific. This differentiation is needed because a JavaServer Faces page must go through the request processing lifecycle where the Faces Context is prepared before the page renders itself.

In short, here is how a Faces navigation event occurs. (We'll cover the details later.) In order for a Faces page to be able to initiate a navigation event or in general submit a form, it must contain a Faces form component (**UIForm**) along with child **UIComponents**, like a Faces button or link, which implement the Faces **ActionSource** interface. When a user clicks on one of these components, a navigation event may be triggered depending on the rules defined in **faces-config.xml**. The JSF request processing lifecycle handles this event with a (default) **NavigationHandler** instance that determines how to process the event based on the navigation rules specified in **faces-config.xml**. It then returns the appropriate view or page based on the outcome of the event and its navigation rule. That's it! Now we'll drill down a bit into what actually happens behind the scenes of a navigation event.

The NavigationHandler—Behind the Scenes

The Faces **NavigationHandler** object is the heart of the navigation model for JavaServer Faces. As mentioned before, a default instance of this is provided by the JSF request processing lifecycle at runtime and is responsible for handling all navigation events. To understand the event handling process, we'll step through the exact flow of events, as shown in Figure 5-2, that occurs when a navigation event, or more specifically an **ActionEvent**, is fired and a subsequent navigation rule is processed.

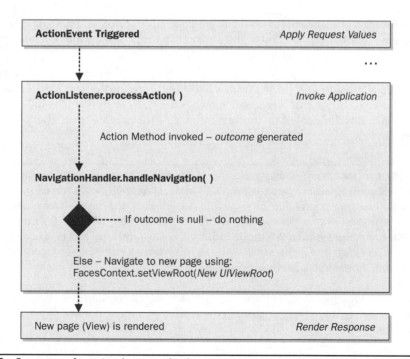

FIGURE 5-2   Sequence of events when a navigation occurs

As you will learn in Chapter 6, any **UIComponent** that can be activated to initiate a form submit, must implement the **ActionSource** interface. Implementing this interface tells the Faces runtime that the component is the source of an **ActionEvent**. The Faces **UICommand** component, which is rendered either as a button or a link by the standard HTML tag library, implements this interface so the Faces developer can rely on this component to trigger an **ActionEvent** when clicked on. The remaining processing of this **ActionEvent** is handled automatically by the Faces runtime, but it's good to know what happens behind the scenes.

After the **ActionEvent** is triggered, if there are no conversion or validation errors in the page, the request processing lifecycle eventually arrives at the Invoke Application phase where the **ActionEvent** is handled by the default **ActionListener** instance and its **processAction()** method. **ActionEvent** extends the standard Java event class **java.util.Event**, and therefore has a **source** property whose value is the ID of the component that was clicked. After the **ActionListener** retrieves the **source** property that identifies the originating component that triggered the event, it processes the source component's **action** property. The value of the **action** property is provided by the page author as either a **static** string or a Faces expression that refers to an *action method*. The action method, which is an instance of **MethodBinding**, returns a **dynamically** derived string value after execution. This string outcome is then handled by the **handleNavigation()** method of the **NavigationHandler** instance, which compares it with the set of navigation rules defined in the application's **faces-config.xml**. Depending on the string outcome and the logic defined in the navigation rules, the **NavigationHandler** does one of the following things:

1. Nothing. The user remains on the same page. This occurs when no navigation rule is successfully matched to the outcome of the action, or the outcome is null.

2. A navigation occurs to a new Faces page by calling **FacesContext.setViewRoot()** with a **UIViewRoot** returned from **ViewHandler.createView()**. This occurs when a Faces navigation rule's outcome matches the static or dynamic value of the action and is designated by the navigation rule to navigate to another Faces-enabled page.

EXPERT GROUP INSIGHT   *You may notice that this event processing model is similar to the one found in standard rich client Java applications. This is no coincidence. The expert group wanted to make the event model as similar as possible to that found in rich clients. It was hoped this would ease development for those familiar with existing rich client UI toolkits. Also, note the key role of the expression language* **MethodBinding** *in action processing and navigation. Enabling the user to easily specify a method that should be called when a button is pressed was the impetus for inventing the concept of* **MethodBinding***.*

When the **NavigationHandler** finishes processing the navigation rule, if successful, a new page will be rendered to the client in the Render Response phase of the request processing lifecycle.

EXPERT GROUP INSIGHT *The Invoke Application phase of the request processing lifecycle was designed to be the place where other frameworks, such as Struts, could plug in to JavaServer Faces applications. This is accomplished by replacing the default **ActionListener** and calling into the Struts navigation machinery. Also, in keeping with the emphasis on extensibility, it is possible to replace or decorate the existing **NavigationHandler**, which allows total customization of the navigation system. One example of the usefulness of this extension point is the ability to have one part of your site built with Faces and another with a different framework, and be able to step cleanly between the two worlds.*

A Note on Faces Action Methods

As you've seen, Faces action methods are user-definable methods that process an event triggered by clicking on buttons, links, or any **UIComponent** that implements **ActionSource** such as **UICommand**. As you may have noticed by now, building action methods to handle user-initiated events is a very common Faces development task. Fortunately, building Faces action methods is quite simple, as they are not defined by any specific API. Instead, any method that has the following characteristics can serve as a Faces action method:

- Must be **public**
- Can accept no arguments
- Must return a string value

As you will see throughout the book, Faces action methods are really the glue that binds the application's user interactive components to the application's server-side logic. In a way, they can be thought of as analogous to Struts Actions in that they are the first bit of code that is executed when a user event occurs. A key difference, however, is that Faces action methods are not directly URL-accessible, such as **http://strutsapp/action.do**.

Building Navigation Rules

Now that you've seen the theory behind Faces navigation, it's time to start putting that theory into practice by defining some Faces navigation rules. JavaServer Faces navigation rules provide a precise way for the developer to define all of the application's navigations. The rules usually reside in the **faces-config.xml** file, or can be configured to reside in a separate file. (An example of how to do this is shown later in this chapter.)

To get a general feel for how navigation rules work, let's take an example from the real world by modeling a simple scenario with a Faces navigation rule: If I'm in the living room, and I'm feeling hungry, I go to the kitchen. If I'm in the living room, and I'm feeling sleepy, I go to the bedroom. This could be modeled with the following navigation rule.

```
<navigation-rule>
  <from-view-id>livingRoom </from-view-id>
  <navigation-case>
    <from-outcome>hungry</from-outcome>
    <to-view-id>kitchen</to-view-id>
  </navigation-case>
```

```
  <navigation-case>
    <from-outcome>sleepy</from-outcome>
    <to-view-id>bedroom </to-view-id>
  </navigation-case>
</navigation-rule>
```

As you can see, navigation rules can easily model many real world or application scenarios. Navigation rules in a more generic form actually have the following structure:

```
<navigation-rule>
  <from-view-id>from_page.jsp</from-view-id>
  <navigation-case>
    <from-action>#{ManagedBean.actionMethod}</from-action>
    <from-outcome>condition 1</from-outcome>
    <to-view-id>/to_page1.jsp</to-view-id>
  </navigation-case>
  <navigation-case>
    <from-action>#{ManagedBean.actionMethod}</from-action>
    <from-outcome>condition 2</from-outcome>
    <to-view-id>/to_page2.jsp</to-view-id>
  </navigation-case>
</navigation-rule>
```

Navigation rules have an optional, single **from-view-id**, which is where the navigation originates. As a peer of the **from-view-id** are 1 to *N* **navigation-case** entries. A **navigation-case** statement has the following child elements:

- **<from-action>**   An action method that returns a custom **String** value such as "Success" or "Failure," which is usually used to indicate if the action method executed successfully. This element along with **from-outcome** is needed for *dynamic navigation* where the output of the action method specified in the **from-action** element is compared to the **from-outcome** value. If a match occurs, the corresponding **to-view-id** location will be navigated to.

- **<from-outcome>**   A **String** value that is passed to the **NavigationHandler** where it is compared with either the output of the corresponding **from-action** or the **action** attribute of a UI component with navigation support such as **commandLink** or **commandButton**.

- **<to-view-id>**   The page to which the user will be navigated upon a successful match of the **from-action** and **from-outcome**.

To get a better feel for building various navigation rules, we'll take a look at a few examples starting with a simple, static navigation.

A Static Navigation Example

This first example shows how to build a simple navigation rule that just links one page to another. Before we begin, it's important to point out that although it's tempting to simply use an HTML **<a href>** tag in static navigation cases, you'll find that standardizing all navigation with JSF navigation rules (no matter how simple) will definitely make the application more manageable in the long run as application size and complexity increases.

Consider two pages, **page1.jsp** and **page2.jsp**. In order for **page1.jsp** to link to a page, you will have to add a **UICommand** UI component onto **page1.jsp**. Normally, the JSP developer does not need to know the underlying UI component, because the standard JSF HTML JSP tag library provides either the **<h:commandButton>** or **<h:commandLink>**, which renders either a button or link with the same **UICommand** UI component. Consider the following **commandButton** example:

```
<h:commandButton value="Proceed to Page2" action="gotopage2" />
```

The key thing to notice is the **action** attribute. For this static navigation, this is the navigation **from-outcome** value that will map to **page2.jsp** in the navigation rule.

Here is an equivalent example using **commandLink**:

```
<h:commandLink  action="gotopage2">
   <h:outputText value="Proceed to Page2"/>
</h:commandLink>
```

Notice the **commandLink** requires a child tag to produce an output similar to how the **<a href...>** tag also requires a body.

Now that an action of the static value **"gotopage2"** has been defined in both the button and link components on the page, the next step is to provide a navigation rule that maps this **from-outcome** value to **/page2.jsp**. Here is the navigation rule required to do this:

```
<navigation-rule>
<from-view-id>/page1.jsp</from-view-id>
  <navigation-case>
    <from-outcome>gotopage2</from-outcome>
    <to-view-id>/page2.jsp</to-view-id>
  </navigation-case>
</navigation-rule>
```

Notice that for this example a **from-action** is not needed; instead, the **from-outcome** is compared to the **action** attribute of the navigation UI component (**commandLink** or **commandButton**).

And that's it. At runtime, clicking on the button or link triggers a navigation to **page2 .jsp**. This is a case of a simple *static* navigation where nothing will change the navigation at runtime. Let's now take a look at a simple *dynamic* navigation rule where a condition will be checked by a Java method and the navigation destination will be dynamically derived.

A Dynamic Navigation Example

This next example shows a typical login example where an action method is used to dynamically determine a navigation case based on values provided in a login form. This example will have the following example pages: **login.jsp**, **success.jsp**, and **failure.jsp**. It will also use **Login.java**, which will be used as a managed bean called **Login**. The **Login** bean is used to temporarily store the user ID and password. **Login** will also contain an action method that will compare the submitted user ID and password values to determine a navigation outcome. Figure 5-3 shows the navigation page flow logic of a simple login application.

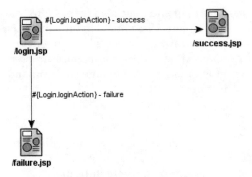

FIGURE 5-3 A simple login application demonstrating dynamic navigation

Let's examine the source code for the **login.jsp** page of this simple example. Notice the usage of two **inputText** components and a **commandButton**.

```
<%@ page contentType="text/html"%>
<%@ taglib uri="http://java.sun.com/jsf/core" prefix="f"%>
<%@ taglib uri="http://java.sun.com/jsf/html" prefix="h"%>
<f:view>
<html>
<head><title>Login</title></head>
<body>
  <h:form>
    <table>
      <tr>
        <td>Userid:</td>
        <td>
          <h:inputText id="userid" value="#{Login.userid}" />
        </td>
      </tr>
      <tr>
        <td>Password:</td>
        <td>
          <h:inputSecret id="password" value="#{Login.password}" />
        </td>
      </tr>
    </table>
    <p><h:commandButton value="Login" action="#{Login.loginAction}" /></p>
  </h:form>
</body>
</html>
</f:view>
```

The key things to notice are that the **inputText** and **inputSecret** fields have *value bindings* to properties of the **Login** managed bean. You'll also notice the **commandButton** has an action binding to a method in the **Login** bean.

The other pages, **success.jsp** and **failure.jsp**, needn't contain any JSF content and can be as simple as:

```html
<html>
  <body>
    <p>Success!</p>
  </body>
</html>
```

The failure JSP page is identical but with a "Failure!" message.

Let's now examine the source code for the **Login** managed bean, which is shown here:

```java
package com.jsfcompref.login;

public class Login {
  String userid;
  String password;

  public Login() { }

  public String getUserid() {
    return userid;
  }

  public void setUserid(String userid) {
    this.userid = userid;
  }

  public String getPassword() {
    return password;
  }

  public void setPassword(String password) {
    this.password = password;
  }

  // Action Method
  public String loginAction() {
    if (userid.equals("guest") && password.equals("welcome"))
      return "success";
    else
      return "failure";
  }
}
```

Notice the **Login** class has corresponding properties **userid** and **password** as well as an action method **loginAction()**. The action method will be invoked when the **commandButton** is clicked. It will return a "success" **String** value if **userid** and **password** equals "guest" and "welcome," respectively. Otherwise, "failure" is returned.

To use **Login** in the JSF application, you must add a reference to it in the **faces-config.xml**.

```xml
<managed-bean>
  <managed-bean-name>Login</managed-bean-name>
  <managed-bean-class>com.jsfcompref.login.Login</managed-bean-class>
  <managed-bean-scope>request</managed-bean-scope>
</managed-bean>
```

Now that the user interface and the backing **Login** bean have been defined, you'll need to define the navigation rule, which is also in the **faces-config.xml** file.

```
<navigation-rule>
  <from-view-id>/login.jsp</from-view-id>
  <navigation-case>
    <from-action>#{Login.loginAction}</from-action>
    <from-outcome>success</from-outcome>
    <to-view-id>/success.jsp</to-view-id>
  </navigation-case>
  <navigation-case>
    <from-action>#{Login.loginAction}</from-action>
    <from-outcome>failure</from-outcome>
    <to-view-id>/failure.jsp</to-view-id>
  </navigation-case>
</navigation-rule>
```

At this point the application is complete with a successful navigation to the **success.jsp** page occurring when "guest" and "welcome" are entered in the login page, and a navigation to **failure.jsp** when anything else is entered in the login page.

Before moving on, you may have noticed how, in addition to setting the **from-outcome** values (as was done in the static example earlier), the navigation rule for the login example also defined a **from-action,** which refers to the action method that will be returning the outcome. It is not always required to provide a **from-action**, but in cases where you have multiple action methods with the same or similar outcomes on the same page, it is best to specify the exact outcome that is expected from a **specific** action method. For example, you might have a login page that has two buttons: one that just logs you in, and a second one that logs you in and immediately performs a service such as checking your account balance. These different login buttons could be bound to two different action methods, **LoginAction()** and **LoginActionCheckBalance()**, but return the same outcome string "success." The only way to differentiate between the two buttons and correctly navigate based on their outcome is to specify the different **from-action** elements in the navigation rule. The following modified navigation rule would correctly handle this situation.

```
<navigation-rule>
  <from-view-id>/login.jsp</from-view-id>
  <navigation-case>
    <from-action>#{Login.LoginAction}</from-action>
    <from-outcome>success</from-outcome>
    <to-view-id>/success.jsp</to-view-id>
  </navigation-case>
  <navigation-case>
    <from-action>#{Login.LoginActionCheckBalance}</from-action>
    <from-outcome>success</from-outcome>
    <to-view-id>/showbalance.jsp</to-view-id>
  </navigation-case>
  <navigation-case>
    <from-action>#{Login.LoginAction}</from-action>
    <from-outcome>failure</from-outcome>
    <to-view-id>/failure.jsp</to-view-id>
  </navigation-case>
</navigation-rule>
```

And here is the code for the second button that is bound to the **LoginActionCheckBalance()** method:

```
<h:commandButton value="Login and Check Balance"
action="#{Login.loginActionCheckBalance}" />
```

Now that you've seen the elements of this dynamic navigation example, it's time to examine the exact sequence of events that occurs when this application is run. After the **login .jsp** page renders the login form to the client, the user enters the values "guest" and "welcome" and then clicks on the Login button. At this point the JSF request processing lifecycle is initiated and passes through both the Apply Request Values and Process Validation phases until it updates the Login bean's properties in the Update Model Values phase.

After updating the bean's values, the Invoke Application phase is entered and the action method **loginAction()** is invoked since it was bound to the **Login commandButton** and the button was clicked. The **loginAction()** method will return "success" because the values "guest" and "welcome" satisfy its **if** condition. At this point the default **NavigationHandler** will consume the returned "success" value and then look for the navigation case that matches the **from-outcome** value of "success" with the **from-action** with the derived value of the method-binding expression **#{Login.loginAction}**. As the match is found, it will select a new view (**success.jsp**) to be rendered using the **to-view-id** value specified in the navigation case and hand the new view to the default **ViewHandler** to render back to the client. In other words, a navigation to the **success.jsp** page will occur. Likewise, if any values are entered in the form other than "guest" and "welcome," the **loginAction()** method would return "failure" and cause a navigation to the **failure.jsp** to occur.

More Sophisticated Navigation Examples

In addition to the simple navigation situations just described, JSF applications usually have more detailed navigation needs. Several examples of more sophisticated navigations are shown in the following sections.

Using Wildcards

An interesting and useful feature of the JavaServer Faces Navigation Model is its ability to handle *wildcard* navigations. Wildcard navigations provide a way to establish a navigation rule for more than one page or **from-view-id**. For example, if a navigation rule has its **from-view-id** set to "*"or "/*", it means that this navigation rule applies to all pages. Another way to apply a navigation rule to all pages is to simply omit the **from-view-id** altogether and the **NavigationHandler** will process the navigation cases for all pages.

If a **from-view-id** is set to something like "/register/*", it means that this navigation rule applies to all pages residing under the **/register** directory.

Consider the example where an application needs a login page to be accessible from all pages. The navigation rule could be as follows:

```
<navigation-rule>
  <from-view-id> * </from-view-id>
  <navigation-case>
  <description>
    Global login rule for any page with a Login button/link
    or any action  method
```

```
    </description>
    <from-outcome>login</from-outcome>
    <to-view-id>/login.jsp</to-view-id>
    </navigation-case>
</navigation-rule>
```

To use this global login rule, any button or link can simply hard-code the action value to "login." Also, if any action method returns the value "login," then this rule will also be invoked.

A navigation rule could handle an error condition where a login is required for any page in the specially designated directory, such as "register/*". If the error condition "login required" is encountered, a **login-required.jsp** page could be navigated to and displayed. For example:

```
<navigation-rule>
    <from-view-id>/register/* </from-view-id>
    <navigation-case>
    <description>
      Login Required error condition for any /register/* page.
    </description>
    <from-action>#{Login.checkLogin}</from-action>
    <from-outcome>login required</from-outcome>
    <to-view-id>/login-required.jsp</to-view-id>
    </navigation-case>
</navigation-rule>
```

Using Redirects

A **<redirect/>** option in a navigation case triggers a slightly different type of navigation. Specifically, the redirect option causes the client browser to request the specified view as opposed to just rendering the response. Recall the Login example from before, where the application did not use redirects in the navigation cases. As the user successfully "logged in" and proceeded to the **success.jsp** page, the URL in the browser would still have the original "...login.jsp.." page in the address bar. This is because the contents of **success.jsp** were simply rendered to the browser without the browser specifically requesting the **success.jsp** page. If a redirect tag is inserted in the navigation case in the form:

```
<navigation-case>
    <from-action>#{Login.loginAction}</from-action>
    <from-outcome>success</from-outcome>
    <to-view-id>/success.jsp</to-view-id>
    <redirect/>
</navigation-case>
```

then the browser is asked via the redirect to request **success.jsp** and the user will actually see "http://.../success.jsp" in the browser's address bar.

Deciding whether to use redirects largely depends on whether what is shown in the address bar of the browser matters or could be confusing if the page referenced no longer matches the page being rendered. Also, if the page that is being navigated to needs to be bookmarked then it is probably best to use a redirect since the browser will remember only the originating page in the bookmark. Another important consideration of when to use redirects is performance. Using a redirect will terminate the current request and cause a new request response cycle to occur. If the page has a very large set of components, this could have a noticeable performance impact. Redirects can also necessitate an extra roundtrip to re-instantiate any request-scoped objects that have disappeared by the next request.

Placing Navigation Rules Outside of faces-config.xml

Since the **faces-config.xml** file primarily holds three distinct types of configurations (managed beans, navigation rules, and everything else), a popular option is to split these separate types of configurations into the separate files: **managed-beans.xml**, **navigation .xml**, and **faces-config.xml** (to hold everything else). To do this split, you simply have to specify a context parameter for the Faces servlet in **web.xml**, as shown here:

```
<context-param>
  <param-name>javax.faces.CONFIG_FILES</param-name>
  <param-value>/WEB-INF/navigation.xml,/WEB-INF/managed-beans.xml
  </param-value>
</context-param>
```

Incidentally, as you will see in Chapter 17 (which covers JSF development in integrated development environments), Sun's Java Studio Creator does this split by default.

Now that you've seen the architectural details behind JavaServer Faces Navigation Model and have stepped through several examples, it's time to look at JavaServer Faces User Interface Component Model in greater detail.

The User Interface Component Model

From the material covered in previous chapters, you should now have a general understanding of how JavaServer Faces is a server-side, component-based architecture for building dynamic Web applications. More importantly, you've seen examples of how Faces Web interfaces are assembled using a collection of both visual and non-visual components, the non-visual ones being the components that perform validation, conversion, or other non-visual tasks, and the visual components being the ones that render a portion of the user interface at runtime.

This chapter will now focus specifically on the Faces user interface component technology by first defining the term "UI component," and then explaining the forces that spurred the creation of component-based Web development. The chapter will then examine the JavaServer Faces user interface component architecture in detail with special attention on how to use it with JSP.

What Are UI Components?

At the outset, it is necessary to define precisely what we mean by the term "UI component." In general, a *component* is a self-contained piece of software with a well-defined user contract that is used by another piece of software. A *user interface component* (UI component) is a specific type of component that displays user interface content. This content ranges from simple input fields or buttons to more complex items, such as trees or datagrids.

In JavaServer Faces, the term *UI component* technically refers to a specific **UIComponent** class that defines the core behavior of the component regardless of how it appears (is rendered) to the client; however, the term is more generally used to describe the entire set of "moving parts" that include both the core **UIComponent** class and other related "helper" components, such as a **Renderer**, **UIComponentTag**, **Validator**, **Converter**, and so on. These different components work together to enable the overall UI component to run in a Faces deployment environment. The helper components, such as **Converter**s and **Validator**s, are also considered Faces components, but they are not UI components.

In general, Faces components represent the time-tested abstraction technique of object-oriented programming theory in which the implementation details of the component are hidden and not important to the page author. Instead he/she simply needs to understand the component's user contract. In other words, the page author simply needs to know what the component does for the user and how to use it. It is not necessary to know the internal workings of the component. Further coverage of the different sub-components (or "moving parts") of UI components are detailed later in the chapter, and numerous examples are provided in Chapter 10.

Because of its emphasis on building user interfaces from reusable and adaptable components, the Faces UI component technology is often compared to Microsoft's ASP.Net component, or *control* (as used in Microsoft's terminology) technology. This is no coincidence since they both represent the most efficient way to build Web user interfaces. However, component-based Web development did not start with ASP.Net and JSF. The following brief history of component-based Web development shows how the trend emerged even before ASP and JSF.

The Rise of Component-Based Web Development

The main benefit of JavaServer Faces is its *standard* component model. The existence of a widely accepted standard component model enables Web developers to choose from a wide variety of components from disparate sources that are tailored to different application domains to build their applications. For example, a developer could obtain a world-class reporting component from Business Objects™, a production-quality GIS mapping component from ESRI™, a feature-rich charting component from ILOG™, and so on, and put them all together into their own application. The ability to create a true, reusable UI component, and package it together in an easily deployable form, is the distinguishing characteristic of a component-based framework. Any framework lacking this characteristic is not component-based.

Of course, Web development wasn't always so easy. Let's review a little Web development history to understand the merits of component-based development and to see why JavaServer Faces has adopted this approach.

As the Web transitioned from a predominantly static environment with simple "home page"–type Web sites to a rich and dynamic environment containing the latest e-commerce applications, Web development technologies have evolved into component-based architectures. This is primarily because of the inherent complications of providing a rich and dynamic end-user experience over a non-synchronous Web/HTTP environment that was designed primarily for static document retrieval. For this reason, Web application development has always been a bit of an art. Because of the lack of a single standard other than HTTP/HTML, Web application development has generally been accomplished through a myriad of different approaches and technologies.

Early Web applications tended to be simplistic in nature, often just displaying small portions of dynamic data using simple CGI back-end processes. These simple back-end processes would also process incoming form values. HTTP and CGI were adequate technologies to handle these basic types of Web applications. As businesses soon saw the advantages of having business applications run over the Web or local TCP/IP intranet networks, traditional client-server applications began transitioning over to Web/HTTP-based architectures. This created an increasing need for more complex user interfaces similar to those that have been around since the beginning of client-server application development. However, because of the lack of standards for building these evermore complex user interfaces for the Web, a number of different approaches have been tried, but with mixed success.

To solve the increasing complexities of building sophisticated user interfaces for the Web, different technologies began to offer a component-centric approach to application development. Technologies such as Cold Fusion and Microsoft's Active Server Pages (ASP) began offering intelligent sets of components to assemble Web applications. With more intelligent Web components, developers could take advantage of pre-built, sophisticated components that took on more user interface responsibilities. For example, a **Datagrid**, which is a common yet fairly sophisticated component in many user interface technologies, can render a grid of dynamic data, possibly from a database, while handling user input gestures to scroll or page through data. Other, more sophisticated components, such as a Javascript-enabled pop-up date picker, offered features that (in most cases) would be too time-consuming to be implemented by hand. As Web application development continued to explode, having pre-built sophisticated Web components reduced Web development complexity and also increased the power of the Web developer to create increasingly sophisticated user interfaces.

As both ASP and other component technologies began to simplify Web application development, the enterprise Java community began to catch up with custom JSP tag libraries and frameworks. In contrast to ASP and other non-Java Web technologies, enterprise Java component technology for Web development has largely been led by Open Source projects through the Apache Jakarta project. For example, the JavaServer Page Standard Tag Library (JSTL), which was basically an amalgamation of helpful Web development custom JSP tag libraries, was developed through the auspices of the Apache Jakarta project. JSTL includes custom tag libraries for handling basic Web development tasks such as rendering and iterating through data, working with XML as well as SQL. JSTL, however, did not offer sophisticated user interface components and JSTL users often had to write a fair amount of code to develop more sophisticated user interfaces using the JSTL tags.

In addition to custom tag libraries, enterprise Java also saw the introduction of complete Web development "frameworks." These provided aid to user interface development and also offered a complete infrastructure for developing Web applications that followed the Model-View-Controller design paradigm. The most notable of these technologies also came from the Apache Jakarta project and is known as Struts. With Struts, a complete infrastructure is provided within the framework including a basic user interface or "presentation"-oriented set of components in the form of custom tag libraries. In contrast to JSTL, however, Struts also provided a Controller servlet and a complete infrastructure for building Web applications fully adherent to the MVC design methodology.

While Struts does provide an MVC framework, it cannot be said to have a true user interface component model. Yes, it is possible to drop in custom tags to do various things such as client-side validation and extended form support, but there really is no single or standard way to package specific UI functionality together into a re-usable component, such as a chart or an e-mail tool. For this reason, Java Web development frameworks such as Struts (along with others including Velocity and WebObjects) may not be considered to offer a true component-centric approach to building user interfaces, while frameworks such as JSF, Tapestry, Wicket, and Echo generally can be.

Aside from JSF, the open source Tapestry, another popular Java Web development framework, provides a component-centric development experience. Tapestry allows Web developers to work in a familiar HTML environment where additional attributes (for example, jwcid) are added to the familiar HTML tags such as **<input >** to allow a set of Java-based components to render different types of sophisticated user interface components. Tapestry also provides a small JSP tag library for integration into JSP applications.

In addition to JSF and other Java Web development frameworks, vendors have also been working hard to provide user interface component-centric development frameworks. For example, Oracle's now deprecated UIX technology, which was originally created for the development of Oracle Applications for the Web and is a forerunner to their ADF Faces technology, provided both a rich set of user interface components as well as the backing technology for a full MVC infrastructure.

The reasons for the rise of component-based Web development frameworks are obvious. They improve productivity by allowing developers to merely assemble Web applications out of ready-to-use sophisticated components as opposed to having to constantly invent their own infrastructure and write their own user interface code.

The Goal of JavaServer Faces UI Components

JavaServer Faces UI components are intended to serve as the prime vehicle by which JavaServer Faces is expected to grow and become truly ubiquitous in Java Web development. Although the Faces specification provides a set of ready-to-use base UI components mainly to allow for building the most general types of user interfaces, the goal behind the UI component architecture was to make it completely extendable so as to empower a growing community of Faces component developers. Although JSF is still a relatively new technology, a new thriving community of Faces component developers is now emerging. These communities include both vendor-supplied and open source developers, and their component libraries complement the base (Standard) JSF components in many unique ways. There now exists a wide variety of third-party component libraries that range from those for general use to those intended for specific uses, such as for charting or mapping applications.

A relatively new open source Faces component library (and implementation) known as *MyFaces* is gaining popularity. MyFaces, shown in Figure 6-1, provides a more powerful

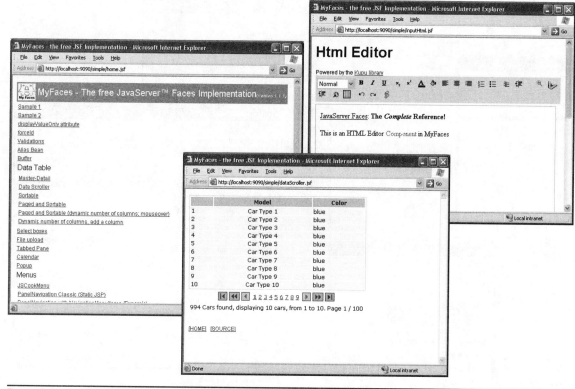

Figure 6-1   Apache MyFaces component library and Faces implementation

component set than the base or Standard components that further simplifies Faces Web development. Oracle's *ADF Faces* component library, shown in Figure 6-2, also provides a set of components that greatly enhances the power of Faces Web developers. In addition to ADF Faces and MyFaces, Sun Microsystems also provides a set of components packaged with its Studio Creator product.

Fortunately, as the JSF component development community continues to grow, some new Web sites are starting to appear that serve as guides to the different third-party components, libraries, and Faces implementations. As shown in Figure 6-3, one of the prime community Web sites to emerge is JSFCentral.com (**http://jsfcentral.com**). At this site you'll find a thorough list of JSF components, component libraries, how-to's, and Faces-related articles.

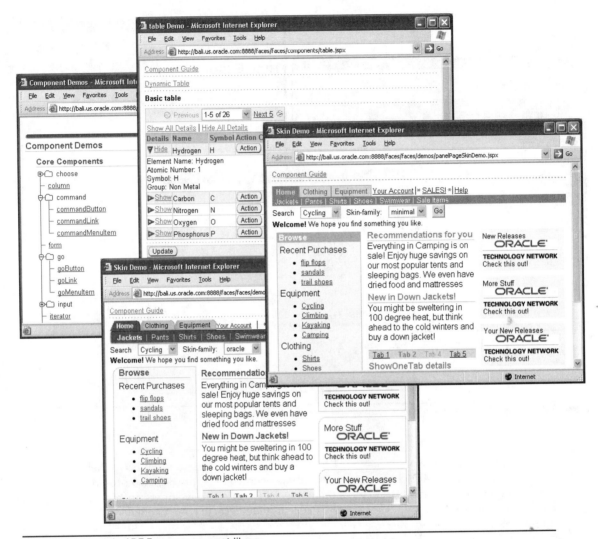

Figure 6-2   Oracle's ADF Faces component library

James Holmes is also now providing community-based Faces-related information at his site: **http://jamesholmes.com/jsf**.

As you gain more experience with JavaServer Faces, you are definitely encouraged to experiment with the various Faces components and libraries referenced at these sites. You will find that the different components provide an extremely useful and thorough understanding of the power and flexibility of the JavaServer Faces technology.

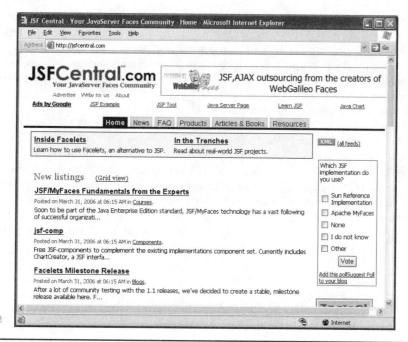

FIGURE 6-3   JSFCentral.com, an online JSF developer's community

Introducing the JSF UI Component Architecture

There are two main types of UI components: those that initiate an action, such as a button, and those that provide data, such as an input field. The behaviors of UI components are described by the distinct *behavioral interfaces* provided by the Faces specification. UI components such as **UICommand** that initiate an action—for example, invoking application logic as the result of a button click—implement the **ActionSource** (or **ActionSource2** in JSF 1.2) interfaces. The other UI components that provide data (that is, allow for data to be submitted to the server), such as **UIInput**, implement either the **ValueHolder** or **EditableValueHolder** interfaces. The **EditableValueHolder** interface allows for components to have their values editable by users.

In addition to implementing either of these two distinct groups of interfaces, UI components (and components in general) also implement various other interfaces that further define their behaviors. Components that need to save their state between requests implement the **StateHolder** interface. **Converter**s, **Validator**s, and **UIComponent**s all implement **StateHolder** since they need to be able to save their state between requests. Components that implement **NamingContainer** require that their children components' identifier IDs are unique. **UIForm** and **UIData** both implement **NamingContainer**.

Aside from understanding the behaviors of the different components, it is important to understand the overall UI component class hierarchy. First, all of the core UI component classes reside in the package **javax.faces.component** and are derived from **UIComponent,** or more directly from **UIComponentBase**. **UIComponentBase** is a convenience class that provides much of the implementation you need for building a component. In general, all of the components extend from **UIComponentBase,** which itself extends **UIComponent.** Figure 6-4 shows the class hierarchy of the core UI components

In addition to the set of core UI components, Faces provides an HTML-friendly set of UI component classes that facilitate Web application development for HTML clients (browsers). The HTML set of components reside in the package **javax.faces.component.html** and are also derived from the same core UI component class hierarchy, but provide a further level of distinction for HTML clients. For example, the **HtmlCommandButton** is a button that renders in HTML (see Note) and extends from the core **UICommand,** which extends **UIComponentBase,** and so on. As another example of the hierarchical nature of UI components, Figure 6-5 shows the class hierarchy of the **HtmlInputText** UI component.

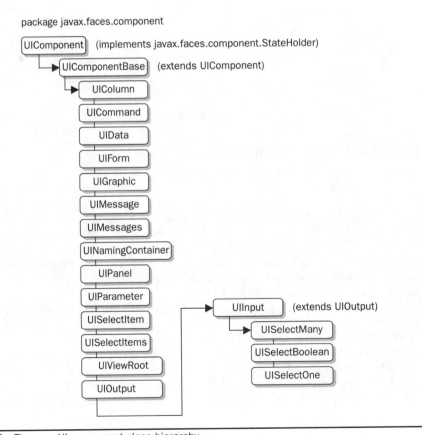

FIGURE 6-4   The core UI component class hierarchy

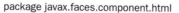

package javax.faces.component.html

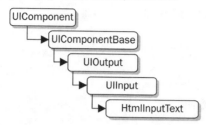

Figure 6-5 The class hierarchy of **HtmlInputText**

Note *Technically speaking,* **HtmlCommandButton** *doesn't really "render" itself in HTML. It actually has convenience methods to set the properties that will be used by an HTML-based* **Renderer***, which happens to be the default renderer used by the Standard component in the reference implementation. The topic of* **Renderers** *and* **Renderkits** *will be covered in more detail in Chapters 10 and 12.*

The UI Component Tree (View)

As first introduced in Chapter 3, Faces solves the inherent incompatibilities between a traditional client/server development process and the stateless Web architecture by providing an infrastructure based on a server-side UI component tree that mirrors exactly what is presented to the user in the client browser. The UI component tree is also known as the **View**. This affords the JSF developer to work on the server-side set of UI components in more of a traditional, event-based mode and let the JSF lifecycle handle the synchronization between the UI component tree on the server and what is rendered to the client browser.

To understand the notion of a server-side UI component tree that mirrors what is presented to the client, consider the JSFReg example again from Chapter 2. As a user makes an initial (non-postback) request to view the registration form, a tree of hierarchical UI components are instantiated on the server that exactly represent what is viewed in the browser. As you recall from Chapter 3, this occurs during the Restore/Create View phase. The subsequent Render Response phase then renders the representation of the registration form to the client by calling a cascading set of **render()** methods on each component that emit the appropriate markup for each respective component to the client. Figure 6-6 illustrates how the server-side UI component tree mirrors what is presented to the user in a client (browser).

Once the UI component tree is in memory, it is updated to reflect any changes in the client between requests, such as new values in input fields or programmatic changes written to access and manipulate any properties of the components. For example, assume an instance (**inputText1**) of a standard Faces input field (**HTMLInputText**, which extends **UIInput**) component. If a new value is entered into the field and subsequently submitted to the server during a postback request, the new value will be applied to the server-side instance of the input field (**inputText1**) during the Apply Request Values phase. You can also alter the same component programmatically through the use of action methods,

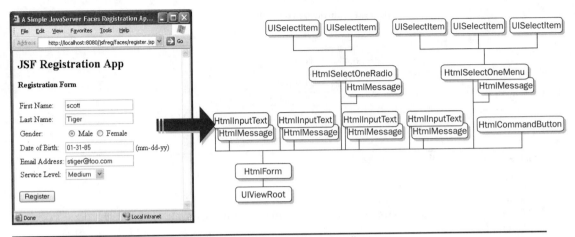

FIGURE 6-6   Faces' server-side UI component tree mirroring what the client sees

PhaseListeners, or any other code that is executed throughout the JSF request processing lifecycle. As an example, the **inputText1** instance can be programmatically set to read only by calling its **setReadonly()** method in an action method that responds to a button click:

```
inputText1.setReadonly(true);
```

As previously mentioned, the **HTMLInputText** component is an extension of the **UIInput** component that can hold a user-entered value because it implements the **EditableValueHolder** interface. In general, each component has a large set of methods that alter the behavior or settings of each component. As an example, the **HTMLInputText** component has numerous methods (both native to the class as well as inherited) that access and/or alter the component's properties. Here are some examples.

getValue( )	Returns the value of the UI component as a **java.lang .Object**. Declared in parent **UIOutput** class.
setValue(java.lang.Object *value*)	Sets the value of the UI component. Also declared in **UIOutput** class.

To eliminate any confusion, it's important to distinguish between the class hierarchy and the server-side UI component tree hierarchy. The server-side UI component tree is a representation of the component layout in a page. It enables programmatic access to the components. For example, the parent UI component **UIForm** has a method **getChildren()**, which returns a **List** of child UI components. Likewise, a UI component also has a **getParent()** method to access its immediate parent component. The hierarchical nature of the component tree is how the JSF lifecycle manages all the components in one operation. Recall from Chapter 3 that the *Render Response* phase calls a cascading set of render methods on each component in order to send back a rendered response to the client. In general, during each new request, the UI component tree is constantly being altered with new values and settings based on the change in state of the UI in the client as changed by the end-user or programmatically on the server.

State Management of UI Components

The UI component tree is fully managed by the **ViewHandler** between requests. However, it is the role of the **StateManager** to preserve the UI component tree in between subsequent requests. It saves the complete status of the component tree using one of several different *state-saving methods* specified as a context parameter (**javax.faces.STATE_SAVING_METHOD**) in the Web application's **web.xml** file. The different state-saving parameters are **server** and **client**.

The **server** parameter causes the application's state to be stored on the server in between requests. This is the default behavior, so this needn't be explicitly specified in the **web.xml**.

The **client** parameter causes the state of the application to be saved on the client. The state information is stored in the form of rendered markup, which is sent back to the client using a hidden input field. For example, the source of the page sent back to the client will contain an input field such as:

```
<input type="hidden" name="com.sun.faces.VIEW" value="H4sIknjsk…" />
```

The state information is then included in the subsequent request as the hidden request parameter. This state-saving method allows the JSF runtime to save the entire application on the client and not on the server.

The UI Component and Its Associated "Moving Parts"

As mentioned earlier in the chapter, the term UI component is often used to describe more than just the core **UIComponent** class, but also its associated helper classes or all the other "moving parts" that work together to serve the end-user in a specific capacity. The following components comprise all of the "moving parts" of a UI component.

The **UIComponent** class captures the abstract meaning of the component, such as: "choose one choice from among several choices," "enter some input," or "display some output." Although the **UIComponent** class can optionally have code to render itself using client- or markup-specific elements (HTML, WML, and so on), it is generally not good practice as **UIComponent**s are meant to avoid any client device–specific information. For maximum flexibility, a separate **Renderer** class is best used for this purpose.

The **Renderer** class is responsible for encapsulating client device–specific content and *rendering* it to the client. Providing this encapsulation in the request/response world of the Web requires two distinct functions: *encoding* a **UIComponent** instance to a specific client device technology, such as HTML or WML, and *decoding* information from the name value pairs in the postback and applying it back to the component for event processing.

EXPERT GROUP INSIGHT *The Expert Group wrestled with the name* **Renderer** *for a long time and ultimately couldn't come up with a better name. One more descriptive but less catchy term considered was "client adapter."*

It is fundamentally important to understand that both the **UIComponent** and **Renderer** can be fully independent and interchangeable so as to offer multiple rendering capabilities for a particular UI component. This is often referred to as "pluggable" rendering and distinguishes Faces from other Web development frameworks. As case in point, Oracle's ADF Faces provides built-in multiple client rendering for its component set. For example, the same ADF Faces table will render in HTML when an HTML browser makes a request; however, the same UI component will render in WML when a PDA makes the same request.

The **UIComponentTag** class along with an associated tag library descriptor (TLD) allows for the usage of UI components and renderers in JSP, but more importantly it is the vehicle by which **Renderer**s or **Renderkit**s (which are families of **Renderer**s) are associated with **UIComponent**s. Figure 6-7 illustrates the relationship between the **UIComponent**, **Renderer**, and **UIComponentTag** classes.

JSF 1.2 TIP   *The* **UIComponentTag** *and* **UIComponentBodyTag** *classes are deprecated as Faces 1.2 provides a new base class,* **UIComponentELTag**.

It is also important to understand UI components can also be used outside the context of JSP. In this case a **UIComponentTag** is not used. Instead, a separate **ViewHandler** can be built to allow for the usage of UI components without JSP. Chapter 13 will provide detailed coverage on how to use JSF components without JSP.

Table 6-1 summarizes the distinct "moving parts" of a usable UI component.

In Chapter 10, we will revisit the specifics of user interface components when we dive deeper into the UI component technology and show how to build custom UI components.

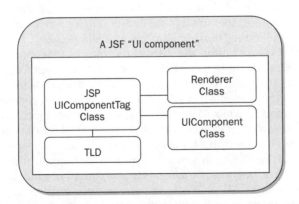

FIGURE 6-7   The relationship between **UIComponent**, **Renderer**, and JSP tag

Component	Purpose
UIComponent	The class that represents the abstract semantics of the component independent of the rendering of the component to a specific client device.
Renderer	An optional class that contains code to render a UI component to a specific client device.
UIComponentTag	The JSP tag handler class that allows the UI component to be used in a JSP. It associates a **Renderer** class or **Renderkit** to be used with a specific **UIComponent**.
Tag Library Descriptor	A standard JSP tag library descriptor (TLD) needed for **UIComponentTag**s.
Associated helper components	An optional collection of helper components such as **Converter**s, **Validator**s, **ActionListener**s, and so on, which provide additional functionality to the UI component. These can be bound to UI components programmatically or through JSP tag attributes.

TABLE 6-1   The Different "Moving Parts" of a Usable JSF UI Component

UI Components and JSP

Since JSP is the most common way to build JSF applications that use UI components, the remainder of this chapter will focus on how UI components are invoked from JSP. The chapter concludes with helpful information on binding UI component instances to UI component tags in JSP pages.

Accessing UI Components Programmatically

As you become more familiar with using UI components in Faces applications, you'll quickly find that working with them involves more than just using their tags in JSP pages. Instead, Faces developers will often need to access and manipulate UI components programmatically.

To fully appreciate this point, consider the following simple example where a JSP page (**hello.jsp**) has three UI components: **InputText**, **OutputText**, and a **CommandButton**. At runtime when the user enters a text value into the input field (**InputText**) and clicks on the button (**CommandButton**), the output field (**OutputText)** is then updated with the value of the text entered into the input field. To meet the requirements of this situation, programmatic access to the UI components is required. Here is the source code for this example. The **hello .jsp** JSP page is as follows:

```
<%@ taglib uri="http://java.sun.com/jsf/html" prefix="h"%>
<%@ taglib uri="http://java.sun.com/jsf/core" prefix="f"%>
<f:view>
  <html>
    <body>
      <h:form>
        <h:inputText />
        <h:commandButton value="Click Me!" />
        <h:outputText value="Hello!" />
      </h:form>
    </body>
  </html>
</f:view>
```

To set the value of the **outputText** component with the value entered in the **inputText** component, an action method can be created that will programmatically get the value of the **inputText** component and set it as the value of the **outputText** field. This action method will reside in a "backing" bean, which will also contain instances of the respective UI components.

Here is the source code of **Hello.java**, which will serve as a backing bean for **hello.jsp**. You'll notice the declared instances of the UI components **HtmlInputText** and **HtmlOutputText** along with the associated getters and setters. These instances allow for programmatic access of the bound UI components.

```
package backing;

import javax.faces.component.html.HtmlCommandButton;
import javax.faces.component.html.HtmlInputText;
import javax.faces.component.html.HtmlOutputText;

public class Hello
{
  private HtmlInputText inputText1;
  private HtmlOutputText outputText1;

  public void setInputText1(HtmlInputText inputText1)
  {
    this.inputText1 = inputText1;
  }

  public HtmlInputText getInputText1()
  {
    return inputText1;
  }

  public void setOutputText1(HtmlOutputText outputText1)
  {
    this.outputText1 = outputText1;
  }

  public HtmlOutputText getOutputText1()
```

```
  {
    return outputText1;
  }
}
```

Here is the managed bean entry for the **Hello.java** class for use as a backing bean for the **hello.jsp** page:

```
<managed-bean>
  <managed-bean-name>backing_hello</managed-bean-name>
  <managed-bean-class>backing.Hello</managed-bean-class>
  <managed-bean-scope>request</managed-bean-scope>
</managed-bean>
```

Here is the JSP page, but now with bindings to the UI component instances declared in the backing bean. This enables programmatic access to the actual components used in the page. It's important to understand that if the UI components in the page were not bound to component instances in a backing bean (as before), the UI component tree would still be created upon request but with separately instantiated components.

```
<h:form>
  <h:inputText binding="#{backing_hello.inputText1}"/>
  <h:commandButton value="Click Me!" />
  <h:outputText value="Hello!"
                binding="#{backing_hello.outputText1}"/>
</h:form>
```

Figure 6-8 illustrates the binding of the UI components referenced in **hello.jsp** to the UI component tree made up of declared instances from the backing bean. Programmatic access to the UI components are enabled through binding them to the tags in the page.

Now that the components used in the page are bound to component instances declared in a managed bean, you can write code to alter/manipulate the properties of the components. For this example, the **outputText** value is set to the value entered in the **inputText** component when the button was clicked. This can be achieved by creating an action method, **commandButton_action()**, which programmatically sets the value of the **outputText**

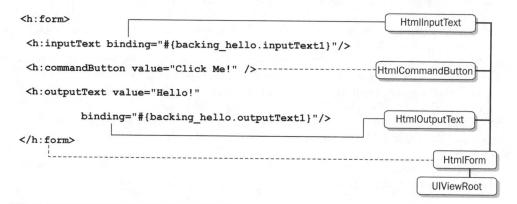

FIGURE 6-8   The UI component tree bound to the components used in the page

to the **inputText**'s value as a result of the button being clicked. This method can also reside in the same **Hello.java** backing bean:

```
public String commandButton_action()
{
  outputText1.setValue(inputText1.getValue());
  return "success";
}
```

The final step needed for this small application to work is to set the **action** attribute of the **commandButton** to the expression referring to the action method. This will ensure that the action method **commandButton_action()** is invoked when the button is clicked. (As you recall from Chapter 3, action methods are actually invoked during the Invoke Application phase of the request processing lifecycle):

```
<h:commandButton value="Click Me!"
           action="#{backing_hello.commandButton_action}"/>
```

Let's review precisely what happens at runtime with this simple application. The end-user makes an initial, non-postback request to view the page **hello.jsp**. The Faces controller servlet handles the request by creating a **UIViewRoot** component and storing it in the **FacesContext**. It then redirects to the **hello.jsp** JSP page. As shown in Figure 6-8, the execution of the JSP page causes the **UIViewRoot** to be populated (into a tree) with children components, as well as causing those components to be rendered to the client as they are added to the component tree. The user then sees the rendered page with an input field, a button, and an output field with an initial "Hello!" value. The component tree is saved for future requests.

JSF 1.2 TIP *In JSF 1.2, the execution of the JSP page only builds the view. The act of rendering the view happens after the JSP page executes. This is important—the knowledge that the entire tree has been built before rendering enables components to avoid problems such as not being able to access another component in the view because it hasn't yet been added to the view.*

The end-user then enters a text value such as "Hello JSF!" into the input field and then clicks the "Click Me!" button, resulting in a postback request being submitted to the JSF application. It again enters the initial Create/Restore phase, but this time it restores the tree from before. It then updates the server-side **InputText1** component with the value "Hello JSF!" during the Apply Request Value phase. Since no validation or conversion is involved nor is a Model bean's property updated since the component was not *value* bound using its **value** attribute, we pass on through to the Invoke Application phase. In this phase the action method **commandButton_action()** is invoked and the **inputText1** component's value is then applied to the **outputText1** component's value. The subsequent Render Response phase renders the current state of the components back to the user. Since no navigation rule was created to handle the "success" value returned from the action method, the same page is rendered.

To get even a better feel for working with UI components programmatically, you could add a call to make the input field read only as the action method executes.

```
outputText1.setValue(inputText1.getValue());
inputText1.setReadonly(true);
return "success";
```

This will change how the input field renders after the submit and it will no longer be editable.

Helpful Advice for Binding UI Components in JSP

The first bit of helpful advice to consider when binding UI components to JSP deals with knowing when and how to use *value binding* and/or *component binding*.

In the previous "Hello JSF" example we took a slight departure from our earlier examples of always value binding to Model bean properties. Recall that JSFReg directly bound the components to the Model **UserBean** by setting the **value** attribute of the UI component to **#{UserBean.firstName}**. This is definitely the right approach if you always want to apply the value of a UI component to a certain Model bean property, but in simple cases you can often work with just the UI components themselves without having to always apply their values to Model bean properties. When a JSF tag representing a UI component is directly bound to an instance of the same type of UI component in a backing bean, direct component binding is preferable. Instead of setting the **value** attribute as before, the **binding** attribute is set with the JSF expression of the instance of the UI component in the backing bean. The same "Hello JSF" example showed that value binding to a Model bean property was not needed. Instead, it was possible to simply work with the values of the components themselves as opposed to value binding them to a separate Model bean property. This is often the case when only working with transient values that do not need to be passed on to the Model.

Using Component Binding—Revisiting the Login Example from Chapter 5

To better understand the difference between value binding and component binding, consider the simple login example presented in Chapter 5. This example contained a login page with UI components value bound to Model bean properties for **userid** and **password** that are both of type **String**:

```
<h:inputText id="userid" value="#{Login.userid}" />
```

and

```
<h:inputSecret id="password" value="#{Login.password}" />
```

As an alternative to value binding the input fields on the page to Model properties, we could instead simply declare **UIInput** properties in a backing bean using:

```
    private HtmlInputText userid;
    private HtmlInputSecret password;
//  Getters and setters for these properties not shown
```

(Both **HtmlInputText** and **HtmlInputSecret** directly extend from **UIInput**.)

In this manner the JSP would instead use component binding to establish a link from the UI components on the page to the UI components declared in the backing bean. The JSP code for this is

```
<h:inputText id="userid" binding="#{Login_Backing.userid}" />
```

and

```
<h:inputSecret id="password" binding="#{Login_Backing.password}" />
```

In this example the backing bean is registered in the **faces-config.xml** with the name "Login_Backing" and contains the **UIInput** declarations.

Similar to the example in Chapter 5, a **loginAction( )** action method is also needed to check the login field values, except it would now be placed in the backing bean. Its code compares the values of the UI component input fields as opposed to comparing the **String** properties of the original **Login** Model bean.

```
// Revised LoginAction Method from Chapter 5
public String loginAction() {
   if (userid.getValue().equals("guest") &&
       password getValue().equals("welcome"))
     return "success";
   else
     return "failure";
}
```

Notice the usage of **getValue( )**. This is because the code has to extract the value from the UI components, **userid** and **password**, whereas before in Chapter 5 it was simply comparing **String** properties in the Model bean. As you can see, this component binding variation of the login example shows how it is possible to simply use UI components in backing beans to hold transient values (such as login credentials) as opposed to passing these values directly onto Model beans. It also shows that placing event handling code, such as **loginAction( )**, into a backing bean is a better coding practice than placing it in a Model bean, which is not really supposed to contain UI-related code.

Final Component Binding Recommendations

The final bit of advice to consider deals with how and when to declare instances of UI components in backing beans. In short, only declare an instance of a UI component in a backing bean when you absolutely need it. You do not need to declare instances for all of the UI components in a page. Doing so tends to overcomplicate your backing bean code. For example, in the earlier "Hello JSF!" example, the UI components **commandButton** and **form** were used in the page along with the **inputText** and **outputText** components. However, the **commandButton** and **form** components did not have any specific code associated with them, so backing bean instances for them were not necessary.

In general, it's important to understand that you do not have to declare instances of all the UI components in a backing bean that are used in a page. You should declare UI component instances in a backing bean only when you need programmatic access to the components referenced in the page. You'll find this practice helpful in keeping your backing bean code as clean as possible.

Here's a final word of caution for those using JSF-enabled IDEs. Several JSF-enabled development environments have the ability to auto-generate UI component instances in backing beans as you drag and drop components onto a page. Although it is often helpful to have the component instances in backing beans generated as you drop them onto a page, one must keep track of this code as it can quickly become hard to manage, especially when numerous components are being used. Pruning of unused (auto-generated) UI component instances is often recommended to keep the backing beans easy to manage.

Converting and Validating Data

This chapter examines in detail two important JSF topics: data conversion and validation. Data conversion is handled by *converters*, while validation is handled by *validators*. The main point of conversion is to guarantee that the application's business logic only deals with data that is of the expected type. By contrast, the main point of validation is to assure that the data has been validated against the application's specific constraints. Systems that make such a guarantee allow for easier-to-develop business logic, since most of the tedious error checking and error handling is done outside of the model tier. You can think of validation and conversion as a protective layer around your business logic that doesn't permit unchecked data to pass through. You saw an example of validation and conversion failures in the sample application in Chapter 2.

At some level, every computer program boils down to data transformation and processing. For example, traditional rich-client development frameworks such as Swing or Motif for the X Window System convert keyboard and mouse input into events delivered to the program's event loop. Batch processing programs read data from files, possibly employing character set transformations, before processing the data. Web applications are no different; they need to convert the value entered by the user, such as "Jan 12, 2003" to a **java.util.Date**. Since the primary transfer protocol between a Web browser and the server is text-based HTTP, Web applications receive most of their data as ASCII text over a TCP socket. In the case of Faces applications, the Servlet API converts this data to the Java Unicode **String** type. While having a Java **String** is an improvement over raw ASCII, more needs to be done to bridge the gap between **String** and the domain model of the application, which deals in terms of objects, such as **Integer**, **Float**, and **java.util.Date**, or primitives, such as **double**, **long**, and **char**. This is the job of the *Faces Converter system*. Conversion is a two-way process by which data is converted from the **String**-based representation of the Servlet API to the **Object**-based representation demanded by the application business logic and back again. Conversion is completely customizable and language-specific, and takes into account the **Locale** in which your application is running.

Getting the data converted into the proper form expected by your application is one thing, but that's still not enough to provide the previously mentioned correctness guarantee to the business logic. It is also necessary to ensure that the data has been validated against some application-specific constraints. This is the job of the *Faces Validation system*. While conversion is a two-way transformation process, validation doesn't transform the data; it only asserts that the data is "correct" given some constraint. Validation is the process by which a piece of converted data has one or more correctness checks applied to it, yielding a Boolean result of whether the data is valid or not. Some basic examples of validation constraints are "this piece of data is required," "this number must be between 1 and 10," and "this credit card number must not be expired."

Some Validation and Conversion Examples

Before describing the details associated with validation and conversion, it's useful to examine some examples that illustrate how the major elements in the conversion and validation system interact with each other, and with the user.

We begin with a simple example that uses a text field with a label and a button, shown next. Assume the data type of the **number** JavaBeans property referred to in the expression **#{bean.number}** is **java.lang.Long**.

```
<p>Enter a number from 1 to 10:
<h:inputText value="#{bean.number}" id="numberField" required="true">
  <f:validateLongRange minimum="1" maximum="10" />
</h:inputText></p>
<h:messages for="numberField" />

<h:commandButton value="Submit" />
```

This produces the following HTML output, which, of course, is rendered by the browser.

```
<p>Enter a number from 1 to 10:
<input type="submit" id="numberField"></input></p>

<input type="submit" value="Submit"></input>
```

If the user clicks Submit with no value entered, the page will be redisplayed with a message stating that a value must be provided, as shown at right.

This is an example of the "**required**" validation facility in action, described later in the chapter. If the user enters a non-number value, the page will be redisplayed with a message stating that the value must be a number, as shown next at right.

This is an example of the implicit conversion facility, described later in the chapter. Because the value entered by the user is stored in the value expression **#{bean.number}**, the system knows the expected type is **java.lang.Long**. Therefore, it is able to apply the **LongConverter** to the value before performing the validation. Implicit converters are available for all Java language primitives and their respective wrapper types, though the set of implicit converters may be extended as described in the section on custom converters.

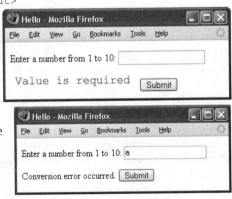

If the user enters a number that is not between 1 and 10, the page will be redisplayed with a message stating that the value must be between 1 and 10, as shown here.

This is an example of using one of the four standard validator tags provided by Faces. The standard validator tags are covered in the section "Using JSP to Associate a Validator with a UIComponent Instance" later in this chapter.

In all cases, the invalid data remains in the text field to aid the user in correcting the error. Also, note that both validation and conversion failures appear to the user in the same way: with a specific message stating what is wrong and how to fix it. While the user doesn't know or care that conversion and validation are distinct processes, it is important for you to understand the distinction: conversion guarantees the data is in the expected type, and validation guarantees that it is valid given the application-specific constraints.

EXPERT GROUP INSIGHT *Some frameworks, such as Tapestry, do not have a separate conversion facility. The Expert Group felt that the expressive power offered by having a separate conversion concept outweighed the complexity it introduced, especially since the implicit conversion facility substantially mitigated the complexity by hiding conversion in many cases.*

The next example uses one of the three standard converter tags.

```
<p>Interest Rate: <h:outputText value="#{rates.prime}}">
  <f:convertNumber type="percentage"/>
</h:outputText>.</p>
```

The following HTML is rendered from this example:

```
<p>Interest Rate: 5.22%.<p>
```

Although all three standard converter tags are explained in detail in the section "Explicit Conversion via JSP Tags" later in the chapter, it is useful to note one point now: Converters can be associated with input or output components, but validators may only be associated with input components. This makes sense because it is impossible for invalid data to enter the system if the developer has properly used the validation system; therefore, there is no need to validate data on output.

The final example in this section shows a reasonably complex application of conversion and validation for an inventory tracking system. The user has to enter a valid Stock Keeping Unit, or SKU, that actually is in the inventory.

```
<h:outputText value="#{bundle.skuLabel}" />
<h:inputText value="#{product.sku}" required="true" id="sku"
  size="8">
    <f:validator validatorId="skuConverter" />
    <f:converter converterId="skuValidator" />
</h:inputText>
<h:message styleClass="errorMessage" for="sku" />
```

This example again shows the "**required**" facility and a custom validator that looks for the item in the inventory. It renders a simple label and text field. Notice that two validators and a converter are attached to the text field. The explicit **skuConverter** ensures that the user has entered something that can be considered an SKU. The required attribute simply states that a value is required, and the **skuValidator** ensures that the item is in the inventory. The **<h:message>** tag directs the system to place the error message, if any, at that point in the page. This example shows how you can extend the Faces framework by providing custom converters and validators that are specific to your business logic needs. Custom converters and validators are dealt with in turn later in the chapter.

Conversion and Validation Under the Covers

Chapter 3 covered the Faces request processing lifecycle in considerable detail, but the portions of the lifecycle that deal with conversion and validation bear repeating here.

Converters are instances of **javax.faces.convert.Converter**, and validators are (usually) instances of **javax.faces.validator.Validator**. As shown in Figures 7-1 and 7-2, conversion (from **String** to **Object**) and validation normally happen during the Process Validations phase of the request processing lifecycle (unless the component has its **immediate** property set to true, in which case they happen during the Apply Request Values phase). Conversion (from **Object** to **String**) happens during the Render Response phase of the request processing lifecycle.

Conversion and validation can be said to have an outcome: success or failure. The outcome alters the flow through the lifecycle. When performing validation, the entire view is traversed by the system and each **UIInput** component is asked to validate itself, which includes performing data conversion. Figure 7-3 shows the components attached to the UI component for validation and conversion.

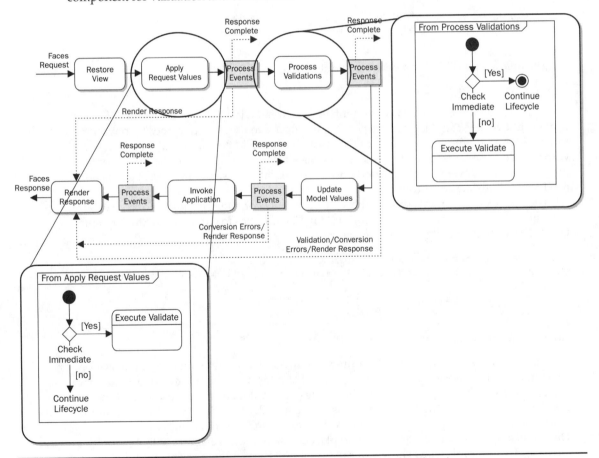

FIGURE 7-1   When conversion and validation happen during the request processing lifecycle

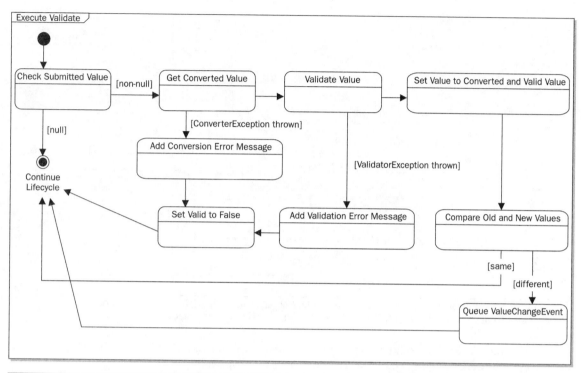

FIGURE 7-2   How conversion and validation are performed

The diagram in Figure 7-3 shows that a **UIOutput** component may have zero or one **Converter** instances associated with it, while a **UIInput**, which is a subclass of **UIOutput**, may have zero or more **Validator** instances associated with it. The means by which these instances are associated with each other may be direct via an instance variable, or indirect, by lookup, or through a **ValueBinding**.

JSF 1.2 **TIP**   *As mentioned in Chapter 4, in JSF 1.2, all occurrences of **javax.faces.el** **.ValueBinding** have been made obsolete, being replaced by **javax.el.ValueExpression**. Keep this in mind when you see occurrences of **ValueBinding** later in this and other chapters.*

Following are the essential elements of the algorithm for doing conversion and validation. Throughout the course of this chapter, the various elements of this algorithm will be examined in detail. At this point, it is necessary to understand only in a general way how the various pieces fit together during the validation process. Keep in mind that this algorithm is performed on each **EditableValueHolder** node in the UI component hierarchy in the page, regardless of the outcome of performing the algorithm on previous nodes.

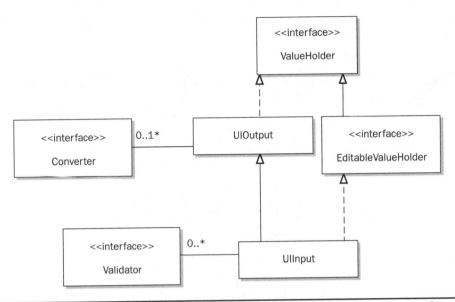

FIGURE 7-3 A UML diagram showing **UIOutput (ValueHolder)**, with zero or one converters, and a subclass **UIInput (EditableValueHolder)**, with zero or many validators attached

There is no way to abort validation processing midway through a view traversal, because the system needs to collect *all* of the error messages in one pass.

1. Obtain the value submitted by the user by calling **getSubmittedValue()** on the **EditableValueHolder** instance of this component. This value was originally retrieved from the incoming request during the Apply Request Values phase of the request processing lifecycle, which is discussed in detail in Chapter 3.

2. Obtain the **Converter** instance to use.

   a. If this component has a **Renderer**, ask it to convert the value.

   b. Otherwise, see if there is a **Converter** instance attached to this component. If so, use it.

   c. Otherwise, if this component's value is bound via a **ValueBinding**, use the type of the **ValueBinding** to create a **Converter** by type.

   d. If none of the previous finds a **Converter**, assume the submitted value is already properly converted and return.

3. Convert the submitted value by calling the **getAsObject()** method on the **Converter** instance.

4. If a **ConverterException** occurs when trying to convert the value, queue the error message, mark the value as invalid, and abort the algorithm.

JSF 1.2 TIP *The* **converterMessage** *property was added to* **UIInput** *to allow the page author to override the standard conversion message enclosed in the* **ConverterException**. *This feature, combined with either the* **f:loadBundle** *tag (described in Chapter 19) or the* **resource-bundle** *element in the* **faces-config.xml** *file (described in Chapter 18), allows the page author to provide fully internationalized conversion messages on a per-instance basis.*

5. Otherwise, proceed to validate the value.

   a. If the value has been marked as "required," yet is empty, queue the required validator failed message, mark the component as invalid, and abort the algorithm. If the value is empty and not required, proceed to step 6.

JSF 1.2 TIP *As mentioned earlier for* **ConverterException**, *a* **requiredMessage** *property was added to* **UIInput** *in JSF 1.2. This allows the page author to override the standard, and not very user-friendly, message shown in response to a failure in the required state of a value.*

   b. Otherwise, call the **validate()** method on each of the **Validator** instances attached to this component instance. If **ValidatorException** is thrown, queue the error message, mark the component as invalid, and abort the algorithm.

   c. If there is a **MethodBinding** for a **Validator** on this instance, invoke it. If the invocation causes an **EvaluationException**, get the cause of the exception. If the cause is an instance of **ValidatorException**, queue the message from the exception, mark the component as invalid, and abort the algorithm.

JSF 1.2 TIP *As mentioned earlier for* **ConverterException**, *a* **validatorMessage** *property was added to* **UIInput** *in JSF 1.2.*

6. If the value is still valid at this point, compare the valid value with the previous value in the component. If the previous value is different from the new value, queue a **ValueChangeEvent**. (Event handling is discussed in Chapter 8.)

7. If the value is not valid, signal a skip to the Render Response phase by calling **renderResponse()** on the current **FacesContext**.

EXPERT GROUP INSIGHT *The initial state of every* **UIInput** *instance is "valid," and the conversion and validation algorithm simply seeks to mark the component as "invalid."*

There are many ways to attach a **Converter** instance, or one or more **Validator** instances, to a **UIInput** component. These are described in detail later in the chapter. Before moving on, it's necessary to mention the final piece of the conversion and validation puzzle: *the message system*. This system allows the page author to control all aspects of the display of conversion and validation error messages in the page in a very flexible manner by using one or more <h:message> or <h:messages> tags. After explaining converters and validators in detail, we'll conclude by exploring the message components.

The Faces Converter System

At the core of the Faces converter system is the **javax.faces.convert.Converter** interface. This interface must be implemented by all objects that want to function as a converter. This section covers in detail the lifetime of converter instances, the standard converters that are available "out-of-the-box," and how converters are associated with **UIComponent** instances. An example of how to write a custom converter is also presented.

   javax.faces.convert.Converter defines the two methods shown next.

```
public Object getAsObject(FacesContext context,
                          UIComponent component,
                          String value)
```

```
public String getAsString(FacesContext context,
                          UIComponent component,
                          Object value)
```

The *context* parameter is the **FacesContext** instance for this request. The *component* parameter is the component whose value is being converted. It is useful for converters to have access to the component so they can query the component's attribute set for any parameters necessary to perform the conversion. The *value* parameter is the value to be converted. Note that it is *not* the responsibility of the converter to modify the component with the converted value. It is advisable that converter implementations don't modify the state of the component.

For all converters, the **getAsString()** method is called during rendering to get the **String** version of the data that is suitable for display in the current rendering technology. The **getAsObject()** method is called during the input processing to convert the value from **String** to the correct model type. If a **ConverterException** is thrown by this method, the component is marked as invalid and the message is extracted from the exception and added to the set of messages on the current **FacesContext**. Afterward, processing continues.

Faces provides the following implementations of **Converter**. A **Converter** instance is registered with the system according to the type of data it can convert, or by a *converter ID*, which is a logical name by which you can refer to the converter. Table 7-1 lists the standard converters, the class they can convert, and their converter ID.

All of the converters shown in Table 7-1 can be used from JSP via the **<f:converter>** tag, described later in the section "Associating a Converter with a UIComponent Instance." The **DateTimeConverter** and **NumberConverter** have their own **<f:convertDateTime>** and **<f:convertNumber>** tags that allow complex configuration parameters to be expressed directly in JSP. These two converters are special in that they provide a gateway to the text formatting capabilities of the **java.text** package. The internal details of these converters as they apply to the calling of their **getAsString()** and **getAsObject()** methods are described in the following

Class in javax.faces.convert	Converts Values of Type	Converter ID
BigDecimalConverter	java.math.BigDecimal	javax.faces.BigDecimal
BigIntegerConverter	java.math.BigInteger	javax.faces.BigInteger
BooleanConverter	java.lang.Boolean boolean	javax.faces.Boolean
ByteConverter	java.lang.Bytebyte	javax.faces.Byte
CharacterConverter	java.lang.Characterchar	javax.faces.Character
DateTimeConverter	java.util.Date java.sql.Date	javax.faces.DateTime
DoubleConverter	java.lang.Doubledouble	javax.faces.Double
FloatConverter	java.lang.Floatfloat	javax.faces.Float
IntegerConverter	java.lang.Integerint	javax.faces.Integer
LongConverter	java.lang.Longlong	javax.faces.Long
NumberConverter	java.lang.Number (for currencies, percentages, and so on)	javax.faces.Number
ShortConverter	java.lang.Shortshor	javax.faces.Short

TABLE 7-1   The Standard Converters

sections. These two converters have several JavaBeans properties that control the conversion process. When using Faces with JSP, the setters for these properties are called by the JSP tag that represents the converter in the page.

DateTimeConverter

The **getAsObject()** method parses a **String** into a **java.util.Date** using an algorithm similar to the following:

1. Examine the argument string. If **null**, return **null**; otherwise, call **trim()** on the argument. If the string ends up being zero length after trimming, return **null**.

2. Use the **Locale** JavaBeans property of this **Converter** instance, if non-**null**. Otherwise, if **Locale** is **null**, use the one from the **UIViewRoot** for this view. This **Locale** will inform the rest of the processing for this method call.

3. If a **pattern** JavaBeans property is specified on this converter instance (by virtue of the converter's **setPattern()** method being called), it must conform to the rules of **java.text.SimpleDateFormat**. The **pattern** property takes precedence over the **type**, **dateStyle**, and **timeStyle** JavaBeans properties.

4. If **pattern** is not specified, parsing takes place based on the value of the **type** property, which must be **date**, **time**, or both.

EXPERT GROUP INSIGHT   *Parsing is non-lenient! The given string must conform exactly to the formatting parameters. Failure to conform causes a conversion error. The Expert Group decided that the original implementation of lenient parsing in the* **SimpleDateFormat** *class of the JDK was incorrect and inconsistently implemented across Java platform vendors. In addition, the so-called "leniency" isn't really lenient in any useful way. Thus, the decision was made to disallow the use of lenient parsing in JSF.*

The **getAsString()** method converts the model tier **Object** to a **String** for rendering using an algorithm very similar to the one described earlier, except that a **null** model tier value is converted to a zero length **String**.

NumberConverter

The **getAsObject()** method parses a **String** into a **java.lang.Number** subclass using an algorithm that is the equivalent of the following:

1. Examine the argument string. If **null**, return **null**; otherwise, call **trim()** on the argument string. If the string ends up being zero length after trimming, return **null**.

2. Use the **Locale** property of this **Converter** instance, if non-**null**. Otherwise, if **Locale** is **null**, use the one from the **UIViewRoot** for this view. This **Locale** will inform the rest of the processing for this method call.

3. If a **pattern** JavaBeans property is specified (by virtue of the **setPattern()** being called), it must conform to the rules of **java.text.DecimalFormat**. The **pattern** property takes precedence over the **type** property.

4. If a **pattern** JavaBeans property is not specified, parsing takes place based on the value of the **type** property, which must be **number**, **percentage**, or **currency**.

5. If the **integerOnly** property is set to true, only the integer part of the **String** is parsed.

The **getAsString()** method converts the model tier **Object** to a **String** for rendering using an algorithm very similar to the one described earlier, except that a **null** model tier value is converted to a zero length string, and the **groupingUsed**, **maxFractionDigits**, **maxIntegerDigits**, **currencyCode**, and **currencySymbol** properties are applied before formatting.

Associating a Converter with a UIComponent Instance

As described in the previous section, each **UIOutput** instance in the view may have zero or one **Converter** associated with it. There are several ways to make that association, and we'll cover each in this section. Since Faces was designed with ease of development in mind, most users will not need to manually associate a converter with a component instance due to the comprehensive list of standard converters that automatically are associated with the component depending on its current value. We call these "implicit converters." In addition to the implicit converter association, there are a number of ways a converter can manually be associated with a component instance: by using one of the standard JSP converter tags, by using a custom converter tag, or programmatically in Java code by calling **setConverter()** on the component instance.

Implicit Conversion

Table 7-2 lists the implicit converters by class. For each entry, there is a corresponding converter instance in the package **javax.faces.convert**. For example, the class **java.lang .Double** has an implicit converter with the fully qualified class name of **javax.faces.convert .DoubleConverter**.

EXPERT GROUP INSIGHT *To help with the JSR goal of making JSF as useful as possible within tools, all of the standard converters adhere to JavaBeans naming conventions for properties. This allows tools to easily add converters to a palette and provide property inspectors for easy customization.*

In order for implicit conversion to occur, the system must be able to discern the type of the value. As you learned in Chapter 3, each **EditableValueHolder** component instance has a

Value Class	Converter
java.math.BigDecimal	javax.faces.convert.BigDecimalConverter
java.math.BigInteger	javax.faces.convert.BigIntegerConverter
java.lang.Boolean	javax.faces.convert.BooleanConverter
java.lang.Byte	javax.faces.convert.ByteConverter
java.lang.Character	javax.faces.convert.CharacterConverter
java.lang.Double	javax.faces.convert.DoubleConverter
java.lang.Float	javax.faces.convert.FloatConverter
java.lang.Integer	javax.faces.convert.IntegerConverter
java.lang.Long	javax.faces.convert.LongConverter
java.lang.Short	javax.faces.convert.ShortConverter

TABLE 7-2   The Implicit Converters

"local value" property, as well as an optional "value binding." The local value is not type-safe, and is always known to the system as being of type **Object**. It is only when a component instance has a value binding that its type is discoverable by the system, thanks to the **getType()** method of the Expression Language API. Components that don't have a value binding cannot have implicit conversion. For example, the first of the two following text fields will have an implicit **Integer** converter associated with it, while the second will not.

```
<h:inputText id="age" value="#{user.age}" />
<h:inputText id="weight" value="10"/>
```

Assuming the **age** JavaBeans property of the **user** managed bean is of type **Integer**, the system will automatically create and use a **javax.faces.convert.IntegerConverter** whenever conversion is required. Conveniently, as you will soon see, it is easy to install additional converters to extend or modify the set of types for which implicit conversion can be performed. Note the absence of an implicit converter for dates. This is because we have no way of knowing if the number should be a Date, a Time, or a Date and Time.

Explicit Conversion via JSP Tags

If you require greater control over conversion than that afforded by implicit conversion, three JSP tags are provided in the **jsf_core** tag library: **<f:convertDateTime>**, **<f:convertNumber>**, and **<f:converter>**. The general form of these tags is shown next. For brevity, some attributes have been omitted. Chapter 19 contains the complete reference. Most of the tag attributes in the following have corresponding JavaBeans properties on the converter instance that sits behind the tag. The setter methods of these properties are called as appropriate.

```
<f:convertDateTime dateStyle="dateStyle"
  locale="locale" pattern="formatPattern" timeZone="timeZone"
  type="type"
  binding="valueExpression"/>

<f:convertNumber currencyCode="code"
  currencySymbol="symbol"
  groupingUsed="boolean" locale="locale"
  pattern="formatPattern" type="type"
  binding="valueExpression" />

<f:converter converterId="converter-id"
  binding="valueExpression" />
```

For **<f:convertDateTime>**, the **dateStyle** attribute must be **short**, **medium**, **long**, **full**, or **default**. If not specified, **default** is assumed. If specified, **locale** must be a value binding expression that evaluates to an instance of **java.util.Locale**, or a literal string that is valid to pass as the first argument to the constructor for **java.util.Locale(String language, String country)**. In this case, the empty string will be passed as the second argument. If locale is not specified, the return value of **FacesContext.getCurrentInstance().getViewRoot() .getLocale()** will be used. If pattern is specified, its value must be a format pattern as used in **java.text.SimpleDateFormat**, or an expression that evaluates to the same. If **timeZone** is specified, its value must be a literal string that is a timezone ID as in the Javadocs for **java.util.TimeZone.getTimeZone()**, or a value binding expression that evaluates to an instance of **java.util.TimeZone**. If not specified, the system timezone is used. If **type** is specified, its value must be **date**, **time**, or **both**. This tells the converter to format or parse the value as a date, a time, or a **DateTime**, respectively. If not specified, **both** is assumed. If **binding** is specified, its value must be a value binding expression that evaluates to an instance of **javax.faces.convert.DateTimeConverter**.

For **<f:convertNumber>**, the **currencyCode**, if specified, must be a literal string that is a valid ISO 4217 currency code (such as USD or EUR), or a value binding expression that evaluates to the same. If not specified, the system currency code is used. If specified, the **currencySymbol** is the actual currency symbol used, such as "$" or "€", or an expression that evaluates to the same. If not specified, the system symbol is used. If specified, the **groupingUsed** must be either true or false. If not specified, **true** is assumed. If specified, **pattern** must be a literal string that is used as the pattern for the underlying **java.text .DecimalFormat** instance, or an expression that evaluates to the same. If not specified, no pattern is used. If specified, the **type** parameter must be **number**, **currency**, or **percentage**. If not specified, **number** is assumed. If specified, the **binding** attribute must be an expression that evaluates to a **javax.faces.convert.NumberConverter** instance.

For **<f:converter>**, the **converterId** attribute is the converter identifier as specified in the config file, such as faces-config.xml. In Faces 1.0 and 1.1, **converterId** was a required attribute, but in 1.2 either the **binding** or **converterId** attribute must be specified. If both are specified, **converterId** is used to create the converter, and the **setValue()** method of the binding is used to store the created converter.

The **<f:convertDateTime>** tag leverages the conversion facilities provided by **java.text .SimpleDateFormat**, the **<f:convertNumber>** tag leverages the conversion facilities provided by **java.text.DecimalFormat**, and **<f:converter>** provides a JSP gateway to look up a converter by its **converter-id**. These three tags are sufficient to cover the conversion needs for all possible datatypes. They are described in detail in Chapter 19, but the following discussion explains how they can be used to control conversion.

The usage pattern for all of the converter tags is to nest them inside the markup for the component to which they should be attached. For example:

```
<h:outputText id="date" value="#{transaction.date}">
  <f:convertDateTime dateStyle="short"/>
</h:inputText>
```

This example associates a **DateTimeConverter** instance with the **HtmlOutputText** instance with the ID **date**. The same pattern is true for the other converter tags.

---

*JSF 1.2 **TIP*** *In JSF 1.2, all of these **Converter** tags provide a **binding** attribute that functions similar to the **binding** attribute on **UIComponent** instances (and the tags that expose them), as described in Chapter 6. Briefly, the **binding** attribute allows you to say that the actual **Converter** instance must come from the result of evaluating an EL expression. This feature enables programmatically configuring a converter instance directly from Java code, and then allows that converter instance to be referred to in many different places. This means you only have to configure the converter attributes once, and avoid the class of bugs that comes from duplicating information in multiple places. Also, the **binding** attribute makes it very easy to add custom converters and validators, as opposed to going through the hassle of adding them to a faces-config.xml file and the attendant JSP tags.*

Before jumping into the tags themselves, let's review the basics of date formatting using **java.text.SimpleDateFormat**. This class is a concrete implementation of **java.text.DateFormat**, which allows parsing dates or times in a language-independent manner. **SimpleDateFormat** applies user-specified parameters to convert a string into a **java.util.Date** instance and back again. These parameters are applied to the **SimpleDateFormat** instance by a variety of methods, as described next. The most basic element of **SimpleDateFormat** is *style*, which is inherited from the superclass, **DateFormat**. The *style* parameter is a symbolic constant passed to the static **getDateInstance()** or **getTimeInstance()** methods on **DateFormat**. This parameter provides a useful abstraction by saying the formatted value will be in **SHORT**, **LONG**, **MEDIUM**, or **FULL** style. The exact meaning of the *style* parameter depends on whether you are dealing with a date, a time, or a date and time. A **SHORT** styled date is 05/26/03, while a **LONG** styled time is 12:30:45 pm. When the maximum level of control is required, use the *pattern* parameter of **SimpleDateFormat**. The pattern is supplied to the instance by calling the **applyPattern()** method. This allows you to specify a format string to control how the date, time, or date and time are output. For example, the pattern string

```
"HH:mm:ss on EEEE ',' MMMM dd ',' yyyy"
```

will produce an output such as this:

```
13:24:21 on Tuesday, April 15, 1997
```

See the Java Platform API documentation for **SimpleDateFormat** for the complete specification of the pattern language. The *timezone* parameter of **DateFormat** allows you to state in which time zone this time should be treated. This is passed as an argument to the **setTimeZone()** method.

The **<f:convertDateTime>** tag exposes the power of the **SimpleDateFormat** class to the JSP Faces user. All of the tag attributes for this tag are value expression enabled. Briefly, the most useful tag attributes are **type**, **style**, and **pattern**. The **type** tag attribute allows you to choose to treat the value as a date, a time, or both. This is used to determine whether **getDateInstance()**, **getTimeInstance()**, or **getDateTimeInstance()** should be used to create the underlying **DateFormat** instance, respectively. The **style** parameter for the underlying **SimpleDateFormat** is specified by providing a **dateStyle** or **timeStyle** tag attribute with values of **SHORT**, **MEDIUM**, **LONG**, or **FULL**. The value of the **pattern** attribute is passed through directly to the underlying **SimpleDateFormat** instance. If you want to force conversion to be a specific **Locale**, the **locale** attribute is provided.

Let's also review the use of **java.text.DecimalFormat** for formatting numbers, including currencies. This class is a concrete implementation of **java.text.NumberFormat** which allows parsing numbers in a language-independent manner. **DecimalFormat** applies user-specified parameters to convert a string into a **java.lang.Number** instance and back again. **DecimalFormat** has many elements, but the main ones of interest to conversion are **pattern** and **groupingUsed** (defined on superclass, **NumberFormat**). As in the **SimpleDateFormat**, the **pattern** parameter provides complete control over the appearance of the number and is applied to the underlying **NumberFormat** instance by calling its **applyPattern()** method. For example, the **pattern** "\u00A4 #.00" says this number should be output as a currency with any number of digits before the decimal separator, and exactly two after it. The currency symbol and decimal separator are, of course, locale-sensitive. The **groupingUsed** JavaBeans property specifies whether a locale-sensitive grouping delimiter should be used—for example, "3,147,295".

The **<f:convertNumber>** tag exposes **java.text.DecimalFormat** to the JSP Faces user. As mentioned earlier, all tag attributes are value expression enabled. The most useful attributes are shown next:

- type
- pattern
- currencyCode
- currencySymbol
- groupingUsed

The **type** attribute can be **number**, **currency**, or **percentage**. The value of this attribute is used to determine if the underlying **NumberFormat** instance should be created using **getNumberInstance()**, **getCurrencyInstance()**, or **getPercentInstance()**, respectively. The **currencyCode** attribute is an ISO 4217 currency code, such as "USD" for U.S. dollar, and "EUR" for European Union Euro. The **currencySymbol** can be used to directly specify the currency symbol, but in JDK 1.4 and beyond, the **currencyCode** takes precedence if specified. The **groupingUsed** attribute is a **boolean** that functions as mentioned in the previous paragraph.

The last of the three standard JSP tags for conversion is **<f:converter>**. This tag allows associating an arbitrary converter with a component using the converter ID lookup mechanism. Previously, we mentioned that converters can be registered and looked up by class. They can also be registered and looked up by **converter-id**, registered in the **faces-config.xml** file for the application. Table 7-1 lists the standard converters and their converter IDs. While it's certainly possible to use the **<f:converter>** tag with the standard converters, it is really intended to provide a gateway to custom converters without requiring the creation of a custom converter tag. For example, the Virtual Trainer example uses a custom **WeightConverter** that consults the user's preferences and displays weights in either metric or English units. For example:

```
<h:inputText id="targetWeight" value="#{user.targetWeight}">
  <f:converter converterId="weight"/>
</h:inputText>
```

Programmatically Associating a Converter with a UIComponent

The final way to associate a **Converter** with a **UIComponent** is programmatically. Nearly all of the JSP tags in Faces serve only to expose the underlying component model to the JSP page author. In the case of the converter tags, this can mean that the **setConverter()** method of a **ValueHolder** instance is called. The existence of a **setConverter()** method means that you can call it directly, if you are so inclined. When using this approach, you must be aware of when in the request processing lifecycle your code is executing. Also, this approach violates the separation of controller from view in the MVC paradigm because a-priori knowledge of the view is required to find the components on which to install the converters. With these cautions, we include this approach here for completeness.

As mentioned earlier, conversion happens twice during the lifecycle, once during the Apply Request Values or Process Validations phase, and again during the Render Response phase.

For JSF 1.2, if you want your **Converter** to be used during the whole lifecycle, try using a **UIViewRoot PhaseListener** registered for the **beforePhase** event of the Render Response phase. This will ensure that the **Converter** is installed before the first rendering and that it remains installed throughout the life of the view thanks to the state management APIs. Once you know when in the lifecycle your converter installing code will execute, it's a matter of creating and installing it in the desired component.

The following example shows how to programmatically create and install a converter on two components in the view. One component uses by-type converter lookup and the other uses by-class converter lookup.

```
FacesContext context = FacesContext.getCurrentInstance();
Converter intConverter = null;
Converter floatConverter = null;
UIComponent component1 = null;
UIComponent component2 = null;
UIViewRoot root = context.getViewRoot();

// Find the components on which we'll install the Converters.
component1 = (ValueHolder) root.findComponent("form" +
                            NamingContainer.SEPARATOR_CHAR +
                            "intComponent");
component2 = (ValueHolder) root.findComponent("form" +
                            NamingContainer.SEPARATOR_CHAR +
                            "floatComponent");

// Create the Converters, one by type, the other by Class.
intConverter =
  context.getApplication().createConverter("javax.faces.Integer");

floatConverter =
  context.getApplication().createConverter(Float.class);

// Install the converters.


component1.setConverter(intConverter);
component2.setConverter(floatConverter);
```

The main point of this example is to show the two variants of **createConverter()** and the use of **setConverter()**.

The Lifetime of a Converter

Even though the Java Platform provides automatic memory management in the form of garbage collection, it is still very important to be mindful of the memory implications of the design decisions that you make as you develop your application. This is particularly important when using a framework, where objects are frequently instantiated on the user's behalf without the user's knowledge. As described in the previous section, each **UIComponent** instance in the view may have zero or one **Converter** associated with it, and there are several ways to make that association. The lifetime implications of these different ways are the subject of this section.

Implicit Conversion

Converters associated with implicit conversion are dynamically created each time they are needed. This might give the appearance of being an unnecessary performance penalty, but actually, implicit conversion is a good thing for performance. The cost of instantiating these kinds of converters is very small, and because they are not attached to the component, there is no state saving and restoring penalty.

Explicit Conversion

All methods of explicit conversion boil down to calling **setConverter()** on the **UIComponent** instance, which makes the converter a part of the component's state, thereby ensuring it will be saved and restored across requests by the state management system. With this approach, the lifetime of the converter is the same as the lifetime of the component instance itself, which is configurable by the application author by setting the server's session timeout value.

Conversion Done by Validators

Some validators also use converters to aid in performing validation. Depending on the implementation of the **Validator**, this may cause a **Converter** instance to be created.

Custom Converters

The real power of the Faces conversion model is its extensibility. In this section, we will provide a complete converter for the Virtual Trainer example. This converter looks up the value of the **weightUnits** preference in the **preferences** object and uses it to convert the weight from the domain model unit, which is kilograms, to the user's preference, which may be kilograms or pounds. We'll start with the converter class and close with the configuration information necessary to hook up the converter to the system.

The converter class for Virtual Trainer is called **WeightConverter**. It implements the **Converter** interface and is shown next. This example is written using the JSF 1.2 API.

```
package com.jsfcompref.trainer.convert;

import javax.faces.convert.Converter;
import javax.faces.convert.ConverterException;
import javax.faces.context.FacesContext;
import javax.faces.application.Application;
import javax.faces.component.UIComponent;

import javax.el.ValueExpression;

import java.util.Locale;
import java.text.NumberFormat;
import java.text.ParseException;

public class WeightConverter implements Converter {

    public static final int UNIT_KILOGRAMS = 0;
    public static final int UNIT_POUNDS = 01;

    private Locale locale = null;

    private NumberFormat formatter = null;
```

```java
public WeightConverter() {
  formatter = null;
  locale = null;
}

private int getUnitFromUserPreferences(FacesContext context) {
  Integer result = null;
  int unit = -1;

  // Look up the user's preference.
  ValueExpression ve =
    context.getApplication().getExpressionFactory().
    createValueExpression("#{currentUser.prefs.weightUnits}");
  try {
    result = (Integer) ve.getValue(context.getELContext());
  }
  catch (Throwable e) {
    // log error
  }

  if(null != result) {
    unit = result.intValue();
  }

  return unit;
}

private getNumberFormat(FacesContext context) {
  if(null == formatter) {
    formatter = NumberFormat.getNumberInstance(getLocale(context));
  }
  return formatter;
}

private Locale getLocale(FacesContext context) {
  Locale locale = this.locale;
  if(locale == null) {
    locale = context.getViewRoot().getLocale();
  }
  return (locale);
}


public Locale getLocale() {
  return (this.locale);
}

public void setLocale(Locale locale) {
  this.locale = locale;
}

public Object getAsObject(FacesContext context,
                          UIComponent component, String value) {
  if(context == null || component == null) {
    throw new NullPointerException();
```

```
  }
  // This example doesn't use the component parameter but we will
  // use it later in the chapter when we explore conversion
  // messages.
  if(null == value || 0 == value.length()) {
    return null;
  }

  int units = getUnitFromUserPreferences(context);
  float floatValue;


  try {
    floatValue = getNumberFormat().parse(value);
  }
  catch (ParseException e) {
    throw new ConverterException(e.getMessage());
  }

  // If the user's preference is English, this String is in
  // pounds.  Get the float value of the pounds
  if(UNIT_POUNDNS == units) {
    floatValue /= 2.2; // convert to kilograms
  }

  return new Float(floatValue);
}

public String getAsString(FacesContext context, UIComponent component,
                          Object value) {
  if(context == null || component == null) {
    throw new NullPointerException();
  }
  // This example doesn't use the component parameter but we will
  // use it later in the chapter when we explore conversion
  // messages.

  if(null == value || 0 == value.length()) {
    return null;
  }

  String result = null;

  int floatValue = ((Float)value).floatValue();
  int units = getUnitFromUserPreferences(context);

  if(UNIT_POUNDNS == units) {
    floatValue *= 2.2; // convert to pounds
  }

  try {
    result = getNumberFormat().parse(new Float(floatValue));
  }
  catch (ParseException e) {
    throw new ConverterException(e.getMessage());
```

```
      }
      if(UNIT_POUNDS == units) {
        result = result + " lbs.";
      }
      else {
        result = result + " kg.";
      }
      return result.trim();
    }
    // This converter has no user-configurable parameters, and thus
    // is stateless.  If we did have user-configurable parameters, we
    // would need to implement the javax.faces.component.StateHolder
    // interface to save and restore the values of these parameters
    // between requests.
}
```

In **WeightConverter**, the **getAsObject( )** method uses the number parsing provided by classes in the **java.text package** to perform the conversion from **String** to **float**. If the user has requested that weights be shown in pounds, the **float** value of pounds is converted to kilograms. The kilogram **float** value is then wrapped in an instance of **java.lang.Float** and returned.

The **getAsString( )** method extracts the **float** primitive from the **Float** wrapper object. If the user has requested that weights be shown in pounds, the **float** value is converted to pounds and the number formatting classes from the **java.text** package are used to format the value into a string, with the units appended.

Helper methods are provided to get the **NumberFormat** and **Locale** instances to use. Pay special attention to the private **getLocale( )** method. It takes a **FacesContext** as a parameter and extracts a **Locale** from the **UIViewRoot** for this view. This is important because the Faces internationalization system ensures that the **UIViewRoot**'s **Locale** is the correct one to use for all language-sensitive operations.

Before **WeightConverter** can be used, it must be hooked up to the system by placing the following in the proper element ordering in the **faces-config.xml**:

```
<converter>
  <description>
    Registers the weight converter using the converter id weight
  </description>
  <converter-id>com.jsfcompref.Weight</converter-id>
  <converter-class>
    com.jsfcompref.trainer.convert.WeightConverter
  </converter-class>
</converter>
```

The XML markup for **WeightConverter** simply identifies the converter by ID and a fully qualified Java class name. This enables the use of the **<f:converter>** tag to attach the converter to **UIComponent** instances in the view. Instead of registering the converter by ID, it is also possible to register the converter by the type of object it can convert. Converters registered in this way can be discovered for use in implicit conversion, which was explained earlier.

The **WeightConverter** can be used from JSP through the **<f:converter>** tag, as shown next:

```
<p>Current Weight <h:outputText value="#{user.currentWeight}">
  <f:converter id="com.jsfcompref.Weight" /> </h:outputText> </p>
```

Note that the **binding** attribute could also be used to good effect in the following:

```
<p>Current Weight <h:outputText value="#{user.currentWeight}">
  <f:converter binding="#{converters.weightConverter} /> </h:outputText> </p>
```

where the expression **#{converters.weightConverter}** points to an instance of our **WeightConverter**.

Now that you've learned about conversion, let's examine validation, which happens immediately after conversion in the flow of the request processing lifecycle.

The Faces Validation System

The **javax.faces.validator.Validator** interface is the foundation of the JSF validation system. As a general rule, this interface is implemented by objects that want to function as a **Validator**. (However, as explained later in this section, not all objects that function as a **Validator** must implement this interface.) This section covers in detail the lifetime of validator instances, the standard validators that are available "out-of-the-box," how validators are associated with **UIComponent** instances, and an example of how to write a custom **Validator**.

The **javax.faces.validator.Validator** interface defines a single method called **validate()**, which is shown next:

public void validate(FacesContext *context*,
                     UIComponent *component*,
                     Object *value*)

As with the converter methods, the *context* parameter is the **FacesContext** instance for this request, the *component* parameter is the component whose value is being validated, and the *value* parameter is the value on which to perform the validation.

This method is called during the Apply Request Values phase if the component has the **immediate** property set, or during the Process Validations phase otherwise. Before calling **validate()**, the component is marked as invalid. The **validate()** method is then passed a value that has been successfully converted. This method must throw a **ValidatorException** if the validation fails. If no such exception is thrown, the system assumes validation has succeeded and marks the component as valid. If the exception is thrown, its message is extracted and added to the set of messages on the current **FacesContext** and processing continues. Standard Faces validators run on the server, though it's possible to write a validator that executes entirely on the client. Even when using client-side validation, it is strongly advisable to perform server-side validation as a double-check against malicious code in the browser.

As with converters, Faces provides a small, but useful set of standard Validator implementations, listed in Table 7-3. Unlike converters, Validator instances are not registered by class, only by **validator-id**. This is because the concept of validation is not tied tightly to an object's type. For example, it is possible for a number to be a valid credit card number, but still be expired. Expired credit cards are of no use to an e-commerce system!

In addition to the validators shown in Table 7-3, Faces also provides a facility to specify that a value is "required," but since this feature is so commonly used, it has been implemented for maximum correctness and simplicity and does not use the regular validation system. Let's examine the standard validators and the "required" facility in detail. The validation messages

validator-id	Tag Handler	Description
javax.faces .DoubleRange	f:validateDoubleRange	Validates that data of type **java.lang .Double** is within a specified range
javax.faces.Length	f:validateLength	Validates that data of type **String** has a length that is within a specified range
javax.faces.LongRange	f:validateLongRange	Validates that data of type **java.lang .Long** is within a specified range

TABLE 7-3 The Standard Validators

used in this section paraphrase the meaning of the message. The real messages will be dealt with later in this chapter in the section "Tie It All Together: Messages in a View."

LongRangeValidator

LongRangeValidator.validate() verifies that the value of the component to which it is attached is within a specified range using an algorithm similar to the following:

1. The argument value has already been converted. This means that it is an instance of **java.lang.Long**. Therefore, the primitive **long** value is extracted.

2. If the user set a maximum parameter for this **Validator** instance, the value is checked against the configured maximum. If the value is greater than the maximum, one of two exceptions must be thrown. First, if the user configured a minimum parameter, then the value is not within the specified range. In this case, a **ValidatorException** with a "not in range" message is thrown. Second, if no minimum parameter is specified, then a **ValidatorException** with a "greater than the specified maximum" message is thrown.

3. If the user set a minimum parameter for this **Validator** instance, the value is checked against the configured minimum. If the value is less than the minimum, one of two exceptions must be thrown. First, if the user configured a maximum parameter, then the value is not in the specified range. In this case, a **ValidatorException** with a "not in range" message is thrown. Second, if no maximum parameter is specified, then a **ValidatorException** with a "less than the specified minimum" message is thrown.

4. If a **NumberFormatException** was thrown during processing, a **ValidatorException** with a "there was a type error during validation" message is thrown.

This class also implements the **equals()** method to allow comparing two instances. The **equals()** method returns true if the other **Validator** is configured with the same parameters values for maximum and minimum. The following example illustrates the use of the **f: validateLongRange** tag, which exposes the **LongRangeValidator** to the JSP page author.

```
<p>Enter a California Zip Code:
  <h:inputText value="#{user.address.zip}" id="zip">
    <f:validateLongRange minimum="90000" maximum="99999" />
  </h:inputText>
<h:message for="zip" /></p>
```

This example asks the user to enter a Zip code in California, which means they must enter a number from 90000 to 99999. A more robust example would also have a custom validator that checks that the Zip code entered is indeed a valid Zip code, since not all numbers between 90000 and 99999 are valid Zip codes in California.

DoubleRangeValidator

The **DoubleRangeValidator** class behaves exactly like the **LongRangeValidator**, except that it operates on **Double** instances instead.

LengthValidator

LengthValidator.validate() verifies that the string length of the data is within a specified range using an algorithm similar to the following:

1. The value has already been converted, which means that you can safely call **toString()** on it.
2. If the user has specified a maximum length parameter and the length of the value is greater than that maximum, throw a **ValidatorException** with the "string is too long" message.
3. If the user has specified a minimum length parameter and the length of the value is greater than that minimum, throw a **ValidatorException** with the "string is too short" message.

This class also implements the **equals()** method to allow two instances to be compared. The **equals()** method returns true if the other **Validator** is configured with the same parameters values for maximum and minimum.

The following example illustrates the use of the **f:validateLength** tag, which exposes the **LengthValidator** to the JSP page author.

```
<p>Credit Card Number:
  <h:inputText value="#{user.creditCard}" id="cc">
    <f:validateLength minimum="16" maximum="16" />
  </h:inputText>
</p>
```

In this example, we require that the user enter exactly 16 characters. Again, a more robust example would include a custom validator that handles things like interspersed dashes and/or spaces and validates the number against a credit card database.

The "required" Facility

The notion of a value being "required" for the user to enter is so common that it receives special treatment in Faces. Recall that any **UIComponent** in the view that can possibly have a user-entered value implements the **EditableValueHolder** interface. This interface has a **boolean** property called **required** whose default value is **false**. The validation processing in **UIInput** checks this property and if no value has been provided by the user, a "value is required" message is added to the set of messages for this **FacesContext** and the component is marked as invalid. If the field is not required, and no value has been provided, no further validation processing happens. This saves the cost of throwing and catching the **ValidatorException** for this common case, and ensures that validation doesn't run on empty values, for the sake of algorithmic correctness.

EXPERT GROUP INSIGHT *Early drafts of the specification included an actual* **Required** *validator instead of the simple* **required** *attribute, but this was removed for performance, convenience, and correctness.*

How to Associate a Validator with a UIComponent Instance

As shown in the UML diagram in Figure 7-2, each **EditableValueHolder** instance in the view may have zero or many **Validator** instances associated with it. There are several ways to make that association, and each is described in this section. Unlike in the case of **Converters**, there is no implicit **Validator** association mechanism. This is because **Validators** don't have the concept of type as a part of their external contract, though **Validators** may indeed need to be aware of the type of the data they are validating to function properly. Two methods are provided for explicitly associating a **Validator** with a **UIComponent** instance: via JSP tags or programmatically. Each **EditableValueHolder** instance maintains a list of **Validator** instances, as well as a special **MethodBinding** property that points to a method that acts like a **Validator**. These two data-stores for **Validator** instances provide lots of flexibility in how to validate your Web application.

Using JSP to Associate a Validator with a UIComponent Instance

There are two ways to associate a **Validator** with a **UIComponent** instance from JSP: using one of the tags from **jsf_core** or using a **MethodBinding** (or **MethodExpression** in Faces 1.2) as the value of the **validator** attribute on one of the component tags directly. This section covers each style in turn.

Faces provides a JSP tag in the **jsf_core** tag library for each of the standard validators. The **<f:validateDoubleRange>**, **<f:validateLongRange>**, and **<f:validateLength>** tags attach the **DoubleRangeValidator**, the **LongRangeValidator**, and the **LengthValidator**, respectively, to the component represented by the component tag in which they are nested. For example:

```
<h:inputText id="zipcode" value="#{user.zipCode}">
  <f:validateLength maximum="5" minimum="5" />
  <f:validateLongRange minimum="90000" maximum="99999" />
</h:inputText>
```

This attaches one **LengthValidator** and one **LongRangeValidator** to the **HtmlInputText** component associated with the **<h:inputText>** tag. The **LengthValidator** has been configured to ensure that the user enters exactly five characters in the text field. The **LongRangeValidator** has been configured to ensure the Zip code is between 90000 and 99999. If the **zipcode** property of the **user** bean is of type **Integer**, implicit conversion will take place as well.

As with converters, Faces also provides a generic **<f:validator>** tag that allows you to associate any **Validator** with the component in which it is nested by giving the **validator-id**. Also, similar to converters and **UIComponent** tags in general, the **Validator** tags offer a "binding" attribute to state that the actual **Validator** instance should come from evaluating an EL expression. (See Chapter 19 for full details on the **Validator** tags and all their attributes.)

Using JSP and the validator Attribute to Associate a Validator with a UIComponent Instance

Unlike conversion, validation is a one-way process, and it only happens once during a run through the request processing lifecycle. These constraints open up the possibility of using the Expression Language to point to a method on an arbitrary JavaBean that adheres to the contract and signature of **Validator.validate()**. The **MethodBinding** class from the EL makes this possible. For example:

```
<h:inputText validator="#{user.validateAge}" value="#{user.age}" />
```

assuming the **user** bean has a method defined like:

```
public void validateAge(FacesContext context, UIComponent component,
                        Object value) {
  // Validation code here
}
```

During the Process Validations phase, when it comes time to validate this component, call the method **validateAge()** on the bean named **user** and assume that it will fulfill the contract of a **Validator**. This late-binding approach saves the instantiation of separate **Validator** instances and can greatly simplify application design by allowing you to put the business logic, and the method to validate it, in the same class.

All of the tags in the **html_basic** tag library that map to **UIComponent**s which implement the interface **javax.faces.component.EditableValueHolder** honor the **validator** attribute. They are

inputHidden	inputSecret	inputText
inputTextarea	selectBooleanCheckbox	selectManyCheckbox
selectManyListbox	selectManyMenu	selectOneListbox
selectOneMenu	selectOneRadio	

Note that using this method of association allows only one **Validator** to be added to the component, but you can still attach multiple validators using the other methods of association.

Programmatically Associating a Validator with a UIComponent Instance

As with converters, the JSP layer for validators is merely a façade around the component model. The JSP tags all result in a call to **addValidator()** on the underlying component instance, and the **required** attribute results in a call to **setRequired(true)** on the component. It is certainly possible to call these methods directly, but as with converters, you must be aware of when in the request processing lifecycle your code to add the validator or set the required attribute will execute.

JSF 1.2 TIP   *If you want your* **Validator** *to be used during the whole lifecycle, try using a* **UIView RootPhaseListener** *registered for the* **beforePhase** *event of the Render Response phase. This will ensure that the* **Validator** *is installed before the first rendering and that it remains installed throughout the life of the view thanks to the state management APIs.*

Once you know when in the lifecycle your validator installing code will execute, it's a matter of creating and adding it to the desired component. The following example shows how to programmatically create and add two different **Validator** instances on a component in the view.

```
FacesContext context = FacesContext.getCurrentInstance();
Validator progressValidator = null;
MethodBinding pointerToValidatorMethod = null;
EditableValueHolder component = null;
UIViewRoot root = context.getViewRoot();


// Find the component on which we'll add the Validator.
component = (EditableValueHolder) root.findComponent("form" +
NamingContainer.SEPARATOR_CHAR + "userComponent");


// Ensure that this component doesn't already have a
// progressValidator.
Validator [] validators = component.getValidators();
boolean found = false;
for(int i = 0; i < validators.length && !found; i++) {
  found = (validators[i] instanceof ProgressValidator);
}
if(found) {
  return;
}

// Create the progressValidator.
progressValidtor = context.getApplication().createValidator("progressValidator");

// Add it to the component.
component.addValidator(progressValidator);

// Ensure that this component doesn't already
// have a validator in its MethodBinding slot.
if(null != component.getValidator()) {
  return;
}

Class params = {FacesContext.class, UIComponent.class, Object.class};
pointerToValidatorMethod =
context.getApplication().createMethodBinding("#{user.validateAge}",
                                    params);
component.setValidator(pointerToValidatorMethod);
```

The main point of this example is to show the use of the **createValidator()**, **addValidator()**, and **setValidator()** methods. Note that we had to take extra care to check if the validator was already added. This is necessary because validators are additive, whereas converters are not.

The Lifetime of a Validator

Due to the lack of implicit validation, it's easier to be aware of the lifetime implications because you always have to take some kind of action to add a **validator**. In all cases, once you take that action, the **Validator** instance persists for the lifetime of the **UIComponent** instance, which is generally limited by the lifetime of the session. If you're worried about excessive object instantiation, a good approach is to use the **MethodBindingValidator** technique as shown in the section "Writing a validation( ) Method That Is Pointed to by a MethodBinding." This places the lifetime constraints squarely into the realm of managed beans.

Custom Validators

Creating custom **Validator** implementations is even more common than creating custom **Converter** instances, partly because the set of standard validators provided by Faces is relatively small, and partly because it is very easy to write a **Validator**. In this section, we'll cover the two ways of implementing a **Validator** and discuss the pros and cons of each.

Implementing the Validator Interface

The first way that you can create a validator is to implement the **Validator** interface. With this approach, it is recommended to keep the validator in its own separate class since you must register it by **validator-id**. Also, instances of the **Validator** can be created automatically so it's best to keep it lightweight. For the Virtual Trainer example, one can imagine a **Validator** that ensures that the client has met all the fitness requirements for participation in an event, according to the opinion of the virtual trainer.

The following class, called **EventRequirementValidator**, provides such an implementation, written using the JSF 1.2 API.

```
package com.jsfcompref.trainer.validator;

import javax.faces.validator.Validator;
import javax.faces.validator.ValidatorException;
import javax.faces.component.UIComponent;
import javax.faces.context.FacesContext;

import javax.el.ValueExpression;


public class EventRequirementValidator extends Object implements Validator {
  public void validate(FacesContext context,
                       UIComponent  component,
                       Object value) throws ValidatorException {
  Boolean hasMetRequirements = null;

  ValueExpression ve =
    application.getExpressionFactory().
    createValueExpression("#{currentUser.status.qualified}");
    try {
      hasMetRequirements = (Boolean) ve.getValue(context.getELContext());
    }
    catch (Throwable e) {
      // log error
    }
    if (!hasMetRequirements.booleanValue()) {
      throw new ValidatorException("You still have more work to do!");
    }
  }
}
```

Before **EventRequirementValidator** can be used, it needs to be identified to the system by putting the following markup into the **faces-config.xml** file.

```
<validator>
  <description>
    Validates that the current user has met the requirements for the event.
  </description>
  <validator-id>eventRequirements</validator-id>
  <validator-class>
    com.jsfcompref.validator.EventRequirementValidator
  </validator-class>
</validator>
```

Note that this **EventRequirementValidator** has no configuration parameters, and thus is essentially stateless. The **validate()** method simply looks up the **qualified** property in the user's **status** bean and throws a **ValidatorException** if it is false. The markup for the validator allows the use of the **<f:validator>** tag to add this validator to any **UIComponent** instance in the view.

Writing a validation( ) Method that is Pointed to by a MethodBinding

The second approach to validation allows any managed bean in your application to function as a **Validator**, without implementing the **Validator** interface or registering the **Validator** in the **faces-config.xml** file. This approach is very useful when you have existing code that you want to retrofit to JSF. You need add only one method and then any **UIComponent** can use that method to perform validation. An example of this approach was shown earlier in this chapter in the section "Using JSP and the **validator** Attribute to Associate a **Validator** with a **UIComponent** Instance."

Tie It All Together: Messages in a View

The previous sections covered the mechanics of conversion and validation, when they happen, their impacts on the request processing lifecycle, the ways to create converters and validators, and how to associate them with the components in your view, but all of that would be for naught were it not for giving user feedback. After all, the point of all this is to tell the user they've done something wrong, and hopefully how to fix it. The way this information flows from the source of the error (a conversion or validation error) to the user is through the **javax.faces.application.FacesMessage** class, the **FacesContext**, and the **UIMessage** or **UIMessages** components. This section covers messages in detail, including how they're created, how to control their display, how to customize the standard messages, and how to add custom messages.

As explained in Chapter 3, the **FacesContext** instance is the per-request object that is the entry point to all of the Faces-specific context information relating to the current run through the request processing lifecycle. The two properties of particular import to conversion and validation are messages and the **UIViewRoot**. The page author doesn't interact with these properties directly, but rather by using the **<h:message>** and **<h:messages>** tags from the **html_basic** tag library. In the interest of completeness, we cover the **FacesContext** message and **UIViewRoot** properties as they relate to conversion and validation.

FacesMessage-Related Methods on FacesContext

The **FacesMessage** class encapsulates a single, localized, human-readable message, typically associated with a particular component in the view, and typically describing a problem in the process of conversion or validation. In addition to the message string itself, a **FacesMessage** has three properties of interest: **severity**, **summary**, and **detail**.

The **severity** property is defined as an inner class of **FacesMessage** with the following logical values: **INFO**, **WARN**, **ERROR**, and **FATAL**. The **severity** property provides additional information to the user about the error and has no effect on the lifecycle. The **summary** and **detail** properties are the actual localized human-readable messages.

The **FacesContext** instance maintains two logical collections of **FacesMessage** instances: a collection of messages that are associated with a component, and those that are not associated with a component. The former is usually the garden-variety conversion and validation message, and the latter may be a message that applies to the form as a whole. These two collections are accessed by the different variants of the **getMessages()** method on **FacesContext**. The variant that takes no arguments returns an **Iterator** of all messages, associated with a component or not. The variant that takes a **clientId** gets messages only associated with the component of that **clientId**, or, if the **clientId** is **null**, gets only messages that are *not* associated with a specific **clientId**. The **FacesContext** also provides a method to return the severity of the most severe message it currently has—**getMaximumSeverity()**, and a method to return an **Iterator** of **clientId**s for which it has messages: **getClientIdsWithMessages()**. Most JSP applications won't need to call these methods directly, but an example to illustrate their use is in order. As you can imagine, the implementations of the renderers for the **h:message** and **h:messages** tags use the **getMessages()** method to get the message or messages to render. Let's go a step further and show an example that directs the application to a special page if there are any messages with a severity of **Severity.FATAL**. To make this happen, we need to hook up an action method to a **UICommand** component. This is the standard way to do navigation in Faces, and is covered in detail in Chapter 5. First, let's show the JSP fragment for the button that submits the form:

```
<h:commandButton action="#{bean.checkForFatalError}" />
```

As explained in Chapter 5, this will cause the **public String checkForFatalError()** method on the managed bean named **bean** to be called when the button is pressed. The return value from this method is fed into the navigation system to determine the next view to display. The implementation of the **checkForFatalError()** method follows.

```
public String checkForFatalError() {
  FacesContext context = FacesContext.getCurrentInstance()
  FacesMessage.Severity severity = context.getMaximumSeverity()
  String result = "next";

  if (null != severity) {
    if (severity == FacesMessage.Severity.SEVERITY_FATAL) {
      result = "fatalError";
    }
  }
  return result;
}
```

This method gets the **FacesContext** for this request, extracts its **maximumSeverity** JavaBeans property, and examines it. If the value is **FacesMessage.Severity.SEVERITY_ FATAL**, it returns the value **fatalError**; otherwise, it returns the value **next**. These two values must be mentioned in a **navigation-rule** in the **faces-config.xml** file for this application, as shown next.

```
<navigation-rule>
  <from-view-id>/form1.jsp</from-view-id>
  <navigation-case>
    <description>Show a special page if any fatal errors are found
    </description>
    <from-outcome>fatalError</from-outcome>
    <to-view-id>/fatalError.jsp</to-view-id>
  </navigation-case>
  <navigation-case>
    <description>The normal page flow</description>
    <from-outcome>next</from-outcome>
    <to-view-id>/form2.jsp</to-view-id>
  </navigation-case>
</navigation-rule>
```

Here we see a single **navigation-rule** element with two **navigation-case** elements inside of it. The first deals with the **fatalError** case, and the second deals with the normal **next** case.

The UIViewRoot and Its Locale Property

The **FacesContext** is the place where you obtain the **UIViewRoot** for the current view. This **UIComponent** subclass is the root node of the tree structure that *is* the view. All of the components in your page are arranged as a tree of children of this root node. This root node has several properties but its **locale** property is of special interest to conversion and validation. The **locale** property is an instance of **java.util.Locale** that is guaranteed to be the right locale for any language-specific processing in this view. Chapter 14 explains how the **locale** property is set by the user and/or by the system, but at this point you need to know only that it is the correct **Locale** to use.

Converters use the locale for many of their methods. For example, the **DateTimeConverter** couldn't get very far unless it knew what separator it should use between numbers in a **SHORT** styled date, or where the year should go. For example, Europeans tend to use 14.05.1995 while Americans prefer 05/14/1995. Because messages are human-readable text, they are localized using the **ResourceBundle** mechanism of the Java platform.

When and How FacesMessage Instances are Created and Added to the FacesContext

There are exactly three times in the request processing lifecycle when the standard components will create a **FacesMessage** instance and add it to the **FacesContext**: when conversion fails, when validation fails, or when the converted and validated data cannot be pushed to the model during the Update Model Values phase. This last case is not likely due to user error, but the user needs to be informed nonetheless. Each case is examined in turn.

A **Converter** signals an error by throwing a **ConverterException**. When creating the exception, the converter has the option of giving a **FacesMessage** to the constructor directly, providing a simple string message, or no message at all. If no **FacesMessage** is provided to the **ConverterException**, a standard "conversion failed" **FacesMessage** is generated. If the **ConverterException** has a string **message** property, its value is used as the **detail** property of the **FacesMessage**. The **severity** of a **Converter FacesMessage** instance is always **ERROR**.

JSF 1.2 TIP   *In Faces 1.2, all of the standard converters have standard messages, but this was simply an omission in earlier revisions of the spec.*

A Validator signals an error by throwing a **ValidatorException**. Unlike the **ConverterException**, the **ValidatorException** must take a FacesMessage in its constructor. The severity of a **Validator FacesMessage** instance is always **ERROR**.

Lastly, if an EL exception is thrown when trying to propagate the value to the model during the Update Model Values phase, the message of the exception is examined. If non-null, a new **FacesMessage** is created with the exception message as the summary. If **null**, a **FacesMessage** is created with a generic error message.

---

*EXPERT GROUP INSIGHT   In all of the preceding cases, we have glossed over how the content of the **FacesMessage** is localized for messages that are built in to the specification. The EG intentionally avoided providing a factory API for **FacesMessage** instances because a generic factory pattern may be included in a future release of the Java platform, and it would be preferable to use that when it is available. Instead of the factory, the EG specified the exact manner in which the Java platform's **ResourceBundle** mechanism must be used to create and populate a **FacesMessage** instance with its localized message content. The following is the algorithm:*

1. *Call the **getMessageBundle()** method on the application. This returns the fully qualified name of the **ResourceBundle** to be used for this application, or null if no such bundle has been set. If null, use **javax.faces.Messages** as the name of the **ResourceBundle**.*

2. *Use the Java platform **ResourceBundle** lookup methods, and the **Locale** from the current **UIViewRoot** to obtain the **ResourceBundle** named from step 1.*

3. *Look in the **ResourceBundle** for a value under the key given by the value of the **messageId** for this **FacesMessage**. If none is found, there is no localized content for this message. Otherwise, use the value as the summary property of the **FacesMessage**. Append the string "_detail" to the **messageId** and look in the **ResourceBundle** for a value under that key. If found, use the value as the detail of the **FacesMessage**.*

4. *Make sure to perform any parameter substitution required on the localized content—for example, if the returned **ResourceBundle** is "Validation Error: Specified attribute is not between the expected values of {0} and {1}," the proper values must be substituted for {0} and {1}, perhaps using **java.text.MessageFormat**.*

How FacesMessages Are Rendered

At long last we have come to the place where the user enters the picture: showing them the errors in their input and how to correct them. In keeping with the JSF component model, there are two standard components that serve as placeholders in the view for messages to appear: **UIMessage** and **UIMessages**. Along with these components, there are renderers in the standard HTML render-kit: **javax.faces.Message** and **javax.faces.Messages**, respectively. Naturally, to show the valid combinations of these components and renderers, there are the **<h:message>** and **<h:messages>** tags in the **html_basic** tag library. As with all of the components in the standard HTML component set, the heavy lifting is done by the renderers, so we'll briefly describe those in this section. We then list the standard message keys for converters and validators, and show how to customize messages and add new ones.

Rendering a Message for a Specific Component in the Page

The **<h:message>** tag places into the view a **UIMessage** component associated with a **javax .faces.Message** Renderer. Whenever the user places a **<h:message>** tag in the page, they are required to provide a **for** attribute that gives the **componentId** of the component for which this tag will display messages. This gives the page author complete freedom to display the messages however they like in the page. The 1.2 version of the specification fixes a problem with earlier versions of JSF in which you couldn't put the **<h:message>** tag in front of the component to which it refers unless both the tag and the component were in the same **<h: form>**. Also in 1.2, a **dir** attribute has been added that lets the page author give a cue to the **Renderer** about the direction of the text, either left to right (LTR) or right to left (RTL). This **Renderer** gets an **Iterator** of messages from the **FacesContext** by calling its **getMessages( )** method, and passing the value of the **for** attribute. Only the first message in the **Iterator** is rendered. (See Chapter 19 for complete information on **<h:message>**.)

Rendering All the Messages in a Page

The **<h:messages>** tag places into the view a **UIMessages** component associated with a **javax.faces.Messages** Renderer. Whenever the user places a **<h:messages>** tag, all messages in the **FacesContext** are displayed, unless the **globalOnly** attribute is set, in which case only messages that are not associated with a given component are displayed. The **layout** attribute can be either **table** or **list**. If **table**, the messages are displayed in an HTML table; if **list**, they are displayed in an HTML unordered list. (Again, see Chapter 19 for complete information on **<h:message>**.)

The Standard Message Keys

Table 7-4 lists the standard message keys in JSF 1.2. The **FacesMessage** instances around which these messages are built are all generated during the Apply Request Values phase if the component has its **immediate** property set, and during the Process Validations phase otherwise. The severity of all these **FacesMessage** instances is **Severity.ERROR**.

Customizing the Content of One of the Standard Messages

The default content for the standard messages is pretty dry and may not be what you want in your application. For example, the standard message for **javax.faces.validator .LengthValidator.MINIMUM** is "Validation Error: Value is less than allowable maximum of "{0}"", which can be pretty cryptic to some. Because of the specification for how **FacesMessage** instances are produced, it is possible to provide your own **ResourceBundle** that is consulted before the standard one, thus allowing you to override any of the standard messages, as well as provide your own for any custom **Converter** or **Validator** implementations you may have. To do this, simply create an **<application>** element in your **faces-config.xml** file (if you don't have one already) and add a **<message-bundle>** element inside of it. Note that DTD and Schema are very ordering-dependent so you must place the message-bundle element in the right order if you have other elements in your **<application>** element. Full details of the element ordering can be found in Chapter 18.

The following is the **<application>** element for the Virtual Trainer:

```
<application>
  <message-bundle>com.jsfcompref.Messages</message-bundle>
  <locale-config>
    <default-locale>en</default-locale>
    <supported-locale>de</supported-locale>
  </locale-config>
</application>
```

messageId	New in 1.2
javax.faces.component.UIInput.CONVERSION	n
javax.faces.component.UIInput.REQUIRED	n
javax.faces.component.UISelectOne.INVALID	n
javax.faces.component.UISelectMany.INVALID	n
javax.faces.converter.BigDecimalConverter.DECIMAL	y
javax.faces.converter.BigIntegerConverter.BIGINTEGER	y
javax.faces.converter.BooleanConverter.BOOLEAN	y
javax.faces.converter.ByteConverter.BYTE	y
javax.faces.converter.CharacterConverter.CHARACTER	y
javax.faces.converter.DateTimeConverter.DATE	y
javax.faces.converter.DateTimeConverter.TIME	y
javax.faces.converter.DateTimeConverter.DATETIME	y
javax.faces.converter.DateTimeConverter.PATTERN_TYPE	y
javax.faces.converter.DoubleConverter.DOUBLE	y
javax.faces.converter.FloatConverter.FLOAT	y
javax.faces.converter.IntegerConverter.INTEGER	y
javax.faces.converter.LongConverter.LONG	y
javax.faces.converter.NumberConverter.CURRENCY	y
javax.faces.converter.NumberConverter.PERCENT	y
javax.faces.converter.NumberConverter.NUMBER	y
javax.faces.converter.NumberConverter.PATTERN	y
javax.faces.converter.ShortConverter.SHORT	y
javax.faces.converter.STRING	y
javax.faces.validator.NOT_IN_RANGE	n
javax.faces.validator.DoubleRangeValidator.MAXIMUM	n
javax.faces.validator.DoubleRangeValidator.MINIMUM	n
javax.faces.validator.DoubleRangeValidator.NOT_IN_RANGE	n
javax.faces.validator.DoubleRangeValidator.TYPE	n
javax.faces.validator.LengthValidator.MAXIMUM	n
javax.faces.validator.LengthValidator.MINIMUM	n
javax.faces.validator.LongRangeValidator.MAXIMUM	n
javax.faces.validator.LongRangeValidator.MINIMUM	n
javax.faces.validator.LongRangeValidator.NOT_IN_RANGE	n
javax.faces.validator.LongRangeValidator.TYPE	n

TABLE 7-4   The Standard Message Keys

This states that the application resource bundle should be **com.jsfcompref.Messages** and that the default locale for the application is English, but German is supported also. (See Chapter 12 for details on internationalizing JSF applications.) All that remains now is to author the **Messages.properties** and **Messages_de.properties** files. The following is a snippet from the **Messages.properties** file. Notice the use of the standard **LengthValidator** to ensure the user's password is at least six characters long.

```
javax.faces.validator.LengthValidator.MINIMUM=\
  Not long enough.  Make it longer!
```

JSF 1.2 TIP *In Faces 1.2, a feature was added where the label of the component with which the message is associated is incorporated in the message string. If you want to support this feature when overriding a standard message, you must keep in mind that element {1} will be substituted with the label. Doing this doesn't make sense for the preceding example, but it's important to keep this in mind.*

There are, of course, cases when you just want to override a standard message for one specific usage of one of the standard **Validators** in your application. This can easily be accomplished using the **MethodBinding** validator approach, as described earlier. In the method functioning as a **Validator**, you can manually call the appropriate standard **Validator**, catch the **ValidatorException**, create your own **FacesMessage** instance with your own message, and pass that to the constructor of a new **ValidatorException**, which you then throw.

JSF 1.2 TIP *You can also override the message using the **requiredMessage**, **converterMessage**, or **validatorMessage** property of **UIInput**. This is exposed as a tag attribute on all of the tags that expose **UIInput** components to the page author.*

Creating Your Own Messages

Creating your own messages is as simple as adding a message key to your properties file, and then following the algorithm in the section "When and How **FacesMessage** Instances Are Created and Added to the **FacesContext**" earlier in this chapter to create the **FacesMessage** instance, and pass it to the constructor of your **ConverterException** or **ValidatorException**. In Chapter 9, you will see how to create a **FacesMessageMaker** class to encapsulate this process. Alternatively, your custom **Validator** could simply just pull the String off of a **ResourceBundle** manually in an application-specific manner.

Now that you've learned the details of conversion and validation, let's examine in depth the Faces Event system in the next chapter.

The JSF Event Model

The JavaServer Faces event model differs from most other Web development technologies because it provides an event-based programming model that is similar to the one used in traditional, thick-client development with Swing or AWT. This enables a much finer degree of control when dealing with complex user interfaces and is well suited for use by traditional client developers. Web developers who may not be fully familiar with this type of event model, which is considerably different than basic HTTP request event (Get/Post) processing, will soon appreciate the level of granularity provided by the Faces event model when dealing with more complex user interfaces.

A High-Level Overview of the JSF Event Model

Before the advent of sophisticated user interfaces, programs tended to execute in a serial fashion. That is, they would start, process data, and exit. When human input was required, the program would prompt the user, using a phrase such as "Enter your name:" and then wait until the data was entered. This simple "question/answer" mechanism constituted programming's first user interface. Although conceptually simple, the effectiveness of this approach was inherently limited. As program/user interactions became more complex a better approach was needed. This need gave rise to the *graphical user interface* (GUI).

The GUI offers a substantially more sophisticated system that is based on user-initiated changes to the various interface elements. To manage these interactions, an event-based mechanism was devised. In this approach, an event is generated when the user changes the state of an interface element. For example, an event is generated when the value of a field is changed or when a button is clicked. The application is then notified of the event and can respond appropriately. For example, an application could be notified of a change in the value of the postal Zip Code field and then react by pre-filling City and State fields with the corresponding city and state names for the given Zip code.

As graphical user interface technologies ranging from the X Window System and the Apple Macintosh to Microsoft Windows began emerging in the late '80s and early '90s, they all had one thing in common: an event-based mechanism for dealing with state changes of user interface elements. In the years preceding the explosion of the Web, these were the dominant technologies for building software user interfaces.

As the Web became the dominant platform for application development, rich, event-based user interface development took a step backward. Because of the loosely connected nature of the Web where clients communicate asynchronously in a much lighter fashion than the traditional user interface technologies, the familiar event-based model regressed to a more primitive form of basic input and output in which a sequence of name value pairs (parameters) are submitted to a server and the application code mainly deals with a single Get or Post event. Gone was the notion of being able to respond to intricate user interface changes.

As the Web gained in popularity, client-based technologies such as JavaScript and DHTML were introduced to improve the end-user experience by allowing the client browser the ability to react to more intricate changes in the state of a user interface element. However, using JavaScript and DHTML has always been a bit of an art mainly because of the dual nature of dealing with client events and dealing with server Get/Post events. There was also the myriad of challenges inherent in getting the application to run in different Web browsers.

NOTE   *Clever use of JavaScript and DHTML in the form of asynchronous calls to the server to pass data back and forth independent of page delivery is becoming popular and is known as Asynchronous JavaScript and XML (AJAX). Examples of how to use AJAX in custom JavaServer Faces components are provided in Chapter 11.*

As mentioned at the start of this chapter, JavaServer Faces distinguishes itself among the different Web technologies by providing an event model that supports a rich, event-based user interface programming style that is similar to that used when developing for AWT or Swing. Using the JSF event model, which is part of the overall JSF request processing lifecycle, you no longer need to be concerned with processing large sets of name/values pairs provided in HTTP Get and Post requests. Instead, you can program to a more traditional event model where user interface elements broadcast changes in state (events) to a respective set of listener objects that then perform the tasks required.

How JSF Events Work

Similar to AWT and Swing, the JavaServer Faces event model architecture borrows concepts from the event model of the JavaBeans specification where "events are a mechanism for propagating state change notifications between a source object and one or more target *listener* objects." So, for example, if the source object was a button and if it were clicked, it would broadcast an event indicating its change in state (i.e., it was clicked) and a corresponding listener object would be able to respond to the event, providing it was designated to listen for the specific type of event that occurred.

It's important to understand that although buttons are pressed or field values are being altered, nothing really happens on the client regarding application state at the instant these changes occur. Instead these changes are evaluated by the request processing lifecycle and are processed according to the rules defined by the lifecycle.

In general, Faces events are used to signify when state changes occur within UI components or within the request processing lifecycle and process them accordingly. Recall from Chapter 6 that all UI components can be broken down into two main branches. The first are those that *initiate an action*, such as a button. These implement the interface **ActionSource** (or **ActionSource2** for JSF 1.2). The second are those that *hold a value*, such as an output or input field. These implement **ValueHolder** or **EditableValueHolder**. The two most common Faces events are patterned after these types of UI components. For **ActionSource** components, an *action event* and a corresponding *action listener* are used to fire and then process events originating from **ActionSource** components, such as when a button is clicked. For UI components that actually hold a value (implement **ValueHolder** or **EditableValueHolder** interfaces), a *value change event* and its associated *value change listener* are used. A value change event and listener can be programmed to react when a value of an input field has changed. Both action events and value change events extend from the generic Faces event **FacesEvent**, which extends from **java.util.EventObject**.

JSF provides another kind of event and listener that goes beyond the scope of events that originate from UI components. To record and process state changes that occur in the request processing lifecycle, *phase events* and *phase listeners* are used. Phase events (implemented by the Java class **PhaseEvent)** are a peer to Faces events (implemented by **FacesEvent**) and also extend from **java.util.EventObject**. Phase events are fired before and after each request processing lifecycle phase. Phase listeners can be written to listen and react to the different phase events that occur during the processing of the lifecycle. Chapters 11 and 15, which cover more advanced custom JSF component development topics, will demonstrate exactly how useful phase listeners can be.

In addition to action events, value change events, and phase events, custom Faces events and event listeners can be written by extending from the base classes provided by Faces. More information on this is provided at the end of the chapter.

The Faces Event Listener Interfaces and Event Classes

The JavaServer Faces event class hierarchy is displayed in Figure 8-1.

To listen to the Faces events, a set of Java interfaces are provided by the Faces environment. Faces event listeners must implement these interfaces, which are illustrated in Figure 8-2.

EXPERT GROUP INSIGHT *Note that* **PhaseEvent** *extends* **java.util.EventObject** *directly while* **ValueChangeEvent** *and* **ActionEvent** *extend from* **FacesEvent**. *The* **PhaseListener** *concept came after the core event model was defined and it was decided to keep the two kinds of events separate in the class hierarchy because the* **FacesEvent** *subclasses all have a* **UIComponent** *as their source, while a* **PhaseEvent** *has the* **Lifecycle** *as its source.*

As we'll explain shortly, exactly when and how Faces events are fired and processed is managed entirely by the JSF request processing lifecycle and there are even ways to manipulate the order of when certain types of events are processed.

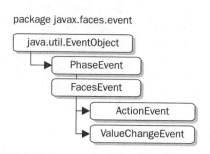

package javax.faces.event

java.util.EventObject
PhaseEvent
FacesEvent
ActionEvent
ValueChangeEvent

FIGURE 8-1   Faces event class hierarchy

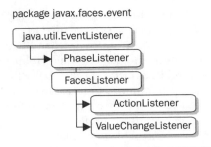

FIGURE 8-2 Faces event listener interface hierarchy

When Are Faces Events Processed?

Figure 8-3 shows when and which types of events are processed throughout the request processing lifecycle.

The following table summarizes the different types of events and when they are processed in the request processing lifecycle.

Event Type	When It Is Processed
ActionEvent	At the completion of the Invoke Application phase unless the **immediate** flag is **true**; then it is processed at the end of the Apply Request Value phase.
ValueChangeEvent	At the completion of the Process Validations phase unless the **immediate** flag is **true**; then it is processed at the end of the Apply Request Value phase.
PhaseEvent	Before or after each lifecycle phase. Can write **PhaseListener** to listen and execute for specific lifecycle phase events.
Faces Event	Superclass of **ActionEvent** and **ValueChangeEvent**. Does not specifically execute in lifecycle.

JSF 1.2 TIP *In JSF 1.2 it is possible to register* **PhaseListeners** *on the* **UIViewRoot** *of the view.* **PhaseEvents** *sent to listeners registered in this way still have the* **Lifecycle** *as their source and have the benefit of being scoped to a particular view, rather than for every view in the application. Phase listeners can be registered on the* **UIViewRoot** *using the* **<f:phaseListener>** *tag or programmatically by calling the* **addPhaseListener()** *method or the* **setBeforePhaseListener()** *or* **setAfterPhaseListener()** *methods. These latter two take a* **MethodExpression** *that points to a method whose signature matches that of the* **afterPhase()** *method of the* **PhaseListener** *interface. The 1.2* **<f:view>** *tag also has attributes* **beforePhaseListener** *and* **afterPhaseListener***, which accept method expression arguments with signatures* **javax.faces.event.PhaseListener** **.beforePhase()** *and* **javax.faces.event.PhaseListener.afterPhase()***, respectively.*

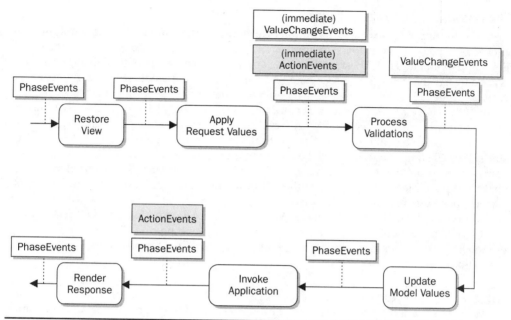

FIGURE 8-3   The processing of events throughout the request processing lifecycle

EXPERT GROUP INSIGHT *The Expert Group spent a lot of time debating the difference between application events and UI events. Generally, an application event is one that changes the state of the application, usually by moving from one page to another, submitting an order, or similar. A UI event was defined to be an event that doesn't change the state of the application, such as clicking on a tab in a tab panel, or expanding or contracting a node in a tree component. While these distinctions are useful concepts, it was ultimately decided not to expose them in the API for simplicity's sake. However, the heritage of these two types of events does live on in the form of the* **ActionListener** *interface, which can loosely be associated with the UI event concept, and the* **action** *mechanism, which can loosely be associated with the application event concept. Both of these are described in this chapter.*

Faces events actually consist of two phases: when the event is fired and when a listening agent acts upon the event. Because the request processing lifecycle handles the firing of the event internally, a complete understanding of what happens behind the scenes is not technically required when building most Faces applications, but still valuable. However, knowing how to write code to handle a Faces event *is* something every Faces developer must understand. The following sections explain both the queuing and handling of Faces action and value change events.

The Anatomy of an Action Event

Consider the simple case of a Faces button (**<h:commandButton/>** or **UICommand**) being clicked on a page. As with any Web application, when the Faces button is clicked, the form is submitted and an HTTP Post is sent to the application server where the JSF application is running. As the JSF request processing lifecycle processes the request, it is in the Apply Request Values phase when the event generated by the button click is queued as an action event. If the HTTP request contains a component ID that matches the ID of the **UICommand** button that was clicked, then the Faces lifecycle knows that the button was clicked.

At this point, the only thing that can be done is to record that the button click occurred since other UI components may still be receiving their updates from other incoming request values. To record the button click event, the Faces lifecycle instantiates an **ActionEvent** object and passes it as an argument to the **UICommand**'s **queueEvent()** method. The event has now been queued for future processing. The Apply Request Values phase will complete and proceed to the other phases, Process Validations and Update Model Values. It isn't until the Invoke Application phase is reached successfully (providing no validation, conversion, or model update errors are encountered), that a corresponding **ActionListener** will process the **ActionEvent**.

NOTE *An **ActionEvent** can actually be processed immediately, that is, during the Apply Request Values phase (instead of waiting until the Invoke Application phase), but only if the **UICommand**'s **immediate** attribute was set to **true**. More information on the effects of setting the **immediate** attribute is provided later in the chapter.*

So far, what has taken place has occurred behind the scenes, being handled automatically by the Faces lifecycle. At this point the **ActionEvent** has been recorded and queued. It is now time for your code to take over. Following the standard operating procedure as per the JavaBeans specification, you must provide an associated **ActionListener** that is listening for the incoming **ActionEvent**.

In general, to handle events in Faces you can write a custom listener class that implements the appropriate interface (**javax.faces.event.ActionListener** for action events) and then bind it to the UI component (in this case, **UICommand**). For action events, it is also possible to just write either an action method or an action listener method. An *action method* is simply a Java method that you can place in a backing bean that takes no arguments and returns a **String**. Action methods are actually handled by a built-in *default **ActionListener*** that takes the returned **String** value from the action method and passes it to the **NavigationHandler** in order to determine if a navigation is warranted. If no navigation is needed after an action event, one can write an action listener method. In contrast to an action method, an *action listener method* simply executes and no navigation is expected as a result of the execution of the method. As a result, the action listener method returns **void** and accepts a single **ActionEvent** as an argument.

An action method is bound to a **UICommand** (or any component that implements **ActionSource**) by setting the **action** attribute with the method expression of the action method. An action listener method is bound in a similar way but to the component's **actionListener** attribute instead.To see examples of both an action method and an action listener method, recall the **confirm.jsp** page in the example application from Chapter 2. In the page there is a **commandButton** whose **action** attribute contains the method expression to invoke the **addConfirmedUser()** method:

```
<h:commandButton value="Confirm"  action="#{UserBean.addConfirmedUser}" />
```

The source of the action method is as follows:

```
public String addConfirmedUser() {
  // This method would call a database or other service and
  // add the confirmed user information.

  System.out.println("Adding new user…");
  return "success";
}
```

As you can see, it follows the standard signature of an action method with no arguments and returns a **String** value. In this example, it simply prints a message to the console and returns "success," but in a real application it would probably call another method that interacts with a database and the returned result would be based on whether the operation succeeded. This returned value is then used to determine if a navigation is needed. For example, if the addition of a new user somehow failed, a "failure" **String** value could be returned and a navigation to an error page could occur. (Of course, a corresponding navigation case would have to be added to **faces-config.xml** for the **NavigationHandler** to handle this.) The key point to remember with an action method is that it relies on the built-in default **ActionListener** to invoke it and then pass this value to the **NavigationHandler** in order to determine if a navigation is needed.

If no navigation was needed after the action event was processed, an action listener method could be used instead of an action method. As mentioned earlier, in contrast to an action method, an action listener method takes a single argument of type **ActionEvent** and has a **void** return type. And instead of binding to the **action** attribute, the action listener method is bound to the UI component's **actionListener** attribute. The following line shows how to bind an action listener method to a Faces **UICommand** button.

```
<h:commandButton value="Confirm"
actionListener="#{UserBean.addConfirmedUserListenerAction}" />
```

And the action listener method could look like this:

```
public void addConfirmedUserListenerAction(ActionEvent ae) {
  // This method would call a database or other service
  // and add the confirmed user information.

  System.out.println("Adding new user…");
}
```

Notice the action listener method takes an **ActionEvent** as its single argument and has a return type of **void**. Other than the fact that an action method has the ability to incur a Faces navigation after execution, uses of action methods and action listener methods are basically identical.

Handling an Action Event Earlier in the Faces Lifecycle

As you recall from earlier in the chapter, action events are normally processed during the Invoke Application phase; however, there are times when you would want the action (or action listener) method to execute earlier, such as before validation during the Apply Request Values phase. For example, you may want to provide a Cancel button that calls a method before validating the field values. To short-circuit the processing of the action event, one simply sets the UI component's **immediate** attribute to **true**.

For example:

```
<h:commandButton value="Confirm"
action="#{UserBean.addConfirmedUser}" immediate="true" />
```

Upon execution, the **addConfirmedUser()** method will execute at the end of the Apply Request Values phase instead of the Invoke Application phase. This short-circuits the normal flow of events and immediately causes the action event to be processed before any validation occurs.

NOTE   *An important point about setting a button's* **immediate** *attribute to* **true** *is that when retrieving another input component's value (using* **getValue()** *in an action/action listener method) as a result of clicking on the button, getting the correct value of that input component is not guaranteed unless the input component's* **immediate** *attribute is also set to* **true**.

The Anatomy of a Value Change Event

Having stepped through what happens during an action event, we'll now step through what happens during a value change event. As you recall from earlier in the chapter, a *value change event* is an event that is used to indicate when a value of a UI component, such as an input field, has changed. In general, value change events handle changes in the values of UI components that implement either **ValueHolder** or **EditableValueHolder** interfaces. A common example of a value change event is when an input field (**UIInput**) has been updated. Recall the scenario earlier in the chapter, where you might want to capture the event when the Zip Code field has been filled in so the server can auto-fill a City field. Another common example is when implementing dependent lists of values in drop-down menus—for example, when an item such as a particular state has been selected in one menu, then the dependent select menu could display the appropriate cities that reside in the chosen state. Handling change events improves the overall usability of a Faces application, and when coupled with a small JavaScript callout (**onchange** or **onclick**) on the client to auto-submit when the change occurs, the user interface can react based on small value change events as opposed to the usual submitting a form or clicking a button.

The behind-the-scenes plumbing of a value change event is basically the same as the action event described earlier. Consider a simple example where a JSP page has a single input field (**UIInput**) and a button (**UICommand**). If the page is run and some text is entered and the button clicked to submit the form, a value change event will be fired. Similar to the action event, the JSF request processing lifecycle will automatically fire a value change event by instantiating a **ValueChangeEvent** object and passing it as an argument to the **UIInput**'s **queueEvent()** method.

Even though the value change event has been fired, there is no code yet to handle the value change method. Similar to action events, this can be done in several ways, ranging from writing a custom value change listener class that implements the **ValueChangeListener** interface, to simply writing a value change listener method that uses the default value change listener provided by the Faces runtime. To react to a value change event, the following method can be used by the default value change listener.

```
public void valueChangeMethod(ValueChangeEvent vce) {
    System.out.println("In valueChangeMethod: A value was changed!");
}
```

This method can reside in a managed bean and be value-bound to an input field (or any UI component that holds a value) using:

```
<h:inputText valueChangeListener="#{backing_bean.valueChangeMethod}"/>
```

When the application is run and a value is entered into the input field and the form is submitted by clicking on the button, the **valueChangeMethod()** will be executed because the value of the input field was changed from its initial empty value to a new value with the entered text. However, unlike the action event in which the event is processed during the Invoke Application phase, value change events are processed in the Process Validations phase. A subsequent re-submission of the form without changing the value in the input field will not cause the value change listener method to execute.

You can cause the value of an input component to be set immediately, before any other input components during the Apply Request Values phase, by setting its **immediate** attribute to **true**. This is needed in certain cases to avoid validation errors when processing value change events. You will see an example of this later in the chapter.

Writing Custom Action and Value Change Listeners

So far you have seen how to write methods that use the default action and value change listeners. These methods were directly associated with UI components by using their **action** or **actionlistener** JSP tag attributes, like this:

```
<h:commandButton value="Confirm"  action="#{UserBean.addConfirmedUser}" />
```

or like this:

```
<h:commandButton value="Confirm"  actionlistener="#{UserBean.addConfirmedUser}" />
```

In addition to using the default listeners, you can write your own action or value change listener classes. These classes simply implement either the **ActionListener** or **ValueChangeListener** interface. The following code is an example of a simple custom action listener class. Notice the **processAction()** method that is overridden to process the actual action event.

```
package com.jsfcompref;

import javax.faces.event.ActionListener;
import javax.faces.event.ActionEvent;

public class MyActionListener implements ActionListener {
  public MyActionListener() {
    }

  public void processAction(ActionEvent ae) {
    System.out.println("MyActionListener is processing an action event!");
  }
}
```

To use the custom action listener class, **MyActionListener**, you can associate it with a UI component using a nested **<f:actionlistener />** tag as follows.

```
<h:commandButton value="Click Me!">
  <f:actionListener type="com.jsfcompref.MyActionListener"/>
</h:commandButton>
```

Notice that in this case the action listener tag uses the **type** attribute to refer directly to the full Java classpath of the custom action listener. As expected, when this page is run and when the button is clicked, the **processAction()** method will execute and print a message to the console.

NOTE *There is a slight limitation with this usage in that there is no ability to configure the* **actionListener** *instance, as it will just be created with default arguments. It is possible, however, to create a custom* **actionListener** *and package it into a reusable JSP tag that exposes its initialization arguments. Oracle's ADF Faces, which is covered in Appendix B, actually provides the* **af:setActionListener** *tag that provides this.*

In a similar fashion, a custom value change listener class that implements the **ValueChangeListener** interface could also be created like this:

```
package com.jsfcompref;

import javax.faces.event.ValueChangeListener;
import javax.faces.event.ValueChangeEvent;

public class MyValueChangeListener implements ValueChangeListener {
  public MyValueChangeListener() {
  }

  public void processValueChange(ValueChangeEvent vce) {
    System.out.println("MyValueChangeListener is processing a value change event!");
  }
}
```

To use the custom value change listener **MyValueChangeListener** class, you can associate it with any UI component that holds a value using a nested **<f:valueChangelistener />** tag as follows.

```
<h:inputText value="foo" ">
  <f:valueChangeListener type="com.jsfcompref.MyValueChangeListener"/>
</h:inputText>
<h:commandButton value="Click me!"/>
```

Similar to the action listener tag, **valueChangeListener** also uses a **type** attribute to refer directly to the value change listener class using its full Java classpath. When the page containing this code is run, the user can then change the current value (from "foo") in the input field and click on the submit button to issue a postback request. During the Apply Request Value phase of the request processing lifecycle, the Faces runtime will see that the value of the input field was changed between the initial and postback request and **MyValueChangeListener**'s. The **processValueChange()** method will execute and print a message to the console.

Many times it is useful to submit a form without requiring the user to click on a submit button. For example, consider the situation in which you want to auto-fill the city and state after a user has entered a Zip code. In this case, setting the JavaScript callout **onchange** attribute of the Zip Code input field to "**this.form.submit()**" will cause the form to be submitted automatically when the field on the client has changed without requiring the user to click on a submit button.

```
<h:inputText value="foo" onchange="this.form.submit();">
  <f:valueChangeListener type="com.jsfcompref.MyValueChangeListener"/>
</h:inputText>
```

After the user enters a value and tabs out of the input field, the JavaScript callout **onchange** will execute the JavaScript function **this.form.submit()** and the form will be submitted by the browser client. Since a value was changed in the field, the custom value change listener (**MyValueChangeListener**) will also execute its **processValueChange()** method as well.

Table 8-1 summarizes the alternate ways to work with action and value change events showing examples using both **<h:commandButton/>** and **<h:inputText/>** UI components:

JSF 1.2 TIP *JSF 1.2 introduces a* **binding** *attribute to the* **f:valueChangeListener** *and* **f:actionListener***. This attribute is analogous to the* **binding** *attribute on* **UIComponent** *tags with the exception that if the* **type** *attribute is also set, then it is used to create the listener instance (rather than the* **binding** *attribute) and the* **binding** *attribute is used to receive the reference to the newly created listener instance. Moreover, the* **binding** *attribute is particularly helpful because you can create multiple reusable listener instances in a backing bean, configure them as you want in code, then reuse them across your app with a single point of maintenance. Or you can create a listener as a managed bean, and have the ability to set properties. This is not possible in JSF 1.1 or 1.0.*

Listener Type	Code Usage Sample
Default action listener with action method	`= <h:commandButton value="Click me!" action="#{ManagedBean.actionMethod}" />`
Default action listener with action listener method	`<h:commandButton value="Click me!" actionlistener="#{ManagedBean.actionListenerMethod}" />`

Custom action listener class	`<h:commandButton value="Click me!" >`
	`<f:actionlistener type="package.CustomActionListener" />`
	`</h:commandButton>`

Default value change listener with value change listener method	`<h:inputText value="foo" valuechangelistener="#{ManagedBean.valueChangeListenerMethod}" />`

Custom value change listener class	`<h:inputText value="foo" >`
	`<f:valueChangeListener type="package.CustomValueChangeListener"/>`
	`</h:inputText>`

TABLE 8-1   Alternative Ways to Use Action and Value Change Listeners

Two Faces Event Examples

To gain a firm understanding of value change listeners, it will be useful to work through two examples. Both examples are based on the Zip code scenario mentioned earlier in the chapter in which City and State fields are automatically filled in after the user provides a value in the Zip Code input field and then tabs out of the Zip Code field. As explained, this mechanism lets the user avoid entering the city and state manually. The first example shows how to implement the basic, auto-fill functionality by using a value change event and listener. This example also shows how to avoid triggering a validation error by using the **immediate** attribute. The second example expands on the first by showing how to conditionally render a portion of the UI also by using a value change listener where a UI component's **rendered** property is toggled when a checkbox is clicked.

Using a Value Change Event to Auto-Fill Fields

For this first example, consider a form with the following input fields: Name, Zip Code, City, and State, like the one shown in Figure 8-4.

The desire is to allow the user to enter a Zip code and have the City and State fields automatically filled in with the matching city and state, as shown in Figure 8-5.

Building this example requires the processing of a value change event that is associated with the Zip Code input field. The event is triggered when the user enters or changes a value, then tabs out of the field. For this example we'll use the default value change listener along with a value change listener method.

The initial source code for the JSP page **autozip.jsp** with the four fields is as follows:

```
<%@ taglib uri="http://java.sun.com/jsf/core" prefix="f"%>
<%@ taglib uri="http://java.sun.com/jsf/html" prefix="h"%>
<f:view>
<html>
<body>
  <h2>Address Form</h2>
  <h:form>
    <h:panelGrid columns="2">
      <h:outputLabel value="Name:"/>
      <h:inputText id="inputname" binding="#{autozip_backing.inputName}"/>
      <h:outputLabel value="Zip Code:"/>
      <h:inputText id="inputzip" binding="#{autozip_backing.inputZip}"/>
      <h:outputLabel value="City:" />
      <h:inputText id="inputcity" binding="#{autozip_backing.inputCity}"/>
      <h:outputLabel value="State:"/>
      <h:inputText id="inputstate" binding="#{autozip_backing.inputState}"/>
      <h:commandButton value="Submit"/>
    </h:panelGrid>
  </h:form>
</body>
</html>
</f:view>
```

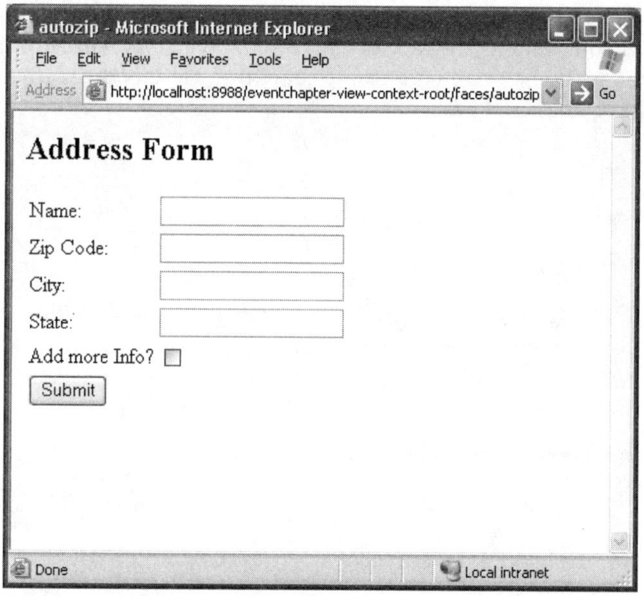

FIGURE 8-4   An example name and address form

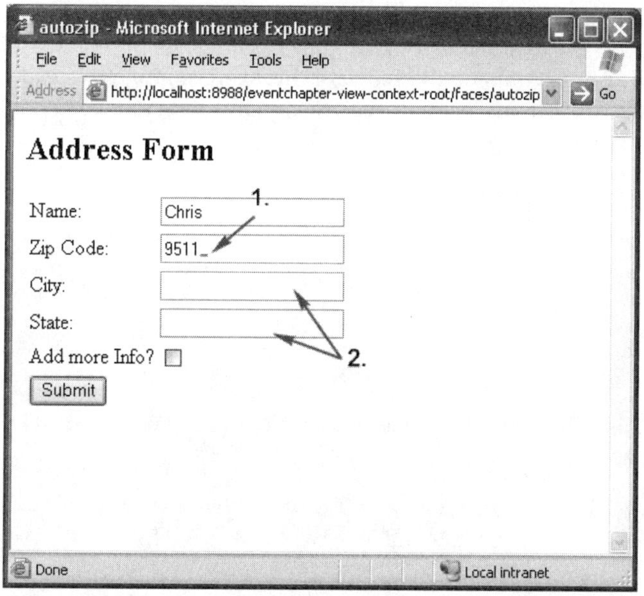

FIGURE 8-5   When a Zip code is entered, the City and State fields are automatically filled in.

The first thing to notice is that each **inputText** component is bound to a set of **HtmlInputText** UI components that are declared in a Java class **AutoZip.java** and registered as a managed bean named **autozip_backing**. Here is the source code for the **autozip_backing** managed bean.

```
public class AutoZip {

  // Declare HtmlInputText components to bind with page components

  private HtmlInputText inputName, inputZip, inputCity, inputState;

// Property setters and getters
  public void setInputName(HtmlInputText inputName) {
    this.inputName = inputName;
  }

  public HtmlInputText getInputName() {
    return inputName;
  }
...
  // The rest of the getters and setters omitted for brevity.
...
}
```

In order to trigger the automatic lookup and filling in of the City and State input fields when a Zip code is entered, a value change listener method is added to the **autozip_backing** managed bean. The logic to actually look up the city and state based on a Zip code is left as a task for the reader and is outside the scope of this exercise, so in this example the value change listener method will just set hard-coded city and state names to the **HtmlInputText** city and state components.

```
public  void autoZipListener(ValueChangeEvent vce) {
  // TODO: implement city/state lookup logic

  // For this example, just hard code to San Jose, California
  inputCity.setValue("San Jose");
  inputState.setValue("California");

}
```

To associate this value change listener method to the Zip Code **inputText** field, the JSP page is modified as:

```
<h:inputText id="inputzip" binding="#{autozip_backing.inputZip}"
  valueChangeListener="#{autozip_backing.autoZipListener}"
  onchange="this.form.submit()"/>
```

Notice the addition of a JavaScript callout **onchange()** with a value of "**this.form .submit()**". Recall that this enables the form to auto-submit itself using JavaScript when the user changes a value and tabs out of the field.

The example will now perform as expected. When a value is entered into the Zip Code field, the form auto-submits itself and values are automatically provided for the City and State fields by the value change listener method. See Figure 8-6.

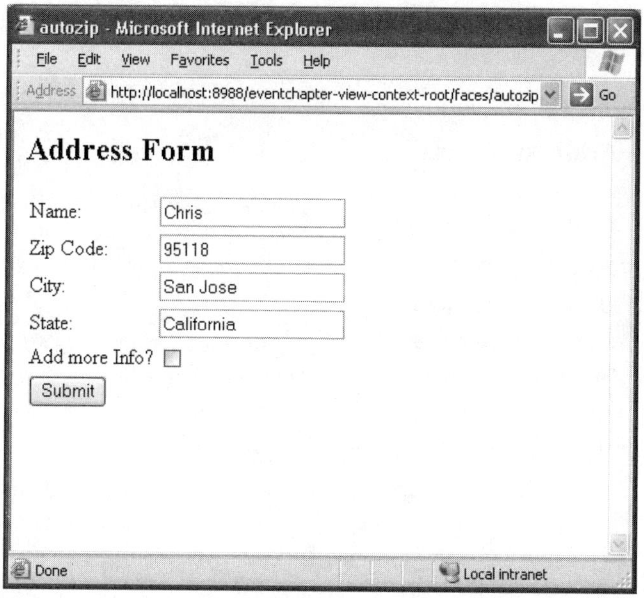

FIGURE 8-6 The form now automatically fills in the City and State fields when a Zip code is provided.

This example works fine as is, but if any validations are added to any of the input fields, the auto-submit could cause a validation error to appear as the user tabs out of the Zip Code field. For example, if the Name field (**inputName**) is changed to be a required field (by setting its **required** attribute to **true**) a validation error will be triggered if the Name field is empty when the form is auto-submitted. This situation is shown in Figure 8-7. Also, in order to show the validation error message, the *inputname* field will need a corresponding **<h:message />** component associated with it.

```
<h:inputText id="inputname" required="true"
binding="#{autozip_backing.inputName}"/>
<h:message for="inputname"/>
```

Now the form has an annoying validation error that is triggered whenever a value is entered into the Zip Code field even before the submit button is clicked. The trick to overcoming this problem is to allow for a form submission to occur without triggering the Process Validations phase of the lifecycle. To do this requires two steps. First, you must set the **immediate** property to **true** on the Zip Code input component and on any other components whose values are being updated by the value change listener (including City and State).

The form input fields now have the following changes:

```
...
<h:inputText id="inputzip" binding="#{autozip_backing.inputZip}"
  valueChangeListener="#{autozip_backing.autoZipListener}"
  onchange="submit()" immediate="true" />
...
<h:inputText id="inputcity" binding="#{autozip_backing.inputCity}" immediate="true" />
...
<h:inputText id="inputstate" binding="#{autozip_backing.inputState}" immediate="true" />
```

FIGURE 8-7 The form with a validation error appearing

The second step you must take to avoid a validation error is to skip the Process Validations phase altogether. This is done by modifying the value change listener code as follows:

```
public  void autoZipListener(ValueChangeEvent vce) {
  // TODO: implement city/state lookup logic

  // For this example, just hard code to San Jose, California
  inputCity.setValue("San Jose");
  inputState.setValue("California");

  // Jump directly to the Render Response phase to avoid validation
  FacesContext context = FacesContext.getCurrentInstance();
  context.renderResponse();
}
```

By calling the **renderResponse()** method of the **FacesContext** in the value change listener, the Process Validations phase will be skipped entirely. The form will now auto-fill the City and State fields when the Zip code is entered without causing a validation error even though the Name field is required.

NOTE *The example shown can be implemented so its behavior is more user-friendly using AJAX. This will prevent the entire page from having to be resubmitted to the client just to see the values of the dependent fields being auto-filled. Techniques for implementing AJAX applications are covered in Chapter 11.*

Extending the Value Change Example

The previous example illustrated a common user interface behavior in which values of one or more input fields are updated as a result of information provided by another input field.

Another very common user interface behavior is to simply change a user interface element property, such as **readonly** or **disabled**. In Faces, this behavior is even easier to implement than the previous example, but is achieved in largely the same manner.

Consider the following enhancement to the Zip code example. To enable the user to enter additional information into the form, another input field called More Info is added. However, this input field will not display initially. Instead, a checkbox labeled "Add more info?" will be included. When the user clicks on the box, it renders the More Info input field (using a new text area) to receive more information. The new input field and checkbox are shown in Figure 8-8.

To implement this new functionality onto the same form in the previous example, you first add the following UI components to the page in between the last field and the submit button. (The **<f:verbatim>** tag is used to maintain three columns in the **PanelGrid**.)

```
...
<h:outputLabel value="Add more Info?"/><h:selectBooleanCheckbox/>
<f:verbatim> </f:verbatim>

<h:outputLabel value="More Info"/><h:inputTextarea id="moreinfo"/>
<h:message for="moreinfo"/>
...
```

NOTE *In a production application, the* **for** *attribute of* **h:outputLabel** *should be set to the* **id** *of the associated input component for accessibility.*

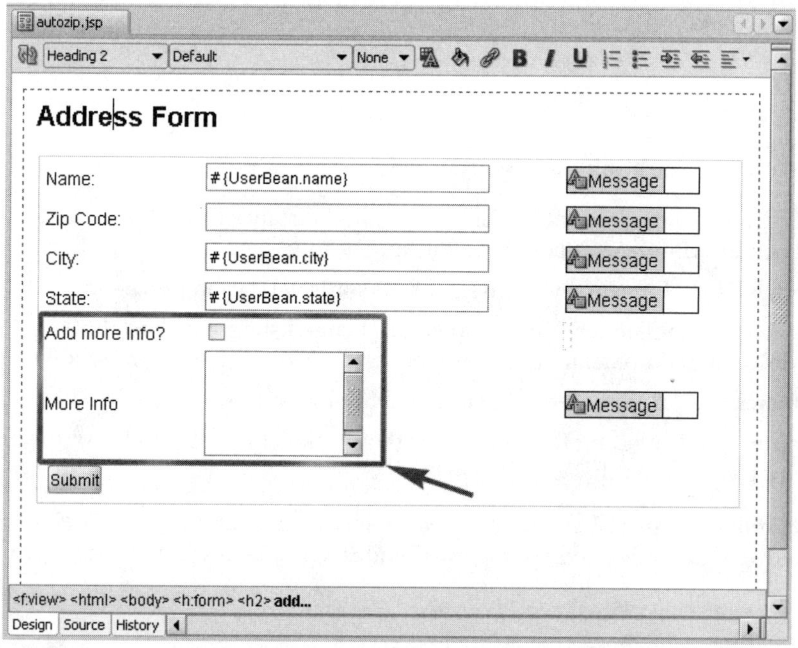

FIGURE 8-8 A new input field that can be rendered conditionally with a checkbox

Because the new UI component tags are added to the JSP page, you must also add declarations for the new components in the **auto_zip** backing bean.

```
private HtmlInputTextarea moreInfo;
private HtmlSelectBooleanCheckbox renderInfoBox;
```

To keep track of the render state of the More Info field, add a **boolean** variable called **infoRendered** and set it initially to **false**:

```
boolean infoRendered = false;
```

In addition to the declarations, you must also add the associated JavaBean getter and setter accessors for each new bean property in order to be able to access/update the properties in the application.

In order to toggle the **infoRendered boolean** variable when the checkbox is clicked, a value change listener method is added to the backing bean. Similar to before, once the value change event is processed, the Render Response phase must be initiated, by calling **renderResponse()**, in order to avoid validations.

```
public void toggleMoreInfo(ValueChangeEvent vce) {
  infoRendered = !infoRendered;
  FacesContext.getCurrentInstance().renderResponse();
}
```

In the JSP page, the new UI component tags are bound to the declarations in the backing bean. The **<h:selectBooleanCheckbox>** tag will have the following modifications:

```
<h:selectBooleanCheckbox binding="#{autozip_backing.renderInfoBox}"
immediate="true"
valueChangeListener="#{autozip_backing.toggleMoreInfo}"
onclick="this.form.submit();"
value="#{autozip_backing.infoRendered}"/>
```

Explanations of the attribute settings follow:

- **binding**   UI component binding to declared instance of **HtmlSelectBooleanCheckbox** in backing bean.
- **immediate**   Immediacy setting, which avoids validation processing.
- **valueChangeListener**   Bound to value change listener method that toggles the **infoRendered boolean** variable to render the More Info field in backing bean.
- **onclick**   JavaScript method to auto-submit the form when the checkbox is clicked.
- **value**   Value binding to synchronize the checkbox with the value of the **boolean** variable to render the *More Info* field.

The More Info output label and text area components must now be modified to render conditionally based on the value of the **infoRendered boolean** variable, as shown next:

```
<h:outputLabel value="More Info:" rendered="#{autozip_backing.infoRendered}"/>
<h:inputTextarea id="moreinfo" binding="#{autozip_backing.moreInfo}"
rendered="#{autozip_backing.infoRendered}"/>
```

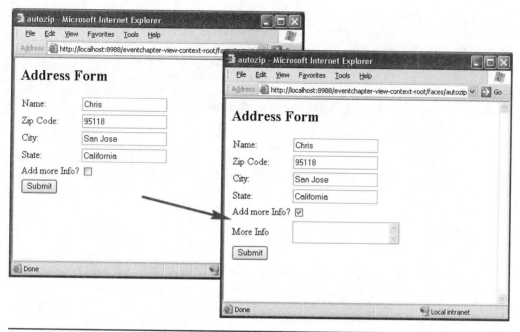

FIGURE 8-9   Toggling the More Info text box with a checkbox

The final step is to change the **autozip_backing** backing bean's **scope** from **request** to **session** in the **faces-config.xml**. Switching the scope of the backing bean to **session** allows the application to preserve the value of the **infoRendered boolean** variable between requests. Otherwise, the variable would constantly be reinitialized to **false** upon each request.

As Figure 8-9 shows, once these changes are complete, the application will work as expected with the new More Info text area field rendering based on the user's selection of the checkbox.

This example has shown how through proper usage of value change events in Faces one can implement a very useful user interface behavior.

Working with Phase Events and Listeners

Recall that in addition to action events and value change events, the other common Faces event is known as the *phase event*. Phase events are events that are processed in between each phase of the Faces request processing lifecycle. Since they have the ability to execute in between the different phases, phase events and their respective phase listeners provide a unique way to jump into the execution of the lifecycle and check or alter values/properties of any object in a Faces application.

Using a PhaseListener to Observe the Faces Lifecycle in Action

One of the most useful and simple things to do is to write a phase listener that executes at every phase in the Faces lifecycle and reports to either a logging facility (or even just to the console) when the different phases of the lifecycle are processed. This type of phase listener is very easy to write and it can be used as a tool to confirm the correct execution of events and phases based on different criteria, such as when certain UI components have their **immediate** property set to **true,** or if a certain listener method short-circuits the lifecycle directly by calling the **RenderResponse()** method of the Faces context.

To build a phase listener to process the phase events that are emitted by the changing of lifecycle phases, simply create a Java class that implements the **PhaseListener** interface. We begin by creating the following skeleton, called **MyPhaseListener.**

```
package com.jsfcompref;
import javax.faces.event.PhaseListener;

public class MyPhaseListener implements PhaseListener {
  public MyPhaseListener() {
  }

  // Implement PhaseListener methods here.

}
```

Next, the methods **beforePhase()**, **afterPhase()**, and **getPhaseId()** must be overridden and implemented. Both the **beforePhase()** and **afterPhase()** methods accept a single argument of type **PhaseEvent** and execute either before or after the phase event is passed to the methods. Each phase event has an associated phase ID and it can be used to pick when to execute the method. Since the **beforePhase()** and **afterPhase()** methods execute for all phase events, if you want to a perform specific action for a single phase of the lifecycle, you can provide some simple logic to check the phase ID of the incoming phase event and then conditionally execute your code based on that check. For example, the following **beforePhase()** method will print a message "Processing new Request!" to the console, but only when it processes a **RESTORE_ VIEW** phase event. The subsequent statement will print a message "before - ..*phase id.*" for all phase events of the lifecycle.

```
public void beforePhase(PhaseEvent pe) {
  if (pe.getPhaseId() == PhaseId.RESTORE_VIEW)
    System.out.println("Processing new Request!");

  System.out.println("before - " + pe.getPhaseId().toString());
}
```

A subsequent **afterPhase()** method can be similarly coded as:

```
public void afterPhase(PhaseEvent pe) {
  System.out.println("after - " + pe.getPhaseId().toString());

  if (pe.getPhaseId() == PhaseId.RENDER_RESPONSE)
    System.out.println("Done with Request!\n");
  }
}
```

Notice how this method prints an *after phase* message for all phases. It also prints a special "Done with Request!" when it encounters the final Render Response phase.

The final method to implement is **getPhaseId()**, which is used to determine which phase this phase listener will process events for. Since it must execute during every phase change, it returns **ANY_PHASE.**

```
public PhaseId getPhaseId() {
  return PhaseId.ANY_PHASE;
}
```

The code to the phase listener is now complete, but to use it in the Faces application, its full classpath must be registered in the **faces-config.xml** as follows:

```
<lifecycle>
  <phase-listener>com.jsfcompref.MyPhaseListener</phase-listener>
</lifecycle>
```

JSF 1.2 TIP *In Faces 1.2 it is also possible to register phase listeners directly on the* **UIViewRoot** *and avoid the necessity of including them in the* **faces-config.xml** *file.*

Once registered in a Faces application, the phase listener will report all of the lifecycle phases being entered during execution of the application. For example, upon an initial, non-postback, request to a Faces application, the output in the console will look like this:

```
...
Processing new Request!
before - RESTORE_VIEW 1
after - RESTORE_VIEW 1
before - RENDER_RESPONSE 6
after - RENDER_RESPONSE 6
Done with Request!
```

This confirms what was presented in Chapter 3 in that during an initial Faces request, where no data is being posted back to the application, the request processing lifecycle simply creates a new view of UI components (in the Restore View phase) and then renders a response to the client.

A subsequent request that now posts form information back to the application will cause the following output since the entire lifecycle will be processed.

```
...
Processing new  Request!
before - RESTORE_VIEW 1
after - RESTORE_VIEW 1
before - APPLY_REQUEST_VALUES 2
after - APPLY_REQUEST_VALUES 2
before - PROCESS_VALIDATIONS 3
after - PROCESS_VALIDATIONS 3
before - UPDATE_MODEL_VALUES 4
after - UPDATE_MODEL_VALUES 4
before - INVOKE_APPLICATION 5
after - INVOKE_APPLICATION 5
before - RENDER_RESPONSE 6
after - RENDER_RESPONSE 6
Done with Request!
```

Once a phase listener like this has been installed, you can observe the effects of several changes that can affect the processing order of the Faces lifecycle. For example, a page with a single **commandButton** that is bound to an action method, which prints out a message "in action method," could have its **immediate** property set to **true.** When the application is run, it will execute the action method at the end of the Apply Request Values phase as opposed to the Invoke Application phase where it would normally execute, as shown next.

```
Processing new  Request!
before - RESTORE_VIEW 1
after - RESTORE_VIEW 1
before - APPLY_REQUEST_VALUES 2
Action event processed...
after - APPLY_REQUEST_VALUES 2
before - RENDER_RESPONSE 6
after - RENDER_RESPONSE 6
Done with Request!
```

In addition to tracking action events, a phase listener such as this could track exactly when a value change listener method executes by simply using a print statement such as "In value change listener method." You can then observe where it executes in the lifecycle. Also recall that in the Zip code example, the value change listener methods also jumped directly to the Render Response phase by calling the **RenderResponse()** method on the Faces context. This will be observable with the same phase listener example.

More detailed examples of the **PhaseListener** facility will be shown in Chapters 10 and 12.

Creating Custom Events and Listeners

As you may have gathered by now, JavaServer Faces is extremely flexible, allowing for customization in numerous ways. Faces events and listeners are no exception, and building custom events and listeners is a fairly straightforward process. You will seldom need to do so, though, because most common Web application development tasks can be handled by the core Faces and phase events provided by the specification. Most often, when a specific need is found for a custom event type, it is within the context of building a complete custom Faces UI component and associated classes because the integration of the custom event type and listener is often tightly coupled.

If the situation does arise in which you must build custom event types and event listeners, here are the steps that you will follow:

1. Decide on a specific purpose for the custom event and listener type. For example, this could be a specialization of a common action or value change event, which fits into the context of usage of the custom component. For instance, a custom table component could implement a custom row change event and listener.

2. Create the custom event type, which must extend, directly or indirectly, **java.util .FacesEvent**. The event's constructor will contain the component (usually custom) with which this event should be associated. Most importantly, the **isAppropriateListener(FacesListener listener)** method must be overridden to inspect the argument **listener** and see if this event applies to the listener. If so, this method returns **true;** otherwise, **false.** This is the single most important method in the custom event and listener API because it alone allows the core JSF runtime to deal with your custom event without knowing the specifics of the event or listener type.

3. Create the custom event listener interface that defines the behavior of the listener. It will extend, directly or indirectly, **FacesListener**.

The details of exactly how an event is bound to specific types of components require an understanding of custom JSF component development, which is covered in Chapters 10, 11, and 12.

Extending
JavaServer Faces

PART

II

CHAPTER 9
Applying JSF: Introducing
the Virtual Trainer Application

CHAPTER 10
Building Custom UI
Components

CHAPTER 11
Building AJAX JSF
Components

CHAPTER 12
Building Non-UI Custom
Components

CHAPTER 13
Alternate View Description
Technology and Facelets

Applying JSF: Introducing the Virtual Trainer Application

In the preceding chapters, you've seen several smaller examples of JavaServer Faces. Now it's time to examine a larger, real-world JSF application that ties together all of the topics covered so far. This example will also provide a firm conceptual foundation that will help you understand the more advanced concepts in the following chapters.

The application is called Virtual Trainer. It is a JSF-based Web application that helps an athlete or casual sports enthusiast train for an event. Virtual Trainer provides a robust introduction to building a complete JSF application because it neatly integrates all of the concepts presented so far, while introducing some new important topics. These include

- Guidance on UI design, page templates, and **subview** usage
- Implementing basic Servlet Filter–based application security
- Displaying and editing multipage tabular data with **dataTable**s
- Implementing **dataTable** column header–based row sorting
- Building drill-down row editing from a **dataTable**
- Constructing a persistence layer using Hibernate
- Internationalizing Faces applications

The Virtual Trainer application presented in this chapter is also downloadable from the online extension and will come in a *pure Java* demonstration version as well as a version that implements a persistence technology. The pure Java demonstration version is used solely as an initial prototype and doesn't require a backend database to test the application.

A Quick Tour of the Virtual Trainer Application

Before looking at exactly how this application was coded, an overview of the Virtual Trainer application is in order. The Virtual Trainer application gives a sports or fitness enthusiast the ability to plan their workout sessions and have them directly relate to actual upcoming athletic events. For example, if a runner wants to train for an upcoming marathon, he or she can create a customized training routine that has a personalized set of individual training or workout sessions that the runner can follow. As the runner fulfills each workout session, he or she can comment on their progress. A human online trainer advisor will also be able to comment and offer encouragement/advice to the user.

The following sections present a quick tour of Virtual Trainer in order to acquaint you with its functionality. It guides you through the following tasks in the application:

- Registering, logging in, and browsing through some of the pre-created training events
- Selecting and updating a specific training event
- Creating and deleting a training event
- Logging out and logging back in as the user **jake**, who is a training advisor
- Updating the training event workout comments that were previously edited by the guest user account

Registering and Logging In to the Virtual Trainer Application

When first accessing the Virtual Trainer application's welcome (**welcome.jsp**) page, you will see a basic information page about the application along with either Login or Register options in the upper-right corner. This is shown in Figure 9-1.

Assuming this is your first time to the Virtual Trainer site, you'll click Register to establish a new account for yourself. This will bring you to the registration page for new accounts. Figure 9-2 shows a properly filled out registration form for a new account.

After you complete the registration and click Register (and assuming no validation errors have occurred), you are automatically logged in to the application with your new account. However, if you log out and need to return to the application, you can click the

Figure 9-1   The Virtual Trainer welcome page

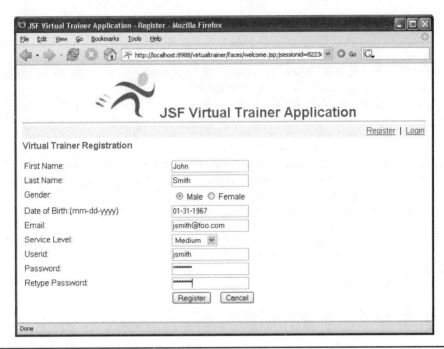

FIGURE 9-2   The Virtual Trainer registration page

Login link in the upper-right corner and be forwarded to the login (**login.jsp**) page (shown in Figure 9-3).

After entering the credentials, you'll then see the main page (shown later in Figure 9-5) where you can create new training events by clicking the Create New Training Event button on the main page.

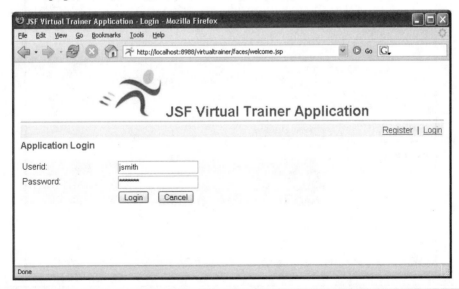

FIGURE 9-3   The Virtual Trainer login page

Creating a New Training Event Workout Plan

The Create Training Event Plan page, as shown in Figure 9-4, allows you to create a workout training plan for a new, upcoming athletic event. First, fill in the event name, type, date, and your respective athletic level. Then choose from a list of online human trainer advisors who will be monitoring your progress as you train for the event.

Once you've finished filling out the form on the Create Training Event Plan page, click Create Event. Virtual Trainer then generates a set of workout sessions based on your age and skill level to help you prepare for the event. At this point, you'll begin your workout routine based on the workout sessions assigned for the event. As you perform your workouts, you'll return to the application to log your progress as each workout session is completed.

In order to get a better feel for dealing with larger sets of training events without having to enter all the information manually, the downloadable version of the Virtual Trainer application provides a guest account that allows anyone to log in and work with preloaded training events and individual workout sessions.

After logging out and logging back in using the guest account, you'll see a preloaded set of training events on the main page, shown in Figure 9-5.

Using the scroller at the bottom of the table of training events, you can page (or scroll) through the different pages of training event data.

Selecting and Updating Training Events

At this point, you can select an individual event and drill down to a single event view page. As shown in Figure 9-6, the event view/edit page displays a single training event in a master-detail form. You can then update the details of the training event and enter information on each workout session.

After you complete a specific workout session, you can check it off and enter any comments about the workout.

FIGURE 9-4 Creating a new Training Event workout plan

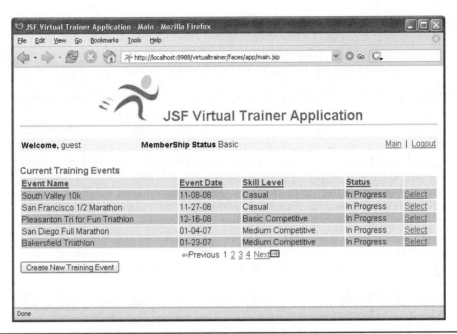

FIGURE 9-5   Browsing multiple training events on the main page

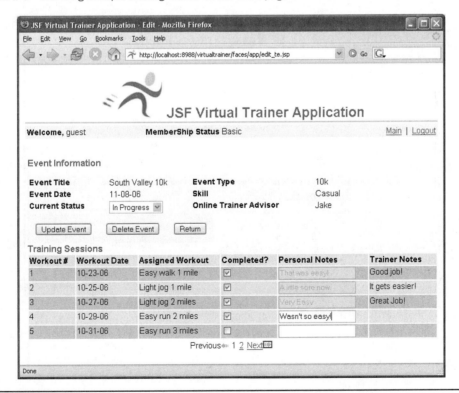

FIGURE 9-6   The edit training event details page

If you decide that you no longer want to train for this event, you can delete the entire training event by clicking the Delete Event button. This causes a confirmation page to be shown that allows you to confirm whether you really want to delete the training event or cancel out of the operation and return to the events edit page.

Logging In as an Online Trainer and Updating Event Workout Comments

As you complete the individual workout sessions and fill in your progress, you can click the Update Event button to update your progress in the application. Your designated online trainer also has the ability to log in to the application and view your progress. The online trainer will be able to provide comments or encouragement throughout your training.

For example, logging in as the user Jake, you will be able to monitor multiple users and offer comments. When logged in as an online trainer, the user interface renders slightly differently with the Membership Status field at the top of the page displaying as Trainer, and the Edit Training page allowing you to edit the trainer's comments, as shown in Figure 9-7.

This concludes the brief walkthrough of the Virtual Trainer application. It is now time to discuss how the application was built by first describing the application requirements and then showing how the individual pages and backing technology were created.

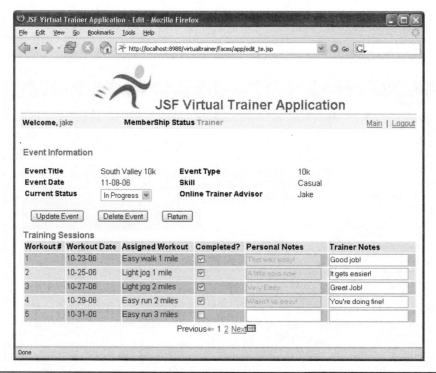

FIGURE 9-7   The online trainer "jake" providing comments

The Virtual Trainer Application Requirements

The following lists the key requirements for the application:

- Application users will have the ability to register new accounts for themselves and log in to the application.
- Users will have ability to create a set of athletic events for which they will be able to train.
- While creating training events, the user will be able to also select an online training advisor who will be able to monitor his or her progress and provide helpful comments along the way.
- Once the athletic training events have been created, an individually customized set of training sessions are generated for each athletic event. These represent individual date-based workout sessions that the user can follow.
- Each individualized training session is assigned with a specific date and will be rendered with a checkbox allowing the user to check off whether he or she performed the specific training session.
- In addition to the checkbox, the user will have an input text field where they can log any specific comments about the training session.
- The online training advisor will also be able to enter comments for each training event as well as to provide guidance.

The Virtual Trainer Application Architecture

In a very simple sense, the application is a classic *master-detail* application where the user can edit a set of items that are related to each other in a master-detail fashion. Figure 9-8 is a UML diagram that provides visual representation of the data model entities of the application. Later in the chapter, you'll see how to build a data access layer that can perform data operations on the data model that could reside in a relational database.

The Virtual Trainer application is comprised of the following elements:

- JSP pages and backing beans
- Navigational page flow
- JSF data model components

Each is described in the following sections.

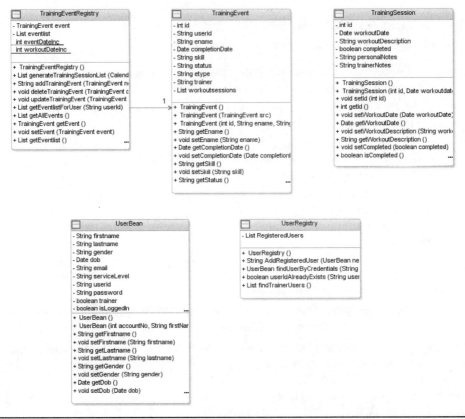

FIGURE 9-8 The data model of the Virtual Trainer application

JSP Pages and Backing Beans

The JSP pages and backing beans used by Virtual Trainer are listed next.

- **index.jsp** This is a non-visual page containing a JSP forward to the **welcome.jsp** page, along with the "faces/" prefix (**<jsp:forward page="faces/welcome.jsp"/>**). This allows the user to immediately forward to the Faces-enabled welcome page without having to manually enter the entire Web address.

- **welcome.jsp** This is the non-authenticated starting point or home page of the application. It provides a high-level introduction to what the application does. It also contains register and login links.

- **login.jsp** The application's login page.

- **Login.java** The backing bean containing the authentication methods **login()** and **logout()**. It is registered in the **faces-config.xml** as **Login_Backing** with a scope of **request**.

- **loginbar.jsp** An included JSP page via a **subview** which presents a basic toolbar for the login and welcome pages.

- **register.jsp**   The application's registration page which allows new users to register themselves to the application.
- **Register.java**   The backing containing the event handler to register a new user. It is registered as **Register_Backing** with a **request** scope.
- **app/main.jsp**   After a successful login, this is the main page of the application. It displays a list of training events that the user has a training plan for. It, along with the remaining pages, resides in the **app** subdirectory.
- **Main.java**   The backing bean for this page, which contains event handler code for creating new training events or selecting an existing one. It is registered as **Main_ Backing** with a **session** scope.
- **app/mainbar.jsp**   An included JSP page via a **subview** which presents a detailed toolbar containing user information as well as logout and main links.
- **app/create_te.jsp**   The training event creation page. It is navigable from the main page.
- **CreateTe.Java**   The backing bean for **create_te.jsp**. Contains an event handler to create a new training event. It's registered as **CreateTe_Backing** with a **request** scope.
- **app/edit_te.jsp**   This allows the user to edit an individual training set of training events. It renders a single athletic event along with a set of multiple training events. This page is where the users will spend a majority of their time logging their individual training activities.
- **EditTe.java**   The backing bean for the edit page. It has event handler code for updating the training event presented on the page. It is registered as **EditTe_ Backing** with a **request** scope.
- **app/delete_te.jsp**   A delete confirmation page that allows users to delete a training event.
- **DeleteTe.java**   Contains the event handler to delete a training event. It is registered as **DeleteTe_Backing** with a **request** scope.

The Navigational Page Flow

Virtual Trainer has various navigational rules associated with the different pages based on the user's interaction. Figure 9-9 provides an illustration of the overall page flow of the application. (Note: This page flow was designed using Oracle's JDeveloper 10.1.3 Java development tool. More information on this and other Faces-enabled tools in Chapter 17.)

As with any standard Faces application, all of the navigation rules for Virtual Trainer are contained within the application's **faces-config.xml**. The navigation rules are comprised of global rules, such as for key pages like **welcome.jsp**, **login.jsp**, **register.jsp**, and **main.jsp**. There are also specific navigation cases per page—for example, from the main page there are navigation cases leading to the event creation page (**create_te.jsp**), edit event page (**edit_te.jsp**), and back to the welcome page via a logout action method.

The JSF Data Model Components

As shown earlier in Figure 9-8, the application's data model consists of a set of managed JavaBeans, which provide data management services.

- **TrainingEvent.java**   A Java class that represents a single athletic event that will be trained for. Its properties contain the event name, type, date, and so on.

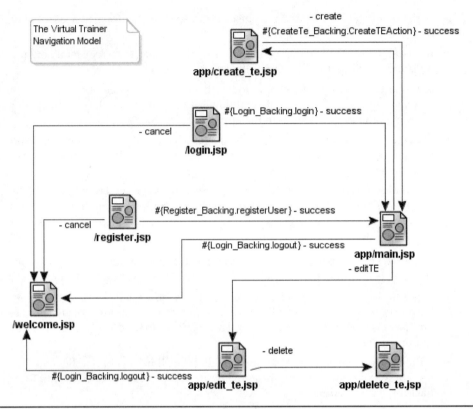

FIGURE 9-9 The Virtual Trainer application's navigational page flow

- **TrainingEventRegistry.java** A Java class which serves as a registry of the different training events. It has several data access methods that allow for the retrieval, editing, and addition of training event items. This class is registered as the managed bean **TrainingEventRegistry** with scope **application**.

- **TrainingSession.java** A Java class that represents a single workout session for a training event. Its properties include **workoutDate**, a Boolean completed flag, personal notes, and trainer notes. Each training event (**TrainingEvent**) is associated with multiple workout sessions (**TrainingSession**).

- **UserBean.java** A Java class that represents a single user of the application. It contains properties such as name, e-mail, and whether or not they are a user or a trainer. (Denoted by the **boolean isTrainer** property.) It is registered as a managed bean as **UserBean** with **session** scope.

- **UserRegistry.java** A Java class that serves as a registry of all the registered users of the application. The **UserRegistry** is used for authentication as well as the registration system. It is registered as **UserRegistry**, and like **TrainingEventRegistry**, it also has a scope of **application**.

Building the Virtual Trainer Application

The next section explains in detail how the Virtual Trainer application is built, starting with the basic page design and culminating with advanced data operations.

Basic Page Layout and Formatting

A very useful approach to follow when starting a Web development project is to first design a prototype in old-fashioned HTML. This approach was used for Virtual Trainer. It was during this phase that a custom Cascading Style Sheet, **vt.css**, was also created to define a consistent look and feel for the entire application. As you'll see shortly, JSF components also come pre-equipped to work well with CSS. It should be noted that in addition to merely providing a look and feel for an application, CSS can also be used to specify the layout of the items on the page. In fact, Sun's Studio Creator, which is one of the JSF-enabled tools detailed in Chapter 17, actually uses CSS to offer absolute positioning as a default layout feature. For the most part, however, HTML tables are still widely used to initially define a page layout.

Once the HTML prototype conveys the general design of the user interface, the HTML pages can then be transformed into JSF-enabled JSP pages. (Incidentally, if you are using Facelets, as described in Chapter 13, you can continue to use plain HTML pages as your actual JSF pages.)

Converting to JSF JSPs simply requires an extension change (**.html** to **.jsp**) and the addition of the JSF taglib directives to the pages. At this point, you have to begin deciding how much HTML will be replaced with JSF components. In general, the HTML tables can be swapped out for JSF layout or container components (such as **panelGrid** and **panelGroup**). It is also possible to continue using HTML tables for layout in your final JSF applications; however, for maximum accessibility it's generally a good practice to use JSF layout/container components.

Another commonly used practice during the design phase of an application is to create a single page template that all other pages will be derived from. While there are many techniques and technologies for page templating, a simple and common approach is to design a single master, or parent template page, that will be used as a starting template for all other pages, thus ensuring a consistent page design and layout. This is the approach that was used for the Virtual Trainer application.

The following is the general page design template for Virtual Trainer:

```
<%@ taglib uri="http://java.sun.com/jsf/core" prefix="f"%>
<%@ taglib uri="http://java.sun.com/jsf/html" prefix="h"%>
<f:view>
  <html>
    <head>
      <title>Virtual Trainer </title>
      <link href="css/vt.css" rel="stylesheet" media="screen"></link>
      <link rel="shortcut icon" href="images/favicon.ico">
    </head>
    <body><h:form>
        <table width="100%" border="0">
          <tr>
```

```
            <td>
              <h1 align="center">
                <h:graphicImage url="/images/vtlogo.jpg"
                                alt="Virtual Trainer Logo"/>
                JSF Virtual Trainer Application
              </h1>
            </td>
          </tr>
          <tr>
            <td >
              <f:subview id="loginbar">
                <jsp:include page="loginbar.jsp"/>
              </f:subview>
            </td>
          </tr>
          <tr>
            <td>
              <h3>(Page Title)</h3>
<!-- Page specific content goes here -->
            </td>
          </tr>
        </table>
      </h:form></body>
  </html>
</f:view>
```

A quick review of this page template code reveals the required JSF taglib directives followed by the CSS reference. A Virtual Trainer shortcut icon is also defined in the header. It serves as a small icon associated with the site/application and is rendered in certain browsers (such as Firefox) in the address bar as well as in the bookmarks.

Moving into the body of the page, you'll see that the rest of the page uses an HTML table to define the overall structure of the page. Again, this structure could also be created using just JSF components, but for this example, an HTML table will suffice.

At the top of the table is the "banner" portion of the page that displays the main logo of the application, **vtlogo.jpg**, along with an **H1**-formatted banner text. At runtime the **H1**-formatted text will render with a line beneath it. This is part of the style associated with **H1** and is specified in the accompanying **vt.css** CSS file.

The other thing to notice is the usage of a JSF **f:subview**. This allows for the inclusion of an external (register and login) portion of content that is used in several pages. In general, JSF **subview**s provide a way to insert reusable portions of content using a **JSP include** in JSF applications.

NOTE *When dealing with **subviews** and parameters, there are some corner cases in JSP that pose problems in passing parameters. These problems have been solved when using technologies such as Facelets or Struts Tiles.*

Recall that JSP **includes** merge Web content at runtime and are also known as dynamic includes. For static includes, where the content is merged at compile time, **subview**s are not needed since the JSF runtime only sees the combined content.

Below the included portion of the page resides the main content area. This is where each page will contain page-specific content. As we step through building all of the pages, we'll start with this page template and fill in this area with page-specific content.

Creating a Simple Authentication System

As you'll see in Chapter 15, creating a truly secure enterprise Web application takes careful planning and coding. However, it is often useful to begin with a simple authentication system that provides basic application-level authentication that can later be enhanced to a more robust architecture without completely redesigning the architecture. This is the approach used by Virtual Trainer.

The application-based authentication employed in Virtual Trainer consists of a login form on a page (**login.jsp**) that obtains user credentials and then checks them against a registry of users. If the user credentials do not exist in the registry, a faces invalid login message is displayed on the form and the user is not permitted to log in to the application.

An additional technique to aid in security is to place all secured pages in a subdirectory. For example, this application places all secure pages in an "/app" subdirectory. This facilitates either application-based or container-managed security to filter out all non-secure requests to pages residing below the secure subdirectory. (Incidentally, the downloadable version of the Virtual Trainer application provides a simple example of application-based security with a Servlet filter to prevent access to the secured "/app/*" pages. The details of how to implement a Servlet filter to secure pages is detailed in Chapter 15.)

The login form that receives the user-entered credentials consists of a two-column **h:panelGrid** component along with child components for the **Userid:** and **Password:** labels. The code for the login form, which is placed in the central content area of the template page, is as follows:

```
<h:messages globalOnly="true" infoClass="LoginError"/>
<h:panelGrid width="70%" columns="3" border="0"
    styleClass="form-bkg">
  <h:outputLabel value="Userid:" for="userid"/>
  <h:inputText required="true" id="userid"
    binding="#{Login_Backing.userid}"/>
  <h:message for="userid" errorClass="ValidateError"/>
  <h:outputLabel value="Password:" for="password"/>
   <h:inputSecret required="true" id="password"
     binding="#{Login_Backing.password}"/>
   <h:message for="password" errorClass="ValidateError"/>
   <f:verbatim> </f:verbatim>
    <h:panelGroup>
      <h:commandButton value="Login"
          action="#{Login_Backing.login}"/>
      <f:verbatim>    </f:verbatim>
      <h:commandButton value="Cancel" immediate="true"
          action="welcome"/>
    </h:panelGroup>
</h:panelGrid>
```

The first thing to notice is the **messages** tag that will display any global messages. Notice that it has a CSS class reference to **LoginError**. This will apply the referenced style contained in the accompanying CSS file (**vt.css**) when an *information* type message arrives, such as when an invalid login occurs. The next component, **h:panelGrid**, serves as a layout container and is specified to have three columns. This means that when rendering, the **h:panelGrid** component will create a new row in the table after every third child component.

As you can see, the login form is comprised of two rows of the components **h:outputLabel**, **h:inputText** (or **h:inputSecret**), and **h:message**. Notice that for the password input field, an **h:inputSecret** component is used so as not to display any characters typed by the user. Also notice each input field has a corresponding **h:message** component. This allows the form to display field-specific validation errors styled with a custom **ValidateError** style, also defined in the main **vt.css** style sheet.

The Virtual Trainer Login page is shown in Figure 9-10 with validation errors.

If no validation errors happen, but instead an application login error occurs, the general **messages** component will display an invalid login error, as shown in Figure 9-11.

It's important to notice that the input fields are bound to UI component instances declared in the page's backing bean using the **binding** attribute. For example:

```
binding="#{Login_Backing.userid}"
```

Recall that using the **binding** attribute to reference a UI component in a managed (backing) bean allows for programmatic access to the bound UI component. In our case, the backing bean, **Login.java**, is registered as a managed bean as "Login_Backing" with a **scope** of type **request**. As you'll see shortly, we can extract the values from the input fields in an action method and then pass them onto an authentication method.

The third row of the login form simply contains an HTML non-breaking space ( ) encapsulated within a **f:verbatim** tag followed by a **panelGroup** containing both Login and Cancel **h:commandButton**s. Inserting a space ( ) in a **f:verbatim** tag ensures that the login button (**h:commandButton**) resides in the middle column. Notice also that a **f:verbatim** tag is also used to separate the Login and Cancel buttons a bit.

FIGURE 9-10   The Virtual Trainer Login page with validation errors

FIGURE 9-11   The Virtual Trainer Login page with an application login error

JSF 1.2 TIP   *The* **panelGrid** *and* **panelGroup** *were originally intended to contain only JSP tags that were JSF components, and not plain HTML (template) text. This is why the* **f:verbatim** *tag is necessary in JSF 1.1. The* **f:verbatim** *tag takes its nested template text and converts it into a* **UIOutput** *component, allowing the* **panelGrid** *and* **panelGroup** *components to lay it out in the expected format. In JSF 1.2, an ease-of-use feature called "content interweaving" automatically converts any template text into* **UIOutput** *components so they can be laid out by components such as the* **panelGrid** *or* **panelGroup***.*

Notice that the **action** attribute of the button refers to the **login** action method that calls an external authentication method to determine if the entered values are valid. The following is the source of the **login** page's backing bean.

```
package com.jsfcompref.trainer.backing;

import com.jsfcompref.trainer.UserBean;
import com.jsfcompref.trainer.UserRegistry;
import com.jsfcompref.trainer.util.UserUtil;
import com.jsfcompref.trainer.util.JSFUtil;

//Remaining import statements omitted for brevity

public class Login {

    private HtmlInputText userid;
    private HtmlInputSecret password;
    private final static String AUTH_USER = "Authorized_User";
```

```java
    public Login() {
    }

    public String login() {
      //Grab UserRegistry Managed Bean

      UserRegistry userRegCopy =
        (UserRegistry)JSFUtil.getManagedObject("UserRegistry");

      // Call findByUserCredentials method
      // Retrieve currentUser which matches credentials
      UserBean currentUser =
        userRegCopy.findUserByCredentials(userid.getValue().toString(),
        password.getValue().toString());

      if (currentUser == null) {
        // login failed
        FacesContext.getCurrentInstance().addMessage(null,
                          new FacesMessage("Invalid Login!"));
        return "failure";
      } else {
        // login success
        UserBean managedUserBean =
          (UserBean)JSFUtil.getManagedObject("UserBean");
        UserUtil.copyUserProperties(currentUser, managedUserBean);
        managedUserBean.setIsLoggedIn(true);

        // Place authorized user token on session to satisfy security filter
        JSFUtil.storeOnSession(FacesContext.getCurrentInstance(),
         AUTH_USER, "Authorized_User");
        return "success";
      }
    }

    public String logout() throws IOException{
      ExternalContext ectx =
          FacesContext.getCurrentInstance().getExternalContext();
      HttpServletResponse response =
          (HttpServletResponse)ectx.getResponse();
      HttpSession session = (HttpSession)ectx.getSession(false);
      session.invalidate();

// Navigate back to welcome page
      FacesContext ctx =  FacesContext.getCurrentInstance();
      Application app = ctx.getApplication();
      app.getNavigationHandler().handleNavigation(ctx,
          "/welcome.jsp", "welcome");


      return null;
    }
// Bean getter and setter methods omitted.
}
```

The first thing to notice about this class is its import of several custom application classes. The **UserBean** class is used to store information about the currently logged-in user. It is maintained in a registry of users in **UserRegistry**. The**UserUtil** utility class has a method that allows for the copying of user properties, while the **JSFUtil** class provides simplified methods to retrieve/update objects from the JSF Managed Bean facility and **HttpSession**. The often used method **JSFUtil.getManagedObject()** uses a Faces variable resolver to resolve the object specified. The code for this method is as follows:

```
public static Object getManagedObject(String objectName){
    FacesContext context = FacesContext.getCurrentInstance();
    Object requestedObject =  context.getApplication().getVariableResolver()
            .resolveVariable(context, objectName);
    return  requestedObject;
}
```

As you can see in the code, when the **login** action method is invoked, an instance of the **UserRegistry** is retrieved from the Managed Bean facility and its **findUserByCredentials()** method is invoked with the values of the **userid** and **password** fields (which were bound to the fields on the page) being passed as arguments. If the **UserRegistry** contains a user matching the provided **userid** and **password**, an instance of a full, matching **UserBean** is returned and the login will proceed successfully. This matching **UserBean** will be copied to a **managedUserBean** object that is maintained as a JSF-managed bean with scope **session**. This bean will be accessible throughout the lifetime of the user's login session and the application will refer to this bean's properties when rendering user-specific information. In addition to copying the user's properties into a **session**-scoped managed bean, an AUTH_USER String token is placed onto the session to disable the security filter (thus allowing access to pages below the "/app" directory). A string value of "success" is then returned, which corresponds to a navigation case and will cause a navigation to the **main.jsp** page. The following is the corresponding navigation-rule in **faces-config.xml**:

```
<navigation-rule>
  <from-view-id>/login.jsp</from-view-id>
  <navigation-case>
    <from-action>#{Login_Backing.login}</from-action>
    <from-outcome>success</from-outcome>
    <to-view-id>/app/main.jsp</to-view-id>
  </navigation-case>
</navigation-rule>
```

However, if the provided **userid** and **password** do not match any user in the registry, a **null** value is returned, a **Faces** message is generated, and a "failure" string is returned. This causes no navigation to occur and the browser will remain on the current page, but now with an "Invalid login!" message rendered by the **h:messages** tag.

Logging Out of the Virtual Trainer Application

A common technique for implementing a J2EE Web application's logout functionality is to clean up any non-committed data and then completely invalidate the **HttpSession**. This is exactly the method used by Virtual Trainer.

The **logout()** method operates simply by invalidating the current user's session. This clears out all **session**-scoped objects in memory. Clearing out the session also removes the AUTH_USER token, so the security filter will once again become active. After invalidating the **session**, it also navigates back to the non-secure welcome page (**/welcome.jsp**) using the Faces navigation handler.

This simple application-based login/logout functionality works great for prototypes; however, as previously mentioned, enterprise security is usually handled in a more robust manner with a more sophisticated security mechanism that could rely on several layers of security. Again, enterprise security with JSF is detailed in Chapter 15.

Before continuing on to the main browse and edit pages, let's review the registration portion of the application, which you'll find is simply an extension from Chapter 2's JSFReg application with a few enhancements.

Revisiting JSFReg—Building the Registration System

Now that we have a simple authentication system, it makes sense to offer functionality that lets people register themselves as valid users of the application. In building a registration system, recall from Chapter 2 the simple JSFReg application. It is now time to incorporate this simple example into the more comprehensive Virtual Trainer application. In short, all we really have to do is import the form onto a **register.jsp** page and provide a comparable backing bean that processes the input and calls a **registerUser** method.

Starting with the same page template from before, the form shown in Figure 9-12 is added to the body content area.

As you can see, this is a typical registration form that behaves in a manner common to most online registration systems. It has built-in validation code to ensure that the e-mail address entered is in the correct format and it also checks to make sure that the two password values entered match each other. There is even validation code to check that the date entered for the user's birthdate is not in the future. The code for the registration form, which also resides in the central content area defined by the page template, is shown next:

```
<h:messages globalOnly="true" infoClass="RegError"/>
<h:panelGrid width="70%" columns="3" border="0">
  <h:outputLabel value="First Name:" for="fname"/>
  <h:inputText required="true" id="fname"
      binding="#{Register_Backing.firstName}"/>
  <h:message for="fname" errorClass="ValidateError"/>
  <h:outputLabel value="Last Name:" for="lname"/>
  <h:inputText required="true" id="lname"
      binding="#{Register_Backing.lastName}"/>
  <h:message for="lname" errorClass="ValidateError"/>
  <h:outputLabel value="Gender:" for="gender"/>
  <h:selectOneRadio required="true" id="gender"
      binding="#{Register_Backing.gender}" >
    <f:selectItem itemLabel="Male" itemValue="male"/>
    <f:selectItem itemLabel="Female" itemValue="female"/>
  </h:selectOneRadio>
  <h:message for="gender" errorClass="ValidateError"/>
  <h:outputLabel value="Date of Birth:(mm-dd-yyyy)" for="dob"/>
  <h:inputText id="dob" required="true"
      binding="#{Register_Backing.dob}" >
    <f:convertDateTime pattern="mm-dd-yyyy"/>
    <f:validator validatorId="pastDateValidate"/>
  </h:inputText>
  <h:message for="dob" errorClass="ValidateError"/>
  <h:outputLabel value="Email:" for="email"/>
  <h:inputText required="true" id="email"
```

```
        binding="#{Register_Backing.email}"
        validator="#{Register_Backing.validateEmail}"/>
   <h:message for="email" errorClass="ValidateError"/>
   <h:outputLabel value="Service Level:" for="level"/>
   <h:selectOneMenu  id="level"
            binding="#{Register_Backing.serviceLevel}">
     <f:selectItem itemLabel="Basic" itemValue="Basic"/>
     <f:selectItem itemLabel="Medium" itemValue="Medium"/>
     <f:selectItem itemLabel="Premium" itemValue="Premium"/>
   </h:selectOneMenu>
   <f:verbatim> </f:verbatim>
   <h:outputLabel value="Userid:" for="userid"/>
   <h:inputText required="true" id="userid"
       binding="#{Register_Backing.userid}"/>
   <h:message for="userid" errorClass="ValidateError"/>
   <h:outputLabel value="Password:" for="password"/>
   <h:inputSecret required="true" id="password"
       binding="#{Register_Backing.password}"/>
   <h:message for="password" errorClass="ValidateError"/>
   <h:outputLabel value="Retype Password:" for="password2"/>
   <h:inputSecret required="true" id="password2"
       binding="#{Register_Backing.passwordCheck}"/>
       validator="#{Register_Backing.validatePassword}"/>
   <h:message for="password2" errorClass="ValidateError"/>
   <f:verbatim> </f:verbatim>
   <h:panelGroup>
     <h:commandButton value="Register"
         action="#{Register_Backing.registerUser}"/>
     <f:verbatim>    </f:verbatim>
     <h:commandButton value="Cancel" action="cancel" immediate="true" />
   </h:panelGroup>
</h:panelGrid>
```

In contrast to the original JSFReg application in Chapter 2, this new version of the registration form uses a three-column **panelGrid** instead of an HTML table to contain the form elements. Each row in the form is made up of label, input field, and corresponding message component to display any validation errors per input field. This version also uses component binding using the **binding** attribute with references to declared instances of like components in the backing bean, whereas the original JSFReg employed value binding (using the **value** attribute) to a JavaBean as a model object. Either approach is acceptable,

Virtual Trainer Registration

First Name:

Last Name:

Gender: Male Female

Date of Birth:(mm-dd-yyyy)

Email:

Service Level: Basic

Userid:

Password:

Retype Password:

Register   Cancel

FIGURE 9-12   The Virtual Trainer application registration form

but setting the **binding** attribute to a UI component declared in a backing bean provides more flexibility by offering programmatic access to the UI component in the page.

You may notice the various validations for the input fields including validation methods for checking the e-mail address as well as checking to see if the passwords matched. An independent **Validator** class is also used in the Date of Birth input field (**<f:validator validatorId="pastDateValidate"/>**) to ensure that the date entered is not in the future. The code for the **pastDateValidate** validator is the following:

```
package com.jsfcompref.trainer.util;
// Import statements omitted

public class PastDateValidator implements Validator {
  public PastDateValidator() {
  }

  public void validate(FacesContext FacesContext,
   UIComponent UIComponent, Object value) throws ValidatorException {
   Date enteredDate = (Date)value;
   Date today = new Date();

   if (today.before(enteredDate)) {
     FacesMessage message =
       new FacesMessage("Entered date must not be in the future!");
     throw new ValidatorException(message);
   }
  }
}
```

In order to use this validator class on the form using the **f:validator** tag, it was registered in the **faces-config.xml** with a **validator-id** of **pastDateValidate**. The rest of the validation logic is provided in the backing bean.

---

*JSF 1.2 TIP JSF 1.2 provides attributes for all Standard input components, which allow for custom converter and validator messages. These can then refer to resource bundles for localized messages (for example, ...**validatorMessage="#{bundle.requiredMessage}"**>). This allows for the placement of these messages in property files as opposed to the validator/converter code. Details on these attributes are provided in Chapter 19.*

The backing bean for the register page, **Register.java**, is somewhat similar to the Login backing bean (**Backing_Login**). It is registered as **Backing_Register** with a **request** scope. Its source is shown next:

```
package com.jsfcompref.trainer.backing;
// Import statements omitted
public class Register {

  private HtmlInputText firstName;
  private HtmlInputText lastName;
  private HtmlSelectOneRadio gender;
  private HtmlInputText dob;
  private HtmlInputText email;
  private HtmlSelectOneMenu serviceLevel;
  private HtmlInputText userid;
  private HtmlInputSecret password;
```

```java
private HtmlInputSecret passwordCheck;

private final static String AUTH_USER = "Authorized_User";

public Register(){
}

public void validateEmail(FacesContext context, UIComponent toValidate,
    Object value) throws ValidatorException {
  String eMail = (String) value;
  if(eMail.indexOf("@")<0) {
    FacesMessage message = new FacesMessage("Invalid email address!");
    throw new ValidatorException(message);
  }
}

public void validatePassword(FacesContext context,
  UIComponent toValidate, Object value) throws ValidatorException {

  String password1 = (String)this.getPassword().getValue();
  String password2 = (String) value;

  if(!password1.equals(password2)) {
    FacesMessage message = new FacesMessage("Passwords do not match!");
    throw new ValidatorException(message);
  }
}

public String registerUser() {
  UserBean newUser = new UserBean();

  newUser.setFirstname(firstName.getValue().toString());
  newUser.setLastname(lastName.getValue().toString());
  newUser.setGender(gender.getValue().toString());
  newUser.setDob((Date)dob.getValue());
  newUser.setEmail(email.getValue().toString());
  newUser.setServiceLevel(serviceLevel.getValue().toString());
  newUser.setUserid(userid.getValue().toString());
  newUser.setPassword(password.getValue().toString());

  UserRegistry ManagedUserRegistry = (UserRegistry)
  JSFUtil.getManagedObject("UserRegistry");

  if (ManagedUserRegistry.AddRegisteredUser(newUser) == null) {
    // userid already exists!

    FacesContext.getCurrentInstance().addMessage(null,
      new FacesMessage("Userid " + newUser.getUserid() +
          " already exists! Please choose another." ));
    newUser = null;

    return(null);
  } else {
    // Is a new user, continue logging in
    UserBean managedUserBean =
```

PART II

```
         (UserBean)JSFUtil.getManagedObject("UserBean");
         UserUtil.copyUserProperties(newUser, managedUserBean);
         managedUserBean.setIsLoggedIn(true);


      // Place AUTH_USER string token on session to disable security filter

         JSFUtil.storeOnSession(FacesContext.getCurrentInstance(),
           AUTH_USER, "Authorized_User");

      FacesContext.getCurrentInstance().addMessage(null,
            new FacesMessage("Registration Successful!"));
      return("main");
   } // Getters and setters omitted.
}
```

As you can see, the Login backing bean contains validation methods for e-mail and passwords validation. The e-mail validation method is the same used in the original JSFReg application. However, the **validatePassword()** is new. It works by comparing the two password values and throwing a validation error if they don't match. This is shown in Figure 9-13.

The most important method in the backing bean is obviously the **registerUser()** action method. The **registerUser()** method constructs an instance of a **UserBean** object and applies the values from the input fields (which are bound to the components in the page). It then passes this onto **addRegisteredUser()**, which places this new object into the **UserRegistry**. Once registered, the user will be able to successfully log in to the application. You'll also notice that if the **userid** already exists in the registry, a **null** value will be returned and the registration will fail and a Faces error message will be displayed. Upon successful registration, however, a Faces message indicating a successful registration to the new user is generated and the user is logged in programmatically and sent to the secured main page, **main.jsp** by returning the String "main", which corresponds to a global navigation rule that specifies a navigation to **/app/main.jsp**.

Building the Browse and Edit Pages of the Virtual Trainer Application

When you log in to the application, the main page of the application (**main.jsp**) is displayed. This page allows you to browse through a list of training events in tabular form. Recall that for each event, there is a corresponding *Select* link that allows you to drill down and edit the specific details of each event. The other actionable object on the page is a button that allows you to create a new training event. Figure 9-14 illustrates the Virtual Trainer application's main page.

Before examining the create and edit pages that are linked to the main page, let's step through how the main browse page (**main.jsp**) is created.

Service Level:	Medium ⌄	
Userid:	jsmith	
Password:		
Retype Password:		*Passwords do not match!*
	Register Cancel	

FIGURE 9-13   A password mismatch validation error

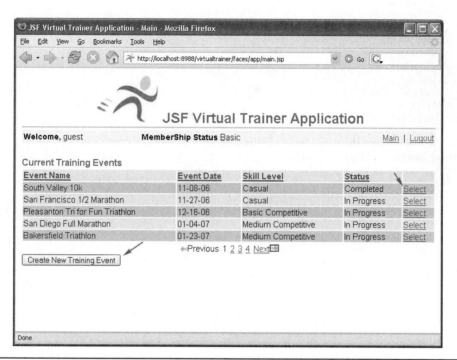

FIGURE 9-14   The main page of the Virtual Trainer application

Creating the Main Browse Page

The most important technique found in the main browse page (**main.jsp**) is its use of the
h:dataTable component and its underlying **UIData** object.

The key purpose of the **main.jsp** page is to display a list of different athletic events
for which workout plans have been created. This list is displayed in a tabular form, so a
standard JSF **h:dataTable** is used. In general, the standard **h:dataTable** component is quite
useful for displaying tabular data but it lacks the capability to page (or *scroll*) through
multiple pages of data. It also lacks the capability to offer column-based sorting of the data;
however, both page-based scrolling and column sorting is implemented in the Virtual
Trainer application and thoroughly explained later in the chapter.

In order to add paging/scrolling functionality to the **h:dataTable**, we will use a custom
JSF component (**ScrollerComponent**), which is accessible in JSP via the tag **t:scroller**.
Incidentally, the **t:scroller** (**ScrollerComponent**) component used in the application is
borrowed from the set of demonstration components provided with the Sun JSF reference
implementation's demonstration samples. Before showing how to use the custom **t:scroller**
component with a standard **h:dataTable**, a basic review of the **h:dataTable** is in order.

Browsing Tabular Data with a dataTable

The standard **h:dataTable** component provides a simple way to iterate over a set of objects
and display them in a tabular form on a page. Its **value** attribute accepts various collection
data types including **Lists**, **Arrays**, and even JDBC **ResultSets**. Recall a simple **h:dataTable**

usage example from Chapter 4 which displays data from a **userBean.sportsInterests** object of type **List**:

```
<h:dataTable value="#{userBean.sportsInterests}" var="row" >
  <h:column>
    <h:outputText value="#{row}"/>
  </h:column>
</h:dataTable>
```

In Virtual Trainer, the main **h:dataTable** displays a **List** of training events (**TrainingEvent** objects) in a tabular format and is a little more complex:

```
<h:dataTable id="eventsTable" rows="5"
    value="#{Main_Backing.trainingEventsForUser}"
    var="te" rowClasses="list-row-odd,list-row-even"
    headerClass="table-header"
    width="100%" binding="#{Main_Backing.data}">
  <h:column rendered="#{UserBean.trainer}">
    <f:facet name="header">
      <h:panelGroup>
        <h:commandLink actionListener="#{Main_Backing.sortByUserId}"
            immediate="true">
          <h:outputText value="User Account"/>
        </h:commandLink>
        <h:graphicImage url="#{Main_Backing.sortUserIdAsc ?
            '/images/arrow-up.gif' : '/images/arrow-down.gif'}"
            rendered="#{Main_Backing.showSortUserIdIcon}"
            height="13"   width="9" />
      </h:panelGroup>
    </f:facet>
    <h:outputText value="#{te.userid}"/>
  </h:column>
  <h:column>
    <f:facet name="header">
      <h:panelGroup>
        <h:commandLink actionListener="#{Main_Backing.sortByEvent}"
              immediate="true">
          <h:outputText value="Event Name"/>
        </h:commandLink>
        <h:graphicImage url="#{Main_Backing.sortEventAsc ?
            '/images/arrow-up.gif' : '/images/arrow-down.gif'}"
            rendered="#{Main_Backing.showSortEventIcon}"
            height="13"   width="9" />
      </h:panelGroup>
    </f:facet>
    <h:outputText value="#{te.ename}"/>
  </h:column>
  <h:column>
    <f:facet name="header">
      <h:panelGroup>
        <h:commandLink actionListener="#{Main_Backing.sortByDate}"
              immediate="true">
          <h:outputText value="Event Date"/>
        </h:commandLink>
        <h:graphicImage url="#{Main_Backing.sortDateAsc ?
```

```
            '/images/arrow-up.gif' : '/images/arrow-down.gif'}"
          rendered="#{Main_Backing.showSortDateIcon}"
          height="13"   width="9" />
      </h:panelGroup>
    </f:facet>
    <h:outputText value="#{te.completionDate}">
      <f:convertDateTime pattern="MM-dd-yy"/>
    </h:outputText>
  </h:column>

// The remaining event data columns are omitted for brevity,
// but they have the same format with a column component containing
// a header facet with a commandLink to execute a sorting action
// listener, as well as a sorting image which renders based on whether
// or not the column is being sorted. Below the header facet is the
// output text field displaying the data.

// The final column simply renders the Select commandLink
// to invoke the edit training event action method.
  <h:column>
    <h:commandLink action="#{Main_Backing.editTrainingEventAction}">
      <h:outputText value="Select" />
    </h:commandLink>
  </h:column>
</h:dataTable>
```

In the Virtual Trainer **h:dataTable** example, notice the **value** attribute is set to **#{Main_Backing.trainingEventsForUser}**, which is an EL reference to the method **getTrainingEventsForUser()** of the **session**-scoped backing bean for **main.jsp**. The **getTrainingEventsForUser()** backing bean method gets the current user's **userid** and first checks to see if the current user's status is of type **trainer**, meaning that this user is classified as an online sports fitness trainer and is authorized to offer training guidance to all registered regular users. If the current user is a trainer, the backing bean method **getAllEvents()** of the **TrainingEventRegistry** (which manages the entire set of **TrainingEvent** objects for the application) is called. The **getAllEvents()** method simply returns the entire **List** of **TrainingEvent** objects for every user back to the page so the current user (who is a trainer) can review and provide training guidance comments to them.

However, if the current user is not a trainer, the backing bean method sends the **userid** as an argument to another **TrainingEventRegistry** method, **getEventlistForUser()**, which returns a filtered **List** of **TrainingEvent** objects corresponding to the user's **userid**. The returned **List** is then sorted and returned to be displayed in the page using the **h:dataTable**.

The code for **main.jsp**'s backing bean method, **getTrainingEventsForUser()** residing in **Main.java**, is the following:

```
public List getTrainingEventsForUser() {
// Get training events for this user, or all if user is a trainer

  List userEventList;
  UserBean managedUserBean=
     (UserBean)JSFUtil.getManagedObject("UserBean");

  // Get user's userid
  String userid = managedUserBean.getUserid();
```

```
TrainingEventRegistry eventRegistry = (TrainingEventRegistry)
        JSFUtil.getManagedObject("TrainingEventRegistry");

// If user is a trainer, return all Training Events,
// else, only return events for the current user.
if (managedUserBean.isTrainer())
  userEventList= eventRegistry.getAllEvents();
else {
  // is not a trainer so call getEventlistForUser
  userEventList=  eventRegistry.getEventlistForUser(userid);
}
// Sort event list
sortEvents(userEventList);

return userEventList;
}
```

The implementation code for the **TrainingEventRegistry** methods **getAllEvents()** and **getEventListForUser()** is dependent on the persistence layer technology; however, a Hibernate-based example is shown later in the chapter in the section "Taking the Next Step—Persisting Virtual Trainer Data."

Returning to the **h:dataTable** attributes, notice that the **var** attribute is set to "te". This is merely an iterator variable and is used to obtain row element data. The **rowClasses** attribute defines the look and feel of the odd and even rows of the rendered table. The two styles, "list-row-odd" and "list-row-even," are provided in the **vt.css** CSS file. The **width** attribute defines the actual width of the rendered HTML table from the **h:dataTable**.

The final **binding** attribute of the **h:dataTable** is worthy of special attention, however, because it is what enables data scrolling and row operations to be performed on the data retrieved for the **h:dataTable** component. The **binding** attribute is set to a declared **javax .faces.component.UIData** instance in the backing bean (**Main_Backing**).

```
<h:dataTable … binding="#{Main_Backing.data}">
```

And the **UIData** declaration in the backing bean is

```
private UIData data = null;
```

Getters and setters for **data** are also needed as well.

The UIData Component

Setting the **binding** attribute of the **h:dataTable** to an instance of **UIData** is important because it provides programmatic access to the underlying data object represented by the **h:dataTable**. This allows the application to traverse rows, define a range of rows to display, and select and edit individual rows.

Incidentally, an **h:dataTable** tag can also have its **binding** attribute set to an instance of **javax.faces.component.html.HtmlDataTable**, which is actually extended from **UIData** and has additional user interface-related methods for managing the appearance of the **dataTable**. However, since Virtual Trainer's main page doesn't need to modify the runtime appearance of the **dataTable**, binding it directly to a **UIData** instance is sufficient. Another reason for not binding directly to **HtmlDataTable** is that you may wish to switch to a non-HTML renderer, and thus the HTML-centric methods provided in **HtmlDataTable** would no longer be suitable.

The **javax.faces.component.UIData** component extends from **javax.faces.UIComponentBase**. Its purpose is to provide full management of tabular or list type data. Some of the most oft-used methods that provide row data management and navigation are shown in Table 9-1.

Having reviewed how the training event data is extracted from the Event Registry and displayed in the **dataTable**, we can now examine Virtual Trainer's *scrolling* feature enhancement, which allows users to scroll through multiple pages of tabular data.

Using a Custom Scroller Component with a dataTable

Similar to sorting, the standard JSF **h:dataTable** does not provide a scrolling capability out of the box. That means it is not possible to scroll through different pages of data presented by the **h:dataTable** without doing some custom coding. Fortunately, giving scrolling capabilities to the standard JSF **h:dataTable** is easily done by adding the custom **scroller** component that is provided with Sun's JSF Implementation as a sample. Of course, it is also possible to implement a scrolling capability purely from scratch using the methods provided by **UIData**, but using the custom **scroller** shows how a custom component can be easily integrated into a Faces application and is therefore included.

The custom **scroller** demonstration component was extracted from Sun's JSF Implementation demonstration samples and integrated into the Virtual Trainer application as a single custom component. The actual code of the custom component is beyond the scope of this chapter; however, custom JSF component development is covered extensively in Chapter 10.

Method	Return Type	Purpose
getRowCount()	int	Return the total number of rows in the underlying data model or −1 if unknown.
getRows()	int	Return the number of rows to be displayed on the page, or zero for all remaining rows in the table.
getRowIndex()	int	Return the zero-relative index of the currently selected row.
getFirst()	int	Return the zero-relative row number of the first row to be displayed. (The first row of the set of rows being displayed.)
getRowData()	Object	Return the data object representing the data for the currently selected row index, if any.
setRowIndex(int rowIndex)	void	Set the zero relative index of the current row, or −1 to indicate that no row is currently selected.
setFirst(int first)	void	Set the zero-relative row number of the first row to be displayed.
setRows(int rows)	void	Set the number of rows to be displayed, or zero to display all rows in the table.

TABLE 9-1   Row Management and Navigation Methods of **UIData**

The custom **t:scroller** component can be used by placing it on the page after the **h:dataTable** component, as shown next.

```
<h:dataTable id="eventsTable" …>
  … dataTable content shown earlier
</h:dataTable>
<!-- Custom Scroller Component -->
<t:scroller navFacetOrientation="NORTH" for="eventsTable"
     actionListener="#{Main_Backing.processScrollEvent}">
  <f:facet name="next">
    <h:panelGroup>
      <h:graphicImage url="/images/arrow-right.gif" />
      <h:outputText value="Next"/>
    </h:panelGroup>
  </f:facet>
  <f:facet name="previous">
    <h:panelGroup>
      <h:outputText value="Previous"/>
      <h:graphicImage url="/images/arrow-left.gif" />
    </h:panelGroup>
  </f:facet>
</t:scroller>
```

Following standard J2EE Web development procedures, the **scroller** component (tag library) must have a taglib directive and assigned prefix:

```
<%@ taglib uri="http://virtualsportstrainer.com/trainercomponents" prefix="t"%>
```

In the preceding **t:scroller** tag usage code, notice that its **actionListener** attribute is set to #{**Main_Backing.processScrollEvent**}. This corresponds to the backing bean method **processScrollEvent()**, which is responsible for handling the event when a user clicks the **scroller** component. The **processScrollEvent()** method relies on two delegate methods to enable scrolling. These are **scroll()** and **processScrollEvent()**.

```
public void processScrollEvent(ActionEvent event) {
  int currentRow = 1;

  UIComponent component = event.getComponent();
  Integer curRow = (Integer) component.getAttributes().get("currentRow");
  if (curRow != null) {
    currentRow = curRow.intValue();
  }
  // scroll to the appropriate page in the ResultSet.
  scroll(currentRow);
}
```

The preceding method responds to the Action Event that is fired when a user clicks the custom **scroller** component in the page. It then calls a **scroll()** method that uses **UIData** methods to scroll to a specific row. (Recall that a **UIData** instance was declared as the variable **data**.)

```
public void scroll(int row) {
```

```
int rows = data.getRows();
if (rows < 1) {
  return; // Showing entire table already
}
if (row < 0) {
  data.setFirst(0);
} else if (row >= data.getRowCount()) {
  data.setFirst(data.getRowCount() - 1);
} else {
  data.setFirst(row - (row % rows));
}
}
```

Also recall that the methods of **UIData** are referenced earlier in Table 9-1. For further information on the **scroller** component (**ScrollerComponent**) used in Virtual Trainer, please consult Sun's Reference Implementation's component samples.

Selecting and Editing a Single Row from a dataTable

After displaying tabular data in a page, the next most common task when working with a table is to provide a way to select an individual row of data and perform data operations on that row. This is sometimes referred to as a *drill down*. Figure 9-15 displays a **dataTable** with its clickable **Select** column.

In short, selecting a single row of data in a **dataTable** requires the following:

- The **dataTable** must be bound to a **UIData** instance in a backing bean.

- The **dataTable** must contain a column that has a child component that implements **ActionSource** such as a **commandLink**.

```
<h:column>
  <h:commandLink action="#{Main_Backing.editTrainingEventAction}">
    <h:outputText value="Select" />
  </h:commandLink>
</h:column>
```

In the action method (**editTrainingEventAction**) of the **commandLink** component, the code uses the **UIData** method **getRowData()** of the bound backing bean property, **data**, to retrieve a single row.

```
public String editTrainingEventAction() {
  TrainingEvent selectedTrainingEvent =
    (TrainingEvent) this.getData().getRowData();
```

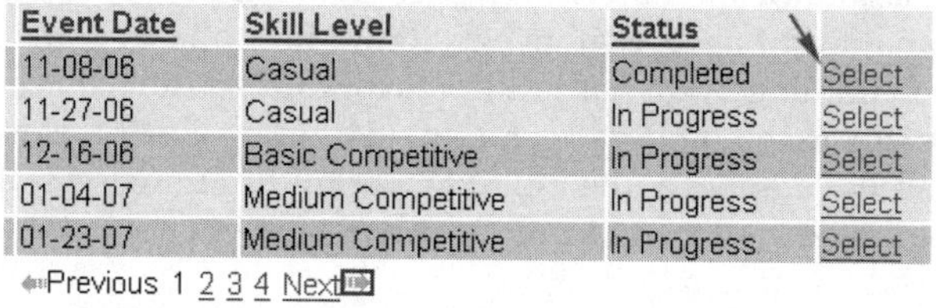

Event Date	Skill Level	Status	
11-08-06	Casual	Completed	Select
11-27-06	Casual	In Progress	Select
12-16-06	Basic Competitive	In Progress	Select
01-04-07	Medium Competitive	In Progress	Select
01-23-07	Medium Competitive	In Progress	Select

Previous 1 2 3 4 Next

FIGURE 9-15   The events **dataTable** with a **Select** column leading to an edit form

As you can see, the method **getRowData()** retrieves the current row that was clicked as an **object**, which can then be typecast with the correct data type. In this case, a single row is of type **TrainingEvent**.

Selecting a Row for Editing

At this point, the application can operate on the current row programmatically; however, once a row is selected, it is common to allow the user to edit the selected data. This can be done by saving the selected row object onto the application's **sessionMap**, which is accessible via **FacesContext.getExternalContext().getSessionMap()**. Once stored, the application can navigate to other pages and access/edit the stored row object.

```
public String editTrainingEventAction(){
  TrainingEvent selectedTrainingEvent =
    (TrainingEvent) this.getData().getRowData();

  FacesContext ctx = FacesContext.getCurrentInstance();

  //Store selected TrainingEvent Row accessible later as #{EditTrainingEvent}
  ctx.getExternalContext().getSessionMap().put("EditTrainingEvent",
   selectedTrainingEvent);

  // go to edit page..
  return "editTE";
}
```

Incidentally there are code examples on the Web which employ a slightly different technique for storing row objects for later editing using **createValueBinding()**:

```
  ValueBinding binding = ctx.getApplication().
     createValueBinding("#{EditTrainingEvent}");
  binding.setValue(ctx, selectedTrainingEvent);
```

This code, along with a corresponding registration of "EditTrainingEvent" in the **faces-config.xml** as a **session**-scoped managed bean, will usually work in JSF 1.1, but will have problems with 1.2. In general, it is best to simply use the **requestMap** or **sessionMap** to temporarily store row objects.

Drilling Down to an Edit Form

After selecting a single row and having it saved it onto the **sessionMap** as "EditTrainingEvent", the application can then navigate to a page that contains an edit form that allows the properties of the row object to be updated. Recall from Chapter 4 that the **sessionMap** (referenced as **sessionScope**) is a supported implicit object in EL, so the selected row can be accessed using #{**sessionScope.EditTrainingEvent**} or simply #{**EditTrainingEvent**}.

In Virtual Trainer, the edit page, **edit_te.jsp**, allows for updates of the selected row's properties. Since each training event has multiple workout sessions, the edit page is actually a master-detail page where the properties of a single training event are displayed in an edit form along with a tabular display of the multiple workout training sessions.

Starting with the single *master* edit form, the training event item is shown in Figure 9-16. The code for the edit form is as follows:

```
<h:outputText value="Event Information" styleClass="PageTitle"/>
<h:messages/>

<h:panelGrid columns="4" width="80%" styleClass="form-bkg"
```

```
             rowClasses="list-row">
<h:outputLabel value="Event Title" styleClass="GUITag" for="ename"/>
<h:inputText id="ename"  value="#{EditTrainingEvent.ename}"/>
<h:outputLabel value="Event Type" styleClass="GUITag" for="etype"/>
<h:inputText id="etype" value="#{EditTrainingEvent.etype}"/>
<h:outputLabel value="Event Date" styleClass="GUITag" for="date"/>
<h:inputText id="date" value="#{EditTrainingEvent.completionDate}">
  <f:convertDateTime pattern="MM-dd-yy"/>
</h:inputText>
<h:outputLabel value="Skill" styleClass="GUITag" for="skill"/>
<h:inputText id="skill" value="#{EditTrainingEvent.skill}"/>
<h:outputLabel value="Current Status" styleClass="GUITag" for="status"/>
<h:selectOneMenu id="status" value="#{EditTrainingEvent.status}">
  <f:selectItem itemLabel="Not Started"
    itemValue="Not Started"/>
  <f:selectItem itemLabel="In Progress"
    itemValue="In Progress"/>
  <f:selectItem itemLabel="Completed" itemValue="Completed"/>
  <f:selectItem itemLabel="Ongoing" itemValue="Ongoing"/>
</h:selectOneMenu>
<h:outputLabel value="Online Trainer Adviser"
    styleClass="GUITag" for="trainer"/>
<h:inputText id="trainer" value="#{EditTrainingEvent.trainer}"/>
</h:panelGrid>

<h:panelGrid columns="3" width="25%" cellpadding="12">
  <h:commandButton value="Update Event"
      action="#{EditTe_Backing.saveTEAction}"/>
  <h:commandButton value="Delete Event"
      action="delete"/>
  <h:commandButton value="Return"
      action="main"/>
</h:panelGrid>
```

The edit portion is straightforward and simply provides information about the selected training event employing **outputText** components with the exception of the event status where a **selectMenu** can be used to update the overall status of the event. Notice that all the fields are value-bound to the **EditTrainingEvent** (row) object that was saved in the

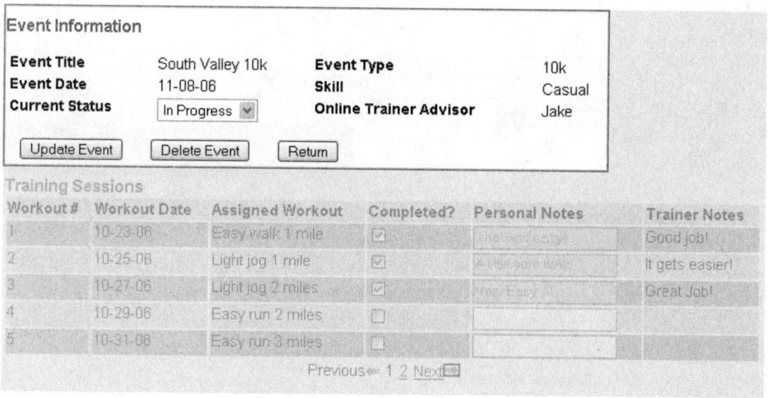

FIGURE 9-16   The training event edit form

editTrainingEventAction() action method. Before discussing the **saveTEAction()** method code, we'll continue on with the detail portion of the page.

In the lower portion of the edit page, shown in Figure 9-17, is the tabular (detail) portion that displays the workout sessions of the training event and also serves as the detail portion of the page.

The following is the source code for the workout sessions portion of the page.

```
<h:outputText value="Training Sessions" styleClass="PageTitle"/>
<h:dataTable id="sessionsTable"
    value="#{EditTrainingEvent.workoutsessions}"
    var="se" rows="5" binding="#{EditTe_Backing.data}"
    rowClasses="list-row-odd,list-row-even"
    headerClass="table-header"width="100%" >
  <h:column>
    <f:facet name="header">
      <h:outputText value="Workout #"/>
    </f:facet>
    <h:outputText value="#{se.id}"/>
  </h:column>
  <h:column>
    <f:facet name="header">
      <h:outputText value="Workout Date"/>
    </f:facet>
    <h:outputText value="#{se.workoutDate}">
      <f:convertDateTime pattern="MM-dd-yy"/>
    </h:outputText>
  </h:column>
  <h:column>
    <f:facet name="header">
      <h:outputText value="Assigned Workout"/>
    </f:facet>
    <h:outputText value="#{se.workoutDescription}"/>
  </h:column>
  <h:column>
    <f:facet name="header">
      <h:outputText value="Completed?"/>
    </f:facet>
    <h:selectBooleanCheckbox value="#{se.completed}" />
  </h:column>
  <h:column>
    <f:facet name="header">
      <h:outputText value="Personal Notes"/>
    </f:facet>
    <h:inputText  value="#{se.personalNotes}" disabled="#{se.completed}"/>
  </h:column>
  <h:column>
    <f:facet name="header">
      <h:outputText value="Trainer Notes"/>
    </f:facet>
    <h:inputText  rendered="#{UserBean.trainer}"
      value="#{se.trainerNotes}"/>
    <h:outputText rendered="#{!UserBean.trainer}"
      value="#{se.trainerNotes}"/>
  </h:column>
</h:dataTable>
```

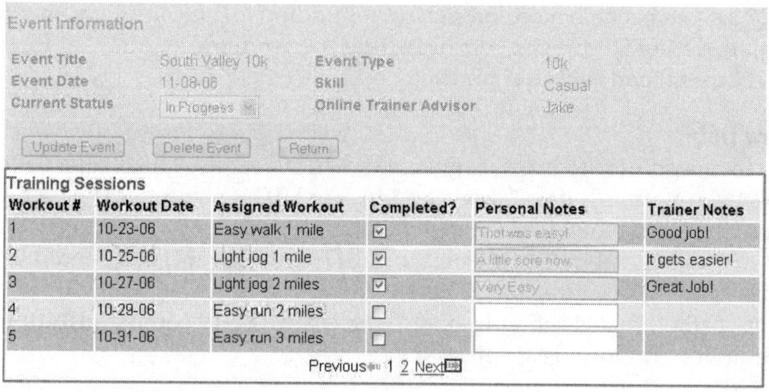

FIGURE 9-17   The detail portion of the page showing individual workout sessions

First off, notice that **dataTable** is value-bound to **EditTrainingEvent.workoutsessions** of type **List**, which is a property of the saved **EditTrainingEvent** row object, as shown next:

```
value="#{EditTrainingEvent.workoutsessions }"
```

Directly beneath the **dataTable** lies another usage of the custom **scroller** component. It's used in exactly the same manner as before on the main page so its code is not shown. You may notice that the **dataTable** also has its **binding** attribute set to #{**EditTe_Backing.data**}, which is also an instance of a **UIData** object in the backing bean. Similar to the main page, the **UIData** instance along with the backing bean scroll methods is necessary for the **scroller** component to function.

Conditionally Rendering UI Components

A subtle yet nice feature of how the table of the workout sessions renders is that when a particular workout session has been completed (that is, the checkbox is checked) the Personal Notes input field changes its rendering from editable to disabled. This is easily achieved by setting the **disabled** attribute to the **boolean** value of the **se.completed** field, as shown next:

```
<h:inputText  value="#{se.personalNotes}" disabled="#{se.completed}"/>
```

The other important conditional-rendering example to notice is the last column, where either an **outputText** or **inputText** is rendered based on whether or not the current user is a trainer. The **rendered** attribute of the component is set to the EL expression of the **boolean** property **trainer**, as in the following:

```
<h:inputText  rendered="#{UserBean.trainer}" value="#{se.trainerNotes}"/>
```

If **UserBean.trainer** is **true**, then the input field is rendered. If **false**, then a corresponding output field is rendered:

```
<h:outputText rendered="#{!UserBean.trainer}" value="#{se.trainerNotes}"/>
```

As you can probably guess, changing the trainer's comment field to editable could also be done by simply using one **inputText** field with its **disabled** attribute set to the **boolean** value determined by whether the user is a trainer. However, for this example, separate UI components are used to show usage of the **rendered** attribute.

In general, as you become more proficient in building JSF applications, you'll find that conditionally rendering UI components by setting the **rendered** attribute to EL expressions is an extremely useful and common practice.

Updating Row Data

So far, we've reviewed how to browse multiple rows of data as well as select, retrieve, and display a specific row from a **dataTable**'s underlying **UIData** object. It is now time to review how to update the edited row data. This is actually very easy. All that is needed is an action method that can take the updated row object (**EditTrainingEvent**) and send it to the update method of the Training Event registry object.

The action method that is action-bound to the *Update Event* **commandButton** that was shown earlier in the edit form is as follows:

```
public String saveTEAction() {
  FacesContext ctx = FacesContext.getCurrentInstance();
  Application app = ctx.getApplication();

  //Get edited TrainingEvent and store locally as "te"
  TrainingEvent te = (TrainingEvent)JSFUtil.
                     getManagedObject("EditTrainingEvent");

  // Get TrainingEventRegistry  - store in "eventRegistry"
  TrainingEventRegistry eventRegistry = (TrainingEventRegistry)
              JSFUtil.getManagedObject("TrainingEventRegistry");

  // Call TE registry method to update registry with edited training event.
  eventRegistry.updateTrainingEvent(te);
  return null;
}
```

The implementation of the code for the **updateTrainingEvent()** method is specific to the persistence technology employed. For an all-Java approach (used in the initial prototype version), the code looks like the following:

```
public void updateTrainingEvent(TrainingEvent updatedTe) {
  int targetEvent = updatedTe.getId();

  if (targetEvent == 0) {
    // This is a new event, so call addTrainingEvent
    addTrainingEvent(updatedTe);
  }
  else {
    for (int i = 0 ;i < eventlist.size() ;i++ ) {
      TrainingEvent te = (TrainingEvent)eventlist.get(i);
      if (te.getId() == updatedTe.getId())
      {
        eventlist.set(i,updatedTe);
        return;
      }
    }
  }
}
```

Essentially, this method extracts the **id** of the updated **TrainingEvent** and first checks to see if it is a new event. If it is, it will call **addtrainingEvent( )** which is also a **TrainingEventRegistry** method. However, if the updated **TrainingEvent** already exists in the registry, then the **eventlist**'s setter is called to update it with the new version. Again the actual implementation of this method, along with **addTrainingEvent( )**, will vary based on the persistence technology. The full code of these registry methods for the Java-only version, as well as persistence-based variations, are available for download. As mentioned earlier, a Hibernate-based example of the **TrainingEventRegistry** is shown later in the chapter.

A Final Observation about dataTables

A final important thing to notice about this edit page example is that building a **dataTable** (or any kind of tabular form) with editable fields is simply a matter of embedding input fields instead of output fields in the **dataTable**. Since the JSF request processing lifecycle processes all of the incoming form parameters automatically, building tables with multiple editable fields is extremely easy since no extra server-side coding is necessary. This is in contrast to other more traditional Web development technologies where each input field that's created on a page requires specific custom code on the server to process the incoming value. Therefore, creating a table with editable fields would obviously take substantially more effort to build.

Deleting a Training Event

Implementing the functionality to delete a **TrainingEvent** object in the **TrainingEventRegistry** is also quite easy. First, recall the button panel in the edit page (**edit_te.jsp**), shown next:

```
<h:panelGrid columns="3" width="25%" cellpadding="12">
  <h:commandButton value="Update Event"
      action="#{EditTe_Backing.saveTEAction}"/>
  <h:commandButton value="Delete Event"
      action="delete"/>
  <h:commandButton value="Return"
      action="main"/>
</h:panelGrid>
```

You see that a **commandButton** is used to initiate an action event **"delete"**. A corresponding navigation case in **faces-config.xml** allows navigation to the delete event page (**delete_te.jsp**). The delete page provides the user with a chance to cancel out of the delete operation. It asks the user if they really want to delete a training event and renders the training event's name, type, and date. The page also contains Delete and Cancel buttons. The relevant code of the delete page is shown next:

```
<h:outputText value="Do you wish to delete this Training Event?"
    styleClass="PageTitle"/>
<h:messages/>

<h:panelGrid  columns="2" styleClass="form-bkg"
        rowClasses="list-row" width="80%">
  <h:outputLabel value="Event Title" styleClass="GUITag" for="ename"/>
  <h:outputText id="ename" value="#{EditTrainingEvent.ename}"/>
  <h:outputLabel value="Event Type" styleClass="GUITag" for="etype"/>
  <h:outputText id="etype" value="#{EditTrainingEvent.etype}"/>
```

```
<h:outputLabel value="Event Date" styleClass="GUITag" for="date"/>
<h:outputText id="date" value="#{EditTrainingEvent.completionDate}">
  <f:convertDateTime pattern="MM-dd-yy"/>
</h:outputText>
</h:panelGrid>

<h:panelGrid columns="2" width="35%" cellpadding="12">
  <h:commandButton value="Delete Event"
     action="#{DeleteTe_Backing.deleteTEAction}"/>
  <h:commandButton value="Cancel"
     action="main" immediate="true"/>
</h:panelGrid>
```

If the user decides to cancel the delete operation, clicking the Cancel **commandButton** sends the user back to the main page (**main.jsp**) via a global navigation rule with **"main"** as the outcome. Again, setting **immediate** to **true** avoids the non-essential request processing phases. If the user wishes to delete the training event, the bound **deleteTEAction()** method is invoked.

The **deleteTEAction()** method code, shown next, is very similar to the previously listed **saveTEAction ()** code except that the **TrainingEventRegistry**'s **deleteTrainingEvent()** method is called at the end instead of **updateTrainingEvent()**.

```
public String deleteTEAction() {
  FacesContext ctx = FacesContext.getCurrentInstance();
  Application app = ctx.getApplication();

  //Get TrainingEvent to be deleted and store locally as "te"
  TrainingEvent te = (TrainingEvent)JSFUtil.
                    getManagedObject("EditTrainingEvent");


  // Get TrainingEventRegistry  - store as "eventRegistry"
  TrainingEventRegistry eventRegistry = (TrainingEventRegistry)
                JSFUtil.getManagedObject("TrainingEventRegistry");

  // Call TE registry method to delete the selected training event.
  eventRegistry.deleteTrainingEvent(te);
  return "main";
}
```

Notice also that the returned **String** value is **"main"**, which corresponds to the global **"main"** navigation rule. This sends the user back to the main page (**main.jsp**) after successful completion of the delete operation.

Creating New Training Events

Now that you've seen how to select, edit, and delete rows of tabular data, it is time to review how to create new row objects. To do this, we return to the **main.jsp** page where the Create New Training Event button resides, and examine the code that executes after clicking it.

In short, creating a new training event is simply a matter of navigating to a page (**create_te.jsp**) and submitting a form that has entries of the new Training Event values. This invokes an action method that instantiates a new **TrainingEvent** object, sets its properties to the properties from the form, and then passes the object as an argument to the **addTrainingEvent()** method of the **TrainingEventRegistry**. The form contained in the **create_te.jsp** page is generally similar to the other forms in the application. However, it does highlight a topic not yet shown in the example application: dynamic select menus.

Implementing Dynamic Select Menus

Dynamic select menus derive their values dynamically at runtime. This differs from static menus, which have hard-coded values. All of the select menus shown so far in the application have had hard-coded values, such as when selecting the gender, the event type, and so on. However, there are many times when you need to retrieve a set of values (dynamically) for a select menu that is only available at runtime. In this example, we will step through how to create a Faces select menu based on dynamic data.

The following is the code for the form in the **create_te.jsp** page that is navigated to when the Create New Training Event button on the main page (**main.jsp**) is clicked. A closer view of this form is shown in Figure 9-18.

In the form, you'll notice that among several static select menus there is also a dynamic select menu (with an **id** of "trainer") that is used to display a list of trainers that is derived at runtime.

```
<h:outputText value="Create Training Event Plan" styleClass="PageTitle"/>
<h:messages globalOnly="true" infoClass="RegError"/>
<h:panelGrid width="70%" columns="3" border="0">
<h:outputLabel value="Event Name:" for="ename"/>
<h:inputText id="ename" required="true"
    binding="#{CreateTe_Backing.ename}"/><h:message for="ename"/>
<h:outputLabel value="Event Type:" for="etype"/>
<h:selectOneMenu  id="etype" binding="#{CreateTe_Backing.etype}" >
  <f:selectItem itemLabel="5k" itemValue="5k"/>
  <f:selectItem itemLabel="10k" itemValue="10k"/>
  <f:selectItem itemLabel="1/2 Marathon"
      itemValue="half_marathon"/>
  <f:selectItem itemLabel="Full Marathon"
      itemValue="full_marathon"/>
  <f:selectItem itemLabel="Triathlon" itemValue="triathlon"/>
  <f:selectItem itemLabel="Weekly" itemValue="weekly"/>
</h:selectOneMenu>
<f:verbatim> </f:verbatim>
<h:outputLabel value="Event Date:(mm-dd-yy)" for="doe"/>
<h:inputText  id="doe" binding="#{CreateTe_Backing.doe}"
    required="true">
  <f:convertDateTime pattern="MM-dd-yy"/>
  <f:validator validatorId="futureDateValidate"/>
</h:inputText><h:message for="doe"/>
<h:outputLabel value="Skill Level:" for="skill"/>
<h:selectOneMenu id="skill" binding="#{CreateTe_Backing.skill}" >
  <f:selectItem itemLabel="Casual" itemValue="casual"/>
  <f:selectItem itemLabel="Basic Competitive"
    itemValue="basic"/>
  <f:selectItem itemLabel="Medium Competitive" itemValue="medium"/>
  <f:selectItem itemLabel="Advanced Competitive - Olympic"
    itemValue="advanced"/>
```

```
</h:selectOneMenu>
<f:verbatim> </f:verbatim>
<h:outputLabel value="Trainer:" id="trainer"/>
<h:selectOneMenu  id="trainer" binding="#{CreateTe_Backing.trainer}">
  <f:selectItems value="#{CreateTe_Backing.trainerList}"/>
</h:selectOneMenu>
<f:verbatim> </f:verbatim>
<h:commandButton value="Create Event"
    action="#{CreateTe_Backing.CreateTEAction}"/>
<h:commandButton value="Cancel" action="cancel" immediate="true" />
</h:panelGrid>
```

Aside from the dynamic select menu, the rest of the form is fairly trivial. The date field uses a similar date validator as was used in the register form. This validator, however, ensures that the date entered for the event is in the future. You'll also notice that each input component is bound to a similar declared UI component in the backing bean, **CreateTe_ Backing**. The **CreateTEAction** action method uses the form values to construct a new instance of a **TrainingEvent** and add it to the **TrainingEventRegistry**. However, before further discussing how the new training event is created, it is important to review exactly how the dynamic **trainer** select menu is implemented.

The dynamic **trainer** menu reshown here

```
<h:selectOneMenu  id="trainer" binding="#{CreateTe_Backing.trainer}">
  <f:selectItems value="#{CreateTe_Backing.trainerList}"/>
</h:selectOneMenu>
```

derives its list of trainers dynamically by having its child component, **f:selectItems**, value-bound to #{**CreateTe_Backing.trainerList**}, which calls the **getTrainerList()** method in the **CreateTe_Backing** bean. This method retrieves an instance of the **UserRegistry** from the managed bean facility and calls its method **findTrainerUsers()** to retrieve a subset **List** of registered users which have their **boolean trainer** property set to **true**. The **getTrainerList()** method uses this returned **List** to construct a **List** of **SelectItem** objects containing the **Firstname**. This list is then returned to the **f:selectItems** on the page. You'll notice also that the **Firstname** value is provided in the **SelectItem()** constructor as both the value (first argument) and the displayed value (second argument) of the select menu.

Create Training Event Plan

Event Name:	San Jose Triathlon
Event Type:	Triathlon
Event Date: (mm-dd-yy)	10-08-06
Skill Level:	Medium Competitive
Trainer:	Jake

Create Event   Cancel

FIGURE 9-18 The create training event form

The following is the full code for the **getTrainerList()** method.

```
public List getTrainerList(){

  UserRegistry userRegistry = (UserRegistry)
      JSFUtil.getManagedObject("UserRegistry");

  List trainers  = userRegistry.findTrainerUsers();
  List selectTrainers = new ArrayList();

  for (int i = 0; i < trainers.size(); i++) {
    UserBean user = (UserBean) trainers.get(i);
    selectTrainers.add(new SelectItem(user.getFirstname(),
        user.getFirstname()));
  }
  return selectTrainers;
}
```

Figure 9-19 shows the rendered output of the dynamically derived trainer advisor select menu.

The code for the **UserRegistry** method **findTrainerUsers()** is not shown here for brevity and because its implementation would again vary based on the persistence technology employed, but it would simply have to return a **List** of all registered users who are of type **trainer**.

The important thing from the JSF user interface's perspective is that the method returns a list of users who are trainers. Again, details on how to implement a persistence-based data layer are provided at the end of the chapter.

Processing the Form Values and Creating a New Training Event

Now, let's turn back to the creation of the new training event. Recall that to create a new training event involves an action method that constructs a new **TrainingEvent** instance using the values of the input fields from the form on the page. The **CreateTEaction** action method, which is invoked via this button

```
<h:commandButton value="Create Event"
    action="#{CreateTe_Backing.CreateTEAction}"/>
```

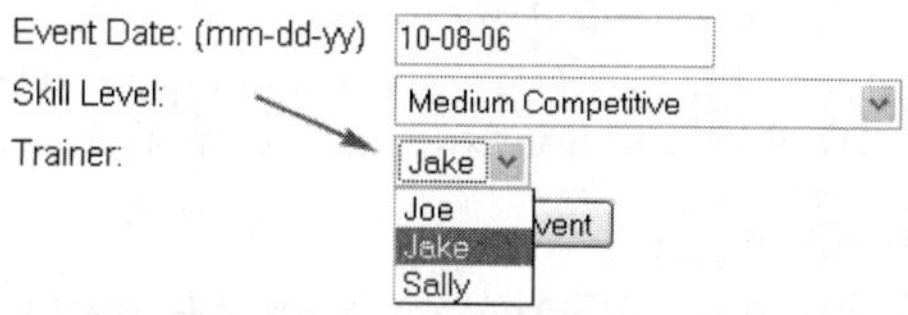

FIGURE 9-19   The dynamic select menu for listing trainer advisors

is trivial and is shown next:

```
public String CreateTEAction(){
  // Create new Training Event
  TrainingEvent newTe = new TrainingEvent();
   newTe.setEname(ename.getValue().toString());
   newTe.setEtype(etype.getValue().toString());
   newTe.setCompletionDate((Date)doe.getValue());
   newTe.setSkill(skill.getValue().toString());
   newTe.setTrainer(trainer.getValue().toString());
   newTe.setStatus("Not Started");

  //Generate a set of training sessions based on the event date and type
  Calendar calendar = new GregorianCalendar();
  calendar.setTime((Date)doe.getValue());

  TrainingEventRegistry eventRegistry = (TrainingEventRegistry)
              JSFUtil.getManagedObject("TrainingEventRegistry");

  List workoutList = eventRegistry.generateTrainingSessionList(calendar,
                                            newTe.getEtype());

  newTe.setWorkoutsessions(workoutList);

  // Get userid info from managed bean
  UserBean currentUser = (UserBean) JSFUtil.getManagedObject("UserBean");
  // and assign to the new training event
  newTe.setUserId(currentUser.getUserid());


  // Add new training event to registry
  eventRegistry.addTrainingEvent(newTe);

  return "success";
}
```

You may notice the event registry method **generateTrainingSessionList()**, which is used to generate a set of workout sessions based on the date of the event and the event type. This is where the Virtual Trainer application could be extended additionally to provide a custom set of workout sessions based on the age, gender, and any other relevant personal information in the user's profile. This method could be implemented purely on the Web-tier or it could interact with a persistence layer. However, for this demonstration, a limited set of different workout sessions will be created based on the event date and event type and code for this method will also remain entirely on the Web-tier and not require interaction with a persistence layer.

Adding the New TrainingEvent Object

Finally, we come to the **TrainingEventRegistry** method **addTrainingEvent()**, which receives a new **TrainingEvent** object filled with data. As before, the implementation of this method also varies based on the persistence technology. However, in the Java-only version, the code to add a new **TrainingEvent** is as follows:

```
// Non persisted Pure Java Demo only
public String addTrainingEvent(TrainingEvent newTE) {
  // Calculate new id when adding event
```

```
// Persistence technologies would handle this automatically
int maxid = 0;

// Determine maximum id in event list
for (int i = 0; i < eventlist.size(); i++) {
  TrainingEvent trainingEvent = (TrainingEvent) eventlist.get(i);
  int currid = trainingEvent.getId();
  maxid = (currid > maxid)?currid:maxid;
}

newTE.setId(maxid + 1);

this.eventlist.add((TrainingEvent) newTE);
return "success";
}
```

Again, this implementation is for the pure Java-only demonstration version. A Hibernate-based persistence implementation of the **TrainingEventRegistry** along with its data management methods, including **addTrainingEvent()**, is shown later in the chapter in the section "Taking the Next Step—Persisting Virtual Trainer Data."

Implementing Sortable Columns

The topic of sortable columns is actually somewhat of an advanced topic when having to implement them on your own. Fortunately, most of the popular third-party component libraries, including MyFaces, Oracle's ADF Faces, and Sun's default component library, now provide out-of-the-box sortable column functionality in their respective table components.

However, this next section discusses how to implement sortable columns from scratch with a standard **dataTable** as a learning exercise and is provided with the Virtual Trainer application. This is shown in Figure 9-20.

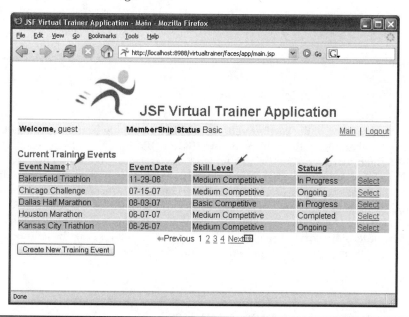

Figure 9-20   Sortable columns in Virtual Trainer

Implementing sortable columns with a **dataTable** can be done primarily in two ways. The first way is to allow the source of the data (such as a database) to sort the data in the data-tier (where the database resides) before sending it to the Faces UI components in the Web-tier or middle-tier. The second way is to implement a sorting functionality where sorting occurs entirely on the middle-tier. There are different reasons for implementing one approach or the other based on several factors. Both are detailed here, however.

Implementing Data-Tier Sorting in Faces

Implementing a sorting capability using the data-tier is relatively easy providing the data-tier server has built-in functionality to sort data, which is usually the case with a relational database. The next thing needed is a set of data access methods which can trigger different queries with the different sorting settings or "order by" clauses. In this sense, the user interface can remain simply a data presentation layer and not have to deal with advanced data manipulation.

Using the data-tier method of sorting simply requires that the user interface provide a way for the user to click table column links (or other UI artifacts) to execute action listener methods which, in turn, call data access methods that, in turn, call data-tier queries with the corresponding sort policy or "order by" clause. Since relational databases usually come with built-in sorting capabilities, the work required to implement this approach lies mainly in just capturing a user's mouse click and determining which column to sort by and what direction. Once these are determined, an appropriate mid-tier method such as **getListSortedByEvents ()** is called to execute the proper data-tier query.

The easiest way to assemble the UI to support column sorting is to place a **commandLink** in a column header and have its **actionListener** attribute bound to an intermediary action listener method that establishes which column to sort by, as well as in what direction. The following UI code can facilitate this.

```
<h:column>
  <f:facet name="header">
    <h:commandLink actionListener="#{Main_Backing.sortByEvent}"
              immediate="true">
      <h:outputText value="Event Name"/>
    </h:commandLink>
  </f:facet>
  <h:outputText value="#{row.ename}"/>
</h:column>
```

The implementation of the **sortByEvent** method in the backing bean can set a global **sortBy** integer variable that designates which column (**SORT_BY_EVENT**) has been selected to be sorted. A **boolean sortEventAsc** variable which keeps track of which direction to sort is also toggled. It is important to note that in order for these values to persist through multiple requests, the parent backing bean (**Main_Backing**) must have its **scope** set to **session**.

The following backing bean code is able to keep track of the sorting options for two columns, **Event** and **Date**. For every new column where sorting is to be implemented, a new **boolean** sort order flag (**sort****Asc**) as well as a static **int** referencing the column (**SORT_BY_****) would be needed in this implementation.

```
public Class Main {
...
// Static SORT_BY_*** constants
private static final int SORT_BY_EVENT = 0;
```

```
private static final int SORT_BY_DATE = 1;
// further SORT_BY constants if needed
...

// global sortBy value - initialized to -1
// At runtime, is set to static SORT_BY_*** values
// based on which column is clicked
private int sortBy = -1;

// boolean sort direction flags
private boolean sortEventAsc = false;
private boolean sortDateAsc = false;
// further boolean sort direction flags if needed...

  public void sortByEvent(ActionEvent ae){
    sortEventAsc = !sortEventAsc;
    sortBy = SORT_BY_EVENT;
  }

  public void sortByDate(ActionEvent ae){
    sortDateAsc = !sortDateAsc;
    sortBy = SORT_BY_DATE;
  }
// further sortBy methods if needed
```

Up to this point, the code shown merely keeps track of which column to sort and in what direction; however, code is also needed to actually execute the appropriate method to retrieve the sorted data. The entry point for this is the **value** attribute of the **dataTable** component.

```
<h:dataTable id="eventsTable"
        value="#{Main_Backing.sortedTrainingEventsForUser}" .../>
```

As you can see, this **dataTable** is bound to the method expression, **getSortedTrainingEventsForUser()**. This method uses a switch statement to call an appropriate data query method based on the sort variables. Its implementation could be

```
public List getSortedTrainingEventsForUser(){
  List sortedEventList;
  TrainingEventRegistry TERegistry =
  (TrainingEventRegistry)JSFUtil.getManagedObject("TrainingEventRegistry");

  switch (sortBy){
    case SORT_BY_EVENT:
      sortedEventList = TERegistry.getListSortedByEvents(sortEventAsc);
      break;
    case SORT_BY_DATE:
      sortedEventList = TERegistry.getListSortedByDateAsc(sortDateAsc);
      break;
      // and so on ...
      ...
    default :
      break;
  }
  return sortedEventList;
}
```

As you can see, a corresponding registry query method is executed based on the value of the **sortBy** variable. The query method also accepts the **boolean** sort direction flag as an argument. This approach requires that a collection of registry methods exist (**getListSortedByEvents()**, **getListSortedByDate()**, and so on) and the implementation of these would depend on the persistence technology used. Although there could be a fair number of these, their code would be very simple since it would largely be based on the same query but with slightly different order by clauses.

This is all that's necessary to implement data-tier–based sorting in a Faces application! At runtime, as a user clicks the column header, this sets the sort variables, and during the page refresh, the **dataTable** will execute its value-bound method to extract the sorted **List** based on the values of the sort variables. This method uses a switch statement to determine which registry method to call in order to receive the properly sorted data.

In our next discussion, we'll examine how to implement sorting based entirely on the Web or server-tier. As you'll see, this approach is very similar, with the exception that the actual sorting is done within the Faces application code as opposed to a database.

Implementing Web-Tier Sorting in Faces

The other technique for implementing sortable columns on a **dataTable** is to not rely on the persistent technology to do the sorting. Instead, the sorting will be performed on the Web-tier using standard Java sorting features available with the Collections utilities.

The implementation of Web-tier sorting is actually very similar to the data-tier sorting—for example, the UI code is exactly the same:

```
<h:column>
  <f:facet name="header">
    <h:commandLink actionListener="#{Main_Backing.sortByEvent}"
            immediate="true">
      <h:outputText value="Event Name"/>
    </h:commandLink>
  </f:facet>
  <h:outputText value="#{row.ename}"/>
</h:column>
```

The action listener methods **sortByEvent()**, **sortByDate()**, and so on, would be identical in that their job is still the same, which is to manage an identical set of global variables that keep track of the sorting behavior:

```
...
  public void sortByEvent(ActionEvent ae){
    sortEventAsc = !sortEventAsc;
    sortBy = SORT_BY_EVENT;
  }
// and so on ...
```

The difference between Web-tier and data-tier sorting lies in how the data is obtained from the data-tier and afterward how it is sorted when it arrives.

For Web-tier sorting, the **dataTable** just uses a generic method to retrieve nonsorted data.

```
<h:dataTable id="eventsTable"
                  value="#{Main_Backing.trainingEventsForUser}"
```

As you saw before, the implementation for the method **getTrainingEventsForUser()** gets an unsorted **List** of training events based on the **userid** of the user. To implement sorting, this method would call a **sort()** method that sorts the **List** before returning it back to the user.

Again, to review the code for **getTrainingEventsForUser()**

```
public List getTrainingEventsForUser(){
// Get training events for this user, or all if user is a trainer

// Initialization code omitted for brevity

// If user is a trainer, return all Training Events,
// else only return events for user.

if (managedUserBean.isTrainer())
  userEventList = eventRegistry.getAllEvents();
else {
// is not a trainer so call getEventlistForUser
userEventList =  eventRegistry.getEventlistForUser(userid);
}
// New! Sort event list
sortEvents(userEventList);

return userEventList;
}
```

As you can see, at the end of the method, just before returning the **List** of events to the user, it is sorted using a **sortEvents()** method. The implementation of this method is somewhat similar to before in that it has a switch statement that determines which column to sort by. It differs from there. Instead of calling a data-tier method to get the sorted data, it calls some local methods to sort the data using **Comparators**. Notice that a conditional expression is used to evaluate whether an ascending or descending **Comparator** based on the **boolean** sort order flag (**sortEventAsc**, **sortDateAsc**, and so on) is sent to the **Collections.sort()** method.

```
private void sortEvents(List TrainingEvents){

  switch (sortBy){
    case SORT_BY_EVENT:
      Collections.sort(TrainingEvents, sortEventAsc ?
          SortTrainingEventAscComparator :
          SortTrainingEventDescComparator);
      break;

    case SORT_BY_DATE:
      Collections.sort(TrainingEvents, sortDateAsc ?
          SortDateAscComparator :
          SortDateDescComparator);
      break;

//     and so on for each column …
```

```
        default :
        break;
      }
   }
```

The topic of **Comparator**s is slightly beyond the scope of this book, but it is easy to see how they operate. The following is the code for the **SortTrainingEventAscComparator**.

```
private static final Comparator SortTrainingEventAscComparator =
    new Comparator(){
      public int compare(Object o1, Object o2){
          String s1 = ((TrainingEvent)o1).getEname();
          String s2 = ((TrainingEvent)o2).getEname();
          return s1.compareTo(s2);
      }
};
```

And next is the code for the **SortDateDescComparator**:

```
private static final Comparator SortDateDescComparator =
    new Comparator(){
        public int compare(Object o1, Object o2){
            Date d1 = ((TrainingEvent)o1).getCompletionDate();
            Date d2 = ((TrainingEvent)o2).getCompletionDate();
            return d2.compareTo(d1);
        }
};
```

For this implementation, two **Comparator**s would be needed per each column that needed sorting support (for ascending and descending).

The **Comparator** simply provides a way to compare different objects. This is then provided to the **Collections.sort** method. The end result is a sorted **Collection**, or in this case a **List** object.

Now that we've examined the code to sort data displayed in a **dataTable**, the following is a simple technique for providing the user with a visual cue regarding which column is being sorted, and in which direction.

Displaying the Sort Behaviors in the Column Header

Indicating which column is being sorted and what direction it is, provides the user with a useful visual clue. This is actually very easy to implement since the data is already available in the backing bean. We merely need to display an appropriate image (or character) that is based on the values of the **session**-scoped sort variables.

We thus return to the event name column portion of the **dataTable**—however, now you'll see an enhancement.

```
<h:column>
  <f:facet name="header">
    <h:panelGroup>
      <h:commandLink actionListener="#{Main_Backing.sortByEvent}"
                immediate="true">
        <h:outputText value="Event Name"/>
      </h:commandLink>
      <h:graphicImage url="#{Main_Backing.sortEventAsc ?
          '/images/arrow-up.gif' : '/images/arrow-down.gif'}"
          rendered="#{Main_Backing.showSortEventIcon}"
          height="13"   width="9" />
    </h:panelGroup>
  </f:facet>
  <h:outputText value="#{row.ename}"/>
</h:column>
```

The obvious enhancement is to add an image component and conditionally set both its **rendered** attribute based on whether this column was selected for sorting, as well as setting its **url** attribute to a conditional expression which derives the correct image based on the value **boolean** sort flag—in this example, **sortEventAsc**.

The **rendered** attribute actually derives its value from a **boolean** getter method **isShowSortEventIcon()** on the backing bean, which is coded as:

```
public boolean isShowSortEventIcon() {
  showSortEventIcon = (sortBy == SORT_BY_EVENT);
  return (showSortEventIcon) ;
}
```

This method returns true if the backing bean **sortBy** variable is equal to the **SORT_BY_ EVENT** static value, or in other words, if the *Event Name* column was selected for sorting. Figure 9-21 displays the Training Events table with the Event Name column selected for sorting.

Subsequently, when the column header is clicked again, the directional arrow changes. This is depicted in Figure 9-22.

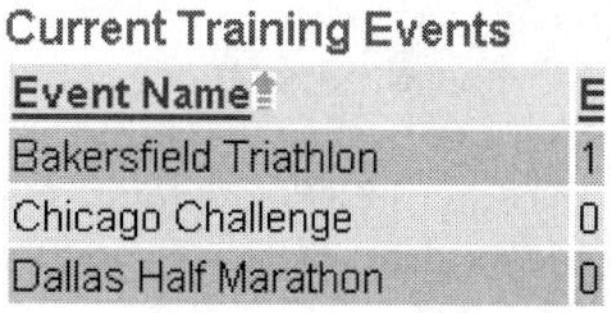

Current Training Events

Event Name	E
Bakersfield Triathlon	1
Chicago Challenge	0
Dallas Half Marathon	0

FIGURE 9-21   Sorting by event names

Current Training Events

Event Name⬇
South Valley 10k
Seattle Coffee Run
Seattle 10k

FIGURE 9-22   Sorting by event names in reverse

Taking the Next Step—Persisting Virtual Trainer Data

So far, Virtual Trainer has been working purely as a pure Java prototype with application data stored in Java objects that are created on the fly as the application is running. However, this was only done during the prototyping phase, leaving the final task of plugging in a persistence technology that can actually store application data. Fortunately, this can be done in a seamless fashion without having to change any user interface code! Thus, we begin our discussion of how to tie in a persistence technology with a JavaServer Faces application.

You may think that adding a new layer of persistence would involve massive recoding of the user interface, but instead no changes are needed since our data access methods will remain the same, just their implementations are changed. Before discussing how this is done, here is a little background on using persistence technologies with J2EE Web applications.

A High-Level Introduction to Using a Persistence Framework

Business applications typically have the need to access data from an object or relational database. Although there are many ways to access this data, such as using the Java Database Connectivity (JDBC) API directly, working with this low-level API can be somewhat cumbersome. Instead, a common and well-established approach to accessing this data is to use a data layer that employs the Data Access Object (DAO) design pattern.

To facilitate the usage of the DAO design patterns, persistence frameworks have substantially gained in popularity in recent years. Although the Java platform has offered the Enterprise JavaBeans (EJB) technology for several years, in recent years technologies such as Oracle's TopLink and the Open Source Hibernate have risen in popularity. The latter frameworks have also become popular because they offer a simple Plain Old Java Object (POJO)-based architecture. The recent introduction of Enterprise JavaBeans version 3 has taken a cue from the popular POJO-based persistence frameworks and is now based on a simplified POJO architecture.

Before discussing the specifics of using a persistence framework, further discussion on how to build a generic *data access layer* that employs the DAO pattern is needed.

Benefits of Building a Data Access Layer

The benefits of building a data access layer are numerous when working on enterprise applications. Most importantly, the data access layer allows for the clean separation of user interface code and business logic. Having a fully independent data access layer of code that performs data operations allows for maximum pluggability of the user interface code. This means that the same data access layer can be loosely coupled with any kind of user interface technology. For example, a JavaServer Faces application, Struts application, or even a Java Swing application could all communicate with the same data access layer.

In short, a data access layer will provide primarily two things: a set of Java objects that represent or are *mapped* to database objects (referred to as *Object Relational Mapping* or *OR Mapping*) and a set of Java objects that have data access methods, such as **add()**, **update()**, or **delete()**, including a collection of query or **find*()** methods.

For example, a Plain Old Java Object (POJO), **Employee.java**, which has properties such as **id** (of type **Integer**), **firstName** (of type **String**), or **lastName** (of type **String**), can represent a database table with similar columns: **id**, **first_name**, and **last_name**.

A data access object for the **Employee** object such as **EmployeeDAO.java** could have generic data access methods, such as **findAllEmployees()**, **findEmployeeById()**, **updateEmployee()**, and so on.

In a generalized fashion, the process for updating an object with a persistence technology usually involves the following:

1. Retrieving a copy of a specific object using a find method. For example:
   Employee: `UpdatedEmployee = EmployeeDAO.findEmployeeById(…);`

2. Updating the retrieved object.
   `UpdateEmployee.setFirstName("Chris");`

3. Calling a persistence method to commit the change and propagate it to the database. For example:
   `EmployeeDAO.updateEmployee(UpdatedEmployee);`

The **updateEmployee** method of **EmployeeDAO** will use the persistence framework's internal methods to commit the change.

Architecture of a JSF Application Using a Data Access Layer and Persistence Technology

Virtual Trainer uses a generic layer of data access objects to communicate to a persistence tier. Figure 9-23 illustrates the architecture strategy that Virtual Trainer employs for accessing/updating training event data. The **TrainingEventRegistry** interface provides a consistent set of methods to interact with the persisted data.

As you can see in the diagram in Figure 9-23, the Virtual Trainer application relies entirely on the data access layer accessed from page backing beans to interact with persistent data.

How to Build a Persistence Layer

In a general sense, using a persistence framework involves mapping the database objects as Java objects and creating data access objects. The process of creating both a set of mapped Java objects and a set of data access objects can be done either by hand or by using a development tool. Fortunately, all of the popular persistence frameworks, including Hibernate and TopLink, have support for auto-mapping and data access code generation capabilities. Even Enterprise JavaBeans have numerous tools that can automatically generate mapping and data access code.

Building a Hibernate Persistence Layer for the Virtual Trainer Application

The following discussion shows how to create a Hibernate-based data access layer, but the methods employed are virtually the same whether working with Hibernate, TopLink, or EJB version 3. The discussion also centers on building just the master-detail portion of the application, which is the set of training events and their associated sets of workout sessions. Building Hibernate persistence of the user registry is not shown but it's trivial since it is a simple, single table/Java class mapping.

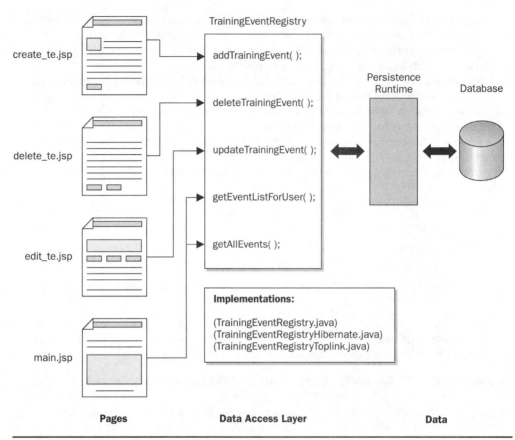

create_te.jsp

TrainingEventRegistry

addTrainingEvent( );

deleteTrainingEvent( );

delete_te.jsp

updateTrainingEvent( );

getEventListForUser( );

edit_te.jsp

getAllEvents( );

Implementations:

(TrainingEventRegistry.java)
(TrainingEventRegistryHibernate.java)
(TrainingEventRegistryToplink.java)

main.jsp

Persistence
Runtime

Database

Pages　　　　**Data Access Layer**　　　　**Data**

FIGURE 9-23　The Virtual Trainer application using a data access layer

The process of object relational mapping involves matching a Java class with a similar database table in structure. The mapping information is usually stored in a separate file that literally maps each database column and data type to a respective Java class's property. There are also different approaches to mapping. One approach is to map existing database tables to new Java classes. This is a common approach when the database structure has already been defined and is referred to as *reverse-engineering* the database tables into a Java persistence layer. The other approach is to *forward-engineer* your Java classes into database objects. This is a logical approach if your application begins as a pure Java prototype.

To get a feel for how database objects and Java classes can be mapped together, consider the Virtual Trainer Java class, **TrainingEvent**, which contains information about a single athletic event with properties such as **ename** (event name), **etype** (event type), and **completionDate** (date of the completion of the event). A corresponding database object could be a table, **TRAININGEVENT** (or **TRAININGEVENTS**), with respective columns **ENAME**, **ETYPE**, and **COMPLETIONDATE**. As you can guess, the challenge to object relational mapping lies in mapping equivalent or similar data types from the Java world to the relational database world. Mapping simple data types such as strings or integers is easily done as databases and Java handle these simple types in a similar manner. There are, however, more complicated mappings such as mapping the Java **boolean** type. Unfortunately, databases do not handle **boolean** data types in the same manner, so persistence technologies have to be aware of the database dialect and provide a solution on the database that emulates the behavior of the Java **boolean** data type.

Another area that can be tricky in object relational mappings deals with handling master-detail relationships, which is the case with the Virtual Trainer application. On the Java side, Virtual Trainer's **TrainingEvent** class has a property, **workoutsessions**, of type **List**. A database equivalent of this requires another table (representing **workoutsessions** data) with a foreign key relationship referring back to the master **TRAININGEVENT** table. The challenge here lies in providing the correct mapping information detailing the master-detail relationship between the two tables and their respective Java class counterparts. This is exactly what was needed for implementing a persistence layer for Virtual Trainer. The remaining discussion focuses on how the Java classes **TrainingEvent** and **TrainingSession** are mapped to respective master-detail database tables.

Since the Java-only version of Virtual Trainer has existing Java objects but doesn't yet have actual database entities representing them, it is possible to have Hibernate generate the necessary DDL to create the database entities based on the Java objects. TopLink also offers this capability. Conversely, had we started with an existing database schema, we could have used Hibernate or TopLink to reverse-engineer the database objects into appropriate Java objects. However, since the Virtual Trainer prototype started from a pure Java prototype, we will use the persistence technology to auto-generate the database entities.

In order to generate a corresponding set of database entities that map to the Java objects, we first need to create mappings of the Java objects so Hibernate will know how to map them to database entities. Again, creating Hibernate mappings can be done automatically using tools, but it is very useful to build your mappings by hand, especially if you are new to Hibernate, so that you fully understand the relationships between your Java objects and the database objects they are mapped to.

Recall the Java class, **TrainingEvent.java**, which has the following properties. (Setters and getters are not shown.)

```
private Long id;
private String ename;
private String etype;
private Date completionDate;
private String skill;
private String status;
private String trainer;
private List workoutsessions;
private String userid;
```

This will have a corresponding Hibernate mapping file, **TrainingEvents.hbm.xml**, which will contain the mappings for the class. The mappings file represents an intermediary representation of the data which can then be applied to multiple different types of database architectures. The Hibernate mapping file is an XML document that can reside in the same location as the **TrainingEvent** class.

The following is the Hibernate mapping file for the **TrainingEvent** class.

```
<?xml version="1.0"?>
<!DOCTYPE hibernate-mapping PUBLIC
        "-//Hibernate/Hibernate Mapping DTD 3.0//EN"
        "http://hibernate.sourceforge.net/hibernate-mapping-3.0.dtd">
```

```
<hibernate-mapping package="com.jsfcompref.trainer">
  <class name="TrainingEvent" table="TRAININGEVENT">
    <id name="id" type="integer">
      <generator class="increment"/>
    </id>
    <property name="ename" />
    <property name="etype" />
    <property name="completionDate" type="timestamp" />
    <property name="skill" />
    <property name="status" />
    <property name="trainer" />
    <property name="userid" />
    <list name="workoutsessions" cascade="all" lazy="false">
      <key column="EVENTNO" not-null="true" />
      <list-index column="EVENTORDER"/>
      <one-to-many class="TrainingSession" />
    </list>
  </class>
</hibernate-mapping>
```

A quick inspection of the mapping file shows that all of the properties have their respective mappings. For simple properties, such as when Java **String** properties match their respective column in name, then a simple **<property>** element with a name attribute is all that is required, although a column name can be specified anyway. However, for the primary key, **id**, of the database table, a special mapping that defines that it's the primary key column and has a unique value (class) generator is needed. For Virtual Trainer, the generator class is set to **increment**, which means that Hibernate is responsible for incrementing the primary key value when new records are added. If on the other hand you wish to allow the database to handle updating the primary key on its own, you can set the generator class to **native**, meaning that it will rely on the database's native, unique value generator such as a sequence. The **completionDate** property maps to a date value on the database; however, databases treat dates differently so a more generic Hibernate **timestamp** can be used. The final element is **<list>**, which maps the Java **List** property and establishes the relationship (one-to-many) and the foreign key (**eventno**) to the detail mapping class (**com.jsfcompref .trainer.TrainingSession**).

Recalling the properties for the **TrainingSession** class:

```
private int id;
private Date workoutDate;
private String workoutDescription;
private boolean completed;
private String personalNotes;
private String trainerNotes;
//An extra property is added which will allow inverse access (many-to-one)
//to the master class TrainingEvent:
private TrainingEvent trainingevent;
```

The Hibernate mapping file for **TrainingSession** is

```
<?xml version="1.0"?>
<!DOCTYPE hibernate-mapping PUBLIC
        "-//Hibernate/Hibernate Mapping DTD 3.0//EN"
        "http://hibernate.sourceforge.net/hibernate-mapping-3.0.dtd">
```

```
<hibernate-mapping package="com.jsfcompref.trainer">
  <class name="TrainingSession" table="TRAININGSESSION">
    <id name="id"  type="integer">
      <generator class="increment"/>
    </id>
    <property name="workoutDate" type="timestamp" />
    <property name="workoutDescription" />
    <property name="completed" type="yes_no" />
    <property name="personalNotes" />
    <property name="trainerNotes" />
    <many-to-one name="TrainingEvent"
          class="TrainingEvent"
          column="EVENTNO" not-null="true"
              insert="false" update="false" />
  </class>
</hibernate-mapping>
```

As you can see, this mapping file is fairly similar to the **TrainingEvent** mapping; however, notice the **boolean** Java type is mapped to the Hibernate **yes_no** type. (The Hibernate runtime will handle this **boolean** value according to the database's architecture.) Also notice the **<many-to-one>** mapping for the **TrainingEvent** property that is mapped back to the master table using the **EVENTNO** foreign key. Finally, notice the insert and update = "false"; this means that updates will occur through the master—meaning that no **TrainingSession** records will be inserted or updated independent of the master **TrainingEvent**.

Creating a Data Access Object

Now that the mappings have been defined for the entity classes for **TrainingEvent** and **TrainingSession**, we can create a Data Access Object whose role is to provide data operations that allow for querying, editing, creating, and deleting data from the mapped objects.

Recall that the **TrainingEventRegistry** class, which is used extensively to operate on the training event data, has the following data access methods:

- **addTrainingEvent( )**
- **deleteTrainingEvent( )**
- **updateTrainingEvent( )**
- **getEventlistForUser( )**
- **getAllEvents( )**

In fact, this class can be transformed into a Java **interface** and a new class, **TrainingEventRegistryHibernate,** which implements the **TrainingEventRegistry** interface. Here is the code for the **TrainingEventRegistry** interface:

```
package com.jsfcompref.trainer;
import java.util.List;

public interface TrainingEventRegistry {
  public Integer addTrainingEvent(TrainingEvent newTE);

  public void deleteTrainingEvent(TrainingEvent deletedTe);

  public void updateTrainingEvent(TrainingEvent updatedTe);
```

```
  public List getEventlistForUser(String userId);

  public List getAllEvents();
}
```

In this manner, the same data access methods can be used by the JSF user-interface portion of the application. The Hibernate implementation (**TrainingEventRegistryHibernate**) of the **TrainingEventRegistry** interface is as follows:

```
package com.jsfcompref.trainer;

// other imports omitted

 import org.hibernate.Query;
import org.hibernate.Session;

import com.jsfcompref.trainer.util.HibernateUtil;

public class TrainingEventRegistryHibernate
    implements TrainingEventRegistry  {

  public TrainingEventRegistry() {
  }

  public Integer addTrainingEvent(TrainingEvent newTE)  {
    Session session = HibernateUtil.getSessionFactory().getCurrentSession();
    session.beginTransaction();
    Integer id = (Integer)  session.save(newTE);

    session.getTransaction().commit();

    return (id);
  }

  public void deleteTrainingEvent(TrainingEvent deletedTe) {
    Session session = HibernateUtil.getSessionFactory().getCurrentSession();
    session.beginTransaction();
    session.delete(deletedTe);
    session.getTransaction().commit();
  }

  public void updateTrainingEvent(TrainingEvent updatedTe) {
    Session session = HibernateUtil.getSessionFactory().getCurrentSession();
    session.beginTransaction();
    session.merge(updatedTe);
    session.getTransaction().commit();
  }

  public List getEventlistForUser(String userid){
    List userlist = null;
    Query q = null;
    Session session = HibernateUtil.getSessionFactory().getCurrentSession();
    session.beginTransaction();
    q = session.createQuery(
        "from TrainingEvent te where te.userid = :teid");
    q.setParameter("teid", userid);
```

```
    return q.list();
  }

  public List getAllEvents() {
    List elist = new ArrayList();
    Session session = HibernateUtil.getSessionFactory().getCurrentSession();
    session.beginTransaction();
    elist = session.createCriteria(TrainingEvent.class).list();

    return elist;
  }


// An extra data access method, even though not used in the application yet.
  public TrainingEvent getTrainingEventById(int id)  {
  TrainingEvent te = null;
  Session session = HibernateUtil.getSessionFactory().getCurrentSession();
  session.beginTransaction();

  te =  (TrainingEvent)session.get(TrainingEvent.class, new Long(id));
  return te;
  }
}
```

Parsing through every line of code and describing exactly how Hibernate provides data access is beyond the scope this book, but with a quick read through the code you can see how to use Hibernate to access/edit mapped data. You'll notice that these methods use a utility class, **HibernateUtil**, that streamlines the data access operations. The code for this class is

```
package com.jsfcompref.trainer.util;

import org.hibernate.*;
import org.hibernate.cfg.*;

public class HibernateUtil {

private static final SessionFactory sessionFactory;
  static {
    try {
      // Create the SessionFactory from hibernate.cfg.xml
      sessionFactory = new
      Configuration().configure().buildSessionFactory();
    } catch (Throwable ex) {
      // Make sure you log the exception, as it might be swallowed
      System.err.println(
          "Initial SessionFactory creation failed." + ex);
      throw new ExceptionInInitializerError(ex);
    }
  }

  public static SessionFactory getSessionFactory() {
      return sessionFactory;
  }
}
```

This class was actually provided by a very useful Hibernate tutorial and is highly recommended for those getting started with Hibernate. It is located at **http://www .hibernate.org/hib_docs/v3/reference/en/html/**.

Some Final Details Before Running a Hibernate Application

In addition to the object entity beans (**TrainingEvent** and **TrainingSession**) and their respective mapping files and Data Access Object (**TrainingEventRegistryHibernate**), to use Hibernate you also need a configuration file that stores the database-specific connection information and configures Hibernate's runtime settings. The following is an example of a Hibernate configuration file for connecting to an Oracle database:

```xml
<?xml version='1.0' encoding='utf-8'?>
<!DOCTYPE hibernate-configuration PUBLIC
    "-//Hibernate/Hibernate Configuration DTD 3.0//EN"
    "http://hibernate.sourceforge.net/hibernate-configuration-3.0.dtd">
<hibernate-configuration>
  <session-factory>
    <!-- Database connection settings -->    <property name="connection.driver_class">
        oracle.jdbc.driver.OracleDriver</property>
    <property name="connection.url">
      jdbc:oracle:thin:@localhost:1521:orcl</property>
    <property name="connection.username">hbtrainer</property>
    <property name="connection.password">hbtrainer</property>
    <!-- JDBC connection pool (use the built-in) -->
    <property name="connection.pool_size">1</property>
    <!-- SQL dialect -->
    <property name="dialect">org.hibernate.dialect.OracleDialect</property>

    <!-- Enable Hibernate's automatic session context management -->
    <property name="current_session_context_class">thread</property>
    <!-- Disable the second-level cache  -->
    <property name="cache.provider_class">
      org.hibernate.cache.NoCacheProvider</property>
     <!-- Echo all executed SQL to stdout -->
     <property name="show_sql">true</property>

     <!-- Drop and re-create the database schema on startup -->
     <property name="hbm2ddl.auto">create</property>

     <mapping resource="com/jsfcompref/trainer/TrainingSession.hbm.xml"/>
     <mapping resource="com/jsfcompref/trainer/TrainingEvent.hbm.xml"/>

  </session-factory>
</hibernate-configuration>
```

First off, in a real application deployment scenario, the database connection information would not be hard-coded into this file. Instead, a JNDI datasource would be used. Also, the connection pool used here is purely for prototyping. Another important setting is the **hbm2ddl.auto** setting. This is a property that when specified with the **create** value will completely refresh the database by dropping and re-creating the objects during each run. This option should only be set during initial runs or when a schema change occurs. Finally, at the end of the file you can see the entries for the two mapping files reviewed earlier.

This concludes the review of using Hibernate for building a persistence layer; for more information on Hibernate, please refer to the **http://www.hibernate.org/** Web site.

Other Persistence Technologies

The preceding discussion of persistence and how it can be implemented for the Virtual Trainer application is meant to describe the general approach to building persistence, with Hibernate being just one of several different technologies that are available for this purpose. The actual Virtual Trainer application that is downloadable in the online extension will provide implementations of the Virtual Trainer application using both the Hibernate and Oracle TopLink persistence technologies. In reviewing the downloadable version, you'll see that the approaches to building persistence are very similar since they all follow a similar POJO and data access architecture. You'll also notice how easy it is to interchange different persistence layers since JSF encourages a solid MVC application design paradigm.

Internationalizing the Virtual Trainer Application

Chapter 14 will cover the topic of internationalization extensively. However, the process for making a multilingual version of the Virtual Trainer application is straightforward and is worth discussing briefly.

The first step in internationalizing a Faces application is to create a resource file such as **UIResources.properties** and place this in the same location as the Java source for the application (**com.jsfcompref.trainer.resources**). This file will contain the translatable **String**s used throughout the application. An example is as follows:

```
# Resource bundle for VirtualTrainer

# Generic Labels etc
title=JSF Virtual Trainer Application
about=About this sample

# Welcome Page
welcome.pageTitle=Welcome
welcome.header=Welcome to the JavaServer Faces Virtual Trainer Application
welcome.description=This application allows a user to …
…
```

A corresponding alternate language version of **UIResources.properties** could be created, such as for the French language: **UIResources_fr.properties**. This would reside in the same location as the default resources file.

```
# French Resource bundle for VirtualTrainer

# Generic Labels etc
title=Management d'Entraînements Sportifs - Basée sur JSF
about=Au sujet de cette application

# Welcome Page
welcome.pageTitle=Bienvenue
welcome.header=Bienvenue à l'Application pour Manager Vos …
…
```

To register this resource as well as the alternate bundles for French and Spanish, you could add the following to the **faces-config.xml**.

```
…
<application>
  <locale-config>
```

```
    <default-locale>en</default-locale>
      <supported-locale>fr</supported-locale>
      <supported-locale>es</supported-locale>
  </locale-config>
</application>
...
```

To use the resources in a JSF page, you must add the JSF standard tag, **f:loadBundle**, in each page where the resource is used.

```
<f:loadBundle basename="com.jsfcompref.trainer.resources.UIResources"
    var="res"/>
```

And finally, to use a resource string in the page, you can refer to the property using an EL expression:

```
<h:outputLabel value="#{res['login.userid']}" />
```

When the application is run, if the client browser specifies a default language of **fr** (French), then the JSF runtime will enable the **fr**-supported locale and the Virtual Trainer application will render in French, as shown in Figure 9-24.

The downloadable version of the Virtual Trainer application has resource bundles for English, French, and Spanish. Virtual Trainer's edit page in the Spanish version is shown in Figure 9-25.

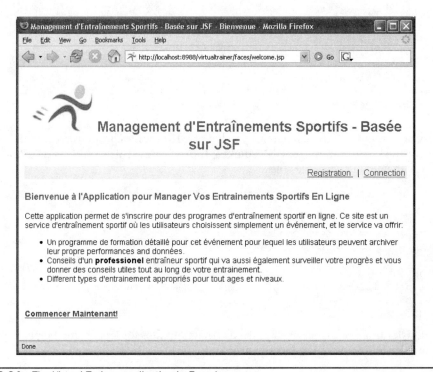

FIGURE 9-24 The Virtual Trainer application in French

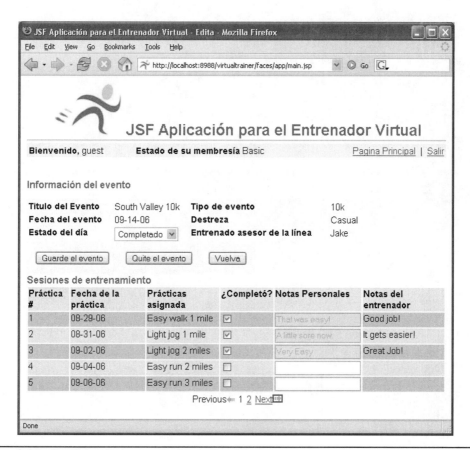

FIGURE 9-25   The Virtual Trainer application in Spanish

Providing resource strings for the UI is actually just a first step towards full internationalization of an application. For example, there are more in-depth changes that are often required, such as localizing the default Date format and so on; however, this is beyond the scope of this book. Chapter 14, however, provides more advanced coverage on how to internationalize a JSF application.

Final Comments on Virtual Trainer

As mentioned at the start of this chapter, the purpose of this walk through the Virtual Trainer development process is to solidify your understanding of the core JSF technologies that are used when building a real Web application. As you move on to the more advanced topics in this book, you may find it helpful to refer back to this chapter, thinking of ways to apply the more advanced techniques to Virtual Trainer.

Readers are also encouraged to download the source code to Virtual Trainer and experiment with the code itself. The downloadable version can be obtained at McGraw-Hill's Web site at **http://www.osborne.com**.

Building Custom UI Components

One of the most compelling and powerful aspects of JavaServer Faces is the development of custom JSF User Interface (UI) components. This is an essential topic for advanced JSF developers because it enables you to extend JavaServer Faces by creating your own JSF components that are tailored to the specific demands of your application.

One of the early goals of JavaServer Faces was to provide a component-centric foundation that the Java community could extend as needed. At the time of this writing, a growing community of JSF component developers is already making great progress on creating new and unique libraries of components that extend the original base components provided in the JSF specification. A quick look at **http://jsfcentral.com** confirms this fact. The new components being created come from both open source and independent vendors. For example, Apache's MyFaces project is a popular open source JSF component library, while leading vendors such as Oracle, Sun, ESRI, JScape, BusinessObjects, and ILOG all have production-quality professional JSF component libraries ready for use in your applications.

As you start learning how to build custom JSF components, don't be surprised if the process seems somewhat complicated at first. This is because JSF components tend to have a fair number of "moving parts" in them. To JSF's credit, this was intentional in order to provide a completely flexible framework that makes no assumptions about the end client. Components can be built to run inside of JSPs or not. They can be built to render in HTML or in other markups such as WML and SVG or even binary. JSF components are even flexible enough to be written so that they can respond dynamically in the appropriate markup dialect based on the request of the client. For example, the same component can render in HTML for a Web browser or in WML for a PDA browser. This is known as *pluggable rendering*. Finally, the JSF component model was designed to enable packaging all the parts of the component, including tool-ready metadata, into a self-contained JAR that can simply be dropped into the **WEB-INF/ lib** directory of a Web application and immediately used in JSP pages without any additional configuration.

It is this extreme flexibility that makes custom component development appear a bit complex at first. However, as you become more experienced at building custom components, you will soon begin to appreciate the flexibility of the API and the extensive benefits it affords them.

Deciding When to Build a Custom UI Component

Before examining the process of building a custom component it is necessary to emphasize that it is something that you won't always need to do. Before deciding to build a custom component, you should first check to see that you are not re-inventing the wheel. You should consider the following before embarking on custom development:

- Customization may not be necessary because the JSF community may already have a solution fulfilling your needs. Consult the component directory section of **http://jsfcentral.com/** or **http://www.jamesholmes.com/JavaServerFaces/** for something that fits your needs.

- Your requirements may not rise to a level that requires a custom component. If the goal is to simply create a dynamic portion of content, you can use subviews, tiles, and so on.

- Certain customization can also be attained without having to build an entirely new UI component. In many cases it is possible to write some custom logic such as a **Validator** or a **Converter** that can then be applied to one of the existing (standard) UI components.

Once an adequate amount of research has been performed and a solution that fits your requirements is still not found, then it is logical to proceed with custom JSF component development.

What Are UI Components?

The term *UI component* as defined in Chapter 6 is an overloaded term meant to communicate a mixture of JSF (sub-) components, working together to serve the end user in a particular protocol or a specific task through a user interface—for example, a custom input field, which has built-in credit card validation. This example UI component would actually consist of a collection of lower-level JSF components, such as a **Converter** or a **Validator**, as well as the other sub-components that provide a representation of the component to the end user. These associated components working together as a usable UI component can be described as the *moving parts* of a UI component.

The Moving Parts of a UI Component

The various moving parts that constitute a JSF UI component, as shown in Figure 10-1, are a collection of the following:

- **UIComponent Class:** A Java class derived from either **UIComponentBase** or directly from **UIComponent**. You can also extend from an existing base **UIComponent** class, such as **UIOutput**. This is the Java class that represents the core behavior of the component. It can optionally contain logic to render itself to a client, or rendering logic can reside in a separate renderer class. It's important to note the distinction between **UIComponent** and "UI component." The first is the actual Java class that provides the core behavior of the component, and the latter is the generic term used by convention meant to describe all of the elements working together to offer the usage of the overall component to the user (such as an input field rendered in HTML with built-in validation and conversion).

- **Renderer Class:** A class that contains code to render a **UIComponent**. It can also contain code to decode the incoming data from a form post. Different rendering classes can provide multiple renderings for the same **UIComponent**. For example, the **UICommand** component can be rendered as a button or a link, depending on the renderer associated with the component. In the former case, a **ButtonRenderer** is used, and in the latter a **LinkRenderer** is used. Renderers can also provide different rendering options for the same **UIComponent** for different client types that accept different markup flavors. For example, a radio button list looks different in a Web browser than it does in a mobile phone.

- **UIComponentTag Class:** A JSP tag handler class that allows the UI component to be used in a JSP. It provides a way for the page author to direct where in the page the component should appear, and allows the page author to customize its appearance by passing attributes in the familiar way one does with HTML. It associates a separate **Renderer** class with a **UIComponent** class. The **UIComponentTag** class is only required for use in a JSP deployment environment. (UI components can also be used in non-JSP environments.)

- **Tag Library Descriptor File:** A standard J2EE JSP tag library descriptor (TLD) file that associates the tag handler class with a tag in a JSP page. (Required only for JSP usage.)

- **Associated Helper Classes:** A collection of standard (included in the JSF RI) or custom helper classes such as **Converter**, **Validator**, and **ActionListener** that can be programmatically bound to UI components (in addition to being associated from inside of a JSP page). For example, a JSF UI input field component can be associated with a built-in number range **Validator** that ensures that a number is within a certain range. These helper classes can also be customized to extend any behavior

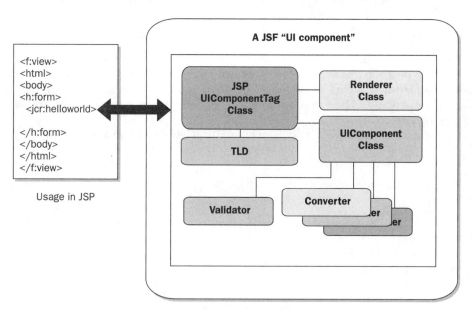

UI Component Elements

FIGURE 10-1 The moving parts of a UI component

not provided out of the box with the JSF reference implementation. For example, a custom credit card **Validator** could be used with a JSF input field to validate credit card numbers or a custom **Converter** could be used to convert currencies.

A Simple Hello World Example

Often the best way to learn a new technology is to begin with a simple, working example—in other words, a "Hello World" program. This is the approach used here. In this section you will see how to build a simple, yet fully functional custom JSF UI component. Although quite short, it introduces the main issues surrounding custom UI component development.

Before showing the actual code needed for our "Hello World" example, let's examine how the component will be used. The name of the component is **HtmlHelloWorld**. A page author will be able to add the custom **HtmlHelloWorld** component to a JSP page and it will render a short message that displays the current date and time. Later, you'll see how to customize it to provide a custom message via one of its properties.

JSF 1.2 TIP   *At the end of this section, you will see an updated version of the component written to take advantage of the features of JSF 1.2 and JSP 2.1.*

Building the HtmlHelloWorld Example

The **HtmlHelloWorld** component consists of the following subcomponents:

- An **HtmlHelloWorld UIComponent** Java class. This is the heart of the UI component. It provides the core functionality of the component, which is to display its message, rendered in HTML.

- An **HtmlHelloWorldTag UIComponentTag** class. This enables the execution of the UI component from a JSP page.

- **components.tld**, a tag library descriptor (TLD) file for the custom JSP tag.

You'll notice that there is no **Renderer** class. For this example, the code that displays (i.e., renders) the hello message is actually embedded in the **HtmlHelloWorld** class. Later examples will show custom UI components with separate **Renderer** classes along with explanations of why and how you would want the rendering code to be in separate classes under certain circumstances.

The source code for the UI component class **HtmlHelloWorld.java** is as follows:

```
package com.jsfcompref.components.component;

import javax.faces.component.UIComponentBase;
import javax.faces.context.FacesContext;
import java.io.IOException;
import javax.faces.context.ResponseWriter;

public class HtmlHelloWorld extends UIComponentBase {
  public String getFamily(){
    return null;
  }

  public void encodeBegin(FacesContext context) throws IOException {
    ResponseWriter writer = context.getResponseWriter();
```

```
      writer.startElement("div", this);
      writer.writeAttribute("style", "color : red", null );
      writer.writeText("HelloWorld! today is: " + new java.util.Date(), null);
      writer.endElement("div");
   }
}
```

The first thing to notice is the name of the class, **HtmlHelloWorld**. This is by convention because this component's default rendering is for an HTML client. As you'll see later in the chapter, UI components and their respective renderers (whether they're embedded in the component or not) have the ability to render in multiple markups such as HTML, WML, and so on.

Referring back to the code, you can see the most important method in this class, **encodeBegin()**, contains the code to render itself to the client. The actual generation of markup (rendering) is performed with a **ResponseWriter** object, which is available from the **FacesContext**. The **ResponseWriter** has various methods to output markup including the ones used here: **startElement()**, **writeAttribute()**, **writeText()**, and **endElement()**. You'll notice the extra **null** arguments in the example. When defined, these extra arguments provide additional component information to development tools to improve the design-time experience. For now you can leave them with **null** values. In addition to the aforementioned **ResponseWriter** methods, it is also possible to use a generic **write()** method that literally dumps any markup directly to the page without requiring writing the elements and attributes separately. This works fine, but can be a bit problematic when having to escape quote characters. For example:

```
writer.write("<div style=\"color : blue\">HelloWorld!</div>");
```

Expert Group Insight   *As mentioned above, the* **ResponseWriter** *concept allows design-time JSF tools to better integrate with the components in the page by allowing the component developer to give hints to the design time environment about the association between the markup in the page and the components in the view. Design-time tools will commonly replace the standard* **ResponseWriter** *with one that "intercepts" this extra information and conveys it to the user in some fashion.*

Note   *As a general tip, although not shown in these preliminary examples, it is considered good practice to also encode an ID attribute for the component. This allows for greater usability with client-side code (JavaScript) that may need to refer or operate on the component by referencing its ID. To render an ID for a component, use: writer.writeAttribute("id", getClientId(context), null);*

In general, the set of rendering methods, including **encodeBegin()**, **encodeEnd()**, and **encodeChildren()**, are the methods for rendering all markup to the client in a hierarchical manner. For example, the **HtmlHelloWorld** component could have had a separate child component to render the date. In this case, all three methods could be used in sequential order to render content ahead of the child component, render the child component, and then render content after the child component.

The other method to notice is the **getFamily()** method. This method returns the general category of which this component is a member. For example, the **UIInput** component belongs to the family **javax.faces.Input**, while the **UICommand** component belongs to the family **javax.faces.Command**. The **family** value is combined with the **rendererType** property to select a **Renderer** from a **RenderKit**. In the case of a component/renderer pairing that renders an HTML input field, the family would be **javax.faces.Input** and the renderer-type would be **javax.faces.Text**. In the case of a component/renderer pairing that renders an HTML button, the family would be **javax.faces.Command** and the renderer-type would be **javax.faces.Button**. In a custom component, the family and renderer-type values can be any string but they must match the corresponding values in the **faces-config** declaration for the component and renderer. The simple **HtmlHelloWorld** example doesn't create a new family of components and renderers, so it can just return a **null** value for now.

The preceding code is essentially all that is necessary for a UI component. The rest of the code is merely the necessary *plumbing* to execute this component in the context of a JSP page. For this, a custom tag class extended from **UIComponentTag** and a tag library descriptor (TLD) is needed. Here is the code for the JSP tag handler class:

```
package com.jsfcompref.components.taglib;
import javax.faces.webapp.UIComponentTag;

public class HtmlHelloWorldTag extends UIComponentTag {

  public String getComponentType() {
    // Associates tag with UI component registered in faces-config.xml
    return "HtmlHelloWorld";
  }

  public String getRendererType() {
    // Since the renderer is embedded in the component, can return null.
    return null;
  }
}
```

In this tag class, the obvious methods to observe are the **getComponentType()**, which associates the tag with the registered name of the **UIComponent** in the **faces-config.xml** file. The tag refers to **HtmlHelloWorld**, so the following registration is necessary in the **faces-config.xml**.

```
<component>
  <component-type>HtmlHelloWorld</component-type>
  <component-class>
    com.jsfcompref.components.component.HtmlHelloWorld
  </component-class>
</component>
```

NOTE *As you become more experienced in developing custom UI components, you'll want to create fully qualified names for component types, such as **com.jsfcompref.HtmlHelloWorld**. Similar to Java packages, this provides greater naming possibilities with its hierarchical structure.*

Returning to the component code, notice also the **getRendererType()** in the tag handler. Since the **HtmlHelloWorld** UI component class contains the code to render itself, **getRendererType()** can return **null**. If we had built a separate renderer class and registered it in **faces-config.xml**, this method would return the registered name of the renderer.

The final component necessary to complete the **HtmlHelloWorld** component is the tag library descriptor file:

```
<?xml version="1.0" encoding="UTF-8" ?>
<taglib xmlns:xsi="http://www.w3.org/2001/XMLSchema-instance"
```

```
xsi:schemaLocation="http://java.sun.com/xml/ns/j2ee
http://java.sun.com/xml/ns/j2ee/web-jsptaglibrary_2_0.xsd" version="2.0"
xmlns="http://java.sun.com/xml/ns/j2ee">
  <description>This is the JSP tag library for the custom
    components chapter.</description>
  <display-name>components</display-name>
  <tlib-version>1.0</tlib-version>
  <short-name>components</short-name>
  <uri>http://jsfcompref.com/demo/components</uri>
<tag>
  <description>Hello World Tag</description>
  <name>helloworld</name>
  <tag-class>
    com.jsfcompref.components.taglib.HtmlHelloWorldTag
  </tag-class>
</taglib>
```

Finally, to use the component, it can be placed in a JSP page with the following source:

```
<%@ page contentType="text/html"%>
<%@ taglib uri="http://java.sun.com/jsf/core" prefix="f"%>
<%@ taglib uri="http://jsfcompref.com/demo/components" prefix="jcr"%>
<f:view>
  <html>
    <head>
      <title>hello</title>
    </head>
    <body>
      <h2>Custom Helloworld component</h2>
      <p><jcr:helloworld /></p>
    </body>
  </html>
</f:view>
```

Notice that the taglib URI, **http://jsfcompref.com/demo/components**, must match the URI defined in the tag library descriptor file. Since **HtmlHelloWorld** doesn't require any attributes, the tag **<jcr:helloworld />** is all that is needed. As with any tag library descriptor, it must be placed in the **WEB-INF** directory of your runtime environment. Figure 10-2 shows what the page looks like at runtime.

Now that we've created a simple, but fully functional component, we can begin adding attributes to the component. Because **HtmlHelloWorld** extends from **UIComponentBase**, **UIComponent** properties from the superclass such as **id**, **binding**, **rendered,** and so on will work automatically once their respective attributes are added to the TLD.

```
...
<attribute>
  <name>id</name>
</attribute>
<attribute>
  <name>binding</name>
</attribute>
<attribute>
  <name>rendered</name>
</attribute>
```

Figure 10-2
Using the custom
HtmlHelloWorld
JSF UI component

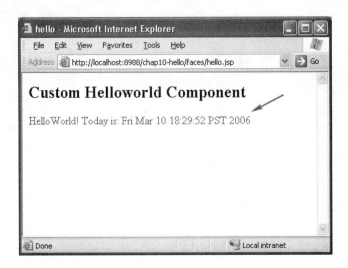

Once these attributes are added to the TLD, they can be used immediately. For example, to test the **rendered** attribute, one can set the value to be false:

```
<jcr:helloworld rendered="false"/>
```

This will cause the UI component to not render in the page.

Adding custom attributes does, however, require adding code to both the **UIComponent** and **UIComponentTag** classes. Let's add an attribute, **hellomsg**, which allows the user to specify a custom message to the component. For this, the following changes to the **UIComponentTag** class are needed:

- Add a JavaBean **String** property, **hellomsg**, which will store the incoming tag attribute. (Actually only the setter method, **setHellomsg()**, is needed.)

- Override the **setProperties()** method. This method will first process the superclass's properties (such as **id**, **binding**, and **rendered**), and then process the incoming tag attribute, **hellomsg**. Processing the tag attribute involves using either the component's **setValueBinding()** or its **getAttributes().put()** method, depending on whether the incoming is a JSF value expression or is just a string value. Once the property is set, the **UIComponent** class will have access to the property. Allowing a tag attribute to accept either a value binding or a literal string value is known as *value-binding enabling* the attribute. In general, it is a good idea to value-binding enable all of your component properties. In JSF 1.2, all properties are value-binding enabled by default.

- Following standard JSP custom development procedure, add a **release()** method to call the superclass's **release()** method and manually reset any attribute variables to **null**.

The updated **HtmlHelloWorldTag** class now has the following source added:

```
...
String hellomsg = null;

protected void setProperties(UIComponent component) {
    // This call to super.setProperties() is VITALLY IMPORTANT!
```

```
  // omitting it will cause the component to break entirely!
  super.setProperties(component);
   if (hellomsg != null) {
    if (isValueReference(hellomsg)) {
      FacesContext context = FacesContext.getCurrentInstance();
      Application app = context.getApplication();
      ValueBinding vb = app.createValueBinding(hellomsg);
      component.setValueBinding("hellomsg", vb);
    }
    else
      component.getAttributes().put("hellomsg", hellomsg);
  }
}

public void setHellomsg(String hellomsg) {
  this.hellomsg = hellomsg;
}

public void release() {
  super.release();
  hellomsg = null;
}
```

The **HtmlHelloWorld UIComponent** just has the following modification:

- Add a **getAttributes()** method call to retrieve the **hellomsg** value from the tag to make it usable in the **UIComponent**.

The **encodeBegin()** method can then use the **hellomsg** value in the **responseWriter** methods to display the message when rendered.

...
```
public void encodeBegin(FacesContext context) throws IOException {
  String hellomsg = (String)getAttributes().get("hellowmsg");
  ResponseWriter writer = context.getResponseWriter();
  writer.startElement("div", null);
  writer.writeAttribute("style", "color : red", null );
  writer.writeText(hellomsg, null);
  writer.endElement("div");
}
```
...

The final changes before testing the component require a change in the TLD to add the new attribute and the actual usage in the JSP page. In the TLD the **hellomsg** attribute is added to the body of the **helloworld** tag:

...
```
<attribute>
  <description>a custom hello message</description>
  <name>hellomsg</name>
</attribute>
```

The JSP page can now define a custom message in the tag.

```
<jcr:helloworld hellomsg="Hello JSF!"/>
```

As the page is run again, the custom message then appears, as Figure 10-3 shows.

FIGURE 10-3
HtmlHelloWorld
using a custom
HelloMessage
attribute

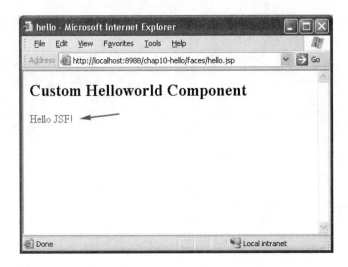

Since **HtmlHelloWorld** now contains code to process a value expression using **isValueReference()**, the custom **hellomsg** attribute supplied in the page can be a JSF EL expression. For example, the code:

```
<jcr:helloworld hellomsg="#{param.msg}"/>
```

will evaluate the expression, allowing the user to provide a request parameter, **msg**, at runtime and have it display as the message. When the page is run with the URL

http://localhost:*port*/faces/*contextroot*/hello.jsp?**msg=HelloAgain!!**

the message in the request parameter will be displayed in the page with the UI component, as shown in Figure 10-4.

Now that **HtmlHelloWord** can accept an attribute, a possible next step is to use the attribute to do something. For example, instead of just printing the value of the **hellomsg** attribute on

FIGURE 10-4
HtmlHelloWorld
using a value
expression

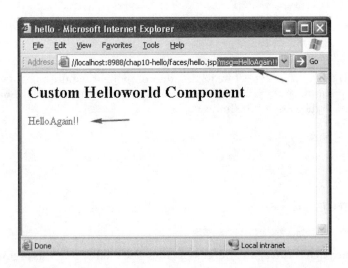

the JSP page, a new attribute such as **stocksymbol** could be added to the component and it could be used as a parameter to a Web service. The returned stock value could then be displayed on the page.

A HelloWorld UI Component That Accepts Form Input

So far, **HtmlHelloWorld** can retrieve attributes provided by the tag and can render (encode) itself to a client. In this next example, we'll create a new version of the component that accepts form input. This new version, called **HtmlHelloInput**, renders an input field and a button. It then processes the incoming value from the input field. In general, the process of handling incoming form values from a UI component is known as *decoding*.

   HtmlHelloInput allows a user to enter some text into the input field and the component will immediately render the entered text onto the page. **HtmlHelloInput** will extend **UIInput** instead of **UIComponentBase**. It also no longer needs to override the **getFamily()** method since it's extending **UIInput**. We will need to declare that this component does not have a specific external renderer because it renders itself. The declaration of the UI component is now:

```
public class HtmlHelloInput extends UIInput {

  public HtmlHelloInput() {
    setRendererType(null);  // this component renders itself
  }
...
```

   The new **HtmlHelloInput** has an **encodeEnd()** method that calls three sub-methods to render the respective sub-element of the UI component.

NOTE *An* **encodeEnd()** *method was used in this case as opposed to an* **encodeBegin()** *from before. In general when a component accepts input, it is best to use an* **encodeEnd()** *because* **encodeBegin()** *can be called before a necessary* **Converter** *is attached.*

```
public void encodeEnd(FacesContext context)
  throws IOException {

  String clientId = getClientId(context);
  encodeInputField(context, clientId + ":inputfield");
  encodeSubmitButton(context, clientId + ":submit");
  encodeOutputField(context);

}
```

   Notice that each sub-element is supplied with a unique identifer (**:inputfield** and **:submit**) that is concatenated with the unique client identification (**clientId**). This will allow the UI component to identify them later during the *decode* process (which parses the incoming submitted data). Let's examine the source for these methods, beginning with **encodeInputField()**, shown here:

```
public void encodeInputField(FacesContext context, String clientId)
  throws IOException  {

  // Render a standard HTML input field
  ResponseWriter writer = context.getResponseWriter();
```

```
writer.startElement("input", this);
writer.writeAttribute("type", "text", null);
writer.writeAttribute("name", clientId, "clientId");
Object value = getValue();
if (value != null)
  writer.writeAttribute("value", value.toString(), "value");
writer.writeAttribute("size", "6", null);
writer.endElement("input");
}
```

Notice the call to **getValue()**. While rendering the input field, the value of the rendered HTML input field is set if the UI component's underlying value is not **null**. Later in the **decode()** method you will see how to set a UI component's value.

The code for **encodeSubmitButton()** and **encodeOutputField()** is shown next:

```
private void encodeSubmitButton(FacesContext context, String clientId)
  throws IOException {
  // render a submit button

  ResponseWriter writer = context.getResponseWriter();
  writer.startElement("input", this);
  writer.writeAttribute("type", "Submit", null);
  writer.writeAttribute("name", clientId, "clientId");
  writer.writeAttribute("value", "Click Me!", null);
  writer.endElement("input");
}

public void encodeOutputField(FacesContext context)
  throws IOException {

  ResponseWriter writer = context.getResponseWriter();
  String hellomsg = (String)getAttributes().get("value");

  writer.startElement("p", this);
  writer.writeText("You entered: " + hellomsg, null);
  writer.endElement("p");
}
```

Notice that **encodeOutputField()** uses an alternate way to retrieve the value of the **hellomsg** attribute, which differs from retrieving the actual value of the overall component, as was done in the **encodeInputField()**.

The final new method is the **decode()** method, which parses the incoming **Request** data after a post-back occurs.

```
public void decode(FacesContext context) {
  Map requestMap = context.getExternalContext().getRequestParameterMap();
  String clientId = getClientId(context);

  String submitted_hello_msg =
    ((String) requestMap.get(clientId+":inputfield"));
  setSubmittedValue(submitted_hello_msg);
}
```

Notice how the decode method uses the unique field identifier **:inputfield** to look up the specific parameter that contains the submitted value in the **requestMap**. Recall that this was assigned in the **encodeInputField()** method.

The **HtmlHelloInput** component also requires a new JSP tag handler and TLD entry. Since the input tag doesn't need to accept an attribute, it has just the code to establish the **ComponentType** and set the **RendererType** to **null**.

```
public class HtmlHelloInputTag extends UIComponentTag {

  public String getComponentType() {
    return "HtmlHelloInput";
  }

  public String getRendererType() {
    // Since renderer is embedded in the component - returns null
    return null;
  }
}
```

Notice the **setProperties()** and **release()** superclass methods no longer need to be overridden. The TLD entry is trivial and resembles the initial **HtmlHelloWorld** example but with a **<tag>** name of **helloinput** along with a **<tag-class>** of **com.jsfcompref.components .taglib.HtmlHelloInputTag**.

Using the **helloinput** tag in JSP is also trivial:

```
<jcr:helloinput />
```

At runtime, the **HtmlHelloInput** component now renders the input, as shown in Figure 10-5.

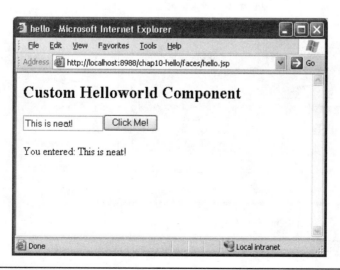

FIGURE 10-5 The HtmlHelloInput component in action

A JSF Stock Quote Component

To make the original **HtmlHelloInput** component more interesting, the component could be altered or a new component based on **HtmlHelloInput** could be created. This new component would present an input field as before but would accept it as a stock symbol and then pass it as an argument in a call to a stock quote Web service. To build a stock quote variation of the **HtmlHelloInput** component, the following tasks need to be done:

- A Web service proxy (or client) has to be created that allows a Java application to make a call to a Web service that returns a current stock quote. Since the Java code needed for Web service proxies/clients tends to be a bit cryptic and somewhat repetitive, it is best to use automatic Web service proxy/client generators, which are provided in many popular Java integrated development environments such as Oracle's JDeveloper or Sun's NetBeans IDE. Once the proxy class is created, it can be instantiated and used in the **UIComponent** code directly, or it can be registered as a Faces-managed bean, making its methods accessible to the Faces application via method binding.

- Once the proxy has been created, the **UIComponent** code can be altered to process a stock **symbol** attribute (as opposed to **hellomsg**). Instead of just displaying a simple message, the current stock price can be displayed. This is accomplished by using the stock symbol as an argument to the stock quote Web service using the proxy.

- Once retrieved, the quote information could be displayed in HTML (or in whatever markup is desired) during the encode process.

The overall architecture for a Web service–enabled stock quote component (**HtmlStockInput**) is illustrated in Figure 10-6.

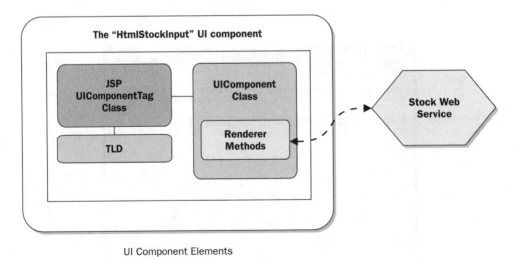

FIGURE 10-6   A Web service–enabled JSF stock quote component

After generating a proxy for the Web service, the decode method can be written to parse the input value and save the stock symbol into the component:

```
public void decode(FacesContext context) {
  Map requestMap = context.getExternalContext().getRequestParameterMap();
  String clientId = getClientId(context);
  String symbol = ((String) requestMap.get(clientId+":inputfield"));
  setSubmittedValue(symbol);
 }
```

In the **encodeOutputField** method a call is then made to the Web service proxy code.

```
public void encodeOutputField(FacesContext context)
   throws IOException  {

  ResponseWriter writer = context.getResponseWriter();

  String symbol = (String)getAttributes().get("value");
  float currentPrice = 0;

  if (null != symbol)  {
  // Use symbol in call to Web Service to get currentPrice
    NetXmethodsServicesStockquoteStockQuotePortClient client = null;
    try  {
      client = new NetXmethodsServicesStockquoteStockQuotePortClient();
    } catch (Exception ex)  {
      ex.printStackTrace();
    }

    currentPrice = client.getQuote(symbol);

    writer.startElement("p", this);
    writer.writeText("Current stock price for " + symbol + " is:" +
      currentPrice, null);
    writer.endElement("p");
  }
}
```

NOTE *The code for the Web service proxy for this example was auto-generated by Oracle JDeveloper 10g. Since Web service proxy code can have application server dependencies, this step is left to the reader. This Web service at* **http://services.xmethods.net/soap/urn:xmethods-delayed-quotes.wsdl** *was active during the writing of this book and is for U.S. stock markets only.*

Usage of the new **stockinput** tag is also trivial:

```
<jcr:stockinput />
```

At runtime the JSF **StockInput** component displays the current stock based on a *symbol* as shown in Figure 10-7.

FIGURE 10-7
Using the custom
JSF **StockInput**
component

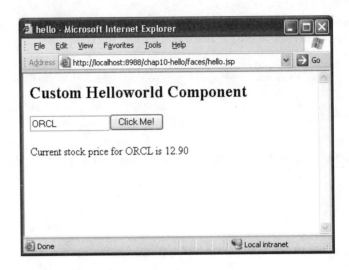

FIGURE 10-7
Using the custom
JSF **StockInput**
component

An InputDate Component with Multiple Renderers

Now that you have seen how to build several basic custom UI components, it's time to examine a slightly more advanced example. In this section, you'll see how to build a custom *date picker* component as shown in Figure 10-8.

Following naming conventions from the JSF Specification, the new date picker component will be called **InputDate**. Instead of embedding the rendering logic into the component, the **InputDate** component will come with two renderers—one for an HTML client and another for a WML client. In order to execute the separate renderers, two JSP tags will be created with their roles being to associate and invoke the **InputDate** component along with the different HTML and WML renderers.

FIGURE 10-8
The **InputDate** UI
component

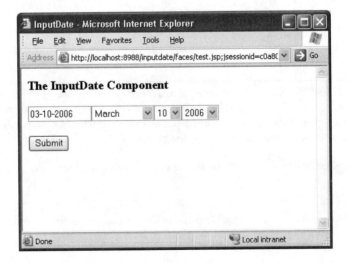

Using the InputDate Component

Using the **InputDate** component in a JSP is quite simple, as shown here:

```
<p>
  <jcr:inputdate value="#{ExampleUser.dob}" size="12"
    startyear="1930" endyear="2020" >
    <f:convertDateTime pattern="MM-dd-yyyy"/>
  </jcr:inputdate>
  <h:commandButton value="Enter"/>
</p>
```

The first thing to notice is that the component is *value-bound* to a managed bean property, **dob** (date of birth), which is of type **java.util.Date**. The other tag attributes, **size**, **startyear**, and **endyear**, are optional but affect the display of the component. The **inputDate** also allows for the use of a standard **Converter** where a specific **DateTime** pattern can be associated with the date. At runtime, the date will render with the pattern "MM-dd-yyyy". (The **commandButton** is purely to allow for a form submission.)

The Code Behind the InputDate Component

When the rendering logic is separated from the actual UI component, the code for a UI component can be rather simple. In this case, the code needed for the **InputDate** component is just enough to extend an existing reference implementation component, **UIInput**, and associate it with a rendering family **InputDateFamily**. The **InputDateFamily** is a family of renderers that will include separate renderers for rendering the **inputDate** component in both HTML and WML. The code for the **InputDate** component is

```
package com.jsfcompref.components.component;

import javax.faces.component.UIInput;
import javax.faces.component.ValueHolder;

public class InputDate extends UIInput implements ValueHolder {

  public String getFamily() {
    return "InputDateFamily";
  }
}
```

As with all custom components, the **InputDate** component also has to be registered in **faces-config.xml**:

```
<component>
  <component-type>InputDate</component-type>
  <component-class>
    com.jsfcompref.components.component.InputDate
  </component-class>
</component>
```

The HtmlInputDateRenderer

As you'll now see, the bulk of the **InputDate** component is in the renderer. It is the role of the renderer to both present the component as well as receive input from the client. As you recall from earlier examples, this is done through encode methods to display the component, and decode methods to parse the incoming form values.

EXPERT GROUP INSIGHT   *The name "renderer" was debated by the expert group since it really doesn't convey the full meaning of what is done. A renderer not only renders the component, it also converts the submitted input from the client into the proper form for the component. As such, another name for renderer was* **ClientAdapter** *but this was discarded as being too cumbersome.*

The core structure of the **HtmlInputDateRenderer** class is as follows. (The code for each method is omitted for brevity and will be shown later.)

```
package com.jsfcompref.components.component;

// import statements omitted

public class HtmlInputDateRenderer extends Renderer {

  public HtmlInputDateRenderer() {
    super();
  }
  private static final String MONTH = ".month";
  private static final String DAY = ".day";
  private static final String YEAR = ".year";

  //Renderer default values
   private static final int defaultInputFieldSize = 10;
   private static final int defaultStartYear = 1980;
   private static final int defaultEndYear = 2025;

  // In a production component, these would be localized names
  static String monthnames[] =
    { "January", "February", "March", "April", "May", "June",
      "July", "August", "September", "October", "November", "December" };

  // Rendering begins here.
  public void encodeBegin(FacesContext context,
        UIComponent component) throws IOException {

  //Declare threadsafe method variables for current month, day & year
  int currMonth, currDay, monthMaxDay, currYear;

  // Initialize current date values
  EditableValueHolder inputdate = (EditableValueHolder)component;
  Calendar tempcal = new GregorianCalendar();

  //  Get current value of Date and apply - if null set date to today
  Date dateval = (Date)inputdate.getValue();
  if (dateval != null)
    tempcal.setTime(dateval);
```

```
  else
    tempcal.setTime(new java.util.Date());

  currMonth = tempcal.get(Calendar.MONTH);
  currDay = tempcal.get(Calendar.DAY_OF_MONTH);
  monthMaxDay = tempcal.getActualMaximum(Calendar.DAY_OF_MONTH);
  currYear = tempcal.get(Calendar.YEAR);

  ResponseWriter writer = context.getResponseWriter();
  String clientId = component.getClientId(context);

  encodeInputField(writer, clientId, context, component);
  encodeMonthSelect(writer, clientId, component, currMonth);
  encodeDaySelect(writer, clientId, component, currDay, monthMaxDay);
  encodeYearSelect(writer, clientId, component, currYear);
  }
  // The bodies of the encode methods and single decode method
  // are omitted here but shown later....
}
```

As you can see in the code, the component's **Date** value is extracted into separate, thread-safe **currMonth**, **currDay**, **monthMaxDay**, and **currYear** variables. However, if the component's **Date** value is null, it sets them to values based on today's date. (The **monthMaxDay** value is used to determine the maximum days in a particular month.)

To ensure thread safety, the date variables (**currMonth**, **currDay** and so on) are declared in the **encodeBegin()** method so they are not instance member variables.

NOTE *In general, thread-safe, non-instance variables should always be used when writing renderer classes.*

The following encode methods render an input field along with drop-down select menus for the month, day, and year. The methods **encodeMonthSelect()** and **encodeDaySelect()** simply generate markup for an HTML select for the maximum days in a month (using **monthMaxDay**) and twelve months, respectively. The **encodeYearSelect()** renders a range of years relative to the current year.

Here is the code for the input field that is rendered with the **encodeInputField()** method.

```
private void encodeInputField(ResponseWriter writer, String clientId,
      FacesContext context, UIComponent component) throws IOException {

  // Render a read-only input field with component's current date value

  writer.startElement("input", component);
  writer.writeAttribute("name", clientId, "clientId");

  Object val = ((UIInput)component).getValue();
  if (val != null) {
    Converter conv = ((UIInput)component).getConverter();
    if (conv != null)
      writer.writeAttribute("value", conv.getAsString(context, component,
        val), "value");
```

```
      else
        writer.writeAttribute("value", val, "value");
    } else
        writer.writeAttribute("value", "", "value");
    Integer size = (Integer)component.getAttributes().get("size");
    if (size != null)
      writer.writeAttribute("size", size, "size");
    else // use default size
      writer.writeAttribute("size", defaultInputFieldSize, "size");
    writer.writeAttribute("readonly", Boolean.TRUE, null);
    writer.endElement("input");
}
```

As you can see, it obtains the converted value of the component value and renders it as the value of the input field. Also notice that this is a read-only input field as it will always accept its value from the select menus.

The code for the **encodeMonthSelect()** method is shown next. Notice the **selected** attribute is rendered when the current month is rendered.

```
private void encodeMonthSelect(ResponseWriter writer, String clientId,
    UIComponent component, int currMonth) throws IOException {

  writer.startElement("select", component);
  writer.writeAttribute("size", "1", null);
  writer.writeAttribute("name", clientId + MONTH, null);

  for (int i = 0; i < 12; i++) {
    writer.startElement("option", component);
    writer.writeAttribute("value", "" + i, null);
    if (i == currMonth)
      writer.writeAttribute("selected", Boolean.TRUE, null);
    writer.writeText(monthnames[i], null);
    writer.endElement("option");
  }
  writer.endElement("select");
}
```

The **encodeDaySelect()** method follows in a similar fashion. Notice it uses the **monthMaxDay** value to render the correct number of days in the month select menu.

```
private void encodeDaySelect(ResponseWriter writer, String clientId,
    UIComponent component, int currDay, int monthMaxDay) throws IOException
{

  writer.startElement("select", component);
  writer.writeAttribute("size", "1", null);
  writer.writeAttribute("name", clientId + DAY, null);

  for (int i = 1; i <= monthMaxDay; i++) {
    writer.startElement("option", component);
    writer.writeAttribute("value", "" + i, null);
    if (i == currDay)
      writer.writeAttribute("selected", Boolean.TRUE, null);
    writer.writeText("" + i, null);
```

```
      writer.endElement("option");
   }
   writer.endElement("select");
}
```

As explained earlier, the **encodeYearSelect()** method has logic that allows the user to specify the range of years to display. Notice the **getAttributes().get()** method calls to retrieve the values passed from the JSP tag. Also notice if the tag does not provide values for the start year and end year, the component renders with default values defined earlier as static class variables (**defaultStartYear** and **defaultEndYear**).

NOTE *In general it is always best to place default values in the rendering code (either in a **Renderer** or **UIComponent**) as opposed to coding them into the JSP tag handler. This ensures that these values can be used outside of a JSP usage (such as with Facelets).*

```
private void encodeYearSelect(ResponseWriter writer, String clientId,
    UIComponent component, int currYear) throws IOException {

  Integer startyear = null;
  Integer endyear = null;

  startyear = (Integer)component.getAttributes().get("startyear");
  if (startyear == null)
    startyear = new Integer(defaultStartYear); //use default value

  endyear = (Integer)component.getAttributes().get("endyear");
  if (endyear == null)
    endyear = new Integer(defaultEndYear); //use default value

  writer.startElement("select", component);
  writer.writeAttribute("size", "1", null);
  writer.writeAttribute("name", clientId + YEAR, null);

  for (int i = startyear.intValue(); i <= endyear.intValue(); i++) {
    writer.startElement("option", component);
    writer.writeAttribute("value", "" + (i), null);
    if (i == currYear)
      writer.writeAttribute("selected", Boolean.TRUE, null);
    writer.writeText("" + i, null);
    writer.endElement("option");
  }
  writer.endElement("select");
}
```

And here is the single **decode()** method, whose job is to parse the incoming data values that have been submitted and apply them to the **Date** value of the component.

```
public void decode(FacesContext context, UIComponent component) {
  EditableValueHolder inputdate = (EditableValueHolder)component;
  Map requestMap = context.getExternalContext().getRequestParameterMap();
  String clientId = component.getClientId(context);

  Calendar calDate = new GregorianCalendar();
  if (requestMap.containsKey(clientId + MONTH) &&
      requestMap.containsKey(clientId + DAY) &&
```

```
      requestMap.containsKey(clientId + YEAR)) {

    //  Set inputDate component with date derived from Request values
    calDate.set(Integer.parseInt((String)requestMap.get(clientId + YEAR)),
                Integer.parseInt((String)requestMap.get(clientId + MONTH)),
                Integer.parseInt((String)requestMap.get(clientId + DAY)));

    inputdate.setSubmittedValue(calDate.getTime());
  } else {
  // Since values not provided in Request, set inputDate to current date
  inputdate.setSubmittedValue(new java.util.Date());
  }
}
```

As you can see, the initial statements of **decode( )** extract the different month, day, and
year values from the **Request**. It uses the unique **clientId** of the component along with
appended identifiers (MONTH, DAY, YEAR) to find the correct input field values. The
individual date values are then applied to a **caldate** object of type **GregorianCalendar**. The
caldate value is then applied to the component. That's it!

Although this date picker is meant purely as a learning example, there are ways it can
be easily improved. For example, it can be made locale-sensitive by checking the locale and
then altering the ordering of the date input select menus. Another way to improve this
component is to employ JavaScript where rich pop-up calendars are possible. Although
we won't extend this component with JavaScript, later in the chapter are examples where
JavaScript is used to enhance the end user experience.

Returning to the **inputDate** component, since the **HTMLInputDateRenderer** class is
separate from the UI component, it must be registered in **faces-config.xml**. In addition to
defining the actual renderer, we'll also define a component-family, to which we will next
add an additional WML renderer:

```
<render-kit>
  <renderer>
    <component-family>InputDateFamily</component-family>
    <renderer-type>HtmlInputDateRenderer</renderer-type>
    <renderer-class>
       com.jsfcompref.components.component.HtmlInputDateRenderer
    </renderer-class>
  </renderer>
</render-kit>
```

NOTE *In the previous code sample, we didn't add either a* **<render-kit-id>** *or a* **<render-kit-
class>** *as child elements of* **<render-kit>**. *Omitting these simply means that the new renderer
class will be added to the default render-kit at runtime. More details on creating custom render-
kits will be provided in Chapter 12.*

The final code required in order to invoke the **HtmlInputDate** component in a JSP page
is the JSP tag. Keep in mind that this is only necessary when the UI component is needed for
use in a JSP page. Later in the book, you'll see how to use JSF outside of JSP. Similar to the
previous JSF custom tag examples, the **HtmlInputDateTag** extends **UIComponentTag**. It

also has properties for **size, value, startyear**, and **endyear**. Getter methods for these properties are not needed for custom tag attributes. The setter methods are also omitted for brevity in the following listing.

```
package com.jsfcompref.components.taglib;

// Import statements omitted for brevity.

public class HtmlInputDateTag extends UIComponentTag {

  // Tag properties
  private String size = null;
  private String value = null;
  private String startyear = null;
  private String endyear = null;

  // Associate component with renderer
  public String getRendererType() { return "HtmlInputDateRenderer"; }
  public String getComponentType() { return "InputDate"; }

  public HtmlInputDateTag() { super(); }

  public void setProperties(UIComponent component) {
    super.setProperties(component);

    // set size
    if (size != null) {
      if (isValueReference(size)) {
        FacesContext context = FacesContext.getCurrentInstance();
        Application app = context.getApplication();
        ValueBinding vb = app.createValueBinding(size);
        component.setValueBinding("size", vb);
      }
    else
      component.getAttributes().put("size", new Integer(size));
    }

    // set value
    if (value != null) {
      if (isValueReference(value)) {
        FacesContext context = FacesContext.getCurrentInstance();
        Application app = context.getApplication();
        ValueBinding vb = app.createValueBinding(value);
        component.setValueBinding("value", vb);
      }
    else
      component.getAttributes().put("value", value);
    }

    // set startyear
    if (startyear != null) {
      if (isValueReference(startyear)) {
        FacesContext context = FacesContext.getCurrentInstance();
```

```
                Application app = context.getApplication();
                ValueBinding vb = app.createValueBinding(startyear);
                component.setValueBinding("startyear", vb);
            }
        else
            component.getAttributes().put("startyear", new Integer(startyear));
        }

        // set endyear
        if (endyear != null) {
            if (isValueReference(endyear)) {
                FacesContext context = FacesContext.getCurrentInstance();
                Application app = context.getApplication();
                ValueBinding vb = app.createValueBinding(endyear);
                component.setValueBinding("endyear", vb);
            }
        else
            component.getAttributes().put("endyear", new Integer(endyear));
            }
        }

    public void release() {
        super.release();
        size = null;
        value = null;
        startyear = null;
        endyear = null;
    }

    // Setter methods for tag properties omitted for brevity.
}
```

The main methods to note in the **HtmlInputDateTag** are the ones that associate the UI component with a renderer: **getComponentType()** and **getRendererType()**, as well as the methods **setProperties()** and **release()**, which allow the tag attributes to be passed to the UI component.

Observing the **setProperties()** more closely you can see that when a tag attribute is provided (and therefore not null), a check is first done to see if it is a *value reference* (such as with a JSF EL expression). If so, a **ValueBinding** object is created using the tag attribute value. The value in the **ValueBinding** object is then applied to the component using **component.setValueBinding()**.

If the tag attribute value, however, is not a value reference, the literal value of the tag attribute is applied directly to the component using the **component.getAttributes().put()** method.

The **release()** method simply resets the tag attribute values to their initial, null states after they've been applied to the component.

NOTE *A listing of the tag library descriptor entry for this tag is omitted for brevity, but it follows the standard J2EE tag library descriptor format.*

A WML InputDate Variation

So far the examples have shown how to build components or renderers that generate HTML markup. This next variation of **inputDate** will serve as a basic introduction on how to build a WML renderer that will allow **inputDate** to render for WML-compliant clients such as PDAs or similar micro-devices. Figure 10-9 shows a WML version of the **inputDate** component viewed in a Palm device.

Building a WML renderer for the **inputDate** component is a straightforward process. All you have to do is build a separate renderer class. Of course, you must also create an entry in **faces-config.xml**, which identifies the external **renderer-kit** and **renderer-family**. (The registration procedure is described in the next section.) Here we will examine the WML renderer code for **inputDate**. The renderer class **WmlInputDateRenderer** is shown here:

```
package com.jsfcompref.components.component;

// Import statements omitted for brevity

public class WmlInputDateRenderer extends Renderer {

  // Class variable declarations are identical to
  // HtmlInputDateRenderer and are omitted.

  public void encodeBegin(FacesContext context,
                          UIComponent component) throws IOException {

    // Thread-safe day, month, year variable declarations and
    // and initializations are identical to HTMLInputDateRenderer
    // and are omitted.

    // The rendering portion of the method is the only part
    // modified for WML. Notice the "card" element.

    ResponseWriter writer = context.getResponseWriter();
    String clientId = component.getClientId(context);

    writer.startElement("card", component);
    writer.startElement("p", component);
    encodeInputField(writer, clientId, context, component);
    encodeMonthSelect(writer, clientId, component);
    encodeDaySelect(writer, clientId, component, monthMaxDay);
    encodeYearSelect(writer, clientId, component);
    writer.endElement("p");
    writer.endElement("card");
  }
```

After rendering the initial **card** and **<p>** start elements, similar rendering methods, including **encodeInputField()**, **encodeMonthSelect()** and so on, are called. The **encodeInputField()** method is almost identical to its HTML counterpart **HtmlInputDateRenderer()**. The only exception is that the **readonly** attribute is not allowed in WML so the statement is removed.

```
writer.writeAttribute("readonly", Boolean.TRUE, null);
```

FIGURE 10-9
Using the WML
version of the
inputDate
component

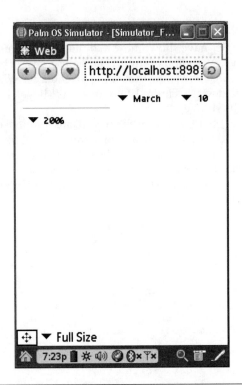

NOTE *For this WML example, leaving the input field editable is okay since its value would be ignored.*

The code for the select rendering methods is almost identical to their respective HTML counterparts. Here is the code for the **encodeMonthSelect( )** method for **WmlInputDateRenderer( )**. Notice that the **selected** and **size** attributes are not included in this method as they are no longer valid attributes of the rendered WML **select** tag.

```
private void encodeMonthSelect(ResponseWriter writer, String clientId,
                    UIComponent component) throws IOException {
  writer.startElement("select", component);
  writer.writeAttribute("name", clientId + MONTH, null);

  for (int i = 0; i < 12; i++) {
    writer.startElement("option", component);
    writer.writeAttribute("value", "" + i, null);
    writer.writeText(monthnames[i], null);
    writer.endElement("option");
  }
  writer.endElement("select");
}
```

The remaining encode methods, **encodeDaySelect( )** and **encodeYearSelect( )**, are also omitted in this code listing since the only difference from their HTML counterparts is that they also do not render the **selected** and **size** attributes. The **decode( )** method has entirely identical code with its HTML counterpart, so it is also not shown.

How to Register Render-Kits and Renderer Families

In order to use the **WMLInputDateRenderer**, it must also be registered in **faces-config.xml**. The new WML renderer can be added to the same component-family, **InputDateFamily**, using the following format:

```
<render-kit>
  <renderer>
    <component-family>InputDateFamily</component-family>
    <renderer type>WmlInputDateRenderer</renderer-type>
    <renderer-class>com.jsfcompref.components.component.WmlInputDateRenderer
    </renderer-class>
  </renderer>
  <renderer>
    <component-family>InputDateFamily</component-family>
    <renderer-type>HtmlInputDateRenderer</renderer-type>
    <renderer-class>
      com.jsfcompref.components.component.HtmlInputDateRenderer
    </renderer-class>
  </renderer>
</render-kit>
```

With both renderers registered in **faces-config.xml** under a single **InputDateFamily**, it will be the job of the respective JSP tags (**HtmlInputDateTag** and **WmlInputDateTag**) to associate a specific renderer with the **inputDate** component. The code

```
public String getRendererType() {
  return "WmlInputDateRenderer";
}

public String getComponentType() {
  return "InputDate";
}
```

can be used in the **WmlInputDateTag** so when the user adds the **<jcr:wmlinputdate>** tag to a JSP page, it will render with the WML renderer. It is common practice to use tags to associate different renderers with the same UI component. For example, **UICommand** in the reference implementation has different renderers associated with different standard JSF JSP tags: **h:commandLink** renders the **UICommand** component with an HTML hyperlink and **h:commandButton** tag renders the same **UICommand** with an HTML button.

Using the **WmlInputDateTag** in a JSP page is done in a fashion similar to the **HtmlInputDate;** however, the JSP page must be WML-compliant.

```
<?xml version="1.0"?>
<!DOCTYPE wml PUBLIC "-//WAPFORUM//DTD WML 1.1//EN"
"http://www.wapforum.org/DTD/wml_1.1.xml"><wml>

<%@ taglib uri="http://java.sun.com/jsf/core" prefix="f"%>
<%@ taglib uri="http://jsfcompref.com/demo/components" prefix="jcr"%>
<f:view>
  <jcr:wmlinputdate value="#{ExampleUser.dob}" size="12" startyear="1930"
    endyear="2020" >
  <f:convertDateTime pattern="MM-dd-yyyy"/>
  </jcr:wmlinputdate>
</f:view>
</wml>
```

FIGURE **10-10**
Running the WML
InputDate in the
Opera WML
Browser

To view the WML-enabled **inputDate** component at runtime, a WML browser such as NetFront, which runs on a PDA device, or Opera, which is a WML-enabled browser that also runs on PCs, can be used. Figure 10-10 shows the **WmlInputDate** component in the Opera browser.

It should be noted that the **WMLInputDateRenderer** example serves only as an introduction to creating different renderers for the same UI component. You might have noticed that there is not a form button for submission. This is because the standard **<h:commandButton>** works for HTML only, thus a separate WML-friendly form and button set of components would also have to be written. Since dealing with form submissions in WML is a little different than in HTML it is beyond the scope of the example, and is left as an exercise for the reader. In general when working with WML, it is recommended that you purchase a book on WML or browse the available online reference materials. A simple Google search yields many helpful resources online.

Dynamically Changing the Renderer at Runtime

Although it is useful to employ JSP tags to associate specific renderers with UI components, there are times when being able to associate the renderer at runtime is even more desirable. For example, a renderer could be chosen at runtime based on the request's client type (**user-agent**). So a PDA client would receive WML markup output and an HTML client browser would receive HTML markup content. Using this approach negates the need to have separate JSP tags. Instead, the same tag can detect the client browser type that is supplied in the request and then dynamically associate the renderer.

In the **UIComponentTag** code, instead of hard-coding a specific **rendererType**, this can be determined at runtime. The **rendererType** can be geared for a specific **user-agent** that is the header value of the client type, which is provided in each **HttpServletRequest**. The following code in a **UIComponentTag** can determine this automatically:

```
public String getRendererType()  {
  // Determine the rendererType dynamically..
  return determineRenderer(FacesContext.getCurrentInstance());
}
```

and the **determineRenderer()** method is as follows:

```
public String  determineRenderer(FacesContext context){
  HttpServletRequest req = (HttpServletRequest)
         context.getExternalContext().getRequest();

  String clientAgent = req.getHeader("user-agent");

  // WML Renderers
  if (clientAgent.indexOf("NetFront") != -1)
    return "WmlRenderer";

  if (clientAgent.indexOf("Opera") != -1)
    return "WmlRenderer";

  if (clientAgent.indexOf("Klondike") != -1)
    return "WmlRenderer";

  // HTML Renderers
  if (clientAgent.indexOf("MSIE") != -1)
    return "HtmlRenderer";

  if (clientAgent.indexOf("Firefox") != -1)
    return "HtmlRenderer";

  // Default
  return "HtmlRenderer";
}
```

Determining the best renderer using the **user-agent** can be a bit of an art and should be tailored to your specific requirements. There are client browsers, such as Opera and NetFront, that can interpret both WML and HTML equally. The Klondike browser, however, will only interpret WML.

NOTE *It should also be mentioned that an alternative way to dynamically switch renderers can be done with separate render-kits using a* **RenderKitFactory***. In this scenario the logic to switch renderers is external to JSP tags so it can be used in non-JSP JSF technologies such as Facelets.*

JSF 1.2 TIP *Supporting multiple render-kits in a single application wasn't fully implemented in JSF 1.0 and 1.1. JSF 1.2 makes the following improvements to enable this feature:*

- *Add a value expression enabled* **renderKitId** *attribute to the* **<f:view>** *tag and* **UIViewRoot** *component.*

- *Modify the state management system to encode the* **renderKitId** *in the response. In the case of HTML, this gets written as a hidden field.*

- *Modify the* **ViewHandler** *(more details on* **ViewHandlers** *are provided in Chapter 12) to inspect the request and discover the* **renderKitId** *encoded by the state management system.*

  With these features, it is possible to easily use more than one render-kit in a single application on a per-view basis.

A Custom Chart Component

The next custom component example demonstrates a component that renders a different type of markup known as Scalable Vector Graphics (SVG) to create dynamic charts. This custom JSF chart component makes it easy to generate dynamic charts based on application data. The end user simply value-binds the chart component with a data object from a managed bean, sets a few other optional attributes, and the component renders an SVG-based chart at runtime as shown in Figure 10-11.

Once you have a basic understanding of SVG syntax, building an SVG rendering chart component is actually very easy. The component essentially has to interpret chart data and render the data graphically using SVG. The chart data could come in any number of forms as long as it contains a series of numeric and label values. For convenience, the chart data in this example will use an **ArrayList** of Faces **SelectItem** objects, each of which contain values and labels. Using the existing Faces **SelectItem** data object provides a perfect value/label data object for our needs and negates having to declare a custom data type. The **ArrayList** of **SelectItems** will be declared in a managed bean and the chart component will be value-bound to it.

As you'll see shortly, rendering chart data in SVG markup using the **ResponseWriter** is as easy as rendering in HTML or WML. The rendering logic in the component simply uses SVG syntax to draw the chart objects based on the data provided.

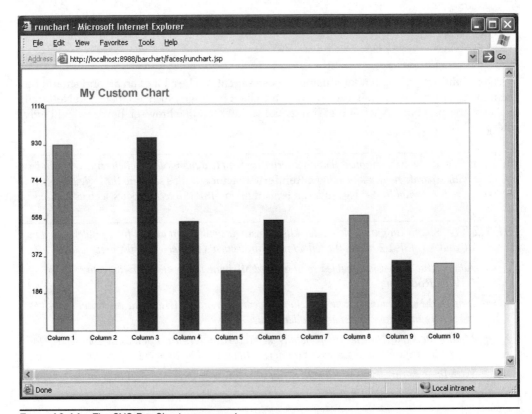

FIGURE 10-11   The SVG Bar Chart component

Preparing the Chart Data Object

Recall that the chart component uses a managed bean with an **ArrayList** of Faces **SelectItems**, each containing name value pairs. This example creates a managed bean, **ChartData,** which generates an **ArrayList** of seven chart (**SelectItem**) objects that contain random values:

```
package com.jsfcompref.data;

import java.util.ArrayList;
import java.util.List;
import javax.faces.model.SelectItem;

public class ChartData {
  public ChartData() {
  }
  List Chartinfo = new ArrayList();

  public List getChartData(){

  //Return a List of 7 chart objects
  for (int i=0; i<7; i++){
    Chartinfo.add(new SelectItem((int)(Math.random() * 1000),
    "Column " + (i+1) ));
  }

  return Chartinfo;
  }
}
```

Obviously, in a real usage, the end user would populate the **List** of **SelectItems** with actual data, which could be from two columns from a database table.

Using the Chart Data Object

To use the JSF chart component, the end user must incorporate the following syntax in a page (**chart.jsp**):

```
<%@ page contentType="image/svg+xml"%>
<%@ taglib uri="http://java.sun.com/jsf/core" prefix="f"%>
<%@ taglib uri="http://jsfcompref.com/demo/components" prefix="jcr"%>
<f:view>
  <jcr:barchart title="My Custom Chart"
    data="#{ExampleChartData.chartData}"/>
</f:view>
```

Notice the content type in the page is **image/svg+xml**. This is necessary to inform the client browser what type of markup is provided in this document. Since this page contains only SVG markup, an ideal usage is to embed this page within another page containing standard HTML content. This can be done by using the HTML **<embed>** statement from another page.

```
<embed id="mychart" src="chart.jsp" type="image/svg+xml" height="500px"
width="1000px" onload="onloadChart(this)" >
```

Rendering an SVG Bar Chart

The main task of the chart component is to parse the chart data and render chart objects in SVG. In contrast to the **inputDate** component, this example puts the rendering code in the UI component itself, as shown here:

```
package com.jsfcompref.components.component;

// Import statements omitted

public class SVGBarChart extends UIOutput  {

  // Chart static variables
  public final static int TITLEOFFSET = 80;
  public final static int CHARTHEIGHT = 341;
  public final static int SCALEPOINTS = 6;
  public final static String CHARTBACKGROUND = "#fdfdfd";
  public final static int CHARTREGIONHEIGHT = 406;
  public final static String CHARTREGIONBACKGROUND = "#fefefe";
  public final static int BARWIDTH = 30;
  public final static int BARMAXPIXELHEIGHT = CHARTHEIGHT - 50;
  public final static int BAROFFSET = 66;
  public final static int INITIALOFFSET = 38;
  public final static int CHARTBASE = 380;
  public final static int CHARTLABELBASE = 394;
  public final static int LABELOFFSET = 10;

  public void encodeBegin(FacesContext context) throws IOException  {
    String title = (String)getAttributes().get("title");
    List chartdata = (List)getAttributes().get("data");
    ResponseWriter writer = context.getResponseWriter();

    renderEmptyChart(writer, chartdata, title);
    renderBars(writer, chartdata);
    writer.write("</svg>");
  }

  public void renderEmptyChart(ResponseWriter writer, List chartdata,
    String title) throws IOException  {
    // Render SVG markup to display an empty chart
  }

  public void renderBars(ResponseWriter writer, List chartdata)
    throws IOException {
    // Render bars using a List chartdata..
  }

  int getMaxBarHeight(List chartdata)  {
    // Helper method to determine maximum bar height.
  }

  String getRandomHexColor()  {
    // Helper method to generate random bar color  }
  }
```

As you can see, the core logic involved in this component is located in the **encodeBegin()** method where the **title** and **chartdata** attributes are collected, and then the chart is rendered using the **ResponseWriter** object.

The first method, **renderEmptyChart()**, displays an empty chart that is scaled using several of the static variables to define the chart dimensions.

```
public void renderEmptyChart(ResponseWriter writer, List chartdata,
  String title) throws IOException
{
  // Perform initial chart dimension calculations
  int scalediv = CHARTHEIGHT/SCALEPOINTS;
  int maxbarheight = getMaxBarHeight(chartdata);
  float magfactor = (float)BARMAXPIXELHEIGHT/maxbarheight;
  int chartWidth = chartdata.size() * (BAROFFSET);
  int chartRegionWidth = chartWidth + 80;
```

Now that the overall chart dimensions have been calculated based on the actual data from **chartdata**, an empty chart can be rendered.

```
// Render empty chart
writer.write("<!DOCTYPE svg PUBLIC \"-//W3C//DTD SVG 1.0//EN\"" +
  "\"http://www.w3.org/TR/2001/REC-SVG-20010904/DTD/svg10.dtd\">\n" +
  "<svg xmlns=\"http://www.w3.org/2000/svg\">\n" +
  "<rect x=\"0\" y=\"0\" width=\"" + chartRegionWidth + "\" height=\"" +
  CHARTREGIONHEIGHT + "\" fill=\"" + CHARTREGIONBACKGROUND + "\"/>\n" +
  "<rect x=\"27\" y=\"39\" width=\"" + chartWidth + "\" height=\"" +
  CHARTHEIGHT + "\" fill=\"" + CHARTBACKGROUND + "\"" +
  "stroke=\"#cccccc\"/>");
chartWidth += 27;
writer.write("<line x1=\"" + chartWidth + "\" y1=\"39\" x2=\"" +
  chartWidth + "\" y2=\"380\" stroke=\"#cccccc\"/>" +
  "<line x1=\"" + chartWidth + "\" y1=\"39\" x2=\"" +
  chartWidth + "\" y2=\"380\" stroke=\"#cccccc\"/>" +
  "<line x1=\"27\" y1=\"39\" x2=\"" + chartWidth + "\"" +
  "y2=\"39\" stroke=\"#cccccc\"/>" +
  "<line x1=\"27\" y1=\"380\" x2=\"27\" y2=\"39\"" +
  "stroke=\"#cccccc\"/>" +
  "<line x1=\"27\" y1=\"380\" x2=\"" + chartWidth + "\" y2=\"380\"" +
  "stroke=\"#000000\"/>" +
  "<line x1=\"27\" y1=\"380\" x2=\"27\" y2=\"39\"" +
  "stroke=\"#000000\"/>");

// Render left scale
int vertspace = scalediv;
for (int i =0; i< SCALEPOINTS ; i++ )  {
  float label =  vertspace/magfactor;
  writer.write("<text xml:space=\"preserve\" x=\"4\" y=\"" +
    (39 + CHARTHEIGHT- vertspace) + "\"" +
    style=\"font:10px sans-serif\" fill=\"#000000\">" +
    (int)label + "</text>");
  writer.write("<line x1=\"23\" y1=\"" + (39 +
    CHARTHEIGHT- vertspace)+ "\" x2=\"27\" y2=\"" +
    (39 + CHARTHEIGHT- vertspace) + "\" stroke=\"#000000\"/>");
```

```
    vertspace += scalediv;
    }
    // Render Chart Title
    writer.write("<text xml:space=\"preserve\" x=\"" + TITLEOFFSET +
      "\" y=\"27\" style=\"font:bold 17px sans-serif\"" +
      "fill=\"#336699\">" + title + "</text>");
}
```

The left scale uses a basic algorithm to calculate the vertical space between scale points based on **scalediv** (scale divisor value). This value is the total height of the chart divided by the number of scale points, which is stored in the static variable **SCALEPOINTS** and is set to 6 for this example. Of course, in a full production version these dimension settings would probably be exposed as component attributes for maximum flexibility. This exercise is left to the reader.

NOTE   *Writing out large amounts of markup using* **ResponseWriter.write( )** *statements as opposed to rendering every element individually using* **ResponseWriter.startElement( )**, **writeAttribute( )**, *and so on won't earn style points, but it does allow for easier rendering of large quantities of markup. Future versions of JSF are planning to address this with an easier solution.*

The final method, **renderBars( )**, loops through the items provided in **chartdata** and renders SVG bars in the chart.

```
public void renderBars(ResponseWriter writer, List chartdata)
    throws IOException  {
    int maxbarheight = getMaxBarHeight(chartdata);
    float magfactor = (float)BARMAXPIXELHEIGHT/maxbarheight;
    int x=INITIALOFFSET;
    float y=0;

    for  (int i = 0; i < chartdata.size(); i++)  {
      SelectItem bar = (SelectItem) chartdata.get(i);
      y = (float) new Integer(bar.getValue().toString()).floatValue();
      y = y * magfactor;

      writer.write("<rect x=\"" + x + "\" y=\"" + (CHARTBASE - y) +
        "\" width=\"" + BARWIDTH + "\" height=\"" + y + "\" fill=\"" +
        getRandomHexColor() + "\" stroke=\"#000000\"/>");
      writer.write("<text xml:space=\"preserve\" x=\"" + (x - LABELOFFSET) +
        "\" y=\"" + CHARTLABELBASE + "\" style=\"font:10px sans-serif\"" +
        "fill=\"#000000\">" + bar.getLabel() + "</text>");
      x = x + BAROFFSET;
    }
}
```

The key areas to note in this method are how the **y** value, which represents the column's height, is retrieved from **chartdata** and then multiplied by a magnification factor (**magfactor**) so that it fits in the chart. This way, both extremely large and small values will generally render with roughly the same size in the chart.

The other key thing to notice is the bar **fill** color where the method **getRandomHexColor()** is called. This method generates a string that represents a random color in hexadecimal red, green, blue (RGB) format—for example, "#5A9CC6".

```
String getRandomHexColor(){
  return "#" + Integer.toHexString((int)(Math.random() * 16777215));
}
```

This method generates an RGB color by taking the hexadecimal string value of the product of **Math.Random()**, which is a random double value greater than or equal to 0 and less than 1.0, and 16777215. The decimal number 16777215 is FFFFFF in hexadecimal.

As before, the final bit of code for this chart example is the JSP tag whose job is to process the two **title** and **data** attributes and apply their values to the chart UI component. It also sets the component type of **SvgBarChart**, which is the name that the UI component will be registered with in **faces-config.xml**. (This step was intentionally omitted for brevity.)

```
package com.jsfcompref.components.taglib;

// Import statements omitted for brevity

public class SvgBarChartTag extends UIComponentTag {
  public SvgBarChartTag(){
  }

  public String title = null;
  public String data = null;

  public String getComponentType() {
    // Associates tag with UI component name in faces-config.xml
    return "SvgBarChart";
  }

  public String getRendererType(){
    // Since renderer is embedded in the component, can return null.
    return null;
  }
  protected void setProperties(UIComponent component) {
    super.setProperties(component);
    // Set title
    if (title != null) {
      if (isValueReference(title))  {
        FacesContext context = FacesContext.getCurrentInstance();
        Application app = context.getApplication();
        ValueBinding vb = app.createValueBinding(title);
        component.setValueBinding("title", vb);
      }
      else
        component.getAttributes().put("title", title);
    }
    if (data != null){
```

```
        if (isValueReference(data)){
           FacesContext context = FacesContext.getCurrentInstance();
           Application app = context.getApplication();
           ValueBinding vb = app.createValueBinding(data);
           component.setValueBinding("data", vb);
        }
        else
           component.getAttributes().put("data", data);
        }
     }
  public void release() {
     super.release();
     title = null;
     data = null;
  }

  // Set methods for properties omitted.
}
```

NOTE *The tag library descriptor for this tag is also omitted for brevity.*

One last point: The same methods just described can be employed to build a variation of the chart component that renders another type of chart, such as a pie chart. You might want to try this on your own.

Using JavaScript in a Custom JSF Component—A Slider Example

As you develop more advanced JSF components, you will no doubt find the need to incorporate JavaScript into the rendered output of a custom component to improve the overall usability or richness of the JSF component. Consider the slider component. Sliders are commonly used in traditional thick client applications; however, since sliders need the ability to sense mouse movements on the client, they are not doable in a Web browser unless JavaScript/DHTML is used. This is because mouse movement events are not transmitted through standard HTTP posts.

The example developed here demonstrates how to encapsulate JavaScript slider code into a custom JSF slider component. In the process, it shows how the end user of the JSF component need not be aware of the underlying JavaScript code required to create a functioning slider component, thus making it extremely easy to use. The example also illustrates how it is possible (even advantageous) to encapsulate complex JavaScript code into a JSF custom component. By doing so, you can greatly simplify overall usage of JavaScript while taking advantage of its superior user interface possibilities.

The slider example, shown in Figure 10-12, allows a user to define the range and the orientation, and then set the output of the slider to an existing **inputText** component (or any component that holds a value).

Figure 10-13 depicts the overall architecture of the core JavaScript slider code.

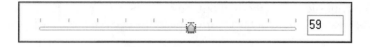

FIGURE 10-12
The JavaScript-
based slider
custom JSF
component

The Challenge of Using Advanced JavaScript

If you've worked with advanced JavaScript at all, you'll know that it can be quite complex
to code and especially debug. The JavaScript slider code is no exception. In order to use the

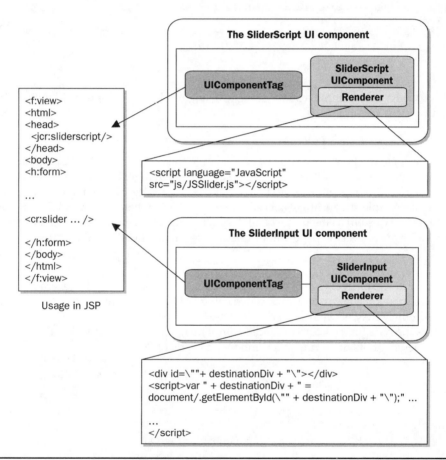

FIGURE 10-13 The overall structure of the JavaScript slider

JavaScript slider directly (without the aid of JSF), the page author is responsible for writing a significant amount of JavaScript code in the body of the HTML page per usage:

```
<div id="slider1">
  <!-- slider goes here -->
</div>
<script>
var slider1 = document.getElementById("slider1");
slider1.appendChild(JSSlider.getInstance("slide2", false, 10, 300,
0, undefined, undefined, "valChangeHandlerslide", false).render());

function valChangeHandlerslide(newStartPercent0To100,
  newEndPercent0To100) {
  var slideVal = Math.round(100*newStartPercent0To100/100);
  document.getElementById("textinput1").value = slideVal;
}
</script>
```

This code is used to apply a slider value to a single HTML text input field with an ID of **textinput1**.

```
<input id="textinput1" type="text" name="textinput1" size="5" />
```

In addition to the JavaScript code being added to the body of the HTML page, any JavaScript functions referred to by this code, such as **valChangeHandlerside()**, must also be added to the HTML page. You can imagine how complex the HTML page could get, especially if multiple sliders are needed in the page! This is where a custom JSF component proves to be very useful as the usage of a JSF slider component, which encapsulates the same slider JavaScript code so the page author doesn't have to deal with it, can be as simple as:

```
<jcr:slider id="slide1" for="in1" maxval="100" length="300" />
```

As you can see, JSF makes usage of the JavaScript slider much easier. In general, JavaScript encapsulation in JSF components makes rich client/AJAX Web development for the page author extremely easy, as we'll also see in the next chapter.

Here is the code for a custom JSF slider component. Again, this example will use a single UI component with its rendering code embedded inside of it.

```
package com.jsfcompref.components.component;
// Import statements omitted

public class SliderInput extends UIComponentBase {
  public SliderInput() {
  setRendererType(null);  // This component renders itself
  }

  String maxval = "100";      // default
  String forid = null;
  String horizontal = "true";  // default
  String length = "300";      // default

  public void encodeBegin(FacesContext context) throws IOException {
    if (getAttributes().get("maxval") != null)
      maxval = (String)getAttributes().get("maxval");
```

```
    if (getAttributes().get("for") != null)
      forid = (String)getAttributes().get("for");

    if (getAttributes().get("horizontal") != null)
      horizontal = (String)getAttributes().get("horizontal");

    if (getAttributes().get("length") != null)
      length = (String)getAttributes().get("length");

    String comp_id = getId();
    String valchangehandler = "valChangeHandler" + comp_id;
    String destinationDiv = "dest" + comp_id;

    // Prepend base client Id to forid
    forid = getBaseClientId(context) + forid;

    ResponseWriter writer = context.getResponseWriter();

    // Render client JavaScript for slider
    writer.write("<div id=\"" + destinationDiv + "\">" +
      "<!-- slider goes here --></div>" +
      "<script>var " + destinationDiv + " = document.getElementById(\"" +
      destinationDiv + "\"); " +
      destinationDiv + ".appendChild(JSSlider.getInstance(\"" +
      comp_id + "\", " + horizontal + ", " +
      "10, " + length + ", 0, undefined, undefined, \"" + valchangehandler +
      "\", false).render());" +
      " function " + valchangehandler +
      "(newStartPercent0To100, newEndPercent0To100) " +
      "{ var slideVal = Math.round(" +
      maxval + "*newStartPercent0To100/100); document.getElementById(\"" +
      forid + "\").value = slideVal; " + "}</script>");
  }

  private String  getBaseClientId(FacesContext context) {
    // Simple method to return "base" of ClientId
    String clientId = getClientId(context);
    return clientId.substring(0, clientId.indexOf(":") + 1);
  }

  public String getFamily() {
    // This component renders itself
    return null;
  }
}
}
```

Obviously, the most important method in this example is the **encodeBegin()** method. The purpose of this method is to render the client portion of JavaScript code shown earlier. The other key thing to notice is that several of the original JavaScript slider (**JSSlider**) attributes are surfaced in the UI component including **maxval**, **horizontal**, and **length**. These allow the end user of the JSF slider component to set the maximum value of the slider, its length, and its orientation.

As with previous examples, to use the JSF component in a JSP page, a corresponding UI JSP tag (**SliderTag**) is needed. Similar to the **<h:message>** tag where its **for** attribute displays

Faces messages for the input component specified, the **for** attribute of the **SliderTag** is the ID of the component that this slider will apply its value to at runtime. Notice also that this tag also refers to the registered name of the **SliderInput** UI component that was registered in **faces-config.xml** as "SliderInput".

```
package com.jsfcompref.components.taglib;

public class SliderTag extends UIComponentTag {
  public SliderInputTag() {
  }

  // Default values are provided in the component renderer, not the tag.
  String For = null;
  String maxval = null;
  String horizontal = null;
  String length = null;

  public String getComponentType(){
  // Associates tag with the UI component registered in the faces-config.xml
  return "SliderInput";
  }

  public String getRendererType() {
  // Renderer is embedded in the component, can return null.
  return null;
  }

  protected void setProperties(UIComponent component){
    super.setProperties(component);
    // set For
    if (For != null) {
      if (isValueReference(For))  {
        FacesContext context = FacesContext.getCurrentInstance();
        Application app = context.getApplication();
        ValueBinding vb = app.createValueBinding(For);
        component.setValueBinding("for", vb);
      }
      else
        component.getAttributes().put("for", For);
    }

    // set maxval
    if (maxval != null) {
      if (isValueReference(maxval)) {
        FacesContext context = FacesContext.getCurrentInstance();
        Application app = context.getApplication();
        ValueBinding vb = app.createValueBinding(maxval);
        component.setValueBinding("maxval", vb);
      }
      else
        component.getAttributes().put("maxval", maxval);
    }

    // set horizontal
```

```
    if (horizontal != null) {
      if (isValueReference(horizontal)) {
        FacesContext context = FacesContext.getCurrentInstance();
        Application app = context.getApplication();
        ValueBinding vb = app.createValueBinding(horizontal);
        component.setValueBinding("horizontal", vb);
      }
      else
        component.getAttributes().put("horizontal", horizontal);
    }
    // set length
    if (length != null) {
      if (isValueReference(length)) {
        FacesContext context = FacesContext.getCurrentInstance();
        Application app = context.getApplication();
        ValueBinding vb = app.createValueBinding(horizontal);
        component.setValueBinding("length", vb);
      }
      else
        component.getAttributes().put("length", length);
    }
  }

  public void setFor(String For) {
    this.For = For;
  }

  public void release()  {
    super.release();
    For = null;
    maxval = null;
    horizontal = null;
    length = null;
  }

// Setter methods omitted.
}
```

Using the JSF Slider Component

The slider component is now ready for use in a JSP. As you recall, this component uses a **for** attribute, which allows it to apply its value to another input field. The following JSP code example shows how to use two slider components along with their respective input field recipients:

```
<h2>Using the JSF Slider Component</h2>
<hr/>
<h:panelGrid columns="2" border="2">
  <jcr:slider id="slide1" for="in1" maxval="100" length="300"
    horizontal="false" />
  <jcr:slider id="slide2" for="in2"  horizontal="false"/>
  <h:inputText size="3" id="in1" value="0" />
  <h:inputText size="3" id="in2" value="0" readonly="true"/>
</h:panelGrid>
<h:commandButton value="Submit"/>
```

Notice the matching **for** attributes; **slide1** applies its value to **inputText** with ID **in1** and **slide2** applies it matched with **inputText in2**. Also notice that the **maxval** and **length** attributes are omitted in the second usage example. This forces the usage of the default values provided in the renderer code.

Adding the Required JavaScript Library

Now that we have a custom JSF UI component that generates some JavaScript code that calls JavaScript slider functions residing in a separate file (**JSSlider.js**), the only remaining thing to do is add the JavaScript reference to **JSSlider.js** to the JSP page using:

```
<script language="JavaScript" src="js/JSSlider.js"></script>
```

This must be placed either in the page header or above the first usage of the code contained in the reference.

Another slightly more elegant solution that hides the usage of JavaScript is to create a custom tag/component that renders the JavaScript reference entry. In this case the usage could be simply to use the following tag instead of the **<script>** reference tag:

```
<jcr:sliderscript />
```

A custom tag to render a script reference also has the benefit of determining the **contextPath** at runtime and prefixing it onto the URL of the resource (for example, src="/**MyJSFApplication**/js/JSSlider.js"). This is considered a best practice when possible.

An even more elegant solution is to bundle the JavaScript reference inside of the JSF slider component itself, providing it renders it only once per page since multiple usages of the slider component with multiple references to the same JavaScript file could cause JavaScript errors in the browser. This can be done by placing an identifier on the **Request** so that during subsequent uses of the same component, it can know not to re-render the JavaScript library reference. Details on how to do this are provided in the next chapter.

Figure 10-14 shows two JSF sliders and their linked input fields at runtime.

Advanced Custom JSF Component Development

We now return to the **HtmlHelloInput** component developed earlier in the chapter as a way to illustrate the more advanced task building custom components that can accept *method expressions* as opposed to just value expressions. Method expressions are introduced in Chapter 2. Here you will see how to build a JSF custom component containing an attribute that accepts method expressions, thus allowing it to execute any method of a JSF managed bean. We will also use this opportunity to show how a JSF 1.2 version of this component can be created.

Updating the HtmlHelloInput UI Component to Use Method Binding

In addition to component properties being value-binding enabled, it is also possible for component properties to be *method-binding* enabled. Method binding enables UI components to execute any managed bean's methods when specified through a component/tag property. An example of a method-binding enabled property is the **action** property of a **UICommand** component when it is used to execute an action method, or in general initiate an action event. Consider the code:

```
<h:commandButton value="Confirm"
           action="#{UserBean.addConfirmedUser}" />
```

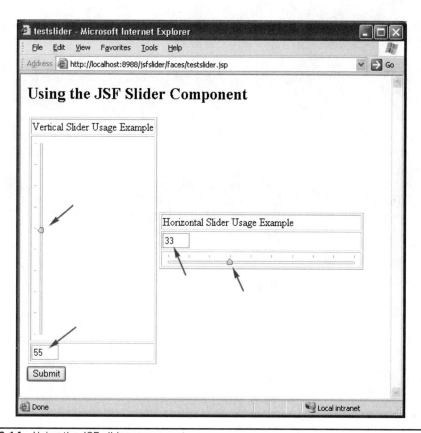

FIGURE 10-14 Using the JSF slider component

We will next update the **HtmlHelloInput** component to support method binding. The modified **HtmlHelloInput** component, called **HtmlHelloInputMB**, will now accept a new attribute value, **msgnotify**. This new attribute contains a method expression pointing to a method that returns **void** and takes two arguments: an instance of **HtmlHelloInputMB** and a **String**. (The first argument just happens to be an **HtmlHelloInputMB**, but it could be of any type.) When the component is posted back, an instance of **HtmlHelloInputMB** and a **String** argument (message) sent to the method pointed at by the method binding.

Before reviewing how to implement method binding in **HtmlHelloInputMB**, we need a managed bean that has a method that accepts the two arguments and returns **void**. The **messageSet()** method in the **MsgListener** class listed below meets the requirements:

```
package com.jsfcompref.example;

public class MsgListener {

String message = null;
HtmlHelloInputMB component = null;
```

```
   public MsgListener() {
   }

   public void messageSet(HtmlHelloInputMB component, String message) {
      System.out.println("Executing messageSet method for component" +
                            component.getId());
      this.component = component;
      this.message = message;
      System.out.println("Input message was: " + message);
   }
}
```

As mentioned earlier, we'll clone the existing **HtmlHelloInput** class and name it **HtmlHelloInputMB**. The "MB" signifies that it takes a method binding argument. Since it will accept a method binding expression, a **MethodBinding** type property must be added to the new **HtmlHelloInputMB** component, as shown here:

```
import javax.faces.el.MethodBinding;

public class HtmlHelloInputMB extends UIInput {

   public HtmlHelloInputMB() {
      setRendererType(null);   // this component renders itself
   }

   // (new) Define a write-only JavaBeans property of type MethodBinding
   private MethodBinding listener = null;

   public void setListener(MethodBinding listener) {
      this.listener = listener;
   }
   ...
```

The new version of **HtmlHelloInputMB** now has a new attribute, **msgnotify**, in the TLD.

```
...
<attribute>
  <description>message method</description>
  <name>msgnotify</name>
  <rtexprvalue>false</rtexprvalue>
  <type>java.lang.String</type>
</attribute>
```

To process this attribute, the tag handler code must also be modified to process this attribute as a method expression.

```
...
String msgnotify = null;

   protected void setProperties(UIComponent component) {
      super.setProperties(component);

      // (new) handle the msgnotify attribute
```

```
      if (msgmethod != null) {
        if (isValueReference(msgnotify)) {
          FacesContext context = FacesContext.getCurrentInstance();
          Application app = context.getApplication();
          Class [] params = {
            HtmlHelloInputMB.class,
            String.class
          };
          MethodBinding mb = app.createMethodBinding(msgmethod, params);
          ((HtmlHelloWorldMB)component).setListener(mb);
        }
        else {
          System.out.println("Error: value of msgnotify attribute " +
                                "must be a MethodBinding.  Was: " +
                                msgnotify);
        }
      }
    }
  }

  public void release() {
    super.release();
    msgnotify = null;
  }

// Setter methods omitted
}
```

As you can see, the new code in **setProperties()** is similar to the other code examples that process tag attributes. However, instead of calling **createValueBinding()**, it calls **createMethodBinding()** with the attribute value, **msgnotify**. The second argument is an array of **java.lang.Class** instance exactly matching the type of the expected method. If the **MethodBinding** method takes no arguments, this second argument may be null. Once the **MethodBinding** object is created, it is set as the value of the **HtmlHelloInputMB**'s **listener** property.

Finally, change the **decode()** method of **HtmlHelloInputMB** to invoke the method as appropriate, as shown here

```
public void decode(FacesContext context) {
  Map requestMap = context.getExternalContext().getRequestParameterMap();
  String clientId = getClientId(context);

  String submitted_msg = ((String)requestMap.get(clientId +
    ":inputfield"));
  setSubmittedValue(submitted_msg);

  // (new) handle the listener attribute, if non-null
  if (null != listener) {
    try {
      Object [] args = {
        this,
        submitted_msg;
      };
```

```
      listener.invoke(context, args);
    }
    // A production quality component would
    // log these messages such as java.util.logging.Logger instead of
    // sending them to standard out.
    catch (javax.faces.el.MethodNotFoundException mnfe) {
      System.out.println("Expecting method that takes a" +
                          "HtmlHelloWorldMB instance and a String. " +
                          "Instead received exception: " +
                          mnfe.getMessage());
    }
    catch (javax.faces.el.EvaluationException ee) {
      // Unwrap the exception to see the cause
      if (null != ee.getCause()) {
        System.out.println(ee.getCause().getMessage());
      }
    }
  }
}
```

The new **decode()** method examines the **listener** instance variable. If non-null, it invokes the method, passing the proper arguments and dealing with any exceptions that may arise.

After registering the new managed bean **ExampleMsgListener** as a managed bean, the JSP usage is

```
<jcr:helloinputmb msgnotify="#{ExampleMsgListener.messageSet}" />
```

When executed, the component will execute the **messageSet()** method and display the following in the console:

```
Executing messageSet method for component …
```

It is now time to discuss how to convert this component so that it runs in JSF 1.2.

Updating the HtmlHelloWorld and HtmlHelloInputMB Components for JSF 1.2

The next set of examples will show how to update two previous examples from JSF version 1.1 to version 1.2. The first component used to illustrate the conversion process is the original **HtmlHelloWorld** that simply printed out a message based on the **hellomsg** attribute. We will use this component to demonstrate how to change to using value expressions. The second component is **HtmlHelloInputMB**. We will use it to show how to convert from a method binding to a method expression.

When considering conversions from JSF 1.1 to 1.2, the main difference with 1.2 is the introduction of the Unified Expression Language into JSP. The Expression Language (EL) used in JSF 1.0 and 1.1 is an extension of the EL first used in the JSP Standard Tag Library (JSTL), and later in JSP versions 1.2 and 2.0. The main user feature brought to the Unified EL by JSF is the notion of deferred vs. immediate expression. (For more details on JSF and EL, refer to Chapter 4.)

The primary impact 1.2 has on the development of custom components is in the area of the JSP tag handler and its tag attributes. The secondary impact is the deprecation of all API methods and classes relating to the JSF 1.1 EL. This includes any methods relating to **ValueBinding** or **MethodBinding**.

Using the **HtmlHelloWorld** component as a first example, let's start with the new TLD declaration required by JSP 2.1. In general, JSF 1.2 and JSP 2.1 use W3C XML Schema to define their config files, and the TLD is no exception. It's important to properly declare the TLD as JSP 2.1. Failure to do so will enable the JSP runtime's backwards compatibility mode and will cause your new style tags to break. The JSP 2.1 TLD declaration must be as follows:

```
<?xml version="1.0" encoding="UTF-8"?>
<taglib xsi:schemaLocation="http://java.sun.com/xml/ns/javaee web-
jsptaglibrary_2_1.xsd" xmlns="http://java.sun.com/xml/ns/javaee"
xmlns:xsi="http://www.w3.org/2001/XMLSchema-instance" version="2.1">
  <description>
    A Custom Tag Library for JSF 1.2 Components exposed to the page
    author via JSP 2.1 tags.
  </description>
  <tlib-version>
    1.0
  </tlib-version>
  <short-name>
    jcr
  </short-name>
  <uri>
    http://jsfcompref.com/demo/components
  </uri>
  <tag>
    <description>Hello World Tag</description>
    <name>helloworld</name>
    <!-- Remaining Tag declaration text omitted -->
     <attribute>
       <description>message method</description>
       <name>hellomsg</name>
       <deferred-value>
         <type>java.lang.String</type>
       </deferred-value>
     </attribute>
  ...
```

Note the use of XML Schema here, instead of DTD. This is required in Java EE 5. (For more on the XML Schema, see Chapter 18.) Also note that the **rtexprvalue** and **type** elements in the **attribute** declaration have been replaced with a single **deferred-value** element, containing the **type**. The **deferred-value** element tells the JSP runtime that the type of the setter in the tag handler must be **javax.el.ValueExpression** and that when the expression evaluates, its type will be **String**.

The type of the **setHellomsg()** method in the **HtmlHelloWorld** tag handler must now be **javax.el.ValueExpression**:

```
private javax.el.ValueExpression hellomsg;
public void setHellomsg(javax.el.ValueExpression hellomsg) {
  this.hellomsg = hellomsg;
}
```

Finally, the **setProperties( )** method must be modified to take the new attribute type into account.

```
protected void setProperties(UIComponent component) {
  // This call to super.setProperties() is VITALLY IMPORTANT!
  // omitting it will cause the component to break entirely!
  super.setProperties(component);

  if (null != hellomsg) {
    component.setValueExpression("hellomsg", hellomsg);
  }
}
```

The same kind of **if-else** clause as in JSF 1.1 is present to determine if the page author used a literal string, such as "hello", or an expression, such as #{param.msg}, as the value of the **hellomsg** attribute. The difference in JSF 1.2 is that no **createValueBinding( )** call is necessary because the JSP runtime hands the tag a **javax.el.ValueExpression** instance in the **setHellomsg( )** method. Also, we are using the **setValueExpression( )** method on the component instead of the **setValueBinding( )** method.

That is all that is required for modifying the original **HtmlHelloWorld** component to be fully 1.2-compliant. Keep in mind that the original 1.1 version will still run in the new 1.2 environment since the 1.2 API is backwards-compatible. However, this example shows the best practice for building the **HtmlHelloWorld** component from scratch for a 1.2 environment.

Let's now return to the **HtmlHelloInputMB** component to show how to revise it to use a method expression for version 1.2.

Modifying the JSF 1.2 HtmlHelloWorldMB Component to Use Method Expressions

The new version of **HtmlHelloWorldMB** will be called **HtmlHelloWorldME**. The name change signifies the key difference from version 1.1 to 1.2 where a **MethodExpression** is used instead of a **MethodBinding**. This conversion is fairly straightforward; let's start with the TLD declaration for the **msgnotify** attribute:

```
<attribute>
  <description>a custom hello message</description>
  <name>msgnotify</name>
  <deferred-method>
    <method-signature>
      void listener(com.jsfcompref.components.component.HtmlHelloInputME,
                    java.lang.String)
    </method-signature>
  </deferred-method>
</attribute>
...
```

Instead of a simple string attribute, we now have a **deferred-method** element. Nested inside we have the required **method-signature** element, which contains the expected signature of the method being pointed to by the method expression. If the signature of the method doesn't match what is specified in the TLD, an error is thrown.

Naturally, the type of the **msgnotify** property in the tag handler for **HtmlHelloInputME** must be changed to be a **MethodExpression**:

```
private javax.el.MethodExpression msgnotify;
public void setMsgnotify(javax.el.MethodExpression msgnotify) {
  this.msgnotify = msgnotify;
}
```

Next, **setProperties()** must be updated accordingly:

```
public void setProperties(UIComponent component) {
  super.setProperties(component);

  // Content omitted

  if (null != msgnotify) {
    ((HtmlHelloInputME)component).setListener(msgnotify);
  }
...
```

Finally, the type of the **listener** property on the **HtmlHelloInputME** component must be changed to be a **MethodExpression** instead of a **MethodBinding** and the **decode()** method updated accordingly.

```
import javax.el.MethodExpression;

public class HtmlHelloInputME extends UIInput {

  public HtmlHelloInputME() {
      setRendererType(null);   // this component renders itself
  }

  // (new) Define a write-only JavaBeans property of type MethodExpression
  private MethodExpression listener = null;

  public void setListener(MethodExpression listener) {
    this.listener = listener;
  }
  // Intervening code omitted
  public void decode(FacesContext context) {
  Map requestMap = context.getExternalContext().getRequestParameterMap();
  String clientId = getClientId(context);

  String submitted_hello_msg =
    ((String) requestMap.get(clientId+":inputfield"));
  setSubmittedValue(submitted_hello_msg);

  // (new) handle the listener attribute, if non-null
  if (null != listener) {
    try {
      Object [] args = {
        this,
        submitted_hello_msg;
      };
```

```
        listener.invoke(context.getELContext(), args);
      }
      // A production quality component would
      // log these messages instead of sending them
      // to standard out.
      catch (javax.el.PropertyNotFoundException pnfe) {
        System.out.println(pnfe.getMessage());
        // Unwrap the exception to see the cause
        if (null != pnfe.getCause()) {
          System.out.println(pnfe.getCause().getMessage());
        }
      }
      catch (javax.el.MethodNotFoundException mnfe) {
        System.out.println("Expecting method that takes a" +
                           "HtmlHelloInputME instance and a String." +
                           "Instead received exception: " +
                           mnfe.getMessage());
      }
      catch (javax.el.ELException ele) {
        System.out.println(ele.getMessage());
        // Unwrap the exception to see the cause
        if (null != ele.getCause()) {
          System.out.println(ele.getCause().getMessage());
        }
      }
    }
  }
}
```

There are two differences between the 1.1 version of **decode()** and this one.

1. The **invoke()** method now takes a **javax.el.ELContext** as its first argument, which must be obtained from the **FacesContext**.

2. The exception types have changed to come from package **javax.el**.

These are the main steps needed to convert a component to run in JSF 1.2. The remainder of the chapter will return to covering JSF 1.1, with JSF 1.2 tips included where appropriate.

Packaging JSF Components into a Self-Contained JAR

The core benefit of JSF components is only realized if they are easy to deploy into an application. By following some simple naming conventions it is possible to produce a single JAR file that can properly describe itself to the JSF runtime. In this case, the only installation necessary is to drop a JAR file into **WEB-INF/lib** and declare the TLD at the top of any JSP page that uses one of the components. To illustrate the process, this section shows how to build a **components.jar** file that will contain all the components presented earlier in the chapter.

Configuration Files

The only configuration files required for a minimal JSF component library are the **faces-config .xml** file for the components, and the TLD file for the taglib that exposes these components to the page author. Note that this particular usage of the **faces-config.xml** file is different than the normal case, where it contains configuration information for the whole application. In the case of a component library, **faces-config.xml** should only contain configuration information for the components themselves, and not require any outside dependencies. These "component-centric" **faces-config.xml** files can indeed contain any valid elements from the **faces-config .xml** syntax, including **phase-listener** and **managed-bean**. This flexibility makes it possible to build very powerful components.

How the JSF Runtime Loads faces-config.xml Files

When a JSF application starts up, the runtime must perform the following steps to load the application configuration resources (**faces-config.xml** files) pertaining to this application. Before doing so, however, it must configure the standard render-kit and any other default behavior such as the **ViewHandler**, **StateManager**, default **ActionListener**, and so on.

1. For each JAR in **WEB-INF/lib**, look inside the JAR and load any **faces-config.xml** files that appear in the **META-INF** directory of that JAR.

EXPERT GROUP INSIGHT   *The order in which these JARs will be encountered by the runtime, and therefore the order in which the* **faces-config.xml** *files will be loaded, is unspecified. An attempt was made to specify this for JSF 1.2, but arriving at a high-quality solution was beyond the scope of the requirements for JSF 1.2. The issue was resolved by reaching an agreement between the Sun and MyFaces implementations to alphabetize the JAR files before they are inspected for their* **META-INF/faces-config.xml** *files.*

2. Look at the value of the servlet initialization parameter called **javax.faces.CONFIG_ FILES**. This value is interpreted to be a comma-separated list of context-relative resource paths that should be loaded as **faces-config.xml** files. Note that the elements of this list can be any resource path, enabling you to name your configuration files anything you like.

3. Look in the Web application for a resource called **/WEB-INF/faces-config.xml**. Load the resource, if present.

If any errors occur anywhere in this process, loading of the files stops and the application does not deploy. If the same definition exists in two different files, either the last one loaded takes precedence, or the contents of the files are merged, depending on the semantics of each individual element. For example, let's say you wanted to override the standard text renderer. You could declare a renderer of type **javax.faces.Text** in the **META-INF/faces-config.xml** file in your **components.jar**. Since the implementation loads the standard render-kit *before* processing the configuration file, the definition would effectively replace the standard one. On the other hand, if you have several files that contain navigation rules listed in the **javax .faces.CONFIG_FILES** initialization parameter, any **navigation-case** elements in those files would be merged in an additive fashion.

How the JSP Runtime Loads TLD Files

Like the **faces-config.xml** files, any JSP tag library descriptor (TLD) files that reside in the **META-INF** directory of any JAR in **WEB-INF/lib** must be loaded by runtime. In JSP this means the tags in the TLD are made available to the JSP pages in the application via the taglib URI given in the TLD. Another useful mechanism is the ability to declare **listener** elements that cause any of the listeners defined by the servlet specification to be loaded and called at the appropriate time in the application's lifecycle. Table 10-1 lists the **Listeners** provided by the servlet specification that can be declared in a TLD.

Listener Name	Description
javax.servlet.ServletRequestEvent	Creates and destroys a **ServletRequest**
javax.servlet.http .HttpSessionListener	Creates and destroys the **HttpSession**
javax.servlet .ServletContextListener	Creates and destroys the **ServletContext**
javax.servlet .ServletRequestAttributeListener	Adds and removes on the attribute set of the **ServletRequest**
javax.servlet .http.HttpSessionAttributeListener	Adds and removes on the attribute set of the **HttpSession**
javax.servlet .ServletContextAttributeListener	Adds and removes on the attribute set of the **ServletContext**

TABLE 10-1 **Listeners** That Can Be Declared in a TLD

Component Classes

Java classes must be packaged in the JAR just as normal—at the top level. Note that this is different than how classes are placed into a WAR file. In the WAR file case, the classes go in **WEB-INF/classes**. In a JSF component JAR, they must go at the normal top level as produced by the standard "jar" command.

Associated Resources

Any non-class resources associated with the components, such as images, stylesheets, and JavaScript files, may be placed anywhere in the JAR, because the responsibility for loading these resources is not covered in the JSF specification. This lack of specificity has left a hole that may be filled in several ways. The MyFaces implementation provides a **Servlet Filter** that must be installed to serve up the static images from the component WAR file. Chapter 11 includes a **PhaseListener** that does exactly this, but for **JavaScript** files.

A JSF Components Package Example: components.jar

This section lists the three elements of a component library—configuration files, Java classes, and associated static resources—by showing how the **components.jar** file is organized. This library contains all the components from this chapter in one easy-to-use package.

Configuration Files

The **META-INF/faces-config.xml** file for **components.jar** is as follows:

```
<?xml version="1.0" encoding="windows-1252"?>
<!DOCTYPE faces-config PUBLIC
    "-//Sun Microsystems, Inc.//DTD JavaServer Faces Config 1.1//EN"
    "http://java.sun.com/dtd/web-facesconfig_1_1.dtd">
<faces-config xmlns="http://java.sun.com/JSF/Configuration">
  <component>
```

```xml
      <component-type>HtmlHelloWorld</component-type>
      <component-class>
        com.jsfcompref.components.component.HtmlHelloWorld
      </component-class>
  </component>
  <component>
      <component-type>HtmlHelloInput</component-type>
      <component-class>
        com.jsfcompref.components.component.HtmlHelloInput
      </component-class>
  </component>
  <component>
      <component-type>HtmlStockInput</component-type>
      <component-class>
        com.jsfcompref.components.component.HtmlStockInput
      </component-class>
  </component>
  <component>
      <component-type>InputDate</component-type>
      <component-class>
        com.jsfcompref.components.component.InputDate
      </component-class>
  </component>
  <render-kit>
      <renderer>
        <component-family>InputDateFamily</component-family>
        <renderer-type>HtmlInputDateRenderer</renderer-type>
        <renderer-class>
          com.jsfcompref.components.renderer.HtmlInputDateRenderer
        </renderer-class>
      </renderer>
      <renderer>
        <component-family>InputDateFamily</component-family>
        <renderer-type>WmlInputDateRenderer</renderer-type>
        <renderer-class>
          com.jsfcompref.components.renderer.WmlInputDateRenderer
        </renderer-class>
      </renderer>
  </render-kit>
  <managed-bean>
    <managed-bean-name>ExampleUser</managed-bean-name>
    <managed-bean-class>com.jsfcompref.example.User</managed-bean-class>
    <managed-bean-scope>request</managed-bean-scope>
  </managed-bean>
  <component>
    <component-type>SvgBarChart</component-type>
    <component-class>
      com.jsfcompref.components.component.SVGBarChart
    </component-class>
  </component>
  <managed-bean>
    <managed-bean-name>ExampleChartData</managed-bean-name>
    <managed-bean-class>
```

```
        com.jsfcompref.example.ChartData
    </managed-bean-class>
    <managed-bean-scope>request</managed-bean-scope>
  </managed-bean>
  <component>
    <component-type>SliderInput</component-type>
    <component-class>
        com.jsfcompref.components.component.SliderInput
    </component-class>
  </component>
  <component>
    <component-type>SliderScript</component-type>
    <component-class>
        com.jsfcompref.components.component.SliderScript
    </component-class>
  </component>
  <component>
    <component-type>HtmlHelloInputMB</component-type>
    <component-class>
        com.jsfcompref.components.component.HtmlHelloInputMB
    </component-class>
  </component>
  <managed-bean>
    <managed-bean-name>ExampleMsgListener</managed-bean-name>
    <managed-bean-class>
        com.jsfcompref.example.MsgListener
    </managed-bean-class>
    <managed-bean-scope>request</managed-bean-scope>
  </managed-bean>
</faces-config>
```

The **META-INF/components.tld** file for **components.jar** is as follows:

```
<?xml version = '1.0' encoding = 'windows-1252'?>
<taglib xmlns:xsi="http://www.w3.org/2001/XMLSchema-instance"
xsi:schemaLocation="http://java.sun.com/xml/ns/j2ee
http://java.sun.com/xml/ns/j2ee/web-jsptaglibrary_2_0.xsd" version="2.0"
xmlns="http://java.sun.com/xml/ns/j2ee">
<description>
  This is the JSP tag library for the custom components chapter.
</description>
<display-name>components</display-name>
<tlib-version>1.0</tlib-version>
<short-name>components</short-name>
<uri>http://jsfcompref.com/demo/components</uri>
  <tag>
    <description>Hello World Tag</description>
    <name>helloworld</name>
    <tag-class>
        com.jsfcompref.components.taglib.HtmlHelloWorldTag
    </tag-class>
    <body-content>empty</body-content>
    <attribute>
      <description>a custom hello message</description>
      <name>hellomsg</name>
```

```xml
        <required>false</required>
        <rtexprvalue>false</rtexprvalue>
        <type>java.lang.String</type>
      </attribute>
      <attribute>
        <name>id</name>
        <required>false</required>
        <rtexprvalue>false</rtexprvalue>
      </attribute>
      <attribute>
        <name>binding</name>
        <required>false</required>
        <rtexprvalue>false</rtexprvalue>
      </attribute>
      <attribute>
        <name>rendered</name>
        <required>false</required>
        <rtexprvalue>false</rtexprvalue>
      </attribute>
    </tag>
    <tag>
      <description>Hello World Input Tag</description>
      <name>helloinput</name>
      <tag-class>
        com.jsfcompref.components.taglib.HtmlHelloInputTag
      </tag-class>
      <body-content>empty</body-content>
      <!-- attributes deleted for brevity -->
    </tag>
    <tag>
      <description>Stock Input Tag</description>
      <name>stockinput</name>
      <tag-class>
        com.jsfcompref.components.taglib.HtmlStockInputTag
      </tag-class>
      <body-content>empty</body-content>
      <!-- attributes deleted for brevity -->
    </tag>
    <tag>
      <description>A simple HTML date picker</description>
      <name>inputdate</name>
      <tag-class>
        com.jsfcompref.components.taglib.HtmlInputDateTag
      </tag-class>
      <body-content>JSP</body-content>
      <!-- attributes deleted for brevity -->
    </tag>
    <tag>
      <description>
        A simple WML date picker
      </description>
      <name>wmlinputdate</name>
      <tag-class>
        com.jsfcompref.components.taglib.WmlInputDateTag
      </tag-class>
      <body-content>JSP</body-content>
```

```
    <!-- attributes deleted for brevity -->
  </tag>
  <tag>
    <description>
      Render SVG Bar Chart.
    </description>
    <name>
      barchart
    </name>
    <tag-class>
      com.jsfcompref.components.taglib.SvgBarChartTag
    </tag-class>
    <body-content>empty</body-content>
    <!-- attributes deleted for brevity -->
  </tag>
  <tag>
    <description>
      render slider
    </description>
    <name>
      slider
    </name>
    <tag-class>
      com.jsfcompref.components.taglib.SliderInputTag
    </tag-class>
    <body-content>empty</body-content>
    <!-- attributes deleted for brevity -->
  </tag>
  <tag>
    <description>
      render slider script include statement
    </description>
    <name>
      sliderscript
    </name>
    <tag-class>
      com.jsfcompref.components.taglib.SliderScriptTag
    </tag-class>
    <body-content>empty</body-content>
  </tag>
  <tag>
    <description>Hello World Input Tag that has Method Binding</description>
    <name>helloinputmb</name>
    <tag-class>
      com.jsfcompref.components.taglib.HtmlHelloInputMBTag
    </tag-class>
    <body-content>empty</body-content>
    <!-- attributes deleted for brevity -->
  </tag>
</taglib>
```

Component Classes

The classes are organized into the following package hierarchy. This grouping of Java classes into **component**, **renderer**, and **taglib** packages is a good practice for extensibility and modularity.

Package com.jsfcompref.components.component
```
HtmlHelloInput
HtmlHelloInputMB
HtmlHelloWorld
HtmlStockInput
InputDate
SVGBarChart
SliderInput
SliderScript
```

Package com.jsfcompref.components.renderer
```
HtmlInputDateRenderer
WmlInputDateRenderer
```

Package com.jsfcompref.components.taglib
```
HtmlHelloInputMBTag
HtmlHelloInputTag
HtmlHelloWorldTag
HtmlInputDateTag
HtmlStockInputTag
SliderInputTag
SliderScriptTag
SvgBarChartTag
WmlInputDateTag
```

Associated Resources

There are several different approaches to packaging any associated resources, such as images, scripts, and stylesheets, into the same JAR as the component classes themselves. This is very desirable from an ease-of-use perspective because it prevents the user from having to place these associated resources in the application server's filesystem in such a way that they are found in the expected place. The MyFaces implementation uses a special Servlet Filter, but this requires extra configuration in the user's **web.xml** file. A better approach is demonstrated in Chapter 11 when we use a **PhaseListener** to serve up the AJAX JavaScript file. This approach can be easily generalized to allow serving all kinds of associated resources, not just JavaScript files.

The Future of JSF Component Metadata

The amount of metadata you can specify with the existing **faces-config.xml** syntax is limited, and not very useful to tools. Two JCP JSRs are now in progress to expand the vocabulary of what metadata can be associated with components. JSR 276, Design-Time Metadata for JavaServer Faces Components, which was spearheaded by Oracle and supported by a majority of JSF IDE vendors, will define an XML Schema that extends the **faces-config.xml** syntax with additional information to help component authors ensure that the components they develop will be useful inside any conformant IDE. It does so by defining static metadata elements that go beyond the minimal set defined in JSF. JSR 273, Design-Time API for JavaBeans, specifies dynamic behavior for components in design-time.

You can think of this as the dynamic counterpart to the work being done in JSR 276. In addition to Oracle JDeveloper, it is hoped that Studio Creator, NetBeans, Eclipse, JetBrains, Borland, and all other Java/JSF IDEs will implement these JSRs when final to make life easier for JSF component developers. This would be an improvement over the current situation, where some tools have begun to create their own proprietary syntax for improving the design-time experience with JSF components.

Building AJAX JSF Components

The term *AJAX* has been bandied about the blogosphere since early 2005, though the technology behind the term is nothing new. It was coined by Mr. Jesse James Garrett of the software consulting firm AdaptivePath. AJAX, which is short for Asynchronous JavaScript and XML, describes a set of practices for building Web applications that result in highly responsive applications that feel more like a "rich client" application instead of a traditional Web application. It is now becoming the technology of choice for a new generation of rich client JSF components that offer the page author unsurpassed power without increasing development complexity. At the same time, it provides a superior, rich client experience for the end user. It is a technology that no JSF developer can afford to ignore.

Introduction to AJAX

AJAX is an acronym for Asynchronous JavaScript and **XMLHttpRequest**. The **XMLHttpRequest** object is a de facto standard object provided by browser-based JavaScript implementations, and when used in an asynchronous fashion it allows the page author to communicate with the Web server in the background of the page, without giving the user any visual cue that this communication is occurring. The Web browser's "spinner" does not spin, the hourglass mouse pointer does not appear, and the browser does not "block" in any way. Using the **XMLHttpRequest** in concert with standard JavaScript and DOM APIs allows the page author to dynamically update the page with arbitrary server-supplied data.

The first implementation of an API for background-based asynchronous communication with the server came from Microsoft in the form of their **XMLHTTP** ActiveX object. This API was later emulated in a compatible fashion by Netscape and other browsers, enabling users to write Web applications that use **XMLHttpRequest** and still run on a variety of browsers while minimizing the amount of browser-dependent code required. It has taken a long time to arrive at the point where most users can be assumed to have a browser capable of AJAX, but as of this writing it's a safe bet.

Even though these technologies had been around for several years their widespread use in Web applications didn't catch on until Google showed the world how powerful a first-class application of AJAX practices can be. The introduction in 2004 of Google's e-mail service, which makes heavy use of **XMLHttpRequest** techniques, inspired a renaissance of interest in JavaScript that ultimately led to what people now call AJAX. Google's map service also leverages AJAX techniques to good effect. As of this writing, the field of innovation is still wide open and the best practices have yet to fully emerge.

Why All the Interest in AJAX?

The software industry has always grappled with the problem of maintenance costs, particularly in large enterprises where huge numbers of users need to have current software updates, bug fixes, and other changes. The problem wasn't so bad in the mainframe days, but with the advent of the PC and the office LAN, things got much worse. Each computing node had its own user-configurable and updateable software stack. Rolling out upgrades to all users was a complex and risky problem. Solving this problem is the main reason for the popularity of Web-deployed applications. Web applications delivered on the promise of downloadable applications that effectively maintained no state information in the client. This enabled administrators to easily upgrade the software with much less risk of downtime for all users.

As shown in the history lesson in Chapter 1, Web applications have been developing in several dimensions. Pertinent to this discussion is the degree to which a Web application resembles a traditional, non-browser-based application in terms of responsiveness and richness of experience. Applets address this problem quite well, but have failed, for a number of technical and non-technical reasons, to achieve widespread adoption. JavaWebStart, a technology that enables distributing, upgrading, and versioning Java applications via the Web, also addresses this problem very well and its use has been steadily growing. However, a JavaWebStart application doesn't run inside the confines of a browser, and many users and IT managers insist that their applications run in a browser. Thus, every Web application framework aspires to be as rich as possible. As Google and others have shown, AJAX makes it possible to bring the Web application experience a lot closer to the rich client experience.

Why JSF and AJAX Are a Perfect Match

As you will see later in this chapter, employing AJAX-only practices by hand is very tricky and error prone, and can be very frustrating for Web developers or page authors. It's particularly difficult dealing with browser quirks to achieve a solution that will run for as many users as possible. For example, the very way in which you obtain a reference to an **XMLHttpRequest** object differs across different browsers, even though the API is the same once you have it. The powerful encapsulation mechanism offered by the Faces component and event model is ideally suited to allow a component developer to provide AJAX-enabled (or *AJAXian*) components that are no more difficult to use than any other normal Faces component.

The remainder of this chapter will cover the fundamentals of AJAX APIs, build on the earlier material of creating custom components by showing how to bring AJAX practices to your component development, review two AJAX JSF component examples, and close with some tips and tricks to ease the pain of developing an AJAXian Faces component. Through the course of covering this material, you will see a fair amount of JavaScript. A thorough treatment of JavaScript is beyond the scope of this book, but an excellent reference is *JavaScript: The Complete Reference, Second Edition* by Thomas Powell (McGraw-Hill, 2004).

AJAX Under the Hood

Before building AJAX-enabled JSF components, it is important to fully understand the core AJAX architecture involved in an AJAX client-server transaction. In its simplest form, AJAX is possible when these two core technologies are present:

- A JavaScript-enabled browser that supports either **XMLHTTP** or **XMLHttpRequest** objects
- An HTTP server technology that can respond in XML or any markup

Since the popular browsers support JavaScript and the necessary **XMLHTTP** request objects and almost any Web server technology can generate XML (or any markup), the core AJAX technology is already widely available. The architecture for an AJAX-only (no JSF involved) application using these technologies is depicted in Figure 11-1.

As you can see in Figure 11-1, an AJAX application in its simplest form is essentially a standard HTML user interface with JavaScript functions to interact with an HTTP server that can generate XML dynamically. Any dynamic Web technology ranging from CGI or servlets to JavaServer Faces, as we'll discuss later, can serve as a server-side AJAX technology. In the user interface, you'll find an HTML page with elements such as an input field, a button, or anything else that can be linked to JavaScript that can communicate via AJAX to a Web server. For example, a button could fire a JavaScript function when pressed and it in turn issues an AJAX request for data. An even more subtle usage would eliminate the button altogether: simply typing in an input field could fire a JavaScript function. This is possible using the JavaScript **onkeyup** event. For example, the input field **searchField** could call a JavaScript function **lookup()** when an **onkeyup** event occurs (i.e., during typing), as shown here:

```
<input type="text" id="searchField" size="20"
       onkeyup="lookup('searchField');">
```

The **lookup()** function could then make an AJAX request for data related to the value in the input field. As you'll see later in the chapter, both of the AJAX examples operate exactly in this fashion where text from an input field is sent to an AJAX-enabled server and a response is then provided to the client without the need for a complete page refresh.

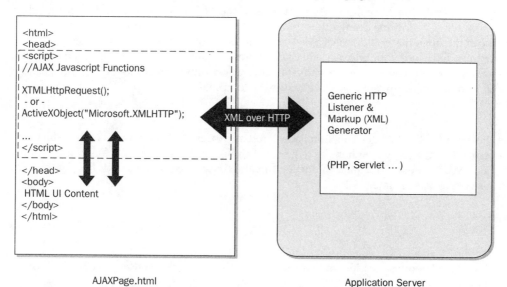

AJAXPage.html   Application Server

FIGURE 11-1   The core AJAX architecture

In addition to responding to user interface interactions like typing or clicking a button, AJAX JavaScript functions can operate independently on their own by using timers—for example, if you want a Web form to have the ability to autosave itself after a certain amount of time has passed.

How to Issue an XML HTTP Request

Now that you know how AJAX JavaScript code can be invoked, let's examine the actual JavaScript code that can issue an XML HTTP request. The following code snippet allows both major browser families (Internet Explorer and Mozilla/Safari) to instantiate respective browser-compatible **XMLHttpRequest** objects, which can then be used to communicate with an AJAX server.

```
if (window.XMLHttpRequest) {
  req = new XMLHttpRequest();
}
else if (window.ActiveXObject) {
  req = new ActiveXObject("Microsoft.XMLHTTP");
}
```

Once the object is instantiated, it can be manipulated in exactly the same manner, regardless of browser type, since it has compatible methods. (A full list of the **XMLHttpRequest** methods and properties is provided in the "AJAX XMLHttpRequest Reference" section at the end of the chapter.)

To initialize a connection to a server, the **open** method is used:

```
req.open("GET", url, true);
```

The first argument is the HTTP method (GET or POST). The second argument is the URL of the server (or form action if using a POST), and the third argument, when **true,** denotes whether the call should be made asynchronously (the "A" in AJAX) or not. This means that the browser can continue doing other things while the request is being fulfilled. A **false** value in the **open** method denotes a non-asynchronous or serial processing. This is not recommended, since your browser will cease operations until the response has been returned.

For asynchronous calls, an **onreadystatechange** call can be made to register a *callback function* that will be invoked once the request is complete:

```
req.onreadystatechange = processXMLResponse;
```

In this example the callback function is declared as **processXMLResponse()**. This function is invoked by the browser when the request is fulfilled and is responsible for taking action on the XML response. The callback function can also be declared inline in the **onreadystatechange** statement:

```
req.onreadystatechange = processXMLResponse() {
  // process request
};
```

Any HTTP request header content can be specified using **req.setRequestHeader.** For example:

```
req.setRequestHeader("Cookie", "someKey=true");
```

Once the **XMLHttpRequest** object (**req**) has been fully initialized, initiating a call to the server can be done using **send()**:

```
req.send(null);
```

For GET requests, a **null** value or empty string (**""**) is used. POST requests contain a string argument with form data. They also require the Content-Type to be set in the header of the request. The following lines show how to perform an AJAX POST to an AJAX server (**/ajaxserver**), with form parameters specified in the **send** call.

```
req.open("POST", "/ajaxserver", true);
req.setRequestHeader("Content-Type", "application/x-www-form-urlencoded";
req.send("name=scott&email=stiger@foocorp.com");
```

The callback function **processXMLResponse** has some code to make sure the request has not errored out. This is accomplished by checking the **readyState** as well as the overall **status** of the HTTP request. (A **readystate** of **4** means the **XMLHttpRequest** is complete and a **status** of **200** means it was a success (as opposed to **404,** etc.).)

```
function processXMLResponse() {
  if (xmlreq.readyState == 4) {
    if (xmlreq.status == 200) {
      // Process the XML response...
    }
  }
}
```

When no error conditions have been encountered, processing the XML response is done using standard JavaScript DOM methods. For example, to extract the employee name, "Joe", from the incoming XML stream:

```
<employee>
  Joe
</employee>
```

one can use **req.responseXML**:

```
var name = req.responseXML.getElementsByTagName("employee")[0];
```

Parsing more complex XML involves iterating through the XML elements using code such as:

```
var elements = req.responseXML.getElementsByTagName("employee");
for (i=0;i<elements.length;i++) {
  for (j=0;j<elements[i].childNodes.length;j++) {
    var ElementData =  elements[i].childNodes[j].firstChild.nodeValue;
  }
}
```

Using XMLHttpRequest with HTML

It should also be stated that the XML response obtained through the **XMLHttpRequest** object need not always be well-formed and valid. This means that the AJAX server can send over HTML content directly to the client. JavaScript code can then retrieve the HTML content by using the **req.responseText** method/property, which simply retrieves the content as a string. The HTML string text can then be used in whatever fashion to alter the page. For example, an HTML stream of:

```
<h3>Hello there!</h3>
<p> This is <cTypeface:Bold>HTML</b></p>
```

could be retrieved into a string using:

```
var HTMLcontent = req.responseText;
```

and then added to a specific **DIV** tag with **id="div1"**.

```
document.getElementById("div1").innerHTML += HTMLcontent;
```

Having stepped through the basics of an AJAX transaction, let's consider a first AJAX example: **DirectorySearch**. This example will first be presented as a pure AJAX-only example without Faces technology. Later you'll see how to turn this and other AJAX examples into AJAX-enabled JSF components, making them much easier to use from a page author's perspective.

DirectorySearch—A First AJAX Example Without JSF

Consider the following **DirectorySearch** example application where the user is presented with a single input text field. When the user begins typing characters into the field, a list of corresponding matches from a fictitious corporation's employee directory appears, as shown in Figure 11-2.

As the user continues typing, the list decreases in size until a best match is found, as depicted in Figure 11-3. The user doesn't even have to click on a Submit button because the page updates itself with the closest matches based on the input so far. This all occurs without requiring a traditional page submission and a complete refresh cycle.

The Architecture of the AJAX(-Only) DirectorySearch

The **DirectorySearch** AJAX example consists of the following elements:

- An HTML page, **directory.html**, that contains:
  - An input text field
  - JavaScript functions that react to the characters entered and invoke an AJAX request, then update the UI with data from the response
- A Java servlet that responds to the AJAX request by sending XML responses

Each is examined next.

The HTML Page

As mentioned earlier in the chapter, the AJAX request is initiated when new text is entered into the input field. This occurs because the input field in the HTML page has an **onkeyup** attribute set with a reference to a JavaScript **lookup()** function.

```
<input type="text" id="searchField" size="20"
     onkeyup="lookup('searchField');">
```

Notice the ID of **searchField** is passed to the **lookup()** function, which then uses this to determine the current value of the field in the callback function.

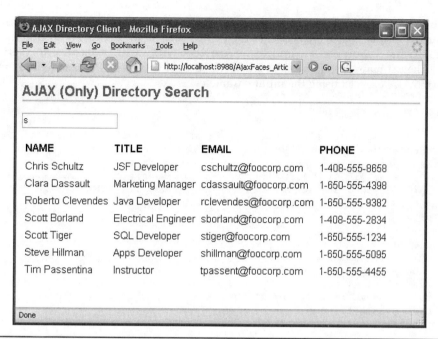

FIGURE 11-2   Entering a character into the AJAX **DirectorySearch**

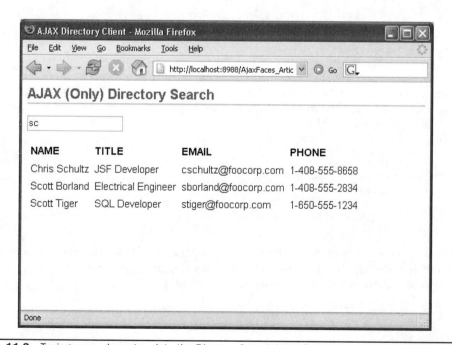

FIGURE 11-3   Typing more characters into the **DirectorySearch** input field

The JavaScript **lookup()** function along with the other functions are embedded inside of a pair of **<script>** tags in the header of the HTML page. In the **lookup()** function shown next, notice that its purpose is to initiate the AJAX call with a URL of **ajaxdirectoryservice**, which is the **url-mapping** of the AJAX servlet. It passes the value of the **searchField** input field to the AJAX servlet using the **input** parameter:

```
<script type="text/JavaScript">

// Note that using global variables to store such things as the
// XMLHttpRequest instance is not a good idea in a production
// environment.  This is because multiple requests from the
// same browser window will overwrite the previously stored value.
// One production grade solution is to use JavaScript "closures",
// which are beyond the scope of this book.
var req;
var writeloc;

function lookup(field) {
  writeloc = field + ":table";
  var searchField = document.getElementById(field);
  var url = "ajaxdirectoryservice?input=" + searchField.value;
  if (window.XMLHttpRequest) {
    req = new XMLHttpRequest();
  }
  else if (window.ActiveXObject) {
    req = new ActiveXObject("Microsoft.XMLHTTP");
  }
  req.open("GET", url, true);
  req.onreadystatechange = processXMLResponse;
  req.send(null);
}
```

Once the request is initiated in asynchronous mode, the **processXMLResponse()** callback function, shown next, will be invoked when the request is complete. This function merely checks to see that the request from the servlet completed successfully and is sent to a data rendering function, **renderTable()**.

```
function processXMLResponse() {
  if (req.readyState == 4) {
    if (req.status == 200) {
      renderTable();
    }
  }
}
```

The data retrieved from the servlet in this example is pure XML and is based on the input text that was supplied to it. For example, if a string of "sc" is sent to the servlet, it will respond with the following matching content in XML:

```
<?xml version = '1.0'?>
<directory>
    <employee>
        <NAME>Chris Schultz</NAME>
        <TITLE>JSF Developer</TITLE>
```

```
        <EMAIL>cschultz@foocorp.com</EMAIL>
        <PHONE>1-408-555-8658</PHONE>
    </employee>
    <employee>
        <NAME>Scott Borland</NAME>
        <TITLE>Electrical Engineer</TITLE>
        <EMAIL>sborland@foocorp.com</EMAIL>
        <PHONE>1-408-555-2834</PHONE>
    </employee>
</directory>
```

The **renderTable()** JavaScript function is as follows:

```
function renderTable()
  {
    xmlDoc = req.responseXML;
    var elements = xmlDoc.getElementsByTagName('employee');
    var table = document.createElement('table');
    table.setAttribute('cellPadding',3);
    table.setAttribute('border',0);
    var tbody = document.createElement('tbody');
    table.appendChild(tbody);
    var h_row = document.createElement('tr');

    for (i=0;i<elements[0].childNodes.length;i++) {
      if (elements[0].childNodes[i].nodeType != 1) continue;
      var t_header = document.createElement('th');
      var headerData =
document.createTextNode(elements[0].childNodes[i].nodeName);
        t_header.appendChild(headerData);
        h_row.appendChild(t_header);
    }
    tbody.appendChild(h_row);

    for (i=0;i<elements.length;i++) {
      var t_row = document.createElement('tr');
      for (j=0;j<elements[i].childNodes.length;j++) {
        if (elements[i].childNodes[j].nodeType != 1) continue;
        var td = document.createElement('td');
        var tdData =
document.createTextNode(elements[i].childNodes[j].firstChild.nodeValue);
        td.appendChild(tdData);
        t_row.appendChild(td);
      }
      tbody.appendChild(t_row);
    }

    // Clear previous table
    var element = document.getElementById(writeloc);
    while(element.hasChildNodes())
      element.removeChild(element.firstChild);

    // Append new table
    document.getElementById(writeloc).appendChild(table);
}
```

The code may seem a bit cryptic, but essentially it just loops through the XML data, constructs a new HTML table with the data in it, and appends it to a specified write location, **writeloc**, which is a DIV defined just below the input text field. The DIV that serves as the write location **writeloc** is defined as:

```
<div id="searchField:table"></div>
```

Also recall that **writeloc** was defined in the **lookup()** function as a concatenation of the **field** name provided and **:table**:

```
writeloc = field + ":table";
```

Before writing the new HTML table, however, the **renderTable()** function removes the old HTML results table just before it appends the new one. The DIV that serves as the write location **writeloc** is defined as:

```
<div id="searchField:table"></div>
```

The AJAXDirectory Servlet

The servlet that responds to the request and processes the incoming **input** parameter is fairly simple and is displayed next.

```
package com.jsfcompref.ajax.servlet;
public class AjaxDirectoryService extends HttpServlet {
  public void init(ServletConfig config) throws ServletException {
    super.init(config);
  }
  public void doGet(HttpServletRequest request,
                    HttpServletResponse response) throws ServletException,
                                    IOException {
    response.setContentType("text/xml");
    response.setHeader("Cache-Control", "no-cache");

    XmlGenerator myXmlGenerator =
      new XmlGenerator(request.getParameter("input"));

    String xmlout = myXmlGenerator.getXmlResponse();
    PrintWriter out = response.getWriter();
    out.write(xmlout);
    out.close();
  }
}
```

Aside from being a typical **HTTPServlet**, the key things to notice are that the content type is set to **text/xml** and a header parameter, **Cache-Control**, is set to **no-cache**. This prevents any of the XML data from being cached by the browser. Notice also the **XMLGenerator** class. This is a custom class that does the XML generation. It can use any technology as long as it can accept a string argument and return an XML data stream as a query result. XPath or XQuery could be used to process these queries. XML-enabled databases such as Oracle and its XML SQL utility can also be used to generate the query response. Since the code varies on how to generate an XML response based on a query string, you can decide how to best perform this task. You may also want to look into the XQuare open source project (formerly known as XQuark), which provides an XML query (XQuery) engine equally across the leading database technologies. (For more information on XQuare, see **http://xquare.objectweb.org/**.)

What's Wrong with the AJAX-Only Version of DirectorySearch?

Although fully functional, there is a potential problem with the architecture of the pure
AJAX-only **DirectorySearch** example application. It forces the page author to bear full
responsibility for making the AJAX transaction work because the AJAX plumbing is
manually constructed using JavaScript in the HTML client. Because of the complexities
involved, this is a task that could overburden a typical page author or Web designer,
especially if the overall user interface is considerably larger. Considering the inherent
difficulties in debugging JavaScript code, this could prove to be a painful task for even the
most technically experienced page author or Web designer. Another complexity that must
be faced is the possibility of having multiple AJAX requests and responses going on in the
page at the same time. It's possible that multiple different servlets would be needed to
handle all the different kinds of responses. Without careful planning, extremely cryptic
conditions can arise that are very difficult to debug.

The ideal solution would be to offer an AJAX-enabled **DirectorySearch** custom JSF
component that the page author can simply drop onto a page and it just works. In this
manner, the page author would not have to code a single line of JavaScript as the JSF
component assumes this responsibility entirely.

Building AJAX-Enabled JSF Components

Most of the remainder of the chapter is devoted to describing how to build AJAX-enabled
JSF components, which provide an extremely easy development experience for the page
author. We will begin by describing the high-level AJAX elements needed when using JSF.

The High-Level Elements of an AJAX System in JSF

Figure 11-4 shows the elements of an AJAX system using JSF and how they work together
during an AJAX transaction. The AJAX JavaScript code (Element 1) converts user interactions
with the rendered UI of the AJAX UI component (Element 2) into parameters on the
XMLHttpRequest and sends them to an AJAX processing server component (Element 3).
The AJAX processing server component can be either independent of the JSF application,
such as with a generic servlet, or integrated into the JSF application, but its job remains the
same: return an AJAX response to the client's AJAX request. The AJAX script, which made
the request, is then responsible for interpreting the AJAX response and updating the
browser page accordingly.

The AJAX Script in the Browser

Similar to the non-JSF AJAX architecture, JavaScript client code is required for interaction
with the AJAX server object. The key difference from the non-JSF AJAX approach is
that the JSF component or application is now entirely responsible for rendering the
script into the browser, thus drastically simplifying AJAX development for the page
author. From the component developer's perspective, however, the key challenge is
implementing a way to render the JavaScript to the client. In HTML there are two
ways the script can be loaded into the browser. The first is inline—that is within the
body of **<script>** tags.

```
<script type="text/JavaScript">
  // This is an inline script.
  document.write("hello world");
</script>
```

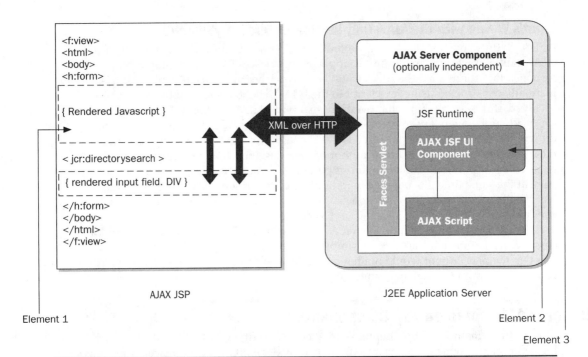

FIGURE 11-4 The high-level elements of an AJAX system in JSF

The second way is by reference—using the **<script>** tag with a **src** attribute that allows the browser to download the script as a separate file:

```
<script type="text/JavaScript" src="ajaxScript.js"></script>
```

NOTE *When using the* **src** *attribute and omitting the nested script content, the closing* **</script>** *tag is optional, but it's a good practice to keep your markup well-formed to ease a possible future transition to XHTML or other XML formats.*

There are pros and cons to both approaches. For example, the latter approach avoids the need to redeploy the application when any JavaScript changes are done since they reside in a **.js** file. Also, most commonly available JavaScript libraries, such as DOJO and Prototype, are distributed in JavaScript files. Loading these by reference allows the browser to store the script content in the browser cache. On the other hand, the former approach is best when custom JavaScript needs to be rendered dynamically with values only available at runtime (such as with the slider example in Chapter 10).

The AJAX JSF examples later in the chapter use both approaches. However, they both also completely hide the JavaScript code from the page author.

The AJAX UI Component

The **UIComponent** subclass plays a key role in an AJAX JSF system. During encoding, this component renders the UI elements for the component itself, such as buttons or input fields. These rendered UI elements provide a way for the end user to trigger any AJAX transactions. In addition to the visible elements initially rendered, the UI component may also render an empty placeholder location such as with a **<DIV>** tag, which can later be used as a writeable location for dynamic content that is generated as a result of the AJAX transactions. Finally, the UI component also renders the AJAX JavaScript, which can be either the full source inline or a **<script>** tag with the **src** attribute as a URL reference to the JavaScript file.

The AJAX Processing Server Component

The last element of the AJAX JSF system is the AJAX Processing Server Component. This element receives AJAX requests from the browser and returns XML responses. An AJAX Faces server component can be implemented as either:

- A fully independent HTTP server object such as a generic servlet, or
- An AJAX server object integrated into the JSF application. This can either be integrated into the AJAX component's **decode()** method or be component-independent but still reside in the JSF application, such as within a **PhaseListener**.

In the **SpellCheckTextArea** example later in the chapter, the **decode()** method in the component serves as the AJAX server component. The other AJAX JSF example, **DirectorySearch**, uses either the **decode()** method or a **PhaseListener** to serve as the AJAX server component.

JSF 1.2 TIP *JSF 1.2 introduced a new feature to define alternate JSF lifecycles specifically for handling AJAX requests. Please see Chapter 12 for details on building a custom lifecycle. Once you have done so, you can simply use an **<init-param>** element in your **web.xml** to identify it as a JSF lifecycle instance to the **FacesServlet**.*

```
<servlet>
  <servlet-name>ajax</servlet-name>
  <servlet-class>javax.faces.webapp.FacesServlet</servlet-class>
  <init-param>
    <param-name>javax.faces.LIFECYCLE_ID</param-name>
    <param-value>com.foo.lifecycle.AJAX_LIFECYCLE_ID</param-value>
  </init-param>
</servlet>
<servlet-mapping>
  <servlet-name>ajax</servlet-name>
  <url-pattern>/faces/*</url-pattern>
</servlet-mapping>
```

*If you have properly configured your custom **LifecycleFactory** as described in Chapter 12, your custom lifecycle will be used instead of the default lifecycle. The details of an AJAX-aware JSF lifecycle are beyond the scope of this chapter, but such an approach is used in the JavaServer Faces Technology Extensions project on java.net: **https://jsf-extensions.dev.java.net/**.*

An AJAX DirectorySearch JSF Component

Let's now convert the original non-JSF AJAX **DirectorySearch** example shown earlier to a JSF UI component. The new JSF version of **DirectorySearch** eliminates the inherent JavaScript complexities that the page author had to deal with earlier. With this new version, the page author simply drops the **<jcr:directorysearch>** tag onto the JSP page to use the component, as shown here:

```
<jcr:directorysearch border="0" />
```

At runtime, the **DirectorySearch** UI component performs its job of providing a directory lookup just like the AJAX-only version. The **DirectorySearch** JSF component also provides attributes that are passed on to the underlying JavaScript. This affords the page author a high degree of control over the component's behavior without having to edit any JavaScript code. For example, the same component can have a different background:

```
<jcr:directorysearch border="0" tablebgcolor="#99EEFF" />
```

This would generate a **DirectorySearch** component with a light blue background.

The AJAX JSF DirectorySearch Architecture

The architecture of the JSF-enabled **DirectorySearch** as depicted in Figure 11-5 is similar to the non-JSF AJAX example from before, except that the JSF component performs the task of rendering the JavaScript directly into the HTML (JSP) page. The JavaScript code then initiates an **XMLHttpRequest** either to the same AJAX servlet that was used before, or to an AJAX server component that essentially contains the same XML generation code that was used in the servlet, but instead integrated into the JSF application. Recall that the AJAX server object could be implemented as a JSF **PhaseListener** or in the **decode()** method of the JSF component itself. Using the existing non-JSF AJAX servlet would be the easiest architecture if your AJAX servlet does not need to interact much with your JSF application data; however, if you want to take advantage of JSF features such as the Expression Language and Managed Beans when building your AJAX server object, it is best to place the code inside the JSF application.

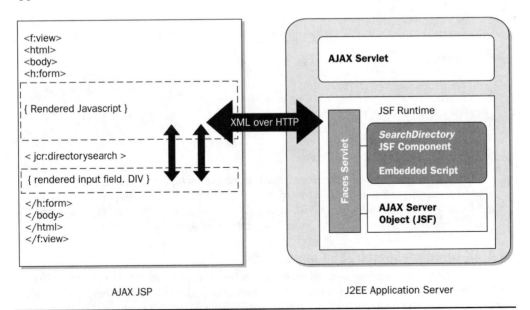

FIGURE 11-5 The AJAX-enabled JSF **DirectorySearch** architecture

The AJAX Script Element for the DirectorySearch Example

For this example, embedding JavaScript inside a JSF component's **encode()** method(s) using the **ResponseWriter** is sufficient. This approach was used previously in the **Slider** and **BarChart** examples of Chapter 10.

The code for rendering the AJAX script for **DirectorySearch** is invoked via the **encodeAjaxJavaScript()** method in the component's **encodeBegin()** method, shown here:

```
public void encodeBegin(FacesContext context) throws IOException  {
  String clientId = getClientId(context);
  encodeAjaxJavascript(context);
  encodeInputField(context, clientId);
}
```

The content of **encodeAjaxJavaScript()** is

```
private void encodeAjaxJavascript(FacesContext context)
throws IOException  {
  String border = (String)getAttributes().get("border");
  String tablebgcolor = (String)getAttributes().get("tablebgcolor");
  // render Ajax-enabled Javascript only once per page
  if (!jsRenderedFlag(context)) {
    // if not rendered yet, go ahead and do it
    ResponseWriter writer = context.getResponseWriter();
    writer.startElement("script", this);
    writer.writeAttribute("type", "text/javascript", null);
    renderLookupFunction(writer);
    render_processXML_function(writer);
    render_renderTable_function(writer, border, tablebgcolor);
    writer.endElement("script");
  }
}
```

The code for **renderLookupFunction()**, which actually generates the JavaScript function **lookup()** in the browser, is presented below in an abbreviated fashion:

```
private void  renderLookupFunction(ResponseWriter writer)
  throws IOException  {
    writer.write("function lookup(field) {\n" +
      "writeloc = field + \":table\";\n" +
      "var searchField = document.getElementById(field);\n" +
      // Remainder of the ResponseWriter output omitted.
      "}\n" );
}
```

The sources for the remaining JavaScript render methods are omitted but are similar to the **renderLookupFunction()** and simply use the **ResponseWriter** to render JavaScript code.

The AJAX UI Component for the DirectorySearch Example

In addition to rendering the AJAX script, the component also renders the core UI element(s) of the component. For the **DirectorySearch** example this is done by using the **encodeInputField()** method, which is also in the component's **encodeBegin()** method.

```
encodeInputField(context, clientId);
```

The UI for **DirectorySearch** is very basic because it is just an input field along with a **<DIV>**, which will serve as the write location for the results from the AJAX transaction.

```
public void encodeInputField(FacesContext context, String clientId)
throws IOException  {
  // render a standard HTML input field along with a DIV
  ResponseWriter writer = context.getResponseWriter();
  writer.startElement("p", this);
  writer.startElement("input", this);
  writer.writeAttribute("type", "text", null);
  writer.writeAttribute("id", clientId, "clientId");
  writer.writeAttribute("size", "20", null);
  writer.writeAttribute("onkeyup", "lookup('" + clientId + "');", null);
  writer.endElement("input");
  writer.endElement("p");
  writer.startElement("div", this);
  writer.writeAttribute("id", clientId + ":table", null);
  writer.endElement("div");
  }
```

Notice that the **lookup()** JavaScript function is included as an attribute of the input field.

The AJAX Server Component for the DirectorySearch Example

As an alternative to using an external servlet to serve as the AJAX server component, the **DirectorySearch** example will embed this functionality inside the component's **decode()** method, as shown here.

```
public void decode(FacesContext context) {
    Map requestMap = context.getExternalContext().getRequestMap();
  HttpServletResponse response = (HttpServletResponse)
    context.getExternalContext().getResponse();
  HttpServletRequest request = (HttpServletRequest)
    context.getExternalContext().getRequest();

  if (requestMap.containsKey("ajaxreq")) {
  // set the header information for the response
  response.setContentType("text/xml");
  response.setHeader("Cache-Control", "no-cache");
  response.setCharacterEncoding("UTF-8");

  try {

    XmlGenerator myXmlGenerator = new
      XmlGenerator(request.getParameter("input"));
    String xmlout = myXmlGenerator.getXmlResponse();
    response.getWriter().write(xmlout);
    response.getWriter().close();
  } catch (IOException e) {
      e.printStackTrace();
    }
  context.responseComplete();
  }
  // Place non-AJAX decode code here…
  }
```

The first thing to notice about this **decode()** method is the code to check if a certain "ajaxreq" (AJAX Request) is one of the request parameters:

```
if (null != request.getParameter("ajaxreq")) {
```

This check allows the **decode()** method to distinguish between AJAX requests (**XMLHttpRequest**) and regular page requests. This approach requires that the JavaScript function making this request must supply this parameter. Another very important request parameter requirement is that the form name must also be passed as a parameter to the JSF application. If this value if not passed, the JSF application will interpret the request as a non-post-back request and the **decode()** method will not be entered. Therefore, the resulting response will be a non-AJAX, complete HTML page. The form name value can be obtained on the client by using **window.document.forms[0].id**.

NOTE *This actually just retrieves the ID of the first form in the page, but this is sufficient to allow the JSF runtime to identify it as a non-post-back request.*

Placing the **formName** along with the **ajaxreq** parameter can be combined with the following JavaScript client code:

```
var formdata = "formName=" + window.document.forms[0].id + "&ajaxreq=true";
```

The **formdata** data is then passed in the **XmlHttpRequest's send()** call with **req .send(formdata)**. Also, because submitting a form always issues a post-back, a different URL (such as **ajaxdirectoryservice**) is not needed for the form's action. Another important bit of information that is often passed as a set of parameters is the current status of the components in the page, or *view state*. This is only needed when the AJAX server component needs access to the UI components of the original view to which the user is now posting back. The next AJAX JSF example in the chapter does, however, show how to do this. The other key thing to notice in the **decode()** method example is the usage of the **HttpServletResponse.getWriter()** method to write the XML directly to the response. Another approach would be to create a custom **ResponseWriter** that is suitable for writing XML.

The final thing to notice is that once the content for the request has been fulfilled, the JSF lifecycle can complete the response immediately so as not to render an entire page by using **context.responseComplete()**.

The other task of the AJAX **DirectorySearch** JSF component is to render the same JavaScript code that was hard-coded directly into the HTML page in the original AJAX-only version. This is accomplished by using the **ResponseWriter** object in the component's **encode()** method. Since this portion is trivial, it is not included in the text but is available on the web site.

In addition to the rendering code, the only remaining sub-component is the JSP tag handler that exposes the UI component to the JSP page. This is also a fairly straightforward step and its code is also available on the web site.

Our next AJAX JSF component example builds on the concepts shown in the **DirectorySearch** example but also shows alternative methods for rendering JavaScript on the client as well as how to process AJAX requests.

An AJAX SpellCheck JSF Component

Similar to the previous AJAX example, this next example falls in line with the guiding philosophy in our usage of AJAX, which is to present to the page author the simplest possible usage model. It therefore also hides all of the complexity of asynchronous JavaScript code behind a Faces component. Our next AJAX example component, **SpellCheckTextArea**, extends **HtmlInputTextArea** and provides a simple AJAX-enabled spell-checking facility. The JSP usage for this is also very simple:

```
<jcr:spellCheckTextArea cols="30" rows="15" value="#{user.interests}" />
```

This component renders a spell-checking panel beneath an HTML **textarea** input field, and allows the user to check the spelling of their text before submitting. As before, the user is not required to put any **<script>** tags anywhere in the page to use this component. When the user presses the Next button (as shown in Figure 11-6), an asynchronous request is made to the server, which causes a **MethodBinding** to be called. This **MethodBinding** points to a method that takes a string and returns an array of suggested spellings. For the sake of simplicity, **<jcr:spellCheckTextArea>** doesn't do anything fancy to highlight the incorrect word or dynamically replace it with the chosen suggestion. This feature has nothing to do with Faces and therefore is left as an exercise for the reader. Rather, the UI simply shows the current misspelled word and lists the suggestions in a simple table, as shown in Figure 11-6.

Similar to the **DirectorySearch** example, the **SpellCheckTextArea** example also shows the power of combining Faces with AJAX techniques while delivering the same ease of development to the page author. We'll now examine the high-level AJAX JSF elements of the **SpellCheckTextArea** example in more detail.

The AJAX Script Element for the SpellCheckTextArea Example

In contrast to rendering AJAX script directly into the page from the component's **encode()** methods, the **SpellCheckTextArea** example uses a **PhaseListener** to deliver the AJAX script instead. In this example, the delivered script is just a reference to an external JavaScript file. It is also conditionally rendered such that only the first usage of the **SpellCheckTextArea**

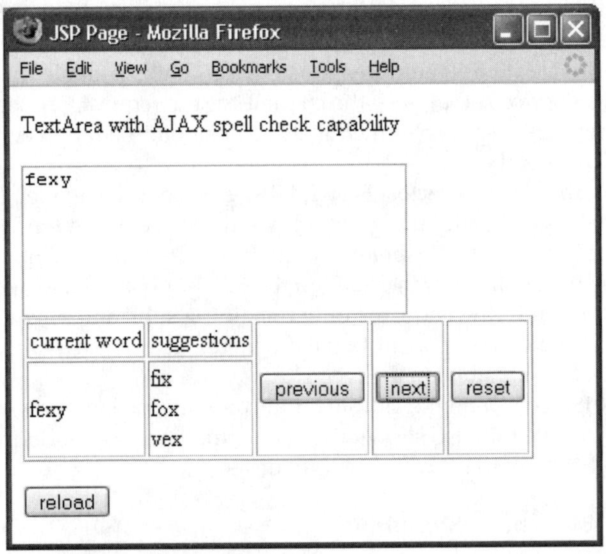

FIGURE 11-6   The AJAX **SpellCheckTextArea** component

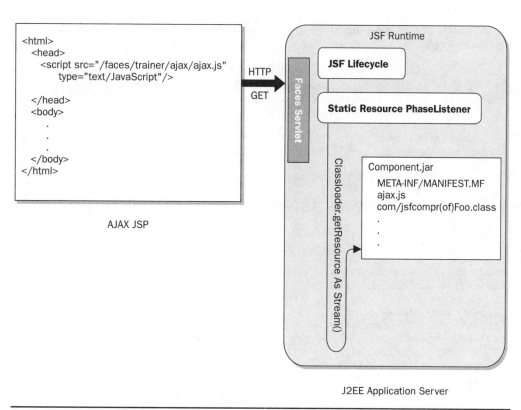

```
<html>
  <head>
    <script src="/faces/trainer/ajax/ajax.js"
        type="text/JavaScript"/>

  </head>
  <body>
        .
        .
        .
  </body>
</html>
```

AJAX JSP

HTTP
GET

Faces Servlet

JSF Runtime

JSF Lifecycle

Static Resource PhaseListener

Classloader.getResource As Stream()

Component.jar
  META-INF/MANIFEST.MF
  ajax.js
  com/jsfcompr(of)Foo.class
  .
  .
  .

J2EE Application Server

FIGURE 11-7   Using a **PhaseListener** to render the AJAX JavaScript

component renders the script since the browser only needs one copy of the AJAX script in memory.

Using a PhaseListener to Deliver the AJAX Script to the Client   Since the AJAX script is just a file reference, in keeping with hiding the JavaScript from the page author, it would be nice to avoid requiring the page author to place the script file at some location on the server's filesystem. Instead, the "file" will be referenced purely as a runtime resource such as "SpellCheckTextArea .ajaxScript". At runtime this script resource will be resolved and the content will be delivered to the client leveraging the existing **FacesServlet** using a **PhaseListener**. This approach, shown in Figure 11-7, allows you to bundle the actual AJAX script file into the same jar file in which the component itself is packaged, preserving the all-important JSF value proposition of "drop the component jar into **WEB-INF/lib** of your application and you're ready to go."

Early in this book, there is an example of how to write a simple **PhaseListener**. This example defines a **SpellCheckPhaseListener** that handles several different processing tasks, one of them being to render the AJAX script. The **SpellCheckPhaseListener** needs to be notified only on the Restore View phase of the lifecycle, so its **getPhaseId()** method looks like this:

```
public PhaseId getPhaseId() {
  PhaseId.RESTORE_VIEW;
}
```

In the case of rendering the AJAX script, the **afterPhase()** event is acted upon during the Restore View phase:

```
public void afterPhase(PhaseEvent event) {
  // If this is restoreView phase and the viewId is the script view id...
  if (-1 != event.getFacesContext().getViewRoot().
      getViewId().indexOf(RENDER_SCRIPT_VIEW_ID)) {
    // render the script
    writeScript(event);
    event.getFacesContext().responseComplete();
  }
}

static final String RENDER_SCRIPT_VIEW_ID = "SpellCheckTextArea.ajaxScript";

private static final String SCRIPT_RESOURCE_NAME =
    "/com/jsfcompref/components/component/ajax.js";

private void writeScript(PhaseEvent event) {
  URL url = getClass().getResource(SCRIPT_RESOURCE_NAME);
  URLConnection conn = null;
  InputStream stream = null;
  BufferedReader bufReader = null;
  HttpServletResponse response = (HttpServletResponse)event.
    getFacesContext().getExternalContext().getResponse();
  OutputStreamWriter outWriter = null;
  String curLine = null;

  try {
    outWriter = new OutputStreamWriter(response.getOutputStream(),
        response.getCharacterEncoding());
    conn = url.openConnection();
    conn.setUseCaches(false);
    stream = conn.getInputStream();
    bufReader = new BufferedReader(new InputStreamReader(stream));
    response.setContentType("text/javascript");
    while (null != (curLine = bufReader.readLine())) {
      outWriter.write(curLine+"\n");
    }
    outWriter.close();

  } catch (Exception e) {
    String message = null;
    message = "Can't load script file:" +
        url.toExternalForm();
    response.sendError(HttpServletResponse.SC_BAD_REQUEST, message);
  }
}
```

The full code for the **SpellcheckPhaseListener** is included on the Web site for this book; however, the **writeScript()** method deserves special attention. This method uses the **ClassLoader** to load the **ajax.js** file and sends it out to the **HttpServletResponse**, making sure to set the **contentType** to **text/javascript** and the **status** to **200**. The call to **responseComplete()** is needed because it tells the Faces lifecycle that the response for this request has been written and no further action need be taken to satisfy this request, thus causing the remaining lifecycle phases to be skipped.

The Content of the SpellCheck AJAX Script and How It Uses XMLHttpRequest   As described above in the **SpellCheckTextArea** component example, all of the AJAX JavaScript code resides in a file called **ajax.js** that is bundled into the **ajaxcomponents.jar** and served up by the **SpellCheckPhaseListener**. The **SpellCheckTextArea** component also renders the HTML markup, which with the provided script starts the process of sending XML requests in response to the user clicking the buttons in the page. We'll look at the component code in detail later. For now, here is the rendered output of the component.

```
<p>
<textarea id="form:textarea" name="form:textarea"
          cols="30" rows="5">
</textarea>
<script type="text/JavaScript"
        src="SpellCheckTextArea.ajaxScript">
</script>

<table border="1">
  <tr>
    <td>current word</td>
    <td>suggestions</td>
    <td rowspan="2">
      <input type="button" value="previous" onclick=
"getSuggestionsForPreviousWord('form:textarea');">
    </td>
    <td rowspan="2">
      <input type="button" value="next" onclick=
"getSuggestionsForNextWord('form:textarea');">
    </td>
    <td rowspan="2">
      <input type="button" value="reset" onclick=
"resetSpellCheck('form:textarea');">
    </td>
  </tr>
  <tr>
    <td id="form:textarea:currentWord"> </td>
    <td id="form:textarea:suggestions"> </td>
  </tr>
</table>
</p>
<p><input type="submit" name="form:_id0"
          value="reload" onclick=
  "clearFormHiddenParams_form(this.form.id);" />
</p>
```

All of the JavaScript functions referenced as the value of **onclick** handlers are defined in the **ajax.js** file. Let's examine **getSuggestionsForPreviousWord( )** to illustrate the necessary actions to send an AJAX request to the server.

```
var theRequest = null;
var isMozilla = false;
var isIE = false;
var gContexts = new Array();
```

```
function getSuggestionsForPreviousWord(clientId) {
  var previousWord = getPreviousWord(clientId);

  var req = prepareRequest(clientId, previousWord);
  req.request.onreadystatechange = processAjaxResponse;
  req.request.send(req.params);

  return false;
}
```

First, some global variables are declared. These variables will be used throughout the **ajax.js** file sent to the browser as requested in the tag:

```
<script type="text/JavaScript" src="SpellCheckTextArea.ajaxScript">
```

Next, note that **getSuggestionsForPreviousWord()** takes the **clientId** of the AJAX component itself. This is very important because without this piece of data it would be impossible to distinguish between multiple instances of the component in the same page. In general, it is a good practice to always pass around the **clientId** of the component to all the JavaScript functions relating to that component. The previous word (**previousWord**) is obtained from the text area. Then the request (shown below) is prepared. The return value from **prepareRequest()** is a JavaScript associative array with two entries. The **req** entry is a two-element JavaScript object. **req.request** is the actual **XMLHttpRequest** JavaScript object. **req.params** is the post data to be sent along with the request. The **onreadystatechange** property in the example is assigned to the callback function, **processAjaxResponse()**.

The content of **getPreviousWord()** and **getContext()** is shown next.

```
function getPreviousWord(clientId) {
  var context = getContext(clientId);
  if (-1 == context.index) {
    context.index = context.words.length - 1;
  }
  return context.words[context.index--];
}

function getContext(clientId) {
  var context = null;

  if (null == (context = gContexts[clientId])) {
    var fieldValue = window.document.getElementsByName(clientId);
    fieldValue = fieldValue[0].value;

    context = new Object();
    context.index = 0;
    context.words = fieldValue.split(' ');
    gContexts[clientId] = context;
  }
  return context;
}
```

The **getPreviousWord()** function calls **getContext()**, which returns another JavaScript associative array that encapsulates the words to be spell checked along with the index of the current word. **getPreviousWord()** simply manipulates the context appropriately.

Next, examine **prepareRequest()**:

```
function prepareRequest(clientId, word) {
  // State submitting code omitted, described later
  var params = "";
  // A truly robust implementation would discern the form number in
  // which the element named by "clientId" exists, and use that as the
  // index into the forms[] array.
  var formName = window.document.forms[0].id;
  // build up the post data
  var ajaxId = clientId + "Ajax";
  var params = params + formName + "=" + formName + "&" + clientId + "=" +
      word + "&" + ajaxId + "=ajax";
  // Again, this is safe to use the 0th form's action because each
  // form in the page has the same action.
  var formAction = window.document.forms[0].action;
  var request = getXMLHttpRequest();

  request.open("POST", formAction, true);
  request.setRequestHeader("Content-Type",
          "application/x-www-form-urlencoded");
  var result = new Object();
  result.request = request;
  result.params = params;

  return result;
}
```

The **prepareRequest()** function takes as arguments the **clientId** of the AJAX component, and the word to be spell checked. These arguments are assembled into name/value pair POST data in the **param** local variable. Also included in the POST data are the view state (omitted here, but explained later), the form name, the client ID, the word to be spell checked, and a special parameter called **ajaxId**, which is expected by the AJAX component on the server to indicate that this request is an AJAX request and not a normal form submit. Once the **param** local variable is properly assembled, the action of the first form in the page is obtained. Note that this will work even if there are multiple JSF forms in the page because the form action is guaranteed by JSF to be the same for each one. As an enhancement from the **DirectorySearch** example, helper method **getXMLHttpRequest()** is used to get the actual **XMLHttpRequest** instance.

```
function getXMLHttpRequest() {
  if (!theRequest) {
    // If this is the mozilla browser
    if (window.XMLHttpRequest) {
      theRequest = new XMLHttpRequest();
      isMozilla = true;
    }
    else if (window.ActiveXObject) {
      theRequest = new ActiveXObject("Microsoft.XMLHTTP");
      isIE = true;
    }
  }
  return (theRequest);
}
```

Recall from before that the code to obtain an **XMLHttpRequest** object must detect the browser family (Mozilla or Internet Explorer) to obtain the correct version. Also note that there is only one actual **XMLHttpRequest** instance in this example. A production quality implementation would need to manage multiple instances using a **clientId** keyed context mechanism similar to what was done with the words in the text area.

Once the request object is attained, the **open()** function is called. Recall that this method takes three arguments: the HTTP method to use for this request, the action to which the request should be sent, and a Boolean parameter indicating if this request should be sent asynchronously or not. As before, this example also posts back to the **FacesServlet,** which always expects the method to be POST. The last argument to **open()** will be **true** again since the "A" in AJAX stands for "asynchronous," after all. After the request has been **open()**ed, the **Content-Type** header is added to ensure the server properly interprets it. The header is the same as before, "application/x-www-form-urlencoded". Finally, a JavaScript **Object** is constructed to hold the initialized **XMLHttpRequest** instance and the parameters to be sent along with it. This **Object** is returned from the **prepareRequest()** method as used in **getSuggestionsForPreviousWord()** above.

The last portion of the AJAX script is the callback function, **processAjaxResponse()**, whose job is to process the returned XML response. For example, when a word such as "ferther" is provided to the **SpellCheckTextArea** component, the XML response below will be returned:

```
<message>
  <suggestions>
    <word>farther</word>
    <word>further</word>
    <word>feather</word>
  </suggestions>
  <currentWord>ferther</currentWord>
  <clientId>form:textarea</currentWord>
<message>
```

Let's examine how the **processAjaxResponse()** method, shown here, takes this message apart and deals with it.

```
function processAjaxResponse() {
  var request = getXMLHttpRequest();
  if (4 == request.readyState) {
    if (200 == request.status) {
      // extract the currentWord from the XML
      var currentWord =
        request.responseXML.getElementsByTagName("currentWord")[0];
      currentWord = currentWord.firstChild.nodeValue;
      // extract the suggested words from the XML
      var wordNodes =
        request.responseXML.getElementsByTagName("suggestions")[0];
      // if there are no suggested words, use an empty array
      if (null == wordNodes) {
        wordNodes = new Array();
      }
      else {
        wordNodes = wordNodes.childNodes;
      }
      // extract the clientId from the XML
```

```
    var clientId =
      request.responseXML.getElementsByTagName("clientId")[0];
    clientId = clientId.firstChild.nodeValue;

    // update the currentWord JavaScript with the value from XML
    var targetElement =
      window.document.getElementById(clientId + ":currentWord");
    targetElement.innerHTML = currentWord;

    // update the suggested words with the value from XML
    targetElement =
      window.document.getElementById(clientId + ":suggestions");
    var wordList = "";
    for (i = 0; i < wordNodes.length; i++) {
      wordList = wordList + wordNodes[i].firstChild.nodeValue +
      "<br />";
    }
    targetElement.innerHTML = wordList;
    }
  }
}
```

Similar to the **DirectorySearch** example, the callback function first checks the **request
.status** value, which is the HTTP response code sent from the server. A value of **200** here
means that everything is okay, and we can read the response from the server. Again, the
XML message is accessed via the **responseXML** property of the **XMLHttpRequest** object.
The callback function also uses standard JavaScript DOM processing techniques here to
extract the important content from the message. Once we've parsed the message, we modify
the DOM of the page in the browser by getting access to the **innerHTML** property for the
currentWord and **suggestions** fields in the table. Recall from the rendered markup at the
beginning of this section that these fields look like this:

```
<tr>
  <td id="form:textarea:currentWord"> </td>
  <td id="form:textarea:suggestions"> </td>
</tr>
```

The **suggestions** field is populated with all the suggested words sent from the server.

The AJAX UI Component for the SpellCheckTextArea Example

Now that you have the ability to easily serve up the AJAX script in response to a request
to the **FacesServlet**, and you have an idea of what is in the AJAX script itself, you need to
generate the actual **<script>** element markup and the **JavaScript** attributes that cause the
AJAX requests to be sent based on user interaction. This is no different from rendering any
other HTML markup as you did earlier in the chapter. In the case of **SpellCheckTextArea**,
we add this logic to the **encodeEnd()** method:

```
public void encodeEnd(FacesContext context) throws IOException {
  getStandardTextareaRenderer(context).encodeEnd(context, this);
  ExternalContext extContext = context.getExternalContext();
  ResponseWriter writer = context.getResponseWriter();
  // Render the main script, only once per page
  if (!extContext.getRequestMap().containsKey("ajaxflag.ajaxScript")) {
    extContext.getRequestMap().put("ajaxflag.ajaxScript", Boolean.TRUE);
    writer.startElement("script", this);
```

```
        writer.writeAttribute("type", "text/JavaScript", null);
        writer.writeAttribute("src", SpellcheckPhaseListener.RENDER_SCRIPT_VIEW_ID,
                        null);
        writer.endElement("script");
}

// Table rendering code omitted
writer.startElement("input", this);
writer.writeAttribute("type",  "button",  "type");
writer.writeAttribute("value",  "previous",  "type");
writer.writeAttribute("onclick", "getSuggestionsForPreviousWord('" +
            clientId + "');", "onclick");
writer.endElement("input");

// More table rendering code omitted
writer.startElement("input", this);
writer.writeAttribute("type",  "button",  "type");
writer.writeAttribute("value",  "next",  "type");
writer.writeAttribute("onclick", "getSuggestionsForNextWord('" +
            clientId + "');", "onclick");
writer.endElement("input");

// More table rendering code omitted
writer.startElement("input", this);
writer.writeAttribute("type",  "button",  "type");
writer.writeAttribute("value",  "reset",  "type");
writer.writeAttribute("onclick", "resetSpellCheck('" +
            clientId + "');", "onclick");
writer.endElement("input");

// More table rendering code omitted
writer.startElement("tr", this);
writer.startElement("td", this);
writer.writeAttribute("id", clientId + ":currentWord", "id");
writer.write(" ");
writer.endElement("td");
writer.startElement("td", this);
writer.writeAttribute("id", clientId + ":suggestions", "id");
writer.write(" ");
writer.endElement("td");
writer.endElement("tr");
```

There are four points of interest in the above code. The first is the usage of a request scoped attribute to prevent the **<script>** element from being rendered more than once per page. This is desirable because once the script has been loaded into the browser, there is no need to re-load it while the browser is on the same page. The second interesting point is the usage of the **RENDER_SCRIPT_VIEW_ID** constant from the **SpellcheckPhaseListener** class. This is a tight coupling between **SpellCheckTextarea** and **SpellcheckPhaseListener**. The rendered script element looks like this:

```
<script type="text/JavaScript" src="SpellCheckTextArea.ajaxScript">
</script>
```

Because the URL from which the JSP page was loaded looks something like

```
http://localhost:8080/spellcheck/faces/spellCheck.jsp
```

the relative URL in the **<script>** element causes the browser to fetch to the URL:

`http://localhost:8080/spellcheck/faces/SpellCheckTextArea.ajaxScript.`

This runs through the Faces lifecycle, and thus causes our **SpellcheckPhaseListener** to be invoked, which in turn returns the AJAX script.

The third interesting point is the liberal sprinkling of **clientId** as a parameter to the **JavaScript** function **getSuggestionsForPreviousWord()**. This is important because it enables multiple instances of the component to reside in a single page, thanks to the ID uniqueness guarantee provided by the JSF runtime.

Finally, note that we render empty **<td>** elements to hold the **currentWord** and **suggestions** values from the server, again making sure to use the **clientId** to distinguish between multiple instances of the spell-check component.

The AJAX Server Component for the SpellCheckTextArea Example

While the **SpellCheckTextArea** component generates the **<script>** tag that loads the AJAX browser script, and the standard **FacesServlet** serves up the script to the browser using the **PhaseListener**, the remaining portion of this example is the AJAX server component, which responds to the AJAX request issued from the script in the browser. Let's now review this in more detail.

Similar to the **DirectorySearch** component where the AJAX server code is integrated into the JSF application, the **SpellCheckTextArea** component example leverages the **FacesServlet** to allow the JSF lifecycle to guide the processing of AJAX requests. As you've seen in the **DirectorySearch** example, this is slightly more complex to develop than an independent generic servlet solution, and there may be higher performance costs if the number of AJAX requests is large. However, the entire AJAX technology is packaged into a single JSF UI Component, thus ensuring easier access to application data (via EL, ManagedBeans, messages) as well as providing a simpler deployment process. The performance cost can also be mitigated by carefully designing your AJAX interactions, and by using a servlet container that can leverage the high-performance **java.nio** package for its network layer, such as the Sun Java System Application Server.

Using the FacesServlet and JSF Lifecycle to Host the High-Level AJAX Processing Server Element   In order for a request from the browser to get into the JSF component lifecycle, the second URL argument of the **open()** call on the **XMLHttpRequest** instance must match the **servlet-mapping url-pattern** defined in the **web.xml** (for example, /faces). There are two ways the JSF request processing lifecycle can be used to orchestrate the AJAX request processing server component: executing within the scope of a view (page) or executing without reference to a specific view. The former involves having the AJAX browser script simulate a form submit with the entire view state, which includes adding the necessary request parameters to allow the JSF lifecycle to restore the entire view and perform processing on it. This approach has the benefit of allowing your components to have access to the entire view while performing the AJAX processing. The latter doesn't ship the component state along with the AJAX request, and therefore the JSF lifecycle cannot access the component state. However, it still can access managed beans and other JSF resources. Let's examine submitting the AJAX request with the component state first, because omitting the component state is simple once you understand how to include it in the first place.

Including the JSF Component View State in the AJAX Request   In the **ajax.js** script, the **prepareRequest()** function is responsible for marshaling the parameters to be sent in the AJAX request, including any view state. The omitted code to pull in the view state is now included here.

```
function prepareRequest(clientId, word) {
  // The following is a dependency on Sun's JSF Implementation.
  // In Faces 1.2, this has been fixed by specifying a value of
  // javax.faces.ViewState as the name of the state field.  A
  // production quality implementation would need to also consider
  // other implementations, such as MyFaces.

  var stateFieldName = "com.sun.faces.VIEW";
  var stateElements = window.document.getElementsByName(stateFieldName);
  var stateValue = null;
  var params = "";

  if (null != stateElements && 0 < stateElements.length) {
    // In the case of a page with multiple h:form tags, there will be
    // multiple instances of stateFieldName in the page.  Even so, they
    // all have the same value, so it's safe to use the 0th value.
    stateValue = stateElements[0].value;
    // We must carefully encode the value of the state array to ensure
    // it is accurately transmitted to the server.  The implementation
    // of encodeURI() in mozilla doesn't properly encode the plus
    // character as %2B so we have to do this as an extra step.
    var uriEncodedState = encodeURI(stateValue);
    var rexp = new RegExp("\\+", "g");
    var encodedState = uriEncodedState.replace(rexp, "\%2B");
    params = stateFieldName + "=" + encodedState + "&";
  }
}
```

The view state code above requires a bit of knowledge about the JSF state management system, but essentially provides the server with the current state of the JSF page (or view component tree). This is only needed when any manipulation of a view component tree is to be done by the AJAX server component.

NOTE *The code provided is actually specific to Sun's implementation of JSF 1.1 because the name of the hidden field for the page state was not standardized until JSF 1.2.*

Generally, the idea is to find the name of the hidden field that contains the page state, if any, and bundle that into the parameters, making sure to encode it properly so the browser doesn't mix things up.

With this approach, the **SpellCheckTextArea** component itself can handle the AJAX processing in its normal **decode()** method, as shown here:

```
public void decode(FacesContext context) {
  ExternalContext extContext = context.getExternalContext();
  String
    clientId = this.getClientId(context),
    ajaxId = clientId + "Ajax",
    ajaxIdVal = (String)
      extContext.getRequestParameterMap().get(ajaxId);
  String [] result = null;
```

```
// Determine if this is an ajax request or a regular Faces request.
if (null == ajaxIdVal || -1 == ajaxIdVal.indexOf("ajax")) {
  // Delegate to standard Textarea Renderer if this is a regular
  // Faces request.
  getStandardTextareaRenderer(context).decode(context, this);
  return;
}

// See if there are any words to check
String value = (String) extContext.getRequestParameterMap().get(clientId);
if (null == value) {
  // If not, return.
  return;
}

try {
  result = (String [])
    getWordServer().invoke(context, new Object [] { value });
} catch (Exception e) {
  System.out.println("Exception: " + e.getMessage());
}
if (null == result) {
  return;
}

HttpServletResponse response = (HttpServletResponse)
context.getExternalContext().getResponse();

// set the header information for the response
response.setContentType("text/xml");
response.setHeader("Cache-Control", "no-cache");

try {
  ResponseWriter writer = Util.getResponseWriter(context);
  writer.startElement("message", this);
  writer.startElement("suggestions", null);
  for (int i = 0; i < result.length; i++) {
    writer.startElement("word", this);
    writer.writeText(result[i], null);
    writer.endElement("word");
  }
  writer.endElement("suggestions");
  writer.startElement("currentWord", this);
  writer.writeText(value, null);
  writer.endElement("currentWord");
  writer.startElement("clientId", this);
  writer.writeText(clientId, null);
  writer.endElement("clientId");
  writer.endElement("message");
} catch (IOException e) {
  // log message…
}
context.responseComplete();

}
```

Similar to the **DirectorySearch** component, the first thing **decode()** checks is the special request parameter, which indicates that it is an AJAX request. In this example it is **ajaxId**. The absence of this parameter causes the component to simply delegate to the standard **Textarea** renderer for the decoding and to return afterward. It then extracts the **clientId** parameter, which is assumed to be the list of words to check, and passes it on to the spell-checking engine. If the server returned any suggestions, the XML message is composed to conform to the syntax expected by the **ajax.js** script. Note that the content type is set to **text/xml** and **Cache-Control** header is set to **no-cache**. These two headers are vitally important. Leaving them out will break the component. Finally, note that **responseComplete()** is called on the context for the same reason it was called on it in **SpellcheckPhaseListener**: to prevent the rendering phase of the request processing lifecycle from happening. This is important because the **ajax.js** script is expecting to receive only the simple XML message, not a full rendered page.

JSF 1.2 TIP *The ability to maintain the component state and context when submitting and processing the AJAX request is essential to using JSF and AJAX together. The previous sections detailed the need for submitting the JSF View State along with the AJAX request. However, there is a special case that must be addressed: iterating components. Consider a data-table with many rows and columns. Let's say we want to update a single cell in that table over AJAX, using, for example, an "in-place editor" widget from a third-party JavaScript library. Recall that the data-table doesn't actually instantiate new components for each row in the table; rather, it uses a "rubber stamp" approach for each row, substituting in the values for each row as the table is rendered.*

```
<h:dataTable id="table" value="#{data.table}" var="row">
  <h:column>
    <h:outputText id="name" value="#{row.userName}" />
  <h:column>
    <h:outputText id="userid" value="#{row.userid}" />
  </h:column>
</h:dataTable>
```

*Regardless of how many rows are in the table, there are only two **outputText** components created and used when the table is rendered. The rendered markup for this table will look something like:*

```
<table>
  <tr>
    <td><div id="table:0:name">John Bigboote</div></td>
    <td><div id="table:0:userid">bigboote</div></td>
  </tr>
  <tr>
    <td><div id="table:1:name">John Small Berries</div></td>
    <td><div id="table:1:userid">jsmallb</div></td>
  </tr>
</table>
```

*Note the funny-looking id attributes of the table cells: **table:1:name**, etc. These clientId values are created by the **UIData** component as the rows of the table are rendered.*

*Let's say we want to replace each **outputText** component with a special AJAX-enabled in-place editor component (the details of this component are beyond the scope of this introductory chapter). Such components typically replace some static text with a text field and a button, submitting the AJAX request when the button is pressed. The JSP markup will look something like this:*

```
<h:dataTable value="#{data.table}" var="row">
  <h:column>
    <ajax:inplaceEditor value="#{row.userName}" />
  <h:column>
    <ajax:inplaceEditor value="#{row.userid}" />
  </h:column>
</h:dataTable>
```

In order for the AJAX request to modify the correct value of the user name based on which cell in which row is edited, the clientId associated with that row must be properly interpreted. Let's say the user clicks on the String "John Smallberries" and clicks OK on the in-place editor text field button. This will cause an AJAX request to be posted back to the **FacesServlet** including a name/value pair like this:

```
table:1:userid="John Ya Ya"
```

When posting back this request, the JSF runtime must be able to locate the individual component representing the **userid** element of the second row in the table. Passing the clientId to **findComponent( )** will not work because the table does not correctly position itself to the desired row. JSF 1.2 introduces the **invokeOnComponent( )** method for this purpose. This method is over-ridden on the **UIData** class to properly position the table before taking action on the component. The syntax for this method is

```
public boolean invokeOnComponent(FacesContext context, String clientId
                    ContextCallback callback) throws FacesException
```

The **ContextCallback** is an interface that you must implement with the following signature:

```
public interface ContextCallback{
  public void invokeContextCallback(FacesContext context,
                                    UIComponent target);
}
```

The general usage pattern is to obtain the **UIViewRoot** from the **FacesContext** and call **invokeOnComponent( )** on it, like this:

```
UIViewRoot root = FacesContext.getViewRoot( );
ContextCallback cb = new ContextCallback( ) {
  public void invokeContextCallback(FacesContext context,
                                    UIComponent target) {
    // Take some action on the component, perhaps setting its value.
  }
};
boolean found = root.invokeOnComponent(context, "table:1:userid", cb);
// found will be true if a matching component was found.
```

Omitting the JSF Component View State from the AJAX Request   Leaving out the component view state when issuing AJAX requests to the **FacesServlet** is also a viable option when the server component does not need access to the page's components at runtime. When this is the case, the AJAX request doesn't need to include the view state information as a request parameter. Under this scenario the AJAX server component can be implemented as a **PhaseListener** as opposed to using a **decode()** method in a component. This approach uses basically the same AJAX server code that was used in the **decode()** method examples from before, but instead it is placed inside of a **PhaseListener**. A complementary example of how to do this is provided in the **DirectorySearch** example and is available on the Web site.

AJAX Tips and Tricks

Debugging a JSF AJAX application may make debugging a regular JSF application look easy. One must directly confront browser incompatibilities. It is common for a component to work fine in one browser but not function at all in another. The Web site **http://www .quirksmode.org/**, named after one of the two modes in which a browser can read an HTML document (the other being strict mode), is a great resource for getting around these incompatibilities. Also, no survey of AJAX tips and tricks would be complete without a reference to Ben Galbraith and Dion Almaer's **http://www.ajaxian.com/**.

For completeness, we also must mention three leading JavaScript libraries that provide advanced JavaScript features that are agnostic to the server side processing, and therefore can be used with JSF.

- **Dojo: http://dojotoolkit.org/** This open source library is a well-documented and robust JavaScript library that includes AJAX processing, a packaging system, and a set of ready-to-use UI Widgets that supplement the ones provided by JSF.

- **Prototype: http://prototype.conio.net/** A competitor to Dojo, this is a smaller library, also open source, with fewer features, but has a lot of buzz going around it due to its association with Ruby on Rails.

- **Zimbra: http://www.zimbra.com/** Zimbra is actually much more than just a JavaScript library, and its other features are not generally germane to JSF; however, they do have a decent AJAX library. Unfortunately, they are not open source as of this writing but have announced plans to go that route.

There are also a number of debuggers and tools available to help in developing an AJAXian application. The most basic is the JavaScript console.

The Mozilla Firefox Web browser has an excellent JavaScript debugger called Venkman (**http://www.mozilla.org/projects/venkman/**). Another Firefox extension is called Greasemonkey (**http://greasemonkey.mozdev.org/**). This enables you to add DHTML to each page to highly customize its behavior in the browser, sometimes providing debugging insight. Internet Explorer users can use the JavaScript debugging functionality in Visual Studio and also make use of the Internet Explorer Developer Toolbar. This download can be obtained by searching the Microsoft Web site for the exact name "**Internet Explorer Developer Toolbar**" (without the quotes).

Finally, when considering deploying an AJAX application, one must consider accessibility concerns. Chapter 14 covers accessibility in detail, but one point deserves special attention here. One of the key guidelines for producing an accessible application is that it should perform well even when JavaScript is turned off. This validity of this guideline is subject to debate, but it is prudent to keep it in mind. As AJAX becomes more and more common, meeting this guideline will become increasingly unreasonable. On the other hand, government-mandated accessibility requirements are not likely to change just because it's possible to build cooler looking applications by ignoring these requirements. Please keep this in mind when developing your AJAX-enabled application.

AJAX XMLHttpRequest Reference

This section provides a brief reference to the functionality of the **XMLHttpRequest** object.

Table 11-1 lists the methods available on the **XMLHttpRequest** object.

Table 11-2 lists the properties on the **XMLHttpRequest** object.

Method	Description
abort( )	Cancels the currently in-progress request. Takes no action if no request is in progress. Returns the instance to the uninitialized state.
getAllResponseHeaders( )	Returns a string of all the response headers received from the server. Each header is in the form Name: Value\r\n where \r\n is a carriage return, followed by a line-feed. The return from this method is only valid after a successful call to **send**( ).
getResponseHeader("*HeaderName*"**)**	Like **getAllResponseHeaders**( ) but only returns the named header.
open("*HTTP Method*", "*URL*"[, *asyncBoolean, username, password*]**)**	Starts the request process but doesn't send the request. HTTP method is generally either GET or POST. URL is the absolute or relative URL to which the request should be sent. If asyncBoolean is true the request is performed asynchronously. Otherwise, it is performed synchronously. If basic authentication is required, the username and password may be provided as well.
send("*params*"**)**	Once the **open**( ) call has been made, the request is sent with this method. The argument is either the POST data to send or DOM object data.
setRequestHeader("*label*", "*value*"**)**	Sets an HTTP request header on the not-yet-sent request. This is typically used to set the **Content-Type** to **application/x-www-form-urlencoded**.

TABLE 11-1   XMLHttpRequest Methods

PART II

Property	Description
onreadystatechange	Points to a JavaScript function that will be called after each state change
readyState	The current state for this instance. This value is changed by the server to indicate the progression of the request through its lifecycle. Every state change will cause the **onreadystatechange** method to be called. Valid values are 0 ⟹ UNINITIALIZED 1 ⟹ LOADING 2 ⟹ LOADED (send has been called, but status and headers are not yet available) 3 ⟹ INTERACTIVE (Some more data is available but not yet ready to read. This state is not well defined) 4 ⟹ COMPLETED (All data is available in either **responseText** or **responseXML** properties)
responseText	Simple string version of the response
responseXML	XML DOM version of the response
status	HTTP response code
statusText	The text accompanying the status code. For example, if the status is 404, the **statusText** will likely be "Not Found"

TABLE 11-2   Properties of the **XMLHttpRequest** Object

Building Non-UI Custom Components

C hapter 10 presented the most popular way to extend Faces, by providing custom UI components that page-authors can easily use. In addition to allowing custom UI components, Faces has many non-UI component extension points that have no visual representation for the end user. These non-UI component extension points are far less frequently used, but when you need to use them, you *really* need to use them. For example, if the existing set of validators and converters doesn't meet your requirements, you need to provide a custom solution, as shown in Chapter 7. In a more advanced case, if you want to seamlessly integrate JSF into an existing persistence scheme, implementing a custom EL resolver is the easiest approach. An example of this scenario is shown later in this chapter when the integration of JSF and the Spring Framework is discussed in the section "ELResolver (JSF 1.2)". Both of these examples can only be accomplished by using one of the non-UI custom component mechanisms described in this chapter.

Non-UI Custom Components and Decoration in JSF

Table 12-1 shows the complete alphabetical listing of the non-UI custom component classes and interfaces defined in the JSF specification. The **Decoratable?** column indicates whether this particular class or interface enables "decorating" the existing implementation rather than wholly replacing it. The concept of decoration is described in the following paragraph.

The XML declaration details for all of the classes shown in Table 12-1 can be found in Chapter 18. The **Decoratable?** column indicates whether or not this particular customizable component is decoratable. The decorator pattern enables a developer to override as much, or as little, functionality of an existing object as desired, while leaving the "rest" to the "real" implementation. The particular implementation of decoration practiced in the JSF specification uses the presence of a single argument constructor in the decorating class to decide if the user wants to leverage decoration or not. For example, Chapter 13 covers in detail the concept of a custom **ViewHandler**. The example used in Chapter 13 is that of Facelets technology, described more fully therein. For now, just know that the class

Class to Extend, or Interface to Implement	Purpose	Decoratable?
ActionListener	Alters what happens when an **ActionEvent** is fired. This occurs when the user presses a button or clicks a link.	Yes
ApplicationFactory	Gains access to the creation of the singleton **Application** instance to alter the way it serves the system.	Yes
Converter	Adds a new way to convert from **String** to a model tier type and back again.	No
ELResolver	The replacement for **VariableResolver** and **PropertyResolver** in the Unified EL (used by JSF 1.2).	No
FacesContextFactory	Takes control of the creation of **FacesContext** instances to alter the way they interact with the rest of the system.	Yes
LifecycleFactory	Adds a new implementation of the request processing lifecycle, or extends or replaces the existing one.	Yes
NavigationHandler	Alters the way navigation between pages is performed.	Yes
PhaseListener	Provides an execution entry point at any particular phase in the request processing lifecycle.	No
PropertyResolver	In JSF 1.1, handles resolving each part of a JSF EL Expression after the initial part.	Yes
RenderKit	Defines a collection of **Renderer** classes designed to adapt a collection of **UIComponent** classes for use in a specific client device type.	No
RenderKitFactory	Gains access to the creation of **RenderKit** instances to alter the way it serves **RenderKit** instances to the system.	Yes
StateManager	Alters the way view state is saved and restored between requests.	Yes
VariableResolver	In JSF 1.1, handles resolving the first part of a JSF EL Expression.	Yes
Validator	Adds a new way to validate correctly converted user-provided data based on application-specific constraints.	No
ViewHandler	Replaces JSP as the view description technology. A custom **ViewHandler** is also useful for other tasks, such as selecting a **RenderKit**, choosing a **Locale**, or gaining access to the timing of view creation.	Yes

TABLE 12-1   The Complete List of Non-View Related Customizable Components in JSF

FaceletViewHandler is a custom **ViewHandler** implementation. The **FaceletViewHandler** class has a single argument constructor that takes an instance of **ViewHandler**, shown next.

```
package com.sun.facelets;

private ViewHandler parent = null;

public FaceletViewHandler(ViewHandler parent) {
  this.parent = parent;
}
```

The XML markup in the **faces-config.xml** file to declare this class to the JSF runtime is as follows:

```
<faces-config>
  <!-- intervening content omitted -->
  <application>
     <view-handler>com.sun.facelets.FaceletViewHandler</view-handler>
  </application>
</faces-config>
```

When the JSF runtime is starting up, the presence of XML elements for any of the decoratable classes from Table 12-1 (such as **view-handler** in the previous Facelet example) will cause the implementation class to be scanned for the presence of a public one-argument constructor with the proper argument type. If one is found, this constructor is used to create the instance, and the "previous" instance is passed to the constructor. It is up to the custom class to choose to save or discard the passed-in "previous" instance. The JSF implementation maintains no reference to it. Instead, the implementation only maintains a reference to the "new" instance. If no public one-argument constructor of the proper type is found, a public zero-argument constructor is used to create the instance. If there is no public zero-argument constructor for the specified class, an error is thrown and the application will not start.

EXPERT GROUP INSIGHT   *Adam Winer, Oracle's representative on the JSF 1.0 Expert Group, was very adamant about the inclusion of decorators wherever possible. His design foresight has significantly helped the extensibility of JSF.*

When running the **FaceletViewHandler** shown earlier in the Sun JSF implementation, the constructor is passed an instance of **com.sun.faces.application.ViewHandlerImpl**, which is saved aside in an instance variable and consulted when needed. Once the **FaceletViewHandler** constructor is returned, the **javax.faces.application.Application**'s **ViewHandler** property is set with the new **FaceletViewHandler** instance, and the previous value is no longer maintained by the runtime.

JSF 1.2 TIP   *JSF 1.2 provides several wrapper classes to ease the burden of decorating one of the previously mentioned classes. These wrappers provide default implementations of all the required methods that simply call through to the wrapped instance. For example, to decorate the* **StateManager** *instance and override only the* **isSavingStateInClient()** *method, you would simply define the following class.*

```
package com.jsfcompref;

import javax.faces.application.StateManager;
```

```
import javax.faces.application.StateManagerWrapper;

public class DecoratedStateManager extends StateManagerWrapper {

  private StateManager previous = null;

  public DecoratedStateManager(StateManager previous) {
    this.previous = previous;
  }

  protected StateManager getWrapped() {
    return previous;
  }

  public boolean isSavingStateInClient(FacesContext context) {
    // This implementation never saves state in client.
    return false;
  }
}
```

Notice the protected **getWrapped()** *method. This is an abstract method on* **StateManagerWrapper** *that you must implement to return the previous instance. Note also that the only* **StateManager** *method overridden is* **isSavingStateInClient()**. *The remaining overrides are handled by the* **StateManagerWrapper** *superclass. JSF 1.2 provides wrappers for* **javax.faces.application** **.StateManagerWrapper, javax.faces.application.ViewHandlerWrapper,** *and* **javax.faces** **.context.ResponseWriterWrapper.**

Non-View Custom Components Explained

The remainder of this chapter provides information or references to information elsewhere in the book for the preceding non-view custom components. The **faces-config** declaration for all of these components is covered in detail in Chapter 18. These components are listed in the order in which it makes the most sense to present them, with the more commonly used extension points first.

PhaseListener

PhaseListeners provide JSF developers with a capability to insert code at any point in the request processing lifecycle. As you saw in Chapters 8 and 10, **PhaseListener**s can be used in multiple ways. Their usages can be purely for analysis by allowing the developer to listen for any application changes at any point in the lifecycle. **PhaseListener**s can also be employed in a production application, such as how a **PhaseListener** was used in Chapter 11 to serve as the heart of the AJAX processing server component. This section lists the ways to add a **PhaseListener** to the application, including the new "per-view PhaseListener" feature in JSF 1.2.

Interface to Implement

In JSF 1.0 and 1.1, a **PhaseListener** is simply a Java class that implements the interface **javax** **.faces.event.PhaseListener**. This interface defines three methods.

```
public PhaseId getPhaseId()
public void beforePhase(PhaseEvent event)
public void afterPhase(PhaseEvent event)
```

The method **getPhaseId()** is called by the runtime to determine which lifecycle phase this listener instance applies to. There are constants in the class **PhaseId** for each of the lifecycle phases, as well as **ANY_PHASE**. Returning **PhaseId.ANY_PHASE** tells the runtime that this listener instance should be called before and after all lifecycle phases. For example:

```
public PhaseId getPhaseId() {
  return PhaseId.ANY_PHASE;
}
```

Likewise, returning **PhaseId.RENDER_RESPONSE** allows the runtime to invoke this **PhaseListener** instance specifically during the Render Response phase. In addition to using **getPhaseId()** to associate a **PhaseListener** with a specific (or any) phase, the interface defines the other methods, **beforePhase()** and **afterPhase()**, which execute both before and after the associated phase, respectively. The developer can then provide custom code inside these methods. For example, the code:

```
public void beforePhase(PhaseEvent pe) {
  if (pe.getPhaseId() == PhaseId.RESTORE_VIEW)
    System.out.println("before - " + pe.getPhaseId().toString());
}
```

will first check to see if the current phase is the Restore View phase, and then will print a simple message to the console indicating that it is executing just before the phase. Obviously, just printing a message indicating the current phase merely scratches the surface of what is possible with a **PhaseListener**. Having access to the entire application at a specific moment in time allows for more creative uses for **PhasesListeners**. In addition to the examples already shown, in Chapter 15 a **PhaseListener** is used to check if a user is logged in when attempting to view a page—if not, the user is redirected to a login page. (Please see Chapter 15 for the full implementation details.) In general, when writing a JSF-centric application, please consider using a **PhaseListener** instead of a Servlet Filter. Nearly anything that can be done in a filter can also be done in a **PhaseListener**, yet **PhaseListeners** have the added benefit of providing access to the entire JSF framework, including the components in the current view, the Expression Language, and the lifecycle itself.

Registering a PhaseListener

When implementing a **PhaseListener**, you must register it by using a **phase-listener** XML element in the **faces-config.xml** file. This element contains a fully qualified Java class name of your **PhaseListener** implementation class. This element is a child of the **lifecycle** element. See Chapter 18 for the **faces-config.xml** syntax for registering a **PhaseListener**.

JSF 1.2 Tip   *JSF 1.2 introduced a new tag to the jsf-core taglibrary,* **f:phaseListener**. *The general form for this tag is shown in Chapter 19 but a usage example is included here for completeness.*

```
<!-- JSP and HTML Declarations omitted -->
<f:view>
  <f:phaseListener binding="#{page1.phaseListener}" />
  <!-- remainder of page omitted -->
</f:view>
```

A per-view **PhaseListener** *is guaranteed only to be invoked when the particular view on which it is declared is going through the lifecycle. The* **f:view** *tag in JSF 1.2 also defines two new*

MethodExpression *attributes called* **beforePhase** *and* **afterPhase** *that must point to public methods that take a* **PhaseEvent** *and return void. These methods are then invoked for every phase except restore view.*

Converter and Validator

Chapter 7 covered converters and validators in detail. Please refer to Chapter 7 for complete information. This section is included here as a reference to the API for providing a custom **converter** or **validator**.

Interfaces to Implement

The interface **javax.faces.convert.Converter** defines the two methods shown next.

```
public Object getAsObject(FacesContext context,
                UIComponent component,
                String value)

public String getAsString(FacesContext context,
                UIComponent component,
                Object value)
```

The **javax.faces.validator.Validator** interface defines a single method called **validate()**, which follows:

```
public void validate(FacesContext context,
                UIComponent component,
                Object value)
```

Registering a Converter or Validator

When implementing a custom converter or validator, you may register them declaratively using **converter** or **validator** elements in the **faces-config.xml** file, or you may register them dynamically at runtime using the API. The **converter** and **validator** elements are direct children of the root **faces-config** element and must be the fully qualified Java class name of the class extending **Converter** or **Validator** respectively. See Chapter 18 for the **faces-config .xml** syntax for registering a **Converter** or **Validator**. See Chapter 7 for any other converter or validator information.

ViewHandler

Chapter 13 covers the custom **ViewHandler** feature in detail. Please refer to Chapter 13 for complete information. This section is included here as a reference to the API for providing a custom **ViewHandler**.

Abstract Class to Extend

The abstract class **javax.faces.application.ViewHandler** defines the following methods.

```
public Locale calculateLocale(FacesContext context);
public String calculateRenderKitId(FacesContext context);
public UIViewRoot createView(FacesContext context, String viewId);
public String getActionURL(FacesContext context, String viewId);
public String getResourceURL(FacesContext context, String path);
```

```
public void renderView(FacesContext context, UIViewRoot viewToRender)
    throws IOException, FacesException;
public UIViewRoot restoreView(FacesContext context, String viewId);
public void writeState(FacesContext context) throws IOException;
```

Registering a ViewHandler

When implementing a custom **ViewHandler**, you may register it declaratively using the **view-handler** element in the **faces-config.xml** file, or you may register it dynamically by calling the **setViewHandler()** method on the **Application** instance. (See the following for more on the **Application** instance). The **view-handler** element is a child of the **application** element in the **faces-config.xml** file. The contents of the **view-handler** element must be the fully qualified Java class name of your **ViewHandler** implementation class. See Chapter 18 for the **faces-config.xml** syntax for registering a **ViewHandler**.

VariableResolver and PropertyResolver

In JSF 1.0 and 1.1, the JSF runtime has default singleton instances of **VariableResolver** and **PropertyResolver** that fulfill the specified requirements to allow JSF EL expressions to be resolved. In JSF 1.2, these two classes have been deprecated with the introduction of the **javax.el.ELResolver** class in the Unified EL. This section covers what these two classes do in JSF 1.0 and 1.1, while the following section covers **ELResolver** in JSF 1.2.

The following example illustrates the central role the **VariableResolver** and **PropertyResolver** play in JSF. For discussion, let's say that the JSF runtime maintains a reference to the **VariableResolver** and **PropertyResolver** using variables **myVariableResolver** and **myPropertyResolver**, respectively. Also, the signatures of the **resolveVariable()** and **getValue()** methods on these classes have been abbreviated for convenience in the discussion shown next. Consider the following JSF EL expression from the Virtual Trainer example in Chapter 9:

```
#{requestScope.user.firstName}
```

To resolve this expression and get its value, the EL implementation in JSF 1.0 and 1.1 breaks this expression down into two parts: **requestScope** and **user.firstName**. The JSF runtime calls **myVariableResolver.resolveVariable("requestScope")**. This method takes the argument string and "resolves" it. In this case, "**requestScope**" is one of the implicit objects, listed in Table 7 of Chapter 4, so the **VariableResolver** instance must return a **java.util.Map** implementation that wraps the attribute set for the current **javax.servlet.ServletRequest**. For the purposes of discussion, let's call this **requestMap**.

With "**requestScope**" successfully resolved to **requestMap**, JSF runtime further breaks down the **user.firstName** part of the expression into its individual parts: **user** and **firstName**. The JSF runtime calls **myPropertyResolver.getValue(requestMap, "user")**. This method will look in the Map for a value under the key "user" and return it. Because we're in the Virtual Trainer example, the **requestMap** has such a value under the key "user", and this value is an instance of **com.jsfcompref.trainer.model.UserBean**. For discussion, let's call this the **userBean**. Finally, the last step in the evaluation of the expression happens when **myPropertyResolver .getValue(userBean, "firstName")** is called. Because **UserBean** is a plain old JavaBean, the **PropertyResolver** looks for a JavaBeans property with the name "**firstName**", which it finds and invokes the **getFirstName()** method, thus returning the first name of the user.

You can now see the pattern of how the expression is continually broken down stepwise into parts, with the result of evaluating step N being fed into the evaluation of step N + 1.

If we were trying to set a value into the expression—for example, as the value of an **h:inputText** field—the last part of the expression would have its **setFirstName()** method called instead of **getFirstName()**. Any expression parts between the first and last parts, however, would still be evaluated exactly as in the "get" case.

You can now see that by enabling the overriding or decoration of **PropertyResolver** and **VariableResolver**, JSF allows extreme customization of the behavior of the EL. Implicit objects can be intercepted or changed. The operation of EL operators "." and [ ] can be changed. The list of things you can do is open ended. The most important aspect to remember when doing a custom **VariableResolver** or **PropertyResolver** is to save and use the previous instance passed into the constructor per the decorator pattern. Failure to do so will cause the EL to stop working.

JSF 1.2 Tip *This loophole was closed in JSF 1.2 where it is impossible to override the behavior of the predefined implicit objects, though it is still possible to introduce new ones. Also, the dependency on the decorator pattern for **VariableResolver** and **PropertyResolver** leaves the developer open to the possibility of introducing serious and difficult-to-understand bugs when he or she tries to decorate one or both of these classes. Neglecting to save and/or use the previous **VariableResolver** or **PropertyResolver** instance when implementing a custom one will cause the entire JSF EL to stop working! This problem has been solved in JSF 1.2 by using a chain of responsibility pattern for **ELResolver** instances instead of the decorator pattern in JSF 1.0 and 1.1.*

Abstract Classes to Extend

For **PropertyResolver**, the abstract class **javax.faces.el.PropertyResolver** must be extended. It defines the following methods.

```
public abstract Object getValue(Object base, Object property)
    throws EvaluationException, PropertyNotFoundException;
public abstract Object getValue(Object base, int index)
    throws EvaluationException, PropertyNotFoundException;
public abstract void setValue(Object base, Object property, Object value)
    throws EvaluationException, PropertyNotFoundException;
public abstract void setValue(Object base, int index, Object value)
    throws EvaluationException, PropertyNotFoundException;
public abstract boolean isReadOnly(Object base, Object property)
    throws EvaluationException, PropertyNotFoundException;
public abstract boolean isReadOnly(Object base, int index)
    throws EvaluationException, PropertyNotFoundException;
public abstract Class getType(Object base, Object property)
    throws EvaluationException, PropertyNotFoundException;
public abstract Class getType(Object base, int index)
    throws EvaluationException, PropertyNotFoundException;
```

For **VariableResolver**, the abstract class **com.sun.faces.el.VariableResolver** must be extended. It defines the following method.

```
public abstract Object resolveVariable(FacesContext context, String name)
    throws EvaluationException;
```

Let's take a real-world example of **VariableResolver** decorating from the source code of the Spring Framework. The following code has been abbreviated. The full version can be downloaded from **www.springframework.org/**. This example allows any JSF EL expression to reference POJOs (plain old Java objects) created by Spring's **BeanFactory** as well as regular JSF managed beans.

```
/*
 * Copyright 2002-2005 the original author or authors.
 *
…

package org.springframework.web.jsf;



import org.springframework.web.context.WebApplicationContext;

/**
 * JSF VariableResolver that first delegates to the original resolver of the
 * underlying JSF implementation, then to the Spring root
 * WebApplicationContext.
 *
 * @author Juergen Hoeller
 */
public class DelegatingVariableResolver extends VariableResolver {

  protected final VariableResolver originalVariableResolver;

  public DelegatingVariableResolver(VariableResolver
                              originalVariableResolver) {
    this.originalVariableResolver = originalVariableResolver;
  }

  protected final VariableResolver getOriginalVariableResolver() {
    return originalVariableResolver;
  }

  public Object resolveVariable(FacesContext facesContext,
                          String name) throws EvaluationException {
    // Ask original resolver.
    Object originalResult = getOriginalVariableResolver().
                          resolveVariable(facesContext, name);
    if (originalResult != null) {
      return originalResult;
    }

    // Ask Spring root context.
    WebApplicationContext wac = getWebApplicationContext(facesContext);
    if (wac.containsBean(name)) {
      return wac.getBean(name);
    }

    return null;
```

```
    }

    protected WebApplicationContext
            getWebApplicationContext(FacesContext facesContext) {
        return FacesContextUtils.getRequiredWebApplicationContext(facesContext);
    }
}
```

The heart of this class is the **resolveVariable()** method required by the **VariableResolver** interface. This method first asks the existing JSF implementation if it can resolve the variable. If not, the Spring **WebApplicationContext** is consulted. Once this **VariableResolver** has been installed in the application, any EL expressions can leverage it without even knowing they are doing so. For example, let's say the bean **shoppingCart** is supplied to the system via Spring's **BeanFactory** and that there is no JSF managed bean with the name **shoppingCart**. Then this expression would cause the **DelegatingVariableResolver** to be consulted: #{shoppingCart.items}.

Registering a VariableResolver or PropertyResolver

A custom **VariableResolver** or **PropertyResolver** may be registered declaratively in the **faces-config.xml** file using the **variable-resolver** and **property-resolver** XML elements, or dynamically at runtime using the **setVariableResolver()** or **setPropertyResolver()** methods on **Application**. The declarative registration is most common and recommended. Both **variable-resolver** and **property-resolver** elements are children of the **application** element in the **faces-config.xml** file. These elements both must contain the fully qualified Java class name of the implementation class for your **VariableResolver** or **PropertyResolver**, respectively. See Chapter 18 for the **faces-config.xml** syntax for registering a **VariableResolver**.

Overriding **PropertyResolver** is much the same as that just shown, but it is less common to do so in practice. As such, this feature is not documented further here.

NOTE *In JSF 1.1, it is perfectly valid to have multiple **property-resolver** or **variable-resolver** elements but not in the same **faces-config.xml** file. The way to work around this restriction is to leverage one of the ways to tell the JSF runtime that there are multiple xml files that should be treated as **faces-config.xml** files. See the section titled "How the JSF Runtime Loads **faces-config.xml** Files" in Chapter 10.*

ELResolver (JSF 1.2)

The previous section covered how the EL can be augmented in JSF 1.1 through the Spring Framework example. In JSF 1.2, **VariableResolver** and **PropertyResolver** have been deprecated, but of course still supported for backwards compatibility. In JSF 1.2, the concepts of **PropertyResolver** and **VariableResolver** have been merged into the Unified EL class **javax.el.ELResolver**. Basically, an **ELResolver** functions as a **VariableResolver** if the first argument to its **getValue()** or **setValue()** method is **null**. Otherwise, it functions as a **PropertyResolver**.

This section shows how to use the JSF 1.2 class **ELResolver** in place of the now-deprecated **PropertyResolver** or **VariableResolver** classes, which were used with JSF 1.1.

The ELResolver Chain of Responsibility

Another change in JSF 1.2 is the removal of the decorator pattern in favor of a *chain of responsibility (CoR)* pattern for extending the EL. The use of the CoR pattern makes it impossible to accidentally break the EL by forgetting to delegate to the existing implementation, as well as making it impossible to redefine implicit objects already defined in the specification. The EL implementation maintains a chain of **ELResolver** instances for various kinds of expression elements. When presented with an expression, the EL implementation walks down the chain for each part of the expression until one of the resolvers in the chain successfully resolves the expression part. This success is signaled by setting a flag: the resolver calling **setPropertyResolved(true)** on the **ELContext** that is passed to every call on every **ELResolver** in the chain. The EL implementation checks the flag by calling **getPropertyResolved()** on the **ELContext** after every call on every resolver in the chain, and if it returns **true**, the next part of the expression is evaluated, starting again at the head of the chain. The **ELResolver** chain is shown in Figure 12-1.

Let's take a generic example (not relating to the Virtual Trainer example) to clarify the resolution process. Let's say we have a request-scoped managed bean named **user** that has a **friends** property whose value is a **Map** of names to other **user** instances. Also, the **user** bean also has a property called **address** that is a **String**. Such an expression could look like #{user. friends.jeff.address}. Assume this is the first time the **user**-managed bean is being resolved and therefore it hasn't yet been instantiated. Before diving into the resolution process for this expression, first some terminology. Each part of the expression is seen by the EL as a **base** object, and a **property** object. For example, when evaluating the last part of the expression, **jeff** is the **base**, while **address** is the property. A special case is the first part of the expression, for which the **base** is **null**.

EXPERT GROUP INSIGHT   *Allowing* **base** *to be* **null** *for the first part of the expression is the key enabling concept that permits the JSF 1.1 concepts of* **VariableResolver** *and* **PropertyResolver** *to be combined into the* **ELResolver**. *If the* **base** *is null, an* **ELResolver** *functions much like a* **VariableResolver**. *Otherwise, it functions as a* **PropertyResolver**.

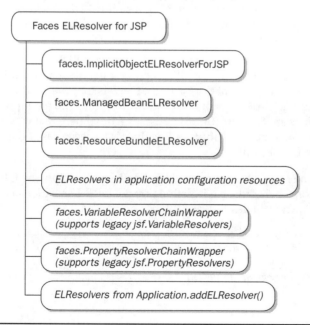

FIGURE 12-1   The **ELResolver** chain from JSP 2.1

The resolution of **#{user.friends.jeff.address}** is as follows:

1. **base** is **null**, property is user.

2. The JSP implementation's **CompositeELResolver** is consulted. This instance is the head of the chain. It doesn't resolve anything on its own.

   a. JSP's **javax.el.ImplicitObjectELResolver** is consulted. Since **user** is not a JSP implicit object, no action is taken, and flow continues down the chain.

   b. Another **CompositeELResolver** is encountered. This one hosts the sub-chain of resolvers for JSF.

   c. JSF's **ImplicitObjectELResolver** is consulted. Since **user** is not a JSF implicit object, no action is taken, and flow continues down the chain.

   d. JSF's **ManagedBeanELResolver** is consulted. Finally, some action is taken! Because **user** is listed as a **managed-bean-name** in the **faces-config.xml** file, this resolver will tell the EL implementation that some action was taken by calling **setPropertyResolved(true)** on the **ELContext** instance, instantiate the managed bean, place it in the proper scope, and return it.

3. **base** is **user**, **property** is **friends**. Now that we have the **user** bean in hand, it's time to resolve its **friends** property. A managed bean is simply a plain old Java object (POJO), but the JSP spec treats POJOs as **JavaBean** instances. Starting again at the top of the chain, each link in the chain is consulted until the **javax.el.BeanELResolver** is reached to perform this resolution. This will call **setPropertyResolved(true)** on the **ELContext**, call the **getFriends()** method on the user bean, and return.

4. **base** is **friends**, **property** is **jeff**. Recall that the **getFriends()** method on the user bean returns a **Map**. Starting at the top, again, we reach the **el.MapELResolver**, which knows how to resolve things on **Map** instances. This resolver calls **setPropertyResolved(true)** on the **ELContext**, looks up the **friends** key in the **Map**, and returns it.

5. **base** is **jeff**; **property** is **address**. Once again, we have a POJO as our base, so the **BeanELResolver** again does the job. It's important to note that the only way the implementation knows to treat the **base** as a POJO is that every other possible way of treating it has yielded no results. In other words, if it's not an implicit object, managed bean, **Map**, **ResourceBundle**, **List**, or **Array**, then treat it as a POJO and see if it works. The **scopedAttributeELResolver** is a special case because it only operates when **base** is **null**.

The **ELResolvers** in Figure 12-1 are defined by the EL specification, the JSP specification, and the JSF specification. Their ordering is defined by the JSP 2.1 specification. The meaning of these resolvers is shown in Tables 12-2 and 12-3.

EXPERT GROUP INSIGHT *The resolvers in Table 12-3 are defined by the JSF 1.2 specification and no public implementation of these classes is provided. This was intentional because the Expert Group didn't want anyone extending the JSF 1.2 resolvers to allow for maximum flexibility in implementation.*

ELResolver in package javax.el	Description	Usage Example
ArrayELResolver	Resolves expression segments that are arrays	#{user.accounts[0]}
BeanELResolver	Resolves JavaBean properties	#{user.name}
CompositeELResolver	Maintains a chain of nested **ELResolver**s	Not Applicable
ImplicitObjectELResolver	Resolves the implicit objects from the JSP specification	#{cookie.userName}
ListELResolver	Resolves expression segments that are **java.util.List** instances	#{user.accounts[0]}
MapELResolver	Resolves expression segments that are **java.util.Map** instances	#{user.propertyMap}
ResourceBundleELResolver	Resolves expression segments that are **java.util .ResourceBundle** instances	#{bundle.key}
ScopedAttributeELResolver	Performs scope search: request, page, session, application	#{user}

TABLE 12-2   **ELResolver** Instances Defined by the EL 1.0 Specification

ELResolver from Faces Specification	Description	Usage Example
ImplicitObjectELResolver	Resolves only the implicit objects defined by JSF—for example, **facesContext** and **view**.	#{FacesContext. viewRoot.locale}
ManagedBeanELResolver	Responsible for instantiating **managed-bean** instances and placing them in the proper scope for future resolution with a scoped attribute **ELResolver**.	#{user.name}
VariableResolverChainWrapper	Responsible for allowing JSF 1.1 style **VariableResolver** instances to continue to work.	#{customImplicitObject. value}
PropertyResolverChainWrapper	Responsible for allowing JSF 1.1 style **PropertyResolver** instances to continue to work.	#{user.name}

TABLE 12-3   **ELResolver** Instances Defined in the JSF 1.2 Specification

ELResolver from Faces Specification	Description	Usage Example
ResourceBundleELResolver	Responsible for returning and/or creating a **ResourceBundle** from information in the **faces-config.xml**. Actual resolution of the key in the bundle happens in the **javax .el.ELResolver**.	#{bundle.name}
ScopedAttributeELResolver	Just like the **javax.el.Scop edAttributeELResolver**, but doesn't resolve page scope.	#{user.name}

TABLE 12-3   ELResolver Instances Defined in the JSF 1.2 Specification *(continued)*

Abstract Class to Extend

An **ELResolver** must extend the abstract class **javax.el.ELResolver** and implement the following methods.

```
public Object getValue(ELContext context,
                    Object base,
                    Object property);
public Class getType(ELContext context,
                    Object base,
                    Object property);
public void setValue(ELContext context,
                    Object base,
                    Object property,
                    Object value);
public boolean isReadOnly(ELContext context,
                        Object base,
                        Object property);
public Iterator getFeatureDescriptors(ELContext context,
                                    Object base);
public Class getCommonPropertyType(ELContext context,
                    Object base);
```

Registering an ELResolver

When implementing an **ELResolver**, you must register it using the **el-resolver** element in the **faces-config.xml** file. The contents of this element must be a fully qualified Java class name of a class that extends **ELResolver**. In JSF 1.2, the **el-resolver** element is a child of the **application** element in the **faces-config.xml** file. See Chapter 18 for the **faces-config.xml** syntax for registering an **ELResolver**.

To illustrate a custom **ELResolver**, and explain how to implement each of the preceding methods, let's examine the **ShaleELResolver** from the Shale framework. This **ELResolver** adds the **jndi** implicit object to the EL. For more on Shale, please see Appendix D.

The **ShaleELResolver** begins as shown next:

```java
/*
 * Copyright 2004-2005 The Apache Software Foundation.
 *
 * License document omitted
 *
 */

package org.apache.shale.faces;

import java.beans.FeatureDescriptor;
import java.util.ArrayList;
import java.util.Iterator;
import javax.el.ELResolver;
import javax.el.ELContext;
import javax.el.PropertyNotFoundException;
import javax.el.EvaluationException;
import javax.faces.el.EvaluationException;
import javax.naming.Context;
import javax.naming.InitialContext;
import javax.naming.Name;
import javax.naming.NameClassPair;
import javax.naming.NameNotFoundException;
import javax.naming.NamingEnumeration;
import javax.naming.NamingException;

/**
 * <p>Shale-specific ELResolver for evaluating JavaServer Faces
 * value and method expressions.  The following special
 * variable names are recognized, and evaluated as indicated:</p>
 * <ul>
 * <li><strong>jndi</strong> - Returns the JNDI context at name
 *    <code>java:comp/env</code> (relative to the initial context
 *    supplied by the container.</li>
 * </ul>
 * <p>All other evaluations are delegated to <code>ELResolver</code>
 * chain.</p>
 *
 */
public class ShaleELResolver extends ELResolver {




    /**
     * <p>Construct a new {@link ShaleELResolver} instance.</p>
     *
     */
    public ShaleELResolver() {

    }
```

```java
/**
 * <p>Variable name to be resolved to our JNDI environment context.</p>
 */
private static final String JNDI_VARIABLE_NAME = "jndi";

// Prevent returning a huge number of results
// from getFeatureDescriptor()
private static final int MAX_TOP_LEVEL_NAMES = 1000;

// --------------------------- VariableResolver Methods

/**
 * <p>Resolve variable names known to this resolver; otherwise,
 * delegate to the ELResolver chain.</p>
 *
 * @param name Variable name to be resolved
 */
public Object getValue(ELContext elContext, Object base,
                       Object property) {
  Object result = null;

  // If we have a non-null base object, function as a PropertyResolver
  if (null != base) {
    if (base instanceof Context) {
      elContext.setPropertyResolved(true);
      Context context = (Context) base;
      try {
        if (property instanceof Name) {
        result = context.lookup((Name) property);
        } else {
          if (null != property) {
            result = context.lookup(property.toString());
          }
        }
      } catch (NameNotFoundException e) {
        // Mimic standard JSF/JSP behavior when base is a Map
        // by returning null
        return null;
      } catch (NamingException e) {
        throw new EvaluationException(e);
      }
    }
  }
  else {
    // function as a VariableResolver
    if (null == property) {
      throw new PropertyNotFoundException("ShaleELResolver: name must
                                          not be null");
    }

    if (JNDI_VARIABLE_NAME.equals(property)) {
      elContext.setPropertyResolved(true);
      try {
        InitialContext ic = new InitialContext();
```

```
        result = (Context) ic.lookup("java:comp/env");
      } catch (NamingException e) {
        throw new EvaluationException(e);
      }
    }
  }
  return result;
}
```

Pay special attention to the **getValue()** method. It is the most often called method on **ELResolver**. Because the **ShaleELResolver** simply adds JNDI capabilities to the EL, a **null base** argument means that it must look at the value of the **property** argument. If it is equal to the string "**jndi**", it sets the **ELResolver's propertyResolved** property to **true**, consults the **InitialContext** from JNDI, and obtains its "java:comp/env" **Context** value and returns it. A non-**null base** argument must be of type **javax.naming.Context**. In this case, the **propertyResolved** property is set to **true**, the **lookup()** method is called on the **Context**, and the value is returned.

Next is the **getType()** method:

```
public Class<?> getType(ELContext elContext, Object base,
                        Object property) {
  if (null != base && base instanceof Context) {
    elContext.setPropertyResolved(true);
    return Object.class;
  }
}
```

The **getType()** method is called by the implementation to determine if a subsequent call to **setValue()** is safe to call without causing a **ClassCastException** to be thrown. In this case, if the base is an instance of **javax.naming.Context**, then any **Object** may be passed as the value.

EXPERT GROUP INSIGHT   *A better name for the* **getType()** *method is* **getTypeForSet()**, *but for historical reasons it is simply called* **getType()**.

The next method is **setValue()**:

```
public void setValue(ELContext elContext, Object base,
      Object property,
      Object value) {
  if (null != base && base instanceof Context) {
      Context context = (Context) base;
    elContext.setPropertyResolved(true);
    try {
      // Mimic standard JSF/JSP behavior when base is a Map
      // by calling rebind() instead of bind()
      if (property instanceof Name) {
        context.rebind((Name) property, value);
      } else {
        context.rebind(property.toString(), value);
      }
    } catch (NamingException e) {
      throw new EvaluationException(e);
    }
  }
}
```

The **setValue()** method is used to enable the all-important "left-hand-side" operation of an expression, discussed in Chapter 4. In this case, it is only valid to set a value in an existing **Context** instance, so the **rebind()** method is called to set the value.

The **isReadOnly()** method, shown next, is called to tell if it is safe to call **setValue()** without fear of a **PropertyNotWritableException** being thrown.

```
public boolean isReadOnly(ELContext elContext,
        Object base,
        Object property) {
  if (base instanceof Context) {
    elContext.setPropertyResolved(true);
    // Mimic standard JSF/JSP behavior when base is a Map
    // by returning false if we cannot tell any better
    return false;
  }
}
```

Next comes the **getFeatureDescriptors()** method:

```
public Iterator getFeatureDescriptors(ELContext elContext,
    Object base) {
  String name = null;
  InitialContext ic = new InitialContext();
  Context context = (Context) ic.lookup("java:comp/env");
  NamingEnumeration<NameClassPair> names = null;
  ArrayList<FeatureDescriptor> featureDescriptors =
      new ArrayList<FeatureDescriptor>();

  if (null == base) {
    name = "";
  } else {
    name = base.toString();
  }

  names = context.list(name);
  try {
    NameClassPair cur = null;
    FeatureDescriptor curDescriptor = null;
    int i = 0;
    while (names.hasMoreElements() && i++ < MAX_TOP_LEVEL_NAMES) {
      cur = names.nextElement();
      curDescriptor = new FeatureDescriptor();
      curDescriptor.setName(cur.getName());
      curDescriptor.setDisplayName(cur.getNameInNamespace());
      curDescriptor.setExpert(true);
      if (null != cur.getClassName()) {
        curDescriptor.setValue(ELResolver.TYPE,
            Class.forName(cur.getClassName()));
      }
      curDescriptor.setValue(ELResolver.RESOLVABLE_AT_DESIGN_TIME,
          true);
      featureDescriptors.add(curDescriptor);
    }
    if (MAX_TOP_LEVEL_NAMES <= i) {
```

```
      // log error
    }
  } catch (NamingException e) {
    throw new EvaluationException(e);
  }
  return featureDescriptors.iterator();
}
```

The **getFeatureDescriptors()** method is used by a design-time tool to allow code completion of expressions at design time. A well-designed custom **ELResolver** will properly implement this method to enable itself to function optimally inside of tools.

Finally, **ShaleELResolver** ends with **getCommonPropertyType()**, shown next. It is also designed to assist tools by returning the "highest" **Class** that this resolver can resolve against the given **base** instance.

```
public Class<?> getCommonPropertyType(ELContext context,
                     Object base) {
  if (null == base) {
    return Context.class;
  }
  return Object.class;
}
}
```

NavigationHandler

The default **NavigationHandler** provided by the JSF implementation is adequate in most cases, but one can imagine some scenarios where supplementing its behavior can be useful. For example, let's suppose you don't like the XML navigation syntax provided by the JSF specification. A custom **NavigationHandler** could be installed to allow for an alternate navigation syntax, for example by using annotations on JSP pages. Such an approach is being investigated for a future version of the JSF specification.

Abstract Class to Extend

A custom **NavigationHandler** must extend the class **javax.faces.application .NavigationHandler** and must define the following method.

public void handleNavigation(FacesContext *context*,
                String *fromAction*,
                String *outcome*);

An implementation of this method must call **context.getViewRoot().getViewId()** and look at the **fromAction** and **outcome** arguments to determine the **viewId** of the next view to be shown, then create it by calling **context.getApplication().createView()**. Before returning, the new **UIViewRoot** is installed by calling **context.setViewRoot()**.

Showing the details of annotation-based **NavigationHandler** as an example of how to implement one is beyond the scope of this section, but a basic description follows. Require the user to provide a backing bean for each page in the application, as is enforced with the Sun JavaStudio Creator tool. Introduce a class level **@FromViewId** annotation to attach to each backing bean class. Introduce a method level **@NavigationCase** annotation, with **fromOutcome** and **toViewId** parameters to attach to each action method in a backing bean. Provide a **ServletContextListener** in your custom component's TLD file that uses the annotation processing tool (apt) included in JDK 1.5 to discover the annotations present in the backing beans. Perhaps you can use a naming convention to make it easier to discover the complete set of backing bean classes. This annotation processor would then build up a data-structure that is used by the custom navigation handler to satisfy **handleNavigation()** requests.

Registering a NavigationHandler

A custom **NavigationHandler** may be registered declaratively in the **faces-config.xml** file using the **navigation-handler** element, or dynamically using the **setNavigationHandler** method on the **Application**. The former is recommended and must contain the fully qualified Java class name of the class extending **NavigationHandler**. The **navigation-handler** element is a child of the **application** element in the **faces-config.xml**. See Chapter 18 for the **faces-config.xml** syntax for registering a **NavigationHandler**.

ActionListener

The **ActionListener** is where the outcome of executing a user action, such as pressing a button, is derived. Once the outcome is obtained, the **ActionListener** is responsible for calling the **NavigationHandler**, which executes the decision-making process based on that outcome. Thus, the **ActionListener** works closely with the **NavigationHandler** but it makes sense to allow them both to be independently replaced. As shown in the previous section, it is sometimes desirable to replace how the navigation decision is made, without changing how the outcome is derived that is passed into the navigation decision-making process. Likewise, it can be convenient to replace just the outcome derivation process without replacing the navigation decision-making process.

Chapter 15 provides an example of how to replace the default **ActionListener** with one that consults the Java platform security model before performing the action. This example only allows the action to complete if the user is properly authenticated and has the proper permissions to execute the action. See the section "Using JAAS Authentication in the Virtual Trainer" in Chapter 15 for details and source code.

Interface to Implement

A custom **ActionListener** must implement the interface **javax.faces.event.ActionListener**, which defines the following method.

```
public void processAction(ActionEvent event)
        throws AbortProcessingException;
```

The **processAction()** method receives the **ActionEvent** emitted from an **ActionSource** component (such as a button), invokes the method binding returned as the value of the **action** property of the **ActionSource** to arrive at the outcome value, and calls the **NavigationHandler** with the resultant outcome.

Registering an ActionListener

A custom **ActionListener** may be registered declaratively using the **action-listener** element in the **faces-config.xml** file, or dynamically using the **setActionListener()** method on **Application**. The former is recommended and must contain the fully qualified Java class name of a class implementing **ActionListener**. The **action-listener** element is a child of the **application** element in the **faces-config.xml**. See Chapter 18 for the **faces-config.xml** syntax for registering an **ActionListener**.

StateManager

A Web Application Framework must provide a solution for managing view state across HTTP requests as the user moves through the application. A *good* Framework will allow the design and implementation of this solution to be customizable and Faces does just that with the **StateManager** API.

   View state management is a complex business and few application developers will have to worry about customizing it. In fact, most use-cases for customizing state management arise for JSF implementers or those taking an existing JSF implementation and customizing it to their needs. For example, one use-case for a custom **StateManager** would be replacing the default implementation with a high-performance one that relies on a database and supports object pooling. Therefore, only a brief overview of the **StateManager** API is provided.

Abstract Class to Extend in JSF 1.1 and 1.0

A custom **StateManager** must extend the abstract class **javax.faces.application .StateManager** and decorate or replace the following methods.

```
    public SerializedView saveSerializedView(FacesContext context);
    protected Object getTreeStructureToSave(FacesContext context);
    protected Object getComponentStateToSave(FacesContext context);
    public void writeState(FacesContext context, SerializedView state)
            throws IOException;
    public UIViewRoot restoreView(FacesContext context, String viewId,
                            String renderKitId);
    protected UIViewRoot restoreTreeStructure(FacesContext context,
                            String viewId,
                            String renderKitId);
    protected void restoreComponentState(FacesContext context,
                            UIViewRoot viewRoot,
                            String renderKitId);
    public boolean isSavingStateInClient(FacesContext context);
```

   A default implementation of **isSavingStateInClient()** is provided that consults the JSF specification-defined **javax.faces.STATE_SAVING_METHOD** servlet context **init** parameter to determine if the state is to be saved in the page (the default) or on the server. The intent of the previous methods is explained by examining the state saving and state restoring process in the context of the request processing lifecycle.

---

*JSF 1.2 TIP   A bug in the JSF 1.1 specification is that the **SerializedView** class itself is not Serializable! When saving the state on the server, this poses problems with containers that need to do session failover within a cluster. This problem was fixed in JSF 1.2 with a redesign of the **StateManager** API which included deprecating all of the JSF 1.1 methods of this class.*

State Saving Using the StateManager in JSF 1.0 and 1.1   As part of the Render Response lifecycle phase, the JSF runtime must call the **saveSerializedView()** method of the **StateManager**. This method returns an instance of the inner class **javax.faces.application .StateManager.SerializedView**, which is a simple structure that encapsulates the tree structure and component state of a view in two **Object**s obtainable from the **getTreeStructure()** and **getComponentState()** methods of **SerializedView**, respectively. The protected helper method **getTreeStructureToSave()** and **getComponentStateToSave()** can be implemented to aid in the creation of the **SerializedView** instance. The meaning of the **treeStructure** and **componentState** properties is implementation-dependent, but tree structure is generally the parent-child relationships of each node in the tree, while component state is the in-depth state of each node of the tree.

Once the **SerializedView** instance is created, the JSF runtime passes it to the **writeState()** method. This method delegates to the **writeState()** method of the **ResponseStateManager** from the current **RenderKit** to write the state in a rendering technology–specific manner—for example, when the **HTML_BASIC RenderKit** writes this state out to a hidden field in the page.

State Restoring Using the StateManager in JSF 1.1 and 1.0   The JSF runtime must call the **restoreView()** method of the **StateManager** to inspect the incoming request and restore the view so that postback processing can occur. As with state saving, the implementation can use the **restoreTreeStructure()**, **restoreComponentState()**, **getTreeStructureToRestore()**, and **getComponentStateToRestore()** methods to aid in the process of restoring the view. The **restoreTreeStructure()** method builds the **UIViewRoot** rooted tree of components. The **restoreComponentState()** method traverses that tree and restores the component state of each node. The respective getters for tree structure and component state may call through to the **ResponseStateManager** to inspect the request in a rendering technology–specific way—for example, the **HTML_BASIC RenderKit** will know to look for a hidden field.

JSF 1.2 TIP   The following sections deal with state management in JSF 1.2.

Abstract Class to Extend in JSF 1.2

In JSF 1.2, all of the methods of **StateManager** except for **restoreView()** and **isSavingStateInClient()** have been deprecated. The inner class **SerializedView** has also been deprecated.

EXPERT GROUP INSIGHT   Special care was taken to ensure that existing, 1.1-style **StateManager** *implementations will continue to function properly.*

Developers wishing to follow the JSF 1.2 patterns must implement the following methods.

```
public Object saveView(FacesContext context);
public void writeState(FacesContext context, Object state)
       throws IOException;
```

These methods leave considerably more up to the implementation than their 1.1 counterparts by not declaring the concepts of tree structure and component state at the API level. As such, no specific description is required for the "save view" and "restore view" behavior, as was the case for the 1.1 versions explained earlier. All you need to know is that **saveView()** is called during the Render Response phase, and **restoreView()** is called during the Restore View phase. Both of these methods must rely on the **ResponseStateManager** from the current **RenderKit** to perform the rendering technology–specific actions regarding state management. The **ResponseStateManager** is covered in the section on **RenderKitFactory** that follows.

Registering a StateManager

A custom **StateManager** may be registered declaratively using the **state-manager** element in the **faces-config.xml** file, or dynamically by calling **setStateManager()** on the **Application**.

The former is recommended and must contain the fully qualified Java class name of a class extending **StateManager**. The **state-manager** element is a child of the **application** element in the **faces-config.xml**. See Chapter 18 for the **faces-config.xml** syntax for registering a **StateManager**.

RenderKit

Chapter 10 demonstrated how to add individual **Renderer** definitions to the standard render-kit, making them immediately available for use by components. A more reusable and well-encapsulated solution is to provide a self-contained **RenderKit**. A **RenderKit** is simply a collection of **Renderers** (usually designed to support the same kind of client device) that is able to render a collection of **UIComponent** classes. A component library may bundle custom components along with the **RenderKit**, or it may simply allow the **Renderers** to render the standard components in the **javax.faces.component** package. In terms of separation of concerns, the JSF architecture allocates the responsibility for all of the rendering technology–specific code to the **RenderKit** and its **Renderers**, while the rendering technology–independent code is the responsibility of the **UIComponent** subclass. An example of rendering technology–specific code is, in HTML, a text field happens to be encoded as **<input type="text" />**, and its value is decoded from the postback as a name=value pair in the POST data or GET query string of the request. An example of rendering technology–independent code is the notion that a component is a "select one choice from many choices" component, and therefore needs some way to represent the selected choice and the possible choices.

There are two main steps to creating a custom **RenderKit**:

1. Defining the **RenderKit** and **Renderer** classes themselves, as well as the XML markup to define them to the JSF runtime

2. Indicating which views in the application use which **RenderKit**

Each is examined in the following.

Step 1: Defining the RenderKit and Renderer Classes

More than anything else, a **RenderKit** is a data-structure that returns a **Renderer** instance given two pieces of information: the component family and the renderer type. These terms were introduced in Chapter 10, but let's recap their meaning. The component family is a logical group of components—for example, "input", "output", or "selectOne". It captures the semantic intent of a component, and in the JSF specification there is exactly one component family declaration for each of the 18 components in the package **javax.faces .component**. The renderer type captures the appearance of the component that this **Renderer** renders. The JSF specification defines renderer types for things like button, checkbox, menu, and textarea. Therefore, the combination of these two pieces of information to select a **Renderer** is the key to JSF's client device independence.

Abstract Class to Extend to Implement a RenderKit   A custom **RenderKit** must extend the abstract class **javax.faces.render.RenderKit** and provide implementations for the following abstract methods.

```
public void addRenderer(String family, String rendererType,
                 Renderer renderer);
public Renderer getRenderer(String family, String rendererType);
public ResponseStateManager getResponseStateManager();
```

```
public ResponseWriter createResponseWriter(Writer writer,
                                           String contentTypeList,
                                           String characterEncoding);
public ResponseStream createResponseStream(OutputStream out);
```

The JSF specification does not define an implementation of **RenderKit** so you must write your own from scratch. Thankfully, both of the major implementations of the JSF specification are available in Open Source with liberal licenses. Sun's implementation of the **RenderKit** is available at **https://javaserverfaces-sources.dev.java.net/source/browse/ javaserverfaces-sources/jsf-ri/src/com/sun/faces/renderkit/RenderKitImpl.java** and is well suited for copying and using in your own application.

Even though the **RenderKit** doesn't support the decorator pattern, it is still possible to provide a simplified **RenderKit** implementation that provides its own (component-family + renderer-type) → **Renderer** mapping and delegates to the standard **HTML_BASIC RenderKit** for the hard stuff (namely, the **getResponseStateManager()**, **createResponseWriter()**, and **createResponseStream()** methods). Note that using this approach restricts your renderers in this **RenderKit** to only outputting the content-types supported by the **HTML_BASIC RenderKit**, which happens to be HTML. The Sun implementation of the **HTML_BASIC RenderKit**, linked previously, also supports XHTML.

```java
package com.jsfcompref.components.renderer;

import java.io.OutputStream;
import java.io.Writer;
import java.util.HashMap;
import java.util.Map;
import javax.faces.FactoryFinder;
import javax.faces.context.FacesContext;
import javax.faces.context.ResponseStream;
import javax.faces.context.ResponseWriter;
import javax.faces.render.RenderKit;
import javax.faces.render.RenderKitFactory;
import javax.faces.render.Renderer;
import javax.faces.render.ResponseStateManager;


/**
 *
 * <p>Provide the simple Map-like behavior of a RenderKit,
 * while delegating to the standard HTML_BASIC RenderKit for the
 * hard stuff.
 */
public class BasicRenderKit extends RenderKit {

  /**
   * A Map of Maps.  Keys are component-family identifiers,
   * values are Maps where the keys are renderer-type identifiers
   * and the values are Renderer instances.
   */

  private Map families;

  private ResponseStateManager responseStateManager = null;
```

```
    private RenderKit htmlBasicRenderKit;

    public BasicRenderKit() {
      families = new HashMap();
    }

    protected RenderKit getHtmlBasicRenderKit() {
      if (null == htmlBasicRenderKit) {
        RenderKitFactory rkFactory = (RenderKitFactory)
        FactoryFinder.getFactory(FactoryFinder.RENDER_KIT_FACTORY);
        htmlBasicRenderKit =
            rkFactory.getRenderKit(FacesContext.getCurrentInstance(),
            RenderKitFactory.HTML_BASIC_RENDER_KIT);
      }
      assert(null != htmlBasicRenderKit);
      return htmlBasicRenderKit;
    }

    public void addRenderer(String family, String rendererType,
        Renderer renderer) {
      Map renderers = null;

      if (null == (renderers = (Map) families.get(family))) {
        renderers = new HashMap();
        families.put(family, renderers);
      }
      assert(null != renderers);
      renderers.put(rendererType, renderer);
    }

    public Renderer getRenderer(String family, String rendererType) {
      Renderer result = null;
      Map renderers = null;
      if (null != (renderers = (Map) families.get(family))) {
        result = (Renderer) renderers.get(rendererType);
      }

      return result;
    }

    public ResponseStateManager getResponseStateManager() {
      return getHtmlBasicRenderKit().getResponseStateManager();
    }

    public ResponseWriter createResponseWriter(Writer writer,
        String contentTypeList,
        String characterEncoding) {
      return getHtmlBasicRenderKit().createResponseWriter(writer,
        contentTypeList, characterEncoding);
    }

    public ResponseStream createResponseStream(OutputStream out) {
      return getHtmlBasicRenderKit().createResponseStream(out);
    }

}
```

As you can see, the **addRenderer()** and **getRenderer()** methods are very simple, and need not be any more complex than this. They simply maintain a nested **Map** data structure, where the outer **Map** goes from **component-family** to the inner **Map**, and the inner **Map** goes from **renderer-type** to **Renderer** instance. The **getResponseStateManager()** returns the **ResponseStateManager** instance used by the **StateManager** as described earlier. Because the implementation details of this class are beyond the scope of this book, we simply leverage the implementation from the **HTML_BASIC RenderKit**. The **createResponseWriter()** method deserves special attention. As shown in Chapter 10 and other chapters, this class provides the abstraction to the client device–dependent markup and is used by individual **Renderer**s to actually write their rendering output to the client. For usage examples of this class, please see Chapter 10. Finally, the **createResponseStream()** method is intended for **RenderKit**s that need to render themselves to a non-textual client device. Unfortunately, there have been no known uses of this method as of this writing.

Registering a RenderKit

Now that you have the **RenderKit** class defined, you need to define individual **Renderer** instances for it. Please see Chapter 10 for an example of a custom **Renderer**. Note that a **Renderer** implementation itself does not necessarily have any knowledge of the **RenderKit** in which it resides, and therefore, it is perfectly fine to reuse the **HtmlInputDateRenderer** as a starting point for your custom **Renderer** implementations. Assuming this has been done and you have all the **Renderer** classes you need for your application, it is now time to examine the **faces-config.xml** markup necessary to declare your **RenderKit** to the JSF runtime. It is shown next:

```
<render-kit>
  <render-kit-id>com.jsfcompref.CustomRenderKit</render-kit-id>
  <render-kit-class>
    com.jsfcompref.components.renderer.BasicRenderKit
  </render-kit-class>

  <renderer>
    <component-family>InputDateFamily</component-family>
    <renderer-type>HtmlInputDateRenderer</renderer-type>
    <renderer-class>
      com.jsfcompref.components.component.HtmlInputDateRenderer
    </renderer-class>
  </renderer>

  <!-- additional renderer elements inserted as needed -->
</render-kit>
```

The preceding **render-kit** declaration will cause the runtime's **RenderKitFactory** (described in the following section) to be populated with an instance of **BasicRenderKit** under the **render-kit-id** of **com.jsfcompref.CustomRenderKit**. This **render-kit-id** is just a plain old **String**, but you can help prevent name clashes by prefixing every public identifier with something reasonably likely to be unique.

Step 2: Indicating Which Views in the Application Use Which RenderKit

In JSF 1.1, support was limited for using multiple **RenderKit**s within a single application.

Expert Group Insight *Hans Bergsten, one of the key contributors to the JSF 1.0 Expert Group, lobbied very hard to fix this issue in a more comprehensive fashion, but his objections were overridden by the schedule pressure to ship the 1.0 specification. This resulted in the simple solution present in JSF 1.0 and 1.1, which has been fixed in a more comprehensive manner in JSF 1.2.*

It is possible to indicate that an alternate **RenderKit** be used to render the entire application by including a **<default-render-kit-id>** element in the **<application>** element of the **faces-config.xml** file, assuming that the **default-render-kit-id** element refers to an actual **render-kit-id** elsewhere in the file, or in another configuration file in the same application. In order to allow for dynamic **RenderKit** selection within a single application in JSF 1.1, a custom **ViewHandler** must be provided that has awareness of which views go with which **render-kit-id** and making sure to pass this **render-kit-id** to the **restoreView()** method of the **StateManager**. Leveraging the decoration technique for **ViewHandler**, shown earlier, we provide a custom **ViewHandler** that delegates to the standard one for all but the **calculateRenderKitId()** and **createView()** methods. As usual, the full code is available online but the following shows the salient parts.

```
package com.jsfcompref.components.application;

import com.jsfcompref.components.util.Util;
import java.io.IOException;
import java.util.Locale;
import java.util.Map;
import java.util.MissingResourceException;
import java.util.ResourceBundle;
import javax.faces.FacesException;
import javax.faces.application.ViewHandler;
import javax.faces.component.UIViewRoot;
import javax.faces.context.FacesContext;
import javax.faces.render.RenderKitFactory;
import javax.servlet.http.HttpServletRequest;

public class JSF11MultiRenderKitViewHandler extends ViewHandler {

  private ViewHandler parent = null;

  /** Creates a new instance of JSF11MultiRenderKitViewHandler */
  public JSF11MultiRenderKitViewHandler(ViewHandler parent) {
    viewsToRenderKitIds = ResourceBundle.getBundle("ViewsToRenderKitIds");
    this.parent = parent;
  }

  ResourceBundle viewsToRenderKitIds = null;

  private ViewHandler getParent() {
    return parent;
  }

  public Locale calculateLocale(FacesContext context) {
    return getParent().calculateLocale(context);
  }

  // Remaining wholly delegated methods omitted for brevity.
```

```java
public String calculateRenderKitId(FacesContext facesContext) {
  // Obtain the viewId from the available request information,
  // as done in the default ViewHandler.
  Map requestMap = facesContext.getExternalContext().getRequestMap();
  String renderKitId = null,
      viewId = (String)
    requestMap.get("javax.servlet.include.path_info");
  if (viewId == null) {
    viewId = facesContext.getExternalContext().getRequestPathInfo();
  }

  if (viewId == null) {
    viewId = (String)
      requestMap.get("javax.servlet.include.servlet_path");
  }

  if (viewId == null) {
    Object request = facesContext.getExternalContext().getRequest();
    if (request instanceof HttpServletRequest) {
      viewId = ((HttpServletRequest) request).getServletPath();
    }
  }

  if (viewId == null) {
    renderKitId = getParent().calculateRenderKitId(facesContext);
  }
  else {
    renderKitId = getRenderKitIdGivenViewId(viewId);
  }
  return renderKitId;
}

public UIViewRoot createView(FacesContext context, String viewId) {
  UIViewRoot result = getParent().createView(context, viewId);
  result.setRenderKitId(getRenderKitIdGivenViewId(viewId));
  return result;
}

private String getRenderKitIdGivenViewId(String viewId) {
  String alternateRenderKitId = null;
  try {
    alternateRenderKitId = viewsToRenderKitIds.getString(viewId);
  } catch (MissingResourceException e) {
    // Set the renderKitId back to the default one
    alternateRenderKitId = RenderKitFactory.HTML_BASIC_RENDER_KIT;
  }
  return alternateRenderKitId;
}
// Rest of class omitted.
```

First, note that this implementation uses a simple properties file, defined at a well-known resource name of **"ViewsToRenderKitIds"**, to hold the mapping of viewIDs to RenderKitIDs. The constructor loads the **ResourceBundle** and stores a reference to the parent **ViewHandler** as described earlier in the section on decoration. The helper method

getRenderKitIdGivenViewId() consults the bundle for a key under the given **viewId**. If there is no value in the bundle under the key for the argument **viewId**, the **RenderKitFactory.HTML_BASIC_RENDER_KIT** is used. This is the RenderKitID of the standard HTML render-kit.

Again, the Virtual Trainer example is employed for the context. For this example, let's use a custom **RenderKit** just for encoding and decoding the **/edit_te.jsp** view. To expose this **RenderKit** to our application, we must declare it in a **faces-config.xml** file somewhere accessible to the application. As shown in the section on packaging at the end of Chapter 10, it is possible the **RenderKit** could be delivered as a self-contained jar file, in which case the **META-INF/faces-config.xml** file would contain the **<render-kit>** declaration. In this example, we'll just put it in the application's main **/WEB-INF/faces-config.xml** file, shown next:

```
<render-kit>
  <render-kit-id>com.jsfcompref.CustomRenderKit</render-kit-id>
  <render-kit-class>
    com.jsfcompref.components.renderer.BasicRenderKit
  </render-kit-class>

  <renderer>

    <component-family>javax.faces.Output</component-family>
    <renderer-type>javax.faces.Text</renderer-type>
    <renderer-class>com.jsfcompref.components.renderer.
      SpecialOutputTextRenderer</renderer-class>
  </renderer>

  <!-- remaining render-kit declarations omitted -->
</render-kit>
```

The online code for the **CustomRenderKit** demonstrates how to effectively "sub-class" the standard **HTML_BASIC RenderKit** and override just select renderers. In this case, we only want to override the renderer that will be used to render **<h:outputText>** components. We use the approach shown in the **SpellCheckTextarea** component from Chapter 11 to obtain the existing standard renderer for the output text component, as shown next.

```
package com.jsfcompref.trainercomponents.renderer;

import com.jsfcompref.trainercomponents.util.Util;
import javax.faces.context.FacesContext;
import javax.faces.context.ResponseWriter;
import javax.faces.render.RenderKitFactory;
import javax.faces.render.Renderer;
import javax.faces.component.UIComponent;
import java.io.IOException;

public class SpecialOutputTextRenderer extends Renderer {

  /** Creates a new instance of RedOutputTextRenderer */
  public SpecialOutputTextRenderer() {
  }

  private Renderer textRenderer = null;
```

```
      private Renderer getStandardTextRenderer(FacesContext context) {
        if (null != textRenderer) {
          return textRenderer;
        }

        textRenderer = Util.getRenderKit(context,
            RenderKitFactory.HTML_BASIC_RENDER_KIT).
            getRenderer("javax.faces.Output", "javax.faces.Text");
        assert(null != textRenderer);

        return textRenderer;
      }

    public void encodeBegin(FacesContext context,
                            UIComponent component) throws IOException {
      ResponseWriter writer = context.getResponseWriter();
      writer.startElement("i", component);
      writer.startElement("blink", component);
      writer.startElement("font", component);
      writer.writeAttribute("color", "red", "color");
      getStandardTextRenderer(context).encodeBegin(context,component);
    }

    public void encodeChildren(FacesContext context,
                               UIComponent component) throws IOException {
      getStandardTextRenderer(context).encodeChildren(context,component);
    }

    public void encodeEnd(FacesContext context,
                          UIComponent component) throws IOException {
      ResponseWriter writer = context.getResponseWriter();
      getStandardTextRenderer(context).encodeEnd(context,component);
      writer.endElement("font");
      writer.endElement("blink");
      writer.endElement("i");
    }

}
```

As in the **SpellCheckTextarea** component from Chapter 11, there is a method that obtains the right **Renderer** from the standard **HTML_BASIC RenderKit**. We override the **encodeBegin()** and **encodeEnd()** methods to wrap the standard markup in markup that makes the rendered text appear red, blinking, and italicized. While you would never want to do this to your users in a real application, this simple example demonstrates a powerful technique for extending the capabilities of an existing **Renderer**. In the online code for this example, you'll see that the rest of the **renderer** declarations in the **CustomRenderKit** simply refer to the existing classes in the Sun Implementation. In other words, the **SpecialOutputTextRenderer** is actually the only **Renderer** defined as a new Java class in the **CustomRenderKit**.

Now that we have the **CustomRenderKit** and **SpecialOutputTextRenderer** inside it, we need to tell the **JSF11MultiRenderKitViewHandler** which views in the Virtual Trainer example application should be rendered with the **CustomRenderKit** using the aforementioned **ViewsToRenderKitIds.properties** file, which is shown next:

```
# The mapping of view-id to render-kit-id.
/edit_te.jsp=com.jsfcompref.CustomRenderKit
```

This file is placed in the **WEB-INF/classes** directory in the trainer application so it is accessible to the **JSF11MultiRenderKitViewHandler**. Now when we cause the **/edit_te.jsp** view to be displayed by clicking an "edit" link from the main page of the application, we can see that all of the **<h:outputText>** tags are rendered in flashing, italicized, red text.

---

*JSF 1.2 TIP In JSF 1.2, a custom **ViewHandler** is no longer necessary to allow different views in the application to be rendered by different **RenderKit**s. Instead, a new **renderKitId** attribute has been added to **<f:view>**. In the case of the **edit-te.jsp** example, you would alter the JSP to look like the following:*

```
<!DOCTYPE HTML PUBLIC "-//W3C//DTD HTML 4.01 Transitional//EN"
"http://www.w3.org/TR/html4/loose.dtd">
<%@ page contentType="text/html;charset=windows-1252"%>
<%@ taglib uri="http://java.sun.com/jsf/core" prefix="f"%>
<%@ taglib uri="http://java.sun.com/jsf/html" prefix="h"%>
<f:view renderKitId="com.jsfcompref.CustomRenderKit">
<!-- The rest of the page is the same as before. -->
```

*The **renderKitId** attribute is **ValueExpression** enabled, so it is possible to introduce even more dynamism into the system by having the **renderKitId** come from the EL, like this: **<f:view renderKitId="#{prefs.renderKitId}" />**. It doesn't take much to see that using custom **RenderKit**s is an effective and simple way to do "skinning" in an application.*

Factories in JSF

The architecture of JSF takes great advantage of several design patterns, as shown earlier in the use of the decorator pattern. A related pattern is the *abstract factory* pattern, which provides an interface for creating families of related or dependent objects without specifying their concrete classes. In JSF, this pattern is implemented in the class **javax.faces .FactoryFinder**, which sends references to factories for creating instances of the following four kinds of classes: **RenderKit**, **FacesContext**, **Lifecycle**, and **Application**. The design of **FactoryFinder** enables replacing the implementation of any of the four kinds of factories.

Table 12-4 lists the types of factories that can be obtained through the **FactoryFinder**, along with the kinds of classes each knows how to create. Table 12-4 also shows which kinds of factories will always return the exact same instance when called any number of times (known as singletons), and those that will return a new and different instance when called.

Factory Class Name	Creates Instances of Class	Returns Singleton?
javax.faces.application .ApplicationFactory	javax.faces.application .Application	Yes
javax.faces.context .FacesContextFactory	javax.faces.context .FacesContext	No
javax.faces.lifecycle.LifecycleFactory	javax.faces.lifecycle.Lifecycle	Yes
javax.faces.render.RenderKitFactory	javax.faces.render.RenderKit	No

TABLE 12-4 Types of Factories Available from **FactoryFinder**, and the Kinds of Classes They Create

To motivate this discussion, recall the initial design requirement of JSF that applications built with JSF must run in a Servlet *or* Portlet container. To enable this, all of the Servlet- or Portlet-specific methods have been extracted in the **ExternalContext** instance that is obtained from the **getExternalContext()** method of **FacesContext.** The **ExternalClass** has many methods that call for different, yet similar, action to be taken when the container is a Servlet container versus a Portlet container. However, the default **FacesContext** implementation required by the JSF specification is only suitable for use in Servlet environments. How then to achieve this required portability? Custom implementations of **FacesContextFactory** and **LifecycleFactory** come to the rescue. The JSF Portlet integration library provides such a class, which we will examine later in this chapter in the section titled "**FacesContextFactory.**" For now, it's necessary to understand the concepts behind these pluggable factories.

Registering a Factory

As will be later shown in Chapter 18, the **faces-config.xml** file may contain a **<factory>** element with sub-elements for any of the four factory classes. This is the primary means by which one would replace a factory instance with a custom implementation. For example, in the Portlet integration library case, we have:

```
<factory>
  <faces-context-factory>
    com.sun.faces.portlet.FacesContextFactoryImpl
  </faces-context-factory>
  <lifecycle-factory>
    com.sun.faces.portlet.LifecycleFactoryImpl
  </lifecycle-factory>
</factory>
```

For completeness, we must also mention a last-resort factory replacement mechanism used by the **FactoryFinder.** If a file exists in the **META-INF/services** directory of any jar in the classpath whose name is equal to any of the fully qualified factory class names in Table 12-4, the contents of that file will be assumed to contain a first line that is a fully qualified class name of a Java class that implements that specific factory. So, to continue the Portlet library example, let's say we have a jar called **factories.jar** that has the following contents:

```
META-INF/MANIFEST.MF
META-INF/services/javax.faces.context.FacesContextFactory
META-INF/services/javax.faces.lifecycle.LifecycleFactory
com/jsfcompref/FacesContextFactoryImpl.class
com/jsfcompref/LifecycleFactoryImpl.class
```

Note that there is no **META-INF/faces-config.xml** file. Further, let's assume that the file **META-INF/services/javax.faces.context.FacesContextFactory** in the jar is a text file that contains only the line:

```
com.jsfcompref.FacesContextFactoryImpl
```

and that the file **META-INF/services/javax.faces.lifecycle.LifecycleFactory** in the jar is a text file that contains only the line:

```
com.jsfcompref.LifecycleFactoryImpl
```

Because there is no **faces-config.xml** file in the jar, the JSF runtime is unable to replace the factory instances using the standard XML mechanism. Therefore, when the runtime asks the **FactoryFinder** to return an instance of **FacesContextFactory**, the **META-INF/services/ javax.faces.context.FacesContextFactory** file is consulted and the custom class **com .jsfcompref.FacesContextFactoryImpl** is returned instead.

Finally, note that methods on **FactoryFinder** are generally never called by developer code. Rather, **FactoryFinder** methods are only invoked by the JSF runtime, though there is no prohibition on user code calling **FactoryFinder**. To that end, we list the methods of **FactoryFinder** next for reference.

public static Object getFactory(String *factoryName*) throws FacesException;
public static void setFactory(String *factoryName*, String *implName*);
public static void releaseFactories() throws FacesException;

The first method returns a factory instance that extends the class given by the **factoryName** argument, as long as the argument is one of the values in the first column in Table 12-4. The second method can be called to replace the factory implementation at runtime whenever needed before the first call to **getFactory()** on that particular factory type. The last method is called to tell the **FactoryFinder** to release all instances of all factories it has created.

RenderKitFactory

Let's examine **RenderKitFactory** first to follow on from the custom **RenderKit** example shown earlier. One use-case for creating a custom **RenderKitFactory** is when you cannot, or do not want to, declare the entire **RenderKit** in XML using the **<render-kit>** and **<renderer>** elements.

Abstract Class to Extend   An instance of **RenderKitFactory** must extend the abstract class **javax.faces.render.RenderKitFactory** and implement the following methods.

public void addRenderKit(String *renderKitId*, RenderKit *renderKit*);
public RenderKit getRenderKit(FacesContext *context*, String *renderKitId*);
public Iterator getRenderKitIds();

For example, suppose you wanted to create a custom **RenderKit** that extended the **HTML_ BASIC RenderKit** and replaced just the **OutputText Renderer** as shown previously, but without specifying any of the XML. The following custom **RenderKitFactory** does just this.

```
package com.jsfcompref.trainercomponents.renderer;

import com.jsfcompref.trainercomponents.renderer.BasicRenderKit;
import java.util.Iterator;
import javax.faces.context.FacesContext;
import javax.faces.render.RenderKit;
import javax.faces.render.RenderKitFactory;

public class ExtendHtmlBasicRenderKitFactory extends RenderKitFactory {

  private String [][] standardRenderKit = {
// The OutputText renderer is intentionally commented out.
//    { "javax.faces.Output", "javax.faces.Text" },
    { "javax.faces.Command", "javax.faces.Button" },
    { "javax.faces.Command", "javax.faces.Link" },
    { "javax.faces.Data", "javax.faces.Table" },
    { "javax.faces.Form", "javax.faces.Form" },
    { "javax.faces.Graphic", "javax.faces.Image" },
    { "javax.faces.Input", "javax.faces.Hidden" },
    { "javax.faces.Input", "javax.faces.Secret" },
```

```
    { "javax.faces.Input", "javax.faces.Text" },
    { "javax.faces.Input", "javax.faces.Textarea" },
    { "javax.faces.Message", "javax.faces.Message" },
    { "javax.faces.Messages", "javax.faces.Messages" },
    { "javax.faces.Output", "javax.faces.Format" },
    { "javax.faces.Output", "javax.faces.Label" },
    { "javax.faces.Output", "javax.faces.Link" },
    { "javax.faces.Panel", "javax.faces.Grid" },
    { "javax.faces.Panel", "javax.faces.Group" },
    { "javax.faces.SelectBoolean", "javax.faces.Checkbox" },
    { "javax.faces.SelectMany", "javax.faces.Checkbox" },
    { "javax.faces.SelectMany", "javax.faces.Listbox" },
    { "javax.faces.SelectMany", "javax.faces.Menu" },
    { "javax.faces.SelectOne", "javax.faces.Listbox" },
    { "javax.faces.SelectOne", "javax.faces.Menu" },
    { "javax.faces.SelectOne", "javax.faces.Radio" }
};


/** Creates a new instance of ExtendHtmlBasicRenderKitFactory */
public ExtendHtmlBasicRenderKitFactory(RenderKitFactory parent) {
  this.parent = parent;
}

private RenderKitFactory parent = null;

public RenderKit getRenderKit(FacesContext facesContext, String renderKitId) {
  RenderKit result = null;
  // First, ask the parent.
  if (null == (result = parent.getRenderKit(facesContext, renderKitId))) {
    // Note that we don't care if renderKitId is null, because we're
    // supposed to throw a NullPointerException if it is.
    if (renderKitId.equals("com.jsfcompref.CustomRenderKit")) {
        result = createAndPopulateBasicRenderKitInstance(facesContext);
        parent.addRenderKit("com.jsfcompref.CustomRenderKit", result);
    }
  }
  return result;
}


private RenderKit createAndPopulateBasicRenderKitInstance(FacesContext context) {
  RenderKit result = new BasicRenderKit();
  RenderKit standard = parent.getRenderKit(context,
      RenderKitFactory.HTML_BASIC_RENDER_KIT);
  int i = 0;
  // For all renderers except outputText, copy from the standard RenderKit.
  for (i = 0; i < standardRenderKit.length; i++) {
    result.addRenderer(standardRenderKit[i][0],
        standardRenderKit[i][1],
        standard.getRenderer(standardRenderKit[i][0],
          standardRenderKit[i][1]));
  }
  // Replace just the outputText renderer.
  result.addRenderer("javax.faces.Output", "javax.faces.Text",
      new SpecialOutputTextRenderer());
  return result;
}
```

```
public void addRenderKit(String renderKitId, RenderKit renderKit) {
  parent.addRenderKit(renderKitId, renderKit);
}

public Iterator getRenderKitIds() {
  return parent.getRenderKitIds();
}

}
```

In the constructor, you see the now familiar decorator pattern at work. The **getRenderKit()** method first delegates to the parent **RenderKitFactory** to satisfy the request. If no **RenderKit** is found for the argument **renderKitId** and the argument is equal to the literal string **com .jsfcompref.CustomRenderKit**, the **createAndPopulateBasicRenderKitInstance()** method is called. This method creates an instance of the class **BasicRenderKit** and leverages the private data-structure called **standardRenderKit** to populate it with renderers from the standard **HTML_BASIC RenderKit** for all renderers **except** the **OutputText Renderer**. This one is handled specifically by adding an instance of **SpecialOutputTextRenderer**. The new **BasicRenderKit** is returned where it is added to the list of **RenderKit**s stored in the parent. The remaining methods, **addRenderKit()** and **getRenderKitIds()**, simply delegate to the parent.

FacesContextFactory

As mentioned at the beginning of this section, one good use-case for providing a custom **FacesContextFactory** is adapting JSF to the Portlet environment. However, this is certainly not the only conceivable use-case. One could also imagine adapting JSF to run inside of a pure Swing application environment, though no one has yet taken this approach. Any such attempt would most likely choose to provide a custom **FacesContextFactory**.

Abstract Class to Extend   A custom implementation of **FacesContextFactory** must extend the abstract class **javax.faces.context.FacesContextFactory** and implement the following method.

> public FacesContext getFacesContext(Object context, Object request,
> Object response, Lifecycle lifecycle)
>   throws FacesException;

Let's examine the simple implementation of this method in the Sun JSF-Portlet integration library, shown next:

```
public FacesContext getFacesContext(Object context,
    Object request,
    Object response,
    Lifecycle lifecycle)
  throws FacesException {
  if ((context == null) || (request == null) ||
      (response == null) || (lifecycle == null)) {
    throw new NullPointerException();
  }

  ExternalContext econtext =
    new ExternalContextImpl((PortletContext) context,
    (PortletRequest) request,
    (PortletResponse) response);

  return (new FacesContextImpl(econtext, lifecycle));
}
```

Here, **getFacesContext()** simply creates an **ExternalContextImpl** instance, casts the **context**, **request**, and **response** arguments to their Portlet interface classes, and passes them on to the **FacesContextImpl** constructor. The implementation details of these classes are not pertinent to this discussion and have been omitted from the text.

LifecycleFactory

The capabilities of this particular JSF extension point are also used in the JSF Portlet integration library; however, the full power of providing additional lifecycles has not yet been fully explored as of this writing.

Abstract Class to Extend   A custom **LifecycleFactory** must extend the class **javax.faces .lifecycle.LifecycleFactory** and implement the following methods.

    public abstract void addLifecycle(String *lifecycleId*, Lifecycle *lifecycle*);
    public abstract Lifecycle getLifecycle(String lifecycileId);
    public abstract Iterator getLifecycleIds();

Like the **RenderKitFactory**, the **LifecycleFactory** maintains a **Map** of **lifecycleIds** to **Lifecycle** instances. In order to take advantage of using a custom **LifecycleFactory**, you must examine the API of the **Lifecycle** class.

    public void addPhaseListener(PhaseListener *listener*);
    public void removePhaseListener(PhaseListener *listener*);
    public PhaseListener[] getPhaseListeners();
    public void execute(FacesContext *context*) throws FacesException;
    public void render(FacesContext *context*) throws FacesException;

The first three methods are simply an implementation of a JavaBeans listener property for **PhaseListener**. The **execute()** method is responsible for running the postback part of the lifecycle, as described in Chapter 3. The **render()** method is responsible only for rendering.

EXPERT GROUP INSIGHT *Initially, there was only an* **execute()** *method, but during development of the specification we realized that a postback to a Portlet limited the postback portion of the request processing lifecycle to only the one Portlet in the page that actually is experiencing the form submit, while every Portlet in the page must re-render itself. Breaking these out into two separate phases allowed this design to be possible.*

Please see Chapter 3 for details on the request processing lifecycle, which will give you insight into ways to provide your own implementation, if desired.

JSF 1.2 TIP *In JSF 1.2, Expert Group member Jacob Hookom, inventor of Facelets, introduced a new way to specify the* **lifecycleId** *for an application with a potential use in AJAX applications: having a different lifecycle for different* **FacesServlet** *instances in the same application. Prior to JSF 1.2, every* **FacesServlet** *in a single Web application was required to share the same* **LifecycleFactory** *and therefore the same kind of* **Lifecycle**. *This was because the only way to specify an alternate lifecycle was through a* **lifecycleId context-param** *in the* **faces-config .xml** *file. Jacob's idea was to also allow an* **init-param** *element to contain a* **lifecycleId**. *By doing this, it's possible to write a custom* **Lifecycle** *implementation that is optimized for handling AJAX requests and responses.*

Application Factory

The final factory class you can replace is the **ApplicationFactory**. The **Application** instance is really the heart of the JSF runtime. It is an application singleton that holds references to many core JSF classes. Some possible use-cases for decorating the **ApplicationFactory** include

- Gaining access to the process by which new **UIComponent** instances are created by overriding or decorating the **createComponent()** method

- Gaining access to the process by which new **Converter** instances are created by overriding or decorating the **createConverter()** method

- Gaining access to the process by which new **Validator** instances are created by overriding or decorating the **createValidator()** method

- Supplementing the **Locale** awareness afforded by the **getSupportedLocales()** method to include other **Locales** without using the XML configuration syntax of the **<locale-config>** element described in Chapter 18. For example, if an application needs to dynamically support a changeable set of **Locales** at runtime without restarting, decorating the **ApplicationFactory** would provide one way to meet this requirement.

In JSF 1.1, **Application** has the JavaBeans properties shown in Table 12-5. Recall that a JavaBeans property is really just a pair of "getter/setter" methods that conform to the following naming conventions. For Read Only properties, only the getter method exists. For Write Only properties, only the setter method exists. For Read/Write methods, both a getter and a setter exist. To derive the name of the getter or setter method given a property name, capitalize the first letter of the property and prefix it with get or set, respectively. For example, for the Read/Write property **actionListener**, the getter is **getActionListener()** and the setter is **setActionListener()**. The type of the property is the return type of the getter method, which must be the same as the argument type of the setter method. Finally, the getter must take no arguments, and the setter method must take only one argument— the same type as the return type of the getter method.

In addition to providing the properties shown in Table 12-5, **Application** also defines the following methods: **createComponent()**, **createConverter()**, **createMethodBinding()**, **createValidator()**, and **createValueBinding()**.

JSF 1.2 adds the properties shown in Table 12-6 and deprecates the **propertyResolver** and **variableResolver** properties. In JSF 1.2, the **createMethodBinding()** and **createValueBinding()** methods are deprecated, and the **evaluateExpressionGet()** has been added.

Abstract Class to Extend   A custom **ApplicationFactory** class must extend the abstract class **javax.faces.application.ApplicationFactory** and must implement the following methods.

```
public Application getApplication();
public void setApplication(Application application);
```

This is simply a Read/Write JavaBeans property of type **Application**. Also, as a final note, it is inadvisable to override the **ApplicationFactory** without using the decorator pattern, because the core nature of the implementation of the **Application** class leads to the introduction of implementation-specific code. Therefore, please use the decorator pattern when overriding the **Application**.

JavaBeans Property	Type	Read Only (RO) or Read/Write (RW)	Description
actionListener	ActionListener	RW	Holds the class responsible for handling actions
componentTypes	Iterator of String	RO	The component types for **UIComponent** instances this application can create on a call to **createComponent(String)**
converterIds	Iterator of String	RO	The converterIds for **Converter** instances this application can create on a call to **createConverter(String)**
converterTypes	Iterator of Class	RO	The types for **Converter** classes this application can create on a call to **createConverter(Class)**
defaultLocale	Locale	RW	The default **Locale** for this application
defaultRenderKitId	String	RW	The default **RenderKitId** for this application
messageBundle	String	RW	The name of the **ResourceBundle** used for application error messages
navigationHandler	NavigationHandler	RW	The **NavigationHandler** for this application
propertyResolver	PropertyResolver	RW	The **PropertyResolver** for this application
stateManager	StateManager	RW	The **StateManager** for this application
supportedLocales	Iterator (on get) Collection (on set)	RW	A **Collection** or **Iterator** of **Locale** instances that are supported by this application
validatorIds	Iterator of String	RO	The validatorIds for **Validators** that can be created by this application on a call to **createValidator(String)**
variableResolver	VariableResolver	RW	The **VariableResolver** for this application
viewHandler	ViewHandler	RW	The **ViewHandler** for this application

TABLE 12-5   **Application** Properties in JSF 1.1

JavaBeans Property	Type	Read Only (RO) or Read/Write (RW)	Description
ELContextListeners	ELContextListener	RW	Allows applications to add a listener to be notified when a new **ELContext** instance is created
ELResolver	ELResolver	RW	Returns the singleton **ELResolver** to be used for resolving all expressions
ExpressionFactory	ExpressionFactory	RO	Returns the **javax.el.ExpressionFactory** for creating **ValueExpression** and **MethodExpression** instances

TABLE 12-6   **Application** Properties Added in JSF 1.2

Alternate View Description Technology and Facelets

JSP pages are the most common way of building a presentation layer in a JavaServer Faces application. Indeed, most of this book assumes the use of JSP for the view description language of JSF applications. The designers of JSF technology acknowledged, however, that JSP is far from being the only game in town, and carefully avoided creating any dependencies on JSP in the core JSF specification. The **ViewHandler** API, and its helper objects, enable the default JSF view description technology to be customized or replaced entirely. This chapter examines the rationale behind providing a custom **ViewHandler**, the principles and mechanics of writing one, and closes with an example of an exciting real-world alternate page description technology known as Facelets.

Motivation for Alternate View Description Technology

The term *view description technology* covers anything related to how you arrange a collection of user interface component instances into a coherent user interface. For Web applications, this generally means the following:

- Use of a markup language, usually HTML or XML

- A mechanism for aggregating chunks of markup together from separate pages to form one logical page, such as JSTL's **c:import** or XML's **XInclude**

- An extension mechanism that allows arbitrary markup to be associated with a user interface component, such as the JSP Custom Tag Library mechanism, or the TagLibrary concept in Facelets

- Some way to correctly handle intermixing markup that represents components and noncomponent markup, also known as "template text"—for example, freely mixing raw HTML and UI components in a page

With the preceding definition, it's easy to see that JSP is certainly a view description technology, but that it also constitutes a lot more when JSP's myriad custom tag libraries are considered. It's also fair to say that JSP is the most popular view description technology in the Java Enterprise platform, in terms of the number of sites deployed using the technology. Even so, good software design focuses on abstractions and loose coupling, so the design of JSF makes no assumptions about using JSP to describe a view.

EXPERT GROUP INSIGHT *Just in case good software design wasn't enough, the Expert Group considered user feedback as a motivator for allowing a pluggable view description technology. Many Web content developers prefer to author using plain HTML. JSP, although providing abstraction from lower-level Servlet development, can still have its technical challenges for nontechnical Web designers. Facelets view description technology allows view descriptions in plain HTML to be first-class JSF pages. Finally, several emerging view description technologies, such as Mozilla XUL and W3C XForms, may gain ground. It would be a great boon to developers if their existing JSF applications were able to take advantage of these things if they catch on.*

Now let's examine the responsibilities of the **ViewHandler** and its relation to the rest of the JSF system in order to provide a conceptual foundation for building a custom **ViewHandler**.

The Relationship of the ViewHandler to the Rest of the JSF System

As mentioned in Chapter 3, the **ViewHandler** plays an important role in fulfilling the requirements of the *Restore View* and *Render View* lifecycle phases. Thus, the **ViewHandler** must interface with the other parts of the system that take part in these phases. The role of the **ViewHandler** in the request processing lifecycle is shown in Figure 13-1.

The Relationship Between ViewHandler, RenderKit, and the Act of View Construction

As Figure 13-2 shows, the concept of the **ViewHandler** is intimately related to the concept of the **RenderKit**, though it is certainly not necessary to have a new **ViewHandler** every time you want to use a different **RenderKit**. In some sense, a **ViewHandler** is like a programming language compiler. It takes a page written in some language, usually a markup language, and turns it into a tree of **UIComponent** instances. If you want to use a different programming language, say in moving from C++ to Java, then you need a different compiler. By analogy, if you want to use a different page description language, using XHTML instead of JSP for example, you need a different **ViewHandler.**

The **ViewHandler** is responsible for deriving the proper **renderKitId** from the incoming request in its implementation of the **calculateRenderKitId()** method. This determines which **RenderKit** is used to process this request. The incoming request also contains information about the natural language to be used to render this response in the form of the **Accept-Lang** HTTP header. The **ViewHandler** must perform an algorithm on the request and derive the correct **Locale** in the **calculateLocale()** method. Finally, the **ViewHandler** is also responsible for returning rendering technology–specific URLs for actions and resources when given a **viewId**. For example, the renderer for the **UIForm** component calls **viewHandler .getActionURL()** to aid in rendering the HTML **action** attribute on the **<form>** tag, while the renderer for the **UIGraphic** component calls **viewHandler.getResourceURL()** to aid in rendering the HTML **src** attribute on the **<img>** tag.

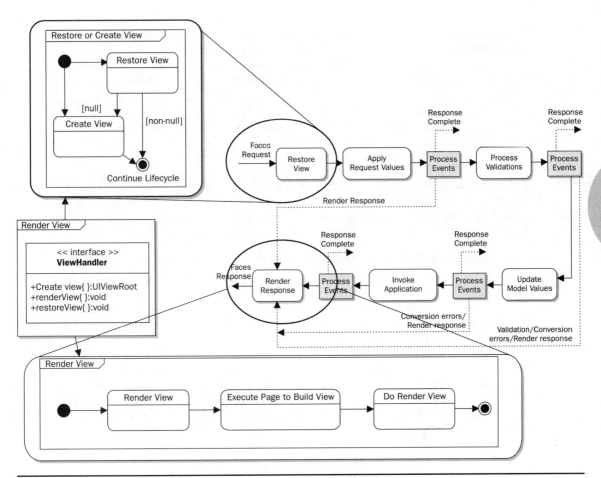

FIGURE 13-1 The role of the **ViewHandler** in the request processing lifecycle

FIGURE 13-2
The relationship
between
ViewHandler
and **RenderKit**

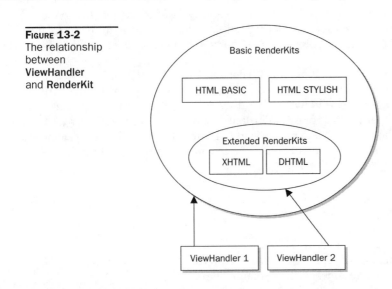

As covered in Chapter 10, all renderers must write their markup using the **ResponseWriter** or **ResponseStream** classes. The specific instances of these classes must be installed on the **FacesContext** during **viewHandler.renderView()**, and the current **RenderKit** is where the **ViewHandler** turns to create instances of a **ResponseWriter** or **ResponseStream**.

EXPERT GROUP INSIGHT   *The specification of the **ViewHandler** was intentionally loose to allow for a wide range of implementation possibilities. For example, the default implementation of the **createView()** method simply creates an empty **UIViewRoot**, with no children, and returns it. This is because the default **ViewHandler** is designed for JSP, which must execute the page in order to construct the view. Because rendering and page execution must occur simultaneously, or nearly simultaneously, in JSP, this action is deferred to the **renderView()** method. Other view description technologies may not have this restriction. For example, imagine a simple XML-based view description technology where the **createView()** method simply loads the XML file for this view, and creates a view of **UIComponent** instances from it.*

The Relationship Between ViewHandler and the State Management System

Figure 13-3 shows the relationship between the **ViewHandler** and the **StateManager**. The **StateManager** API was covered in detail in Chapter 12, but it makes sense to review it from the perspective of the **ViewHandler**. The **restoreView()** method is responsible for returning a **UIViewRoot** that is the root of a view which is identical to the view rendered to the client the last time the **renderView()** method was called.

The default implementation of **restoreView()** calls through to **StateManager** API to accomplish this task, but it is not required to do so. On the state saving side, the **writeState()** method of the **ViewHandler** is called by the rendering system to inject the state into the rendered output. Naturally, the manner in which this is accomplished is very specific to the rendering technology which can cause some tight coupling between the **ViewHandler** and **StateManager** implementations.

How to Build and Install a Custom ViewHandler

This section shows how to build a simple **ViewHandler**. This **ViewHandler** will not actually perform any of the view functions itself. Instead, it delegates all of its functionality to the default **ViewHandler**. This approach makes it easy to illustrate the steps required to create a custom **ViewHandler**. It also gives you a skeleton that you can use to develop your own **ViewHandler**.

As with many things in the Java EE platform, a custom **ViewHandler** is declared using XML. The **ViewHandler** is declared within the **<application>** element of the **faces-config .xml** file. There must be, at most, one **ViewHandler** declaration in this element because there is only one **ViewHandler** per Faces application instance. As you will see in Chapter 18, the ordering of elements in the **faces-config.xml** file is important. If the **<application>** element is present, it must be the first child element of the **<faces-config>** element, as shown next.

```
<faces-config>
  <application>
    <view-handler>com.jsfcompref.vtlib.util.
      TrainerViewHandler</view-handler>
  </application>
  <!-- the rest of the faces-config content -->
```

There are two approaches to providing a custom **ViewHandler** to JSF, known as *decoration* and *replacement*. These concepts are explained next.

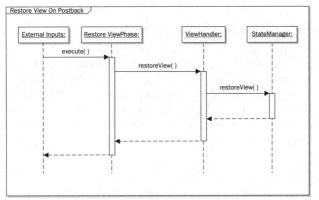

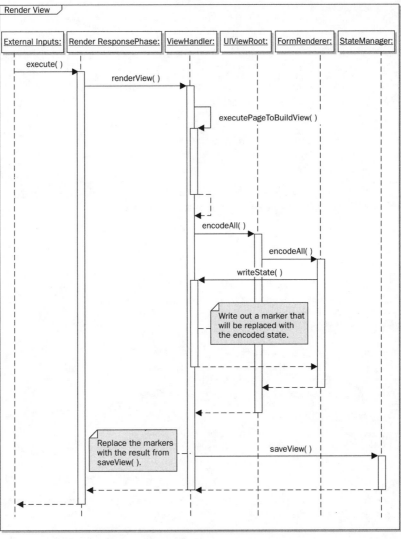

FIGURE 13-3 The relationship between **ViewHandler** and **StateManager**

Using Decoration for the Custom ViewHandler

As you learned in Chapter 12, many of the replaceable components in Faces allow the user to extend the existing implementation using the decorator design pattern. To recap this concept, the decorator design pattern enables a developer to override as much or as little functionality of an existing object as desired. The Faces specification requires the JSF runtime to guarantee that a custom **ViewHandler** declared in the **faces-config.xml** file be passed the default **ViewHandler** in its constructor when the JSF runtime is starting up. The following example shows how this is done in Faces 1.1.

```java
import javax.faces.application.ViewHandler;

public class TrainerViewHandler extends ViewHandler {
  private final ViewHandler parent;

  public TrainerViewHandler(ViewHandler parent) {
    this.parent = parent;
  }

  public Locale calculateLocale(FacesContext context) {
    return this.parent.calculateLocale(context);
  }

  public String calculateRenderKitId(FacesContext context) {
    return this.parent.calculateRenderKitId(context);
  }

  public UIViewRoot createView(FacesContext context, String viewId) {
    return this.parent.createView(context, viewId);
  }

  public String getActionURL(FacesContext context, String viewId) {
    return this.parent.getActionURL(context, viewId);
  }

  public String getResourceURL(FacesContext context, String path) {
   return this.parent.getResourceURL(context, path);
  }

  public void renderView(FacesContext context,
                         UIViewRoot viewToRender)
    throws IOException, FacesException {
    this.parent.renderView(context, viewToRender);
  }

  public void restoreView(FacesContext context,
                          String viewId) {
    this.parent.restoreView(context, viewId);
  }

  public void writeState(FacesContext context) throws IOException {
    this.parent.writeState(context);
  }
}
```

This **ViewHandler** does nothing itself. Instead, it simply delegates to the previous implementation for all methods. However, you can adapt this skeleton to create your own **ViewHandler** by implementing one or more of the methods. The important thing to observe about the preceding code is that it has a constructor that takes one argument, the existing **ViewHandler**. Observe that there are eight public methods defined on **ViewHandler**. In practice, a custom **ViewHandler** may delegate to the previous implementation for most of those methods. The methods for which delegation is not practical are covered in the section later in this chapter titled "The Design, Architecture, and Implementation of Facelets."

To clarify how the decorator pattern is implemented, let's examine how the JSF runtime handles the processing of the preceding **faces-config.xml** file with the custom **ViewHandler** declaration.

How the JSF Runtime Implements the Decorator Pattern

Figure 13-4 shows the steps taken by the JSF runtime to implement the decorator pattern. Before the JSF runtime loads any **faces-config.xml** files from the user, the runtime initializes its own set of default implementations for all the replaceable objects, including **ViewHandler**. For this discussion, we'll refer to the default **ViewHandler** as **DefaultViewHandler**. During startup, whenever the JSF implementation comes across a **faces-config.xml** file with a **<view-handler>** element, it inspects that class for a public constructor that takes one argument of type **ViewHandler**. In this case, the **TrainerViewHandler** does have such a constructor. The JSF runtime invokes the constructor and passes **DefaultViewHandler** as the argument. Because **TrainerViewHandler** wants to leverage the **DefaultViewHandler** instance to do the work of all the methods, it keeps a reference to **DefaultViewHandler** in an instance variable. The JSF runtime replaces its reference to **DefaultViewHandler** with a reference to the new **TrainerViewHandler**. As far as the runtime knows, **DefaultViewHandler** no longer exists. In other words, the custom **ViewHandler** may choose to observe the decorator pattern or not. If it doesn't keep a reference to the **DefaultViewHandler**, the custom **ViewHandler** is said to "replace" the **DefaultViewHandler** rather than "decorate" it.

Another way for a custom **ViewHandler** to handle replacement is to offer only a public no-argument constructor. In this case, the JSF runtime will simply use that constructor to make the new instance and replace the **DefaultViewHandler**. This process continues as the **faces-config.xml** files are loaded until all startup processing is complete.

Decoration in JSF 1.2

As the preceding section shows, the decorator pattern greatly reduces the difficulty of providing a custom **ViewHandler**, but you still have to provide implementations for every abstract method on the **ViewHandler** class. In Faces 1.2, an additional convenience to ease decoration is provided: the wrapper pattern. This pattern obviates the need to laboriously override all the abstract methods of **ViewHandler**. For example, consider the following.

```
import javax.faces.webapp.ViewHandlerWrapper;

public class TrainerViewHandler extends ViewHandlerWrapper {

  private ViewHandler oldViewHandler = null;

  public TrainerViewHandler(ViewHandler oldViewHandler) {
    this.oldViewHandler = oldViewHandler;
  }
```

```
public ViewHandler getWrapped() {
    return oldViewHandler;
}
}
```

You still must provide a public one-argument constructor that takes a **ViewHandler**, and a corresponding **getWrapped()** method that returns that argument. The **ViewHandlerWrapper**

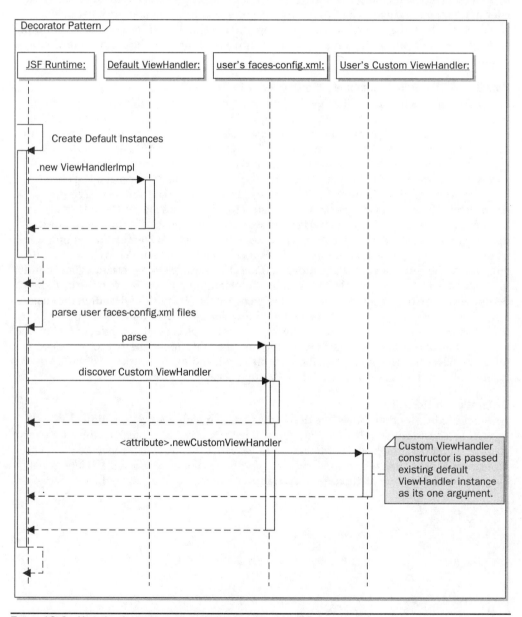

Figure 13-4 How the decorator pattern is implemented in JSF

class provides implementations of all the abstract methods on **ViewHandler** that call your **getWrapped()** method, as in the following:

```
public void renderView(FacesContext context, UIViewRoot viewToRender)
  throws IOException, FacesException {
  getWrapped().renderView(context, viewToRender);
}
```

This little trick of object-oriented programming eliminates the need to manually override all the **ViewHandler** abstract methods.

JSF 1.2 Tip *The 1.2 version of the JSF specification also provides wrappers for* **StateManager** *and* **ResponseWriter***, in addition to* **ViewHandler***.*

The previous discussion covered the mechanics of building a custom **ViewHandler**. The interesting part, of course, is in the details of what methods to override, and what to do in those methods. These details are described in the chapter's later section titled "The Design, Architecture, and Implementation of Facelets."

General Considerations When Writing a Custom ViewHandler

Because **ViewHandler** is a singleton (a class that allows only one object instance per application), its methods are accessed by many threads simultaneously. Therefore, the developer must take the usual precautions to ensure thread safety. In particular, they should take great care not to store any per-request state as instance variables, and protect any initialization steps by either putting them in the constructor, known as *eager initialization*, or in a synchronized block that effectively executes only once per request, known as *lazy initialization*. Before we jump into the specifics of Facelets, let's look at an example that illustrates a thread safety consideration. In general, Facelets uses lazy initialization where possible to allow for faster startup times. The following is an example of thread safety from the **FaceletViewHandler**.

```
private boolean initialized = false;

public void renderView(FacesContext context, UIViewRoot viewToRender) {
  throws IOException, FacesException {
  // Lazy initialize so we have a FacesContext to use.
  if (!this.initialized) {
    this.initialize(context);
  }
  // Rest of method omitted.
}

protected void initialize(FacesContext context) {
  synchronized (this) {
    if (!this.initialized) {
      log.fine("Initializing");
      // rest of initialization logic omitted
      this.initialized = true;
      // Rest of method omitted.
    }
  }
}
```

Let's examine the thread safety implications of this code. To guard against the unlikely possibility of two different browsers accessing the site simultaneously before requests from any other browsers access the site, the checking and setting of the **initialized** instance variable is done inside a synchronized block.

The Facelets View Description Technology

This section presents a brief but thorough guide to using Facelets view description technology, invented by JSF Expert Group member Jacob Hookom. It also examines the implementation of Facelets to illustrate the details of creating a custom view description technology in Faces. (Additional information on Facelets can be found at **https://facelets .dev.java.net/**.)

The Power of Templating in Faces

The terms "templating" and "composition" are used interchangeably to describe building a single logical page view for the user out of several separate files. Consider the following pseudo-code in a fictional markup language:

```
<!-- This is the main page for the application

<f:view>
<include name="menubar" file="menubar.xml" user="#{currentUser}" />

<include name="sidebar" file="sidebar.xml" user="#{currentUser}"/>

<include name="summary" file="summary.xml" user="#{currentUser}"/>
</f:view>
```

This shows the power of using a composition mechanism. The constituent parts—**menubar**, **sidebar**, and **summary**—can be reused in multiple pages and their display can be customized by "passing in" parameters, optionally leveraging the EL. Naturally, we expect that any Faces components contained within the included files will be added to the **UIViewRoot** and function as expected.

While it is possible to use JSP's **jsp:include** and **<%@ include %>**, and JSTL's **c:import** to do templating, these approaches have some drawbacks in the current version of the JSP and JSF specs. For example, it is impossible to pass parameters from the host file to the included file. The **<jsp:param>** feature doesn't work for JSF because it stores its content in page scope, which is not supported in JSF. Furthermore, the current implementations of the containers can cause unexpected replication of the included content. These drawbacks go beyond being mere bugs in a particular container's implementation.

Facelets addresses these problems by providing a simple, EL-aware, templating mechanism with full support for JSF's component model that supports parameter passing. So let's recast the previous pseudo-code using Facelets.

```
<!DOCTYPE html PUBLIC "-//W3C//DTD XHTML 1.0 Transitional//EN"
"http://www.w3.org/TR/xhtml1/DTD/xhtml1-transitional.dtd">
<html xmlns="http://www.w3.org/1999/xhtml"
      xmlns:ui="http://java.sun.com/jsf/facelets"
      xmlns:h="http://java.sun.com/jsf/html">
<!-- This is the main page for the application
```

```
<ui:include src="menubar.xml">
  <ui:param name="user" value="#{currentUser}"/>
</ui:include>

<ui:include src="sidebar.xml">
  <ui:param name="user" value="#{currentUser}"/>
</ui:include>

<ui:include src="summary.xml">
  <ui:param name="user" value="#{currentUser}"/>
</ui:include>
```

We'll cover templating using Facelets in depth later in the chapter; however, for now, this example is a template that can be used by any page in the application. It provides for a menu bar, a side bar, and a summary. It shows that included documents are passed a **user** parameter to customize their display. Now let's examine some similarities and differences between JSP and Facelets to build a conceptual understanding of the technology.

Similarities and Differences Between JSP and Facelets

From a high level, Facelets and JSP are very similar. As far as core JSF is concerned, they are both just view description technologies. In fact, you can use both JSP and Facelets in a single application because the Facelets **ViewHandler** will delegate any requests it doesn't understand to the default **ViewHandler**, which uses JSP. As you'd expect, there are significant similarities between the two, as shown in Table 13-1, but the differences, displayed in Table 13-2, are more telling.

The two most important differences between Facelets and JSP are the ability to author JSF pages in plain HTML, and the ability to do first class templating. In fact, Facelets was created in response to user demand for these two features. The remaining differences reflect how Facelets was designed with JSF in mind, rather than for JSP, which was designed well before JSF was invented. The remainder of this chapter covers the details of Facelets from a perspective of how it differs from JSP.

View Description Concept	Facelets	JSP
Pages authored in XML	Yes, or XHTML	Yes, the JSP XML syntax
Leverages a page compiler concept	XML is parsed into a **TagHandler** object tree which is executed. There is no bytecode generation.	XML is translated into Java, then compiled into a .class and executed.
Uses the unified EL	Yes	Yes (JSP 2.1)
Supports the concept of tag libraries (taglibs)	Yes	Yes
Supports the concept of tag files	Yes	Yes
Dynamic tag attributes	Required	Optional

TABLE 13-1   Some Similarities Between Facelets and JSP

View Description Concept	Facelets	JSP
Authors pages using raw HTML	Yes, with **jsfc** attribute or **TagDecorators**	No
Supports Faces-aware parameter passing to templated content	Yes	No
Expressions that reference other expressions work appropriately	Yes, built in to the **FaceletContext**.	Yes, but only in JSP 2.1 and must be specified explicitly or set twice.
Tag lifecycle	All tag instances are stateless, only one instance of each tag per application.	Stateful tags are pooled.
Built-in templating engine	Yes	No (only has simple include capabilities)
Tags perform rendering and other display-related tasks	No, tags just help to build the **UIComponent** tree.	Yes, and there is a wide variety of third-party taglibs available to help in rendering the view.
Mature, proven technology with vast industry support and wide range of vendor choice	No	Yes
Taglibs can have a single Java class access point	Yes, the TagLibrary interface	No

TABLE 13-2   Differences Between Facelets and JSP

Taglibs in Facelets

As mentioned in Chapter 10, it is strongly recommended that a JSP custom tag that represents a Faces **UIComponent**, **Converter**, or **Validator** perform only three responsibilities, which are shown in Table 13-3. As you would expect, the same three responsibilities are also asked of a Facelets tag.

Of course, it's possible for a custom tag to do much more than this, but putting any additional functionality into your JSP tag layer will result in a component that is only usable with JSP. In contrast to JSP tag handlers for **UIComponents**, Facelets tag handlers for **UIComponents** are designed to do the preceding three things and nothing more. These constraints allow the Facelets tag library concept to be much simpler than its JSP counterpart.

Implementing a Facelets Taglib

As mentioned earlier, both Facelets and JSP have the concept of tag libraries. JSP taglibs are declared to the container in a Tag Library Descriptor file, or TLD. The TLD lists the tags in the taglib, describes the valid attributes for each tag, and associates a Java class or tag file with each tag, called a Tag Handler.

Facelets also has a tag library descriptor, but its syntax is much simpler than its JSP counterpart. It's a good practice to always name your Facelet taglib file with a **.taglib.xml**

Responsibility	Example
Create a logical association between a **component-type**, such as **javax.faces .Input**, and a **renderer-type**, such as **javax.faces.Text**.	Consider the tag **h:inputText**. This tag associates a **javax.faces.Input component-type** with a **javax.faces.Text renderer-type**.
Convey tag attributes from JSP or Facelets page into properties or attributes on the **UIComponent**.	The **maxlen** and **required** tag attributes in the tag **<h:inputText required="true" maxlen="6" />** are converted into method calls **setRequired(true)** and **getAttributes( ) .put("maxlen", 6)** on the **UIInput** associated with the tag.

Aid in constructing the **UIComponent** hierarchy, rooted at **UIViewRoot**.	This markup declares a **UIForm** to be a child of the **UIViewRoot**:
	`<f:viewRoot>`
	`  <h:form>`
	`    <!—other tags omitted`
	`  </h:form>`
	`</f:viewRoot>`

TABLE 13-3   The Responsibilities of a JSP or Facelet Tag in Faces

extension and place it in the **META-INF** directory of the WAR file for your application. Facelets also looks in the value of the Servlet **context-param** named **facelets.LIBRARIES** for a semicolon-delimited list of context-root relative pathnames to the **taglib.xml** file. Facelet taglibs can be described in two ways: entirely in XML with no Java code, or mostly in Java code. The sole purpose of a Facelets taglib is to expose **UIComponents**, **converters**, and **validators** to the page author. Facelets also supports exposing EL functions to the page author, but these are beyond the scope of this chapter. The XML syntax for describing a **UIComponent**, **converter**, and **validator** is as follows.

```
<!DOCTYPE facelet-taglib PUBLIC
    "-//Sun Microsystems, Inc.//DTD Facelet Taglib 1.0//EN"
    "http://java.sun.com/dtd/facelet-taglib_1_0.dtd">

<facelet-taglib>
  <namespace>http://jsfcompref.com/vtlib</namespace>
  <tag>
    <tag-name>spellCheck</tag-name>
    <component>
      <component-type>vtlib.SpellCheckTextarea</component-type>
      <renderer-type>com.jsfcompref.SpellCheckRenderer</renderer-type>
    </component>
  </tag>
  <tag>
    <tag-name>validateEventRequirements</tag-name>
    <validator>
      <validator-id>com.jsfcompref.vtlib.validator.
                    EventRequirementValidator</validator-id>
    </validator>
```

```
    </tag>

    <tag>
      <tag-name>convertWeight</tag-name>
      <converter>
        <converter-id>vtlib.WeightConverter</converter-id>
      </converter>
    </tag>
</facelet-taglib>
```

No further Java code or XML markup is needed to create a tag library. The Facelets system provides the actual tag handler implementations based on the previous markup. This taglib declares three tags in the **vtlib** namespace: **spellCheck**, **validateEventRequirements**, and **convertWeight**. You can see that some of the XML elements are exactly the same as in the **faces-config.xml** file for a custom component (Chapter 10), converter, or validator (Chapter 7). Furthermore, notice that the previous markup fulfills requirement 1 of what a tag must do to support Faces.

If you choose to define your Facelets taglib in Java code, rather than in XML, you must tell the system the fully qualified class name of the Java class that implements the **com.sun .facelets.tag.TagLibrary** interface:

```
<!DOCTYPE facelet-taglib PUBLIC
    "-//Sun Microsystems, Inc.//DTD Facelet Taglib 1.0//EN"
    "http://java.sun.com/dtd/facelet-taglib_1_0.dtd">

<facelet-taglib>
    <library-class>
      com.jsfcompref.vtlib.VTLibrary
    </libraryclass>
</facelet-taglib>
```

This markup declares the class **VTLibrary** as a Facelets taglib. The **TagLibrary** interface is very simple:

```
public interface TagLibrary {
    public boolean containsNamespace(String ns);
    public boolean containsTagHandler(String ns, String localName);
    public TagHandler createTagHandler(String ns, String localName,
    public boolean containsFunction(String ns, String name);
    public Method createFunction(String ns, String name);
}
```

Facelets provides an abstract class implementation of this interface, **com.sun.facelets .tag.AbstractTagLibrary**. All that a custom taglib must do is create a subclass of this class with a no-argument constructor that adds the components to the library. The following is an example:

```
package com.jsfcompref.vtlib;

import com.sun.facelets.tag.AbstractTagLibrary;

public final class VTLibrary extends AbstractTagLibrary {

    public final static String Namespace = "http://jsfcompref.com/vtlib";
```

```
public VTLibrary() {
  super(Namespace);
  addComponent("spellCheck", "vtlib.SpellCheckTextarea",
              com.jsfcompref.SpellCheckRenderer.class.getName());
  addConverter("convertWeight", "vtlib.WeightConverter");
  addValidator("validateEventRequirements",
    com.jsfcompref.vtlib.validator.EventRequirementValidator.class.getName());

  }
}
```

This taglib is identical to the XML-declared version shown previously.

Facelets also supports a concept of tag files that's analogous to JSP's tag files. In XML, a tag file is declared like the following:

```
<tag>
  <tag-name>hello</tag-name>
  <source>tags/helloparam.xhtml</source>
</tag>
```

While the XHTML implementing the tag file may look like that shown next:

```
<ui:composition xmlns:ui="http://java.sun.com/jsf/facelets">
  hello #{param}
</ui:composition>
```

And a usage of the **hello** tag looks like:

```
<vtlib:hello param="#{user.firstName}"/>
```

Finally, Facelets does allow you to define custom tag handlers in Java, but the details of doing this are beyond the scope of this discussion.

You can see that the Facelets tag library mechanism, while simple, is very powerful when combined with the JavaServer Faces Framework. Exploiting the full power of Facelets with JSF is also beyond the scope of this discussion, but examples of doing so may be found at **https://facelets.dev.java.net/**.

Using a Facelets Taglib

Taglibs in Facelets are declared in the page using XML namespaces. Facelets pages may be authored in any XML dialect, but to enable the convenience of direct viewing in a Web browser, it is easy to author them in XHTML. The following is a basic XHTML file that can serve as the basis for your Facelets pages.

```
<!DOCTYPE html PUBLIC "-//W3C//DTD XHTML 1.0 Transitional//EN"
"http://www.w3.org/TR/xhtml1/DTD/xhtml1-transitional.dtd">
<html xmlns="http://www.w3.org/1999/xhtml"
      xmlns:ui="http://java.sun.com/jsf/facelets"
      xmlns:f="http://java.sun.com/jsf/core">
  <h:form>
    First Name: <h:inputText value="#{user.firstName}" /><br />
    Last Name: <input type="text" jsfc="h:inputText"
                      value="#{user.lastName}" />
    <h:commandButton value="submit" />
  </h:form>
</html>
```

Note that it declares all the necessary taglibs as attributes in the **<html>** element. Facelets provides taglibs for the **h:**, **f:**, and jstl **c:** tag libraries. Once the taglib is declared, it operates exactly as in JSP. Note the plain HTML **<input type="text">** element with the **jsfc** attribute. You can apply this attribute to any piece of markup to associate the component identified by the value of the attribute with that piece of markup in the page. Any attributes present on the plain HTML tag are passed to the underlying component just as if you had used a regular **h:inputText** style tag. The purpose of the **jsfc** attribute is similar to the **jwcid** attribute in Tapestry, and delivers the same value of allowing nondeployed previews of the look and feel of your pages, as well as increased tool friendliness with non-JSP aware tools.

Templating with Facelets

There are two main perspectives in templating with Facelets: the **template** file and the **template client** file. These are shown in Figure 13-5.

The template client is the file whose name actually corresponds to a **viewId**, such as **greeting.xhtml**. The template client employs one or more templates to achieve reuse of page content.

Let's illustrate templating with Facelets by rewriting the **register.jsp** page from the JSFReg application in Chapter 2 using Facelets templates. As indicated at the beginning of this section, one of the main values of templating is the reuse of page designs in multiple pages of your application. Let's define a simple template that could be used in every page in the Virtual Trainer application: **lnf-template.xhtml** (which stands for "look and feel" template).

```
<!DOCTYPE html PUBLIC "-//W3C//DTD XHTML 1.0 Transitional//EN"
"http://www.w3.org/TR/xhtml1/DTD/xhtml1-transitional.dtd">
<html xmlns="http://www.w3.org/1999/xhtml"
      xmlns:ui="http://java.sun.com/jsf/facelets">
<head>
  <meta http-equiv="Content-Type"
        content="text/html; charset=windows-1352" />
  <title><ui:insert name="title">Placeholder Title</ui:insert></title>
  <link href="css/vt.css" rel="stylesheet" media="screen" />
</head>
<body>
  <table width="100%" border="0">
    <tr>
      <td height="89">
        <h1 align="center">
           <img src="images/logo.jpg" width="92"
                height="110" />JSF Virtual Trainer Application</h1>
      </td>
    </tr>
    <tr>
      <ui:insert name="body">Placeholder Body</ui:insert>
    </tr>
  </table>
</body>
</html>
```

The first thing you'll notice is that this is a regular XHTML page with an additional namespace of "ui" defined, and two usages of the **ui:insert** tag from that namespace. These two **<ui:insert>** tags state that the contents of this element will be replaced with something

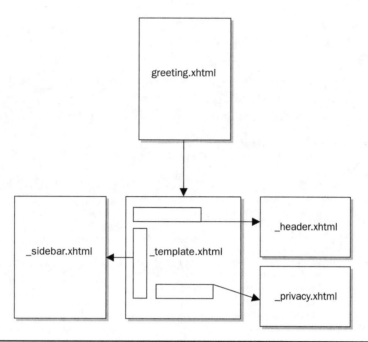

Figure 13-5   The template and the template client

else when the page is compiled. Let's now examine the page that contains the markup referred to by the **<ui:insert>** tags, **register.xhtml**, the template client to the **lnf-template .xml** file.

```
<!DOCTYPE html PUBLIC "-//W3C//DTD XHTML 1.0 Transitional//EN"
"http://www.w3.org/TR/xhtml1/DTD/xhtml1-transitional.dtd">
<html xmlns="http://www.w3.org/1999/xhtml"
      xmlns:ui="http://java.sun.com/jsf/facelets"
      xmlns:h="http://java.sun.com/jsf/html"
      xmlns:f="http://java.sun.com/jsf/core">

<body>
<ui:composition template="/lnf-template.xhtml">
<ui:define name="title">
  JavaServer Faces Virtual Trainer Application Registration
</ui:define>

<ui:define name="body">

  <table width="70%">

    <tr>
      <td width="40%">First Name:</td>
      <td width="60%">
        <input type="text" jsfc="h:inputText" required="true"
               id="fname"
               value="#{UserBean.firstname}" />
        <h:message for="fname"/>
```

```
        </td>
      </tr>

      <tr>
        <td width="40%">Last Name:</td>
        <td width="60%">
          <input type="text" jsfc="h:inputText"
                 value="#{UserBean.lastname}" required="true"
                 id="lname" />
          <h:message for="lname"/>
          <span jsfc="h:message" for="fname">Message</span>
        </td>
      </tr>

      <tr>
        <td width="40%">Gender:</td>
        <td width="60%">
          <h:selectOneRadio type="radio"
                 value="#{UserBean.gender}" required="true" id="gender">
            <input type="radio" jsfc="f:selectItem"
                   itemLabel="Male" itemValue="male" />
            <input type="radio" jsfc="f:selectItem"
                   itemLabel="Female" itemValue="female" />
          </h:selectOneRadio>
          <h:message for="gender"/>
        </td>
      </tr>

      <tr>
        <td width="40%">Date of Birth:</td>
        <td width="60%">
          <h:inputText value="#{UserBean.dob}" id="dob" required="true" >
            <f:convertDateTime pattern="mm-dd-yy"/>
          </h:inputText>(mm-dd-yy)
         <h:message for="dob"/> </td>
      </tr>

      <tr>
        <td width="40%">Email Address:</td>
        <td width="60%">
          <h:inputText value="#{UserBean.email}" required="true"
            validator="#{UserBean.validateEmail}" id="email"/>
          <h:message for="email"/>
       </td>
      </tr>

      <!-- Remainder of rows deleted for brevity -->

    </table>

</ui:define>
</ui:composition>
  </body>

</html>
```

The main content of this page is enclosed in a **<ui:composition>** tag. In a template client page using **<ui:composition>**, anything outside of the bounds of a **<ui:define>** tag is ignored and is not included in the rendered output. Also, note that although this example doesn't show it, a template client file can itself act as a template and leverage other files as template clients.

Guide to Facelets Templating Tags

Facelets provides six tags in the **ui:** tag library to perform templating, each with special features. This section serves as a guide and reference to these tags. Each section heading lists the general form for the tag.

ui:composition
<ui:composition template=*"optionalTemplate"*>

The **ui:composition** tag is used in files acting as a template client, and is the fundamental enabler for templating in Facelets. This tag indicates to the Facelets system that the enclosing children should be grafted into the **UIComponent** hierarchy at that point in the page. Optionally, it declares a template to which the enclosed content should be applied using the **template** attribute. Generally, **<ui:composition>** causes the child components to be created as direct children of the **UIViewRoot**, as would be the case in the example in Figure 13-6.

There's no need to explicitly use the **<f:view>** tag in Facelets because the Facelet markup serves no other purpose than to generate the **UIComponent** tree.

As you can see in Figure 13-6, Facelets provides several tags designed for use with **<ui:composition>**. The details of these are described next.

ui:decorate
<ui:decorate template=*"requiredTemplate"*>

The **<ui:decorate>** tag provides the same feature as **<ui:composition>**, but it causes any content surrounding the **<ui:decorate>** tag to be included in the page, rather than be trimmed, as in the case of **<ui:composition>**. This enables taking any element in the page, and applying it to a template. Also, observe that the **template** attribute is required in this tag. This tag is useful when you have a series of items in one page that require the same appearance. If you were to use **ui:composition**, the output around the tags would be trimmed, which is not desirable in this case.

ui:define
<ui:define name=*"requiredName"*>

The **<ui:define>** tag is used in files acting as a template client, inside of a **<ui:composition>** tag, to define a region that will be inserted into the composition at the location given by the **<ui:insert>** tag with the corresponding name for the **<ui:define>** tag. Figure 13-7 shows **<ui:define>** in action.

ui:insert
<ui:insert name=*"optionalName"*>

The **<ui:insert>** tag is used in files acting as a template to indicate where the corresponding **<ui:define>** in the template client is to be inserted. If no name is specified, the body content of the **<ui:insert>** tag is added to the view.

ui:include
<ui:include src=*"requiredFilename"*>

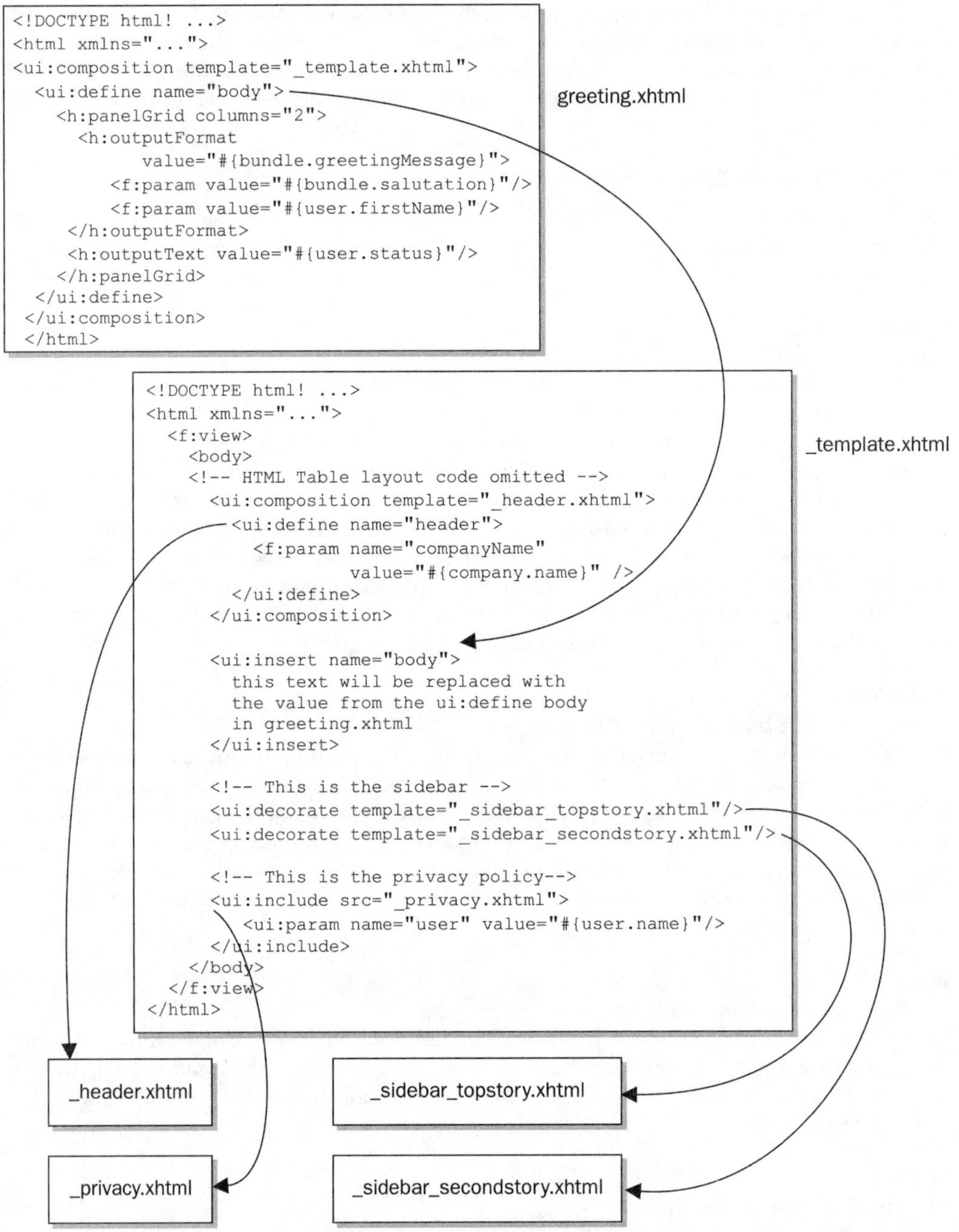

```
<!DOCTYPE html! ...>
<html xmlns="...">
<ui:composition template="_template.xhtml">
  <ui:define name="body">
    <h:panelGrid columns="2">
      <h:outputFormat
          value="#{bundle.greetingMessage}">
        <f:param value="#{bundle.salutation}"/>
        <f:param value="#{user.firstName}"/>
      </h:outputFormat>
      <h:outputText value="#{user.status}"/>
    </h:panelGrid>
  </ui:define>
</ui:composition>
</html>
```

greeting.xhtml

```
<!DOCTYPE html! ...>
<html xmlns="...">
  <f:view>
    <body>
    <!-- HTML Table layout code omitted -->
      <ui:composition template="_header.xhtml">
        <ui:define name="header">
          <f:param name="companyName"
                   value="#{company.name}" />
        </ui:define>
      </ui:composition>

      <ui:insert name="body">
        this text will be replaced with
        the value from the ui:define body
        in greeting.xhtml
      </ui:insert>

      <!-- This is the sidebar -->
      <ui:decorate template="_sidebar_topstory.xhtml"/>
      <ui:decorate template="_sidebar_secondstory.xhtml"/>

      <!-- This is the privacy policy-->
      <ui:include src="_privacy.xhtml">
        <ui:param name="user" value="#{user.name}"/>
      </ui:include>
    </body>
    </f:view>
</html>
```

_template.xhtml

_header.xhtml

_sidebar_topstory.xhtml

_privacy.xhtml

_sidebar_secondstory.xhtml

FIGURE 13-6 **<ui:composition>** in action

The eminently useful tag **<ui:include>** is combined with the **<ui:param>** tag to enable the parameterized inclusion of pages. This tag may be present in templates or template clients. For example, consider the following in a template file called **header.xml**:

```
<html xmlns="http://www.w3.org/1999/xhtml"
      xmlns:ui="http://java.sun.com/jsf/facelets">
<body>
  <ui:include src="userWelcome.xhtml"><ui:param name="details"
                   value="#{user}"/></ui:insert>
 </body>
</html>
```

The following is the **userWelcome.xhtml** file:

```
<xml xmlns="http://www.w3.org/1999/xhtml"
      xmlns:ui="http://java.sun.com/jsf/facelets"
      xmlns:h="http://java.sun.com/jsf/html"
      xmlns:f="http://java.sun.com/jsf/core">
Welcome, #{details.honorific} #{details.firstName} #{details.lastName}!
</xml>
```

Note that the **<ui:param>** tag passes the **#{user}** expression to the **userWelcome.xhtml** file.

ui:param
<ui:param name="*requiredName*" value="*requiredValue*">

The **<ui:param>** tag is used exclusively inside of **<ui:include>** tags to define name/value pairs that are available via the EL in the included page. Both the **name** and **value** attributes may be literal strings or EL expressions. See the previous tag for an example.

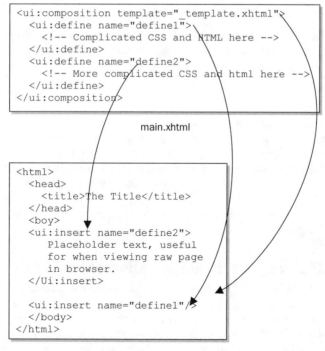

Figure 13-7   **<ui:define>** in action

Guide to Non-Templating Facelets Tags

To complete our discussion of using Facelet tags, let's examine the remaining four tags in the Facelets **ui:** tag library—**<ui:component>**, **<ui:fragment>**, **<ui:remove>**, and **<ui:debug>**.

ui:component

<ui:component id="*optionalComponentId*"
                    binding="*optionalValueExpression*">

As mentioned earlier, the **jsfc** attribute can be placed on raw HTML markup to indicate that this piece of markup corresponds to a particular **UIComponent** instance in the tree. The **<ui:component>** tag has an optional **id** attribute that will be set into the **id** property of the component. If not specified, a page-unique ID is generated. The optional **binding** attribute is a **ValueExpression** that refers to a JavaBeans property whose type is a **UIComponent**. This is exactly the same as the **binding** attribute on JSP JSF component tags. If the **ValueExpression** has no initial value, an appropriate **UIComponent** instance is created automatically and set into the **ValueExpression**. Any markup occurring outside of the **<ui:component>** tag is not included in the view.

ui:fragment

<ui:fragment id="*optionalComponentId*"
                    binding="*optionalValueExpression*">

The **<ui:fragment>** tag is the same as **<ui:component>** except that it wraps a series of components inside a single parent component before the parent is added to the tree.

ui:remove

<ui:remove>

The **<ui:remove>** tag is mainly used during development to "comment out" a portion of the markup in order to prevent it from actually ending up in the view. **<ui:remove>** has no attributes and may appear anywhere in the page where it is valid to have a component or something that represents a component.

ui:debug

<ui:debug hotkey="*optionalHotKey*" />

This astoundingly useful tag will enable a hot key that pops up a new window displaying the component tree, any scoped variables currently active, and other useful debugging information. You have to set the **facelets.DEVELOPMENT context-param** in your web.xml to enable this to work. If *optionalHotKey* is not specified, pressing CTRL-SHIFT-D will pop up the debug window.

Now that you have seen how to use Facelets, let's examine how Facelets implements an alternate view description technology.

The Design, Architecture, and Implementation of Facelets

This section explains the design, architecture, and some of the implementation details of Facelets. Understanding how Facelets works is valuable because it enables you to use Facelets as a model when developing your own custom view description technology.

Figure 13-8 shows the UML class diagram of the core **com.sun.facelets** package. Classes that are not in this package are shown with their fully qualified class names. Classes from the private implementation of Facelets are shown in gray.

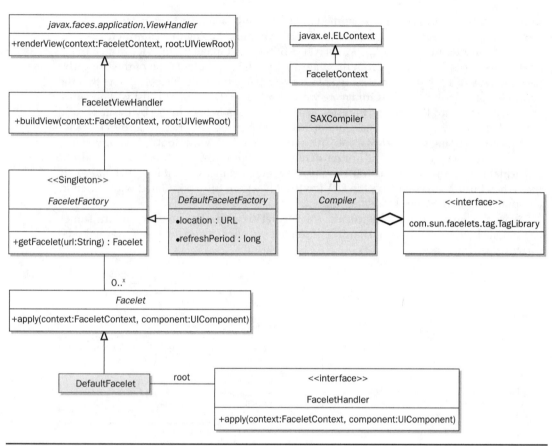

Figure 13-8 The UML class diagram of the core Facelets architecture

Let's step through the flow of control for an initial request to render a page defined in Facelets. As described in Chapter 3, during the *Render* lifecycle phase, the **renderView()** method is called on the **ViewHandler**. This method takes the argument **UIViewRoot**, which in the case of an initial request has no children, and does two things with it:

1. Populates it with **UIComponent** children as defined in the view description technology
2. Renders the newly constructed view to the client

The default **ViewHandler** in JSF 1.1 did these two things together, which caused many problems described in Chapter 3. The default **ViewHandler** in JSF 1.2 does these two things separately.

In the case of an application using Facelets, the default **ViewHandler** has been replaced with an instance of the **FaceletViewHandler**. Naturally, to fulfill the first requirement of the **renderView()** method the protected **buildView()** method is called. All of the Facelets-specific processing is done inside this method and its helpers. In **buildView()**, the **FaceletViewHandler** calls its **FaceletFactory** to create an instance of the root **Facelet** for this **viewID**. The implementation of this process is handled by the **DefaultFaceletFactory** instance. This class performs the loading of the XHTML file and compiles it using the **Compiler**.

The **Compiler** turns the collection of XHTML files that make up the view into a tree of **Facelet** instances. You can see from the diagram that the implementation of the **Compiler** uses the SAX API provided by the Java platform to parse the XML file. Also, note that the compiler contains a list of **TagLibrary** instances for the application. This list will always include the standard Facelets tag libraries, plus any additional ones in use by the application. Given this tree of **Facelet** instances, the **buildView()** method simply calls **apply()** on the root **Facelet**, passing the **UIViewRoot**. This will cause the **UIViewRoot** to be populated, thus accomplishing requirement 1 of **renderView()**. Figure 13-9 illustrates how a collection of **Facelet** pages corresponds to a hierarchy of **Facelet** instances, but it is sufficient to know that when **buildView()** returns, the **UIViewRoot** has been fully populated with the child components for that view, templates and all.

Once the view has been constructed, the **FaceletViewHandler** does exactly the same thing done by the default **ViewHandler**: it renders the view using the standard methods provided by the Faces API.

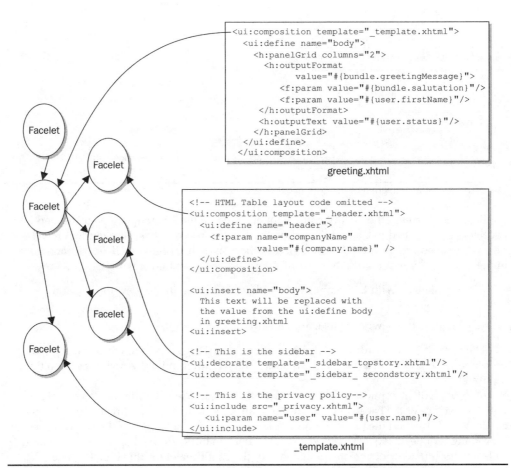

greeting.xhtml

_template.xhtml

Figure 13-9 A collection of template files and how they correspond to **Facelet** instances

ViewHandler Methods Explained

Thanks to the decorator pattern, developers who want to customize JSF with their own **ViewHandler** need only provide actual method implementations where the functionality to be offered differs from that provided by the default implementation. This section lists the abstract methods of **ViewHandler**, explains the behavior of the default implementation, gives some ideas for why you'd want to override the method with your own behavior, and indicates whether the method is overridden by Facelets.

public abstract Locale calculateLocale(FacesContext *context*)

Default Behavior   Performs a matching algorithm (described in Chapter 12) to find the best match **Locale** between the supported **Locale**s of the application, and the **Locale**s requested by the user-agent.

Why Override?   If the existing algorithm is insufficient or undesirable in some way.

Overridden in Facelets?   No.

public abstract String calculateRenderKitId(FacesContext *context*)

Default Behavior   In JSF 1.1, this method always returned the default **RenderKitId**. In JSF 1.2, this method consults the request parameter map for a parameter named by the value of the symbolic constant **javax.faces.render.ResponseStateManager.RENDER_KIT_ID_ PARAM**. If present, the value of the parameter is returned. If not present, the default **RenderKitId** is returned.

Why Override?   To supplant the **RenderKit** selection algorithm with something else. For example, you may want to interrogate the **User-Agent** header and choose a render-kit based on a particular browser's capabilities.

Overridden in Facelets?   No.

public abstract UIViewRoot createView(FacesContext *context*, String *viewId*)

Default Behavior   Simply creates an empty **UIViewRoot** with no children and initializes its **locale** and **renderkit** properties using the previously mentioned methods.

Why Override?   If your custom **ViewHandler** wants to leverage a static file to describe the view, such as Mozilla XUL, this method is where a pool of existing views is populated and consulted for maximum performance. This strategy is employed by the Tapestry web framework from Jakarta. Using this strategy prevents the view hierarchy from being altered during runtime, so examine the tradeoffs between performance and flexibility carefully.

Overridden in Facelets?   No.

public abstract String getActionURL(FacesContext *context*, String *viewId*)

Default Behavior   Translates a **viewId** into a URL suitable for selecting that **view** as the result of an HTTP request. This method is used when rendering the HTML **form** element to aid in outputting the value of the **action** attribute.

Why Override?   The JSF Portlet integration library overrides this method to interpose the Portlet ID parameter into the URLs. This is a key enabler for allowing JSF applications to run well inside of Portlets.

Overridden in Facelets?   No.

public abstract String getResourceURL(FacesContext *context*, String *path*)

Default Behavior   Similar to **getActionURL()**, this method translates a path into a URL suitable for resolving against the currently running JSF application.

Why Override?   The JSF Portlet integration library overrides this method to interpose the Portlet ID into resource URLs, such as the value of the **src** attribute for **<img>** tags.

Overridden in Facelets?   No.

public abstract void renderView(FacesContext *context*, UIViewRoot *viewToRender*) throws IOException, FacesException

Default Behavior   This is the most important method in **ViewHandler** and does the most work. Its job is to take the argument **UIViewRoot**, which was created by a previous call to **createView()**, and render it to the browser. The default implementation in JSF 1.2 leverages JSP to populate the **UIViewRoot** with children as described in the JSP page, and then traverses the view to render each child to the browser.

Why Override?   Most custom **ViewHandler** implementations will want to override this method; it is the heart of providing an alternate view description technology.

Overridden in Facelets?   Yes.

public abstract UIViewRoot restoreView(FacesContext *context*, String *viewId*)

Default Behavior   Delegate to the **restoreView()** method of **StateManager** (described in Chapter 11).

Why Override?   If you want to provide custom state management, but do not want to conform to or leverage the **StateManager** API.

Overridden in Facelets?   No.

public abstract void writeState(FacesContext *context*) throws IOException

Default Behavior   Due to one of the complexities of handling multiple forms in a single JSF view, this method writes out a state marker into the buffer containing the output of rendering. When the tree is completely rendered, the markers are replaced with the actual state of the view. This enables the view to be properly restored regardless of which form was submitted, because each form contains the complete state of the view.

Why Override?   For the same reason one would override **restoreView()**.

Overridden in Facelets?   Yes.

    This chapter has presented the concepts behind providing a custom view description technology, and has explained how Facelets implements these concepts. The next chapter examines, in detail, two significantly less esoteric matters: internationalization and accessibility.

PART

Applying JavaServer Faces

CHAPTER 14
Localization and
Accessibility with
JavaServer Faces

CHAPTER 15
Securing JavaServer Faces
Applications

CHAPTER 16
Automated Testing and
Debugging of JavaServer
Faces Applications

Localization and Accessibility with JavaServer Faces

This chapter covers two features important to the creation of many Web sites: localization and accessibility. When effectively applied, both enable your Web application to be accessed by large numbers of users throughout the global marketplace. Localization and accessibility are examined together because they both share some common implementation techniques.

Localization

Localization is the process by which an application is adapted to meet the requirements of a specific geographic region of the world, also known as a *locale*. This includes a wide range of considerations, including culture, language, currency, typesetting, and so on. Localization is often abbreviated L10n because there are ten letters between the "l" and the "n" in the word "localization."

A closely related term to localization is *internationalization*, which is commonly abbreviated as i18n. (Localization is abbreviated with a capital *L*, but internationalization is abbreviated with a lowercase *i* because the lowercase *l* looks like a number 1, but there is no such confusion with the letter *i*.) Internationalization is what happens during software development to ease the process of localization; ideally, localization should require no programming at all. With JavaServer Faces, all of the internationalization work has already been done for you, so localizing your application is literally as easy as authoring your **ResourceBundle**s and possibly setting some **dir** and **lang** attributes on your markup. This section covers how to perform localization on a Faces application, including an example of localizing the Virtual Trainer application.

Some Benefits of the Localization Facilities Provided by JavaServer Faces

Let's begin by examining some of the benefits of the internationalization facility provided by Faces. Like many things in JSF, the way to handle localization is the same as for any other Java applications—Web-based or otherwise: using **ResourceBundle**s. Unlike desktop Java applications, though, the Web offers unprecedented reach, allowing users from all around the globe to concurrently access a single instance of an application. Faces takes advantage of the user-configurable language information sent by a Web browser with each request to choose the best locale among the choices available to the application. The Faces internationalization system allows you to declare exactly which locales are supported by your application, even down to different variants of the same language. For example, you could have an application localized for Austrian German and German German such that users from Austria would see a greeting of "*Gruß Gott*", while users from Germany would see "*Guten Tag*".

In addition to the standard Java platform techniques of using **ResourceBundle**s, Faces provides several ways to expose your **ResourceBundle**s to the Faces runtime via the Expression Language. A simple JSP example shows how easy it is:

```
<f:view>
  <f:loadBundle basename="com.jsfcompref.trainer.Resources" var="bundle" />

  <h:form>
    <p><h:outputText value="#{bundle.greeting}" />
    <h:outputText value="#{user.firstName}" />
  </h:form>
</f:view>
```

This example shows the use of the **f:loadBundle** tag to associate a request-scoped variable called **bundle** with the **ResourceBundle** that uses the base name of **com.jsfcompref.trainer.Messages**.

In this example, the resource bundle is located under **com/jsfcompref/trainer** in the file **Resources.properties**. The general form for defining a **ResourceBundle** in a properties file is **<basename>_<language>_<country>_<variant>**. The **basename** portion is a fully qualified Java class name. As with actual **.java** files, the real filename is only the last part of the fully qualified class name; the previous parts of the fully qualified Java class name come from the directory structure. The meaning of the **language**, **country**, and **variant** extensions is explained later in the chapter, but for now, just know that these extensions tell the Java runtime to what **Locale** object this **ResourceBundle** applies. Also, note that the **language**, **country**, and **variant** parameters are optional. Their absence means this **ResourceBundle** is to be used as a fallback in case no better match for the requested locale can be found. For this example, the different resource files for this example could look like:

Resources.properties:

```
greeting=Hello
titleMale=Mr.
...
```

Resources_fr.properties:

```
greeting=Bon Jour
titleMale=Monsieur.
...
```

Resources_de.properties:

```
greeting=Guten Tag
titleMale=Herr
...
```

Resources_de_at.properties:

```
greeting= Gruß Gott
titleMale=Herr
...
```

Once this association is made, you can refer to any key within that bundle using an EL expression that starts with **bundle** (or whatever you choose for the value of **var**). The text after the first dot is interpreted as the key in the bundle. You may wonder how to refer to **ResourceBundle** keys that contain dots. No worries, the square bracket EL syntax can be used in that case. For example, if there was a bundle key called **home.directory** you could refer to it with the expression #{**bundle.home['directory']**}. There are other ways to use **ResourceBundle**s in Faces which will be covered in detail later in the chapter in the section "How to Expose ResourceBundles to JSF."

Another example of the usefulness of localization in Faces is the **FacesMessage** system described in Chapter 7. These messages are presented to the user when a conversion or validation error occurs in the page, and naturally they can also be localized.

A JSF Localization Example

Before looking at the details of localization with JSF, it's helpful to work through a complete example. This section shows how to localize the JSFReg example from Chapter 2. Because localization is best kept to the presentation layer, let's start by examining the localization needs of the three JSP pages that comprise the JSFReg application. Table 14-1 lists the pages and their localization needs.

When localizing an existing application, it's a good practice to perform a similar analysis to determine the localization needs. Of course, it is preferable that the application be developed with localized labels to begin with, but this is not always possible. From the analysis, we see that the localization needs of JSFReg are pretty simple, and can all be addressed with a **ResourceBundle**. A real-world application will likely have more complex needs, such as the capability to dynamically switch locales while using the application, and also support right-to-left text, such as Arabic. Figure 14-1 portrays the various elements of a localized JSF application.

Creating the ResourceBundles

The way localization is done in Java is through the use of the **java.util.ResourceBundle** class. Several ways exist to create an instance of **ResourceBundle** and make it available to

Application Page	Localization Needs
main.jsp	Title, Sub title, Link text
register.jsp	Title, Sub title, First Name label, Last Name label, Gender label, Male label, Female Label, Date of Birth label, Email address label, Date of Birth pattern, Date of Birth pattern label, Service Level label, Service Level labels, Button label
confirm.jsp	In addition to the localization needs from **register.jsp**, **confirm.jsp** requires a Confirmation label, and button labels for "edit" and "confirm".

TABLE 14-1   The Localization Needs of the JSFReg Application

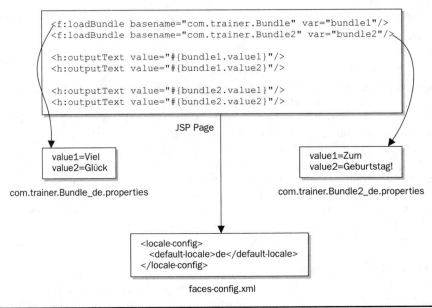

```
<f:loadBundle basename="com.trainer.Bundle" var="bundle1"/>
<f:loadBundle basename="com.trainer.Bundle2" var="bundle2"/>

<h:outputText value="#{bundle1.value1}"/>
<h:outputText value="#{bundle1.value2}"/>

<h:outputText value="#{bundle2.value1}"/>
<h:outputText value="#{bundle2.value2}"/>
```

JSP Page

```
value1=Viel
value2=Glück
```
com.trainer.Bundle_de.properties

```
value1=Zum
value2=Geburtstag!
```
com.trainer.Bundle2_de.properties

```
<locale-config>
  <default-locale>de</default-locale>
</locale-config>
```
faces-config.xml

FIGURE 14-1 A localized JSF application

your application. This chapter only explains the use of a properties file as the means for authoring a **ResourceBundle**, while the act of making it available to your application is handled by the Faces runtime, as described next. The following **Resources_de.properties** file shows the keys and values for the German version of the localized messages.

```
title=Ein Einfaches JavaServer Faces Ausrichtung Anwendung
subtitle= Ausrichtung Anwendung
inviteRegistriationLink=Klicken Sie Hier um anzumelden
registrationLabel=Anmeldeformular
firstName=Vorname:
lastName=Nachname:
genderLabel=Sex:
genderMale=Mann
genderFemale=Frau
birthday=Geburtstag:
datePattern=dd.MM.yy
emailAddress=Email Adresse:
serviceLevel=Bedienungsqualit\u00e4t
serviceLevelBasic=einfach
serviceLevelMedium=mittlerer
serviceLevelPremium=erstklassig
registerButton=anmelden
confirmationLabel=Best\u00e4tigung
editButton=\u00c4ndern
confirmationButton= Best\u00e4tigen
```

Simple applications can afford to put all the localized resources in one bundle, but more complex applications may want to break out the bundles by page or function.

Making the ResourceBundles Available to the Application

Recall from the section on "Assembling the JSFReg Application" in Chapter 2 the list of files and where they reside in the directory structure of the Web application. **ResourceBundle** instances are loaded into the VM using the regular Java **ClassLoader** facility; therefore, they must reside in a subdirectory of the **WEB-INF/classes** directory that matches the package hierarchy in which the **ResourceBundle** is to reside. In this example, the bundle will reside in

```
C:\JSFReg\web\WEB-INF\classes\com\jsfcompref\
    trainer\Resources_de.properties
```

A more complex application requiring multiple **ResourceBundles** would probably have all the bundles in a separate package, such as **com.jsfcompref.trainer.bundles**.

Declaring the Supported Locales for the Application

In order for Faces to find the right **Locale** instance for the user, given his or her language settings in the browser, you must tell the Faces runtime what is the default locale and supported locales. This is done in the **<application>** method of the **faces-config.xml** file.

```
<application>
  <locale-config>
    <default-locale>en</default-locale>
    <supported-locale>de</supported-locale>
    <supported-locale>fr</supported-locale>
    <supported-locale>es</supported-locale>
  </locale-config>
</application>
```

The preceding declaration states that the default locale is English, while German, French, and Spanish are supported. The ordering of elements in the **<locale-config>** element is important, as described next in the section on how Faces chooses the right locale.

Localizing the JSP Pages

The final step in localizing the application is to modify the JSP files to use the **ResourceBundle** instead of hard-coded label values. We will only include the **register.jsp** page, because the process of changing the rest of the pages is exactly the same.

```
<%@ page contentType="text/html"%>
<%@ taglib uri="http://java.sun.com/jsf/core" prefix="f"%>
<%@ taglib uri="http://java.sun.com/jsf/html" prefix="h"%>
<f:view>
 <f:loadBundle var="bundle" basename="com.jsfcompref.trainer.Resources" />
 <html>
  <head><title><h:outputText value="#{bundle.title}" /></title></head>
    <body>
      <h:form>
        <h2><h:outputText value="#{bundle.subtitle}" /></h2>
        <h4><h:outputText value="#{bundle.registrationLabel}" /></h4>
        <table>
         <tr>
          <td><h:outputText value="#{bundle.firstName}" /></td>
          <td>
           <h:inputText id="fname" value="#{UserBean.firstName}" required="true"/>
           <h:message for="fname"/>
          </td>
         </tr>
```

```
         <tr>
          <td><h:outputText value="#{bundle.lastName}" /> </td>
          <td>
           <h:inputText id="lname" value="#{UserBean.lastName}"
                      required="true" />
           <h:message for="lname"/>
          </td>
         </tr>
         <tr>
          <td><h:outputText value="#{bundle.genderLabel}" /></td>
          <td>
       <h:selectOneRadio id="gender" value="#{UserBean.gender}"  required="true"/>
        <f:selectItem itemLabel="#{bundle.genderMale}"
                     itemValue="male"/>
        <f:selectItem itemLabel="#{bundle.genderFemale}"
                     itemValue="female"/>
       </h:selectOneRadio>
       <h:message for="gender"/>
          </td>
         </tr>
         <tr>
          <td><h:outputText value="#{bundle.birthday}" /></td>
          <td>
           <h:inputText value="#{UserBean.dob}" id="dob" required="true" >
            <f:convertDateTime pattern="#{bundle.datePattern}"/>
           </h:inputText> (<h:outputText value="#{bundle.datePattern}" />)
           <h:message for="dob"/>
          </td>
         </tr>
         <tr>
          <td><h:outputText value="#{bundle.emailAddress}" /></td>
          <td>
           <h:inputText id="email" value="#{UserBean.email}" required="true"
             validator="#{UserBean.validateEmail}"/>
           <h:message for="email"/>
          </td>
         </tr>
         <tr>
          <td><h:outputText value="#{bundle.serviceLevel}" /></td>
          <td>
           <h:selectOneMenu value="#{UserBean.serviceLevel}">
            <f:selectItem itemLabel="#{bundle.serviceLevelBasic"
                         itemValue="basic"/>
            <f:selectItem itemLabel="#{bundle.serviceLevelMedium}"
                         itemValue="medium"/>
            <f:selectItem itemLabel="#{bundle.serviceLevelPremium}"
                         itemValue="premium"/>
           </h:selectOneMenu>
          </td>
         </tr>
        </table>
        <p><h:commandButton value="#{bundle.registerButton}" action="register" /></p>
      </h:form>
    </body>
   </html>
</f:view>
```

The first thing to notice about this example is the **<f:loadBundle>** tag. This tag just associates the name **bundle** with the **ResourceBundle** in your **WEB-INF/classes** directory. Note that all the English template text has been replaced by **<h:outputText>** components with **value** attributes pointing to the appropriate **ResourceBundle** key using the EL. Also, the value of the **itemLabel** attribute in the **<h:selectOneRadio>** and **<h:selectOneMenu>** tags has been replaced with similar EL expressions. Finally, note the value of the **pattern** attribute on the **<f:convertDateTime>** also comes from the bundle. If you opt not to use the **pattern** attribute, you can use the **dateStyle** attribute, which will derive a **pattern** value from the **Locale**. The localized JSFReg page is displayed at right.

The Details Behind Faces Localization and Internationalization

Now that you have worked through an example, it is time to examine the details of localization. Let's begin by reviewing the string representation of a **Locale** and how that concept applies to the name of a **ResourceBundle**. A **Locale** is broken down into three parts: language, country, and variant. The string representation of a **Locale** uses a two-letter ISO 639 code for the language, a two-letter ISO 3166 code for the country, and a vendor-specific code for the variant, all separated by dashes or underscores. For example, **fr_CA** indicates the French language as spoken in Canada. A file name for a **ResourceBundle** defined as a properties file consists of four parts, a required **basename**, and optional language, country, and variant parts. For example, the **ResourceBundle com.jsfcompref.trainer.Resources_de_AT.properties** has **com.jsfcompref.trainer.Resources** as the basename, **de** as the country, and **at** as the language.

Now let's take a closer look at the **<locale-config>** element, shown next:

```
<application>
  <locale-config>
    <default-locale>en</default-locale>
    <supported-locale>de_at</supported-locale>
    <supported-locale>de_de</supported-locale>
    <supported-locale>fr</supported-locale>
    <supported-locale>es</supported-locale>
  </locale-config>
</application>
```

The **<locale-config>** element is the one place where the developer tells the JSF runtime which languages are supported by the application. This differs from JSP and JSTL where the presence or absence of bundles for a particular locale is used to determine which languages are supported.

Expert Group Insight   *The <locale-config> element is used to make the determination because no* **ResourceBundle**s *will have been loaded by the time the determination is needed; therefore, they cannot be examined for their locality. Also, it's possible that the JSF implementation may be localized for more languages than your application, and you don't want the application to display messages for any languages other than the ones you know your application supports.*

How the Correct Locale Is Determined

It is useful to understand the details of the algorithm for determining the correct locale based on the user's preferences sent by the browser. Most browsers allow the user to configure a priority list of languages in which pages should be rendered. Figure 14-2 illustrates this configuration in the Firefox Web browser.

These settings are sent to the server in the **Accept-Language** and **Accept-Charset** HTTP headers, which are exposed to the JSF runtime via the Servlet API.

During the *Restore View* phase of the request processing lifecycle, the **calculateLocale()** method is called on the **ViewHandler**, which causes the following algorithm to be performed and the result set as the **locale** property of the **UIViewRoot** for this view. Note that if you need to provide a different algorithm for selecting the locale, it is very easy to do so using the custom **ViewHandler** techniques described in Chapter 13.

For each language entry "**preferred**" sent in the **Accept-Language** header by the browser:

1. For each entry "**supported**" in the list of **supported-locale**s from the **faces-config .xml** file:

   a. If **preferred** is exactly equal to **supported**, consider it a match and return.

   b. If the language portion of **preferred** is equal to the language portion of **supported**, and **supported** has no country defined, consider it a match and return.

2. If no match is found in the **supported-locale**s list:

   a. If preferred is exactly equal to the **default-locale**, consider it a match and return.

   b. If the language portion of **preferred** is equal to the language portion of **default-locale**, and **default-locale** has no country defined, consider it a match and return.

If no match is found with the previous algorithm for any of the **preferred** languages sent in the **Accept-Language** header, and if there is a **<default-locale>**, use it. Otherwise, just use **Locale.getDefault()**.

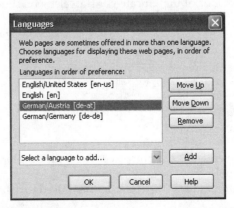

Figure 14-2   The languages and character encoding dialog in Firefox

Let's work through some examples to clarify the algorithm. Let's say the user prefers **de_ ch, en,** and **fr** as his or her language priorities, and the **<locale-config>** is as listed previously. First, we consider **de_ch**. It's not exactly equal to any of the **supported-locale**s or the **default-locale**, so we continue on to **en**. This doesn't match any of the **supported-locale**s, but it does match the **default-locale**, so it is considered a match and the page is rendered in English. Let's remove the **default-locale** from the **locale-config** and re-evaluate the algorithm. Again, **de_ch**, has no match, so we continue. The same goes for **en**. We now come to **fr**. There is an exact match in the **supported-locale** list, so the page is rendered in French.

The user can override the **Locale** determined by the previous algorithm either by calling **setLocale()** on the **UIViewRoot** directly, or by giving a **locale** attribute to the **<f:view>** tag, like in the following:

```
<f:view locale="en_US" >
```

The **locale** attribute is **ValueExpression**-enabled, so the following is also valid:

```
<f:view locale="#{prefs.locale}">
```

provided that the expression evaluates to a **Locale** instance or a string representation of a **Locale** instance as described earlier.

How the Correct Character Encoding Is Determined

There is considerable confusion regarding meanings of the terms "charset," "character encoding," and "character code." Let's clear up some of that confusion before explaining how these terms relate to Web applications in general and Faces applications in particular. The whole point of localization is to display your application so that it can be understood by users from specific geographic regions. Since the Web is still mainly a textual medium, the elements that make up text are very important. Let's say that the elements that make up text in a natural language are called *characters*. A collection of characters grouped together in some logical fashion is called a *character repertoire*. No specific computer representation or even sort order is implied by the concept of a character repertoire; it's purely a human concept. A character repertoire is usually presented by giving the names of the characters and a visual representation of each one. A *character code* is a big list of the characters in a character repertoire, with a non-negative integer number, known as a *code position*, assigned to each character. Synonyms for code position are *code point, code number, code element,* and *code set value*. With the introduction of the concept of character code comes the notion of the characters being sorted. For example, Morse code lists each letter in the English alphabet in alphabetical order, followed by the numerals 0 through 9, followed by some control characters. Finally, a *character encoding* is another big list, this time of the *code positions* in a *character code* with a sequence of binary numbers known as *octets* associated with each. ASCII is probably the best known character encoding. It is also a character code because each code position is also its encoding—for example, the letter *a* is at code position 97, and it is also encoded as the number 97. Figure 14-3 illustrates the concepts of repertoire, code, and encoding.

Generally, the only concept you have to understand is character encoding. The declaration of a character encoding is what allows the big sequence of bytes that comprise a Web page to be turned into meaningful localized human-readable text. Without a character encoding, the browser would have no way to know how it should interpret the bytes for display. The most common encoding for computer systems is, of course, ASCII, but this encoding doesn't travel well because it only contains characters for English. The most common character encoding for the Web is called ISO-8859-1, also known as Latin 1. This encoding is a superset of ASCII, but also includes characters for Western and Northern European Languages.

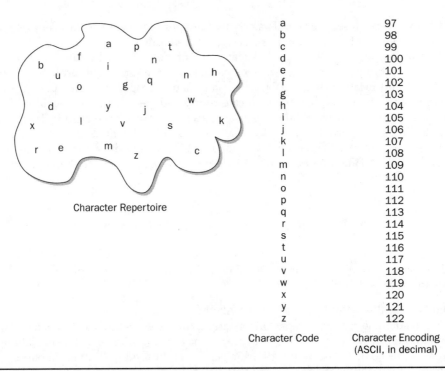

		Character Code		Character Encoding (ASCII, in decimal)

Character	Code
a	97
b	98
c	99
d	100
e	101
f	102
g	103
h	104
i	105
j	106
k	107
l	108
m	109
n	110
o	111
p	112
q	113
r	114
s	115
t	116
u	117
v	118
w	119
x	120
y	121
z	122

FIGURE 14-3   Character repertoire, character code, and character encoding

Other popular encodings are Shift_JIS for Japanese, Big5 for Chinese, ISO-8859-6 for Arabic, and UTF-8 for the Unicode encoding. UTF-8 is growing in popularity because it allows a single document to use nearly any world language without having to switch encodings.

Now that you understand why character encodings are important in general, let's see why they are important to the Web. Because the HTTP protocol of the Web is a request/ response protocol, it is vitally important that the character encoding used to render a Web page with an HTML **form** element to the browser be the same as the character encoding used to submit the form to the browser. This is done by passing character encoding information along with the request and response. As with the language of the document, the character encoding is sent via an HTTP header. In this case, the encoding is sent as a parameter to the **Content-Type** header. Generally, for the Web, **Content-Type** is **text/html** for HTML pages, **application/xhtml+xml** for XHTML documents, and **text/xml** for XML documents. So, to say that a Web page is presented as HTML using the UTF-8 encoding, the **Content-Type** header would be

```
Content-Type: text/html; charset=UTF-8
```

Note that the name of the parameter is **charset** even though it refers to a character encoding. This header travels along with the Web page when it is sent from the server to the browser, and with the form submit when it is sent from the browser back to the server.

Now, let's answer the question of how the correct character encoding is set. In JSP, the user may leverage a page directive to set the **Content-Type** and character encoding, as shown next:

```
<%@ page contentType="text/html; charset=UTF-8" %>
```

In addition, it is often useful to include a **meta** tag in the **<head>** element with the same information:

```
<meta http-equiv="Content-Type" content="text/html; charset=UTF-8" />
```

These actions cause the response character encoding to be set as desired. The JSF framework will discover the character encoding value set in this manner and store it in the session. When the form postback occurs, the request character encoding is set with the information stored in the session **before** the request is interpreted. In this way, the proper interpretation of the postback is achieved.

How to Expose ResourceBundles to JSF

As shown earlier in the chapter, the **f:loadBundle** tag is an easy way to make localized labels available for use in your JSP pages.

EXPERT GROUP INSIGHT *The Expert Group went through considerable debate regarding interoperation with JSTL's* **<fmt:setBundle>** *tag and JSF's* **<f:loadBundle>** *tag. Because JSF is a higher-level abstraction than what is provided by JSTL, it was decided that* **<fmt:setBundle>** *should not be used in JSF applications. Instead, one aspect of the work that was done by* **<fmt: setBundle>**, *that of propagating a* **Locale** *to the JSP layer, is done by JSF. Also, it is better to expose the* **ResourceBundle** *properties via the EL for greater flexibility.*

The nicest thing about **f:loadBundle** is its ease of use. Just declare that the tag and all the keys in the bundle are exposed for use anywhere you can use the EL. Unfortunately, there is a performance impact because the **ResourceBundle** must be reloaded on each request since this tag simply exposes the **ResourceBundle** as a **Map** in a request-scoped attribute. Also, when using JSF and AJAX, the JSP page may not be available on the AJAX postback; therefore, we need some other way to expose **ResourceBundle**s to the application. For more on using JSF and AJAX, please see Chapter 11.

JSF 1.2 TIP *In JSF 1.2, an additional element was added to the* **application** *element:* **resource-bundle**. *This allows* **ResourceBundle**s *to be declared at the application level, avoiding the performance hit of loading the bundle for each request. More importantly, localized values may now be obtained without using JSP, and on phases other than "render response." This is vital for AJAX applications, where there is often no JSP page when processing the postback. As with* **<f:loadBundle>**, *the* **ResourceBundle** *declared in this way is accessible via the EL. An example declaration of the* **<resource-bundle>** *element follows:*

```
<application>
  <resource-bundle>
    <base-name>com.jsfcompref.ApplicationBundle</base-name>
    <var>appBundle</var>
  </resource-bundle>
  <locale-config>
    <!—Locale config as above -->
  </locale-config>
</application>
```

This declaration allows the bundle to be referenced inside JSP pages like in the following:

```
<h:outputText value="#{appBundle.message}" />
```

where **message** *is a key inside the* **ResourceBundle** *called* **ApplicationBundle**.

Internationalization Issues for Custom Components

The JSF framework is fully internationalized so that users can simply perform the task of localization. However, when authoring your own components, you must perform internationalization so that your components have the same level of localizability that users expect from the JSF framework. You should consider three main areas:

- Locale-specific component attributes—for example, a calendar component that uses a Gregorian character for some locales, and a Muslim character if the locale is Arabic.

- Localized **FacesMessage** data for when errors such as validation or conversion problems occur.

- Any tool-specific metadata, such as what will be shown in an IDE when a developer is working with your component—for example, the **<description>** element in the **faces-config.xml** for the component.

Locale-specific component attributes are largely a matter of the design of your component. JSF provides the component developer a guarantee that the **UIViewRoot** has already been populated with the proper **locale** property so that your component can simply query that property whenever it needs a **Locale** instance.

Localized **FacesMessage** data pertains mainly to **FacesMessage** instances generated in response to conversion or validation errors generated by the component during the request process lifecycle. The details of the **FacesMessage** mechanism are described in Chapter 7.

Tool-specific metadata is a special case because the localization is performed by the component developer, not the component user. Let's work through an example that shows how the custom **WeightConverter** of the Virtual Trainer example provides localized data to an IDE. Recall the XML declaration of the converter, from Chapter 7:

```
<converter>
  <description>
    Registers the weight converter using the converter id weight
  </description>
  <converter-id>weight</converter-id>
  <converter-class>
    com.jsfcompref.trainer.convert.WeightConverter
  </converter-class>
</converter>
```

Here, we want to localize the **<description>** element. This is done using the **xml:lang** XML attribute. The localized version of the converter declaration is shown next:

```
<converter>
  <description xml:lang="en">
    Registers the weight converter using the converter id weight
  </description>
  <description xml:lang="de">
    Registriert den Gewichtkonverter mit dem
    Konverterkennzeichnung Gewicht
  </description>
  <converter-id>weight</converter-id>
  <converter-class>
    com.jsfcompref.trainer.convert.WeightConverter
  </converter-class>
</converter>
```

Accessibility

Accessibility in the context of Web applications is the quality of an application that makes it usable by people with disabilities. In keeping with the tradition of silly abbreviations for this sort of thing, accessibility is sometimes abbreviated as a11y. The Web has always been intended to be accessible and all of the standards that make up the Web have very good support for accessibility. Faces leverages the existing accessibility features of the Web to make it very easy to create accessible applications that comply with such laws as Section 508 in the United States.

Why Accessibility Is Important

One of the most attractive things about Web application development is the ability to reach a large number of people with a single technology investment. To extend the application's reach as far as possible, it is good practice, and good citizenship, to make your application accessible to people operating in circumstances that may be very different from the common case. The Web Content Accessibility Guidelines (WCAG), offered by the W3C (**http://www.w3.org/TR/WCAG10/**), bring the issue of accessibility into focus using some of the following points. In the WCAG, accessibility means allowing people to access your application who

- May not be able to see, hear, move, or process certain types of information at all.
- May have difficulty reading or comprehending text.
- May not have, or be able to use, a keyboard or mouse.
- May have a text-only screen, or a slow Internet connection.
- May be in a situation where their eyes, ears, or hands are busy or unavailable for manipulating the software.
- May have an old version of a browser, a different browser, or a different operating system.

Notice that this list includes far more situations than just people with disabilities. For example, many experienced computer users (as well as users with typing-related injuries) prefer to use keyboard shortcuts instead of using the mouse. Note that "different browser" and "different operating system" are specifically called out. This is important to consider when deciding whether or not to use a flashy feature offered only on one OS or browser. The point is that accessibility is all about extending the reach of your application.

While your particular application requirements may not call for complete accessibility, in some cases it is required by law. Section 508 of the United States Rehabilitation Act requires that when Federal agencies develop, procure, maintain, or use electronic and information technology, they shall ensure that this technology allows individuals with disabilities to have access to, and use of, information that is comparable to that provided to individuals without disabilities. Other countries have similar laws.

Guidelines for Providing Accessibility in JSF Applications

The aforementioned WCAG lists 14 recommendations to achieve compliance with Section 508 and to provide accessibility in general. The standard JSF components are required to comply with these guidelines in all the markup they generate, and any well-designed third-party component will do the same. In this section, we list only the guidelines that are pertinent to the development of custom JSF **UIComponents**. Other kinds of JSF components, such as converters and validators, usually do not have accessibility considerations because they have no specific graphical user interface of their own.

Before jumping into the guidelines, let's stress one fundamental point about accessibility: *consistency is very important*. For example, if you provide **accesskey** and **tabindex** settings for one page in your application, you must do the same for all the pages in the application. Making only part of your application accessible is almost as bad as having none of it accessible at all. One approach to consistency is to provide a copy of your entire site that is designed for accessibility. A great example of a site using such an approach is the "Hurricane Science and Safety" site at **http://meted.ucar.edu/hurrican/strike/**. This approach also allows you to comply with some of the more difficult guidelines, such as "avoid the use of JavaScript" and "don't use pop-up windows."

Give a Text Equivalent to Nontextual Content

The most important guideline is also the easiest to follow: give a text equivalent to nontextual content. Because it is the most important guideline, it is the first one listed in the WCAG. A common example is the **alt** attribute for the **h:commandButton** and **h:graphicImage** components. For example, HTML provides the **alt** attribute on the **<img>** element, and Faces exposes this on the **h:graphicImage** tag, as shown next.

```
<h:graphicImage src="#{bundle.nextButtonImage}"
                alt="#{bundle.nextButtonAltText}" />
```

Note that we've also localized this example. You can, of course, use literal strings instead of expressions. Naturally, the **alt** attribute is only necessary on the button when using an image for the button. Another approach is to provide a **description link** immediately next to the nontextual content. This is a simple HTML link to another page containing only a description of the nontextual content and no other content. Use this approach when you have more information that is appropriate for an **alt** attribute.

Use Markup and Stylesheets Properly

It is important to use markup and stylesheets properly. This is Guideline 3 in the WCAG. HTML has its roots in SGML (Standard Generalized Markup Language) and, as such, allows some level of separation between document content, structure, and presentation. From the WCAG:

> *The content of a document refers to what it says to the user through natural language, images, sounds, movies, animations, etc. The structure of a document is how it is organized logically (e.g., by chapter, with an introduction and table of contents, etc.)... The presentation of a document is how the document is rendered (e.g., as print, as a two-dimensional graphical presentation, as a text-only presentation, as synthesized speech, as Braille, etc).*

Although HTML provides limited capability for combining these three aspects of a document (content, structure, and presentation), it is best to separate them as much as possible. For example, avoid using HTML tables for layout in your custom components. This confuses screen readers, making it impossible for the user to understand what the component is trying to convey. A better approach is to use a CSS stylesheet associated with your component to do the layout and styling. Of course, if your component does actually display tabular data, such as a custom **dataTable** component, the use of HTML tables is entirely appropriate. The HTML table element provides many accessibility features which are leveraged in full by the renderer behind the standard **h:dataTable** tag.

Clarify Natural Language Usage

You should clearly specify what natural language is being used. This is Guideline 4 in the WCAG. Here is where accessibility and localization overlap. You can use the localization techniques described earlier whenever the natural language changes within the scope of your application. For example, let's say your page contains content in the default language, as well as in French. An HTML **<span lang="fr">** could be used to denote the French sections. Also, it is a good practice to include a **Content-Language** header in your documents. The easiest way to do that is through the **<meta>** tag in the HTML **<head>** element:

```
<meta http-equiv="Content-Language"
      content="fr" />
```

Ensure That Pages Featuring New Technologies Transform Gracefully

When using a new or not widely supported technology (such as Scalable Vector Graphics, as of print time for this book) you must make sure that the feature transforms gracefully when the new technology is not supported. This is Guideline 6 in the WCAG. The most relevant aspect of this guideline involves the use of JavaScript in your pages. To make your application as accessible as possible, avoid the use of JavaScript. In many cases, this is a rather impractical recommendation, yet the W3C guidelines recommend it nonetheless. One strategy for complying with this guideline is to have a separate set of pages for the accessible content, in which no JavaScript is used.

JSF 1.2 TIP   In earlier versions of JSF, no restriction was placed on which tags could cause JavaScript to be generated, although the Sun Implementation only happened to generate it to handle the **<h:commandLink>** *tag. In JSF 1.2, the spec has been tightened to state that only this component may generate JavaScript.*

Ensure User Control of Time-Sensitive Content Changes

You must ensure user control of time-sensitive content changes. This is WCAG Guideline 7. Screen readers are unable to read moving text, such as marquees, blinking text, scrolling text, and so on. So, if your JSF component generates such text, make sure to provide an accessible way to turn it off. Also, avoid using auto-page refresh, such as with the **HTTP-EQUIV=refresh**. Auto-refresh is confusing because it can cause the user to lose track of where they are in the application.

Design for Device Independence

Device independence is a crucial part of accessibility. This is Guideline 9 in the WCAG. The **RenderKit** mechanism of JSF is ideally suited to meeting this guideline. But another dimension of device independence is how it applies to which input device is being used to interact with the page. In general, pages that are entirely keyboard-accessible are handled well by accessibility tools. To achieve this, always define a logical tab ordering of components using the **tabindex** attribute, and provide keyboard shortcuts to important components using the **accesskey** attribute.

The common technique of using pop-up windows in Web applications hampers accessibility. Thus, pop-up windows should be avoided.

Use the Label Element

Use the label element to ensure that the user agent can convey the relationship between a label and an input element. This is WCAG Guideline 10. JSF supports this guideline through the **Label** renderer associated with the **h:outputLabel** tag, for example:

```
<h:outputLabel value="#{bundle.firstName}" for="firstName" />
<h:inputText id="firstName" value="#{user.firstName}" />
```

JSF 1.2 TIP *In earlier versions of JSF, the label had to reside in the same **h:form** as the component it is labeling. With the new tree creation mechanism in JSF 1.2, this restriction is no longer present. However, it is good practice to have the label immediately precede the component it is labeling.*

Using the **outputLabel** tag generates markup that accessible user-agents can leverage to convey the meaning of the text field. In this case, it is a text field intended to store the user's first name.

Context and Orientation Information

The wise use of context and orientation information is vital to the successful creation of accessible Web pages. This is Guideline 12 in the WCAG. Leverage as much of the logical grouping and contextual information provided by HTML as is sensible for your application. For example, let's say you have a custom component that renders a set of form controls that are interrelated. Such as an "accept license" component that renders a radio button list with buttons for "accept" and "decline." The rendered content for the component should use the **fieldset** and **legend** elements. The JSP markup for such a component may look like:

```
<user:licenseDialog id="acceptDecline"
     acceptAction="accept" declineAction="decline"
                    label="#{bundle.licenseLabel}" tabindex="5"/>
```

But the rendered output may look like:

```
<fieldset>
  <legend>Accept or Decline License</legend>
  <span tabindex="5">
  <input type="radio" name="acceptDecline" id="accept:0"
         value="Accept"/>
  <input type="radio" name="acceptDecline" id="accept:1"
         value="Decline"/>
  </span>
</fieldset>
```

Naturally, much has been omitted from this component for the purpose of discussion.

This completes our survey of the WCAG for JSF. While Faces does a lot to help with accessibility, the overall accessibility of your application is still largely up to you, the developer.

Securing JavaServer Faces Applications

This chapter explains how to secure your JavaServer Faces application. At the outset, it is important to state that computer security in general, and Web security in particular, are very large topics. In this chapter, we examine the issue only as it relates to JSF. We begin with an introduction to some high-level security concepts, followed by a review of the fundamentals of the security features provided by the Java EE Platform Web tier. Fortunately, everything you already know about Java EE Platform Security applies to JSF applications as well. The chapter will close by presenting a simple JSF-based framework for securing a JSF Web application, using the Virtual Trainer as an example. Throughout, you'll see how effectively leveraging JSF streamlines the process of adding security.

Aspects and Implementation of Web Application Security

Web application security can be broken down into three main aspects.

- **Authentication**   Proving to the system that a user's identity is authentic. In other words, "you are who you say you are."

- **Authorization**   Granting access to certain parts of the system based on the user's identity. This is sometimes referred to as *role-based access control* because each user is associated with one or more roles, and the roles dictate what actions the user may take. In other words, "we know who you are; now, what are you allowed to do?"

- **Data Security**   Ensuring that interactions between the user and the system cannot be observed by unauthorized parties. In other words, "we know who you are, what you're allowed to do, and now, let's prevent people from snooping on you while you do it."

Not all applications need all three aspects; customer requirements will dictate which of the three are needed. For example, an intranet application that runs on a secure LAN does not require data security because all the communications on the LAN are already assumed to be secure. Also, some of the aspects may be combined. Consider an application that doesn't require authentication for general use, yet has a portion of the application that only administrators may access. In this case, the user must be *authenticated* as an administrator, and then *authorized* to perform functions that normal users cannot. You can see that applying security to a Web application is an art that requires merging customer requirements with the aspects of authentication, authorization, and data security.

The implementation of the aspects of Web security is generally broken down into two areas: *container managed* and *application managed*. An application is said to use container-managed security when it relies on the security features provided by the container. For many applications, this is all that is needed. This chapter will cover the fundamentals of container-managed security in the following section. Application-managed security is when the application itself provides some or all of the security features. Application-managed security is often built on top of the features of container-managed security and is used when container-managed security alone fails to meet the security requirements. Application-managed security will be covered at the end of the chapter in the section "Application-Managed Security with JavaServer Faces."

Container-Managed Security

This section provides an overview of the security features provided by the Java EE Platform (formerly known as J2EE) Web tier. The discussion will be guided by presenting each of the three aspects of Web application security and how each is addressed in the Web tier. All of the container-managed security features are configured using entries in the Web deployment descriptor, the **web.xml** file.

Container-Managed Authentication

Many applications require only container-managed authentication security. The Web tier provides three features to implement this aspect: basic, form-based, and client certificate. (A fourth version of authentication is provided, called digest, but it is not widely supported and therefore is not discussed further.) You tell the container which kind of authentication you are using by placing a **<login-config>** element inside of the **<web-app>** element in the **web.xml** file. Recall that the ordering of elements inside of the **<web-app>** element is significant and the application may fail to deploy if you don't follow the proper ordering as dictated in the DTD or schema. The following example configures basic authentication for the application:

```
<web-app>
  <!-- intervening elements omitted -->
  <security-constraint>
    <!-- contents omitted, see discussion on Authorization -->
  </security-constraint>
  <login-config>
    <auth-method>BASIC</auth-method>
    <realm-name>UserDatabase</realm-name>
  </login-config>
  <!-- intervening elements omitted -->
</web-app>
```

The details of the **<security-constraint>** element are left to the section on authorization, but for now, just know that this element allows you to control which parts of your application are subject to authentication.

The Servlet API provides several methods on **HttpServletRequest** to interface with the container-managed authentication system, regardless of which method (basic, form, digest, or client certificate) is used. These are shown in Table 15-1.

Method Name	Return Type	Purpose
getAuthType( )	String	Returns a string showing which authentication type is in use, or **null** if the request is unauthenticated.
getRemoteUser( )	String	Returns the username of the user making this request, or **null** if the request is unauthenticated.
getUserPrincipal( )	Principal	Returns a **java.security.Principal** instance representing the currcnt user. **Principal** is a simple interface, implementations of which are provided by the underlying security system to represent the user while allowing a flexible security implementation.
isUserInRole(String role)	boolean	Returns **true** if the user making this request is included in the argument **role**. Otherwise, it returns **false**.

TABLE 15-1   **HttpServletRequest** Authentication Methods

These methods provide one way to build application-managed security on top of the existing security infrastructure of the Web tier. We'll revisit these API methods in the section "Container-Managed Authorization and the Concept of Roles" with an example of how to integrate container-managed security elements into application-managed security.

Let's examine each of the four implementations of container-managed authentication in the Java EE Web tier.

Basic Authentication and the Concept of a "Realm"

Basic authentication has been around since the beginning of the Web. Indeed, it was defined in the HTTP 1.0 specification way back in 1996. The basic authentication scheme also introduced the notion of "realm" which you saw earlier as **<realm-name>** in the **web.xml** excerpt. A realm is an opaque string interpreted by the server to identify a data store for resolving username and password information. The *implementation of the realm concept is not standard*; different containers implement it differently. In the Apache Tomcat container, a simple plain text XML file is used to configure the **UserDatabase** realm, the **<TOMCAT-HOME>/conf/ tomcat-users.xml** file:

```
<tomcat-users>
  <role name="trainer" />
  <role name="user" />
  <user name="administrator" password="admin" roles="trainer" />
  <user name="edburns"  password="pass" roles="user"  />
</tomcat-users>
```

The Sun Java System Application server provides **file**, **admin-realm**, and **certificate** realms, as well as support for JAAS (Java Authentication and Authorization Service), all of which have their own configuration mechanisms. Oracle's OC4J (Oracle Containers for J2EE) has its own **jazn-data.xml** configuration file which is also a JAAS Descriptor. All of these files contain realm definitions with associated users and roles.

Basic authentication is not secure because the username and password information are sent via Base64 encoded plain text as the value of the **Authorization** HTTP header. (Unfortunately, the name of the header is "Authorization," but the service it performs is authentication.) Base64 encoding is a well-known algorithm that converts binary data into plain ASCII text by breaking the binary data down into 6-bit chunks and converting each one to an ASCII character. There is no encryption element to the Base64 encoding algorithm, therefore this data can easily be examined by packet sniffers and other network intrusion technologies.

To make basic authentication secure, a secure transport layer must be employed. Please see the section on "Container-Managed Data Security" for more on this topic. When using basic authentication, the browser presents a pop-up dialog to the user asking them to provide their username and password, as shown in Figure 15-1.

While basic authentication may not be secure, there are some instances in which it is sufficient for user requirements, such as when the entire application resides on a secure network and when prototyping.

Form-Based Authentication

Form-based authentication is so called because you must author a Web page with a form in it that provides the UI to the login page of the application. Form-based authentication was designed well before JSF came along and makes assumptions about the server-side processing of the authentication that are not entirely compatible with the design of JSF. It is certainly possible to use the standard form-based authentication technique to provide authentication to a JSF application, but an ideal solution would use a custom component to hide the details from the page author. This section will show one way to build such a component. We will use the component to illustrate the use of form-based authentication. First though, let's return to the **<login-config>** element of the **web.xml** file.

```
<login-config>
  <auth-method>FORM</auth-method>
  <realm-name>UserDatabase</realm-name>
  <form-login-config>
    <form-login-page>/faces/login.jsp</form-login-page>
    <form-error-page>/faces/loginError.jsp</form-error-page>
  </form-login-config>
</login-config>
```

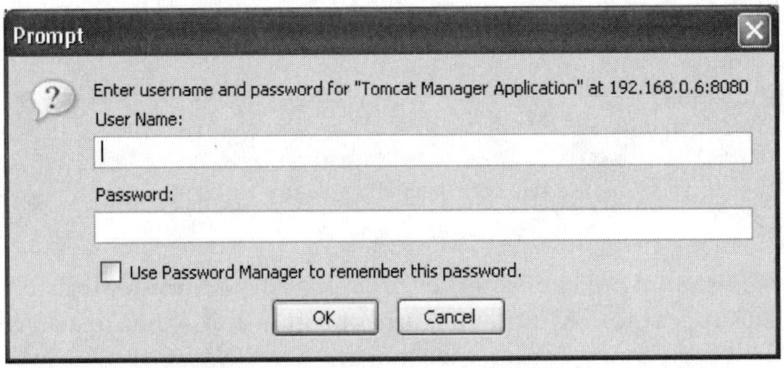

FIGURE 15-1   A browser's basic authentication dialog

Assuming the **<security-constraint>** element is correctly defined to cover the parts of the application that you want to be subject to authentication, any attempts to access these pages without first going through the login page will fail, and the user will be redirected to the login page. Let us now show the portion of the **login.jsp** page using the custom **vt: formBasedLogin** component. This component hides the details of the container-managed, form-based login mechanism. Most notably, it hides the awkward and non-JSF-based **j_ security_check** syntax required for container-managed form-based login.

```
<p>Please Login to access this part of the site.</p>
<vt:formBasedLogin userNameLabel="Username:"
                   passwordLabel="Password:"
                   buttonLabel="Login" />
```

The **loginError.jsp** page is just a plain old Web page (it need not be a JSF or even JSP) that is shown when the login has failed for some reason. For this reason, we need not discuss it here, except to say that it is useful to provide a "try again" link that allows the user to try to log in again.

Recall from Chapter 10 that a JSF component consists of several parts: the JSP tag, the **UIComponent** subclass, and an optional **Renderer** to provide device independence. For brevity, this example omits the **Renderer** and places the rendering logic straight in the **UIComponent** subclass. The source code for the JSP tag is straightforward and conforms to the practices described in Chapter 10—namely, the JSP tag only serves as a way to expose the **UIComponent** to the page author, and allow the page author to configure the instance of the component using tag attributes. The complete source code for the JSP tag is included in the online code for this book. Now that we've dispensed with the **Renderer** and the JSP tag, let's list the source for the **FormBasedLoginComponent**.

```
package com.jsfcompref.vtlib.component;

import java.io.IOException;
import javax.faces.component.UIOutput;
import javax.faces.context.FacesContext;
import javax.faces.context.ResponseWriter;
import javax.faces.el.ValueBinding;

public class FormBasedLoginComponent extends UIComponentBase {

  public FormBasedLoginComponent() {
  }

  public String getFamily() { return "vtlib.FormBasedLogin"; }

  public void encodeEnd(FacesContext context) throws IOException {
    ResponseWriter writer = context.getResponseWriter();
    writer.startElement("form", this);
    writer.writeAttribute("method", "post", null);
    writer.writeAttribute("action", "j_security_check", null);

    // Using Tables for Layout violates WCAG guideline 5.
    // A production quality implementation would use CSS for layout.
    writer.startElement("table", this);
```

```
// Userid row
writer.startElement("tr", this);

writer.startElement("td", this);
writer.startElement("label", this);
writer.writeAttribute("for", "j_username", null);
writer.writeText(this.getUsernameLabel(), "usernameLabel");
writer.endElement("label");
writer.endElement("td");

writer.startElement("td", this);
writer.startElement("input", this);
writer.writeAttribute("type", "text", null);
writer.writeAttribute("name", "j_username", null);
writer.writeAttribute("id", "j_username", null);
writer.endElement("td");

writer.endElement("tr");

// Password row
writer.startElement("tr", this);

writer.startElement("td", this);
writer.startElement("label", this);
writer.writeAttribute("for", "j_password", null);
writer.writeText(this.getPasswordLabel(), "passwordLabel");
writer.endElement("label");
writer.endElement("td");

writer.startElement("td", this);
writer.startElement("input", this);
writer.writeAttribute("type", "password", null);
writer.writeAttribute("name", "j_password", null);
writer.endElement("td");

writer.endElement("tr");

// Button row
writer.startElement("tr", this);
writer.startElement("td", this);
writer.startElement("input", this);
writer.writeAttribute("type", "reset", null);
writer.writeAttribute("name", "reset", null);
writer.writeAttribute("value", getResetButtonLabel(),
    "resetButtonLabel");
writer.endElement("td");
writer.startElement("td", this);
writer.startElement("input", this);
writer.writeAttribute("type", "submit", null);
writer.writeAttribute("name", "submit", null);
writer.writeAttribute("value", getButtonLabel(), "buttonLabel");
writer.endElement("td");
writer.endElement("tr");
writer.endElement("table");
```

```
    writer.endElement ("form");

  }

  public void encodeChildren(FacesContext context) throws IOException {
  }

  public void encodeBegin(FacesContext context) throws IOException {

  }

  private String usernameLabel;
  private static String defaultUsernameLabel = "Username:";

  public String getUsernameLabel() {
if (this.usernameLabel != null) {
  return (this.usernameLabel);
}
ValueBinding vb = getValueBinding("usernameLabel");
if (vb != null) {
  return ((String) vb.getValue(getFacesContext()));
} else {
  return (defaultUsernameLabel);
}

  }

  public void setUsernameLabel(String usernameLabel) {
    this.usernameLabel = usernameLabel;
  }

  // JavaBeans properties for passwordLabel,
  // buttonLabel, and resetButtonLabel
  // are omitted from this listing, but
  // are present in the online code.  The implementation
  // of these properties is exactly the same as for
  // the usernameLabel property.

}
```

This is a very simple but useful component. Basically, it just generates the required markup for form-based authentication, providing parameters to control the values of the label, as follows.

```
<form method="post" action="j_security_check">
<table>
  <tr>
    <td>Username:</td>
    <td><input type="text" name="j_username"></td>
  </tr>
  <tr>
    <td>Password:</td>
    <td><input type="password" name="j_password"></td>
  </tr>
```

```
<tr>
  <td><input type="reset" name="reset" value="Reset"></td>
  <td><input type="submit" name="submit" value="Login"></td>
</tr>
</table>
</form>
```

The important thing to note is that **vt:formBasedLogin** must not be nested within an **<h:form>** tag because the component itself generates the HTML **<form method="post" action="j_security_check">**. The **j_security_check**, **j_username**, and **j_password** HTML attribute values are required by container-managed authentication. Also, note that the **FormBasedLoginComponent** does not implement the **saveState()** and **restoreState()** methods because these are only useful when JSF manages the postback. This is not the case with form-based authentication.

Certificate Authentication

Client certificate authentication is the most secure of the standard forms of container-managed security. Unfortunately, even though parts of setting up certificate authentication are standardized, a complete implementation requires significant vendor-specific configuration steps. Therefore, this section presents a higher-level view of performing authentication using certificates than was provided for basic or form-based authentication.

We must first introduce the concept of public key cryptography before we can explain the concept of an identity certificate. The easiest way to share data securely is to encrypt it using some scheme and share the password with the party with whom you want to share the data. Of course, the matter of sharing the password securely is a problem, but let's just say you can tell the person directly. While the shared password scheme is easy to understand and implement, it doesn't scale to large numbers of users without compromising security. Public key cryptography, also called public key infrastructure, or PKI, solves the problem by breaking the concept of a password into two parts, a "public key" and a "private key." The archetypal analogy to describe PKI involves two people—Alice and Bob—who want to send messages to each other through the postal mail. In order for Alice to send a message to Bob securely, Alice asks Bob to send her his open padlock, to which only Bob has the key. Alice then puts the message in the box and locks it with Bob's padlock, sending it in the mail. When Bob receives the box he can open the box with his key and see the message. Conversely, when Bob wants to send a message to Alice, he needs Alice's open padlock. In PKI, the padlock is the public key, and the key for the padlock is the private key. This situation is depicted in Figure 15-2.

In order to share data with someone, you need their public key and your private key; therefore, it is desirable to distribute your public key as widely as possible. That's where the "infrastructure" in public key infrastructure really comes in. When padlocks (public keys) are freely distributed, the problem is verifying that Alice's padlock really belongs to Alice and not some malicious postman who opened the mail and replaced Alice's padlock with his own, only to intercept the return package and open the box. The authenticity of a public key is determined using an "identity certificate."

When speaking of Internet security, an "identity certificate" is an electronic document originating from a trusted source that vouches for the authenticity of a public key. The source from which the certificate originates is known as the certificate authority (CA), and there are a handful of such bodies in business around the world today. CACert, Thawte, and VeriSign are three popular CAs. To bring the matter back to Web applications, servers and clients may

FIGURE 15-2 Public key infrastructure

possess their own public keys, and identity certificates to vouch for them, to encrypt all the traffic between client and server. Because Web applications are by nature interactive, clients must authenticate themselves to servers as well as servers to clients. This is known as two-way authentication and is the standard practice when using client certificate authentication. Once the certificates have been authenticated, the public keys are used to establish a secure transport connection, such as with the Secure Sockets Layer (SSL). Whenever you see a URL that begins with **https:**, you're using SSL.

To enable client certificate authentication, you need to put the following in your **login-config** element:

```
<login-method>
  <auth-method>CLIENT-CERT</auth-method>
  <realm-name>admin-realm</realm-name>
</login-method>
```

Unfortunately, this is where the standardization ends. Please consult your container's documentation for how to complete the implementation of client certificate authentication.

Container-Managed Authorization and the Concept of Roles

Now that we have discussed how users prove their identities to the Web application, let's examine how the Web application designer can restrict access to various parts of the application. The **<security-constraint>** element in the **web.xml** file is used to provide this feature.

```
<web-app>
  <!-- intervening elements omitted -->
  <security-constraint>
    <web-resource-collection>
      <web-resource-name>trainer modules</web-resource-name>
      <url-pattern>/admin/*</url-pattern>
    </web-resource-collection>
    <auth-constraint>
      <role-name>trainer</role-name>
    </auth-constraint>
  </security-constraint>
  <login-config>
    <auth-method>BASIC</auth-method>
    <realm-name>UserDatabase</realm-name>
  </login-config>
  <!-- intervening elements omitted -->
</web-app>
```

The preceding XML states the following about the application. This Web application may have zero or more security constraints. Each security constraint contains zero or more collections of pages, and access to any of the pages is predicated on the user being a member of the specified role. A user's membership in a role is determined using some form of authentication method. The previous **web.xml** excerpt says, "Users that try to access any page inside of the top-level **admin** directory must be authenticated using basic authentication, with the authentication database being provided by the container-specific **UserDatabase**. Once authenticated, they must be a member of the **trainer** group in order to be allowed to see the page." Each of the elements related to authorization in **<security-constraint>** is described in Table 15-2.

You may ask, if the only interesting element inside of **<auth-constraint>** is **<role-name>**, why do we need the **<auth-constraint>** element? This is to distinguish the role from the **<user-data-constraint>** element, which dictates which transport-level security is to be used to protect the resources in the collection. More on **<user-data-constraint>** in the next section.

Container-Managed Data Security

The last aspect of Web application security is **Data Security**. Generally, this aspect builds on top of **authentication** and **authorization**, but this need not necessarily be the case. For example, any user may view the Web page for Sun's JSF implementation on **java.net** at **https://javaserverfaces.dev.java.net/**, but in order to file issues in the issue tracker, or take any other actions, the user must have the appropriate authentication and authorization. As with all aspects of container-managed security, data security is configured using the

Element Name	Contained in Element	Description
web-resource-collection	security-constraint	A collection of content in your Web application. Typically, this means a collection of JSP pages and the images, scripts, and other content used by those pages. You must have at least one **<web-resource-collection>** inside your **<security-constraint>** element.
web-resource-name	web-resource-collection	A human-readable name you can attach to the collection. There must be exactly one **<web-resource-name>** per **<security-constraint>** element.
url-pattern	web-resource-collection	A pseudo regular-expression style syntax for grouping pages together. For example, the url-pattern /admin/* includes pages inside the admin directory. You can also use a file extension as a url-pattern—for example, /*.jsp is a url-pattern that identifies all JSP files in the root directory of the Web application. There may be zero or more **<url-pattern>** elements in the **<web-resource-collection>** element. The absence of a **<url-pattern>** means the constraint doesn't apply to any resource.
auth-constraint	security-constraint	Contains zero or more **<role-name>** elements. If any of the elements is the asterisk character (*), all users are granted access to the resources defined in the **<web-resource-collection>**.
role-name	auth-constraint	The name of a role defined in a container-specific fashion. For example, in elements in the **tomcat-users.xml** file as described earlier.

TABLE 15-2   Elements in **<security-constraint>**

web.xml file. Let's complete our example from the trainer by stating that all trainer pages be transmitted between server and client using data security.

```
<web-app>
  <!-- intervening elements omitted -->
  <security-constraint>
    <web-resource-collection>
      <web-resource-name>trainer modules</web-resource-name>
      <url-pattern>/admin/*</url-pattern>
    </web-resource-collection>
    <auth-constraint>
```

```
      <role-name>trainer</role-name>
   </auth-constraint>
   <user-data-constraint>
     <transport-guarantee>CONFIDENTIAL</transport-guarantee>
   </user-data-constraint>
  </security-constraint>
  <login-config>
   <auth-method>BASIC</auth-method>
   <realm-name>UserDatabase</realm-name>
  </login-config>
  <!-- intervening elements omitted -->
</web-app>
```

The only new element here is **<user-data-constraint>** and its child **<transport-guarantee>**. Valid values for **<transport-guarantee>** are **NONE, INTEGRAL,** and **CONFIDENTIAL**. Generally, the latter two imply SSL. In order to use SSL on your server you must give it an identity certificate and public/private key pair (described earlier in the section titled "Certificate Authentication") using container-specific techniques.

A Small Security Improvement in the Virtual Trainer

Now that you understand container-managed security, let's look at a simple example that shows how to integrate it into your application. Recall the four security methods on **HttpServletRequest** from Table 15-1: **getAuthType(), getRemoteUser(), getUserPrincipal(),** and **isUserInRole(String role)**. Let's take the common example of showing or hiding content on the page based on whether or not the user is in a certain role. In the Virtual Trainer application, let's say we want to provide an "edit" link for the list of events only if the user is in the "trainer" role. The easiest way to do this is to provide a Boolean read-only JavaBeans property in a request-scoped managed bean that uses the **isUserInRole()** method of the Servlet API. For example, consider the **isUserIsTrainer()** method shown next.

```
public boolean isUserIsTrainer() {
  FacesContext context = FacesContext.getCurrentInstance();
  Object request = context.getExternalContext().getRequest();
  boolean result = false;
  if (request instanceof HttpServletRequest) {
    result = ((HttpServletRequest)request).isUserInRole("trainer");
  }
  else if (request instanceof PortletRequest) {
    result = ((PortletRequest)request).isUserInRole("trainer");
  }
  return result;
}
```

Notice that we are taking care to consider that this application may run in a Portlet environment. The **ExternalContext** class is intended to handle this for you by wrapping commonly used methods.

Once you have the **userIsTrainer** JavaBeans property, you can access it via the EL as the value of the **rendered** attribute to show or hide parts of the page:

```
<h:dataTable value="#{events.data}" var="event">
  <h:column>
    <h:outputText value="#{event.name}" />
```

```
    </h:column>
    <h:column rendered="#{user.userIsTrainer}">
      <h:commandLink action="editEvent" />
    </h:column>
  </h:dataTable>
```

Note that we had to name the method **isUserIsTrainer** in order to be able to refer to it as **#{user.userIsTrainer}** from the EL. This is because of JavaBeans naming conventions. Specifically, for Boolean properties the leading "is" in the method name is omitted.

Application-Managed Security with JavaServer Faces

Container-managed security provides several advantages over application-managed security. Perhaps the two most important are convenience and peace of mind. The convenience comes from just using what the specifications and containers provide. The peace of mind comes from using features that have been implemented by security professionals and vetted by the competitive marketplace. However, if the constraints of container-managed security don't fit your customer's requirements, or if you are simply the type of person who likes to control all the variables yourself, application-managed security is for you. Obviously, it is possible and advisable to build your application-managed security solution on top of existing container-managed facilities, as shown in some of the examples in the remainder of the chapter.

This discussion of application-managed security follows the same three aspects of security as container managed: authentication, authorization, and data security. We will examine each aspect and present some approaches for implementing each using an application-managed approach.

Reviewing the Virtual Trainer

The Virtual Trainer application, presented in its entirety in Chapter 9, demonstrated a simple, yet adequate implementation of application-managed security. Let's review the security in the Virtual Trainer and see how it can be improved. Please refer to Chapter 9 for more details about the parts of the Virtual Trainer not relating to security.

The Virtual Trainer relies on "security through obscurity" by only publishing the URL of the first page in the application: **index.jsp**. This page has links to other pages for login and registration. There is nothing in the Virtual Trainer to prevent a user from going directly to a page "inside" of the application if they happen to know the URL—for example, **http://somehostname.com/faces/main.jsp**. To prevent this sort of thing, application-managed authorization is required. (You'll see an example of an application-managed authorization scheme that uses Servlet Filters in the section "Servlet Filters and Authorization.") Assuming the user does first register and then log in to the application, the application-managed authentication mechanism pushes the user ID and password fields into a session-scoped managed bean, **Authentication_Backing**, and uses an action handler, a **MethodBinding** on the **Authentication_Backing** bean, to perform the application-managed lookup of the user ID and password. If the login is successful, a session-scoped managed bean, **UserBean**, is created and its **loggedIn** property is set to **true**.

This approach, while simple, is rather flexible, and only requires a few modifications to make it more production-ready. In addition to providing an authorization scheme (including roles), the authentication process should be placed under transport level data security (that is, SSL) and a "remember me" feature should be added. A final step would be to call out to some external data source, such as JNDI or JAAS, for authentication rather than using the home-grown managed bean solution. Let's briefly state the plan for improving the Virtual Trainer, then we'll examine each step in detail.

1. Implement forced login via a Servlet Filter.
2. Implement forced login via a PhaseListener.
3. Implement "remember me" feature.
4. Show how to cleanly leverage the existing security infrastructure of the Java platform.

Obviously there is no one "right" way to achieve security in a Faces application, and the decisions you take to achieve it will probably differ from the preceding list. These steps are simply an example to show one way of doing it.

Servlet Filters and Authorization

The Servlet Filter concept, implemented in version 2.3 of the Servlet specification, and refined in 2.4, allows for one or more **Filter** implementations to operate on the request before it is processed by a **Servlet** or a JSP page. With Faces, this means the filters act before the request hits the **FacesServlet**. The timing of filters before Servlets is important because it allows using the filter to check for the login state of the user before granting access to their intended page, as shown in Figure 15-3.

Let's augment the Virtual Trainer application with a **ForcedLoginFilter** that requires the user to log in, or register and then log in, before being able to access the application. It does

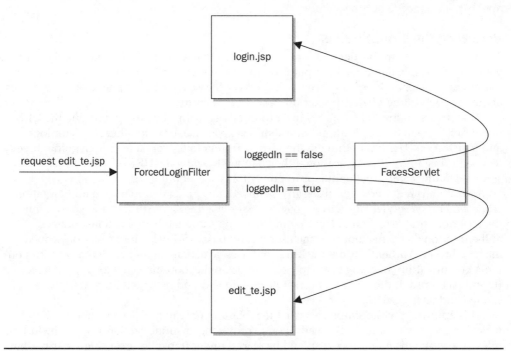

FIGURE 15-3   Using filters to implement forced login

this by forwarding the user to the main entry page if either of the two following conditions is met.

- The user is not logged in
- The requested page is not one of the pages an unauthenticated user is allowed to access.

The first step in using a Servlet Filter for this purpose is to declare it in **web.xml** file and pass it the appropriate initialization parameters.

```
<filter>
  <description>Require that the user log in before accessing any page
    other than the entry pages </description>
  <filter-name>ForcedLoginFilter</filter-name>
  <filter-class>com.jsfcompref.trainer.util.ForcedLoginFilter</filter-class>
  <init-param>
    <param-name>com.jsfcompref.trainer.LoginURI</param-name>
    <param-value>/faces/index.jsp</param-value>
  </init-param>
  <init-param>
    <description>ViewIDs for which this filter must not
      forward back to the login page.</description>
    <param-name>com.jsfcompref.trainer.NoForwardViewIds</param-name>
    <param-value>register.jsp login.jsp index.jsp</param-value>
  </init-param>
</filter>
<filter-mapping>
  <filter-name>ForcedLoginFilter</filter-name>
  <url-pattern>*.jsp</url-pattern>
  <dispatcher>REQUEST</dispatcher>
  <dispatcher>FORWARD</dispatcher>
</filter-mapping>
```

By this time, most of the **web.xml** syntax should be self-evident but the **filter-mapping** and **init-param** elements require an explanation. The **filter-mapping** element is applied to the **url-pattern *.jsp**. This is important because we don't want the filter acting on requests for CSS, image, or JavaScript files. The first **init-param**, which is **com.jsfcompref.trainer .LoginURI**, gives the request URI of the page to forward to when the filter's login requirements are not satisfied. Note that the **LoginURI** string is prefixed by **com.jsfcompref.trainer**. When declaring public names, it is a very good idea to disambiguate as much as possible. A convenient way of doing disambiguation is to follow the Java fully qualified class naming conventions. The remaining parameter, **com.jsfcompref.trainer.NoForwardViewIds**, tells the **ForcedLoginFilter** which Faces view IDs must not be protected by the filter. This is analogous to specifying a **web-resource-collection** using container-managed authentication, but in this case we are stating that *all* view IDs except for these three require authentication. The remaining **web.xml** syntax for filters is boilerplate code that needs no further discussion.

The actual implementation of the **ForcedLoginFilter** has a few subtleties that are discussed next. The required filter methods **init( )** and **destroy( )** have been omitted for brevity. They are present in the online code for this chapter.

```
package com.jsfcompref.trainer.util;

import com.jsfcompref.trainer.model.UserBean;
```

```java
import java.io.IOException;
import java.util.Iterator;

import javax.servlet.Filter;
import javax.servlet.FilterChain;
import javax.servlet.FilterConfig;
import javax.servlet.RequestDispatcher;
import javax.servlet.ServletException;
import javax.servlet.ServletRequest;
import javax.servlet.ServletResponse;
import javax.servlet.http.HttpServletRequest;
import javax.servlet.http.HttpSession;

public class ForcedLoginFilter implements Filter {

  private String [] noForwardViewIds = null;

  public ForcedLoginFilter() {
  }

  private static boolean checkLoginState(ServletRequest request,
                              ServletResponse response)
  throws IOException, ServletException {
    boolean isLoggedIn = false;
    HttpSession session =
      ((HttpServletRequest)request).getSession(false);

    UserBean managedUserBean = null;
    // If there is a UserBean in the session, and it has
    // the isLoggedIn property set to true.
    if (null != session &&
      (null != (managedUserBean = (UserBean)
          session.getAttribute("UserBean")))) {
      if (managedUserBean.isIsLoggedIn()) {
        isLoggedIn = true;
      }
    }
    return isLoggedIn;
  }

  public void doFilter(ServletRequest request,
                      ServletResponse response,
                      FilterChain chain)
    throws IOException, ServletException {

    Throwable problem = null;
    boolean isLoggedIn = false;

    isLoggedIn = checkLoginState(request, response);

    // If this invocation of the filter is forwardable
    // and we are not logged in.
    if (isForwardable((HttpServletRequest) request)
        && !isLoggedIn) {
      String loginURI =
```

```
        getFilterConfig().
        getInitParameter("com.jsfcompref.trainer.LoginURI");
    loginURI = (null != loginURI) ? loginURI :
                DEFAULT_LOGIN_URI;
    RequestDispatcher requestDispatcher =
        request.getRequestDispatcher(loginURI);
    // Force the login
    requestDispatcher.forward(request, response);

    return;
  } else {
    try {
      chain.doFilter(request, response);
    } catch(Throwable t) {
      // A production quality implementation will
      // deal with this exception.
    }
  }
}

/**
 * <p>Returns true if this filter is not
 * processing the login postback
 * and the filter is not already on the
 * callstack for this request.</p>
 */

private boolean isForwardable(HttpServletRequest request) {
  boolean onCallstack = true,
      isNoForwardViewId = false;
  String noForwardViewId = null,
       requestURI = null;
  Iterator noForwardViewIdIter = null;
  if (null ==
      request.
      getAttribute("com.jsfcompref.ForcedLoginFilter.OnStack")) {
    request.setAttribute("com.jsfcompref.ForcedLoginFilter.OnStack",
        Boolean.TRUE);
    onCallstack = false;
  }

  requestURI = request.getRequestURI();
  noForwardViewIdIter = getNoForwardViewIds(request);
  // Iterate over the list of noForwardViewIds and bail out if
  // the current requestURI contains a match
  while (!isNoForwardViewId && noForwardViewIdIter.hasNext()) {
    noForwardViewId = (String) noForwardViewIdIter.next();
    isNoForwardViewId = (-1 != requestURI.indexOf(noForwardViewId));
  }

  if (isNoForwardViewId) {
    return false;
  }

  if (onCallstack) {
```

```
        return false;
    }
    return true;
}


/**
 * <p>Returns an Iterator over the contents of the
 * NoForwardViewIds init parameter, or the empty
 * iterator if that parameter is not specified.</p>
 */
Iterator getNoForwardViewIds(HttpServletRequest request) {
  Iterator result = null;

  if (null == noForwardViewIds) {
    synchronized (this) {
      noForwardViewIds = new String[0];
      String viewIdList =
        getFilterConfig().
        getInitParameter("com.jsfcompref.trainer.NoForwardViewIds");
      if (null != viewIdList) {
        try {
          noForwardViewIds = viewIdList.split(" ");
        } catch (Exception e) {
        }
      }
    }
  }
  final String [] viewIds = noForwardViewIds;
  result = Arrays.asList(noForwardViewIds).iterator();

  return result;
}

  private static final String DEFAULT_LOGIN_URI = "/faces/index.jsp";
}
```

Let's start with the **doFilter()** method. This is the primary entry point called by
the Servlet container. The first thing it does is call **checkLoginState()**, which contains
application-specific knowledge about how the Chapter 9 version of the Virtual Trainer
maintains its login status: by storing a managed bean that is an instance of **UserBean** in
the session under the key **UserBean**, and by setting the Boolean property **isLoggedIn** to
true on that bean. Therefore, if there is no session, or the **UserBean** doesn't exist in the
session, or the **isLoggedIn** property is **false**, the user is not logged in and **checkLoginState()**
returns **false**. This is straightforward.

The first subtlety comes in the **isForwardable()** method. This method does two things:

- Protects against infinite recursion by storing a request scope attribute that
  effectively disables the filter if it is called multiple times on the same callstack.

- Consults the previously mentioned **NoForwardViewIds** initialization parameter
  and effectively disables the filter if the current request URI contains one of the **view
  IDs** for which forwarding should not be performed.

Note the synchronized block around the initialization parameter lookup and the use
of the **String.split()** method introduced in JDK 1.4. These operations are somewhat costly,

and since the value of the initialization parameter does not change during the lifetime of the filter instance, it is safe to cache the value. A production-quality implementation should give more consideration to performance.

Now that the two cases mentioned at the beginning of the section have been handled, we can move on to the mechanics of actually performing the forward. If we do need to forward to the login page, the **doFilter()** method looks up the appropriate URI from the value of the **LoginURI** initialization parameter. If the parameter is **null**, a default value of **/faces/index.jsp** is used. This is a problem because it hard-codes the specific mapping of the **FacesServlet** used by this instance of the application, **/faces**, when the user may employ any arbitrary mapping allowable by the Servlet Spec. This is why the value is configurable using a parameter. Once the proper **LoginURI** value has been obtained, **RequestDispatcher .forward()** is called, which will cause the user to see the main page for the application. If it turns out that is not necessary to forward to the login page, the normal processing of the request is resumed by calling **chain.doFilter()**.

PhaseListeners and Authorization

A simpler approach to force the user to log in that is more Faces-centric is to use a **PhaseListener**. This idea was originated by Aaron L. Bartell on the JSF-developers mailing list and is adapted here to suit the Virtual Trainer. Recall from Chapter 12 how **PhaseListener** instances are installed and declared in the **faces-config.xml**. In this case, they are installed in the **faces-config.xml** that accompanies the **trainercomponents** JSF component library.

```
package com.jsfcompref.trainercomponents.util;

import java.io.IOException;
import javax.faces.application.NavigationHandler;
import javax.faces.context.FacesContext;
import javax.faces.event.PhaseEvent;
import javax.faces.event.PhaseId;
import javax.faces.event.PhaseListener;
import com.jsfcompref.trainer.util.*;

/**
 *
 * <p>The idea to use a PhaseListener for this was taken from
 * Aaron L. Bartell on the JSF-developers mailing list.</p>
 */
public class ForcedLoginPhaseListener implements PhaseListener {

  /** Creates a new instance of ForcedLoginPhaseListener */
  public ForcedLoginPhaseListener() {
  }
  public PhaseId getPhaseId() {
    return PhaseId.RESTORE_VIEW;
  }

  public void afterPhase(PhaseEvent event) {
    FacesContext context = event.getFacesContext();

    // Check to see if they are on the login page.
    boolean onLoginPage = (-1 != context.getViewRoot().getViewId().
```

```
        lastIndexOf("login")) ? true : false,
        isLoggedIn = false;
    try {
      isLoggedIn = ForcedLoginFilter.checkLoginState(context.
        getExternalContext().getRequest());
    }
    catch (Exception e) {
      // A production-quality implementation would log the exception
    }
    if (!onLoginPage && !isLoggedIn) {
      context.getApplication().getNavigationHandler().
          handleNavigation(context, null, "login");
    }
  }

  public void beforePhase(PhaseEvent event) {
  }
}
```

This technique shows a novel approach to using the **NavigationHandler** programmatically, but introduces a possibly undesirable coupling between the application's page flow as specified in the **faces-config.xml** file and the component, which expects a **navigation-rule** for the **from-outcome** named **login** to exist.

Now that we've implemented a basic but secure container-managed authentication scheme, let's move on to providing role-based access control using managed beans.

Implementing a "Remember Me" Feature

A popular feature of Web applications that require security is a simple checkbox, often with the label Remember Me, that causes the Web site to automatically log the user in, or populate the user ID and password fields in the UI with the proper values the next time they return to the site. Here, you'll see how to extend the Chapter 9 Virtual Trainer with this useful feature.

As with many things in Faces, this problem is best solved with a custom **UIComponent**. This particular design for the **RememberMeLoginComponent** takes advantage of several subtleties of advanced JSF custom component techniques, so we will cover the component in detail. While not all of the source code for the component will be shown in this text, the complete code is available in the online code for this book. The operation of the **RememberMeLoginComponent** is shown in Figure 15-4.

The **RememberMeLoginComponent** extends the **FormBasedLoginComponent** shown earlier in the chapter and adds a checkbox below the row of buttons. It is a composite component, containing several other components, but is presented to the page author

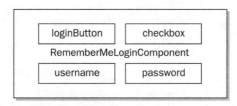

FIGURE 15-4   The **RememberMeLoginComponent** in operation

as a single component. The first time a user encounters the login page using the **RememberMeLoginComponent**, they have the option of checking the checkbox. If they do so, and if the login is successful, a **Cookie** is set into the response. The next time they visit the login page, the **RememberMeLoginComponent** examines the cookie and pre-populates the fields of the login page with the saved username and password values.

The page author experience of using this component is very simple and was designed to be dropped into the existing login page from the trainer application. Recall that the original login page used component bindings for the username and password fields, and a **MethodBinding** for the button action, all of which were exposed on the backing bean called **Authentication_Backing**. The **rememberMeLogin** exposes **usernameBinding**, **passwordBinding**, and **buttonAction** attributes for the component bindings and method bindings, respectively. These three attributes are required, but additional optional attributes are provided to allow localization. The general form for the tag follows:

```
<vt:rememberMeLogin id="optionalId" usernameLabel="Username: "
    passwordLabel="Password: " buttonLabel="Login"
    resetButtonLabel="Reset"
    usernameBinding="#{Authentication_Backing.userid}"
    passwordBinding="#{Authentication_Backing.password}"
    buttonAction="#{Authentication_Backing.login}"/>
```

As with any JSF component, there are the usual parts: JSP tag, the **UIComponent** subclass, and the **Renderer**. For simplicity, we have absorbed the **Renderer** into the **UIComponent** subclass, though a production implementation would surely want to break it out, considering the rendering-intensive nature of this component. In addition to the usual three parts, there is an additional **RememberMePhaseListener**. This is necessary because the action of the component depends on the validity of the login. Only if the login is successful do we want to set the cookie. This is a perfect application for a component-specific **PhaseListener**, registered for the Render Response phase of the lifecycle, and taking action on the **beforePhase** event therein.

The following is an outline of the **RememberMeLoginComponent**'s operation. An explanation of each part of the outline, with code examples, is presented in the following sections.

- **RememberMeLoginComponent**
  - Lifecycle and State Management
  - Rendering Behavior
  - Properties
- **RememberMeLoginTag**
- **RememberMePhaseListener**
  - Interaction with the Virtual Trainer Login Scheme
  - Interaction with the Servlet API

RememberMeLoginComponent: Lifecycle and State Management

This component is a composite component, as shown in the UML diagram in Figure 15-5.

In noncomposite JSF components, the view description technology, such as JSP, is responsible for instantiating the **UIComponent**s and adding them into the view. With a

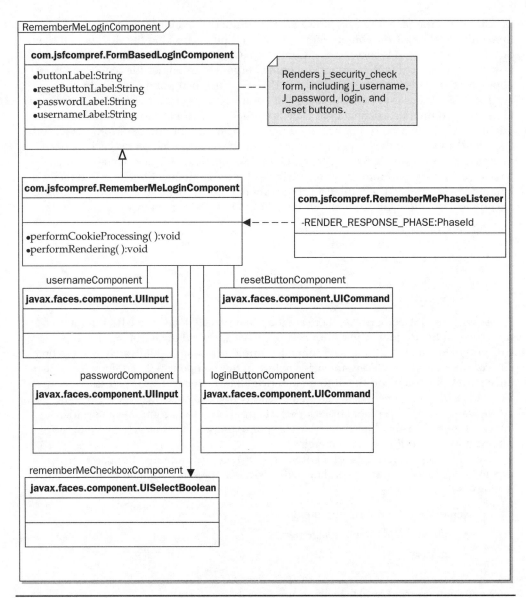

FIGURE 15-5   The class diagram of the **RememberMeLoginComponent**

composite component, that responsibility now belongs to the component itself. This presents a subtlety involving state management. As shown in Chapter 11, the user can choose to have the application save its state in the client or on the server in an implementation-dependent manner. Some implementations of the state management API cause new instances of the components in the view to be created on each run through the lifecycle; therefore, care must be taken to avoid adding the child components on restore. The following is the class declaration, constructor, initialization, and **StateHolder** methods from **RememberMeLoginComponent:**

```
package com.jsfcompref.trainercomponents.component;

import com.jsfcompref.trainercomponents.util.Util;
import java.io.IOException;
import java.util.List;
import java.util.Map;
import javax.faces.component.UICommand;
import javax.faces.component.UIComponent;
import javax.faces.component.UISelectBoolean;
import javax.faces.component.UIInput;
import javax.faces.component.UIViewRoot;
import javax.faces.component.html.HtmlCommandButton;
import javax.faces.component.html.HtmlSelectBooleanCheckbox;
import javax.faces.context.FacesContext;
import javax.faces.context.ResponseWriter;
import javax.faces.el.ValueBinding;
import javax.servlet.http.Cookie;
import javax.servlet.http.HttpServletRequest;

public class RememberMeLoginComponent extends FormBasedLoginComponent {

  public RememberMeLoginComponent() {
    buildLoginComponents();
  }

  private void buildLoginComponents() {
    // reset button
    HtmlCommandButton reset = new HtmlCommandButton();
    reset.setImmediate(true);
    reset.getAttributes().put("type", "reset");
    reset.setValue(getResetButtonLabel());
    setResetButtonComponent(reset);

    // login button
    setLoginButtonComponent(new HtmlCommandButton());
    getLoginButtonComponent().setValue(getButtonLabel());

    // checkbox
    setRememberMeCheckboxComponent(new HtmlSelectBooleanCheckbox());
  }

  public Object saveState(FacesContext context) {
    Object [] state = new Object[6];
    state[0] = super.saveState(context);
    state[1] = saveAttachedState(context, getUsernameComponent());
    state[2] = saveAttachedState(context, getPasswordComponent());
    state[3] = saveAttachedState(context, getLoginButtonComponent());
    state[4] = saveAttachedState(context, getResetButtonComponent());
    state[5] = saveAttachedState(context,
        getRememberMeCheckboxComponent());
    return null;
  }
  public void restoreState(FacesContext context, Object state) {
    Object [] stateArray = (Object []) state;
    super.restoreState(context, stateArray[0]);
    setUsernameComponent((UIInput)
      restoreAttachedState(context, stateArray[1]));
```

```
      setPasswordComponent((UIInput)
        restoreAttachedState(context, stateArray[2]));
      setLoginButtonComponent((UICommand)
        restoreAttachedState(context, stateArray[3]));
      setResetButtonComponent((UICommand)
        restoreAttachedState(context, stateArray[4]));
      setRememberMeCheckboxComponent((UISelectBoolean)
        restoreAttachedState(context, stateArray[1]));
    }

  private void initializeComponent(UIComponent oldC, UIComponent newC) {
    List children = getChildren();
    UIViewRoot root = FacesContext.getCurrentInstance().
        getViewRoot();
    if (null != oldC) {
      children.remove(oldC);
    }
    newC.setId(root.createUniqueId());
    children.add(newC);
  }

  private javax.faces.component.UIInput usernameComponent;

  public javax.faces.component.UIInput getUsernameComponent() {

    return this.usernameComponent;

  }

  public void setUsernameComponent(javax.faces.component.UIInput usernameComponent) {
    initializeComponent(getUsernameComponent(), usernameComponent);
    usernameComponent.setId("userid");
    this.usernameComponent = usernameComponent;
  }

  // Similar getters and setters exist for the passwordComponent,
  // loginButtonComponent, resetButtonComponent, and
  // rememberMeCheckboxComponent properties.

// … Remainder of code below.
```

Let's take a moment to examine the state management implications of this code, since this area often causes developers some pain. Note that the constructor unconditionally calls **buildLoginComponents()** to create the buttons and the checkbox as children of itself. As mentioned in Chapter 10, this practice is undesirable, but sometimes unavoidable, as is the case with this composite component. Let's review why modifying the state of the component from its constructor is undesirable. When JSF processes the postback from a browser, the first thing it does is restore the view to its previous state. Depending on the state management implementation, this may cause the constructor of each component in the view to be called, followed by a call to the **restoreState( )** method. Therefore, if the component state is modified in any way in the constructor, the **restoreState()** method must take those modifications into account when applying the restored state.

Strict adherence to the OO principle of always using accessor methods instead of instance variables makes it possible to encapsulate this behavior in the **initializeComponent()** method, which is called from every component property setter, such as **setUsernameComponent()** or **setLoginButtonComponent()**. Look at the **initializeComponent()** method and note that it takes two arguments, the old component, which may be **null**, and the new component. This method removes the old component from the view, before adding the new one. As mentioned in Chapter 10, each component must have an ID that is unique within the scope of its closest ancestor component that is a **NamingContainer**. This method also initializes the new component with a generated unique ID, from **UIViewRoot.createUniqueId()**. Note that the setter for the **usernameComponent** property overwrites this unique ID with the hard-coded ID of **userid**. This is necessary to adhere to the contract for JAAS integration, described in the section "Leveraging JAAS from a JSF Application."

There is one remaining hitch in the implementation of the **saveState()** and **restoreState()** methods: this component is a composite component and it needs to make sure to save the state of its constituent components. There is a pair of special static methods in the **UIComponent** base to handle this case. **saveAttachedState()** saves the state of an attached object associated with a component, and **restoreAttachedState()** does the same on the restore side.

Returning to the **buildLoginComponents()** method, we can see that the **type** attribute of the reset button is set to **reset** so that an HTML **<input type="reset">** is generated. The remainder of the method just adds the Submit button and the checkbox by which the user indicates their desire to have the application "remember" their user ID and password.

The remaining two methods relating to lifecycle are **getComponentFamily()** and **getRendersChildren()** and have been described in Chapter 10. The **getRendersChildren()** returns **true** because the **RememberMeLoginComponent** is responsible for handling the rendering of its children.

RememberMeLoginComponent: Rendering Behavior

The encoding behavior of the component is basically the same as **FormBasedLoginComponent**, but an additional element is added: a checkbox and a label, as illustrated next.

The benefit of this component is its capability to interact with the **Cookie** class in the Servlet API to save the value of the user ID and password if requested. The rendering code for the component is listed next.

```
// ...

public boolean getRendersChildren() {
  return true;
```

```
  }
  public void encodeBegin(FacesContext context) throws IOException {
    getPasswordComponent().getAttributes().put("redisplay", Boolean.TRUE);
  }

  public void encodeChildren(FacesContext context) throws IOException {
  }

  public void encodeEnd(FacesContext context) throws IOException {
    performCookieProcessing(context);
    performRendering(context);
  }
  public static final String COOKIE_NAME =
   "com.jsfcompref.RememberMeCookie";
  public static final String USERNAME_PASSWORD_DELIMITER =
    "com.jsfcompref.CookieDelimiter";

  private void performCookieProcessing(FacesContext context) {
    // Initialize the state to be everything is null.
    getRememberMeCheckboxComponent().setValue(Boolean.FALSE);
    getUsernameComponent().setValue(null);
    getUsernameComponent().setLocalValueSet(false);
    getUsernameComponent().setSubmittedValue(null);
    getPasswordComponent().setValue(null);
    getPasswordComponent().setLocalValueSet(false);
    getPasswordComponent().setSubmittedValue(null);

    // A production quality implementation would not expose the
    // component to the Cookie API, but perhaps encapsulate the
    // cookie behavior on the PhaseListener.

    Map cookieMap = context.getExternalContext().getRequestCookieMap();
    if (cookieMap.containsKey(COOKIE_NAME)) {
      Cookie c = (Cookie) cookieMap.get(COOKIE_NAME);
      String value = c.getValue();

      // If the user wants to be remembered
      if (0 < value.length()) {
        // Check the checkbox
        getRememberMeCheckboxComponent().setValue(Boolean.TRUE);
        // A production quality implementation would require the cookie
        // to be decrypted.
        assert(null != value);
        int i = value.indexOf(USERNAME_PASSWORD_DELIMITER);
        assert(-1 != i);
        String username =  value.substring(0, i),
            password = value.substring(i +
                       USERNAME_PASSWORD_DELIMITER.length());
        getUsernameComponent().setValue(username);
        getPasswordComponent().setValue(password);
      }
    }
  }

  private void performRendering(FacesContext context) throws IOException {
```

```
ResponseWriter writer = Util.getResponseWriter(context);

// A production-quality implementation will want to do some
// refactoring with the superclass FormBasedLoginComponent to
// avoid the needless duplication of the below table generation
// code.

// Using Tables for Layout violates WCAG guideline 5.
// A production-quality implementation would use CSS for layout.
writer.startElement("table", this);

// Userid row
writer.startElement("tr", this);

writer.startElement("td", this);
writer.writeText(this.getUsernameLabel(), "usernameLabel");
writer.endElement("td");

writer.startElement("td", this);
encodeAllComponent(context, getUsernameComponent());
writer.endElement("td");

writer.endElement("tr");

// Password row
writer.startElement("tr", this);

writer.startElement("td", this);
writer.writeText(this.getPasswordLabel(), "passwordLabel");
writer.endElement("td");

writer.startElement("td", this);
encodeAllComponent(context, getPasswordComponent());
writer.endElement("td");

writer.endElement("tr");

// Button row
writer.startElement("tr", this);
writer.startElement("td", this);
encodeAllComponent(context, getResetButtonComponent());
writer.endElement("td");
writer.startElement("td", this);
encodeAllComponent(context,  getLoginButtonComponent());
writer.endElement("td");
writer.endElement("tr");

// checkbox row
writer.startElement("tr", this);
writer.startElement("td", this);
writer.write(" ");
writer.endElement("td");
writer.startElement("td", this);
encodeAllComponent(context, getRememberMeCheckboxComponent());
writer.writeText(this.getRememberMeLabel(), "rememberMeLabel");
```

```
    writer.endElement("td");
    writer.endElement("tr");

    writer.endElement("table");
}

private void encodeAllComponent(FacesContext context,
    UIComponent component) throws IOException {

  // suppress rendering if "rendered" property on the component is
  // false.
  if (!component.isRendered()) {
    return;
  }

  // Render this component and its children recursively
  component.encodeBegin(context);
  if (component.getRendersChildren()) {
    component.encodeChildren(context);
  } else {
    Iterator kids = getChildren(component);
    while (kids.hasNext()) {
      UIComponent kid = (UIComponent) kids.next();
      encodeAllComponent(context, kid);
    }
  }
  component.encodeEnd(context);
}

protected Iterator getChildren(UIComponent component) {

  List results = new ArrayList();
  Iterator kids = component.getChildren().iterator();
  while (kids.hasNext()) {
    UIComponent kid = (UIComponent) kids.next();
    if (kid.isRendered()) {
      results.add(kid);
    }
  }
  return (results.iterator());

}
```

The first thing to note is that this component returns **true** from **getRendersChildren()**. This tells the Faces runtime that this component is taking responsibility for rendering its children. (See Chapter 10 for more on the **getRendersChildren()** method.)

The **encodeBegin()** method simply takes the password component, provided by the user via the **passwordComponent** binding attribute, and sets its **redisplay** property to true. Without this property being set, JSF can't populate this field automatically with the saved password. Note that the more natural place to set the **redisplay** property is in the **buildLoginComponents()** method, but the property cannot be set there because the component binding doesn't happen until the **setProperties()** method is called, which happens after the component is instantiated. The **encodeChildren()** is overridden to take no action because that logic has been deferred to **encodeEnd()**. **encodeEnd()** is where all the real work happens, which is broken down into two submethods: **performCookieProcessing()** and **performRendering()**.

performCookieProcessing() first clears the login panel and checkbox. Then it uses the **ExternalContext**'s **CookieMap**, which exposes the cookies sent by the browser as a **Map**, to check for the existence of the cookie named by the value of the constant **COOKIE_NAME**. Note again that the cookie name is prefixed with **com.jsfcompref** to guard against the chance of overwriting someone else's cookie. If the cookie named **COOKIE_NAME** exists, and has a positive length, we can assume it was placed there by this component on a prior request, and then must set the value of the checkbox to be **true**. The cookie is then taken apart and the username and password extracted, and set as the current value of the username and password components. Note that these values are saved in unencrypted clear text for this example, but a production solution will need to provide encryption for the data. If the cookie does not exist, **performCookieProcessing()** takes no action.

performRendering() is very similar to the **encodeBegin()** method of **FormBasedLoginComponent**. The main difference is that actual **UIComponents** are used to handle the rendering of the actual text fields, buttons, and the checkbox. The **encodeAllComponent()** helper method handles this delegation by recursively rendering the children of the argument component while honoring the **rendersChildren** setting of each child.

The decode processing of the input fields and the button is handled by the JSF runtime because these components are added to the tree. We don't need to explicitly decode them ourselves. The postback cookie processing is deferred to the **RenderResponse** phase using a **PhaseListener**, described next, but one crucial step must be taken during the normal **decode()** as is shown in the following.

```
public void decode(FacesContext context) {
  context.getExternalContext().getRequestMap().put(COOKIE_NAME,  this);

}
```

Here the actual **RememberMeLoginComponent** instance is stored in the **RequestMap** so the **PhaseListener** can have access to it in a threadsafe manner. This is necessary because a single **PhaseListener** instance is used for all requests from all users in the application, and therefore must be thread safe. Since the Servlet specification guarantees that request processing all happens on a single thread, the **RequestMap** is a great place to store things that need to be thread safe.

RememberMeLoginComponent: Properties

The **RememberMeLoginComponent** extends **FormBasedLoginComponent** primarily to inherit its **usernameLabel**, **passwordLabel**, **buttonLabel**, and **resetButtonLabel** JavaBeans string properties. In addition, this component adds a **rememberMeCheckboxLabel** String property, the **usernameComponent** and **passwordComponent** JavaBeans **UIInput** properties, and the String **buttonAction** JavaBeans property.

During encoding, this component will check for the existence of a specific cookie in the request. The cookie will only be present if the user checked the "remember me" checkbox on a previous visit to the site. If present, the cookie is examined and the user ID and password are extracted from it and set as the value of the **userid** and **password** components in the tree. This approach is straightforward and works well in JSF 1.1 and 1.2.

RememberMeLoginTag

For every component property configurable by the page author, there must be a corresponding JavaBeans property in the custom JSP tag for that component. As described in Chapter 10, there are two parts to satisfy this requirement:

- A write only, or read/write JavaBeans property of the correct type, as specified in the TLD for the tag.
- Some action in the **setProperties()** method that conveys the value of that property as provided by the page author to the actual **UIComponent** instance that sits behind the tag.

Both of these parts were described in Chapter 10, but we're reviewing the second part because this is the most important method of a JSP custom tag for a JSF component. The action of this method is no different than that taken in the custom components in Chapter 10.

```
package com.jsfcompref.trainercomponents.taglib;

import com.jsfcompref.trainercomponents.component.RememberMeLoginComponent;
import com.jsfcompref.trainercomponents.util.ConstantMethodBinding;
import javax.faces.FacesException;
import javax.faces.application.Application;
import javax.faces.component.UIComponent;
import javax.faces.component.UIInput;
import javax.faces.context.FacesContext;
import javax.faces.el.MethodBinding;
import javax.faces.el.ValueBinding;
import javax.faces.el.ReferenceSyntaxException;

public class RememberMeLoginTag extends FormBasedLoginTag {
// …

protected void setProperties(UIComponent component) {
  super.setProperties(component);
  RememberMeLoginComponent comp =
      (RememberMeLoginComponent) component;
  FacesContext context = getFacesContext();
  Application application = context.getApplication();
  ValueBinding vb = null;
  MethodBinding md = null;
  String action = this.getButtonAction();

  if (null != rememberMeLabel) {
    // if this is an expression
    if (isValueReference(rememberMeLabel)) {
      try {
        vb = application.createValueBinding(rememberMeLabel);
        comp.setValueBinding("rememberMeLabel", vb);
      }
    catch (ReferenceSyntaxException rse) {
      // log exception
      }
    }
    else {
```

```
          comp.setRememberMeLabel(rememberMeLabel);
     }
   }

   // Hook up the bindings
   try {
     vb = application.createValueBinding(getUsernameBinding());
     comp.setUsernameComponent((UIInput) application.
         createComponent(vb, context, "javax.faces.HtmlInputText"));
     vb = application.createValueBinding(getPasswordBinding());
     comp.setPasswordComponent((UIInput) application.
         createComponent(vb, context, "javax.faces.HtmlInputSecret"));
     if (isValueReference(action)) {
       MethodBinding mb = FacesContext.getCurrentInstance().
           getApplication().createMethodBinding(action, null);
       comp.getLoginButtonComponent().setAction(mb);
     } else {
       comp.getLoginButtonComponent().
           setAction(new ConstantMethodBinding(action));
     }

   }
   catch (Exception e) {
     throw new FacesException(e);
   }

}
```

The first thing a custom **setProperties( )** method must do is call **super.setProperties( )**, passing the same **UIComponent** argument passed to this instance. Not doing this will probably cause your custom component to break. In this case, the **super** call processes the attributes inherited from **FormBasedLoginComponent**. It then does exactly the same thing with the **rememberMeLabel** property.

After the simple properties are propagated to the **RememberMeLoginComponent**, the **usernameBinding**, **passwordBinding**, and **buttonAction** properties are dealt with. These last three properties are listed as **required** in the TLD entry for the tag, so the JSP page will not compile unless the page author provides values for these.

The first two properties are **ValueBinding** properties whose type is **UIComponent**, also known as a component binding. The user must provide a valid value expression as the value of these two attributes, and the type of that expression must be **UIComponent**. Note that **Application.createComponent( )** is called from inside the argument to the setter of the **usernameComponent**, and **passwordComponent** properties, passing the **ValueBinding** as an argument to **createComponent( )**. **createComponent( )** takes the argument **ValueBinding** and component type and instantiates a component of the given type and sets its value into the **ValueBinding** by calling its **setValue( )** method. In the Virtual Trainer, this causes the **setUserid( )** and **setPassword( )** methods of the **Authentication_Backing** managed bean to be called. This step is crucial because it establishes the link between the **RememberMeLoginComponent** and the Virtual Trainer's existing login mechanism.

The final tag property, **buttonAction**, is a **MethodBinding** expression or literal string that is passed on to the **action** property of the **UICommand** component representing the login button in the panel. As such, the JSP tag must examine the value of the **buttonAction** property to see if it is an expression. If so, a **MethodBinding** is created for the expression using the

Application.createMethodBinding() method. If not, a special **ConstantMethodBinding** is created. The **ConstantMethodBinding** simply allows the user to directly type in an outcome, such as "success", into the JSP page as the value of the **buttonAction** property, and allows the "success" value to be conveyed to the navigation system, as described in Chapter 5. In either case, the **MethodBinding** is set into the button component's **action** property.

RememberMePhaseListener

The last piece of the **RememberMeLoginComponent** is the **RememberMePhaseListener**. This component exists solely to defer the setting of the cookie into the response until we can be sure that the user logged in successfully. Figure 15-6 shows the lifecycle implications of the login process.

Let's look at the code for **RememberMePhaseListener**.

```java
package com.jsfcompref.trainercomponents.component;

import com.jsfcompref.trainer.util.ForcedLoginFilter;
import javax.faces.context.ExternalContext;
import javax.faces.event.PhaseEvent;
import javax.faces.event.PhaseId;
import javax.faces.event.PhaseListener;
import javax.servlet.http.Cookie;
import javax.servlet.http.HttpServletResponse;


public class RememberMePhaseListener implements PhaseListener {
  public RememberMePhaseListener() {
  }

  public PhaseId getPhaseId() {
    return PhaseId.RENDER_RESPONSE;
  }

  public void beforePhase(PhaseEvent event) {
    ExternalContext extContext = event.getFacesContext().getExternalContext();
    RememberMeLoginComponent remember = null;
    Cookie c = null;  // c is for Cookie
    boolean isLoggedIn = false;
    String username, password;
    HttpServletResponse response =
        (HttpServletResponse) extContext.getResponse();

    // if the checkbox was checked
    if (extContext.getRequestMap().
      containsKey(RememberMeLoginComponent.COOKIE_NAME)) {
      try {
        isLoggedIn = ForcedLoginFilter.
            checkLoginState(extContext.getRequest());
      }
      catch (Throwable e) {
      }
      if (isLoggedIn) {
        remember = (RememberMeLoginComponent)
          extContext.getRequestMap().
            get(RememberMeLoginComponent.COOKIE_NAME);
```

```
Object value = remember.getRememberMeCheckboxComponent().getValue();
if (null != value && value.toString().equals("true")) {
  assert(null != remember.getUsernameComponent());
  assert(null != remember.getPasswordComponent());
  username = remember.getUsernameComponent().getValue().toString();
  password = remember.getPasswordComponent().getValue().toString();
  assert(null != username);
  assert(null != password);
  // fabricate and add the cookie
  c = new Cookie(RememberMeLoginComponent.COOKIE_NAME,
      username +
      RememberMeLoginComponent.USERNAME_PASSWORD_DELIMITER +
      password);
}
}
// If the user is not logged in, or they elected not to be remembered
if (null == c) {
  // clear out the value
  c = new Cookie(RememberMeLoginComponent.COOKIE_NAME, "");
  c.setMaxAge(0); // delete this cookie
}
else {
  c.setMaxAge(604800);
}
response.addCookie(c);
}
}
}
```

The setup and lifecycle for this **PhaseListener** are as described in Chapter 12. In this case, we want to take action during the **beforePhase()** event of the **RenderResponse** lifecycle phase.

The real work of the **beforePhase()** method takes place only if this run through the lifecycle is for a postback request that passed through the **decode()** method of the **RememberMeLoginComponent**. Recall that this method stored a reference to the **RememberMeLoginComponent** instance in the **RequestMap**. Here, the existence of that

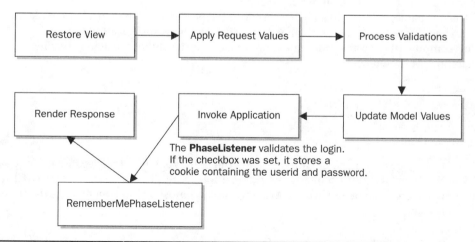

FIGURE 15-6   Login processing and the request processing lifecycle

instance in the Map is checked. If it is not present, no action is taken. If it is present, the static **checkLoginState** method of the **ForcedLoginFilter** component uses the Virtual Trainer's login scheme to check if the login was successful. If so, the next step determines if the user checked the checkbox, indicating their desire to have the login information remembered. If so, the user ID and password are extracted from the components and set as the value of a cookie. Otherwise, an empty cookie is created. In all cases, a cookie is added to the response. This is necessary because the Servlet API provides no way to remove a cookie from the browser's cookie store, so if the user decides they want to have the system forget the cookie value, the best we can do is clear out sensitive information from the cookie's value.

Leveraging JAAS from a JSF Application

We will conclude this chapter by showing how to enhance the Virtual Trainer example by leveraging the standard security infrastructure of the Java platform. From its inception, the Java platform has treated security as a first-class concern. Indeed, one of the first benefits of Java was to securely bring dynamic behavior to Web-deployed applications. Over the years, the implementation and API to security has evolved, but the core principals have improved and become steadily more secure. Therefore, choosing to build your application-managed security on top of the standard Java security features is a very safe bet.

A term often applied to Java security is JAAS, which is short for Java Authentication and Authorization Service. JAAS started out as an optional package in JDK 1.3 but has become a core part of the Java platform as of JDK 1.4. As the name implies, JAAS covers the first two of the three main aspects of security: authentication and authorization. Let's explore one way to integrate JAAS-style authentication and authorization into the Virtual Trainer application.

Using JAAS Authentication in the Virtual Trainer

While it would certainly be possible to call into the JAAS layer directly from the Virtual Trainer's application logic—for example, from the **UserRegistry** bean—a more reusable solution is to encapsulate the JAAS interface in a custom **ActionListener**. This approach decouples the security completely from your application and takes advantage of the intended use of the **ActionListener** extension hook.

The mechanics of providing such an **ActionListener** are described in Chapter 12, but let's review briefly here. The first step is to modify the **faces-config.xml** file for the **trainercomponents** reusable component library so that it includes the **action-listener** declaration, as shown next.

```
<application>
  <action-listener>
    com.jsfcompref.trainercomponents.util.JAASActionListener
  </action-listener>
</application>
```

Then, leverage the decorator pattern, as described in Chapter 12, to delegate most of the work to the "real" **ActionListener** by providing a constructor that saves a reference to it. Following the constructor, the **processAction()** method must be implemented, as described in the following.

```
...
  private ActionListener parent = null;
```

```java
public void processAction(ActionEvent event)
  throws AbortProcessingException {
  FacesContext context = FacesContext.getCurrentInstance();
  ValueHolder comp = null;
  String userid = null, password = null;
  JAASHelper jaasHelper = new JAASHelper();

  // Check to see if they are on the login page.
  boolean onLoginPage = (-1 != context.getViewRoot().getViewId().
      lastIndexOf("login")) ? true : false;
  if (onLoginPage) {
    if (null != (comp = (ValueHolder)
      context.getViewRoot().findComponent("form:userid"))) {
      userid = (String) comp.getValue();
    }
    if (null != (comp = (ValueHolder)
      context.getViewRoot().findComponent("form:password"))) {
      password = (String) comp.getValue();
    }
    // If JAAS authentication failed
    if (!jaasHelper.authenticate(userid, password)) {
      context.getApplication().getNavigationHandler().
        handleNavigation(context, null, "login");
      return;
    }
    else {
      // Subject must not be null, since authentication succeeded
      assert(null != jaasHelper.getSubject());
      // Put the authenticated subject in the session.
      context.getExternalContext().getSessionMap().put(JAASSubject,
        jaasHelper.getSubject());
    }
  }
  parent.processAction(event);
  // use JAAS to perform viewId level authorization
  // The ForcedLoginPhaseListener already forced the user to log in
  // before reaching this page.
  Subject subject = (Subject) context.getExternalContext().
     getSessionMap().get(JAASSubject);
  assert(null != subject);
  // If the user doesn't have permission to view this viewId
  if (!jaasHelper.hasPermissionToAccessViewId(subject, context.
     getViewRoot().getViewId())) {
    // Put error messages in the request
    Map requestMap = context.getExternalContext().getRequestMap();
    requestMap.put("userid", userid);
    requestMap.put("requiredPermission", "trainer");
    requestMap.put("viewId", context.getViewRoot().getViewId());
    // Redirect to the insufficientPermissions page
    context.getApplication().getNavigationHandler().
        handleNavigation(context, null, "insufficientPermissions");
  }
}
```

The first thing to note is that part of the usage contract for **JAASActionListener** is the requirement that the username and password components be nested inside a **UIForm** named "form", and be named "userid" and "password", respectively. This expedient measure allows the **JAASActionListener** to easily extract the user-provided values for username and password so that they can be passed on to the **JAASHelper** class. The second thing to note about the usage contract is the requirement that the application provide a navigation rule for the outcome "login" that causes the user to be directed to the login page if the authentication failed. In the failure case, **processAction()** is not called until after redirecting to the "login" outcome using **NavigationHandler**. If authentication succeeded, the **Subject** is stored in the session for later access. The **java.security.Subject** is the Java class that represents the user to the runtime. (We'll cover **Subject** in greater detail in the section on JAAS authentication.) Finally, the parent **processAction()** method is called to do the normal action handling. Note that this causes the existing application-managed authentication, as described in Chapter 9, to take place. A production-quality implementation would probably remove the application-managed authentication in favor of using JAAS, rather than just supplementing it, as we have done here.

Let's examine the **JAASHelper** class.

```
public class JAASHelper {

  LoginContext loginContext = null;

  public JAASHelper() {
  }

  public boolean authenticate(String userid, String password) {
    boolean result = false;
    try {
      loginContext = new LoginContext("FileLogin",
          new LoginCallback(userid, password));
      loginContext.login();
      result = true;
    }
    catch (LoginException e) {
      // A production-quality implementation would log this message
      result = false;
    }
    return result;
  }

  public Subject getSubject () {
    Subject result = null;
    if (null != loginContext) {
      result = loginContext.getSubject();
    }
    return result;
  }

  public static class LoginCallback implements CallbackHandler {
    private String userName = null;
    private String password = null;
```

```
    public LoginCallback(String userName, String password) {
      this.userName = userName;
      this.password = password;
    }

    public void handle(Callback[] callbacks) {
       for (int i = 0; i< callbacks.length; i++) {
         if (callbacks[i] instanceof NameCallback) {
           NameCallback nc = (NameCallback)callbacks[i];
           nc.setName(userName);
         } else if (callbacks[i] instanceof PasswordCallback) {
           PasswordCallback pc = (PasswordCallback)callbacks[i];
           pc.setPassword(password.toCharArray());
         }
       }
    }
  }
}
```

The **authenticate( )** method uses the class **java.security.auth.login.LoginContext** to perform the login. The **login( )** method of this class will throw a **LoginException** if the login fails for any reason. This exception is caught by **authenticate( )** and it responds by setting **result** to **false**. If no exception is thrown, **result** is set to **true**. **authenticate( )** ends by returning the value of **result**.

The two arguments to the **LoginContext** constructor are the most important part of this example. The first, the literal string "FileLogin", refers to an implementation of the **javax .security.auth.spi.LoginModule** interface. This interface is implemented by a provider of a particular implementation of authentication technology—for example, JNDI, LDAP, or database. In this example, we use a free software implementation called "tagish" that provides a simple file-based authentication scheme. The implementation comes from John Gardner and can be found at **http://free.tagish.net/jaas/**. Providing a **LoginModule** implementation is beyond the scope of this chapter, but we must illustrate how to use one, once it has been provided. This is the beauty of JAAS—the authentication technology itself is separated from the rest of the system. In other words, if you want to plug in LDAP, do it by providing a custom **LoginModule**.

The JVM is made aware of the existence of a **LoginModule** implementation either through a **-D** flag, or via a modification to the **JAVA_HOME/jre/lib/java.security** file. In our case, we use the former option:

```
-Djava.security.auth.login.config==
D:/Projects/trainer/chapterCode/ch14/trainer/src/resources/tagish.login
```

Note the use of forward slashes instead of the standard Windows backslashes. Also note the "==" instead of just one "=". The format of this file is prescribed by JAAS:

```
FileLogin
{
  com.tagish.auth.FileLogin required
pwdFile="D:/Projects/trainer/chapterCode/ch14/trainer/src/resources/passwd";
};
```

The **FileLogin** identifier must match the argument to the **LoginContext** constructor. The first element inside the **FileLogin** declaration is the fully qualified class name of the class implementing **LoginModule**. In our application, we have bundled **tagish.jar**, which contains this class, into the **WEB-INF/lib** directory of the application. The **required** flag tells the system that the login must succeed, and whether it succeeds or fails, the login must still proceed down the **LoginModule** chain. Other valid values for this flag are **requisite**, **sufficient**, and **optional** and are described in the javadocs for the class **javax.security.auth .login.Configuration**. The **pwdFile** argument is an implementation-specific parameter to the code in **tagish.jar** that tells it where to find its password file. The format of this file is also implementation-specific and for the trainer application looks like:

```
username:MD5 Hash Of Password:group*
```

The specific file for the Virtual Trainer follows:

```
# Passwords for com.tagish.auth.FileLogin

jfitness:5a64edabc9358c603103053a3c600a88:user
stiger:40be4e59b9a2a2b5dffb918c0e86b3d7:user
guest:084e0343a0486ff05530df6c705c8bb4:user
jake:1200cf8ad328a60559cf5e7c5f46ee6d:user:trainer
```

Obviously, a simple MD5 hash of the password is not at all secure and a production-quality implementation would use an actual encryption algorithm. For the purposes of security, MD5 is just as secure as Base64 encoding, described earlier in the chapter, which is to say, not at all secure. A handy MD5 hash calculator can be found at **http://bfl.rctek.com/ tools/?tool=hasher**. Note that user **jake** is a member of the **user** and **trainer** groups, while all the other users are simply members of the **user** group. Groups will come into play in the next section.

The second argument to the **LoginContext** constructor is an implementation of the **javax.security.auth.callback.CallbackHandler** interface. The **LoginCallback** implementation saves the username and password ultimately originating from the **userid** and **password** components in its constructor and uses standard boilerplate code to propagate them to the JAAS system.

Using JAAS Authorization in the Virtual Trainer   A detailed review of JAAS authorization is beyond the scope of this book, but we will show just enough to get you started. These classes are displayed in Figure 15-7. After authentication, the logged-in user is associated with an instance of **Subject**. As shown in the previous section, the **Subject** is stored in the session for easy access elsewhere in the application. A **Subject** has a set of **Principal**s, otherwise known as groups. Each **Principal** has zero or more **Permission**s associated with it that govern what a **Subject** with that **Principal** is allowed to do. In the Virtual Trainer example, the subject **jake** has the **user** and **trainer** principals. Users with the **trainer** principal are allowed to access pages that normal users may not access. **Subject** instances can also have **Credential**s associated with them for things such as public/private key pairs for a public key infrastructure, or certificates for certificate-based authentication.

The **tagish** library provides an implementation of **Principal** sufficient for our needs in the form of the **com.tagish.auth.TypedPrincipal** class. The Java platform provides a concrete **BasicPermission** class that applications can extend to define their own subclass. In our case, we define **ViewIdPermission** to represent permission to access a given view ID.

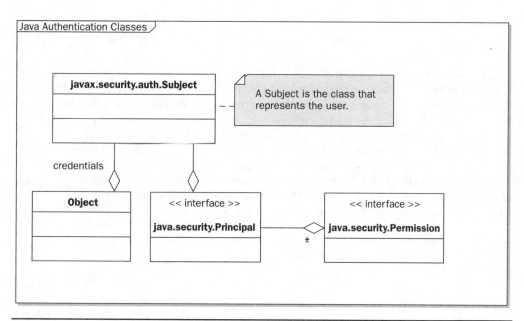

FIGURE 15-7   Java authorization classes

A production-quality implementation will want to extend **Permission** directly and provide robust behavior for view ID pattern matching. The listing for **ViewIdPermission** follows.

```
public class ViewIdPermission extends BasicPermission {

  public ViewIdPermission(String viewId) {
    super(viewId);
  }

  public ViewIdPermission(String viewId, String actions) {
    super(viewId, actions);
  }

}
```

You can see that this subclass adds no value over the **BasicPermission** class and is included here mainly to show where a production implementation would extend.

The valid principal types, and the permissions each one has, are defined in a policy file declared to the VM in a similar manner to the way the login configuration was declared earlier, via a **-D** option, or via modifying the **java.security** file. As in the previous, we choose the former option.

```
-Djava.security.auth.policy==
D:/Projects/trainer/chapterCode/ch14/trainer/web/WEB-INF/trainer.policy
```

The format of the file is defined by JAAS:

```
grant Principal com.tagish.auth.TypedPrincipal "trainer" {
  permission com.jsfcompref.trainercomponents.util.ViewIdPermission "*";
};
```

```
grant Principal com.tagish.auth.TypedPrincipal "user" {
  permission com.jsfcompref.trainercomponents.util.ViewIdPermission "/main.jsp";
};
```

The preceding policy file defines two **Principal**s, "trainer" and "user", and grants some **ViewIdPermission**s to each. The trainer is allowed to access any view ID as indicated by the "*" declaration. The user is only allowed to access the "/main.jsp" view ID. Note that we don't need to list the login and logout view IDs because they are explicitly excluded from the authorization scheme by the **JAASActionListener** implementation. The limitation of our simple **ViewIdPermission** implementation is evident here because we have to modify this policy file to explicitly grant the "user" access to any view IDs they must view.

Once the **Principal**s and **Permission**s have been defined and declared, the **JAASActionListener** and **JAASHelper** classes must be extended to use them. First, let's rewrite the **processAction()** method to include this feature.

```
public void processAction(ActionEvent event)
   throws AbortProcessingException {
   FacesContext context = FacesContext.getCurrentInstance();
   UIOutput comp = null;
   String userid = null, password = null;
   JAASHelper jaasHelper = new JAASHelper();

   // Check to see if they are on the login page.
   boolean onLoginPage = (-1 != context.getViewRoot().getViewId().
      lastIndexOf("login")) ? true : false;
   if (onLoginPage) {
     if (null != (comp = (UIOutput)
       context.getViewRoot().findComponent("form:userid"))) {
       userid = (String) comp.getValue();
     }
     if (null != (comp = (UIOutput)
       context.getViewRoot().findComponent("form:password"))) {
       password = (String) comp.getValue();
     }
     // If JAAS authentication failed
     if (!jaasHelper.authenticate(userid, password)) {
       context.getApplication().getNavigationHandler().
          handleNavigation(context, null, "login");
       return;
     }
     else {
       // Subject must not be null, since authentication succeeded
       assert(null != jaasHelper.getSubject());
       // Put the authenticated subject in the session.
       context.getExternalContext().getSessionMap().put(JAASSubject,
          jaasHelper.getSubject());
     }
   }
   parent.processAction(event);
   // use JAAS to perform viewId level authorization
   // The ForcedLoginPhaseListener already forced the user to log in
   // before reaching this page.
   Subject subject = (Subject) context.getExternalContext().
```

```
        getSessionMap().get(JAASSubject);
    assert(null != subject);
    // If the user doesn't have permission to view this viewId
    if (!jaasHelper.hasPermissionToAccessViewId(subject, context.
        getViewRoot().getViewId())) {
      // Redirect to the insufficientPermissions page
     context.getApplication().getNavigationHandler().
        handleNavigation(context, null, "insufficientPermissions");

   }
}
```

The first part of the method is unchanged from the previous section. We have added code after the **parent.processAction(event)** call to handle authorization. First, the **Subject** is retrieved from the session. Then, the static **hasPermissionToAccessViewId()** method is called on **JAASHelper**, passing the **Subject** and the view ID. If **hasPermissionToAccessViewId()** returns false, we navigate to the "insufficientPermissions" outcome using the **handleNavigation()** method of **NavigationHandler**. Note that the last argument to the **handleNavigation()** is hard-coded to the value "insufficientPermissions". This constitutes an implicit usage contract requirement in the necessity of the user to declare an **insufficientPermissions navigation-rule outcome** and associated JSP page to show when the user doesn't have permission to access the given view ID. Let's now examine the implementation of **hasPermissionToAccessViewId()**.

```
public static boolean hasPermissionToAccessViewId(Subject subject,
                                                  String viewId) {
  boolean result = true;
  final Permission perm = new ViewIdPermission(viewId);
  final SecurityManager sm;
  if (System.getSecurityManager() == null) {
    sm = new SecurityManager();
  } else {
    sm = System.getSecurityManager();
  }
  try {
    Subject.doAsPrivileged(subject, new PrivilegedExceptionAction() {
      public Object run() {
        sm.checkPermission(perm);
        return null;
      }
    },null);
    result = true;
  } catch (AccessControlException ace) {
    result = false;
  } catch (PrivilegedActionException pae) {
    result = false;
  }


  return result;
}
```

This standard code obtains or creates a **SecurityManager** for use later in the method. It then calls the static **doAsPrivileged()** method, passing the argument **Subject** and an inner class **PrivilegedExceptionAction** subclass that asks the **SecurityManager** if the currently executing code has the argument **Permission**. If the code does not have the permission, either an **AccessControlException** or **PrivilegedActionException** will be thrown, in which case it returns false from **hasPermissionToAccessViewId()**. Otherwise, it returns **true**.

To Learn More about Security

As mentioned at the beginning of the chapter, computer/network security is a very large topic. This book covers only the part that relates to JSF. Those readers who are interested in gaining broader knowledge of the subject should read *Hacking Exposed, Fifth Edition* (McGraw-Hill/Osborne, 2005) by Stuart McClure et al.

Automated Testing and Debugging of JavaServer Faces Applications

As with the previous chapter on security, the topic of this chapter is a broad and deep one, with many books, articles, and dissertations written about it. A thorough coverage of the general topic of automated testing and debugging is certainly beyond the scope of this book. Instead, we will cover the state of the art as currently practiced, giving particular examples used in real-world JSF projects.

This chapter is about automated testing: the practice of writing tests in such a way that they can be re-executed automatically, with little or no manual intervention. Of course, there is a place for manual testing, but Web applications are particularly well suited to automated testing due to their markup-based interfaces. Therefore, manual testing is not covered. Many different areas can be tested in a Web application; one can test for valid markup, browser incompatibilities, link integrity, spelling, responsiveness, performance—the list can go on and on. This chapter focuses on two areas: application correctness and stress testing. The former tests if the application is doing what it is supposed to do, while the latter tests that it is performing at acceptable levels while doing so.

In the first part of the chapter, we review the basics of software testing as applied to JSF applications. We will cover some of the terminology of testing and show you how to do a popular development technique that is closely related to testing: test driven development. The second part of the chapter will give an overview of several current Web testing technologies that have emerged as standard testing tools. Special attention will be given to freely available open-source tools. In the third part of the chapter, we apply the knowledge from the previous two parts and show how to write unit and system tests for a JSF application. We close the chapter with a section somewhat unrelated to automated testing, but arguably even more useful: debugging JSF applications. By the time you finish this chapter, you'll be able to confidently develop automated tests and debug them (as well as debugging your application in general) using current best practices.

A Review of Software Testing Terminology

Before examining the practice of automated testing of Java Web applications, let's review some of the basics of software testing that apply in this domain. The whole point of testing is to maximize software quality by minimizing bugs in the code. The role of testing in a software project depends on many factors, ranging from the size of the team to the desired quality goals for the project and, of course, the amount of time in the schedule. One indisputable fact is this: testing happens. Whether it is done by the development team or by the end user, testing does happen. It is far better to do testing as early as possible in the development cycle to reduce the cost of fixing bugs, as you can see from Figure 16-1.

From the beginning of software engineering, there have been many different methodologies and practices aimed at reducing bugs. Some have focused on preventing bugs from being introduced in the first place, while others have focused on finding bugs as soon as possible after they are introduced. One technique currently popular, especially among enterprise Java developers, is the extreme programming practice of test driven development (TDD). This practice implies performing testing at the earliest possible point in the software development lifecycle: as the code is being written, feature by feature. TDD yields such great results that the authors have chosen to include a section on doing TDD with JSF later in this chapter.

There are different kinds of tests for different parts of the software development lifecycle, as shown in Figure 16-2.

Of course, Figure 16-2 depicts an overly simplistic view of the software lifecycle, and different methodologies and practices present the lifecycle in vastly different ways. Also, there are more kinds of tests than those pictured here, such as acceptance, usability, performance, scalability, security, and so on. However, the basic four of unit, integration, system, and stress tests cover a lot of ground and illustrate techniques found in most of the other kinds of tests. Let's examine the basic four and how they apply to JSF applications.

The cost of fixing a bug as a function of time

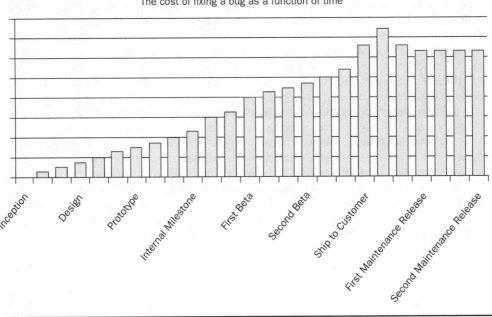

FIGURE 16-1 The cost of fixing a bug as a function of time

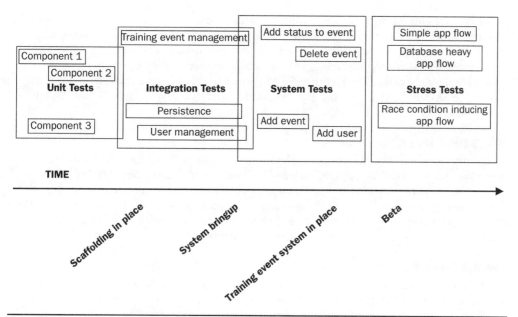

FIGURE 16-2   Some of the software lifecycle, and some of the tests that are appropriate during the lifecycle

Unit Testing

Unit testing is the finest grained kind of testing discussed here. A well-written single unit test will exercise all of the things that can possibly happen to a single class, in isolation from other classes from the same application. This includes verifying that expected things happen when given both "normal" and "abnormal" inputs. Unit tests are often called "black box" tests because they traditionally don't take implementation details for granted. However, just as often unit tests are written as "white box" tests, which *do* take individual implementation details into account. Unit testing is the only kind of testing for which a white box approach is recommended. Higher-level tests all use black box techniques. Regardless of white or black box, the challenge with unit tests is allowing them to run in isolation, which requires some careful thought when designing the application. A common strategy is called "mock objects" and requires the creation of dummy classes with which the class being tested can interact. One possible arrangement of mock objects for the **SpellCheckTextAreaComponent**, described in Chapter 11, is shown in Figure 16-3.

In JSF, custom **UIComponent**, **Renderer**, **Converter**, and **Validator** classes are well suited to being unit tested, and we'll show some examples of this later in the chapter.

There are many benefits to having a large library of high-quality unit tests for your application. Most importantly, they can provide some peace of mind when making changes

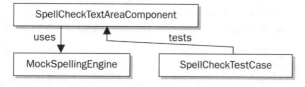

FIGURE 16-3   A class being unit tested with the aid of mock objects

to the system—for example, when performing refactoring. If the unit tests passed before and after making the changes, you know at least that things are probably no worse than they were before you started changing things. Unit tests used in this capacity are known as *regression tests*. Unit testing can also allow new team members to ramp up more quickly on a system by providing small chunks of easily executable example code. In general, it is difficult to repeatedly deliver a production-quality system of any complexity without using unit testing.

Integration Testing

By definition, unit testing misses out on a large class of bugs that arise when the units are assembled into a larger subsystem, such as "training event management" or "persistence." This is the realm of the integration test. Integration tests are seldom done in white box style because doing so would be too burdensome to maintain as the system evolves over time. With JSF, integration tests generally don't need to know about individual components, but rather exercise the portion of the Web application that is devoted to a particular functional area.

System Testing

As shown in Figure 16-2, there is overlap between integration and system testing, particularly when it comes to Web applications. As the name implies, system testing works on the entire application, just as a real user would. System tests are often scenario-based, such as "add user to the application" or "complete a training event." These are also black box tests because they use only human-accessible interfaces of the application.

Stress Testing

Stress testing generally only applies to multiuser applications, such as Web applications, and is a kind of *load testing* where the entire system is placed under unusually heavy loads to verify that it performs as required. The loads can be varied but usually they involve large numbers of simultaneous users doing as much as they possibly could do with the system in the shortest amount of time. Stress testing may be nothing more than system tests scaled up to many users, or it could consist of just throwing a large number of simple requests at the application simultaneously.

Test Driven Development

Like most things in extreme programming, the idea behind test driven development is simple and pragmatic. It is based on this fact: No one knows the code any better than the developer who wrote it, and at no point in time do they know the code any better than when they just wrote it. The idea is also based on the practice of incremental or iterative development: functionality is gradually added to the module until the user requirements have been met. TDD is the subject of many other books, and two good ones are *Extreme Programming Installed* by Ron Jeffries et al. and *Test Driven Development: by Example* by Kent Beck. The following is an overview of the steps of test driven development.

1. Write just enough of the module (generally a class, or a class and an interface) so that it compiles. This really could be a constructor and a few methods.

2. Write an automated test case that calls the methods on the module from the previous step.

3. Run the test, and observe that it fails (you haven't implemented anything yet!).

4. Refactor and clean up the code to prepare for adding features so that the test passes.

5. Go back to step 2, but add more code to the test each time, exercising more features until all features in the module are implemented and tested.

At this point, you can see that TDD is just as much a method of designing software as it is about testing software. One way to think about it is that you are designing software with a byproduct of having a complete, high-quality set of unit tests suitable for regression testing when you're done.

Tools for the Automated Testing of Web Applications

As mentioned earlier, Web applications by nature are well suited to automated testing. This has caused a proliferation of tools, both free and commercial, to ease the task of testing your Web application. There are many fine tools available, but this chapter focuses on a few of the most popular open-source ones, which also are used in the test library for Sun's JSF implementation. These are shown in Figure 16-4. Even if you don't use these particular tools in practice, this discussion will illustrate the important concepts of Web testing and provide a basis for comparison with other tools.

It's important to make a distinction between testing reusable custom JSF components (such as UI components, converters, and validators) and testing a Web application that uses those components. The former are testable with unit test techniques, using technologies such as JUnit and Cactus, while the latter are generally best tested with integration, system, or stress testing, using technologies such as HTMLUnit and JMeter. All of these techniques and technologies are described in the following sections.

JUnit, the Most Popular Automated Testing Technology for the Java Platform

JUnit is a test framework built by some of the originators of the Extreme Programming software development technique, Kent Beck and Erich Gamma. It was designed to be unobtrusive and easy to use and extend. Judging by its popularity the design goals were achieved. For example, all of the major IDEs have support for writing and executing JUnit tests, as do the two most popular Java software build tools, ant and maven. A tutorial on using JUnit from these and other tools is beyond the scope of this book. One thing to keep in mind is that configuring your development environment and tools with JUnit can be tricky, so be prepared to spend some effort on this one-time operation.

Let's get started with a simple unit test that does some things with the **WeightConverter** from Chapter 7. JUnit provides a base class that each test case you define can extend: **junit**

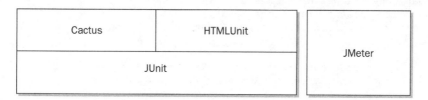

Figure 16-4   Automated testing tools used in the Sun JSF implementation

.framework.TestCase. Here is a complete JUnit test suite containing tests for each of the two important methods of **WeightConverter**. There are many different ways to write JUnit tests; this is the one used on the JUnit tests for the Sun JSF implementation.

```java
package com.jsfcompref.trainercomponents.convert;

import com.sun.faces.mock.MockFacesContext;
import javax.faces.component.html.HtmlInputText;
import javax.faces.context.FacesContext;
import junit.framework.*;

public class WeightConverterJUnitTest extends TestCase {

  public WeightConverterJUnitTest(String testName) {
    super(testName);
  }

  public static Test suite() {
    TestSuite suite = new TestSuite(WeightConverterJUnitTest.class);

    return suite;
  }

  WeightConverter toTest = null;
  HtmlInputText input = null;
  FacesContext context = null;

  protected void setUp() throws Exception {
    toTest = new WeightConverter();
    input = new HtmlInputText();
    context = new MockFacesContext();
  }

  protected void tearDown() throws Exception {
    toTest = null;
    input = null;
    context = null;
  }

  public void testGetAsObject() throws Exception {
    System.out.println("testGetAsObject");

    Object result = toTest.getAsObject(context, input, "30 lbs");
    float convertedWeight = 13.636364f;
    assertTrue(result instanceof Float);
    assertEquals(convertedWeight, ((Float)result).floatValue());
  }

  public void testGetAsString() throws Exception {
    System.out.println("testGetAsString");

    String result = toTest.getAsString(context, input, new
Float(13.636364f));
```

```
        assertEquals("30 lbs.", result);

    }

}
```

This is slightly more complex than a "hello world" test case, but at least it does something useful. It tests that the default desired unit is kilograms, and that passing in the string **"30 lbs."** to the **getAsObject()** method of **WeightConverter** returns a **Float** with the value of 13.636364. It also tests that the converse is true with the **getAsString()** method. Note that we have marked each of these methods as throwing **Exception**. This is a convenient trick to avoid the need for **try catch** blocks in each test method. Any exceptions thrown will cause the test to fail. As often happens in unit testing, the actual test is pretty straightforward. In this case, more work actually goes into creating the environment in which the test can run—otherwise known as "the test fixture"—and this is where JUnit shines.

Let's examine the JUnit-specific part of this test case. First, consider the constructor. **TestCase** has two constructors, one with no-arguments and one that takes a **String** argument. The former is intended just to allow serialization, and the latter is intended to provide the string that is shown when the test is running. JUnit takes advantage of the Java reflection API to define several naming conventions to ease the test development process. First, if you define a **suite()** method as shown earlier, JUnit will automatically consider each method you define in your test that returns **void**, takes no arguments, and starts with the string **test** to be an individual test. In this case, this means the **testGetAsObject()** and **testGetAsString()** methods will be automatically added to the suite and run by the test runner, described next. Finally, note the **setUp()** and **tearDown()** methods. JUnit will call the **setUp()** method before each test method is invoked, and call the **tearDown()** method after each test method is invoked. In **WeightConverterJUnitTest,** we are using these methods to instantiate the instance variables needed for each test case. Most production testing environments will create one or more **TestCase** subclasses to serve as the base classes for the bulk of the unit tests. When building a production test library, strive to make the tests easy to maintain by leveraging good OO practices and refactoring techniques.

When using plain old JUnit for testing, it is necessary to create "mock" objects to represent the parts of the system required by the code under test. Sun's implementation of JSF 1.2 provides a **jsf-extensions-test-time.jar** that contains a collection of mock objects in the package **com.sun.faces.mock** for doing unit testing on JSF components. Generally, the most important mock object is the **MockFacesContext**, which we use in this test case to pass to the **getAsString()** and **getAsObject()** methods. The Sun JSF mock object library contains mock objects for all of the standard JSF artifacts. Consult the documentation for this project at **https://jsf-extensions.dev.java.net/** for complete details on how to use these in your test cases.

Once the test case has been built, it's time to run it. Like everything else in JUnit, there are several ways to do it. Here we document the two most popular techniques: via ant using the **<junit>** task, and via ant using the **TestRunner** UI. Let's discuss the former first.

```
<path id="classpath">
  <pathelement location="${commons-beanutils.jar}"/>
  <pathelement location="${commons-collections.jar}"/>
  <pathelement location="${commons-digester.jar}"/>
  <pathelement location="${commons-logging.jar}"/>
  <pathelement location="${jsf-api.jar}"/>
  <pathelement location="${jstl.jar}"/>
```

```
    <pathelement location="${standard.jar}"/>
    <pathelement location="${build}/${appName}/WEB-INF/classes"/>
    <pathelement location="${servlet.jar}"/>
    <pathelement location="${jsp.jar}"/>
    <pathelement location="${junit.jar}"/>
    <pathelement location="${build.test}/${}"/>
    <pathelement location="${build}/classes/${}"/>
</path>

<target name="test" depends="buildLibTest">
  <mkdir dir="${test.results.dir}"/>

  <junit printSummary="no" fork="yes"
        haltonfailure="yes" haltonerror="yes">
    <jvmarg line="${debug.jvm.args}"/>
    <classpath  refid="classpath"/>
    <formatter   type="xml" usefile="true"/>
    <batchtest todir="${test.results.dir}">
      <fileset    dir="${build.test}/${}"
            includes="**/*Test.class"/>
    </batchtest>
  </junit>
</target>
```

Complete documentation on ant may be found at **http://ant.apache.org/**. The **path** element contains the complete classpath for the test run. These tend to be pretty inclusive and often involve trial and error to make sure everything needed is included. Note the **jvmarg** element. This is a convenient technique for enabling source-level debugging of JUnit tests. The value of the **${debug.jvm.args}** property is the list of arguments to turn on debugging in the JVM that is running the test. For example, "**-Xdebug -Xrunjdwp:transport=dt_socket,address=8000,server =y,suspend=n**" will turn on debugging in Sun's JVM. The **classpath** element inside the **junit** element refers to the **path** element defined earlier. The **formatter** element tells the file format for the test results, which can be interpreted by a number of tools for display and analysis. The **batchtest** element directs the test output to files in the specified directory. Because we are using the XML formatter, these files will be named **TEST-<fully-qualified-class-name-of-test>.xml**. For example, the **WeightConverterJUnitTest** will have its results in the file **TEST-com .jsfcompref.trainercomponents.convert.WeightConverterJUnitTest.xml**. Finally, the **fileset** element collects the files matching the pattern **"**/*Test.class"** and passes them to the **batchtest** element. This pattern says, for all subdirectories of the directory specified in the **dir** element, find all files that end in **Test.class**. Naturally, this catches **WeightConverterJUnitTest.class**.

For those desiring a GUI to running tests, JUnit provides AWT and Swing versions. As it happens, it's easiest to run these through ant, rather than at the command line, simply due to ant's classpath management mechanism.

```
<target name="test.ui" depends="buildLibTest">
  <mkdir dir="${test.results.dir}"/>

  <java failonerror="yes" dir="${build.test}/${}" fork="yes"
        classname="junit.swingui.TestRunner">
    <jvmarg line="${debug.jvm.args}"/>
    <classpath  refid="classpath"/>
  </java>
</target>
```

This will cause the **TestRunner** swing UI, shown next, to search the classpath for JUnit tests and provide a UI for running them.

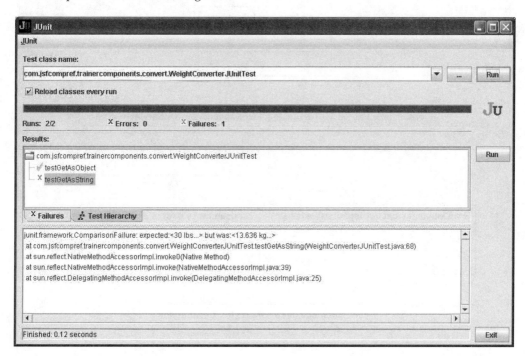

NOTE *For more information on using JUnit, see* **http://www.junit.org/**.

Cactus, Server-Side Automated Unit Testing

Jakarta Cactus (**http://jakarta.apache.org/cactus/**) extends the capabilities of JUnit to enable running JUnit tests inside of a J2EE Web container. The primary benefit of this approach is to remove the need for mock objects, instead allowing the use of real objects to provide the test fixture. However, an unfortunate side effect is the complexity of requiring a real Servlet/JSP container in order to run the tests. The Sun and Apache implementations of JSF use Cactus for some of their automated testing. If you're using the Sun JSF 1.2 implementation, you can use the **jsf-extensions-test-time.jar** from **https://jsf-extensions.dev.java.net/** to help in writing server-side automated tests of JSF applications. This section shows how to leverage the classes in this package to test JSF classes on the server side.

As mentioned previously, Cactus is an extension of JUnit. It provides two classes that extend JUnit's core **TestCase** class for testing Servlet and JSP-based classes. The **jsf-extensions-test-time** package extends these Cactus classes and adds JSF capabilities to each, as shown in Figure 16-5.

JspFacesTestCase extends Cactus's **JspTestCase** and is used for classes that need access to JSP-specific classes, such as the **PageContext**. **ServletFacesTestCase** extends Cactus's **ServletTestCase** and is used for classes that need access to the Servlet API–specific classes.

Let's modify the earlier **WeightConverterJUnitTest** to run on the server side. Since JSF converters don't need to access the JSP API, we can make our test case extend

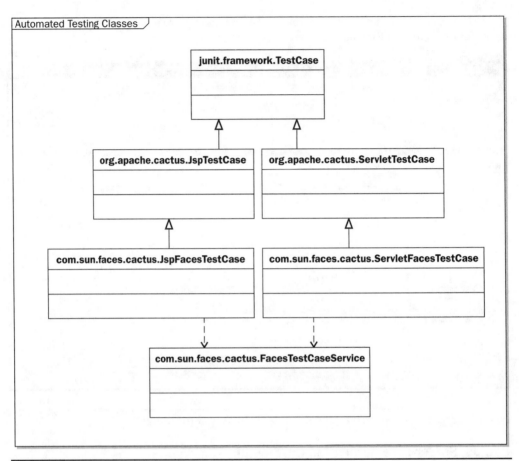

FIGURE 16-5   Test classes in JUnit, Cactus, and **jsf-extensions-test-time**

ServletFacesTestCase. We don't need to change much from the JUnit version, as shown next.

```
package com.jsfcompref.trainercomponents.convert;

import com.sun.faces.cactus.ServletFacesTestCase;
import javax.faces.component.html.HtmlInputText;
import junit.framework.Test;
import junit.framework.TestSuite;

public class WeightConverterCactusTest extends ServletFacesTestCase {

  public WeightConverterCactusTest(String testName) {
    super(testName);
  }

  public static Test suite() {
    TestSuite suite = new TestSuite(WeightConverterCactusTest.class);
```

```
      return suite;
   }

   WeightConverter toTest = null;
   HtmlInputText input = null;

   public void setUp() {
     super.setUp();
     toTest = new WeightConverter();
     input = new HtmlInputText();
   }

   public void tearDown() {
     toTest = null;
     input = null;
     super.tearDown();
   }

   public void testGetAsObject() throws Exception {
     System.out.println("testGetAsObject");

     Object result = toTest.getAsObject(getFacesContext(), input, "30 lbs");
     float convertedWeight = 13.636364f;
     assertTrue(result instanceof Float);
     assertEquals(convertedWeight, ((Float)result).floatValue());
   }

   public void testGetAsString() throws Exception {
     System.out.println("testGetAsString");

     String result = toTest.getAsString(getFacesContext(), input, new
Float(13.636364f));
     assertEquals("30 lbs.", result);

   }
}
```

First, the **setUp()** and **tearDown()** methods must call their superclass implementations manually. This is because most of the work of the Cactus and **jsf-extensions-test-time** framework happens as a result of these two methods. Second, note that the **FacesContext** instance variable is no longer present. This has been replaced with a call to the **getFacesContext()** accessor method from the **ServletFacesTestCase** class. This call returns a real **FacesContext** instance that is running within the scope of a real HTTP request, not a mock object as with the JUnit version. This is possible because the Cactus tests run as part of a real Web application, which can be configured with the full set of artifacts as in the production application.

The Cactus framework and the **ServletFacesTestCase** base class do a lot of work to ensure that the test environment is equivalent to the production environment. Unfortunately, the task of setting up Cactus to run is rather tricky, so please consult the downloadable code for this chapter which includes the ant build scripts to run the cactus tests with the simple command **ant cactus.test**. Finally, the **jsf-extensions-test-time** library provides a number of useful facilities for testing JSF components and applications, including capturing the rendered output and comparing it to a known "golden" file to verify that things are rendering as expected.

HTMLUnit: Testing the Virtual Trainer Application Flow

One of the oldest methods of test automation is the framework that impersonates a user. In the days of green-screen applications, this sort of testing was easy because the interface was entirely textual. With the advent of graphical user interfaces, the task became more difficult because the location of the UI elements became a lot harder to detect and therefore to test. However, when the Web came along, and user interfaces were again textual (though this time in HTML), it was again possible to easily simulate the user action by impersonating a browser. There are currently several competing open-source automated system test technologies, jWebUnit, HTTPUnit, and HTMLUnit to name a few. The Sun JSF implementation uses HTMLUnit and has found it to fit the bill quite well, though don't let that stop you from trying other testing frameworks. Regardless of which you settle on, the concept is always the same: there is some programmatic way to describe the interactions between the browser and the server.

The **jsf-extensions-test-time** project provides a base class, **HtmlUnitFacesTestCase**, that is tailored to testing JSF applications. We can extend this class to produce a simple test that logs in and logs out of the trainer application.

```
package com.jsfcompref.trainer;

import com.gargoylesoftware.htmlunit.html.HtmlAnchor;
import com.gargoylesoftware.htmlunit.html.HtmlSubmitInput;
import com.gargoylesoftware.htmlunit.html.HtmlPage;
import com.gargoylesoftware.htmlunit.html.HtmlPasswordInput;
import com.gargoylesoftware.htmlunit.html.HtmlTextInput;
import com.sun.faces.htmlunit.HtmlUnitFacesTestCase;
import java.util.List;
import junit.framework.Test;
import junit.framework.TestSuite;

public class TrainerHtmlUnitTest extends HtmlUnitFacesTestCase {

  public TrainerHtmlUnitTest(String name) {
    super(name);
  }

  public static Test suite() {
    return (new TestSuite(TrainerHtmlUnitTest.class));
  }

  public void testLoginLogout() throws Exception {
    HtmlPage page = getPage("");
    HtmlAnchor login = page.getFirstAnchorByText("Login");
    page = (HtmlPage) login.click();
    List inputs = getAllElementsOfGivenClass(page, null,
                                        HtmlTextInput.class);
    HtmlTextInput loginField = (HtmlTextInput) inputs.get(0);
    inputs = getAllElementsOfGivenClass(page, null,
                                   HtmlPasswordInput.class);
    HtmlPasswordInput passwordField = (HtmlPasswordInput) inputs.get(0);
    loginField.setValueAttribute("jake");
    passwordField.setValueAttribute("jake");
    List buttons = getAllElementsOfGivenClass(page, null,
                                      HtmlSubmitInput.class);
```

```
    page = (HtmlPage) ((HtmlSubmitInput) buttons.get(0)).click();
    HtmlAnchor logout = page.getFirstAnchorByText("Logout");
    page = (HtmlPage) logout.click();
    login = page.getFirstAnchorByText("Login");
    assertNotNull(login);

  }

}
```

Note that the first method invoked is **getPage()**. This method is provided by the superclass and uses the system properties **host**, **port**, and **context.path** to build the URL to which the argument to **getPage()** is appended. The system properties are set in the build system, which can be inspected in the download area for this chapter. In this case, the derived URL is **http://localhost:8080/trainer/**. As shown in Chapter 9, this causes the browser to be forwarded to the URL **http://localhost:8080/trainer/faces/index.jsp**. HTMLUnit automatically handles the request and response traffic necessary to handle the HTTP 302 redirect sent by the server. This is one of the useful features of HTMLUnit, but it can be disabled by calling **client.setRedirectEnabled(false)**. The **client** instance variable is provided by the **HtmlUnitFacesTestCase** base class and is useful for setting a number of properties for each client request to be made to the server.

After having obtained the **HtmlPage**, it can be searched for a link with the link text of "Login". At this point, a fragility in this method of testing becomes apparent. For one thing, extra work must be done to handle localized values. For another, if the design of the page changes to use a button instead of a link, this test will fail. The point is that there is a tight coupling between the test script and the UI of the application. This can be mitigated to some extent by using the **getHtmlElementById()** method on the **HtmlPage** class. This solves the localization problem, but we still have to know the types of the elements. This is one of the weaknesses of using a strongly typed language like Java to write test scripts. In any case, once the login link has been retrieved, calling **click()** on it yields another **HtmlPage**.

At this point, the **getAllElementsOfGivenClass()** method provided by the **HtmlUnitFacesTestCase** is used to obtain the userid and password text fields. Note that this method returns a list, so the list must be dereferenced to get the actual text fields. A smarter way to write this test case would take advantage of the class hierarchy of HTMLUnit instead of having the password and userid fields be strongly typed all the way down to their lowest class. For each field, the value is set using the **setValueAttribute()** method, in this case, to the trainer value "jake". Then a reference to the **HtmlSubmitInput** button is obtained, which is assumed to be the first and only button on the page, and this button is clicked. Once on the main page, a link with the link text of "Logout" is found and then clicked. Back on the main page, a link with the link text of "Login" is retrieved and its existence is verified.

This is a simple test case, but it shows the power of a system like **HtmlUnit**, where the DOM of the page is exposed programmatically. With judicial use of the **HtmlUnit** API, it is possible to write maintainable test cases that traverse the entire breadth of the application.

An important consideration is the role of JavaScript in the application. Components that make heavy use of JavaScript, such as AJAX components, pose special problems for automated testing. HTMLUnit has some support for JavaScript by virtue of its embedded JavaScript engine. Therefore, it is possible to work around most of the challenges of testing AJAX components but the practice of doing so is still evolving and beyond the scope of this section.

Load Testing and Profiling a JSF Application

We conclude our survey of automated Web testing technologies with JMeter, a popular open-source load testing package that is capable of simulating large numbers of users simultaneously accessing a Web application. Load testing will tell when application performance degrades below acceptable levels, but to discover *why* the application performance degrades, a profiling tool is required. The Profiler tool for the cost-free, open-source **NetBeans 5 IDE** from Sun Microsystems is used to gather profiling data and show how the trainer application can be enhanced to make it perform better.

Using Apache JMeter to Generate Load

First, let's examine how to use JMeter to record and execute a simple test case that covers a basic scenario in the trainer application, as follows.

1. Log in as the default trainer, jake.

2. Review the existing training events by paging through them using the scroller component.

3. Edit the last event on the last page of events to show that all the training sessions have been completed.

4. Return to the main page.

5. Create a new training event with a faulty date and submit it, causing a conversion error.

6. Fix the conversion error and resubmit the event.

7. Log out of the application.

Let's establish some terminology before continuing. A JMeter test case is called a "test plan" and it consists of one or more "thread groups" and one or more "listeners." A JMeter thread group contains a list of steps, or "samples" in JMeter terminology, to execute the test plan and can be configured to set the number of simultaneous threads JMeter uses to run the test plan. In this way, JMeter simulates a load placed on the server by multiple users accessing the application at the same time. A JMeter listener is an element inside of a test plan that gathers and reports data about the execution of the tests. There are many listeners provided with the JMeter application but only the "graph results" listener is examined for brevity. There are also many different kinds of samples to cover the entire breadth of testing distributed applications, but the only one of interest to JSF applications is the HTTP sampler.

The process of building a JMeter test plan consists of creating the list of HTTP sampler requests that simulate the user running through the application scenario. This can be done by hand, but it is rather impractical to do so. JMeter provides a built-in HTTP proxy server at which one can point one's Web browser to "record" the user's interaction with the Web server. The recorded steps are converted into HTTP sampler requests that can be executed at will by JMeter. Let's see how to use the proxy to build a test plan that executes the mentioned scenario. These steps are based on the "recording tests" tutorial at the JMeter Web site.

Instructions for downloading and installing JMeter are found in its project documentation. The binaries and documentation can be found at **http://jakarta.apache.org/jmeter/**. Once the application has been downloaded and installed, the GUI can be run from the **bin** directory using one of the provided **jmeter** scripts, depending on one's operating system. The basic JMeter UI is shown next.

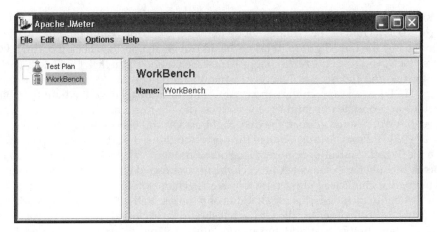

Select the "Test Plan" node in the tree view on the left of the UI. Change the value of the **Name** field in the right panel to reflect the trainer application—for example, by changing it to "trainer". Right-click the renamed "trainer" node in the tree view and choose Add | Thread Group, as shown next.

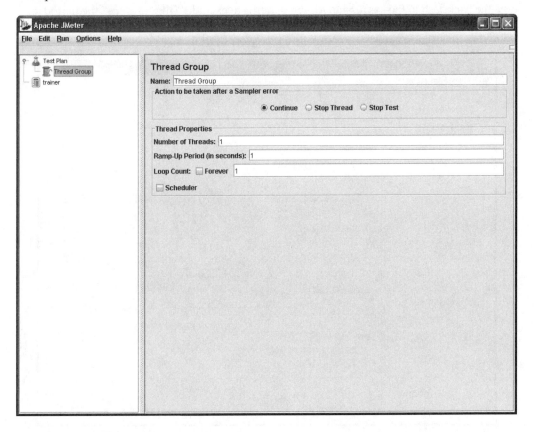

Most of the configuration steps require the right-click mouse action. The Thread Group will show up as a child of the "trainer" node in the tree. Use the **Name** field in the right panel to rename the thread group to **Jake's Basic Traversal**, and then click the Thread Group in the tree view; you'll see the node change names. Select and right-click the "Jake's Basic…" node in the tree and choose Add | Config Element | Http Request Defaults. In the **protocol** field, add **HTTP**, in all caps. In the server name, add **localhost**. Leave the **path** field blank, and add the appropriate port number for your server—in this case, **8080**.

Select the **WorkBench** node in the tree. Right-click it and choose Add | Non-Test Elements | HTTP Proxy Server. Change the port to an unused port—for example, 9090. Change the **Target Controller** option list to choose trainer | Jake's Basic Traversal. In the **Patterns to Include** panel, choose **Add**, click the newly created line in the UI, and enter in .*. That's the period character followed by the asterisk character. This is a regular expression that tells JMeter to include URLs for all kinds of requests. In the **Patterns to Exclude** panel, choose **Add** and add entries for the URLs that should be excluded from the proxy. This is generally images. In this case, add entries for .*\.**gif**, .*\.**jpg**, .*\.**jpeg**, .*\.**ico**, and .*\.**png**. This excludes the commonly encountered images, importantly also excluding the **favicon .ico** image requested by most browsers. Excluding images allows you to get a better idea of the responsiveness of the application since most browsers will have cached the images after the first time through the program, but the JMeter HTTP client does no caching. Also, note the backslash in the expression for the patterns to exclude. This "escapes" the period character so it must be matched literally, a common regular expression practice. The following illustration shows the completed proxy configuration.

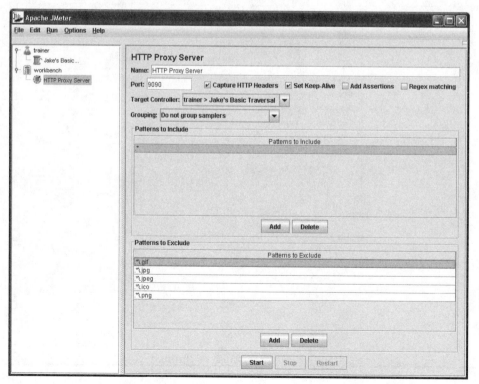

Click the **Start** button and then bring up a Web browser so it can be configured to use the proxy, and then use to execute the steps of the test plan. For Internet Explorer, go to the Tools menu and select the Internet Options item. In the resulting dialog, choose the Connections tab, and the LAN settings button on that tab. In the Proxy Server panel, check the checkbox that says "Use a proxy server for your LAN" and make sure the "Bypass proxy server for local addresses" box is *not* checked. Fill in localhost and 9090 as the host and port. For Mozilla Firefox, go to the Tools menu and choose the Options item. Click the General button in the left icon list and then click the Connection Settings button. Choose the Manual proxy configuration radio button and check the checkbox labeled "Use the same proxy for all protocols". Then fill in localhost and 9090 as the host and port. Make sure the "No proxy for" box does not contain localhost or 127.0.0.1. You are now ready to use the JMeter proxy and your Web browser to "record" your test case.

Make sure the trainer application is installed in your Web server as described in Chapter 9. Then enter this address into your browser's address bar: **http://localhost:8080/trainer/** and press ENTER. At this point, run through the preceding application scenario listed at the beginning of this section, making sure to log in as "jake" first. Once completed, return to JMeter and click the **Stop** button in the proxy panel. Then, select the top-level trainer node in the tree and choose File | Save Test Plan As to save the test plan. The final Test Plan should look something like the following illustration.

Note the URL paths prefixed by **/trainer** underneath the **Jake's Basic Traversal** node. These are the HTTP requests that make up the traversal through the application. Clicking each one allows inspecting the HTTP request parameters sent with each request, if so desired.

The final step in creating the test plan is to sprinkle in some random timings between the requests to increase realism. Right-click the **Jake's Basic Traversal** item and choose Add | Timer | Uniform Random Timer. If desired, modify the **Random Delay Maximum** field appropriately. Drag the Uniform Random Timer element up the tree until the **/trainer/** node is highlighted. Release the button and choose **Insert After** in the pop-up menu that appears. Repeat this step to include a Uniform Random Timer after each request in the tree, making sure to select the **Jake's Basic Traversal** node after each insertion. This action causes each insertion to happen at the end of the list of requests. Make sure to save the test plan when done. The final product is shown next.

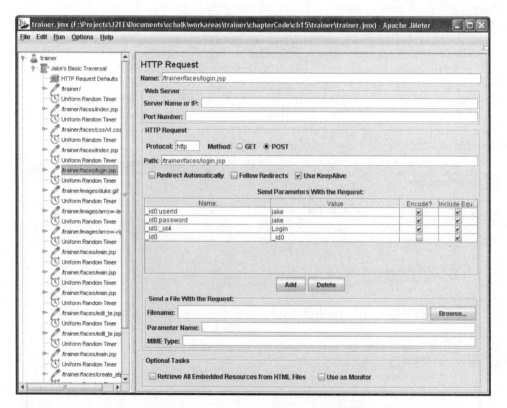

Note that this scenario relies on the **jake** userid being logged in several times at once. A production-quality test would have to create different userids for each thread and allow them to be used during the execution of the test.

It is a good practice to quit and restart JMeter at this point to ensure everything has saved correctly. Once JMeter restarts, open the saved test plan. Select the **Jake's Basic Traversal** node in the tree and alter the **Number of Threads** parameter to be 30 and the **loop count** to be 5. The former parameter tells JMeter how many simultaneous threads on which to execute the steps in that thread group. The latter parameter tells how many times within each thread to run through the steps of the thread group. The **Ramp Up Period**, which is set to 30, tells JMeter how long to take before starting up all the threads.

In order to see what's going on in the server, it is necessary to attach one or more listeners to the thread group. Right-click the **Jake's Basic Traversal** node and choose Add |

Listener | Graph Results. You are now ready to run the test. Choose Run | Start from the main menu, then select the **Graph Results** node in the tree to see the results as they come in. The results are shown in Figure 16-6.

You can see that throughput increased nearly linearly as the number of threads ramped up, but then fell off precipitously at the end of the test. This dropoff is due to the number of test threads ending in a staggered fashion, just as they started, due to the ramp-up time of 30. There are many other listeners to gather other kinds of data about the responsiveness of the application, but examining them in detail goes beyond the scope of this book.

Using the NetBeans 5 Profiler on Your JSF Application

We conclude our coverage of JMeter with a brief look at the other side of load testing: profiling. Profiling is where the detailed runtime characteristics of the application under load are examined and performance problems are identified. There are many excellent tools in production to profile applications including the JSF-enabled Oracle JDeveloper reviewed later in Chapter 17 in the section "Oracle JDeveloper." For this chapter, however, we will examine the NetBeans Profiler available for free for use with the open-source and freely available NetBeans 5 IDE from Sun Microsystems. As with JMeter, downloading and installing NetBeans and the Profiler are not covered here, but the documentation and binaries are available at **http://www.netbeans.org/**. Once the IDE and the Profiler have been installed, it's time to re-run the JMeter tests, but this time under the Profiler.

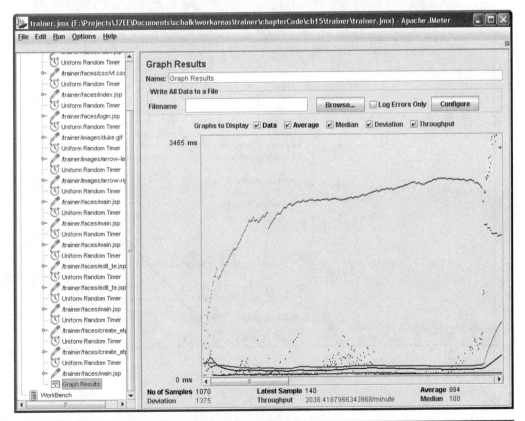

FIGURE 16-6   Graph results from running the JMeter test

If possible, it's a good idea to run the JMeter invocation on another machine on the same LAN as the server, because running JMeter, the Tomcat server, the IDE, and the Profiler all on one machine may be too much to ask of the hardware, and it may skew test results unnecessarily. When running JMeter on another machine, the HTTP Request Defaults node must be modified to include the IP address of the server on your LAN, instead of **localhost** as was used earlier. This is accomplished by selecting the **HTTP Request Defaults** node underneath **Jake's Basic Traversal** and changing the **Server Name or IP** field appropriately. JMeter also provides a very useful feature to drive several computers on a LAN to direct traffic to the same server. This allows load testing at levels that exceed the network capacity of a single host. The details of this exercise are beyond the scope of this section, but this feature is definitely good to know.

With the JMeter task safely relegated to another machine on the LAN, it's time to configure the NetBeans Profiler. Before using the Profiler, a one-time automatic configuration process must be undertaken by choosing Profile | Advanced Commands | Run Profiler Calibration, then selecting the installed JDK to configure. Once calibration is complete, start the server by choosing the **Runtime** tab in the navigator, expanding the **Servers** node, right-clicking the **Bundled Tomcat** node, and choosing **Start in Profile Mode**. Choose **OK** on the dialog that pops up to start the server. The server starts up and waits for the Profiler to attach, as shown next.

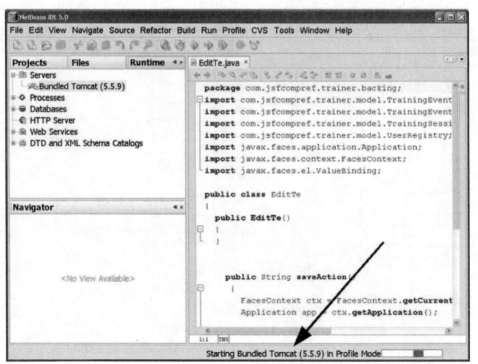

Attach the Profiler by selecting Profile | Attach Profiler from the main menu. A dialog appears that allows you to choose the profiling task. The options are shown in Table 16-1.

We will begin with **Analyze Performance.** To best illustrate this feature, it is necessary to make a CPU-consuming change to a frequently called method in the Virtual Trainer so that the Profiler can show where the problem lies. To do this, add the following code to the **TrainingEventRegistry** constructor.

```
StringBuffer buf = new StringBuffer(1000);
for (int j = 0; j < 20; j++) {
  buf.delete(0, 1000);
  for (int i = 0; i < 1000; i++) {
    buf.append("h");
    String foo = null;
    try {
      foo.length();
    }
    catch (NullPointerException e) {
      foo = e.getMessage();
    }
  }
}
```

Profiling Task	Description
Monitor Application	Provides a window displaying the high-level characteristics of the application as it runs, including heap size, amount of allocated heap space, number of threads, and thread status (running, waiting, and so on).
Analyze Performance	Enables drilling down to a specific class or classes to get performance information about that class, including hotspots.
Analyze Code Fragment Performance	Chooses a particular segment of code to watch. When that code executes, performance data is gathered and shown.
Analyze Memory Usage	Shows statistics on object creation and garbage collection.
Run Custom Profiling	Enables creating and selecting a custom profiling configuration. Useful when the previous configurations do not provide the desired behavior.

TABLE 16-1 Profiling Tasks in the NetBeans Profiler

From the **Attach Profiler** dialog, choose the **Analyze Performance** button. Once this option is selected, change the **Filter** menu option to **Quick Filter...** and the dialog box appears as shown here.

This feature enables only profiling classes from selected packages. In this case, the **Inclusive** filter type is selected and the classes **com.jsfcompref.***, **com.sun.faces.***, **javax.faces.***, **javax.servlet.***, and **com.sun .faces.*** are selected to be profiled. Click **OK** on the **Set Quick Filter** dialog, then choose **Attach** back on the **Attach Profiler** dialog. Once the server has fully started, go over to the JMeter machine and start the tests. It's

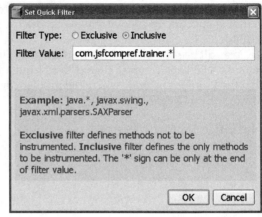

possible to see live results by clicking the **Live Results** button in the **Profiler** tab, but the most useful thing to do is to wait for the JMeter test to complete, then shut the Tomcat server down and allow NetBeans to generate a summary report. The **Combined** tab shows both call stack and method hotspots. Hotspots are places in the code where much time is spent and which may be good targets for optimization. In the following illustration, we have applied a filter to the hotspot view to only show **com.jsfcompref.** classes, revealing that the **TrainingEventRegistry** constructor is the culprit.

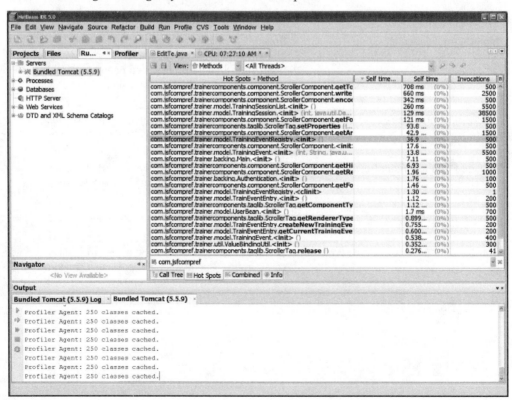

Another useful profiling metric is **Analyze Memory Usage**. This allows the developer to see how many instances of each class are created during the test run of the application. The usage of this metric is self-explanatory and need not be examined further here except to point out that it is very useful.

This section has only given you a taste of load testing and profiling of JSF applications, but it is a starting point from which to launch further learning.

Debugging JSF Applications

As much as one would like to believe otherwise, bugs happen and even test driven development can't prevent bugs from entering the system in all cases. Therefore, debugging JSF applications is an important skill, proficiency at which will save time and money. This section covers two different techniques for debugging JSF applications: *with* a source-level debugger; and *without* using a source-level debugger. Naturally, both methods have appropriate uses and many times both will be used simultaneously. For instructional clarity, the two techniques are covered separately. Non-debugger debugging will be covered first, with specific attention given to the Sun and Apache JSF implementations. Source-level debugging will be covered using Sun Microsystems NetBeans IDE and the Eclipse foundation's Eclipse IDE. There are many other fine IDEs available, but these two were chosen to highlight here due to their popularity and open-source nature. Chapter 17 will cover developing with visual tools in more detail.

Debugging JSF Applications Without a Source-Level Debugger

Of course, the most common approach to non-debugger debugging is the simple print statement inserted liberally throughout the code. This approach has many well-documented problems, including bad style, an inability to select which kinds of messages should be output, a propensity to clutter the code, the possibility of forgetting to remove the statements before shipping to the customer, and a tendency towards having incoherent information spewed to the console, the meaning of which is lost over time. A marginally better approach is to use a logging mechanism. This solves most of the problems of print statement–style debugging but still requires discipline to get the greatest usefulness from the technology. When authoring your JSF application, it's a good idea to take advantage of the logging facilities in the **java.util.logging** package in JDK 1.4 and later or the Jakarta Commons Logging package in cases where the standard logging API cannot be used. The javadocs for **java.util.logging** include some useful guidelines, such as the different classes of consumers of logging information, and the kind of information they consume, as summarized in Table 16-2.

These are only high-level guidelines and are not programmatically enforced in the logging API. It is up to you as to how to apply the logging API to best meet your needs, but keep in mind that once a system gets deployed to the customer, the usage of the logging facility is one of the most valuable aspects of the system and it is well worth your time to learn to use the logger proficiently.

Logging Using the java.util.logging Facility

The Sun JSF 1.1 implementation uses Jakarta Commons Logging because it is targeted to run with a minimum JDK requirement of 1.3. Commons Logging is really just a thin API on top of either the JDK 1.4 (and later) logging, or the **Jakarta Log4J** logging system. The benefit of Commons Logging is that it provides a single API to your application while enabling the underlying logging technology to be swapped out at runtime. For example, when running on JDK 1.3 and earlier, Log4J can be used, but the preferred option is to

Logging Information Consumer	Kind of Information Logged
End User and System Administrator	Global system information, such as resource consumption, database connection status, and Web service interaction status.
Field Service Engineers	Finer-grained information targeted within individual subsystems, requires some knowledge of the implementation itself.
Development Organization	When the Field Service Engineer cannot fix the problem with the available information, the development organization gets involved, and they need even finer-grained information, not intended for use by the end user.
Individual Developers	This is the most fine-grained logging information, intended for an individual developer to understand their own code.

TABLE 16-2 Logging Information Consumers and the Information They Consume

use the JDK 1.4 logging if possible. A brief example of logging with the **java.util.logging** package is shown next.

```
package com.jsfcompref.trainer.model;

import java.util.logging.Level;
import java.util.logging.Logger;

// other imports omitted

public class TrainingEventRegistry {
  // other details omitted...

  private static Logger log = Logger.getLogger("com.jsfcompref",
      "com.jsfcompref.trainer.messages.Resources");

  public TrainingEventRegistry() {
    // populate list
    if (eventlist == null) {
      if (log.isLoggable(Level.FINE)) {
        log.fine("Event list was null - populating TE list");
      }
    }
    // other details omitted
  }
}
```

This example modifies the **TrainingEventRegistry** class, which formerly employed **System.out.println()** to use the JDK 1.4 and later logging API. The **Logger.getLogger()** call uses the two-argument version. The first argument is the name of the logger. This value would be placed in the **logging.properties** file. In this case, the entry would be

```
com.jsfcompref.level = FINE
```

The second argument is the name of a **ResourceBundle**, should localized logging messages be desired. The next interesting call is **log.isLoggable()**. This prevents the logging from being generated unless that specific level (or a level that supercedes that level) is specified by the user. The levels come from constants on the **java.util.logging.Level** class. Valid levels in descending order of verbosity are

- SEVERE (least verbose)
- WARNING
- INFO
- CONFIG
- FINE
- FINER
- FINEST (most verbose)

Finally, the **log.fine( )** call actually outputs the message. The argument to this message is either the literal message string, or a key in the **ResourceBundle** given in the call to **Logger.getLogger( )**.

Logging Using the Jakarta Commons Logging Facility

Repeating the preceding example with commons-logging instead, we have the following:

```
package com.jsfcompref.trainer.model;

import org.apache.commons.logging.Log;
import org.apache.commons.logging.LogFactory;

// other imports omitted

public class TrainingEventRegistry {
  // other details omitted...

  private static final Log log =
     LogFactory.getLog(TrainingEventRegistry.class);

  public TrainingEventRegistry() {
    // populate list
    if (eventlist == null) {
      if (log.isDebugEnabled()) {
        log.debug("Event list was null - populating TE list");
      }
    }
    // other details omitted
  }
}
```

This code is obviously very similar to the **java.util.logging** example except that the **LogFactory** takes a Java class, there are individual **is<Level>Enabled( )** methods rather than the single **isLoggable( )** method, the names of the levels are different, and there are fewer of them. The levels provided by Jakarta Commons Logging are

- fatal (least verbose)
- error
- warn

- info

- debug

- trace (most verbose)

Configuring the Sun JSF 1.1 Implementation to Use Log4J

The main problem with Log4J over **java.util.logging** is the difficulty of its configuration. One must place the proper jars in the classpath, and properly define the location and content of the configuration file to get everything working. The following steps worked with Tomcat.

1. Bundle **commons-logging.jar** version 1.0.4 and **log4j-1.2.12.jar** into your application's **WEB-INF/lib** directory.

2. Prepend the **commons-logging.jar** to the **bootclasspath** and tell commons-logging to use Log4J by setting the **JAVA_OPTS** environment variable to something like the following:

```
"-Xbootclasspath/p:D:\Files_2k\commons-
logging-1.0.4\commons-logging.jar
-Dorg.apache.commons.logging.Log=org.apache.
commons.logging.impl.Log4JLogger"
```

3. Tell Log4J where its configuration file is by setting the **CATALINA_OPTS** environment variable to something like this:

```
-Dlog4j.configuration=
file:d:/Projects/J2EE/trainer/chapterCode/ch15/
trainer/log4j.properties
```

4. Fill out the **log4j.properties** with sensible debug scoping information. Please consult the Log4J documentation for details at **http://logging.apache.org/log4j/ docs/manual.html**. The following configuration causes all log messages from the Sun Implementation to be sent to a file.

```
# Set the root logger to only show "FATAL" errors, and declare
# a logger called JSF
log4j.rootLogger=FATAL, JSF

# Set the JSF logger to use the File Appender and tell it the file
# to which it should append.
log4j.appender.JSF=org.apache.log4j.FileAppender
log4j.appender.JSF.File=d:/Projects/trainer/chapterCode/
ch15/trainer/trainer.log
# Use one of many layout options. This is required
log4j.appender.JSF.layout=org.apache.log4j.PatternLayout
log4j.appender.JSF.layout.ConversionPattern=%-4r %-5p [%t] %37c %3x - %m%n

# Output all log messages for the sun JSF impl.

log4j.logger.com.sun.faces=DEBUG
```

The most useful line in this config file is the last one. It tells Log4J, and commons-logging, to only output messages originating from the Sun JSF implementation. The syntax of this line is a bit confusing. The first part, **log4j.logger.**, says that this is a logger declaration. The part after **log4j.logger.**, but before the **=**, is a Java package or class on which logging information should be output. After the **=** comes the level declaration. When writing code, the developer must attach a level to each logging statement that represents the granularity of the statement being logged. Valid levels are **DEBUG, INFO, WARN, ERROR**, and **FATAL**. Generally these levels correspond to decreasing amounts of verbosity. For example, turning on the **DEBUG** level will produce the most copious and verbose output, while turning on the **FATAL** level will only produce logging in the case of a fatal error (provided that the developer adhered to logging best practices when writing logging statements).

Configuring the Sun JSF 1.1 Implementation to Use JDK Logging

When using JDK 1.4 and later, it is preferred to use the Java platform standard debugging system over Log4J. The configuration is very similar and can be affected with the following steps.

1. Edit **$JRE_HOME/lib/logging.properties** and add the following lines:

```
com.sun.faces.level = ALL
javax.faces.level = ALL
```

2. Modify the **CATALINA_OPTS** environment variable to ensure commons-logging is used with the **Jdk14Logger**:

```
-Dorg.apache.commons.logging.Log=
org.apache.commons.logging.impl.Jdk14Logger
```

As with Log4J, the logging output can be redirected to a file and filtered to specific Java packages and classes.

JSF 1.2 TIP *With JSF 1.2, commons-logging is no longer used since the minimum required JDK is 1.5, which includes the standard JDK logging API. Therefore, step 2 shown earlier is not necessary with JSF 1.2.*

Logging Classes in the Sun JSF Implementation

Table 16-3 lists the classes and packages with useful logging information in the Sun JSF 1.1 implementation.

Class Relative to com.sun.faces	Kind of Logging Information
application.ActionListenerImpl	Prints out the component ID for the action being processed
application.ApplicationAssociate	Managed Bean Lifecycle Information
application.ApplicationImpl	Property information for application-scoped classes
application.NavigationHandlerImpl	Gives insight into navigation
application.StateManagerImpl	State management
application.ViewHandlerImpl	Related to rendering the view; useful for debugging path mapping issues
config	Reading **faces-config.xml** files
el	EL evaluation
lifecycle	Traversal through the request processing lifecycle
renderkit	The rendering process

TABLE 16-3   Logging-Enabled Classes and Packages in the Sun JSF 1.1 and 1.2 Implementation

Class Name	Actions or Type of Logging Information
javax.faces.webapp.FacesServlet	High-level lifecycle events
org.apache.myfaces.application.ApplicationImpl	Property set null checking messages
org.apache.myfaces.application.jsp.JspStateManagerImpl	Serialization status
org.apache.myfaces.application.jsp.JspViewHandlerImpl	Mapping information
org.apache.myfaces.application.NavigationHandlerImpl	Navigation logging
org.apache.myfaces.config.FacesConfigurator	Resource loading
org.apache.myfaces.context.portlet.PortletExternalContextImpl	Print out the content character encoding
org.apache.myfaces.context.servlet.ServletExternalContextImpl	Print out the content character encoding
org.apache.myfaces.el	EL messages
org.apache.myfaces.lifecycle.LifecycleImpl	Print out messages as the lifecycle is traversed
org.apache.myfaces.portlet.MyFacesGenericPortlet	Lifecycle status
org.apache.myfaces.util.bundle.BundleUtils	Warn when a resource isn't found
org.apache.myfaces.util	Messages relating to utility classes, including the **DebugUtil** class

TABLE 16-4   Logging-Enabled Classes and Packages in the Apache MyFaces JSF 1.1 Implementation

Logging Classes in the Apache MyFaces Implementation

The Apache MyFaces implementation also uses commons-logging, and offers the logging-enabled classes shown in Table 16-4.

Additional Non-Debugger Debugging Techniques for JSF Applications

The **PhaseListener** interface can be used to produce phase-specific debugging information. This approach has the advantage that the listener can be removed from the system when no longer needed simply by removing the **phase-listener** declaration in the **faces-config.xml** file. Implementing and installing a **PhaseListener** was covered in Chapter 12 but another example is shown here which you will find particularly useful when debugging: a **PrintTreePhaseListener**. This class prints out the view hierarchy from the **UIViewRoot**.

```
package com.sun.faces.systest.model;

import javax.faces.event.PhaseListener;
import javax.faces.event.PhaseId;
import javax.faces.event.PhaseEvent;

import com.sun.faces.util.DebugUtil;
import javax.faces.context.FacesContext;

public class PrintTreePhaseListener extends Object implements PhaseListener {
```

```
public void afterPhase(PhaseEvent event) {
  DebugUtil.printTree(FacesContext.getCurrentInstance().getViewRoot(),
                      System.out);
}

public void beforePhase(PhaseEvent event) {

}

public PhaseId getPhaseId() {
  return PhaseId.ANY_PHASE;
}
}
```

This class simply makes use of the **DebugUtil** class in the Sun implementation, which currently only has one useful method, **printTree()**. The first argument is the **UIComponent** from which to start printing, and the second is a **PrintStream** to which the tree should be printed.

The MyFaces implementation also has a **DebugUtils** class which has a **printView()** method that takes exactly the same arguments as the Sun **printTree()** but has been refactored to expose its individual helper methods **printComponent()** and **printAttribute()**. A **traceView()** method is also provided that only takes the action of calling **printTree()** if **log.isTraceEnabled()**.

Source-Level Debugging with Eclipse

This section is a tutorial on how to debug the Virtual Trainer application running on top of the Sun JSF implementation using the Eclipse IDE. It was written with version 3.1 of the Eclipse SDK, which can be downloaded from **http://www.eclipse.org/**. Let's assume the Virtual Trainer, Eclipse, and version 1.1 of the Sun JSF implementation are all installed and properly configured. We choose version 1.1 of the Sun JSF implementation because not every developer has the latitude to use JDK 1.5, which is required for JSF 1.2

We begin by building a project to host the Sun JSF implementation. Choose File | New | Project. Select the **Java Project** node and choose **Next**. In the **Project Name** field, enter **sun-jsf-1.1** and click **Next**. In the **Java Settings** window, highlight the **sun-jsf-1.1** node and click the **Link Additional Source to Project** button as shown in Figure 16-7.

Click the **Browse...** button next to the **Linked Folder Location** field and browse through the file system to the **javaserverfaces-sources/jsf-api/src** directory inside your JSF 1.1 implementation, then click **OK**. You may receive a **Source Folder Added** message dialog saying "To avoid overlapping, the project is removed as source folder..." Just click **OK** in this dialog. In the **Folder Name** field, rename this to **jsf-api**, instead of the default of **src**. Select the **sun-jsf-1.1** node again and do the same for the **javaserverfaces-sources/jsf-ri/src** directory, setting the **Folder Name** to **jsf-impl**. When both **jsf-api** and **jsf-impl** folders have been added, click **Finish**.

Perform the same steps to create a project for the Virtual Trainer sample application, making sure to add the sources for the **chapterCode/ch15/trainer/src/java** directory. Name the project **trainer**. When the **sun-jsf-1.1** and **trainer** projects have been created, the Eclipse IDE should look like Figure 16-8.

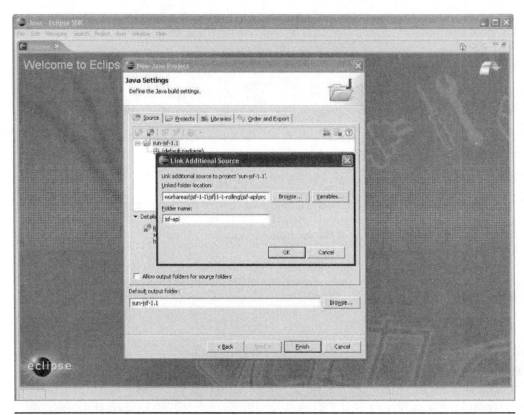

FIGURE 16-7 The Eclipse Java Settings Wizard page

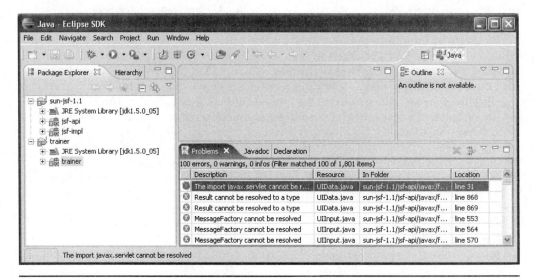

FIGURE 16-8 The Eclipse IDE with the **sun-jsf-1.1** and **trainer** projects opened

The final step in the process is linking the two projects together so breakpoints can be found, and then setting the breakpoints. Right-click the **trainer** node and choose the **Properties** item. Select the **Projects** tab and click the **Add** button. Select the **sun-jsf-1.1** node and click **OK**. We will set two breakpoints, one in the core JSF implementation, and the other in the trainer application. We will then demonstrate that these breakpoints get hit and allow the full range of debugging features of the NetBeans IDE. Expand the tree view in the upper left of the UI to show **sun-jsf-1.1 | jsf-impl | com.sun.faces.lifecycle | LifecycleImpl .java**. Double-click this node and the source file will be shown in the IDE. Look at the **Outline** tab panel in the right of the IDE. This shows the classes in the **LifecycleImpl** class. Double-click the **render()** method and the IDE will show that method. Place the cursor on the

```
if (context == null)
```

line, and choose Run | Toggle Line Breakpoint from the main menu. This sets a breakpoint on the current line.

Go through the same steps to set a breakpoint on the

```
if (eventlist == null)
```

line in the **TrainingEventRegistry** constructor by choosing **trainer | ch15 | com.jsfcompref .trainer.model | TrainingEventRegistry**.

You are now ready to run Tomcat and attach the debugger. Set the **JPDA_TRANSPORT** environment variable to be **dt_socket** and start Tomcat with the command **catalina jpda run**. Look in the console output of the server for the line **Listening for transport dt_socket at address:** and write down the port number. Back in the Eclipse IDE, choose Run | Debug… from the main menu. The **Create, Manage, and Run Configurations** dialog appears. In the **Configurations** panel, select **Remote Java Application** and click the **New** button below the **Configurations** panel. In the **Project** field, enter something like **trainer** and in the **Port** field enter the port noted earlier and press the **Apply** and then **Debug** buttons. An **Errors in Project** dialog may appear. Choose **YES**.

Go to the browser and visit **http://localhost:8080/trainer/**. The **LifecycleImpl.render()** breakpoint will be hit. Remove the breakpoint by selecting the source code line in the debugger editor and choosing Run | Toggle Line Breakpoint. Then choose Run | Resume from the main menu. As you browse through the application, eventually the **TrainerEventRegistry** constructor breakpoint will be hit. Remove this breakpoint and resume.

This may not seem like much, but the ability to debug anywhere in your application, and also into the underlying JSF implementation, is very useful and can get you past many of the hurdles you will encounter.

Source-Level Debugging with NetBeans

This section takes a brief look at how to use the NetBeans 5 IDE from Sun Microsystems to debug the Virtual Trainer application. For contrast with the previous example in Eclipse, we'll use the Apache MyFaces 1.1.1 implementation as our JSF runtime and demonstrate debugging into the MyFaces source code, as well as the Virtual Trainer source code. NetBeans 5 can be obtained from **http://www.netbeans.org/** and MyFaces 1.1.1 can be obtained from **http://myfaces.apache.org/**.

The online code for the book shows how to configure the build environment to use the MyFaces implementation instead of the Sun JSF implementation to build the Virtual Trainer.

Assuming NetBeans 5, MyFaces 1.1.1 source and binary, and the **trainer.war** with MyFaces bundled in are all installed and ready to go, let's continue.

The first step is to build a NetBeans project around the MyFaces source code. Start up NetBeans 5 and choose File | New Project… from the main menu. In the **Categories** panel, select **General** and in the **Projects** panel choose **Java Project with Existing Sources**, then click the **Next** button. On the **Name and Location** wizard page, enter **myfaces-1.1.1** into the **Name** field and create a new directory, entering its value into the **Project Folder** field. Make sure the **Set as Main Project** box is not checked. Click **Next**.

This next step, **Existing Sources**, is where you define to NetBeans the source directories of the MyFaces project. In the **Source Package Folders** area, click **Add Folder** and add each of the directories shown in the following window. Of course, the location on your hard disk of the **myfaces-1.1.1-src** directory will most likely differ from that shown in the image.

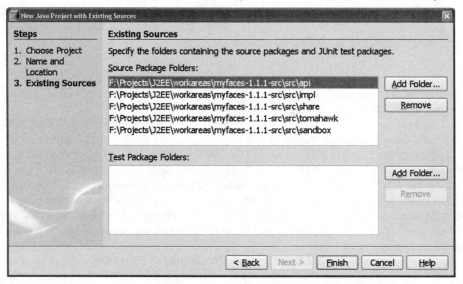

Note that each of these directories is the super-directory of a top-level directory tree for java source files. For example, inside the **myfaces-1.1.1-src\impl** directory are **javax** and **org** directories. It is very important that the directories in the **Source Package Folders** list all are direct super-directories of the top-of-class hierarchy. If this is not the case, you will be unable to set breakpoints and step into code. Once all the directories have been added, click **Finish**. Follow the same steps to create a new project for the Virtual Trainer application, mounting the source directories as appropriate for this chapter.

Now that the trainer and myfaces projects are open inside of NetBeans, you are ready to set some breakpoints, one in the myfaces source code, the other in the Virtual Trainer application. In the upper-left corner of the NetBeans IDE, you will see a tab panel showing different views on the currently opened projects.

- The **Projects** tab shows a logical view of your project. This view understands concepts such as Java packages and classes, Web pages, and other programmatic concepts.

- The **Files** tab shows the physical file system view of the project.

- The **Runtime** tab allows you to control the embedded HTTP server, among other development container options.

- If you have installed the profiler as discussed previously in the chapter, you will see a **Profiler** tab that allows you to control the profiler.

The IDE is shown in the following illustration.

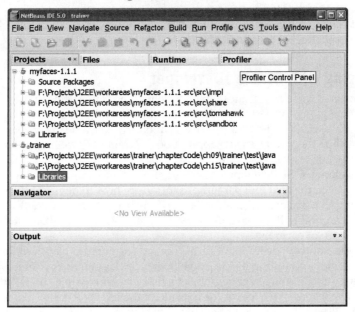

Open the **myfaces** node in the tree view in the **Projects** tab and expand it to show the **org.apache.myfaces.lifecycle.LifecycleImpl.java** node inside the **myfaces-1.1.1-src\ impl** directory. Select the **LifecycleImpl.java** node. The **Navigator** window, below the **Projects** tab, shows the methods in that class. Double-click the **render()** method and the source code opens up to that method. Put the cursor on the **isResponseComplete()** line and right-click and choose **Toggle Breakpoint** from the pop-up menu.

Return to the **Projects** tab and open up the **trainer** project and expand the view to select the **com.jsfcompref.trainer.model.TrainingEventRegistry.java** file. Double-click the constructor for that class in the Navigator and set a breakpoint on the following line.

```
if (eventlist == null) {
```

You are now ready to run the server and test the application. Go to the **Runtime** tab and expand the **Servers** node to select the **Bundled Tomcat** node. Right-click this node and choose **Properties**. In the **Server Manager** dialog, choose the **Startup** tab. Look at the **Debugger Transport** section. If you are using Windows, you'll want to choose the **Shared Memory Name** radio button, filling in a simple string in the text field, such as **jdbconn**. Otherwise, the shared memory debugging transport is unavailable and you'll have to take note of the socket port. Click **Close** and return to the **Runtime** tab. Right-click the **Bundled Tomcat** node and this time choose **Start in Debug Mode.** The server will start up. Make sure Virtual Trainer is installed using the usual Tomcat webapp installation methods. From the main menu choose Run | Attach Debugger and click **OK**. Go to a browser and browse to Virtual Trainer—for example, at **http://localhost:8080/trainer/**. The breakpoint in **LifecycleImpl.render()** should be hit, and show up as green in the debugger.

At this point, you can mouse over variables and see their values, and many more options are available from the Window | Debugging menu. Please consult the NetBeans documentation to discover the full power of the NetBeans debugger. Right-click the line with the breakpoint and choose **Toggle Breakpoint**. This will remove the current breakpoint. From the Run menu, choose Continue. Go back to the browser, log in as userid **jake** password "jake", and press the **login** button. You will now hit the second breakpoint, in the **TrainingEventRegistry** constructor.

JSF JSP Debugging with Oracle JDeveloper

One of the benefits of using an advanced IDE for debugging is that some of them even have the ability to offer debugging support throughout the entire lifecycle of a running Web application including both JSP execution and Java source execution. We conclude the chapter with a brief look at how to debug the Virtual Trainer application JSP content as well as Java source using Oracle JDeveloper 10*g*.

Oracle JDeveloper's JSF development experience will be examined in more detail in Chapter 17; however, the next few paragraphs introduce how to debug both JSP and Java source code using an advanced JSF-enabled Java IDE such as JDeveloper. NetBeans, JavaStudio Creator, Eclipse, and other IDEs have this capability, but we focus on JDeveloper here to increase the breadth of coverage.

We'll forgo the source code importation aspect and assume you have a running version of the Virtual Trainer application inside JDeveloper's development environment. Since JDeveloper supports JSP source debugging, let's first mark a few lines in the **edit_te.jsp** (Edit Training Event) page by clicking the left side of the JSP code editor to insert a few breakpoints. As Figure 16-9 shows, notice that JDeveloper's visual JSP editor also shows the page in its runtime appearance.

By inserting breakpoints in the JSP source code, at runtime, the execution of the JSP will halt at the line specified and allow for full inspection of all runtime variables. After inserting JSP breakpoints, you can switch to the Java code editor and, in the same fashion, insert breakpoints in the **EditTe.java** class which serves as a backing bean to the **edit_te.jsp** page. (See Figure 16-10.)

Now that debug points have been put in both JSP and Java source, you can start the application in debug mode. This will launch JDeveloper's internal J2EE server (OC4J) and invoke a browser to access the application. After you log in to the application and then click one of the **Edit** links for a specific Training Event, the debugger will halt execution and JDeveloper will return to the forefront and display the source in debug mode. At this point, you can step through the lines of the JSP line by line or resume execution until the next debug point. While the application is halted, you can inspect all the application's objects in memory at this current moment using the debugger's various windows. (See Figure 16-11.) Of most use is the Smart Data debugger window. It provides the developer with a live view of the most pertinent application data at runtime. The other debugger windows are useful, as well as the call Stack window, which shows the call stack for the current thread.

For this run-through, click the **Resume** button to continue rendering the page in the browser. At this point, the focus is back on the browser and you can change a value in the Edit Training Event form, such as the status or the online trainer advisor, and then click the **Update** button. As the action method in the **EditTe.java** backing bean executes, it will again halt at the second debug point, as shown in Figure 16-12.

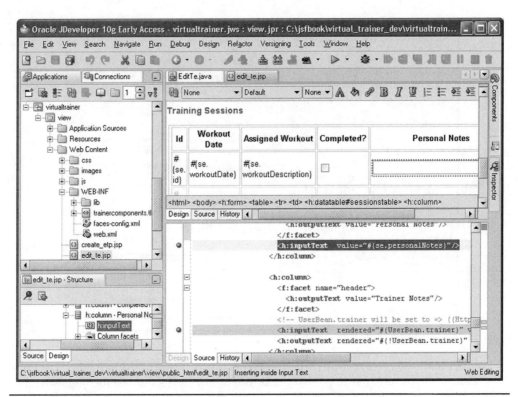

FIGURE 16-9   Inserting JSP breakpoints in JDeveloper

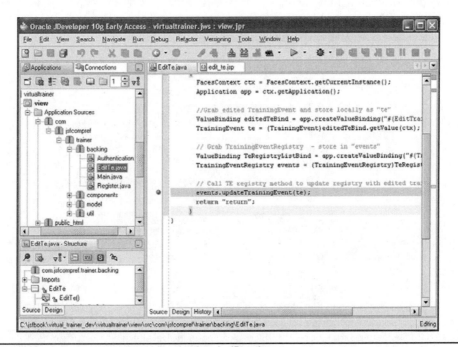

FIGURE 16-10   Inserting Java source breakpoints in JDeveloper

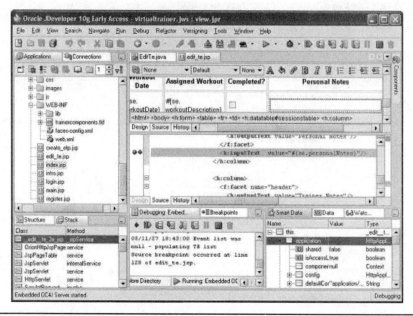

FIGURE 16-11   Debugging a JSF JSP in JDeveloper

At this point, you can drill down into the **events.updateTrainingEvent** method (or any other method) by clicking the Step Into button. You can step back out of a method using the Step Out button of the debugger. You might want to experiment with these features a bit more on your own before moving on.

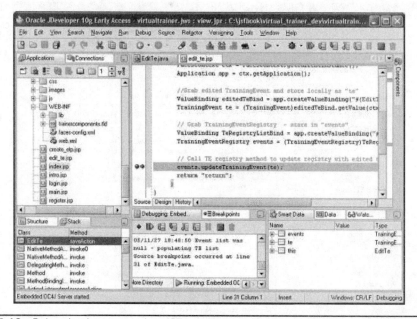

FIGURE 16-12   Debugging Java source in a JSF backing bean in JDeveloper

JavaServer Faces Tools and Libraries

IV PART

CHAPTER 17
Developing JSF Applications with Visual Development Environments

CHAPTER 18
The JavaServer Faces Configuration File

CHAPTER 19
The Standard JSF Component Library

CHAPTER 20
The MyFaces Implementation and Component Library

Developing JSF Applications with Visual Development Environments

Given the strong tools and development support offered by multiple vendors, it is easy to think that JSF *requires* a visual Integrated Development Environment (IDE) to be used successfully. This, however, is a misconception. As explained in Chapter 2, it is relatively easy to download and set up a JSF development environment without the use of an IDE. On the other hand, the JSF development experience can be substantially enhanced through the use of an IDE. For this reason, several top-notch Faces-enabled IDEs are examined here. The key strengths of these development environments tend to lie in the following areas:

- **Visual design of JSF pages**   This allows the Faces developer to visually design pages using an editor that provides an approximation of the runtime view of the pages during development.

- **Visual design of the navigation model**   A visual navigation model design tool, or page flow editor, allows the developer to visually design the navigation model of the application by drawing lines and connecting pages as opposed to just editing the **faces-config.xml** file directly.

- **Visual databinding**   This feature allows the developer to associate UI components with data objects in a visual manner.

- **Productive code generation**   These features improve the productivity of the Faces developer by automatically generating certain pieces of code, such as backing beans.

- **Other productivity features**   Such as an enhanced **faces-config.xml** console editor.

The remainder of this chapter examines several of the most popular JSF-enabled development environments. These include

- Sun Java Studio Creator
- BEA Workshop Studio

- Oracle JDeveloper 10*g*
- IBM Rational Web Developer
- Exadel Studio Pro

To show how each development environment compares with the others, a simple Faces application will be built in all of them, with a focus towards addressing the aforementioned key areas. In certain cases, special attention will be given to features that showcase some of the product's unique strengths.

The Application

The example application to be built in the different development environments is a subset of the Virtual Trainer application introduced in Chapter 9. In this version, a welcome page (**welcome.jsp**) provides a navigation to a login page (**login.jsp**), which checks a user's credentials. A successful login will forward to a destination page (**table.jsp**) where tabular data is displayed. This is depicted in Figure 17-1.

To build this application, several Java classes will be made available to each JSF IDE. These include

- **TrainingEvent.java**   Represents a single object or row of a Virtual Trainer training event. The properties include the event name, event type completion date, and so on.

- **TrainingEvents.java**   Has a property of type **List** that contains **TrainingEvent** objects.

- **TrainingEventsLogin.java**   Contains code to authenticate a user by checking **userid** and **password** properties in an action method.

In addition to the Java classes, master-detail database tables (**trainingevents** and **trainingsessions**) that contain similar training event and workout session data are also available for building user interfaces that interact with a backend database. Two files that help define the look and feel (**vt.css** and **vtlogo.jpg**) are also provided for this simple application.

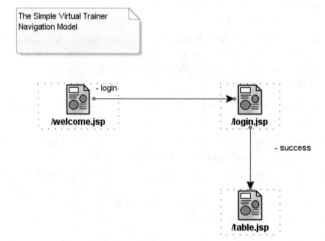

FIGURE 17-1   The simplified Virtual Trainer application

Sun Java Studio Creator

We begin our look at JSF IDEs with Sun Java Studio Creator. Java Studio Creator is Sun's effort to provide a JSF-centric development environment that provides a productive, visual development experience not unlike Microsoft Visual Basic or Visual Studio, without abandoning the most common Java development features you'd expect with any Java IDE. At the time of this writing, the current version of Studio Creator is 2.0, which is easily downloadable using your free Sun Developer Network account. Once installed, it occupies approximately 600 megabytes on the file system. Further details on Java Studio Creator can be found at **http://www.sun.com/software/products/jscreator/**.

Getting Familiar with Java Studio Creator

As you first start Studio Creator, you'll notice the wide variety of tutorials and samples accessible. You'll also notice that a bundled PointBase database is available, which makes the samples ready to run. To learn the basics of Studio Creator, you can definitely make use of these tutorials and samples. For our purposes, though, we'll create a new Web Project from scratch.

Creating a New JSF Web Project

After completing the New JSF Web Project Wizard, which allows for the selection of project name, location, and default Java package, you'll notice that the file system has a new empty JSF Web project that contains the following:

- **page1.jsp**   An initial starter JSF-enabled JSP document (XML) with starter code. This empty page comes preloaded with taglib directives for the JSF core, standard, and Sun's default Web UI component library.

- **resources/**   A subdirectory with a starter **stylesheet.css**.

- **WEB-INF/**   A subdirectory with a **web.xml** file that defines **faces-config.xml** with delegate files for the navigation model (**navigation.xml**) and for the managed beans (**managed-beans.xml**). The **web.xml** file also comes preloaded with several additional entries for use with Sun's default Web UI component library. These include a file upload (**FileUpload**) filter, **ExceptionHandler** servlet, and a **ThemeServlet**.

- **sun-web.xml**   An additional configuration file for use with Sun's default Web UI components.

In addition to the extra items provided in the Web root directory, Studio Creator also creates several JavaBeans. Three are general-purpose beans registered with the different Faces scope settings as denoted by their names: **RequestBean1.java**, **SessionBean1.java**, and **ApplicationBean1.java**. A backing bean called **Page1.java** is also created. It serves as the event handler for the JSP page **Page1.jsp** and has declared UI component instances for Sun's UI component's **com.sun.rave.web.ui.component.Body**, **Form**, **Head**, **Html**, **Link**, and **Page**. In general, Studio Creator tightly couples every page with a backing bean Java class, which handles all the user interface events from the page and provides the page with data access to external sources.

A quick inspection of the initial **Page1.jsp** (or any new JSP page) reveals that Creator uses a JSP (XML) document along with a combination of the Standard components and Sun's default UI component library, as shown next:

```
<?xml version="1.0" encoding="UTF-8"?>
<jsp:root version="1.2"
    xmlns:f="http://java.sun.com/jsf/core"
    xmlns:h="http://java.sun.com/jsf/html"
    xmlns:jsp="http://java.sun.com/JSP/Page"
    xmlns:ui="http://www.sun.com/web/ui">
  <jsp:directive.page contentType="text/html;charset=UTF-8"
    pageEncoding="UTF-8"/>
  <f:view>
    <ui:page binding="#{Page1.page1}" id="page1">
      <ui:html binding="#{Page1.html1}" id="html1">
        <ui:head binding="#{Page1.head1}" id="head1">
          <ui:link binding="#{Page1.link1}" id="link1"
                   url="/resources/stylesheet.css"/>
        </ui:head>
        <ui:body binding="#{Page1.body1}" id="body1"
              style="-rave-layout: grid">
          <ui:form binding="#{Page1.form1}" id="form1"/>
        </ui:body>
      </ui:html>
    </ui:page>
  </f:view>
</jsp:root>
```

The Design Environment

As shown in Figure 17-2, after creating a new project, you'll notice that the visual design editor is shown in *grid layout* mode. Studio Creator is unique in this regard in that it defaults to a grid layout, which means that the editor supports *absolute positioning* of the components on the page. Grid layout and absolute positioning is achieved through usage of CSS styles defining position information for each component on the page. This differs from the more common flow layout that Web applications or HTML, in general, uses as a default.

Creator's designer also has the option of switching to a more traditional flow layout by toggling the **page-layout** property in the properties editor for the overall page. Changing this property modifies the **style** attribute Sun's **body** component, as shown next:

```
<ui:body binding="#{Page1.body1}" id="body1" style="-rave-layout: grid">
```

A noticeable change seen when you switch to flow layout is that a cursor appears and the visual editor then accepts typing directly onto the canvas.

At the top of the visual editor, you'll notice three button toggles for switching from Design, JSP, and Java, as shown here. Clicking Java will open the provided backing bean in a Java source editor.

Clicking the JSP toggle switches to a color-highlighted JSP source code editor, which provides JSP code completion along with

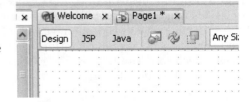

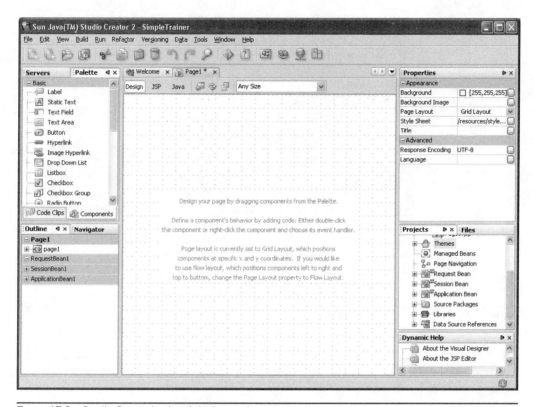

FIGURE 17-2   Studio Creator's visual design environment

collapsible code regions (referred to in Sun's documentation as *code folding*). The JSP code editor also provides a very helpful *tag completion* feature, shown in Figure 17-3, where matching tags appear in a menu after typing the initial characters. In addition to tag completion, there is also *tag attribute completion* where after a tag has been typed, a list of attributes appears in a menu. Creator even provides a help window below on the selected attribute.

Creator's Java source code editor is also feature-rich with code folding, code completion, syntax coloration, automatic error detection, and several refactoring options.

Building the Simple Virtual Trainer Application in Studio Creator

To start building the simplified version of the Virtual Trainer application, a new welcome page (**welcome.jsp**) is created. For this page, we will use Creator's default **grid** layout with absolute positioning. To build the banner portion of the welcome page, we'll use Creator's default set of UI components (although the Standard components are also available on the Palette). For the image, we use **<ui:image>**, and for the banner text, a **<ui:staticText>** component. Since the default **grid** layout has been applied, the components have their style attribute set to define their location on the page:

```
<ui:image binding="#{welcome.image1}" id="image1" style="left: 24px; top: 24px;
position: absolute" url="/resources/vtlogo.jpg"/>
```

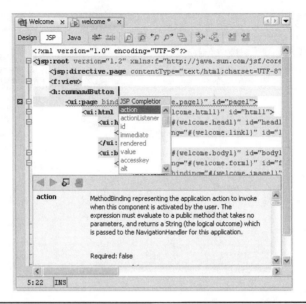

FIGURE 17-3   Studio Creator's JSP code editor

Notice also that the **binding** attribute is set to an auto-generated **image1** component of type import **com.sun.rave.web.ui.component.ImageComponent**, which is declared in the backing bean (**Welcome.java**), as shown next:

```
private ImageComponent image1 = new ImageComponent();
```

This illustrates a very important feature to be aware of: when any UI component is dropped onto the page, it will automatically have its **binding** attribute set to a component declaration that is automatically generated in the backing bean for the page. Studio Creator prefers to manage these components and even places warnings against modifying the Creator-managed code in the generated code.

Building the Navigation Model

To productively build the Faces navigation model, there is a Faces *Page Navigation* page flow design view (shown in Figure 17-4). With this view, you can design the overall application navigation model as well as create new pages. From the Page Navigation window, you can create the entire navigation model as well as starter pages (**login.jsp** and **table.jsp**). To create a new page in the Page Navigation window, right-click the diagram and select **New Page...**

Creating navigation rules is simply a matter of dragging lines from one page to another. The navigation view also offers a Source toggle button, which allows direct editing of the navigation model using an XML editor. To quickly edit the new login page, you can double-click the page in the navigation view and jump to the JSP editor.

To build the login form shown in Figure 17-5 on the page, we will use a standard **<h:panelGrid>** component to contain two Sun **<ui:label>** components, along with input components: **<ui:textField>** and a **<ui:passwordField>**. To complete the page, a **<ui:button>** tag is added to the page to allow the form to be submitted. A **<ui:messageGroup>** tag, which renders any system/error messages, is also added.

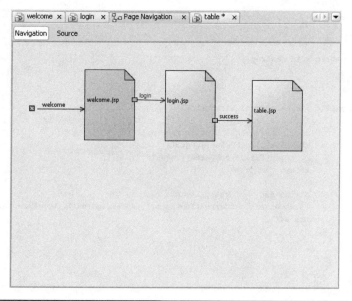

FIGURE 17-4   The Studio Creator page flow navigator

A nice feature in the visual editor is that when the button is double-clicked, an action method is auto-generated and bound to the button. As shown in Figure 17-6, you are then placed inside of the auto-generated action method. This behavior is reminiscent of Microsoft's Visual Basic or Visual Studio. For our application, double-click the button and add the simple login code. After manual editing, the completed method checks the values of the two input UI components and returns "success" if they both equal "jake".

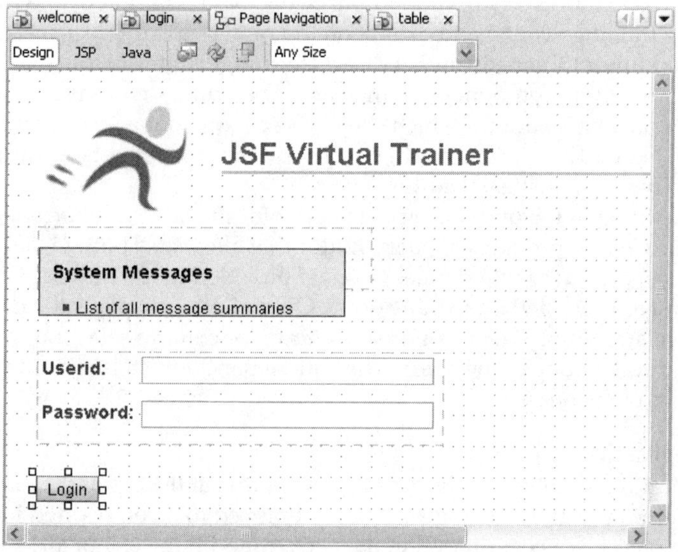

FIGURE 17-5   The Simple Virtual Trainer's login page in Studio Creator

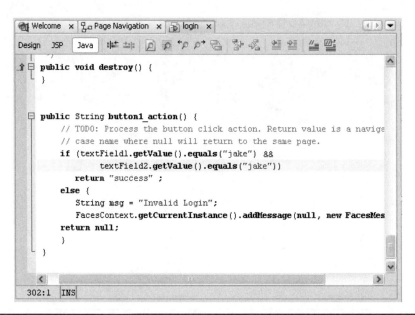

FIGURE 17-6 Creating an action method that's bound to a button in Studio Creator

Since Studio Creator is based on Sun's more general-purpose Java IDE, NetBeans, it has a high-quality Java source code editor with code completion capabilities that include collapsible code regions (also known as code folding).

To build the **table.jsp** page, we'll opt for using Sun's more advanced **<ui:table>** to display the training event data. As the **<ui:table>** component is dropped onto the page, it will render in a generic, non-databound form. Then we'll open the Servers window, which has a registry of Data Sources where connections to databases are stored, and drag a database table (containing training events) and drop it on top of the **<ui:table>**. This action creates a usable **javax.sql.rowset.CachedRowSet** object (**trainingeventsRowSet**) and makes it available to the **<ui:table>** component on the page. The **<ui:table>** rendered in the visual editor then takes on an appearance which shows the column data-types of the actual data. This is shown in Figure 17-7. At this point, we can edit the generated table directly, removing or reordering columns in the visual editor.

If any extra editing of the underlying data object for the table (*trainingeventsRowSet*) is needed, Studio Creator provides a Query Editor that allows for both visual and direct editing of the database query that defines the data provided to the RowSet data object.

As shown in Figure 17-8, the top pane of the Query Editor displays the database tables as well as their relationships. The second pane allows for column selection, while the third pane allows for direct editing of the query. The bottom pane (which is currently empty) will display the results of the query.

Running the Application

To run the application, simply click the green arrow button at the top of the main menu. This makes sure that the application is compiled and deployed to an embedded instance of the Sun application server, which is started in the background if it was not already started. When the application has been successfully deployed to the server, a browser will appear

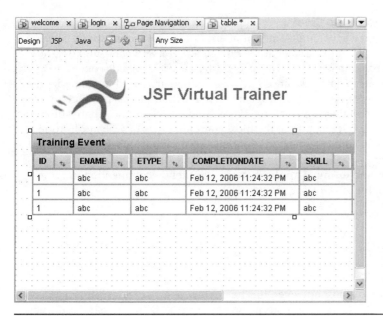

FIGURE 17-7   Databinding the **<ui:table>** component

and the default start page will show in the browser. The initial **page1.jsp** is set as the default start page, but you can reset it to any page you want by selecting it in the projects view window and then right-clicking it and selecting Set as Start Page. To run the application in debug mode, choose Run | Debug from the main menu. This will shut down the server (if running) and restart it in debug mode.

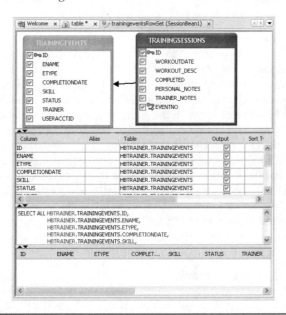

FIGURE 17-8   Java Studio Creator's Query Editor

Final Observations with Java Studio Creator

It is obvious that Sun has put a substantial amount of effort into Studio Creator by offering many extra features, especially in the area of auto-code generation and choosing to tightly couple its JSP pages with backing beans as well as the three clearly defined scope-managed beans for managing application data. Advanced Java developers may find the high degree of code generation a little excessive, but Sun appears to be positioning this product more to new JSF developers who are coming from a Visual Basic/Studio background where automatic code generation enables very fast creation of the most common types of Web application artifacts. Finally, this example application exercise of building a simple login and databound table application is really just scratching the surface of the features in Studio Creator. Stepping through its many tutorials and example applications is definitely recommended to get a better overall feel for what Studio Creator provides.

BEA Workshop Studio

In late 2005, BEA acquired the M7 corporation along with its Eclipse-based NitroX development tools. The NitroX tool family has since been renamed to *BEA Workshop* and includes the tools *Workshop for JSF* and *Workshop Studio*. Both of these tools offer visual design support for JSF applications; however, for this review, just Workshop Studio will be used. Further details on BEA Workshop Studio and the overall BEA Workshop product family can be found at **http://www.bea.com**.

Getting Familiar with BEA Workshop Studio

Downloading a 15-day trial version of BEA Workshop Studio is very easy. At the time of this writing, the current version of Workshop Studio was 3.0. It offers a full version 120-megabyte download, which includes the Eclipse IDE, or just the Workshop Studio plug-in, which is only 80MB. When installing the full version, it will occupy less than 200MB, which makes it have one of the smallest footprints of all the JSF IDEs available.

Creating a New Web Project

Creating a new Web Application Project in Workshop Studio provides options that allow the user to specify the JSP version (1.2 or 2.0), whether or not you want to use Enterprise JavaBeans version 3.0, as well as whether or not the project will use Hibernate. In contrast to Studio Creator, once a project is created, the files created are fairly minimal. There is, of course, a **web.xml** file configured with the Faces servlet. There are also some MyFaces configuration entries since MyFaces is one of the default component libraries available out of the box with BEA Workshop Studio. An initial page, **index.jsp**, is provided by default and it simply has a JSP forward pointing to another auto-created page, **/pages/welcome.jsp**. The intention being that the location of all JSF pages should be placed under the **/page** directory, which is actually good coding style especially when establishing security that is based on directory structure. Another nice feature is the resource bundle properties file that is created and added to the project. In fact, the **welcome.jsp** has several **outputText** components that refer to resources in the bundle. For persistence support, checking the Hibernate Support checkbox will provide a starter **hibernate.cfg.xml** file.

The Workshop Studio Design Environment

To get started with the new Web project, you can open the **/pages/welcome.jsp** and you'll see the JSP visual editor in its default mode, which shows both the JSF source and visual designer. This is shown in Figure 17-9.

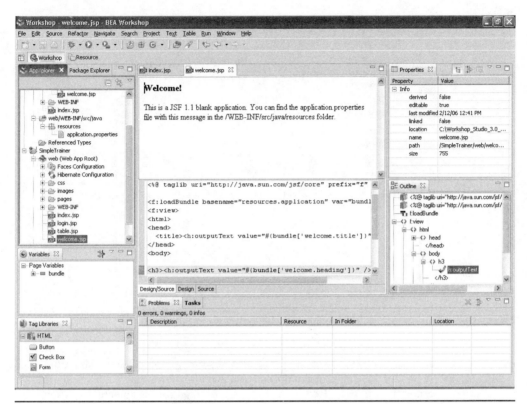

FIGURE 17-9   BEA Workshop's visual design environment

Similar to Studio Creator, it also has three buttons. However, in this case they are Design, Source, and the combined Design/Source (default). The visual editor behaves much like a traditional HTML designer but with JSF component rendering. A grid layout feature using CSS absolute positioning like Studio Creator is not offered.

When working directly with the JSP code editor, you'll quickly see how helpful it is. Although the JSP code editor lacks collapsible regions (code folding), it does have very snappy tag completion and tag attribute completion capabilities.

Building the Simple JSF Trainer Application

Building the pages of the JSF trainer application is done by launching a new *Web Artifact* Wizard, which can be invoked from the main menu or by the context menu. To create our Web pages, choose the JSF Page Web Artifact to generate a Faces-enabled JSP page. In addition to allowing you to set the name of the page, it also allows you to select a resource bundle, from which it will insert a standard **<f:loadBundle>** tag into your page.

After building the initial pages of the (simple) Trainer application, it is possible to build navigation rules by opening the application's **faces-config.xml** file in the Faces Configuration editor, shown in Figure 17-10. This editor provides a console user interface for the efficient editing of the **faces-config.xml** elements. It is also possible to visually edit the navigation model using a page flow navigation tool that is accessible by clicking the **Navigation** tab at the bottom left.

FIGURE 17-10 The Faces config and navigation editor in BEA Workshop Studio

Clicking the Navigation tab at the bottom of the editor displays a visual navigation model (shown in Figure 17-11); however, it only displays navigation rules one at a time.

Filling out the rest of the pages in the application is merely a matter of editing them visually and inserting the various JSF components from the Tag Libraries palette. For example, to build the Login page (shown in Figure 17-12), a simple **panelGrid** was dropped onto the

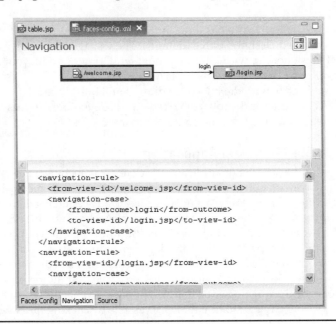

FIGURE 17-11 The visual navigation rule editor

FIGURE 17-12   Designing JSF pages in BEA Workshop Studio

page and the Standard **outputLabel**, **inputText**, and **inputSecret** components were dropped inside of the **PanelGrid**. Incidentally, Workshop Studio also provides the Apache MyFaces (Tomahawk) tags on its palette in addition to the Standard JSF tags.

Editing Java Source in BEA Workshop Studio

Since the simple Trainer application contains several JavaBeans, we relied on BEA Workshop's underlying Eclipse-based Java source code editors to build the beans necessary for the application. Using Eclipse for Java editing is extremely easy and the Virtual Trainer beans were quickly created from scratch.

Registering them as Faces-managed beans can either be done directly in the **AppXplorer** project window, or by using the Faces configuration editor. Once registered, you can use a simple EL binding editor to select properties or methods from the managed bean and apply them to component attributes. For example, in building the final page of the application (**table.jsp**), simply drop a standard **dataTable** from the palette onto the page. This causes a wizard to be invoked and allows for the databinding of the table attributes, including the child *column* components. This wizard relies on a small JSF EL Binding dialog that allows you to select EL accessible items and apply their values to UI component attributes. This is shown in the illustration at right.

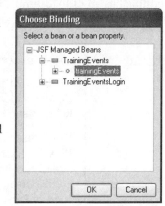

As shown in Figure 17-13, once finished, the table is rendered in the JSP page in a single-row approximation of its runtime appearance.

To run the application, an external server such as Tomcat or Weblogic must be configured. BEA Workshop will then use this server to run the applications being developed. This is configured at install time.

FIGURE 17-13   A databound dataTable component

Viewing Different Locales in the Visual Editor

With regard to building multilingual applications, BEA Workshop has a unique feature that is worth mentioning: It is possible to visually design JSF pages in different locales. How does this work? In general, as you design your pages in visual editors, you are actually *browsing* the components much like a typical browser. This means that the visual editor could have the ability to send locale information in the **Request** to the components, and in turn have the components respond in the appropriate locale (language).

This is, in fact, what BEA Workshop Studio's visual editor has the capability to do. It gives you the ability to view the JSP pages in the different languages and immediately fix any localization design issues related to internationalization. Changing the locale in the visual editor can be done by choosing Text | Resource Locale... from the main menu and then selecting a locale from the drop-down list. This is enabled when the page you are editing has an **<f:loadBundle>** tag in it, and a message bundle, along with separate nondefault locales, are defined in the application's **faces-config.xml**.

Recall that to use a resource in a JSF page requires using EL such as:

```
<h:outputText value="#{bundle['welcome.title']}"/>
```

Setting this EL value is very easy in Workshop Studio because a special EL picker along with a Resources pane allows for easy selection of resource keys, as shown in the illustration at left.

Final Observations with BEA Workshop Studio

BEA's Workshop Studio provides a familiar development experience for those already acquainted with the Eclipse development platform. In contrast to Studio Creator, BEA Workshop does not have the same auto-generation of code and advanced databinding features. Instead, it relies on the developer to create most of the necessary code artifacts. This is not necessarily a bad thing because more experienced Java developers often want to be responsible for all code in their applications.

Overall, despite having an extremely lightweight footprint, Workshop Studio has some very compelling development features, such as its AppXRay feature that tracks and synchronizes changes to all files in a JSF application, as well as the visual development support for different locales.

Oracle JDeveloper 10g

Having been one of the major backers of Java and JavaServer Faces in particular, Oracle provides a formidable Java development environment, which also has strong support for JSF development. At the time of this writing, Oracle's current production version of JDeveloper is JDeveloper 10g Release 3 (10.1.3), and it is offered in the following three bundles:

- **JDeveloper 10g Studio**   Contains all the features of the J2EE version, plus the Oracle ADF Framework
- **JDeveloper 10g J2EE version**   Supports enterprise visual J2EE development with support for JSF, EJB version 3, Struts, and even UML modeling
- **JDeveloper 10g Java version**   A lightweight Java source code editor and compiler

Downloading and installing JDeveloper 10g is easily done since it is packaged into a single zip file (the Studio version is approximately 333MB in size). Installation simply requires unzipping the zip file, and since it is free, there is no trial license or expiration. Further details on Oracle JDeveloper can be found at **http://www.oracle.com/technology/products/jdev**.

Getting Familiar with JDeveloper

In contrast to the previously discussed tools, Oracle JDeveloper (shown in Figure 17-14) is a full-fledged Java IDE. That is, it can be used to build any kind of Java-related object, ranging from Enterprise JavaBeans and Web Services to Java Applets and Swing Applications. In addition to support for general Java-related development, it also has specialized support for JavaServer Faces in the areas of productive visual development of Faces applications.

Creating a New Application and Web Project

To get started building Web applications with JDeveloper, invoke the Application Creation Wizard, which creates a *workspace* serving as a high-level container module that can hold multiple *projects*. In essence, a JDeveloper workspace is analogous to an enterprise J2EE application which can be archived as an *Enterprise Archive* (*EAR*) file and contain multiple *JAR* files, as well as Web applications archived in *WAR* files. JDeveloper projects can be considered analogous to J2EE Web applications.

The Application Creation Wizard (shown here) allows you to specify a common package prefix for all classes created in this application workspace. The wizard also allows you to select an application template, which can generate an initial set of subprojects along with starting code.

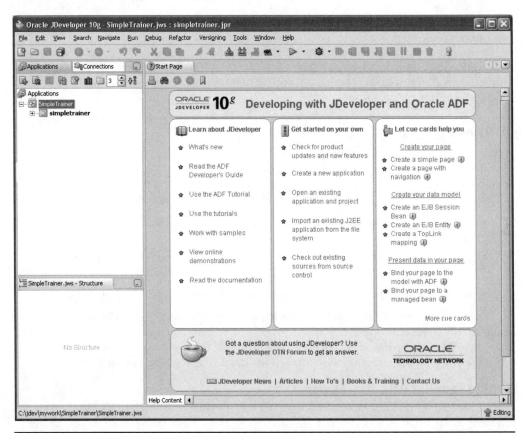

FIGURE 17-14   Oracle JDeveloper 10g Release 3 (10.1.3)

For example, an application template labeled "JSF EJB" exists. When selected, it pre-creates a workspace with two subprojects: Model and ViewController. The Model project is empty upon creation, but in accordance with the MVC design pattern, it is where you would place your EJB (Model) code. The ViewController project contains all View- (and Controller-) related code (this is where your JSF Web application will reside). Notice in the illustration at right that the ViewController project is loaded with a starter **faces-config.xml** and a preconfigured **web.xml**.

Since you specified that this application is to use JSF and EJB technologies, it will filter the many wizard selection options down to a subset of wizards that pertain to JSF and EJB development. This makes it a lot easier to select the right code generation wizard since there is a wide variety to choose from in the Studio version of JDeveloper, where the set of code generation/starter wizards range in technologies from Web Services to UML modeling.

For our purposes—creating the simplified version of the Virtual Trainer—we needn't use an application template. Instead, we can just select No Template [All Technologies] (shown in Figure 17-15). This will create an empty workspace where no specific technologies have yet been chosen for the application.

Once the new workspace has been created, a New Empty Project dialog appears. This is where the Virtual Trainer application will actually reside. Choosing a name of **simpletrainer** as a project name, we now have an empty project and can begin adding Web application elements to it.

A first task is to write the Java classes: **TrainingEvent**, **TrainingEvents**, and **TrainingEventsLogin**. This is easily done using JDeveloper's Java source code editor, which has exceptionally strong core Java-editing features, such as refactoring, syntax coloration, code completion, collapsible regions (code folding), automatic error detection, and code improvement features that include prompted package importing.

After creating the Training Event classes in the project, the JSF-enabled JSP pages were added. Creating new JSF JSP pages can be done in two ways in JDeveloper. The traditional way is to invoke the JSF JSP Wizard and create a new JSF-enabled JSP page, as shown in Figure 17-16.

JDeveloper's JSF JSP Wizard creates a new JSP page but also adds any necessary items required to run it, such as a new **faces-config.xml** and a **web.xml** (configured to run a Faces application). The wizard also allows users to specify which J2EE version, JSP/Servlet 1.2/2.3 or 2.0/2.4 depending on whether the project already has defined the J2EE level. Two other smaller features in the JSF JSP Wizard include the ability to choose between creating an XML JSP document with extension, **.jspx**, or the more commonly used non-XML (**.jsp**). The second feature allows the user to define whether the JSP will be used in a mobile device. This will preset the visual editor to adhere to the specific screen dimensions of several well-known mobile devices.

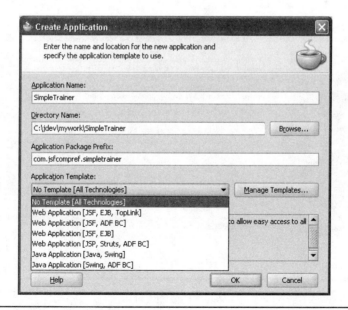

FIGURE 17-15   Creating an application with no templates

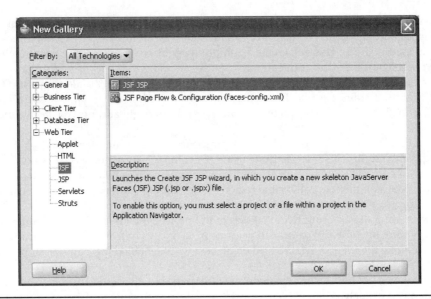

FIGURE 17-16   JDeveloper's JSF JSP Wizard

JDeveloper's Optional Component Binding Feature

A feature definitely worth mentioning is JDeveloper's optional *component binding* feature. When turned on, it behaves in a manner similar to Studio Creator in that it will automatically create a backing bean for the JSP page, as shown in Figure 17-17.

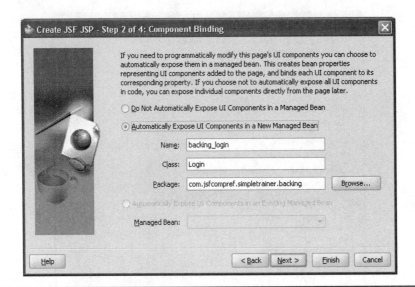

FIGURE 17-17   JDeveloper's optional component binding feature

Automatic component binding also means that whenever a UI component is dropped onto a JSF JSP page, a corresponding UI component declaration of a like component instance will be inserted inside the backing bean for the page. For example, if you drop an **inputText** onto your page name **login.jsp**, the following code:

```
private HtmlInputText inputText1;
```

along with its setter and getter,

```
public void setInputText1(HtmlInputText inputText1) {
  this.inputText1 = inputText1;
}
public HtmlInputText getInputText1() {
  return inputText1;
}
```

is added to the backing bean, **Login.java**. This bean is also automatically registered with a default name, **backing_login**, and the **inputText** component in the page is bound to this declared UI component in the backing bean:

```
<h:inputText binding="#{backing_login.inputText1}" id="inputText1"/>
```

In addition to creating a new class for a backing bean, a third option is available where the user can select an already existing backing bean from which to generate the UI component declaration.

In addition to offering the option of automatic component binding to a page at creation time, it is also possible to toggle this option on or off at any time by selecting the **Page Properties…** item in the Design menu on the main toolbar, selecting the Component Binding tab.

In general, having the component binding feature turned on can be very useful if you always want the components on your page to be bound to declared instances of the component in a backing bean. However, sometimes automatically generating code is not preferable for developers who want to be in full charge of all code in their application. In this case, you can simply opt out and not choose to turn on automatic component binding. You will then assume the responsibility of declaring and manually binding the page components with any backing bean instances of like components. Recall that binding a UI component on a page to a backing bean is not always required and should really only be done when you actually need to do something with the component instance in the backing bean.

Designing the Navigation Model Using JDeveloper's JSF Navigation Modeler

Similar to other tools discussed in this chapter, JDeveloper provides a design tool that enables users to create a JSF navigation model entirely visually, from a bird's-eye point of view, as opposed to editing the navigation rules and cases directly in the application's **faces-config.xml**. Accessing JDeveloper's JSF navigation modeler is done by opening the application's **faces-config.xml** file and clicking the Diagram tab on the lower left of the modeler. Pages or navigation elements can either be dropped from the JSF Navigation Diagram palette on the right, or existing pages in the project can be dragged and dropped from the application explorer on the left.

PART IV

Creating navigation cases simply involves clicking JSF Navigation Case on the palette and then connecting two pages with a line. As opposed to using the JSF JSP Wizard, as shown earlier, creating new JSF JSP pages can also be done by dragging a JSF page from the JSF Navigation Diagram palette onto the diagram. You'll notice that as you drop a new page onto the diagram, it will appear with a yellow caution sign on it. This simply means that it is a new page that exists only in the diagram and has yet to be generated. This is shown for the **table.jsp** page in Figure 17-18. To actually generate the page, double-click the page, which will launch the same JSF JSP Wizard as before. Figure 17-18 also shows that notes can be added to the navigation diagram.

As you can see, building the navigation model and the initial pages for the simple Virtual Trainer application is very easy when using the navigation modeler and JSF JSP Wizard. However, there are times when you need to edit the **faces-config.xml** in a more direct fashion, such as when manually adding managed beans, components, and the like. In this case, JDeveloper also provides a console-type editor for **faces-config.xml**. This editor, shown in Figure 17-19, can be accessed by clicking the Overview tab (next to Diagram) at the bottom of the page.

As you can see in the figure, creating entries in **faces-config.xml** can be done by registering them using the Faces configuration editor. For developers who are more comfortable editing XML directly, JDeveloper also provides access to a powerful XML editor by clicking the Source tab. The XML editor offers collapsible code regions as well as tag completion capabilities. It's shown in Figure 17-20.

Having examined the various **faces-config** friendly visual design editors in JDeveloper, it's time to move on to designing the JSF pages.

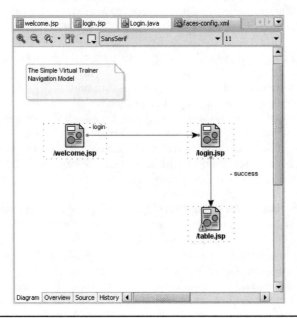

FIGURE 17-18   JDeveloper's Faces navigation modeler

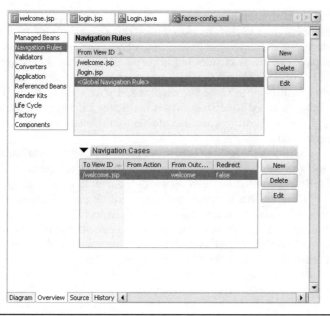

FIGURE 17-19   JDeveloper's Faces configuration editor

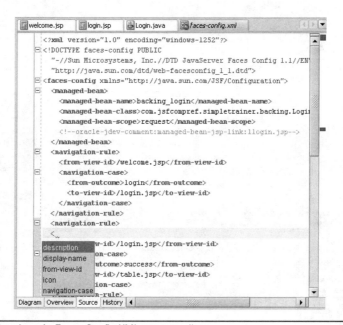

FIGURE 17-20   JDeveloper's Faces-Config XML source editor

The JSP Visual Design Environment

Similar to the other JSF IDEs, Oracle JDeveloper provides a visual design editor for JSP, HTML, and, most importantly, JSF-enabled JSP pages. In general, JDeveloper's visual editor supports the ability to edit pages with any custom tag library and have the tag appear in its runtime state in the visual editor. This means that you could even develop your own custom tag library and have its runtime appearance be displayed in the visual editor. This ability to render the tags in the visual editor also allows it to display JSF tags and their underlying UI components in the visual editor. This also means that JDeveloper can visualize any JSF tag/component library.

For example, in addition to the Standard Core and HTML JSF libraries, any third-party library, such as MyFaces or Oracle's own extended ADF Faces component library, can be visualized in the JSP visual editor. Another aspect of the overall visual design environment is that all editing of the elements in either the source editor, visual editor, or even the Structure Window on the lower left and the Property Inspector on the lower right are all synchronized visually. That is, when you select a component in the visual editor, the corresponding source code is selected along with the component in the Structure Pane. This is illustrated in Figure 17-21 where the JDeveloper visual design environment is shown.

You'll also notice in Figure 17-21 that it is possible to edit both in the source and with the visual editor simultaneously. This is done by selecting Window | Split Document on the main menu.

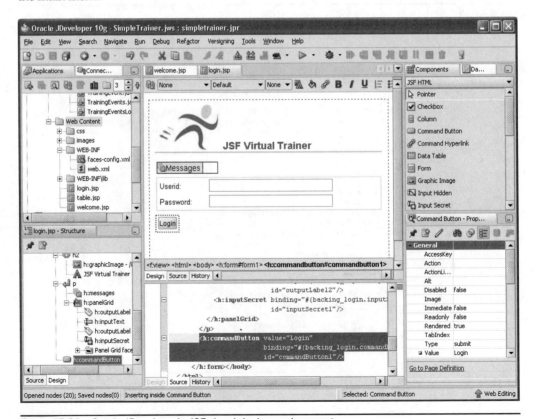

FIGURE 17-21 Oracle JDeveloper's JSF visual design environment

The JSP source editor also supports the most popular features found in the other JSF IDEs. This includes collapsible code regions and tag completion, as shown next.

In addition to tag completion, JDeveloper's JSP source editor provides attribute completion, shown in the illustration at right, where entering a space invokes a selection menu of available choices for attributes of the tag.

Code Generation via the Visual Editor

Similar to Studio Creator, JDeveloper offers an option to automatically generate event handling code. For example, when a JSF (**ActionSource**) UI component, such as a **commandButton**, is double-clicked in the visual editor, a dialog will appear that can auto-generate an action method. This dialog provides an auto-generated method name (**commandButton1_action**), but the name can also be overridden in the dialog. For the example application, we use **login_action**. Clicking OK will generate the method; thus, the Java source editor will be invoked and the cursor placed in the new action method code, as shown here.

```
public String login_action() {
    // Add event code here...

    return null;
}
```

In addition to generating the action method, the button that was double-clicked will have its **action** attribute set to the EL expression of the action method:

```
<h:commandButton id="commandButton1" value="Login"
    binding="#{backing_login.commandButton1}"
    action="#{backing_login.login_action}"/>
```

Subsequent double-clicks of the same button in the visual editor will cause the Java editor to be invoked and the cursor to be placed in the same action method.

Binding UI Component Attributes with the EL Binder Dialog

A common feature of most JSF IDEs is to provide a dialog that helps generate the appropriate JSF EL expression based on the data available to the application. This is possible using JDeveloper's general EL binder dialog, which allows for the easy selection of any EL-accessible data, and will have a corresponding EL expression generated and placed in a UI component attribute. To see the EL binder in action, assume you want to value-bind one of the input components to a property of a separate JavaBean—for example, if you added a new managed bean, **UserBean**, with properties **userid** and **password**. If it was registered as a managed bean with the name "user_bean" you could value-bind it to an input component with this statement:

```
<h:inputText binding="#{backing_login.inputText1}"
        value="#{user_bean.userid}"/>
```

To do this with the EL binder, select the input component in the visual editor. Then, in the Property Inspector window on the lower right, locate the **value** attribute and click the Databind button, which is located at the top of the Property Inspector window and resembles a cylinder. This causes the EL binder dialog to appear, as shown in Figure 17-22.

Once the dialog appears, generating the appropriate JSF EL expression is done by double-clicking any object in the tree on the left. The EL expression can also be *hand-coded* in the small window on the right.

In general, using the EL binder allows you to quickly generate the appropriate EL expression based on all data accessible to JSF EL, including managed bean properties, methods, or other implicit objects.

In addition to the EL binder dialog, it is also possible to invoke the EL code completion feature simply by typing the EL expression directly into the JSP source and pausing. This causes a code completion EL menu to appear, from which selections can be made, as shown next.

```
<h:inputText binding="#{backing_login.inputText1}" id="inputTex
        value="#{user_bean.|}"/>
<h:outputLabel value="Passwo
        binding="#{be     gin.outputLabel2}"
        id="outputLabe
```

```
password
userid
```

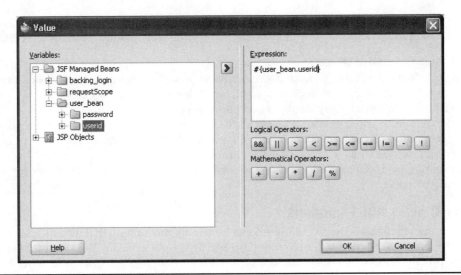

FIGURE 17-22 JDeveloper's EL binder dialog

Building DataBound Tables

Continuing to build the simple version of the Virtual Trainer application, the final page, **table.jsp**, contains a **dataTable** of individual training events. Recall from earlier in the book that building a usable **dataTable** involves binding the parent **dataTable** component along with providing a set of child **column** components. Like the other JSF IDEs, JDeveloper has a wizard for generating this code in an efficient manner. Invoking JDeveloper's **dataTable** Wizard is done by dragging a **dataTable** from the palette onto a page. Once invoked, the wizard allows for the selection of the EL source for the value of the table as well as the selection of column component types and table header values, as shown in Figure 17-23.

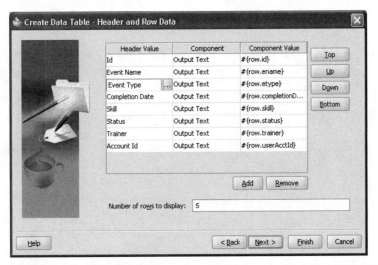

FIGURE 17-23 The **dataTable** Wizard in JDeveloper

Once the wizard completes, it will generate the appropriate code in the page and the visual editor will render the table in a simulated runtime way, as shown in Figure 17-24.

Other Code Generation Wizards

In addition to the **dataTable** Wizard, JDeveloper also provides other quick code generation wizards for compound UI components that have children such as the select menus (**selectOneMenu**, **selectManyMenu**...) and **panelGrid**.

A final point worth mentioning about the code generation wizards in JDeveloper is that they are re-entrant. That is, you can select a component that was created by the wizard (such as a **dataTable**), and then (right-click) select **Properties...** from the context menu. This will reinvoke the same wizard used to create the component UI component and allow you to update any values.

Using Oracle's ADF Framework

Before completing this overview of JDeveloper it is worth mentioning that the Studio version of JDeveloper (as opposed to the smaller J2EE and Java versions) contains a middle-tier development framework known as the Application Development Framework, or ADF.

Oracle's ADF technology provides a way to access and manipulate data from different middle-tier technologies in a simple and consistent way. Oracle ADF supports various middle-tier technologies such as Enterprise JavaBeans, Oracle TopLink, and Oracle Business Components, as well as Web Services and even simple POJO data objects. By supporting these technologies, a developer can visually design middle-tier logic, as well as declaratively build a user interface visually without having to manually write code to interact with these middle-tier technologies. With ADF, the developer essentially performs two tasks: 1) builds a middle-tier with a technology of choice; and 2) uses ADF's visual tools, such as the Data Control palette, to create a user interface that allows data interaction with the middle-tier.

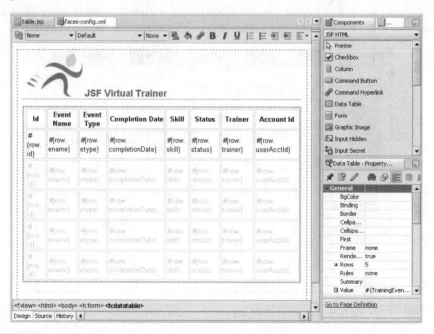

FIGURE 17-24   A rendered **dataTable** in JDeveloper's visual editor

Step 1: Building a Middle-Tier and Binding to the Presentation with ADF

To build a middle-tier in JDeveloper, you can choose from technologies such as Enterprise JavaBeans, Oracle TopLink, Oracle Business Components, Web Services, and/or simple Java POJO classes. The details of these technologies go beyond the scope of this book. However, to get a feel for developing an application with ADF, we'll create an EJB 3 middle-tier to use with ADF.

For quickly generating Enterprise JavaBeans, JDeveloper provides a set of wizards. For our application, assume that you have a database table (**trainingevents**) containing a list of athletic events you wish to train for. You would create an EJB entity bean using the CMP Entity Beans from Tables Wizard to select the database table and generate the appropriate entity bean code for the table (**Trainingevent**). You would then use the Create EJB Session Bean Wizard to create a bean that will serve as a façade to the entity bean. This bean will contain the data operations necessary to interact with the **Trainingevent** entity bean—and its underlying database table. Figure 17-25 shows the EJB Session Bean Wizard generating the data methods for our session bean.

Step 2: Building the Presentation Tier with ADF

Once the session bean has been created, it can be selected in the application navigator, and an ADF Data Control can be created. This will generate a small XML file behind the scenes that will register the EJB session bean with the ADF framework. This causes the EJB session bean to appear in the ADF Data Control Palette. At this point, a developer can drag and drop any data item from the Data Control Palette, as shown in Figure 17-26, and add it to the page. This will launch a corresponding wizard to generate user interface code depending on what was dropped onto the page. If a single field or property is dropped onto the page, a single input or output field will be generated. If a method such as **findAllTrainingevents()**, which has a return type of **Trainingevent**, is dragged onto the page, a corresponding set of wizard options will appear, allowing the user to create a tabular or form type user interface to interact with the data.

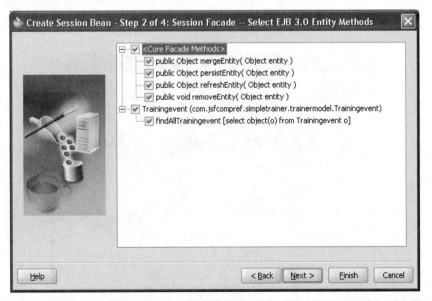

FIGURE 17-25 Generating a session bean façade in JDeveloper

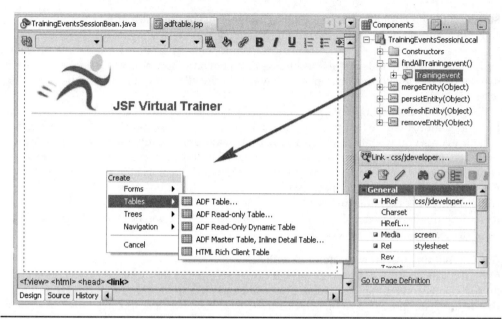

FIGURE 17-26 Drag and drop databinding from the ADF Data Control Palette

Selecting **ADF Read-only Table...** will launch a simple wizard (shown in Figure 17-27) that gathers information about the ADF table to be generated. Notice the similarity to the more generic **dataTable** wizard. Also notice that we can choose to enable row selection (Enable selection) as well as column sorting (Enable sorting).

Once the wizard is complete, it will generate the appropriate user interface artifact. In this case, we chose to create a table of data that allows for column sorting and row selection. You may notice that the table already has a certain *look and feel* associated with it. This is because the default user interface generation technology uses the ADF Faces library of

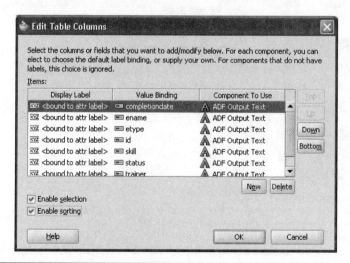

FIGURE 17-27 The ADF Table Wizard

components. ADF Faces has a built-in *skinning* technology where it is possible to create different types of application-level looks.

If the developer still prefers to generate only with Standard JSF components (Core, HTML), he or she can set an option in the ADF View options of the project properties to also allow for the generation of user interface artifacts using the standard JSF components.

Once the user interface artifact is generated, it will render in the visual editor, as shown in Figure 17-28.

Some Final Words on Oracle ADF

While the previous example showed an example using Enterprise JavaBeans, it's important to understand that Oracle ADF can also be used with other middle-tier technologies such as Oracle TopLink, Oracle Business Components, or Web Services, each of which has its own respective code-generation wizards. However, building a user interface to interact with these different data sources follows the same process of using the Data Control Palette and dragging and dropping the data onto the page and generating appropriate user interface artifacts.

A Word Regarding ADF Faces

Before concluding this discussion of ADF, it's important to highlight a few things with regard to the default user interface technology used with ADF: *ADF Faces*. As you saw when creating a databound table with ADF, the actual table component used was an ADF Faces table, which belongs to the ADF Faces component library. A standard **dataTable** could have also been generated using the drag and drop operation from the Data Control Palette, but the ADF Faces table was chosen instead to illustrate the benefit of features like automatic column sorting, data scrolling, and row selection.

The ADF Faces component library, like any other third-party JSF component library, works within the standard JSF specification but offers additional capabilities over the standard or base components provided in the specification. JDeveloper, however, doesn't

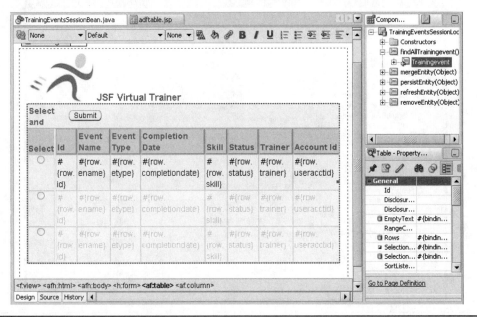

FIGURE 17-28 The finished ADF table

care which JSF component library developers choose to build applications and provides both the ADF Faces library and the standard (JSF Core and JSF HTML) libraries on its palette. You can use any combination of either of these when building applications.

A final thing to mention about the ADF Faces component library and Oracle's ADF framework: although they work great together, they are not mutually dependent on each other. The ADF Faces JSF component library can stand on its own and can be used with any kind of middle-tier technology. Likewise Oracle ADF framework can work with any Java-based user interface technology. For more information on Oracle's ADF Faces, please refer to Appendix B.

Adding Custom Tag Libraries/Components to JDeveloper

In addition to offering built-in design support for both the Standard JSF components and ADF Faces, you can also add other custom tag or component libraries to JDeveloper simply by registering the component library's tag file. JDeveloper allows this by providing a registry of JSP tag libraries, shown in Figure 17-29, from which users can add/edit. The tag library registry is accessed from the main menu by choosing **Tools** | **Manage Libraries...** For example, the MyFaces component library can easily be added to the palette by using the JSP tag library registry and registering the jar file of the library. Notice also in Figure 17-29 the checkbox Execute Tags in JSP Visual Editor. This allows JDeveloper to render the components in the visual editor at design time.

Running and Debugging with JDeveloper Embedded OC4J

To run a JSF application, or any specific JSP page in JDeveloper, you can right-click a JSP page in the Application Navigator window and choose the Run option. To debug a JSP page/ application, instead of selecting Run, you would select Debug. (JDeveloper even supports

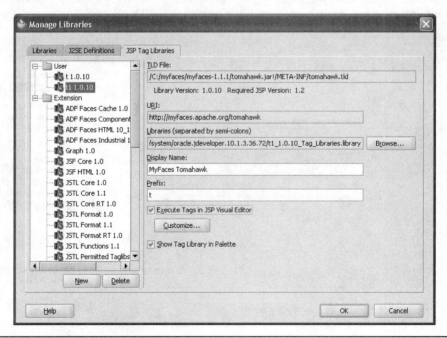

FIGURE 17-29 Managing JSP tag libraries in JDeveloper

JSP source debugging in addition to Java source debugging, because the JSP source editor allows for the insertion of breakpoints in JSP source code.)

Running or debugging a Web application is possible by using JDeveloper's embedded OC4J J2EE application server, which serves as the heart of the larger Oracle Application server. Once the server is started, an external browser is launched and pointed to the URL of the running page/application. At this point, the server can remain running, or the developer can shut down or restart it whenever needed.

Deploying a JSF Application from JDeveloper
Once the application is tested, it can be deployed to any J2EE-compliant application server in two ways. The first is to deploy the application to a separate WAR (Web Archive) or EAR (Enterprise Archive) file and then use the application server's management utilities to deploy the application from the saved archive. The other option is to deploy directly to a running instance of an application server. JDeveloper supports direct deployment to Oracle's Application Server, Stand Alone OC4J, Weblogic, JBoss, and Tomcat.

Final Observations with JDeveloper
The preceding walkthrough really serves as an introduction to the JSF-related features in JDeveloper 10g. Remember that JDeveloper 10g is also a complete enterprise Java IDE, as opposed to a JSF-only development environment, and contains many other development features that apply to enterprise Java, Web services, and relational databases.

IBM Rational Web Developer
Among the many products that IBM offers for software development, IBM's Rational Web Developer Version 6.0 most resembles the other IDEs reviewed in this chapter. Rational Web Developer is the slightly smaller cousin to Rational Application Developer and has evolved from the earlier Websphere Application Developer (5.1.2), which was one of the first IDEs to offer integrated JSF support. As such, it is focused primarily on JSF Web application development as opposed to the more general Rational Application Developer, which has a superset of features including UML design, Crystal Reports development, and so on.

Although Rational Web Developer is smaller than Rational Application Developer, it is the true goliath among the IDEs reviewed in this chapter. You'll need at least 5GB of free disk space when downloading a 60-day trial version from the Web. This is because you download the software in pieces using IBM's Download Director.

You then build an image of the software using a downloaded utility. Once the image is built, you can then install from that image—hence the need for 5GB. Once entirely installed, the IDE uses approximately 3.4GB.

For further information on Rational Web Developer and IBM's other development products, visit **http://www.ibm.com/developerworks/rational/products/rwd/**.

Getting Familiar with IBM Rational Web Developer
Once Rational Web Developer is installed, you are treated to a solid JSF visual development environment (shown in Figure 17-30), which has the familiar feel of the Eclipse development environment, along with features somewhat similar to Sun's Studio Creator.

The Rational Web Developer Design Environment
To get started in Rational Web Developer, you create a Dynamic Web Project from the main menu. As shown in Figure 17-31, the Dynamic Web Project Wizard allows you to set a number

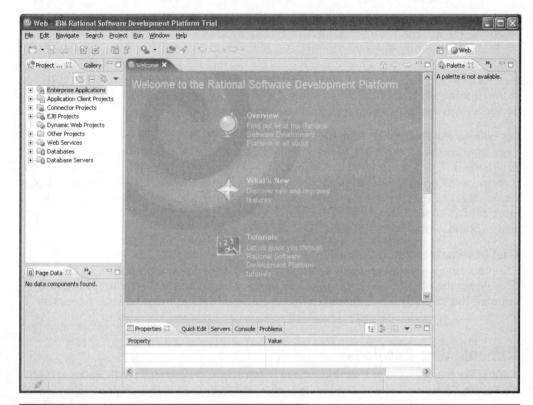

of project options such as the Servlet version (2.2, 2.3, 2.4), target server (the default is
Websphere Application Server v6.0), and a deployment project into which you can package
your Web project.

After creating a new Dynamic Web Project, Rational Web Developer does not yet assume
you will be building a Faces application, so there is no default **faces-config.xml**, nor a starter
Faces page. In the application's WEB-INF directory, you'll see a standard **web.xml** file as
well as some extra IBM databinding files, **ibm-web-bnd.xmi** and **ibm-web-ext.xmi**. These
additional files help enable databinding features in the application. The Faces-specific items
of the project (such as the **faces-config.xml**) will be added once a Faces JSP page is created.

Building the Simple JSF Trainer Application

Since the Java source editing features are basically the same as the other Eclipse-based IDEs,
for this review we will just import existing Java sources from the file system as opposed to
creating any application-related Java sources from scratch.

Importing Resources

To get started we import some existing Virtual Trainer Java classes using the Import… feature,
which is common to all Eclipse-based tools. For this application, we can pull in the Java
sources from a file system–based location.

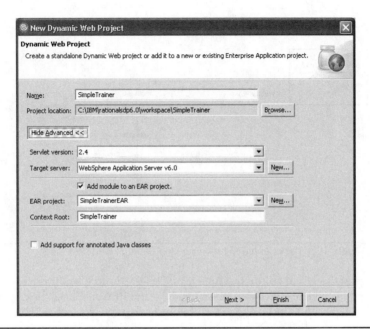

FIGURE 17-31   Creating a new Dynamic Web Project in Rational Web Developer

The **vt.css** style sheet and **vtlogo.jpg** image files can also be imported using the same file importation utility.

Creating New JSF Pages and Designing the Navigation Model

To Faces-enable the project and build our first JSF page, we use the Faces JSP File Wizard. Once a Faces-enabled JSP page is created (for example, **welcome.jsp**), the project is then configured as a Faces application with a **faces-config.xml** file and a configured **web.xml** file. In addition to creating the JSF JSP page, Rational Web Developer also automatically creates a backing bean (**Welcome.java**) and registers it as a managed bean.

Again similar to the other JSF IDEs, there is a visual editor for designing the navigation rules for the entire application. This is referred to in Rational Web Developer simply as the Web Diagram, as shown in Figure 17-32. When open, you can design the navigational page flow in almost exactly the same way as the other navigation page flow editors.

Once the Web Diagram is open, you can drag and drop any JSP pages from the Project Explorer or you can create it by dragging a Web page from the Palette and double-clicking it to launch the Faces JSP File Wizard. You can create navigation rules (and cases) by connecting pages using a Connection item on the Palette.

In contrast to Exadel Studio Pro and JDeveloper, there are no tabs on the Web Diagram that allow you to switch to editing **faces-config.xml** in a console-type editor (or XML source editor).

Designing JSF Pages in Rational Web Developer

Rational Web Developer's JSP Visual Editor is a very solid HTML and JSP visual editor regardless of JSF. It most resembles JDeveloper's visual editor because it allows for pure HTML design and formatting as well as providing rendering for Faces components in the visual editor.

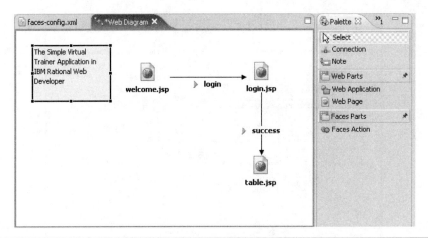

At the base of the visual editor are three tabs: Design, Source, and Preview. Not surprisingly, the JSP source editor resembles Exadel's and BEA's. It lacks the code folding feature of JDeveloper and Studio Creator, but does have basic tag completion.

Building the Login Page and Table Page

A login form can be built in a fashion similar to that used by the other IDEs. However, Rational Web Developer has a slightly unique approach to both registering a Java class as a managed bean and making its data accessible from the JSF page. In contrast to tools like BEA Workshop Studio and Oracle JDeveloper, where you first register a Java class as a managed bean and then bind one of its properties to a UI component attribute, Rational Web Developer offers an option on its palette where you can drag a JavaBean item from the Palette onto the JSP page in the visual editor. This invokes a wizard (shown in Figure 17-33) that both registers a Java class in the **faces-config.xml,** as well as creates a set of methods in the page's backing bean to access the managed bean. In addition to this, it also launches a wizard that allows you to define a user interface in the page based on the bean's properties.

In the same wizard, you can then auto-generate a form in your page based on the bean's properties, as shown in Figure 17-34. This will generate a form with prebound input fields based on what was chosen in the wizard.

For the Virtual Trainer page, **table.jsp,** it is possible to drag and drop a JavaBean from the palette onto the page and create a prebound **dataTable** using the same Add JavaBean Wizard. In the wizard, you would select the **TrainingEvents** bean that has a method that returns a list of **TrainingEvent** objects. As mentioned earlier, this action both registers the bean as a managed bean in the **faces-config.xml** file and makes the managed bean accessible to the backing bean of the page. This is achieved by inserting a method into the page that accesses the managed bean. It's shown next:

```
public com.jsfcompref.simpletrainer.TrainingEvents getTrainingevents() {
  if (trainingevents == null) {
    trainingevents = (TrainingEvents) getFacesContext().getApplication()
      .createValueBinding("#{trainingevents}").getValue(getFacesContext());
  }
  return trainingevents;
}
```

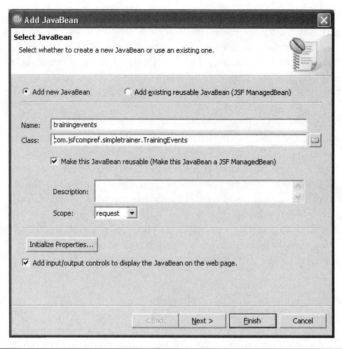

FIGURE 17-33   Adding a JavaBean to a page, as well as the **faces-config.xml**

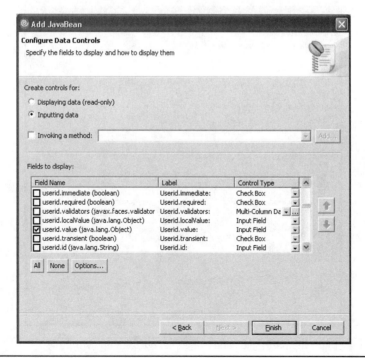

FIGURE 17-34   Creating a "data control" based on a JavaBean

Now that the backing bean (*page code* in IBM's terminology) has a method that accesses the managed bean, any UI component can then be bound to it. For example, a **dataTable** could be created and manually bound to this method from the backing bean. Or using the same Add JavaBean Wizard in the next step, it is possible to generate a **dataTable** to display the **TrainingEvent List** objects. This is shown in Figure 17-35.

Once complete, the JSP page will then have generated the **dataTable** UI component on the page, as shown in Figure 17-36.

In the same way that a JavaBean was used to generate a user interface, dynamic data from a database can also be used to generate a user interface artifact. In addition to JavaBean, the palette also contains *Relational Record* and *Relational Record List*, which makes data from either a single database row or a set of rows (respectively) usable on a page.

Dragging Relational Record List onto the page invokes a wizard that first allows you to select a database table from a named connection. You can then select columns to display in the page, as shown in Figure 17-37.

Once the generated **dataTable** is inserted into the JSP page, it can then be customized using the Properties view window at the bottom. In the example shown in Figure 17-38, a Paging option is added to the table, which lets you page through multiple pages of data at runtime.

Running the Simple JSF Virtual Trainer Application

Running the application, or any specific page, is done by right-clicking a JSP in the Project Explorer and selecting Run | Run On Server. This will launch the embedded Websphere Application Server and point a built-in browser window to the page that was chosen to run (as shown in Figure 17-39).

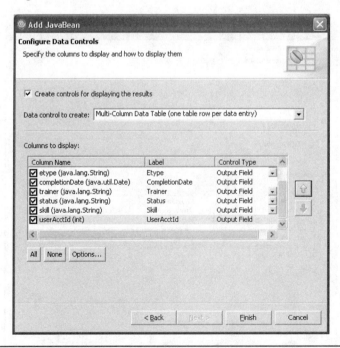

Figure 17-35   Generating the **dataTable** code using the Add JavaBean Wizard

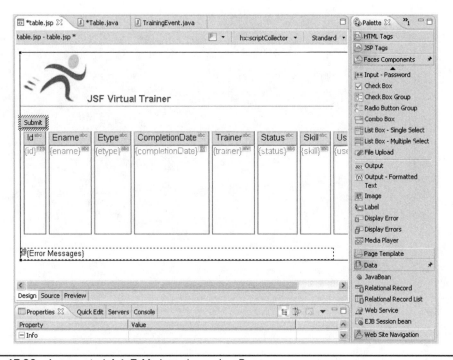

FIGURE 17-36 A generated **dataTable** based on a JavaBean

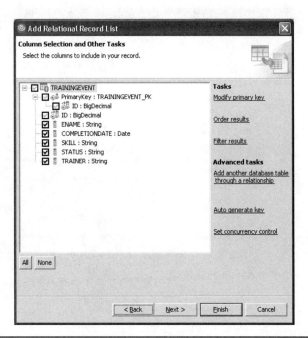

FIGURE 17-37 Adding a relational record list

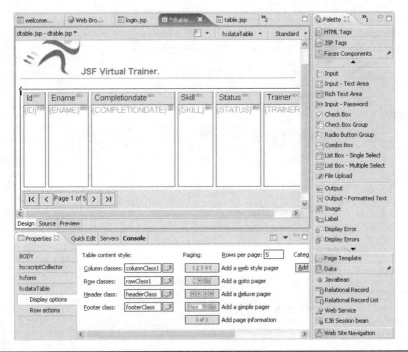

FIGURE 17-38   A databound **dataTable** in IBM Rational Web Developer

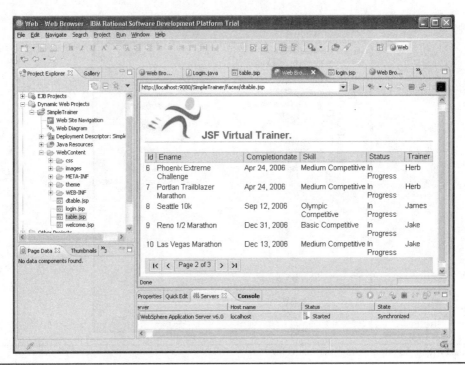

FIGURE 17-39   Running the **table.jsp** page which queries data from a database

Like the other Eclipse-based tools, it is possible to register other server configurations in addition to the preconfigured Websphere server. However, native configuration support is only offered for Websphere server types (as opposed to other vendor's servers).

How Databinding Works: Some Words on SDO

The databound pages work using a middle-tier technology called Service Data Objects (SDOs). An SDO is not so different from Oracle's ADF framework since it is designed to simplify and unify the way in which applications handle data. Using SDO, applications can interact and manipulate data from different types of data sources, including relational databases, XML data sources, and Web services.

By using the wizards in Rational Web Developer, the underlying SDO plumbing is automatically created behind the scenes, but a quick look at the backing bean code as well as the file system shows that for each data entity (such as the **TrainingEvents** database table) there is a metadata file which contains information about the database object. For example, **trainingevents.xml** has the following structure:

```
<?xml version="1.0" encoding="UTF-8"?>
<com.ibm.websphere.sdo.mediator.jdbc.metadata:Metadata xmi:version="2.0"
 xmlns:xmi="http://www.omg.org/XMI"
 xmlns:com.ibm.websphere.sdo.mediator.jdbc.metadata=
"http:///com/ibm/websphere/sdo/mediator/jdbc/metadata.ecore"
 rootTable="//@tables.0">
  <tables schemaName="TRAINER" name="TRAININGEVENT">
    <primaryKey columns="//@tables.0/@columns.0"/>
    <columns name="ID" type="9"/>
    <columns name="ENAME" type="4" nullable="true"/>
    <columns name="COMPLETIONDATE" type="10" nullable="true"/>
    <columns name="SKILL" type="4" nullable="true"/>
    <columns name="STATUS" type="4" nullable="true"/>
    <columns name="TRAINER" type="4" nullable="true"/>
  </tables>
</com.ibm.websphere.sdo.mediator.jdbc.metadata:Metadata>
```

The necessary SDO plumbing code is also added to the page's backing bean so it will be able to pull data from the data source and render/update it from the page.

Final Observations on IBM Rational Web Developer

Overall IBM's Rational Web Developer provides a compelling Faces development environment. In addition to offering a strong visual page editor and navigation modeler, it has some powerful features for auto-generating data-bound page artifacts. Again, like the other IDE reviews, the features mentioned here just scratch the surface of all of what is available in Rational Web Developer, and users are encouraged to look into the many tutorials available in the product.

Exadel Studio Pro

Besides the Java heavyweights Sun, BEA, Oracle, and IBM, smaller companies are having success in providing a sleek and productive development environment for JSF. Much like the previously independent M7 Corporation, the Exadel Corporation succeeds in providing an exceptionally nimble and flexible development environment worthy of notice.

Exadel Studio Pro is another Eclipse JSF+ development environment with strong
support for productive and visual development of JSF applications. Exadel Studio Pro
represents Exadel's latest tool offering which is a merging of previous products geared for
Struts and JSF development separately. The previous products were named Exadel Struts
Studio and Exadel JSF Studio, respectively. At the time of this writing, the current products
available from Exadel are Exadel Studio (version 3.0), which is free, and Exadel Studio Pro
(version 3.5), which currently costs $199 (USD). The Pro version contains the visual page
editor and Hibernate mapping tools and is described in the following section.

To try out Exadel Studio Pro on your own, a 15-day trial version is easily downloaded and
occupies less than 300MB once installed. Further details can be found at **http://exadel.com/**.

Getting Familiar with Exadel Studio Pro

As with other Eclipse-based development environments, Exadel Studio Pro's JSF design
environment, shown in Figure 17-40, has that same familiar Eclipse feel.

The Exadel Studio Pro Design Environment

The Exadel Studio Pro JSF design environment resembles other JSF IDEs; however, its
default design mode shows both the JSP source and visual designer.

Building the Simple JSF Trainer Application

To appreciate a similar development experience for comparison purposes, let's create the
same simplified Virtual Trainer application in Exadel Studio Pro.

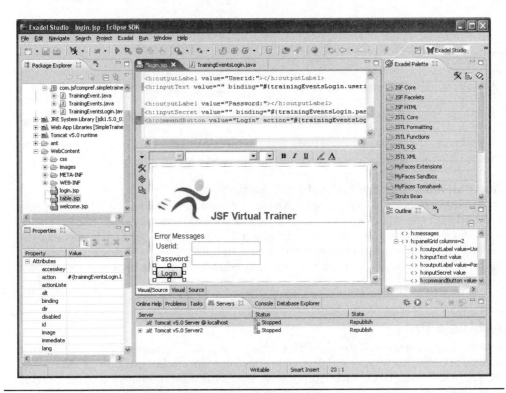

FIGURE 17-40   The Exadel Studio Pro JSF design environment

Creating a New Web Project

Creating a new JSF project is done by selecting the new JSF Project Wizard from the main menu. This is shown in Figure 17-41.

Exadel's JSF Project Wizard allows JSF developers great flexibility in their choice of JSF environments. These include

- JSF 1.0 Reference Implementation (from Sun)
- JSF 1.1_01 Reference Implementation (from Sun)
- JSF 1.1_01 with Facelets
- MyFaces 1.1.1
- MyFaces 1.1.1 with Shale

The JSF Project Wizard also provides two application templates, JSFBlank and JSFKickStart, to help you get started. For our purposes, let's use the JSFBlank template, because it will generate a J2EE Web project along with a **faces-config.xml** file and a configured **web.xml** file.

As you may have noticed, Exadel distinguishes itself from the other JSF IDEs by offering integrated support of the popular open-source Facelets technology. For Facelets enthusiasts, this is a real bonus. More information on Facelets can be found in Chapter 13.

Similar to other Eclipse-based development environments, building or importing the Virtual Trainer application Java classes (**TrainingEvent**, **TrainingEvents**, and **TrainingEventLogin**) can be done very easily by using the core Java development features or the Import feature.

JSF-enabled JSP pages can be built either directly from a wizard or from the Faces-config Graphical Editor, which provides similar page flow editing, as well as console-based editing of **faces-config.xml**. Exadel's Faces-Config Graphical Editor most closely resembles JDeveloper's faces-config editor in that it has three panes: Diagram, Tree, and Source.

FIGURE 17-41   Invoking Exadel's JSF Project Wizard

To build a JSF page using a wizard, Exadel provides a generic JSP File Wizard, which can create a JSP page with support for any of the technologies handled by Exadel Studio. This is specified in a wizard page that allows for the selection of the JSP tag libraries provided by the different technologies (JSF, Struts, Shale, and so on). To preload a JSP with the necessary JSF **<f:view>** tags, the developer chose to create the page from a JSF template called JSFBasePage.

The other method of creating JSF pages is to edit the **faces-config.xml** file in the graphical editor. To do so, in the Diagram view, click the View Template button on the left. This will prompt a quick JSF (or View) page creation wizard where a new JSF page can be created. Similar to JDeveloper, pages that have already been created can easily be added to the faces configuration (navigation) diagram by simply dragging and dropping them from the file explorer on the left onto the diagram. Also similar to JDeveloper, adding a navigation rule (and case) can be done by first clicking the Create New Connection button on the left side of the diagram and then connecting two pages in the diagram. This inserts a new navigation rule and case into the application's **faces-config.xml** source.

For our simple Virtual Trainer application, quickly building the initial pages and navigation rules can be done very easily using the page wizard and Faces-Config Graphical Editor, as shown in Figure 17-42.

Using the Tree View of the Graphical Faces Configuration Editor

Similar to JDeveloper and BEA Workshop Studio, Exadel Studio Pro provides a console-based way to edit the faces configuration file. This is accessed by clicking the Tree tab at the bottom of the page when editing a **faces-config.xml** file. This action invokes a similar configuration console, as shown in Figure 17-43.

Using the Faces Config Editor, we can register the three training event classes as managed beans. Finally, clicking the Source tab opens the Faces configuration file in an XML editor which also supports tag completion (but not collapsible code regions).

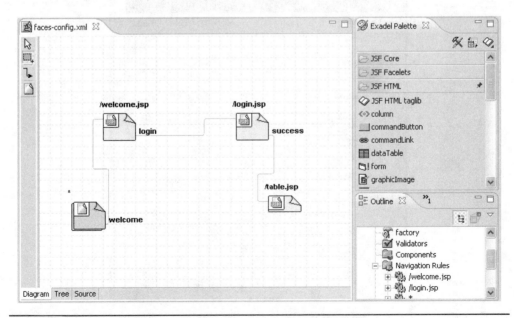

FIGURE 17-42 Building JSF pages and navigation rules in Exadel Studio Pro

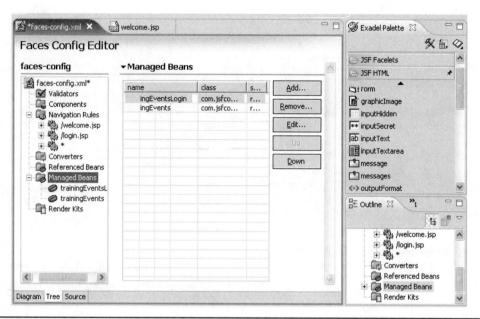

FIGURE 17-43   Exadel Studio's Faces configuration editor

Visually Designing JSF Pages in Exadel Studio Pro

To design the actual content in the pages, like the other JSF tools, Exadel Studio Pro provides an exceptional visual editor for JSP. After creating new empty JSF pages using the JSFBasePage template, UI components are added by dragging the components from the palette onto the page. Also like JDeveloper, components can be dragged and dropped from the palette onto the Outline view (window). Sometimes it is easier to drop directly to the outline window because it ensures the exact position of the component relative to the other components. Dropping on the page sometimes causes the component to be in an incorrect position. This is a not a big problem because the JSP source editor is never far away. Similar to BEA Workshop Studio, Exadel's JSP editor has three tabs: Visual/Source, Visual, and Source.

In contrast to JDeveloper, Workshop Studio, and Studio Creator, Exadel's JSP source editor does not offer collapsible code regions (code folding) but it does offer both tag completion (shown next):

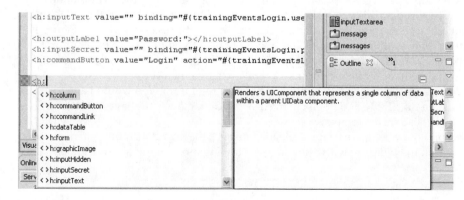

and JSF tag attribute completion for EL, as shown here.

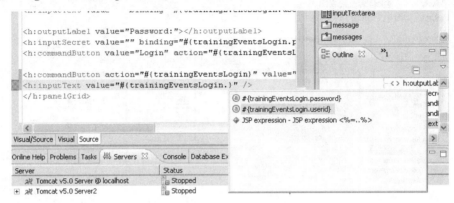

Using Exadel Studio Pro's EL Binder

In addition to using the attribute completion feature in the source editor, it is easy to bind

attributes in the visual editor. First, click a component in the visual editor. Then, shift over to the Properties window and click the property to which you want to add an EL expression. A small "…" button appears on the right side of the property. Clicking it invokes a simple JSF EL dialog window, as shown in the illustration at right, which allows you to select the appropriate EL accessible object. Clicking OK excuses the window and inserts the JSF EL expression into the attribute's value field.

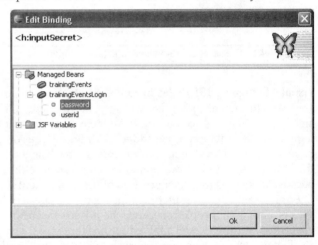

Binding a dataTable

Similar to JDeveloper and BEA Workshop Studio, dragging and dropping a compound component such as a **dataTable** invokes a wizard that has the ability to bind the **dataTable** itself, as well as the generating child columns. Exadel's **dataTable** dialog, shown in Figure 17-44, allows for the generation of columns but does not permit you to specify the column's component type. Instead, it defaults to **outputText** for all the columns. It does, however, allow you to add, edit, or remove columns as well as change their order.

Unlike JDeveloper, Exadel's **dataTable** dialog is not re-entrant. You would have to delete the existing **dataTable** and re-create it. Also, the dialog does not have an option to generate table headers (or footers).

As shown in Figure 17-45, once the dialog is finished, the new **dataTable** is generated and is rendered in the JSP page with a single row showing its column value attributes.

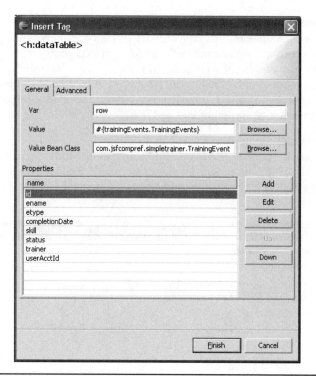

FIGURE 17-44   Exadel's **dataTable** dialog

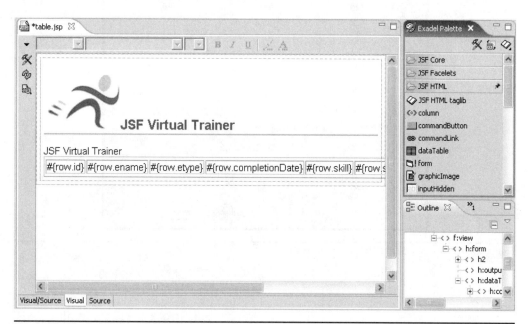

FIGURE 17-45   A databound **dataTable** in Exadel Studio Pro

Running the Simple JSF Virtual Trainer Application

To run the application, Exadel maintains a registry of JSP containers while providing a default Tomcat-based runtime environment. Exadel supports configurations for many of the popular J2EE Servers, as shown in Figure 17-46.

Once a server has been configured, it can be started. A built-in Web browser is invoked as the server starts. Accessing a Web page from the server is done by entering the URL of the page into the browser, as shown in Figure 17-47.

Hibernate Within Exadel Studio Pro

It should be mentioned that like BEA Workshop Pro, Exadel Studio Pro integrates Hibernate Tools support into the IDE. This allows developers to use the Eclipse-based tools for creating Hibernate-based persistence. Some of the Hibernate features include the capability to

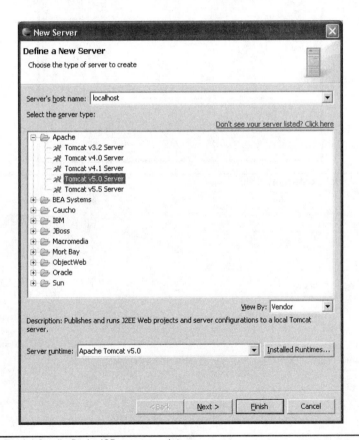

FIGURE 17-46   Exadel Studio Pro's JSP server registry

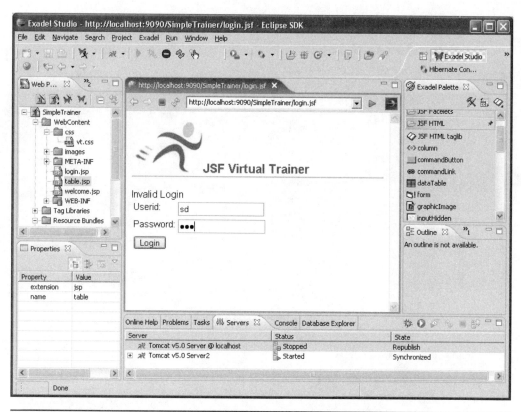

FIGURE 17-47 Running the simple JSF Virtual Trainer application in Exadel Studio Pro

automatically generate Data Access Object classes for persistent entities, the capability to automatically generate DDL files, and an easy configuration user interface for both XML and Hibernate configuration files.

Final Observations on Exadel Studio Pro

Overall, Exadel Studio Pro provides a solid and extremely flexible JSF development environment without a large footprint. Similar to BEA Workshop, Exadel Studio Pro is probably more geared towards Java developers who want maximum control of their code and who feel comfortable writing most of it. It does strike a happy medium though, by offering simple code generation features such as the **dataTable** generation dialog. Also, its integrated support of Facelets is no doubt one of its most compelling features.

The JavaServer Faces Configuration File

One of the core benefits of using the JavaServer Faces framework is that a great deal of your application's configuration can be specified declaratively in an external configuration file instead of being hard-coded into the application. This greatly simplifies development because many changes can be made to the application without having to recompile any code. Upon application startup, JavaServer Faces loads its configuration file(s) and creates a series of configuration objects that correspond to the settings in the file. JavaServer Faces then uses those configuration objects to guide its behavior.

EXPERT GROUP INSIGHT *As of the JSF 1.2 release, XML configuration files are falling out of fashion in favor of naming convention– or annotation-based configuration. Expect future versions of JSF to leverage these kinds of approaches for configuration details, eliminating the need for some or all of the XML.*

The JavaServer Faces configuration file is XML-based and its format is governed by either a Document Type Definition (DTD) file or an XML schema file, depending on the version of JSF in use. JSF versions 1.0 and 1.1 use a DTD to govern the format of their configuration files; versions 1.2 and later use XML schema. The DTDs and XML schema specify how the configuration elements must be ordered in the file, what settings are required, and so on. Each JSF configuration file declares its conformance to a DTD or XML schema by having either a **DOCTYPE** definition or an XML schema definition at the top of the file. Following is the **DOCTYPE** definition for JSF version 1.0 configuration files that makes use of the 1.0 DTD:

```
<!DOCTYPE faces-config PUBLIC
  "-//Sun Microsystems, Inc.//DTD JavaServer Faces Config 1.0//EN"
  "http://java.sun.com/dtd/web-facesconfig_1_0.dtd">

<faces-config>
  <!-- Configuration file contents go here. -->
</faces-config>
```

Next is the **DOCTYPE** definition for JSF version 1.1 configuration files:

```
<!DOCTYPE faces-config PUBLIC
  "-//Sun Microsystems, Inc.//DTD JavaServer Faces Config 1.1//EN"
  "http://java.sun.com/dtd/web-facesconfig_1_1.dtd">

<faces-config>
  <!-- Configuration file contents go here. -->
</faces-config>
```

Finally, the definition shown next specifies the XML schema for JSF version 1.2 configuration files:

```
<faces-config xmlns="http://java.sun.com/xml/ns/javaee"
  xmlns:xsi="http://www.w3.org/2001/XMLSchema-instance"
  xsi:schemaLocation="http://java.sun.com/xml/ns/javaee/web-facesconfig_1_2.xsd"
  version="1.2">
  <!-- Configuration file contents go here. -->
</faces-config>
```

Notice that for XML schema there is no **DOCTYPE** declaration. The XML schema being used is defined via the **xmlns:xsi** and **xsi:schemaLocation** attributes of the root element (**<faces-config>**) of the configuration file. Also note that all of the other Java EE config files, such as the **web.xml**, and Tag Library Descriptors (TLDs) are now governed by XML schema instead of DTDs as of Java EE version 5.

When JSF reads a configuration file, its XML parser uses the **DOCTYPE** definition to determine the DTD or schema with which the XML file must conform. If configured to do so, the XML parser will validate the XML file's conformance to the DTD or XML schema and prevent application startup if an error occurs, such as out of order elements, or poorly formed XML markup.

Understanding XML DTDs

Before examining each of the elements in this library, it's necessary to review how XML DTDs work. DTDs originated in 1971 as one of the core constructs of IBM's Generalized Markup Language (GML). GML was later standardized to produce Standard Generalized Markup Language (SGML), which is considered to be the mother of all markup languages, including HTML and XML. DTDs specify a set of elements and attributes that make up a specific XML document type. DTDs also specify the order in which elements must be placed in the file, and the relationship between elements. For example, an element definition defines what other elements can be nested inside of it, how many occurrences can be nested, and in what order the nesting can occur. Additionally, DTDs define which element attributes are required and which are optional.

Each element described in this chapter has a "DTD Definition" section that lists the element's definition from the JSF configuration file DTD.

NOTE *Elements that were introduced in JSF 1.2 do not have a definition inside one of the JSF configuration file DTDs because JSF 1.2 configuration files are governed by an XML schema. However, in order to represent the proper ordering and constraints on how elements are used, a schema-equivalent DTD definition is specified for the 1.2 elements.*

The definitions will be similar to the one shown in the following snippet:

```
<!ELEMENT navigation-case (description*, display-name*, icon*,
from-action?, from-outcome?, to-view-id, redirect?)>
```

This example defines a **navigation-case** element and the elements that can be nested inside of it. According to the definition, the element can have nested **description**, **display-name**, **icon**, **from-action**, **from-outcome**, **to-view-id**, and **redirect** elements. The question mark (?) and asterisk (*) characters following the nested elements' names indicate the number of times the nested element can be nested. The question mark character indicates that the element can be nested zero or one time. The asterisk character indicates that the element can be nested zero or more (unlimited) times. A plus (+) character (not shown in the previous example) indicates that the element must be nested at least once and as many times as you'd like. The lack of a trailing character means that the element must be nested exactly once and no more. To specify that any element can be nested inside of a defined element, the **ANY** keyword is used. An example of this is shown here:

```
<!ELEMENT attribute-extension ANY>
```

If no elements should be nested inside the defined element, **EMPTY** will be used to denote that:

```
<!ELEMENT redirect EMPTY>
```

Finally, if the element does not accept any nested elements and is used to specify a value, **#PCDATA** will be used to denote that:

```
<!ELEMENT action-listener (#PCDATA)>
```

Understanding XML Schemas

XML Schema was developed by W3C and made an official recommendation in 2001. XML Schema was developed to solve some problems with DTDs, such as providing an XML syntax for describing the document itself, rather than the different, non-XML notation of the DTD, and providing a way to associate concrete data types with markup elements. Unfortunately, W3C XML Schema ended up being very obtuse and difficult to understand, and went way beyond solving just the above problems. Nevertheless, it is the standard chosen for describing XML documents in Java EE 5 so it's important to understand how it works.

XML schemas work much the same way that DTDs do. XML schemas specify a set of elements and attributes that make up a specific XML document type along with specifying the order in which elements must be placed in the file, and the relationship between elements. Additionally, XML schemas define which element attributes are required and which are optional. The main difference between a DTD and an XML schema is that XML schemas are themselves an XML document. Because of this, XML schemas offer a much richer format for defining an XML document type. This allows for a more specific definition of the format that an XML document type must have.

Understanding How Configuration Files Are Processed

At Web application startup, JSF implementations use a standardized algorithm for locating and loading configuration files. The locating and loading of configuration files is completed before any requests can be processed by the Web application. If any of the configuration files being loaded has an XML parsing error, the application startup process will be aborted and the application will not be accessible.

Following is the process and order in which configuration files are located and loaded.

- Check for the existence of a **/META-INF/faces-config.xml** file in each **.jar** file accessible by the servlet context class loader and load it if it exists. This means all **.jar** files in the **WEB-INF/lib** directory will be scanned, and this is how custom JSF components can declare themselves to the JSF runtime. See Chapter 10 for more on building a self-contained JSF component library jar.

- Check for the existence of a **javax.faces.CONFIG_FILES** context parameter in the application's **web.xml** deployment descriptor and, if it exists, load the list of comma-delimited files it specifies. The following example configuration file illustrates the use of the **javax.faces.CONFIG_FILES** context parameter:

```
<!DOCTYPE web-app PUBLIC
    "-//Sun Microsystems, Inc.//DTD Web Application 2.3//EN"
    "http://java.sun.com/dtd/web-app_2_3.dtd">

<web-app>
    <display-name>Example</display-name>
    <description>Example Application</description>
    <context-param>
      <param-name>javax.faces.CONFIG_FILES</param-name>
      <param-value>
         /WEB-INF/test1-faces-config.xml,
         /WEB-INF/test2-faces-config.xml,
         /WEB-INF/test3-faces-config.xml
      </param-value>
    </context-param>
    <servlet>
      <servlet-name>Faces Servlet</servlet-name>
      <servlet-class>javax.faces.webapp.FacesServlet</servlet-class>
      <load-on-startup>1</load-on-startup>
    </servlet>
    <servlet-mapping>
      <servlet-name>Faces Servlet</servlet-name>
      <url-pattern>*.faces</url-pattern>
    </servlet-mapping>
</web-app>
```

Note that the JSF Configuration files listed in the **param-value** element can be located anywhere in the Web application; they are not required to be underneath the **WEB-INF** directory. It is just a useful convention to put such things in the **WEB-INF** directory. Also, the files can be named anything you choose, they need not be named **faces-config.xml**.

- Check for the existence of a **/WEB-INF/faces-config.xml** file and load it if it exists.

The Faces Configuration Elements

Table 18-1 lists and describes each of the elments used to configure the JSF configuration file. Additionally, the table specifies the cardinality (or number of times an element must be nested inside its parent element) for each element and the versions of JSF configuration files the elements apply to.

Element	Description	Cardinality	JSF Versions
action-listener	Specifies the fully qualified class name of a **javax.faces.event.ActionListener** implementation class that will replace the JSF implementation's default action listener implementation.	Zero to unlimited	1.0, 1.1, 1.2
application	Encapsulates the set of elements that specify application configuration details. All of the sub-elements of this element are used for replacing or decorating per-application singleton classes, such as the **ViewHandler** or the **NavigationHandler**.	Zero to unlimited	1.0, 1.1, 1.2
application-extension	Encapsulates any elements specific to a JSF implementation for the **application** element. See "Extension Elements" section.	Zero to unlimited	1.2
application-factory	Specifies the fully qualified class name of a **javax.faces.application.ApplicationFactory** implementation class that will replace the JSF implementation's default application factory implementation.	Zero to unlimited	1.0, 1.1, 1.2
attribute	Encapsulates the set of elements used to specify the details for an attribute.	Zero to unlimited	1.0, 1.1, 1.2
attribute-class	Specifies the fully qualified class name for an attribute's value.	Once	1.0, 1.1, 1.2
attribute-extension	Encapsulates any elements specific to a JSF implementation for a given **attribute** element. See "Extension Elements" section.	Zero to unlimited	1.0, 1.1, 1.2
attribute-name	Specifies the logical name for an attribute under which the attribute's value will be stored.	Once	1.0, 1.1, 1.2
base-name	Specifies the fully qualified class name of a **javax.util.ResourceBundle** instance that will be registered with the JSF application with a logical name specified by an associated **var** element.	Once	1.2
component	Encapsulates the set of elements used to specify the details for a UI component.	Zero to unlimited	1.0, 1.1, 1.2
component-class	Specifies the fully qualified class name for a UI component.	Once	1.0, 1.1, 1.2
component-extension	Encapsulates any elements specific to a JSF implementation for a given **component** element. See "Extension Elements" section.	Zero to unlimited	1.0, 1.1, 1.2
component-family	Specifies the component family to which a renderer will be linked.	Once	1.0, 1.1, 1.2
component-type	Specifies the logical name for a UI component.	Once	1.0, 1.1, 1.2

PART IV

TABLE 18-1   The Complete List of Elements of the JSF Configuration File

Element	Description	Cardinality	JSF Versions
converter	Encapsulates the set of elements used to specify the details for a converter.	Zero to unlimited	1.0, 1.1, 1.2
converter-class	Specifies the fully qualified class name for a converter implementation.	Once	1.0, 1.1, 1.2
converter-extension	Encapsulates any elements specific to a JSF implementation for a given converter element. See "Extension Elements" section.	Zero to unlimited	1.2
converter-for-class	Specifies the fully qualified class name for which a converter will be associated.	Once	1.0, 1.1, 1.2
converter-id	Specifies the logical name for a converter.	Once	1.0, 1.1, 1.2
default-locale	Specifies the default locale for the JSF application.	Zero or once	1.0, 1.1, 1.2
default-render-kit-id	Specifies the logical name of a render kit that will replace the JSF implementation's default render kit.	Zero to unlimited	1.0, 1.1, 1.2
default-value	Specifies the default value for an attribute or a property.	Zero or once	1.0, 1.1, 1.2
description	See "Metadata Elements" section.	Zero to unlimited	1.0, 1.1, 1.2
display-name	See "Metadata Elements" section.	Zero to unlimited	1.0, 1.1, 1.2
el-resolver	Specifies the fully qualified class name of a **javax.el.ELResolver** implementation class that will replace the JSF implementation's default expression language resolver implementation.	Zero to unlimited	1.2
faces-config	Is the root element for the JSF configuration file and thus encapsulates all other elements in the file.	Once	1.0, 1.1, 1.2
faces-config-extension	Encapsulates any elements specific to a JSF implementation for the **faces-config** element. See "Extension Elements" section. *Note: This element was created to host application metadata that is global in scope.*	Zero to unlimited	1.2
faces-context-factory	Specifies the fully qualified class name of a **javax.faces.context.ApplicationFactory** implementation class that will replace the JSF implementation's default faces context factory implementation.	Zero to unlimited	1.0, 1.1, 1.2
facet	Encapsulates the set of elements used to specify the details for a facet.	Zero to unlimited	1.1, 1.2

TABLE 18-1   The Complete List of Elements of the JSF Configuration File *(continued)*

Element	Description	Cardinality	JSF Versions
facet-extension	Encapsulates any elements specific to a JSF implementation for the **facet** element. See "Extension Elements" section.	Zero to unlimited	1.1, 1.2
facet-name	Specifies the logical name for a facet.	Once	1.1, 1.2
factory	Encapsulates the set of elements that specify factory configuration details.	Zero to unlimited	1.0, 1.1, 1.2
factory-extension	Encapsulates any elements specific to the JSF implementation for the **factory** element. See "Extension Elements" section.	Zero to unlimited	1.2
from-action	Specifies an action reference expression that must have been executed in order to have the associated navigation case selected.	Zero or once	1.0, 1.1, 1.2
from-outcome	Specifies the logical outcome value that an action method must generate in order to have the associated navigation case selected.	Zero or once	1.0, 1.1, 1.2
from-view-id	Specifies the view ID that a navigation rule applies to.	Zero or once	1.0, 1.1, 1.2
icon	See "Metadata Elements" section.	Zero to unlimited	1.0, 1.1, 1.2
key	Specifies the key for a map entry defined by the **map-entry** element.	Once	1.0, 1.1, 1.2
key-class	Specifies the fully qualified class name of an object type that all keys will be converted to before being added to a map defined by a **map-entries** element.	Zero or once	1.0, 1.1, 1.2
large-icon	See "Metadata Elements" section.	Zero or once	1.0, 1.1, 1.2
lifecycle	Encapsulates the set of elements that specify lifecycle configuration details.	Zero to unlimited	1.0, 1.1, 1.2
lifecycle-extension	Encapsulates any elements specific to a JSF implementation for the **lifecycle** element. See "Extension Elements" section.	Zero to unlimited	1.2
lifecycle-factory	Specifies the fully qualified class name of a **javax.faces.lifecycle.ApplicationFactory** implementation class that will replace the JSF implementation's default lifecycle factory implementation.	Zero to unlimited	1.0, 1.1, 1.2
list-entries	Encapsulates a list of values that will be used to populate a **java.util.List** instance or an array that will serve as the value for a managed property or to populate a managed bean that is itself an instance of **java.util.List**.	Once	1.0, 1.1, 1.2

TABLE 18-1   The Complete List of Elements of the JSF Configuration File *(continued)*

PART IV

Element	Description	Cardinality	JSF Versions
locale-config	Encapsulates the set of elements that specify the application's locale configuration details.	Zero to unlimited	1.0, 1.1, 1.2
managed-bean	Encapsulates the set of elements used to specify the details for a managed bean.	Zero to unlimited	1.0, 1.1, 1.2
managed-bean-class	Specifies the fully qualified class name for a managed bean.	Once	1.0, 1.1, 1.2
managed-bean-extension	Encapsulates any elements specific to the JSF implementation for a given **managed-bean** element. See "Extension Elements" section.	Zero to unlimited	1.2
managed-bean-name	Specifies the logical name for a managed bean.	Once	1.0, 1.1, 1.2
managed-bean-scope	Specifies the Web application scope in which the managed bean will be stored when it is instantiated.	Once	1.0, 1.1, 1.2
managed-property	Encapsulates the set of elements used to specify the details for a managed bean's property.	Zero to unlimited	1.0, 1.1, 1.2
map-entries	Encapsulates a set of key-value pairs that will be used to populate a **java.util.Map** instance that will serve as the value for a managed property or to populate a managed bean that is itself an instance of **java.util.Map**.	Once	1.0, 1.1, 1.2
map-entry	Encapsulates a key-value pair that makes up an entry for a map defined by a **map-entries** element.	Zero to unlimited	1.0, 1.1, 1.2
message-bundle	Specifies the fully qualified base name of a resource bundle that will be used for the JSF application.	Zero to unlimited	1.0, 1.1, 1.2
navigation-case	Encapsulates the set of elements that specify navigation case configuration details.	Zero to unlimited	1.0, 1.1, 1.2
navigation-handler	Specifies the fully qualified class name of a **javax.faces.application.NavigationHandler** implementation class that will replace the JSF implementation's default navigation handler implementation.	Zero to unlimited	1.0, 1.1, 1.2
navigation-rule	Encapsulates the set of elements that specify navigation rule configuration details.	Zero to unlimited	1.0, 1.1, 1.2
navigation-rule-extension	Encapsulates any elements specific to the JSF implementation for a given **navigation-rule** element. See "Extension Elements" section.	Zero to unlimited	1.2
null-value	Indicates that the property defined by the enclosing element must be initialized to **null**.	Once	1.0, 1.1, 1.2

TABLE 18-1 The Complete List of Elements of the JSF Configuration File *(continued)*

Element	Description	Cardinality	JSF Versions
phase-listener	Specifies the fully qualified class name of a **javax.faces.event.PhaseListener** implementation class that will be notified of all phase changes during the JSF request processing lifecycle.	Zero to unlimited	1.0, 1.1, 1.2
property	Encapsulates the set of elements used to specify the details for a property.	Zero to unlimited	1.0, 1.1, 1.2
property-class	Specifies the fully qualified class name for a property's value.	Zero or once	1.0, 1.1, 1.2
property-extension	Encapsulates any elements specific to a JSF implementation for a given **property** element. See "Extension Elements" section.	Zero to unlimited	1.0, 1.1, 1.2
property-name	Specifies the logical name for a property.	Once	1.0, 1.1, 1.2
property-resolver	Specifies the fully qualified class name of a **javax.faces.el.PropertyResolver** implementation class that will replace the JSF implementation's default property resolver implementation.	Zero to unlimited	1.0, 1.1, 1.2
redirect	Indicates that the associated navigation case to view ID URL should be navigated to using an HTTP redirect instead of the standard View Handler processing.	Zero or once	1.0, 1.1, 1.2
referenced-bean	Encapsulates the set of elements used to specify the details for a referenced bean.	Zero to unlimited	1.0, 1.1, 1.2
referenced-bean-class	Specifies the fully qualified class name of an external bean that is supposed to be available to the JSF application at runtime by existing in one of the Web application scopes (request, session, or application).	Once	1.0, 1.1, 1.2
referenced-bean-name	Specifies the logical name for a referenced bean.	Once	1.0, 1.1, 1.2
render-kit	Encapsulates the set of elements used to specify the details for a render kit.	Zero to unlimited	1.0, 1.1, 1.2
render-kit-class	Specifies the fully qualified class name for a render kit implementation.	Zero or once	1.0, 1.1, 1.2
render-kit-extension	Encapsulates any elements specific to a JSF implementation for the **render-kit** element. See "Extension Elements" section. *Note: This element was created to host metadata that applies to the entire render kit, not to just one renderer.*	Zero to unlimited	1.2

PART IV

TABLE 18-1   The Complete List of Elements of the JSF Configuration File *(continued)*

Element	Description	Cardinality	JSF Versions
render-kit-factory	Specifies the fully qualified class name of a **javax.faces.render.RenderKitFactory** implementation class that will replace the JSF implementation's default render kit factory implementation.	Zero to unlimited	1.0, 1.1, 1.2
render-kit-id	Specifies the logical name for a render kit.	Zero or once	1.0, 1.1, 1.2
renderer	Encapsulates the set of elements used to specify the details for a renderer.	Zero to unlimited	1.0, 1.1, 1.2
renderer-class	Specifies the fully qualified class name for a renderer implementation.	Once	1.0, 1.1, 1.2
renderer-extension	Encapsulates any elements specific to a JSF implementation for a given renderer element. See "Extension Elements" section.	Zero to unlimited	1.0, 1.1, 1.2
renderer-type	Specifies the logical name for a renderer.	Once	1.0, 1.1, 1.2
resource-bundle	Encapsulates the set of elements that specify resource bundle configuration details.	Zero to unlimited	1.2
small-icon	See "Metadata Elements" section.	Zero or once	1.0, 1.1, 1.2
state-manager	Specifies the fully qualified class name of a **javax.faces.application.StateManager** implementation class that will replace the JSF implementation's default state manager implementation.	Zero to unlimited	1.0, 1.1, 1.2
suggested-value	Specifies the suggested value for an attribute or a property.	Zero or once	1.0, 1.1, 1.2
supported-locale	Specifies a locale supported by the JSF application.	Zero to unlimited	1.0, 1.1, 1.2
to-view-id	Specifies the view ID for a view that will be displayed if the navigation case associated with that view ID is selected.	Once	1.0, 1.1, 1.2
validator	Encapsulates the set of elements used to specify the details for a validator.	Zero to unlimited	1.0, 1.1, 1.2
validator-class	Specifies the fully qualified class name for a validator.	Once	1.0, 1.1, 1.2
validator-extension	Encapsulates any elements specific to a JSF implementation for a given validator element. See "Extension Elements" section.	Zero to unlimited	1.2
validator-id	Specifies the logical name for a validator.	Once	1.0, 1.1, 1.2
value	Specifies the literal value or value binding expression that generates a value for a list entry, managed property, or map entry.	Once	1.0, 1.1, 1.2

TABLE 18-1   The Complete List of Elements of the JSF Configuration File *(continued)*

Element	Description	Cardinality	JSF Versions
value-class	Specifies the fully qualified class name of an object type that all values will be converted to before being added to a list defined by a **list-entries** element or a map defined by a **map-entries** element.	Zero or once	1.0, 1.1, 1.2
var	Specifies the logical name for a resource bundle instance that will be registered with the JSF application.	Once	1.2
variable-resolver	Specifies the fully qualified class name of a **javax.faces.el.VariableResolver** implementation class that will replace the JSF implementation's default variable resolver implementation.	Zero to unlimited	1.0, 1.1, 1.2
view-handler	Specifies the fully qualified class name of a **javax.faces.application.ViewHandler** implementation class that will replace the JSF implementation's default view handler implementation.	Zero to unlimited	1.0, 1.1, 1.2

TABLE 18-1   The Complete List of Elements of the JSF Configuration File *(continued)*

EXPERT GROUP INSIGHT   *The *-extension elements may contain any well-formed XML, but JCP JSR 276 is currently in process at the time of this writing. This JSR is called "Design Time Metadata for JSF Components" and will specify an XML schema for the contents of the *-extension elements that will provide a richer vocabulary for components to describe themselves to IDEs.*

The remainder of this chapter discusses each element in detail, including a complete description of the element, the element's DTD definition, a table that lists the element's usage rules, and a usage example for the element. In the tables that describe each element's usage rules, pay special attention to the JSF Versions rule, which specifies the JSF versions to which the given element is applicable. Also note that the DTD definitions included in this section include JSF 1.2 elements, even though these elements are not defined in any formal DTD. This was done for expediency because DTDs are far more human-readable than XML schemas.

The action-listener Element

The **action-listener** element is used to specify the fully qualified class name of a **javax.faces .event.ActionListener** implementation class that will replace the JSF implementation's default action listener implementation. The action listener is called during the Invoke Application phase of the JSF request processing lifecycle and is responsible for processing **javax.faces .event.ActionEvent** events. The **action-listener** element provides the ability to override the default JSF event processing by plugging in a custom **ActionListener**. More detail on the application of this element can be found in Chapter 11. An example **ActionListener** is shown in Chapter 14.

DTD Definition
Following is the DTD definition for the **action-listener** element:

```
<!ELEMENT action-listener (#PCDATA)>
```

Usage Rules

Rule	Value
JSF Versions	1.0, 1.1, 1.2
Parent Elements	application
Child Elements	None
Uniqueness Constraints	None

Example Usage
The following example illustrates the usage of the **action-listener** element:

```
<faces-config>
  <application>
    <action-listener>
      com.example.jsf.TestActionListener
    </action-listener>
  </application>
</faces-config>
```

The application Element
The **application** element is used to encapsulate the set of elements that specify application singleton classes, such as overriding or decorating the default **ViewHandler** or **ActionListener**. This element has no other use than to denote the beginning and end of the application configuration details.

DTD Definition
Following is the DTD definition for the **application** element:

```
<!ELEMENT application ((action-listener|default-render-kit-id|
message-bundle|navigation-handler|view-handler|state-manager|
el-resolver|property-resolver|variable-resolver|locale-config|
resource-bundle|application-extension)*)>
```

Usage Rules

Rule	Value
JSF Versions	1.0, 1.1, 1.2
Parent Elements	faces-config
Child Elements	action-listener, application-extension, default-render-kit-id, el-resolver, locale-config, message-bundle, navigation-handler, property-resolver, resource-bundle, state-manager, variable-resolver, view-handler
Uniqueness Constraints	None

Example Usage

The following example illustrates the usage of the **application** element:

```
<faces-config>
  <application>
    <action-listener>
      com.example.jsf.TestActionListener
    </action-listener>
    <state-manager>
      com.example.jsf.TestStateManager
    </state-manager>
  </application>
</faces-config>
```

The application-factory Element

The **application-factory** element is used to specify the fully qualified class name of a **javax .faces.application.ApplicationFactory** implementation class that will replace or decorate the JSF implementation's default application factory implementation. The application factory is used to retrieve and store a **javax.faces.application.Application** instance for the current Web application. See Chapter 11 for more details.

DTD Definition

Following is the DTD definition for the **application-factory** element:

```
<!ELEMENT application-factory (#PCDATA)>
```

Usage Rules

Rule	Value
JSF Versions	1.0, 1.1, 1.2
Parent Elements	factory
Child Elements	None
Uniqueness Constraints	None

Example Usage

The following example illustrates the usage of the **application-factory** element:

```
<faces-config>
  <factory>
    <application-factory>
      com.example.jsf.TestApplicationFactory
    </application-factory>
  </factory>
</faces-config>
```

The attribute Element

The **attribute** element is used to encapsulate the set of elements specifying the details for an attribute. This element has no other use than to denote the beginning and end of an attribute's configuration details.

There are four ways that the **attribute** element can be used, as listed here and shown later in the "Example Usage" section.

- An attribute can be defined for a UI component by nesting **attribute** elements inside the **component** element.

- An attribute can be defined for a converter by nesting **attribute** elements inside the **converter** element.

- An attribute can be defined for a renderer by nesting **attribute** elements inside the **renderer** element.

- An attribute can be defined for a validator by nesting **attribute** elements inside the **validator** element.

---

*EXPERT GROUP INSIGHT   All of these usages convey information intended for use at design time, such as by a tool. For example, it is useful to know that the **UIOutput** component has a **value** attribute, and that the **javax.faces.Messages** renderer has a **layout** attribute. A tool would use this information to populate a palette of options. The content of these elements has no runtime meaning; however, any XML errors will prevent the application from deploying at runtime.*

DTD Definition

Following is the DTD definition for the **attribute** element:

```
<!ELEMENT attribute ((descriptionGroup? | (description*, display-name*,
icon*)), attribute-name, attribute-class, default-value?, suggested-value?,
attribute-extension*)>
```

Usage Rules

Rule	Value
JSF Versions	1.0, 1.1, 1.2
Parent Elements	component, converter, renderer, validator
Child Elements	attribute-class, attribute-extension, attribute-name, default-value, description (1.0, 1.1), descriptionGroup (1.2), display-name (1.0, 1.1), icon (1.0, 1.1), suggested-value *Note: The parenthetical numbers represent the JSF versions that the corresponding child element applies to if the child element does not apply to all JSF versions.*
Uniqueness Constraints	None

Example Usage

As mentioned, there are four ways that the **attribute** element can be used. The first way, shown here, defines an attribute for a UI component:

```
<faces-config>
  <component>
    <component-type>
      com.example.jsf.TestComponent
    </component-type>
    <component-class>
      com.example.jsf.UITestComponent
    </component-class>
    <attribute>
      <attribute-name>testAttribute</attribute-name>
      <attribute-class>java.lang.String</attribute-class>
    </attribute>
  </component>
</faces-config>
```

The following is the second way to use the **attribute** element:

```
<faces-config>
  <converter>
    <component-for-class>
      java.lang.Long
    </component-for-class>
    <component-class>
      com.example.jsf.LongConverter
    </component-class>
    <attribute>
      <attribute-name>testAttribute</attribute-name>
      <attribute-class>java.lang.String</attribute-class>
    </attribute>
  </converter>
</faces-config>
```

The third way to use the **attribute** element is shown here:

```
<faces-config>
  <render-kit>
    <renderer>
      <component-family>
        javax.faces.Data
      </component-family>
      <renderer-type>
        javax.faces.Table
      </renderer-type>
      <renderer-class>
        com.sun.faces.renderkit.html_basic.TableRenderer
      </renderer-class>
      <attribute>
        <attribute-name>testAttribute</attribute-name>
        <attribute-class>java.lang.String</attribute-class>
      </attribute>
    </renderer>
  </render-kit>
</faces-config>
```

The fourth and final way to use the **attribute** element is shown here:

```
<faces-config>
  <validator>
    <validator-id>
      javax.faces.Length
    </validator-id>
    <validator-class>
      javax.faces.validator.LengthValidator
    </validator-class>
    <attribute>
      <attribute-name>testAttribute</attribute-name>
      <attribute-class>java.lang.String</attribute-class>
    </attribute>
  </validator>
</faces-config>
```

The attribute-class Element

The **attribute-class** element is used to specify the fully qualified class name for an attribute's value—for example, **java.lang.String** for string values and **java.lang.Integer** for an integer value.

DTD Definition

Following is the DTD definition for the **attribute-class** element:

```
<!ELEMENT attribute-class (#PCDATA)>
```

Usage Rules

Rule	Value
JSF Versions	1.0, 1.1, 1.2
Parent Elements	attribute
Child Elements	None
Uniqueness Constraints	None

Example Usage

The following example illustrates the usage of the **attribute-class** element:

```
<faces-config>
  <validator>
    <validator-id>
      javax.faces.Length
    </validator-id>
    <validator-class>
      javax.faces.validator.LengthValidator
    </validator-class>
    <attribute>
      <attribute-name>testAttribute</attribute-name>
      <attribute-class>java.lang.String</attribute-class>
```

```
      </attribute>
    </validator>
</faces-config>
```

The attribute-name Element

The **attribute-name** element is used to specify the logical name for an attribute under which the attribute's value will be stored.

DTD Definition

Following is the DTD definition for the **attribute-name** element:

```
<!ELEMENT attribute-name (#PCDATA)>
```

Usage Rules

Rule	Value
JSF Versions	1.0, 1.1, 1.2
Parent Elements	attribute
Child Elements	None
Uniqueness Constraints	None

Example Usage

The following example illustrates the usage of the **attribute-name** element:

```
<faces-config>
  <validator>
    <validator-id>
      javax.faces.Length
    </validator-id>
    <validator-class>
      javax.faces.validator.LengthValidator
    </validator-class>
    <attribute>
      <attribute-name>testAttribute</attribute-name>
      <attribute-class>java.lang.String</attribute-class>
    </attribute>
  </validator>
</faces-config>
```

The base-name Element

The **base-name** element is used to specify the fully qualified class name of a **javax.util** **.ResourceBundle** instance that will be registered with the JSF application with a logical name specified by an associated **var** element.

EXPERT GROUP INSIGHT   *This element was added in JSF 1.2 to provide application-scoped localization exposed via the EL. Prior to this feature it was only possible to define* **ResourceBundles** *on a per-view basis using the* **f:setBundle** *element.*

DTD Definition

Following is the DTD definition for the **base-name** element:

```
<!ELEMENT base-name (#PCDATA)>
```

Usage Rules

Rule	Value
JSF Versions	1.2
Parent Elements	resource-bundle
Child Elements	None
Uniqueness Constraints	None

Example Usage

The following example illustrates the usage of the **base-name** element:

```
<faces-config>
  <application>
    <resource-bundle>
      <base-name>
        com.example.jsf.TestResources
      </base-name>
      <var>testResources</var>
    </resource-bundle>
  </application>
</faces-config>
```

The component Element

The **component** element is used to encapsulate the set of elements specifying the details for a UI component. This element has no other use than to denote the beginning and end of the UI component details.

DTD Definition

Following is the DTD definition for the **component** element:

```
<!ELEMENT component ((descriptionGroup? | (description*, display-name*,
icon*)), component-type, component-class, facet*, attribute*, property*,
component-extension*)>
```

Usage Rules

Rule	Value
JSF Versions	1.0, 1.1, 1.2
Parent Elements	faces-config

Rule	Value
Child Elements	attribute, component-class, component-extension, component-type, description (1.0, 1.1), descriptionGroup (1.2), display-name (1.0, 1.1), facet, icon (1.0, 1.1), property *Note: The parenthetical numbers represent the JSF versions that the corresponding child element applies to if the child element does not apply to all JSF versions.*
Uniqueness Constraints	None

Example Usage

The following example illustrates the usage of the **component** element:

```
<faces-config>
  <component>
    <component-type>
      javax.faces.Input
    </component-type>
    <component-class>
      javax.faces.component.UIInput
    </component-class>
  </component>
</faces-config>
```

The component-class Element

The **component-class** element is used to specify the fully qualified class name for a UI component implementation. The implementation must extend from the **javax.faces .component.UIComponent** abstract base class.

DTD Definition

Following is the DTD definition for the **component-class** element:

```
<!ELEMENT component-class (#PCDATA)>
```

Usage Rules

Rule	Value
JSF Versions	1.0, 1.1, 1.2
Parent Elements	component
Child Elements	None
Uniqueness Constraints	None

Example Usage

The following example illustrates the usage of the **component-class** element:

```
<faces-config>
  <component>
```

```
   <component-type>
      javax.faces.Input
   </component-type>
   <component-class>
      javax.faces.component.UIInput
   </component-class>
  </component>
</faces-config>
```

The component-family Element

The **component-family** element is used to specify the component family that a renderer will be linked to. Component families are used to group families of components together and are used along with renderer types to uniquely identify a specific rendering.

DTD Definition

Following is the DTD definition for the **component-family** element:

```
<!ELEMENT component-family (#PCDATA)>
```

Usage Rules

Rule	Value
JSF Versions	1.0, 1.1, 1.2
Parent Elements	renderer
Child Elements	None
Uniqueness Constraints	None

Example Usage

The following example illustrates the usage of the **component-family** element:

```
<faces-config>
  <render-kit>
    <renderer>
      <component-family>
         javax.faces.Command
      </component-family>
      <renderer-type>
         javax.faces.Button
      </renderer-type>
      <renderer-class>
         com.sun.faces.renderkit.html_basic.ButtonRenderer
      </renderer-class>
    </renderer>
  </render-kit>
</faces-config>
```

The component-type Element

The **component-type** element is used to specify the logical name for a UI component. The logical name is used to register the UI component with JSF so that it can later be accessed by the same logical name.

DTD Definition

Following is the DTD definition for the **component-type** element:

```
<!ELEMENT component-type (#PCDATA)>
```

Usage Rules

Rule	Value
JSF Versions	1.0, 1.1, 1.2
Parent Elements	component
Child Elements	None
Uniqueness Constraints	None

Example Usage

The following example illustrates the usage of the **component-type** element:

```
<faces-config>
  <component>
    <component-type>
      javax.faces.Input
    </component-type>
    <component-class>
      javax.faces.component.UIInput
    </component-class>
  </component>
</faces-config>
```

The converter Element

The **converter** element is used to encapsulate the set of elements specifying the details for a converter. This element has no other use than to denote the beginning and end of the converter details.

DTD Definition

Following is the DTD definition for the **converter** element:

```
<!ELEMENT converter ((descriptionGroup? | (description*, display-name*,
icon*)), (converter-id | converter-for-class), converter-class, attribute*,
property*, converter-extension*)>
```

Usage Rules

Rule	Value
JSF Versions	1.0, 1.1, 1.2
Parent Elements	faces-config
Child Elements	attribute, converter-class, converter-extension (1.2), converter-for-class, converter-id, description (1.0, 1.1), descriptionGroup (1.2), display-name (1.0, 1.1), icon (1.0, 1.1), property *Note: The parenthetical numbers represent the JSF versions that the corresponding child element applies to if the child element does not apply to all JSF versions.*
Uniqueness Constraints	None

Example Usage

The following example illustrates the usage of the **converter** element:

```
<faces-config>
  <converter>
    <converter-for-class>
      java.lang.Double
    </converter-for-class>
    <converter-class>
      javax.faces.convert.DoubleConverter
    </converter-class>
  </converter>
</faces-config>
```

The converter-class Element

The **converter-class** element is used to specify the fully qualified class name for a converter implementation. The implementation must implement the **javax.faces.convert.Converter** interface.

DTD Definition

Following is the DTD definition for the **converter-class** element:

```
<!ELEMENT converter-class (#PCDATA)>
```

Usage Rules

Rule	Value
JSF Versions	1.0, 1.1, 1.2
Parent Elements	converter
Child Elements	None
Uniqueness Constraints	None

Example Usage
The following example illustrates the usage of the **converter-class** element:

```
<faces-config>
  <converter>
    <converter-for-class>
      java.lang.Double
    </converter-for-class>
    <converter-class>
      javax.faces.convert.DoubleConverter
    </converter-class>
  </converter>
</faces-config>
```

The converter-for-class Element
The **converter-for-class** element is used to specify the fully qualified class name for which a converter will be associated. JSF uses two mechanisms for associating converters: by ID (logical name) with the **converter-id** element, or by registering the converter to a corresponding class with the **converter-for-class** element.

DTD Definition
Following is the DTD definition for the **converter-for-class** element:

```
<!ELEMENT converter-for-class (#PCDATA)>
```

Usage Rules

Rule	Value
JSF Versions	1.0, 1.1, 1.2
Parent Elements	converter
Child Elements	None
Uniqueness Constraints	Values for this element must be unique within the configuration file.

Example Usage
The following example illustrates the usage of the **converter-for-class** element:

```
<faces-config>
  <converter>
    <converter-for-class>
      java.lang.Double
    </converter-for-class>
    <converter-class>
      javax.faces.convert.DoubleConverter
    </converter-class>
  </converter>
</faces-config>
```

The converter-id Element

The **converter-id** element is used to specify the logical name for a converter. The logical name is used to register the converter with JSF so that it can later be accessed by the same logical name. JSF uses two mechanisms for associating converters: by ID (logical name) with the **converter-id** element, or by registering the converter to a corresponding class with the **converter-for-class** element.

DTD Definition

Following is the DTD definition for the **converter-id** element:

```
<!ELEMENT converter-id (#PCDATA)>
```

Usage Rules

Rule	Value
JSF Versions	1.0, 1.1, 1.2
Parent Elements	converter
Child Elements	None
Uniqueness Constraints	Values for this element must be unique within the configuration file.

Example Usage

The following example illustrates the usage of the **converter-id** element:

```
<faces-config>
  <converter>
    <converter-id>
      javax.faces.Boolean
    </converter-id>
    <converter-class>
      javax.faces.convert.BooleanConverter
    </converter-class>
  </converter>
</faces-config>
```

The default-locale Element

The **default-locale** element is used to specify the default locale for the JSF application. JSF uses locale information to retrieve all localized resources for the application. JSF uses the default locale setting if another locale is not specified (e.g., via the browser). The locale value specified with the **default-locale** element must be in the following format:

> language_country_variant

The *language, country,* and *variant* arguments of the locale definition must be separated by either an underscore (_) or a hyphen (-). The *country* and *variant* arguments are optional. The *language* argument must be specified using a valid two-letter ISO-639 language code (e.g., "en" for English or "es" for Spanish). The *country* argument must be specified using a valid uppercase two-letter ISO-3166 country code (e.g., "US" for United States or "CA" for

Canada). The *variant* argument is for a vendor- or browser-specific code (e.g., "WIN" for Windows or "MAC" for Macintosh). For a listing of each of the ISO language and country codes, visit their respective specification Web sites listed here:

> **http://www.unicode.org/unicode/onlinedat/languages.html**
> **http://www.unicode.org/unicode/onlinedat/countries.html**

To illustrate the rules of locales, consider the following example locale definitions:

- **en**   English
- **en_US**   United States English
- **en_US_WIN**   United States English on Windows
- **es**   Spanish
- **es_MX**   Mexican Spanish
- **es_MX_MAC**   Mexican Spanish on Macintosh

DTD Definition

Following is the DTD definition for the **default-locale** element:

```
<!ELEMENT default-locale (#PCDATA)>
```

Usage Rules

Rule	Value
JSF Versions	1.0, 1.1, 1.2
Parent Elements	locale-config
Child Elements	None
Uniqueness Constraints	None

Example Usage

The following example illustrates the usage of the **default-locale** element:

```
<faces-config>
  <application>
    <locale-config>
      <default-locale>en</default-locale>
      <supported-locale>es</supported-locale>
      <supported-locale>fr_FR</supported-locale>
    </locale-config>
  </application>
</faces-config>
```

The default-render-kit-id Element

The **default-render-kit-id** element is used to specify the logical name of a render kit that will replace the JSF implementation's default render kit. The default render kit is responsible for rendering views via the view handler. The **default-render-kit-id** element provides the ability to override the default JSF view rendering by plugging in a custom render kit.

DTD Definition

Following is the DTD definition for the **default-render-kit-id** element:

```
<!ELEMENT default-render-kit-id (#PCDATA)>
```

Usage Rules

Rule	Value
JSF Versions	1.0, 1.1, 1.2
Parent Elements	application
Child Elements	None
Uniqueness Constraints	None

Example Usage

The following example illustrates the usage of the **default-render-kit-id** element:

```
<faces-config>
  <application>
    <default-render-kit-id>
      testRenderKit
    </default-render-kit-id>
  </application>
</faces-config>
```

The default-value Element

The **default-value** element is used to specify the default value for an attribute or a property. Default values differ from suggested values in that default values will be assigned to an attribute or property whereas suggested values are only suggestions and may or may not be applied to an attribute or property.

DTD Definition

Following is the DTD definition for the **default-value** element:

```
<!ELEMENT default-value (#PCDATA)>
```

Usage Rules

Rule	Value
JSF Versions	1.0, 1.1, 1.2
Parent Elements	attribute, property
Child Elements	None
Uniqueness Constraints	None

Example Usage

There are two ways that the **default-value** element can be used. The first way, shown here, defines a default value for an attribute:

```
<faces-config>
  <component>
    <component-type>
      com.example.jsf.TestComponent
    </component-type>
    <component-class>
      com.example.jsf.UITestComponent
    </component-class>
    <attribute>
      <attribute-name>testAttribute</attribute-name>
      <attribute-class>java.lang.String</attribute-class>
      <default-value>testDefaultValue</default-value>
    </attribute>
  </component>
</faces-config>
```

The following is the second way to use the **default-value** element to define a default value for a property:

```
<faces-config>
  <converter>
    <component-for-class>
      java.lang.Long
    </component-for-class>
    <component-class>
      com.example.jsf.LongConverter
    </component-class>
    <property>
      <property-name>testAttribute</property-name>
      <property-class>java.lang.String</property-class>
      <default-value>testDefaultValue</default-value>
    </property>
  </converter>
</faces-config>
```

The el-resolver Element

The **el-resolver** element is used to specify the fully qualified class name of a **javax.el .ELResolver** implementation class that will replace the JSF implementation's default expression language resolver implementation. The expression language resolver is called each time an expression must be resolved. The **el-resolver** element provides the ability to override the default JSF expression language resolving by plugging in a custom **ELResolver**. For more on this topic, see Chapter 11.

DTD Definition

Following is the DTD definition for the **el-resolver** element:

```
<!ELEMENT el-resolver (#PCDATA)>
```

PART IV

Usage Rules

Rule	Value
JSF Versions	1.2
Parent Elements	application
Child Elements	None
Uniqueness Constraints	None

Example Usage

The following example illustrates the usage of the **el-resolver** element:

```
<faces-config>
  <application>
    <el-resolver>
       com.example.jsf.TestELResolver
    </el-resolver>
  </application>
</faces-config>
```

The faces-config Element

The **faces-config** element is the root element for the JSF configuration file and thus encapsulates all other elements in the file. This element has no other use than to denote the beginning and end of the configuration data.

DTD Definition

Following is the DTD definition for the **faces-config** element:

```
<!ELEMENT faces-config ((application|factory|component|converter|
managed-bean|navigation-rule|referenced-bean|render-kit|lifecycle|
validator|faces-config-extension)*)>
```

Attributes

Attribute	Description	Required
version	Specifies the JSF implementation version that the configuration file is for. Note: This attribute was introduced in JSF 1.2 and does not apply to previous versions.	Yes

Usage Rules

Rule	Value
JSF Versions	1.0, 1.1, 1.2
Parent Elements	None

Rule	Value
Child Elements	application, component, converter, faces-config-extension (1.2), factory, lifecycle, managed-bean, navigation-rule, referenced-bean, render-kit, validator *Note: The parenthetical numbers represent the JSF versions that the corresponding child element applies to if the child element does not apply to all JSF versions.*
Uniqueness Constraints	Because this element is the root element for the JSF configuration file, it must occur only once.

Example Usage
The following example illustrates the usage of the **faces-config** element:

```
<faces-config>
  <application>
    <action-listener>
      com.example.jsf.TestActionListener
    </action-listener>
  </application>
</faces-config>
```

The faces-context-factory Element

The **faces-context-factory** element is used to specify the fully qualified class name of a **javax.faces.context.ApplicationFactory** implementation class that will replace the JSF implementation's default faces context factory implementation. The faces context factory is used to retrieve a **javax.faces.context.FacesContext** instance for the current Web application.

DTD Definition
Following is the DTD definition for the **faces-context-factory** element:

```
<!ELEMENT faces-context-factory (#PCDATA)>
```

Usage Rules

Rule	Value
JSF Versions	1.0, 1.1, 1.2
Parent Elements	factory
Child Elements	None
Uniqueness Constraints	None

Example Usage
The following example illustrates the usage of the **faces-context-factory** element:

```
<faces-config>
  <factory>
    <faces-context-factory>
```

```
          com.example.jsf.TestFacesContextFactory
       </faces-context-factory>
   </factory>
</faces-config>
```

The facet Element

The **facet** element is used to encapsulate the set of elements specifying the details for a facet. This element has no other use than to denote the beginning and end of the facet details.

There are two ways that the **facet** element can be used, as listed here and shown later in the "Example Usage" section.

- A facet can be defined for a UI component by nesting **facet** elements inside the **component** element.

- A facet can be defined for a renderer by nesting **facet** elements inside the **renderer** element.

DTD Definition

Following is the DTD definition for the **facet** element:

```
<!ELEMENT facet ((descriptionGroup? | (description*, display-name*,
icon*)), facet-name, facet-extension*)>
```

Usage Rules

Rule	Value
JSF Versions	1.1, 1.2
Parent Elements	component, renderer
Child Elements	description (1.0, 1.1), descriptionGroup (1.2), display-name (1.0, 1.1), facet-extension, facet-name, icon (1.0, 1.1) *Note: The parenthetical numbers represent the JSF versions that the corresponding child element applies to if the child element does not apply to all JSF versions.*
Uniqueness Constraints	None

Example Usage

As mentioned, there are two ways that the **facet** element can be used. The first way, shown here, defines a facet for a UI component:

```
<faces-config>
  <component>
    <component-type>
      com.example.jsf.TestComponent
    </component-type>
```

```
      <component-class>
        com.example.jsf.UITestComponent
      </component-class>
      <facet>
        <facet-name>header</facet-name>
      </facet>
    </component>
</faces-config>
```

The following is the second way to use the **facet** element:

```
<faces-config>
  <render-kit>
    <renderer>
      <component-family>
        javax.faces.Output
      </component-family>
      <renderer-type>
        javax.faces.Text
      </renderer-type>
      <renderer-class>
        com.sun.faces.renderkit.html_basic.TextRenderer
      </renderer-class>
      <facet>
        <facet-name>header</facet-name>
      </facet>
    </renderer>
  </render-kit>
</faces-config>
```

The facet-name Element

The **facet-name** element is used to specify the logical name for a facet. The logical name is used to register the facet with JSF so that it can later be accessed by the same logical name.

DTD Definition

Following is the DTD definition for the **facet-name** element:

```
<!ELEMENT facet-name (#PCDATA)>
```

Usage Rules

Rule	Value
JSF Versions	1.1, 1.2
Parent Elements	facet
Child Elements	None
Uniqueness Constraints	None

Example Usage

The following example illustrates the usage of the **facet-name** element:

```
<faces-config>
  <component>
    <component-type>
      com.example.jsf.TestComponent
    </component-type>
    <component-class>
      com.example.jsf.UITestComponent
    </component-class>
    <facet>
      <facet-name>header</facet-name>
    </facet>
  </component>
</faces-config>
```

The factory Element

The **factory** element is used to encapsulate the set of elements that specify factory configuration details. This element has no other use than to denote the beginning and end of the factory configuration details.

DTD Definition

Following is the DTD definition for the **factory** element:

```
<!ELEMENT factory ((application-factory|faces-context-factory|
lifecycle-factory|render-kit-factory)*)>
```

Usage Rules

Rule	Value
JSF Versions	1.0, 1.1, 1.2
Parent Elements	faces-config
Child Elements	application-factory, faces-context-factory, lifecycle-factory, render-kit-factory
Uniqueness Constraints	None

Example Usage

The following example illustrates the usage of the **factory** element:

```
<faces-config>
  <factory>
    <application-factory>
      com.example.jsf.TestApplicationFactory
    </application-factory>
    <lifecycle-factory>
      com.example.jsf.TestLifeCycleFactory
    </lifecycle-factory>
  </factory>
</faces-config>
```

The from-action Element

The **from-action** element is used to specify an action reference expression that must have been executed in order to have the associated navigation case selected.

DTD Definition

Following is the DTD definition for the **from-action** element:

```
<!ELEMENT from-action (#PCDATA)>
```

Usage Rules

Rule	Value
JSF Versions	1.0, 1.1, 1.2
Parent Elements	navigation-case
Child Elements	None
Uniqueness Constraints	None

Example Usage

The following example illustrates the usage of the **from-action** element:

```
<faces-config>
  <navigation-rule>
    <from-view-id>/main.jsp</from-view-id>
    <navigation-case>
      <from-action>#{loginForm.execute}</from-action>
      <from-outcome>success</from-outcome>
      <to-view-id>/details.jsp</to-view-id>
    </navigation-case>
  </navigation-rule>
</faces-config>
```

The from-outcome Element

The **from-outcome** element is used to specify the logical outcome value that an action method must generate in order to have the associated navigation case selected.

DTD Definition

Following is the DTD definition for the **from-outcome** element:

```
<!ELEMENT from-outcome (#PCDATA)>
```

Usage Rules

Rule	Value
JSF Versions	1.0, 1.1, 1.2
Parent Elements	navigation-case
Child Elements	None
Uniqueness Constraints	None

PART IV

Example Usage

The following example illustrates the usage of the **from-outcome** element:

```
<faces-config>
  <navigation-rule>
    <from-view-id>/main.jsp</from-view-id>
    <navigation-case>
      <from-outcome>details</from-outcome>
      <to-view-id>/details.jsp</to-view-id>
    </navigation-case>
  </navigation-rule>
</faces-config>
```

The from-view-id Element

The **from-view-id** element is used to specify the view ID that a navigation rule applies to. If a navigation rule does not specify a from view ID with this element, the navigation rule will apply to all view IDs. Similarly, an asterisk (*) can be used to signify a global navigation case.

DTD Definition

Following is the DTD definition for the **from-view-id** element:

```
<!ELEMENT from-view-id (#PCDATA)>
```

Usage Rules

Rule	Value
JSF Versions	1.0, 1.1, 1.2
Parent Elements	navigation-rule
Child Elements	None
Uniqueness Constraints	None

Example Usage

The following example illustrates the usage of the **from-view-id** element:

```
<faces-config>
  <navigation-rule>
    <from-view-id>/main.jsp</from-view-id>
    <navigation-case>
      <from-outcome>details</from-outcome>
      <to-view-id>/details.jsp</to-view-id>
    </navigation-case>
  </navigation-rule>
</faces-config>
```

The key Element

The **key** element is used to specify the key for a map entry defined by the **map-entry** element. Keys specified by the **key** element will be converted to the object type specified by an associated **key-class** element if present. If the **key-class** element is not present for the encompassing **map-entries** element, all keys for the map will be converted to **java.lang.String**.

DTD Definition

Following is the DTD definition for the **key** element:

```
<!ELEMENT key (#PCDATA)>
```

Usage Rules

Rule	Value
JSF Versions	1.0, 1.1, 1.2
Parent Elements	map-entry
Child Elements	None
Uniqueness Constraints	None

Example Usage

The following example illustrates the usage of the **key** element:

```
<faces-config>
  <managed-bean>
    <managed-bean-name>
      testManagedBean
    </managed-bean-name>
    <managed-bean-class>
      com.example.jsf.TestManagedBean
    </managed-bean-class>
    <managed-bean-scope>
      session
    </managed-bean-scope>
    <managed-property>
      <property-name>testProperty</property-name>
      <map-entries>
        <key-class>java.lang.Integer</key-class>
        <map-entry>
          <key>1000</key>
          <value>testValue1</value>
        </map-entry>
        <map-entry>
          <key>2000</key>
          <null-value/>
        </map-entry>
      <map-entries>
    </managed-property>
  </managed-bean>
</faces-config>
```

The key-class Element

The **key-class** element is used to specify the fully qualified class name of an object type that all keys will convert to before being added to a map defined by a **map-entries** element. If this element is not nested inside a **map-entries** element, all map entry keys will default to **java.lang.String** as their object type.

DTD Definition
Following is the DTD definition for the **key-class** element:

```
<!ELEMENT key-class (#PCDATA)>
```

Usage Rules

Rule	Value
JSF Versions	1.0, 1.1, 1.2
Parent Elements	map-entries
Child Elements	None
Uniqueness Constraints	None

Example Usage
The following example illustrates the usage of the **key-class** element:

```
<faces-config>
  <managed-bean>
    <managed-bean-name>
      testManagedBean
    </managed-bean-name>
    <managed-bean-class>
      com.example.jsf.TestManagedBean
    </managed-bean-class>
    <managed-bean-scope>
      session
    </managed-bean-scope>
    <managed-property>
      <property-name>testProperty</property-name>
      <map-entries>
        <key-class>java.lang.Integer</key-class>
        <map-entry>
          <key>1000</key>
          <value>testValue1</value>
        </map-entry>
        <map-entry>
          <key>2000</key>
          <null-value/>
        </map-entry>
      <map-entries>
    </managed-property>
  </managed-bean>
</faces-config>
```

The lifecycle Element
The **lifecycle** element is used to encapsulate the set of elements that specify lifecycle configuration details. This element has no other use than to denote the beginning and end of the lifecycle configuration details.

DTD Definition

Following is the DTD definition for the **lifecycle** element:

```
<!ELEMENT lifecycle (phase-listener*)>
```

Usage Rules

Rule	Value
JSF Versions	1.0, 1.1, 1.2
Parent Elements	faces-config
Child Elements	phase-listener
Uniqueness Constraints	None

Example Usage

The following example illustrates the usage of the **lifecycle** element:

```
<faces-config>
  <lifecycle>
    <phase-listener>
      com.example.jsf.TestPhaseListener
    </phase-listener>
  </lifecycle>
</faces-config>
```

The lifecycle-factory Element

The **lifecycle-factory** element is used to specify the fully qualified class name of a **javax.faces.lifecycle.LifecycleFactory** implementation class that will replace the JSF implementation's default lifecycle factory implementation. The lifecycle factory is used to store and retrieve **javax.faces.lifecycle.Lifecycle** instances for the current Web application as well as to retrieve a list of the IDs for lifecycles supported by the factory.

DTD Definition

Following is the DTD definition for the **lifecycle-factory** element:

```
<!ELEMENT lifecycle-factory (#PCDATA)>
```

Usage Rules

Rule	Value
JSF Versions	1.0, 1.1, 1.2
Parent Elements	factory
Child Elements	None
Uniqueness Constraints	None

Example Usage

The following example illustrates the usage of the **lifecycle-factory** element:

```
<faces-config>
  <factory>
    <lifecycle-factory>
      com.example.jsf.TestLifecycleFactory
    </lifecycle-factory>
  </factory>
</faces-config>
```

The list-entries Element

The **list-entries** element is used to encapsulate a list of values that will be used to populate a **java.util.List** instance or an array that will serve as the value for a managed property or to populate a managed bean that is itself an instance of **java.util.List**.

DTD Definition

Following is the DTD definition for the **list-entries** element:

```
<!ELEMENT list-entries (value-class?, (null-value|value)*)>
```

Usage Rules

Rule	Value
JSF Versions	1.0, 1.1, 1.2
Parent Elements	managed-bean, managed-property
Child Elements	null-value, value, value-class
Uniqueness Constraints	None

Example Usage

The following example illustrates the usage of the **list-entries** element to populate a managed property's value with a **java.util.List** instance:

```
<faces-config>
  <managed-bean>
    <managed-bean-name>
      testManagedBean
    </managed-bean-name>
    <managed-bean-class>
      com.example.jsf.TestManagedBean
    </managed-bean-class>
    <managed-bean-scope>
      session
    </managed-bean-scope>
    <managed-property>
      <property-name>testProperty</property-name>
```

```
   <list-entries>
      <value>1000</value>
      <value>2000</value>
   <list-entries>
  </managed-property>
 </managed-bean>
</faces-config>
```

The second way to use the **list-entries** element is shown here:

```
<faces-config>
  <managed-bean>
    <managed-bean-name>
      testManagedBean
    </managed-bean-name>
    <managed-bean-class>
      com.example.jsf.TestManagedBean
    </managed-bean-class>
    <managed-bean-scope>
      session
    </managed-bean-scope>
    <list-entries>
      <value>1000</value>
      <value>2000</value>
    <list-entries>
  </managed-bean>
</faces-config>
```

This example populates a managed bean that is itself an instance of **java.util.List**.

The locale-config Element

The **locale-config** element is used to encapsulate the set of elements that specify the application's locale configuration details. This element has no other use than to denote the beginning and end of the locale configuration details.

DTD Definition

Following is the DTD definition for the **locale-config** element:

```
<!ELEMENT locale-config (default-locale?, supported-locale*)>
```

Usage Rules

Rule	Value
JSF Versions	1.0, 1.1, 1.2
Parent Elements	application
Child Elements	default-locale, supported-locale
Uniqueness Constraints	None

Example Usage

The following example illustrates the usage of the **locale-config** element:

```
<faces-config>
  <application>
    <locale-config>
      <default-locale>en</default-locale>
      <supported-locale>es</supported-locale>
      <supported-locale>fr_FR</supported-locale>
    </locale-config>
  </application>
</faces-config>
```

The managed-bean Element

The **managed-bean** element is used to encapsulate the set of elements specifying the details for a managed bean. Managed beans are beans that JSF manages for an application by providing lifecycle services. Managed beans are instantiated and populated by JSF at runtime as needed. For detailed information on managed beans, see Chapter 4.

DTD Definition

Following is the DTD definition for the **managed-bean** element:

```
<!ELEMENT managed-bean ((descriptionGroup? | (description*, display-name*,
icon*)), managed-bean-name, managed-bean-class, managed-bean-scope,
(managed-property* | map-entries | list-entries))>
```

Usage Rules

Rule	Value
JSF Versions	1.0, 1.1, 1.2
Parent Elements	faces-config
Child Elements	description (1.0, 1.1), descriptionGroup (1.2), display-name (1.0, 1.1), icon (1.0, 1.1), list-entries, managed-bean-class, managed-bean-extension, managed-bean-name, managed-bean-scope, managed-property, map-entries *Note: The parenthetical numbers represent the JSF versions that the corresponding child element applies to if the child element does not apply to all JSF versions.*
Uniqueness Constraints	None

Example Usage

The following example illustrates the usage of the **managed-bean** element:

```
<faces-config>
  <managed-bean>
    <managed-bean-name>
      testManagedBean
    </managed-bean-name>
```

```
    <managed-bean-class>
      com.example.jsf.TestManagedBean
    </managed-bean-class>
    <managed-bean-scope>
      session
    </managed-bean-scope>
    <managed-property>
      <property-name>testProperty</property-name>
      <value>testValue</value>
    </managed-property>
  </managed-bean>
</faces-config>
```

The managed-bean-class Element

The **managed-bean-class** element is used to specify the fully qualified class name of a managed bean.

DTD Definition

Following is the DTD definition for the **managed-bean-class** element:

```
<!ELEMENT managed-bean-class (#PCDATA)>
```

Usage Rules

Rule	Value
JSF Versions	1.0, 1.1, 1.2
Parent Elements	managed-bean
Child Elements	None
Uniqueness Constraints	None

Example Usage

The following example illustrates the usage of the **managed-bean-class** element:

```
<faces-config>
  <managed-bean>
    <managed-bean-name>
      testManagedBean
    </managed-bean-name>
    <managed-bean-class>
      com.example.jsf.TestManagedBean
    </managed-bean-class>
    <managed-bean-scope>
      session
    </managed-bean-scope>
    <managed-property>
      <property-name>testProperty</property-name>
      <value>testValue</value>
    </managed-property>
  </managed-bean>
</faces-config>
```

The managed-bean-name Element

The **managed-bean-name** element is used to specify the logical name for a managed bean. The logical name is used to register the managed bean with JSF so that it can later be accessed by the same logical name.

DTD Definition

Following is the DTD definition for the **managed-bean-name** element:

```
<!ELEMENT managed-bean-name (#PCDATA)>
```

Usage Rules

Rule	Value
JSF Versions	1.0, 1.1, 1.2
Parent Elements	managed-bean
Child Elements	None
Uniqueness Constraints	Values for this element must be unique within the configuration file.

Example Usage

The following example illustrates the usage of the **managed-bean-name** element:

```
<faces-config>
  <managed-bean>
    <managed-bean-name>
      testManagedBean
    </managed-bean-name>
    <managed-bean-class>
      com.example.jsf.TestManagedBean
    </managed-bean-class>
    <managed-bean-scope>
      session
    </managed-bean-scope>
    <managed-property>
      <property-name>testProperty</property-name>
      <value>testValue</value>
    </managed-property>
  </managed-bean>
</faces-config>
```

The managed-bean-scope Element

The **managed-bean-scope** element is used to specify the Web application scope that the managed bean will be stored in when it is instantiated. The values this element accepts are **request**, **session**, **application**, or **none**. A value of **none** indicates that the managed bean should be instantiated, but not be stored in a Web application scope. Using **none** is helpful in the scenario of dynamically creating trees of related objects.

DTD Definition

Following is the DTD definition for the **managed-bean-scope** element:

```
<!ELEMENT managed-bean-scope (#PCDATA)>
```

Usage Rules

Rule	Value
JSF Versions	1.0, 1.1, 1.2
Parent Elements	managed-bean-scope
Child Elements	None
Uniqueness Constraints	None

Example Usage

The following example illustrates the usage of the **managed-bean-scope** element:

```
<faces-config>
  <managed-bean>
    <managed-bean-name>
      testManagedBean
    </managed-bean-name>
    <managed-bean-class>
      com.example.jsf.TestManagedBean
    </managed-bean-class>
    <managed-bean-scope>
      session
    </managed-bean-scope>
    <managed-property>
      <property-name>testProperty</property-name>
      <value>testValue</value>
    </managed-property>
  </managed-bean>
</faces-config>
```

The managed-property Element

The **managed-property** element is used to encapsulate the set of elements specifying the details for a managed bean's property. This element has no other use than to denote the beginning and end of a managed property's configuration details.

DTD Definition

Following is the DTD definition for the **managed-property** element:

```
<!ELEMENT managed-property ((descriptionGroup? | (description*,
display-name*, icon*)), property-name, property-class?, (map-entries|
null-value|value|list-entries))>
```

Usage Rules

Rule	Value
JSF Versions	1.0, 1.1, 1.2
Parent Elements	managed-bean
Child Elements	description (1.0, 1.1), descriptionGroup (1.2), display-name (1.0, 1.1), icon (1.0, 1.1), list-entries, map-entries, null-value, property-class, property-name, value *Note: The parenthetical numbers represent the JSF versions that the corresponding child element applies to if the child element does not apply to all JSF versions.*
Uniqueness Constraints	None

Example Usage

The following example illustrates the usage of the **managed-property** element:

```
<faces-config>
  <managed-bean>
    <managed-bean-name>
      testManagedBean
    </managed-bean-name>
    <managed-bean-class>
      com.example.jsf.TestManagedBean
    </managed-bean-class>
    <managed-bean-scope>
      session
    </managed-bean-scope>
    <managed-property>
      <property-name>testProperty</property-name>
      <value>testValue</value>
    </managed-property>
  </managed-bean>
</faces-config>
```

The map-entries Element

The **map-entries** element is used to encapsulate a set of key-value pairs that will be used to populate a **java.util.Map** instance that will serve as the value for a managed property or to populate a managed bean that is itself an instance of **java.util.Map**.

DTD Definition

Following is the DTD definition for the **map-entries** element:

```
<!ELEMENT map-entries (key-class?, value-class?, map-entry*)>
```

Usage Rules

Rule	Value
JSF Versions	1.0, 1.1, 1.2
Parent Elements	managed-bean, managed-property
Child Elements	key-class, map-entry, value-class
Uniqueness Constraints	None

Example Usage

The following example illustrates the usage of the **map-entries** element to populate a managed property's value with a **java.util.Map** instance:

```
<faces-config>
  <managed-bean>
    <managed-bean-name>
      testManagedBean
    </managed-bean-name>
    <managed-bean-class>
      com.example.jsf.TestManagedBean
    </managed-bean-class>
    <managed-bean-scope>
      session
    </managed-bean-scope>
    <managed-property>
      <property-name>testProperty</property-name>
      <map-entries>
        <map-entry>
          <key>testKey1</key>
          <value>1000</value>
        </map-entry>
        <map-entry>
          <key>testKey2</key>
          <null-value/>
        </map-entry>
      <map-entries>
    </managed-property>
  </managed-bean>
</faces-config>
```

The second way to use the **map-entries** element is shown here:

```
<faces-config>
  <managed-bean>
    <managed-bean-name>
      testManagedBean
    </managed-bean-name>
```

```
  <managed-bean-class>
    com.example.jsf.TestManagedBean
  </managed-bean-class>
  <managed-bean-scope>
    session
  </managed-bean-scope>
  <map-entries>
    <map-entry>
      <key>testKey1</key>
      <value>1000</value>
    </map-entry>
    <map-entry>
      <key>testKey2</key>
      <null-value/>
    </map-entry>
  <map-entries>
  </managed-bean>
</faces-config>
```

This example populates a managed bean that is itself an instance of **java.util.Map**.

The map-entry Element

The **map-entry** element is used to encapsulate a key-value pair that makes up an entry for a map defined by a **map-entries** element.

DTD Definition

Following is the DTD definition for the **map-entry** element:

```
<!ELEMENT map-entry (key, (null-value|value))>
```

Usage Rules

Rule	Value
JSF Versions	1.0, 1.1, 1.2
Parent Elements	map-entries
Child Elements	key, null-value, value
Uniqueness Constraints	None

Example Usage

The following example illustrates the usage of the **map-entry** element:

```
<faces-config>
  <managed-bean>
    <managed-bean-name>
      testManagedBean
    </managed-bean-name>
    <managed-bean-class>
      com.example.jsf.TestManagedBean
    </managed-bean-class>
    <managed-bean-scope>
      session
    </managed-bean-scope>
```

```
      <managed-property>
        <property-name>testProperty</property-name>
        <map-entries>
          <map-entry>
            <key>testKey1</key>
            <value>testValue1</value>
          </map-entry>
          <map-entry>
            <key>testKey2</key>
            <null-value/>
          </map-entry>
        <map-entries>
      </managed-property>
    </managed-bean>
</faces-config>
```

The message-bundle Element

The **message-bundle** element is used to specify the fully qualified base name of a resource bundle that will be used for the JSF application. The value specified with this element must use Java's dot (.) package notation to separate directories and the resource bundle file name. Here is an example:

```
dir1.dir2.dir3.ResourceBundleFileName
```

Note that the **.properties** extension of the resource bundle file name should not be included in the value specified with the **message-bundle** element. JSF automatically appends that to the file name at runtime along with any locale information that might be necessary.

DTD Definition

Following is the DTD definition for the **message-bundle** element:

```
<!ELEMENT message-bundle (#PCDATA)>
```

Usage Rules

Rule	Value
JSF Versions	1.0, 1.1, 1.2
Parent Elements	application
Child Elements	None
Uniqueness Constraints	None

Example Usage

The following example illustrates the usage of the **message-bundle** element:

```
<faces-config>
  <application>
    <message-bundle>
      com.example.jsf.TestResources
    </message-bundle>
  </application>
</faces-config>
```

The navigation-case Element

The **navigation-case** element is used to encapsulate the set of elements that specify navigation case configuration details. This element has no other use than to denote the beginning and end of the navigation case configuration details.

DTD Definition

Following is the DTD definition for the **navigation-case** element:

```
<!ELEMENT navigation-case ((descriptionGroup? | (description*,
display-name*, icon*)), from-action?, from-outcome?, to-view-id,
redirect?)>
```

Usage Rules

Rule	Value
JSF Versions	1.0, 1.1, 1.2
Parent Elements	navigation-rule
Child Elements	description (1.0, 1.1), descriptionGroup (1.2), display-name (1.0, 1.1), from-action, from-outcome, icon (1.0, 1.1), redirect, to-view-id *Note: The parenthetical numbers represent the JSF versions that the corresponding child element applies to if the child element does not apply to all JSF versions.*
Uniqueness Constraints	None

Example Usage

The following example illustrates the usage of the **navigation-case** element:

```
<faces-config>
  <navigation-rule>
    <from-view-id>/main.jsp</from-view-id>
    <navigation-case>
      <from-outcome>details</from-outcome>
      <to-view-id>/details.jsp</to-view-id>
    </navigation-case>
  </navigation-rule>
</faces-config>
```

The navigation-handler Element

The **navigation-handler** element is used to specify the fully qualified class name of a **javax .faces.application.NavigationHandler** implementation class that will replace the JSF implementation's default navigation handler implementation. The navigation handler is called during the Invoke Application phase of the JSF request processing lifecycle and is responsible for managing the navigation between views in a JSF application. The **navigation-handler** element provides the ability to override the default JSF navigation handling by plugging in a custom **NavigationHandler**.

DTD Definition
Following is the DTD definition for the **navigation-handler** element:

```
<!ELEMENT navigation-handler (#PCDATA)>
```

Usage Rules

Rule	Value
JSF Versions	1.0, 1.1, 1.2
Parent Elements	application
Child Elements	None
Uniqueness Constraints	None

Example Usage
The following example illustrates the usage of the **navigation-handler** element:

```
<faces-config>
  <application>
    <navigation-handler>
      com.example.jsf.TestNavigationHandler
    </navigation-handler>
  </application>
</faces-config>
```

The navigation-rule Element

The **navigation-rule** element is used to encapsulate the set of elements that specify navigation rule configuration details. This element has no other use than to denote the beginning and end of the navigation rule configuration details.

DTD Definition
Following is the DTD definition for the **navigation-rule** element:

```
<!ELEMENT navigation-rule ((descriptionGroup? | (description*, display-name*,
icon*)), from-view-id?, navigation-case*)>
```

Usage Rules

Rule	Value
JSF Versions	1.0, 1.1, 1.2
Parent Elements	faces-config
Child Elements	description (1.0, 1.1), descriptionGroup (1.2), display-name (1.0, 1.1), from-view-id, icon (1.0, 1.1), navigation-case *Note: The parenthetical numbers represent the JSF versions that the corresponding child element applies to if the child element does not apply to all JSF versions.*
Uniqueness Constraints	None

Example Usage
The following example illustrates the usage of the **navigation-rule** element:

```
<faces-config>
  <navigation-rule>
    <from-view-id>/main.jsp</from-view-id>
    <navigation-case>
      <from-outcome>details</from-outcome>
      <to-view-id>/details.jsp</to-view-id>
    </navigation-case>
  </navigation-rule>
</faces-config>
```

The null-value Element
The **null-value** element is used to indicate that the property defined by the enclosing element must be initialized to null. Note that the **null-value** element does not accept any values and is to be used as an empty element, as shown here:

```
</null-value>
```

There are three ways that the **null-value** element can be used, as listed here and shown later in the "Example Usage" section.

- A list entry can be initialized to null by nesting a **null-value** element inside the **list-entries** element.

- A managed property of a managed bean can be initialized to null by nesting a **null-value** element inside the **managed-property** element.

- A map entry can be initialized to null by nesting a **null-value** element inside the **map-entry** element.

DTD Definition
Following is the DTD definition for the **null-value** element:

```
<!ELEMENT null-value EMPTY>
```

Usage Rules

Rule	Value
JSF Versions	1.0, 1.1, 1.2
Parent Elements	list-entries, managed-property, map-entry
Child Elements	None
Uniqueness Constraints	None

Example Usage
As mentioned, there are three ways that the **null-value** element can be used. The first way, shown here, defines a null entry for a list:

```
<faces-config>
  <managed-bean>
    <managed-bean-name>
      testManagedBean
    </managed-bean-name>
    <managed-bean-class>
      com.example.jsf.TestManagedBean
    </managed-bean-class>
    <managed-bean-scope>
      session
    </managed-bean-scope>
    <managed-property>
      <property-name>testProperty</property-name>
      <list-entries>
        <value>testValue1</value>
        <null-value/>
        <value>testValue3</value>
      <list-entries>
    </managed-property>
  </managed-bean>
</faces-config>
```

The following is the second way to use the **null-value** element for instantiating a managed property to null:

```
<faces-config>
  <managed-bean>
    <managed-bean-name>
      testManagedBean
    </managed-bean-name>
    <managed-bean-class>
      com.example.jsf.TestManagedBean
    </managed-bean-class>
    <managed-bean-scope>
      session
    </managed-bean-scope>
    <managed-property>
      <property-name>testProperty</property-name>
      <null-value/>
    </managed-property>
  </managed-bean>
</faces-config>
```

The third and final way to use the **null-value** element is shown here:

```
<faces-config>
  <managed-bean>
    <managed-bean-name>
      testManagedBean
    </managed-bean-name>
    <managed-bean-class>
      com.example.jsf.TestManagedBean
    </managed-bean-class>
```

```
      <managed-bean-scope>
        session
      </managed-bean-scope>
      <managed-property>
        <property-name>testProperty</property-name>
        <map-entries>
          <map-entry>
            <key>testKey1</key>
            <value>testValue1</value>
          </map-entry>
          <map-entry>
            <key>testKey2</key>
            <null-value/>
          </map-entry>
        <map-entries>
      </managed-property>
    </managed-bean>
</faces-config>
```

This example shows how to initialize a map entry to null.

The phase-listener Element

The **phase-listener** element is used to specify the fully qualified class name of a **javax.faces .event.PhaseListener** implementation class that will be notified of all phase changes during the JSF request processing lifecycle.

DTD Definition

Following is the DTD definition for the **phase-listener** element:

```
<!ELEMENT phase-listener (#PCDATA)>
```

Usage Rules

Rule	Value
JSF Versions	1.0, 1.1, 1.2
Parent Elements	lifecycle
Child Elements	None
Uniqueness Constraints	None

Example Usage

The following example illustrates the usage of the **phase-listener** element:

```
<faces-config>
  <lifecycle>
    <phase-listener>
      com.example.jsf.TestPhaseListener
    </phase-listener>
  </lifecycle>
</faces-config>
```

The property Element

The **property** element is used to encapsulate the set of elements specifying the details for a property. This element has no other use than to denote the beginning and end of a property's configuration details.

There are three ways that the **property** element can be used, as listed here and shown later in the "Example Usage" section.

- A property can be defined for a UI component by nesting **property** elements inside the **component** element.

- A property can be defined for a converter by nesting **property** elements inside the **converter** element.

- A property can be defined for a validator by nesting **property** elements inside the **validator** element.

DTD Definition

Following is the DTD definition for the **property** element:

```
<!ELEMENT property ((descriptionGroup? | (description*, display-name*,
icon*)), property-name, property-class, default-value?, suggested-value?,
property-extension*)>
```

Usage Rules

Rule	Value
JSF Versions	1.0, 1.1, 1.2
Parent Elements	component, converter, validator
Child Elements	default-value, description (1.0, 1.1), descriptionGroup (1.2), display-name (1.0, 1.1), icon (1.0, 1.1), property-class, property-extension, property-name, suggested-value *Note: The parenthetical numbers represent the JSF versions that the corresponding child element applies to if the child element does not apply to all JSF versions.*
Uniqueness Constraints	None

Example Usage

As mentioned, there are three ways that the **property** element can be used. The first way, shown here, defines a property for a UI component:

```
<faces-config>
  <component>
    <component-type>
      com.example.jsf.TestComponent
    </component-type>
    <component-class>
      com.example.jsf.UITestComponent
```

```
      </component-class>
      <property>
        <property-name>testProperty</property-name>
        <property-class>java.lang.String</property-class>
      </property>
    </component>
</faces-config>
```

The following is the second way to use the **property** element:

```
<faces-config>
  <converter>
    <component-for-class>
      java.lang.Long
    </component-for-class>
    <component-class>
      com.example.jsf.LongConverter
    </component-class>
    <property>
      <property-name>testProperty</property-name>
      <property-class>java.lang.String</property-class>
    </property>
  </converter>
</faces-config>
```

The third and final way to use the **property** element is shown here:

```
<faces-config>
  <validator>
    <validator-id>
      javax.faces.Length
    </validator-id>
    <validator-class>
      javax.faces.validator.LengthValidator
    </validator-class>
    <property>
      <property-name>testProperty</property-name>
      <property-class>java.lang.String</property-class>
    </property>
  </validator>
</faces-config>
```

The property-class Element

The **property-class** element is used to specify the fully qualified class name for a property's value—for example, **java.lang.String** for string values and **java.lang.Integer** for an integer value.

DTD Definition

Following is the DTD definition for the **property-class** element:

```
<!ELEMENT property-class (#PCDATA)>
```

Usage Rules

Rule	Value
JSF Versions	1.0, 1.1, 1.2
Parent Elements	property
Child Elements	None
Uniqueness Constraints	None

Example Usage

The following example illustrates the usage of the **property-class** element:

```
<faces-config>
  <validator>
    <validator-id>
      javax.faces.Length
    </validator-id>
    <validator-class>
      javax.faces.validator.LengthValidator
    </validator-class>
    <property>
      <property-name>testProperty</property-name>
      <property-class>java.lang.String</property-class>
    </property>
  </validator>
</faces-config>
```

The property-name Element

The **property-name** element is used to specify the logical name for a property under which the property's value will be stored.

DTD Definition

Following is the DTD definition for the **property-name** element:

```
<!ELEMENT property-name (#PCDATA)>
```

Usage Rules

Rule	Value
JSF Versions	1.0, 1.1, 1.2
Parent Elements	property
Child Elements	None
Uniqueness Constraints	None

Example Usage

The following example illustrates the usage of the **property-name** element:

```
<faces-config>
  <validator>
    <validator-id>
      javax.faces.Length
    </validator-id>
    <validator-class>
      javax.faces.validator.LengthValidator
    </validator-class>
    <property>
      <property-name>testProperty</property-name>
      <property-class>java.lang.String</property-class>
    </property>
  </validator>
</faces-config>
```

The property-resolver Element

The **property-resolver** element is used to specify the fully qualified class name of a **javax .faces.el.PropertyResolver** implementation class that will replace the JSF implementation's default property resolver implementation. The property resolver is used to process value binding expressions and is called each time a value binding expression must be resolved. The **property-resolver** element provides the ability to override the default JSF property resolving by plugging in a custom **PropertyResolver**.

DTD Definition

Following is the DTD definition for the **property-resolver** element:

```
<!ELEMENT property-resolver (#PCDATA)>
```

Usage Rules

Rule	Value
JSF Versions	1.0, 1.1, 1.2
Parent Elements	application
Child Elements	None
Uniqueness Constraints	None

Example Usage

The following example illustrates the usage of the **property-resolver** element:

```
<faces-config>
  <application>
    <property-resolver>
      com.example.jsf.TestPropertyResolver
    </property-resolver>
```

```
    </application>
</faces-config>
```

The redirect Element

The **redirect** element is used to indicate that the associated navigation case's to-view-id URL should be navigated to using an HTTP redirect instead of the standard View Handler processing.

DTD Definition

Following is the DTD definition for the **redirect** element:

```
<!ELEMENT redirect EMPTY>
```

Usage Rules

Rule	Value
JSF Versions	1.0, 1.1, 1.2
Parent Elements	navigation-case
Child Elements	None
Uniqueness Constraints	None

Example Usage

The following example illustrates the usage of the **redirect** element:

```
<faces-config>
  <navigation-rule>
    <from-view-id>/main.jsp</from-view-id>
    <navigation-case>
      <from-outcome>details</from-outcome>
      <to-view-id>/details.jsp</to-view-id>
      <redirect/>
    </navigation-case>
  </navigation-rule>
</faces-config>
```

The referenced-bean Element

The **referenced-bean** element is used to encapsulate the set of elements specifying the details for a referenced bean. Referenced beans are external beans that are supposed to be available to a JSF application at runtime by existing in one of the Web application scopes (request, session, or application). This element has no other use than to denote the beginning and end of the referenced bean details.

DTD Definition

Following is the DTD definition for the **referenced-bean** element:

```
<!ELEMENT referenced-bean ((descriptionGroup? | (description*,
display-name*, icon*)), referenced-bean-name, referenced-bean-class)>
```

Usage Rules

Rule	Value
JSF Versions	1.0, 1.1, 1.2
Parent Elements	faces-config
Child Elements	description (1.0, 1.1), descriptionGroup (1.2), display-name (1.0, 1.1), icon (1.0, 1.1), referenced-bean-class, referenced-bean-name *Note: The parenthetical numbers represent the JSF versions that the corresponding child element applies to if the child element does not apply to all JSF versions.*
Uniqueness Constraints	None

Example Usage

The following example illustrates the usage of the **referenced-bean** element:

```
<faces-config>
  <referenced-bean>
    <referenced-bean-name>
      TestReferencedBean
    </referenced-bean-name>
    <referenced-bean-class>
      com.example.jsf.TestReferencedBean
    </referenced-bean-class>
  </referenced-bean>
</faces-config>
```

The referenced-bean-class Element

The **referenced-bean-class** element is used to specify the fully qualified class name of an external bean that is supposed to be available to the JSF application at runtime by existing in one of the Web application scopes (request, session, or application).

DTD Definition

Following is the DTD definition for the **referenced-bean-class** element:

```
<!ELEMENT referenced-bean-class (#PCDATA)>
```

Usage Rules

Rule	Value
JSF Versions	1.0, 1.1, 1.2
Parent Elements	referenced-bean
Child Elements	None
Uniqueness Constraints	None

Example Usage
The following example illustrates the usage of the **referenced-bean-class** element:

```
<faces-config>
  <referenced-bean>
    <referenced-bean-name>
      TestReferencedBean
    </referenced-bean-name>
    <referenced-bean-class>
      com.example.jsf.TestReferencedBean
    </referenced-bean-class>
  </referenced-bean>
</faces-config>
```

The referenced-bean-name Element
The **referenced-bean-name** element is used to specify the logical name for a referenced bean. The logical name is used to register the referenced bean with JSF so that it can later be accessed by the same logical name.

DTD Definition
Following is the DTD definition for the **referenced-bean-name** element:

```
<!ELEMENT referenced-bean-name (#PCDATA)>
```

Usage Rules

Rule	Value
JSF Versions	1.0, 1.1, 1.2
Parent Elements	referenced-bean
Child Elements	None
Uniqueness Constraints	None

Example Usage
The following example illustrates the usage of the **referenced-bean-name** element:

```
<faces-config>
  <referenced-bean>
    <referenced-bean-name>
      TestReferencedBean
    </referenced-bean-name>
    <referenced-bean-class>
      com.example.jsf.TestReferencedBean
    </referenced-bean-class>
  </referenced-bean>
</faces-config>
```

The render-kit Element
The **render-kit** element is used to encapsulate the set of elements specifying the details for a render kit. This element has no other use than to denote the beginning and end of the render kit details.

PART IV

DTD Definition

Following is the DTD definition for the **render-kit** element:

```
<!ELEMENT render-kit ((descriptionGroup? | (description*, display-name*,
icon*)), render-kit-id?, render-kit-class?, renderer*, render-kit-extension*)>
```

Usage Rules

Rule	Value
JSF Versions	1.0, 1.1, 1.2
Parent Elements	faces-config
Child Elements	description (1.0, 1.1), descriptionGroup (1.2), display-name (1.0, 1.1), icon (1.0, 1.1), render-kit-class, render-kit-extension (1.2), render-kit-id, renderer *Note: The parenthetical numbers represent the JSF versions that the corresponding child element applies to if the child element does not apply to all JSF versions.*
Uniqueness Constraints	None

Example Usage

The following example illustrates the usage of the **render-kit** element:

```
<faces-config>
  <render-kit>
    <render-kit-id>test</render-kit-id>
    <render-kit-class>
      com.example.jsf.TestRenderKit
    </render-kit-class>
    <renderer>
      <component-family>
        javax.faces.Data
      </component-family>
      <renderer-type>
        javax.faces.Table
      </renderer-type>
      <renderer-class>
        com.sun.faces.renderkit.html_basic.TableRenderer
      </renderer-class>
    </renderer>
  </render-kit>
</faces-config>
```

The render-kit-class Element

The **render-kit-class** element is used to specify the fully qualified class name for a render kit implementation. The implementation must extend the **javax.faces.render.RenderKit** abstract base class.

DTD Definition
Following is the DTD definition for the **render-kit-class** element:

```
<!ELEMENT render-kit-class (#PCDATA)>
```

Usage Rules

Rule	Value
JSF Versions	1.0, 1.1, 1.2
Parent Elements	render-kit
Child Elements	None
Uniqueness Constraints	None

Example Usage
The following example illustrates the usage of the **render-kit-class** element:

```
<faces-config>
  <render-kit>
    <render-kit-id>test<render-kit-id>
    <render-kit-class>
      com.example.jsf.TestRenderKit
    </render-kit-class>
    <renderer>
      <component-family>
        javax.faces.Data
      </component-family>
      <renderer-type>
        javax.faces.Table
      </renderer-type>
      <renderer-class>
        com.sun.faces.renderkit.html_basic.TableRenderer
      </renderer-class>
    </renderer>
  </render-kit>
</faces-config>
```

The render-kit-factory Element
The **render-kit-factory** element is used to specify the fully qualified class name of a
javax.faces.render.RenderKitFactory implementation class that will replace the JSF
implementation's default render kit factory implementation. The render kit factory is
used to store and retrieve **javax.faces.render.RenderKit** instances for the current Web
application as well as to retrieve a list of the IDs for render kits supported by the factory.

DTD Definition
Following is the DTD definition for the **render-kit-factory** element:

```
<!ELEMENT render-kit-factory (#PCDATA)>
```

Usage Rules

Rule	Value
JSF Versions	1.0, 1.1, 1.2
Parent Elements	factory
Child Elements	None
Uniqueness Constraints	None

Example Usage

The following example illustrates the usage of the **render-kit-factory** element:

```
<faces-config>
  <factory>
    <render-kit-factory>
      com.example.jsf.TestRenderKitFactory
    </render-kit-factory>
  </factory>
</faces-config>
```

The render-kit-id Element

The **render-kit-id** element is used to specify the logical name for a render kit. The logical name is used to register the render kit with JSF so that it can later be accessed by the same logical name.

DTD Definition

Following is the DTD definition for the **render-kit-id** element:

```
<!ELEMENT render-kit-id (#PCDATA)>
```

Usage Rules

Rule	Value
JSF Versions	1.0, 1.1, 1.2
Parent Elements	render-kit
Child Elements	None
Uniqueness Constraints	None

Example Usage

The following example illustrates the usage of the **render-kit-id** element:

```
<faces-config>
  <render-kit>
    <render-kit-id>test<render-kit-id>
    <render-kit-class>
      com.example.jsf.TestRenderKit
```

```
        </render-kit-class>
        <renderer>
          <component-family>
            javax.faces.Data
          </component-family>
          <renderer-type>
            javax.faces.Table
          </renderer-type>
          <renderer-class>
            com.sun.faces.renderkit.html_basic.TableRenderer
          </renderer-class>
        </renderer>
    </render-kit>
</faces-config>
```

The renderer Element

The **renderer** element is used to encapsulate the set of elements specifying the details for a renderer. This element has no other use than to denote the beginning and end of the renderer details.

DTD Definition

Following is the DTD definition for the **renderer** element:

```
<!ELEMENT renderer ((descriptionGroup? | (description*, display-name*,
icon*)), component-family, renderer-type, renderer-class, facet*,
attribute*, renderer-extension*)>
```

Usage Rules

Rule	Value
JSF Versions	1.0, 1.1, 1.2
Parent Elements	render-kit
Child Elements	attribute, component-family, description (1.0, 1.1), descriptionGroup (1.2), display-name (1.0, 1.1), facet, icon (1.0, 1.1), renderer-class, renderer-extension, renderer-type *Note: The parenthetical numbers represent the JSF versions that the corresponding child element applies to if the child element does not apply to all JSF versions.*
Uniqueness Constraints	None

Example Usage

The following example illustrates the usage of the **renderer** element:

```
<faces-config>
  <render-kit>
    <renderer>
```

```
      <component-family>
        javax.faces.Data
      </component-family>
      <renderer-type>
        javax.faces.Table
      </renderer-type>
      <renderer-class>
        com.sun.faces.renderkit.html_basic.TableRenderer
      </renderer-class>
    </renderer>
  </render-kit>
</faces-config>
```

The renderer-class Element

The **renderer-class** element is used to specify the fully qualified class name for a renderer implementation. The implementation must extend from the **javax.faces.render.Renderer** abstract base class.

DTD Definition

Following is the DTD definition for the **renderer-class** element:

```
<!ELEMENT renderer-class (#PCDATA)>
```

Usage Rules

Rule	Value
JSF Versions	1.0, 1.1, 1.2
Parent Elements	renderer
Child Elements	None
Uniqueness Constraints	None

Example Usage

The following example illustrates the usage of the **renderer-class** element:

```
<faces-config>
  <render-kit>
    <renderer>
      <component-family>
        javax.faces.Data
      </component-family>
      <renderer-type>
        javax.faces.Table
      </renderer-type>
      <renderer-class>
        com.sun.faces.renderkit.html_basic.TableRenderer
      </renderer-class>
    </renderer>
  </render-kit>
</faces-config>
```

The renderer-type Element

The **renderer-type** element is used to specify the logical name for a renderer. The logical name is used to register the renderer with JSF so that it can later be accessed by the same logical name.

DTD Definition

Following is the DTD definition for the **renderer-type** element:

```
<!ELEMENT renderer-type (#PCDATA)>
```

Usage Rules

Rule	Value
JSF Versions	1.0, 1.1, 1.2
Parent Elements	renderer
Child Elements	None
Uniqueness Constraints	None

Example Usage

The following example illustrates the usage of the **renderer-type** element:

```
<faces-config>
  <render-kit>
    <renderer>
      <component-family>
        javax.faces.Data
      </component-family>
      <renderer-type>
        javax.faces.Table
      </renderer-type>
      <renderer-class>
        com.sun.faces.renderkit.html_basic.TableRenderer
      </renderer-class>
    </renderer>
  </render-kit>
</faces-config>
```

The resource-bundle Element

The **resource-bundle** element is used to encapsulate the set of elements that specify resource bundle configuration details. This element has no other use than to denote the beginning and end of the resource bundle configuration details.

DTD Definition

Following is the DTD definition for the **resource-bundle** element:

```
<!ELEMENT resource-bundle (descriptionGroup?, base-name, var)>
```

PART IV

Usage Rules

Rule	Value
JSF Versions	1.2
Parent Elements	application
Child Elements	base-name, descriptionGroup, var
Uniqueness Constraints	None

Example Usage

The following example illustrates the usage of the **resource-bundle** element:

```
<faces-config>
  <application>
    <resource-bundle>
      <base-name>
        com.example.jsf.TestResources
      </base-name>
      <var>testResources</var>
    </resource-bundle>
  </application>
</faces-config>
```

The state-manager Element

The **state-manager** element is used to specify the fully qualified class name of a **javax.faces .application.StateManager** implementation class that will replace the JSF implementation's default state manager implementation. The state manager is called during the Restore View and Render Response phases of the JSF request processing lifecycle and is responsible for storing and retrieving the state of current view between HTTP requests. The **state-manager** element provides the ability to override the default JSF state management by plugging in a custom **StateManager**.

DTD Definition

Following is the DTD definition for the **state-manager** element:

```
<!ELEMENT state-manager (#PCDATA)>
```

Usage Rules

Rule	Value
JSF Versions	1.0, 1.1, 1.2
Parent Elements	application
Child Elements	None
Uniqueness Constraints	None

Example Usage

The following example illustrates the usage of the **state-manager** element:

```
<faces-config>
  <application>
    <state-manager>
      com.example.jsf.TestStateManager
    </state-manager>
  </application>
</faces-config>
```

The suggested-value Element

The **suggested-value** element is used to specify the suggested value for an attribute or a property. Suggested values differ from default values in that suggested values may or may not be assigned to an attribute or property whereas default values will be assigned to an attribute or property.

DTD Definition

Following is the DTD definition for the **suggested-value** element:

```
<!ELEMENT suggested-value (#PCDATA)>
```

Usage Rules

Rule	Value
JSF Versions	1.0, 1.1, 1.2
Parent Elements	attribute, property
Child Elements	None
Uniqueness Constraints	None

Example Usage

There are two ways that the **suggested-value** element can be used. The first way, shown here, defines a suggested value for an attribute:

```
<faces-config>
  <component>
    <component-type>
      com.example.jsf.TestComponent
    </component-type>
    <component-class>
      com.example.jsf.UITestComponent
    </component-class>
    <attribute>
      <attribute-name>testAttribute</attribute-name>
      <attribute-class>java.lang.String</attribute-class>
      <suggested-value>testSuggestedValue</suggested-value>
    </attribute>
  </component>
</faces-config>
```

The following is the second way to use the **suggested-value** element to define a suggested value for a property:

```
<faces-config>
  <converter>
    <component-for-class>
      java.lang.Long
    </component-for-class>
    <component-class>
      com.example.jsf.LongConverter
    </component-class>
    <property>
      <property-name>testAttribute</property-name>
      <property-class>java.lang.String</property-class>
      <suggested-value>testDefaultValue</suggested-value>
    </property>
  </converter>
</faces-config>
```

The supported-locale Element

The **supported-locale** element is used to specify a locale supported by the JSF application. JSF uses locale information to retrieve all localized resources for the application. JSF uses the default locale setting if another locale is not specified (e.g., via the browser). The locale value specified with the **supported-locale** element must be in the following format:

language_country_variant

The *language, country*, and *variant* arguments of the locale definition must be separated by either an underscore (_) or a hyphen (-). The *country* and *variant* arguments are optional. The *language* argument must be specified using a valid two-letter ISO-639 language code (e.g., "en" for English or "es" for Spanish). The *country* argument must be specified using a valid uppercase two-letter ISO-3166 country code (e.g., "US" for United States or "CA" for Canada). The *variant* argument is for a vendor- or browser-specific code (e.g., "WIN" for Windows or "MAC" for Macintosh). For a listing of each of the ISO language and country codes, visit their respective specification Web sites listed here:

http://www.unicode.org/unicode/onlinedat/languages.html
http://www.unicode.org/unicode/onlinedat/countries.html

To illustrate the rules of locales, consider some of the following example locale definitions.

- **en**   English
- **en_US**   United States English
- **en_US_WIN**   United States English on Windows
- **es**   Spanish
- **es_MX**   Mexican Spanish
- **es_MX_MAC**   Mexican Spanish on Macintosh

DTD Definition

Following is the DTD definition for the **supported-locale** element:

```
<!ELEMENT supported-locale (#PCDATA)>
```

Usage Rules

Rule	Value
JSF Versions	1.0, 1.1, 1.2
Parent Elements	locale-config
Child Elements	None
Uniqueness Constraints	None

Example Usage

The following example illustrates the usage of the **supported-locale** element:

```
<faces-config>
  <application>
    <locale-config>
      <default-locale>en</default-locale>
      <supported-locale>es</supported-locale>
      <supported-locale>fr_FR</supported-locale>
    </locale-config>
  </application>
</faces-config>
```

The to-view-id Element

The **to-view-id** element is used to specify the view ID for a view that will be displayed if the navigation case that the view ID is associated with is selected.

DTD Definition

Following is the DTD definition for the **to-view-id** element:

```
<!ELEMENT to-view-id (#PCDATA)>
```

Usage Rules

Rule	Value
JSF Versions	1.0, 1.1, 1.2
Parent Elements	navigation-case
Child Elements	None
Uniqueness Constraints	None

Example Usage
The following example illustrates the usage of the **to-view-id** element:

```
<faces-config>
  <navigation-rule>
    <from-view-id>/main.jsp</from-view-id>
    <navigation-case>
      <from-outcome>details</from-outcome>
      <to-view-id>/details.jsp</to-view-id>
    </navigation-case>
  </navigation-rule>
</faces-config>
```

The validator Element

The **validator** element is used to encapsulate the set of elements specifying the details for a validator. This element has no other use than to denote the beginning and end of the validator details.

DTD Definition
Following is the DTD definition for the **validator** element:

```
<!ELEMENT validator ((descriptionGroup? | (description*, display-name*,
icon*)), validator-id, validator-class, attribute*, property*,
validator-extension*)>
```

Usage Rules

Rule	Value
JSF Versions	1.0, 1.1, 1.2
Parent Elements	faces-config
Child Elements	attribute, description (1.0, 1.1), descriptionGroup (1.2), display-name (1.0, 1.1), icon (1.0, 1.1), property, validator-class, validator-extension (1.2), validator-id *Note: The parenthetical numbers represent the JSF versions that the corresponding child element applies to if the child element does not apply to all JSF versions.*
Uniqueness Constraints	None

Example Usage
The following example illustrates the usage of the **validator** element:

```
<faces-config>
  <validator>
    <validator-id>
      javax.faces.Length
    </validator-id>
```

```
    <validator-class>
      javax.faces.validator.LengthValidator
    </validator-class>
  </validator>
</faces-config>
```

The validator-class Element

The **validator-class** element is used to specify the fully qualified class name for a validator implementation. The implementation must implement the **javax.faces.validator.Validator** interface.

DTD Definition

Following is the DTD definition for the **validator-class** element:

```
<!ELEMENT validator-class (#PCDATA)>
```

Usage Rules

Rule	Value
JSF Versions	1.0, 1.1, 1.2
Parent Elements	validator
Child Elements	None
Uniqueness Constraints	None

Example Usage

The following example illustrates the usage of the **validator-class** element:

```
<faces-config>
  <validator>
    <validator-id>
      javax.faces.Length
    </validator-id>
    <validator-class>
      javax.faces.validator.LengthValidator
    </validator-class>
  </validator>
</faces-config>
```

The validator-id Element

The **validator-id** element is used to specify the logical name for a validator. The logical name is used to register the validator with JSF so that it can later be accessed by the same logical name.

DTD Definition

Following is the DTD definition for the **validator-id** element:

```
<!ELEMENT validator-id (#PCDATA)>
```

PART IV

Usage Rules

Rule	Value
JSF Versions	1.0, 1.1, 1.2
Parent Elements	validator
Child Elements	None
Uniqueness Constraints	Values for this element must be unique within the configuration file.

Example Usage

The following example illustrates the usage of the **validator-id** element:

```
<faces-config>
  <validator>
    <validator-id>
      javax.faces.Length
    </validator-id>
    <validator-class>
      javax.faces.validator.LengthValidator
    </validator-class>
  </validator>
</faces-config>
```

The value Element

The **value** element is used to specify the literal value or value binding expression that generates a value for a list entry, managed property, or map entry.

DTD Definition

Following is the DTD definition for the **value** element:

```
<!ELEMENT value (#PCDATA)>
```

Usage Rules

Rule	Value
JSF Versions	1.0, 1.1, 1.2
Parent Elements	list-entries, managed-property, map-entry
Child Elements	None
Uniqueness Constraints	None

Example Usage

There are three ways that the **value** element can be used. The first way, shown here, uses the **value** element to specify list entry values:

```
<faces-config>
  <managed-bean>
    <managed-bean-name>
      testManagedBean
    </managed-bean-name>
    <managed-bean-class>
      com.example.jsf.TestManagedBean
    </managed-bean-class>
    <managed-bean-scope>
      session
    </managed-bean-scope>
    <managed-property>
      <property-name>testProperty</property-name>
      <list-entries>
        <value>1000</value>
        <value>#{myBean.myProperty}</value>
      <list-entries>
    </managed-property>
  </managed-bean>
</faces-config>
```

The second way to use the **value** element is for a managed property and is shown here:

```
<faces-config>
  <managed-bean>
    <managed-bean-name>
      testManagedBean
    </managed-bean-name>
    <managed-bean-class>
      com.example.jsf.TestManagedBean
    </managed-bean-class>
    <managed-bean-scope>
      session
    </managed-bean-scope>
    <managed-property>
      <property-name>testProperty</property-name>
      <value>testValue</value>
    </managed-property>
  </managed-bean>
</faces-config>
```

Following is the third way to use the **value** element:

```
<faces-config>
  <managed-bean>
    <managed-bean-name>
      testManagedBean
    </managed-bean-name>
    <managed-bean-class>
      com.example.jsf.TestManagedBean
    </managed-bean-class>
```

```
<managed-bean-scope>
  session
</managed-bean-scope>
<managed-property>
  <property-name>testProperty</property-name>
  <map-entries>
    <map-entry>
      <key>testKey1</key>
      <value>1000</value>
    </map-entry>
    <map-entry>
      <key>testKey2</key>
      <null-value/>
    </map-entry>
  <map-entries>
  </managed-property>
  </managed-bean>
</faces-config>
```

The value-class Element

The **value-class** element is used to specify the fully qualified class name of an object type that all values will be converted to before being added to a list defined by a **list-entries** element or a map defined by a **map-entries** element. If this element is not nested inside a **list-entries** or **map-entries** element, all list or map entry values will default to **java.lang .String** as their object type.

There are two ways that the **value-class** element can be used, as listed here and shown later in the "Example Usage" section.

- To specify the fully qualified class name of an object type for list entry values by nesting **value-class** elements inside the **list-entries** element.

- To specify the fully qualified class name of an object type for map entry values by nesting **value-class** elements inside the **map-entries** element.

DTD Definition

Following is the DTD definition for the **value-class** element:

```
<!ELEMENT value-class (#PCDATA)>
```

Usage Rules

Rule	Value
JSF Versions	1.0, 1.1, 1.2
Parent Elements	list-entries, map-entries
Child Elements	None
Uniqueness Constraints	None

Example Usage

As mentioned, there are two ways that the **value-class** element can be used. The first way, shown here, defines the value class for a list:

```
<faces-config>
  <managed-bean>
    <managed-bean-name>
      testManagedBean
    </managed-bean-name>
    <managed-bean-class>
      com.example.jsf.TestManagedBean
    </managed-bean-class>
    <managed-bean-scope>
      session
    </managed-bean-scope>
    <managed-property>
      <property-name>testProperty</property-name>
      <list-entries>
        <value-class>java.lang.Integer</value-class>
        <value>1000</value>
        <value>2000</value>
      <list-entries>
    </managed-property>
  </managed-bean>
</faces-config>
```

The following is the second way to use the **value-class** element for defining the value class for a map:

```
<faces-config>
  <managed-bean>
    <managed-bean-name>
      testManagedBean
    </managed-bean-name>
    <managed-bean-class>
      com.example.jsf.TestManagedBean
    </managed-bean-class>
    <managed-bean-scope>
      session
    </managed-bean-scope>
    <managed-property>
      <property-name>testProperty</property-name>
      <map-entries>
        <value-class>java.lang.Integer</value-class>
        <map-entry>
          <key>testKey1</key>
          <value>1000</value>
        </map-entry>
        <map-entry>
```

```
            <key>testKey2</key>
            <null-value/>
         </map-entry>
      <map-entries>
    </managed-property>
  </managed-bean>
</faces-config>
```

The var Element

The **var** element is used to specify the logical name for a resource bundle instance that will be registered with the JSF application. The resource bundle instance can then be later accessed by a call to the **javax.faces.application.Application.getResourceBundle()** method passing in the value specified by the **var** element.

DTD Definition

Following is the DTD definition for the **var** element:

```
<!ELEMENT var (#PCDATA)>
```

Usage Rules

Rule	Value
JSF Versions	1.2
Parent Elements	resource-bundle
Child Elements	None
Uniqueness Constraints	None

Example Usage

The following example illustrates the usage of the **var** element:

```
<faces-config>
  <application>
    <resource-bundle>
      <base-name>
        com.example.jsf.TestResources
      </base-name>
      <var>testResources</var>
    </resource-bundle>
  </application>
</faces-config>
```

The variable-resolver Element

The **variable-resolver** element is used to specify the fully qualified class name of a **javax .faces.el.VariableResolver** implementation class that will replace the JSF implementation's default variable resolver implementation. The variable resolver is used to process value binding expressions and is called each time a value binding expression must be resolved. The **variable-resolver** element provides the ability to override the default JSF variable resolving by plugging in a custom **VariableResolver**.

DTD Definition

Following is the DTD definition for the **variable-resolver** element:

```
<!ELEMENT variable-resolver (#PCDATA)>
```

Usage Rules

Rule	Value
JSF Versions	1.0, 1.1, 1.2
Parent Elements	application
Child Elements	None
Uniqueness Constraints	None

Example Usage

The following example illustrates the usage of the **variable-resolver** element:

```
<faces-config>
  <application>
    <variable-resolver>
      com.example.jsf.TestVariableResolver
    </variable-resolver>
  </application>
</faces-config>
```

The view-handler Element

The **view-handler** element is used to specify the fully qualified class name of a **javax.faces .application.ViewHandler** implementation class that will replace the JSF implementation's default view handler implementation. The view handler is called during the Restore View and Render Response phases of the JSF request processing lifecycle and is responsible for managing response generation and the saving and restoring of the state for each view. The **view-handler** element provides the ability to override the default JSF view handling by plugging in a custom **ViewHandler**.

DTD Definition

Following is the DTD definition for the **view-handler** element:

```
<!ELEMENT view-handler (#PCDATA)>
```

Usage Rules

Rule	Value
JSF Versions	1.0, 1.1, 1.2
Parent Elements	application
Child Elements	None
Uniqueness Constraints	None

Example Usage

The following example illustrates the usage of the **view-handler** element:

```
<faces-config>
  <application>
    <view-handler>
      com.example.jsf.TestViewHandler
    </view-handler>
  </application>
</faces-config>
```

Extension Elements

Many of the Web application frameworks preceding JSF fell short from a configuration perspective because they made it cumbersome, or in some cases impossible, to extend their configuration files. The limited extensibility of these files is due to the files being governed by rigid DTD or XML schema specifications. JSF configuration files, conversely, were designed from the beginning to be extensible.

JSF solved the extensibility problem by adding extension points throughout the configuration file that allow proprietary XML elements to be inserted. These extension points allow individual JSF implementations to make use of proprietary configuration data without requiring a separate configuration file. More importantly, the extension points prevent the various implementations that utilize proprietary elements from impacting other implementations that might not recognize the proprietary elements. An implementation that does not recognize the proprietary elements will simply ignore any elements nested inside the extension elements. The extension points also provide a mechanism for you to extend the configuration data for your own applications if so desired.

The following table lists each of the extension points in the JSF configuration file. The Parent Element column specifies the parent element that acts as an extension point and the Extension Element column specifies the name of the child element in which proprietary elements can be nested.

Parent Element	Extension Element
application	application-extension
attribute	attribute-extension
component	component-extension
converter	converter-extension
faces-config	faces-config-extension
facet	facet-extension
factory	factory-extension
lifecycle	lifecycle-extension
managed-bean	managed-bean-extension
navigation-rule	navigation-rule-extension
property	property-extension
render-kit	render-kit-extension
renderer	renderer-extension
validator	validator-extension

The following example illustrates how extension elements are used to add proprietary configuration data to a JSF configuration file.

```
<faces-config>
  <application>
    <application-extension>
      <proprietary-tag-a>value a</proprietary-tag-a>
      <proprietary-tag-b>value b</proprietary-tag-b>
      <proprietary-tag-c>value c</proprietary-tag-c>
    </application-extension>
  </application>
</faces-config>
```

A particular JSF implementation or application that does not recognize the **proprietary-tag-a**, **proprietary-tag-b**, and **proprietary-tag-c** elements will simply ignore them altogether.

Metadata Elements

Several of the elements for the JSF configuration file give you the option to nest metadata elements. The metadata elements exist solely for adding extra information to the configuration file that will be displayed in GUI tools and the like; JSF implementations

themselves ignore the metadata elements. The following table lists the elements that
support nesting of metadata elements.

attribute
component
converter
facet
managed-bean
managed-property
navigation-case
navigation-rule
property
referenced-bean
render-kit
renderer
resource-bundle
validator

Most of the metadata elements do not have any attributes, thus you simply add text
between their opening and closing elements to specify their value, as shown here:

```
<validator>
  <description>Validator that validates credit card numbers.</description>
  <display-name>Credit Card Validator</display-name>
  <icon>
    <small-icon>small.gif</small-icon>
    <large-icon>large.gif</large-icon>
  </icon>
  <validator-id>CreditCardValidator</validator-id>
  <validator-class>com.example.jsf.CreditCardValidator</validator-class>
</validator>
```

The **display-name** and **description** elements are the only metadata elements that have
attributes. These elements both have a single attribute: **xml:lang**. The **xml:lang** attribute is
used to specify the language of the element's value. The following snippet illustrates this
use for Spanish:

```
<display-name xml:lang="es">Nombre de la Exhibición</display-name>
<description xml:lang="es">Descripción</description>
```

The language specified with the **xml:lang** attribute is a lowercase two-letter code for a language as defined by the ISO-639 standard. A listing of these codes can be found online at **http://www.unicode.org/unicode/onlinedat/languages.html**.

The following table lists and describes each of the metadata elements.

Element	Description
description	Defines descriptive text for the enclosing element.
display-name	Defines a short description (or name) for the enclosing element.
icon	Encapsulates an instance of the **large-icon** and the **small-icon** elements.
large-icon	Defines the location for a large (32 × 32 pixel) icon to associate to the enclosing element. The icon may be in either GIF, JPG, or PNG format. (Note that the PNG format is not supported for versions prior to JSF 1.2.)
small-icon	Defines the location for a small (16 × 16 pixel) icon to associate to the enclosing element. The icon may be in either GIF, JPG, or PNG format. (Note that the PNG format is not supported for versions prior to JSF 1.2)

Editing Configuration Files with Faces Console

As you can imagine, trying to remember every element's list of attributes as well as its proper order inside the configuration file can be cumbersome. If you make a mistake in typing any of the element's or attribute's names, your JSF application will not be configured properly. To ease the creation and modification of JSF configuration files, you can use any of the tools mentioned in Chapter 16 as well as Faces Console, which is covered in Appendix A. Faces Console, shown in Figure 18-1, is a stand-alone Java Swing application that provides a graphical editor for JSF configuration files. Additionally, Faces Console can be used as a plug-in with several major Java IDEs, providing a seamless JSF development experience.

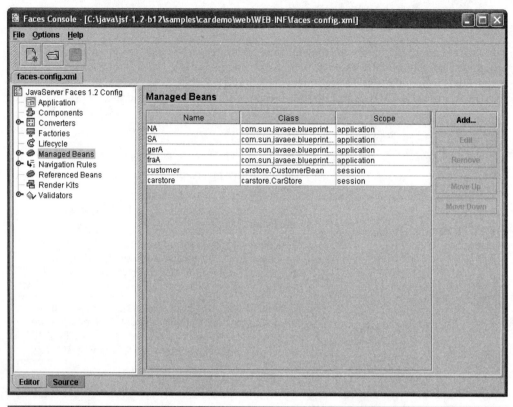

FIGURE 18-1 Faces Console

Faces Console is free and can be downloaded from **http://www.jamesholmes.com/ JavaServerFaces/**, which has all the information you need to configure it to work with your favorite Java IDE. Additionally, Appendix A contains a quick reference for installing and using Faces Console.

The Standard JSF Component Library

This chapter serves as a reference to the *standard* JSF component library. This library must be provided by any implementation that adheres to the JSF specification. The standard JSF library consists of two parts: the *core* library and the *HTML* library. The core library provides common application development utilities in the areas of validation, conversion, internationalization, and overall application development. It is important to note that the core library is not specific to HTML clients and that none of the components in the core library have any visual representation for the end user. The HTML library, however, is specifically for HTML clients and provides a set of widgets rendered in HTML that are common in most Web applications, such as text fields, buttons, checkboxes, and so on.

A Brief Review of JSF and JSP Tag Nomenclature

Since Faces provides technology to be used within JSP, having a good understanding of custom JSP terminology and nomenclature is in order. The following is a quick review of the various terms associated with custom JSP technology, which Faces relies upon. Understanding these terms will be helpful since the remaining reference chapters dealing with custom JSF component libraries use them extensively.

Term	Description
JSP Action	JSP actions are elements that can create and access programming language objects and affect the output stream. The JSP 2.1 specification defines a set of approximately 16 standard actions that must be provided by any compliant JSP implementation. These include **<jsp:useBean>**, **<jsp:setProperty>**, and so on.
JSP Tag	JSP tags are responsible for invoking the underlying JSP actions. JSP actions are invoked by JSP tags in a JSP page. The terms "JSP tag" and "JSP action" are often used synonymously.
Custom JSP Action	Custom JSP actions can be developed in addition to the standard actions provided in the JSP specification. Development of custom actions has been supported since JSP version 1.1.
Custom JSP Tag	Similar to standard JSP tags and actions, a custom JSP tag allows for the invocation of a custom JSP action.

Term	Description
Custom JSP Tag Library	A collection of custom actions and custom tags, along with a tag library descriptor (tld) file. To use JSF within JSP, custom JSP tag libraries are used.
JSF UIComponent	An underlying Java class (**UIComponent**) that defines the behavior of a JSF user interface element. A **UIComponent** can have code that renders itself embedded in them, or it can use a separate **Renderer** class.
JSF Renderer	An optional Java class (**Renderer**) that is used to *render* a user interface element. It works in concert with an associated **UIComponent** class. It is optional because **UIComponent** classes can include code to render themselves.
JSF JSP Tag	A custom JSP tag that extends **UIComponentTag** and provides a JSP-based method of invocation of an associated **UIComponent** and (optionally) a JSF **Renderer**. (For more details on custom JSF UI component development, see Chapter 10.)

Acquiring and Installing the Standard Libraries

The standard JSF component libraries are part of the specification and also come with any standard JSF implementation such as Sun's reference implementation or the MyFaces implementation. Chapter 2 provides detailed instructions on how to download Sun's reference implementation along with how to install and integrate it into your Web applications.

What You Get (Binary)

The jar files you get when downloading Sun's JSF reference implementation are **jsf-api.jar** and **jsf-impl.jar**. These are accompanied by a set of Jakarta Commons jar files that JSF is dependent on.

> **JSF 1.2 TIP** *As of JSF 1.2, the JSF binaries are a part of the Java EE container and are no longer available as a separate download. Rather, one must use the JSF implementation provided by your container, such as Sun's Java System Application Server version 9.*

What You Get (Source)

The source for the standard components is available, but is not provided in the reference implementation. Instead, the reference implementation source code is available from the **javaserverfaces-sources** project of **java.net** at **ttps://javaserverfaces-sources.dev.java.net/**. A free user ID at **java.net** along with access to the **javaserverfaces-source** project is required, however.

The Core and HTML Component Library Reference

This next section serves as a comprehensive reference for the standard core component library.

The Standard Core Library

The standard core library is accessible in JSP via a JSP tag library with a URI of **http://java.sun.com/jsf/core** and default prefix of **f**. A quick reference of the standard core library is provided in Table 19-1.

Component/Tag*	Description
actionListener	Allows you to register an **actionListener** instance on the **UIComponent** associated with the closest parent **UIComponent** custom action.
attribute	Allows you to set an attribute or **ValueExpression** into the **UIComponent** associated with the closest parent **UIComponent** custom action. An attribute is simply a name/value pair in the map returned by **UIComponent.getAttributes( )**.
convertDateTime	Installs a **DateTimeConverter** instance on the **UIComponent** associated with the closest parent **UIComponent** custom action.
convertNumber	Installs a **NumberConverter** instance on the **UIComponent** associated with the closest parent **UIComponent** custom action.
converter	Installs a named **Converter** instance on the **UIComponent** associated with the closest parent **UIComponent** custom action.
facet	Adds a named **facet** to the **UIComponent** associated with the closest parent **UIComponent** custom action.
loadBundle	Inserts a resource bundle localized for the locale of the current view, and exposes it (as a **Map**) in the request attributes for the current request. This makes the contents of the **ResourceBundle** available via the expression language.
param	Adds a child **UIParameter** component to the **UIComponent** associated with the closest parent **UIComponent** custom action. Some components, such as **commandLink,** convert nested **param** tags into URL query parameters.
phaseListener (1.2 only)	The **PhaseListener** is a JSF 1.2-only component tag that adds a **PhaseListener** instance to the **UIViewRoot** associated with the closest parent **UIViewRoot** custom action.
selectItem	Adds a child **UISelectItem** component to the **UIComponent** associated with the closest parent **UIComponent** custom action.
selectItems	Adds a child **UISelectItems** component to the **UIComponent** associated with the closest parent **UIComponent** custom action.
setPropertyActionListener (1.2 only)	Registers an **ActionListener** instance on the **UIComponent** associated with the closest parent **UIComponent** custom action. This **actionListener** will cause the value given by the **value** attribute to be set into the **ValueExpression** given by the **target** attribute.
subview	Container action for all JSF core and component custom actions used on a nested page included via **<jsp:include>** or any custom action that dynamically includes another page from the same Web application, such as JSTL's **<c:import>**. Note: In JSF 1.2, a subview is not required for includes.
validateDoubleRange	Registers a **DoubleRangeValidator** instance on the **UIComponent** associated with the closest parent **UIComponent** custom action.

TABLE 19-1   The Standard Core Library Quick Reference

PART IV

Component/Tag*	Description
validateLength	Registers a **LengthValidator** instance on the **UIComponent** associated with the closest parent **UIComponent** custom action.
validateLongRange	Registers a **LongRangeValidator** instance on the **UIComponent** associated with the closest parent **UIComponent** custom action.
validator	Registers a named **Validator** instance on the **UIComponent** associated with the closest parent **UIComponent** custom action.
valueChangeListener	Registers a **ValueChangeListener** instance on the **UIComponent** associated with the closest parent **UIComponent** custom action.
verbatim	Registers a child **UIOutput** instance on the **UIComponent** associated with the closest parent **UIComponent** custom action which renders nested (HTML/XML/Markup) content.
view	Container for all JSF core and custom components used on a page.

* For some tags, there is actually no underlying **UIComponent** and the tag operates on its own.

TABLE 19-1 The Standard Core Library Quick Reference *(continued)*

A detailed reference for the tags/components referenced in Table 19-1 follows next.

The actionListener Tag

Tag name: <f:actionListener>
UIComponent class: **n/a**
Component type: **n/a**

The **actionListener** tag associates an **actionListener** with the closest parent **UIComponent**.

Attributes

Attribute	Type	Description	Required
type	String	A fully qualified Java class name of an **ActionListener** to be created and registered	Yes (1.1)No(1.2)*
binding (JSF 1.2 only)	ValueExpression	A **ValueExpression** expression that evaluates to an object that implements **javax.faces.event .ActionListener**	No*

* In JSF 1.2, either a type or a binding must be provided.

Example Usage

```
<f:actionListener type="fully-qualified-classname" binding="value
Expression"/>
```

JSF 1.2 TIP *If type and binding are both specified, the type is used to instantiate the class and the binding is employed as the target of a "set" operation where the value will be the created*

ActionListener *instance. This is useful if you want to manage your listener instances manually yet still allow them to be created from code referenced from the JSP page.*

The attribute Tag

Tag name: **<f:attribute>**
UIComponent class: **n/a**
Component type: **n/a**

The **attribute** tag adds an attribute with a specified name and string value to the component whose tag it is nested inside, if the component does not already contain an attribute with the same name. This tag creates no output to the page currently being created. Attributes are stored in the **Map** returned by **UIComponent.getAttributes()**. Note that values stored in this map are persisted as a part of the component's state when the view is saved and restored across postbacks.

JSF 1.2 TIP *In JSF 1.2, EL expressions are not stored in the Map returned by* **UIComponent** *.getAttributes(), instead they are stored via* **setValueExpression()**.

Attributes

Attribute	Type	Description	Required
name	String	The name of the component attribute to be set	Yes (1.1) No (1.2)
value	Object	The value of the component attribute to be set	Yes (1.1) No (1.2)

Example Usage

```
<f:attribute name="employeeNo" value="#{bean.empno}" />
```

The convertDateTime Tag

Tag name: **<f:convertDateTime>**
UIComponent class: **n/a**
Component type: **n/a**

The **convertDateTime** tag creates and configures an instance of the converter registered with the ID **javax.faces.DateTime** and associates it with the closest parent **UIComponent**. In general, it's used to convert between **String** and **java.util.Date** values.

Attributes

Attribute	Type	Description	Required
dateStyle	String	Formatting style that determines how the date component of a date string is to be formatted and parsed. Applied only if type is "date" or "both". Valid values are "default" (default), "short", "medium", "long", and "full".	No

Attribute	Type	Description	Required
locale	String	Locale with specific styles for dates and times used during formatting or parsing. If not specified, the Locale returned by **FacesContext .getViewRoot( ).getLocale( )** will be used. Value must be either a **ValueExpression** that evaluates to a **java.util.Locale** instance, or a string that is valid to pass as the first argument to the constructor **java. util.Locale(String language, String country)**. The empty string is passed as the second argument.	No
pattern	String	A custom formatting pattern that determines how the date/time string should be formatted and parsed.	No
timeStyle	String	A predefined formatting style that determines how the time component of a date string is to be formatted and parsed. Applied only if type is "time" or "both". Valid values are "default" (default), "short", "medium", "long", and "full".	No
timeZone	String	A time zone used to interpret any time information in the date string. Value must be either a ValueExpression that evaluates to a **java.util .TimeZone** instance, or a string that is a timezone ID as described in the javadocs for **java.util.TimeZone .getTimeZone( )**.	No
type	String	Specifies whether the string value will contain a date, time, or both.	No
binding (1.2 only)	ValueExpression	A **ValueExpression** expression that evaluates to an object that implements **javax.faces.convert.Converter**.	No

Example Usage

```
<h:inputText id="hiredate" value="#{employee.hireDate}">
  <f:convertDateTime dateStyle="full"/>
</h:inputText>
```

Pattern Formats

A pattern of symbols determines what the formatted date and time looks like. Examples of locale-sensitive date and time pattern formats are "EEE, MMM d, yyyy" and "h:mm a", which generate the output "Thu, Apr 9, 1998" and "6:15 PM" if the U.S. locale is specified. See the Java class **java.text.SimpleDateFormat** for more information about date and time patterns and symbols.

The convertNumber Tag

Tag name: **<f:convertNumber>**
UIComponent class: **n/a**
Component type: **n/a**

The **convertNumber** tag creates and configures an instance of the converter registered with the ID **javax.faces.Number**. Associates it with the closest parent **UIComponent**. In general, it's used to convert between **String** and **java.lang.Number** values.

Attributes

Attribute	Type	Description	Required
currencyCode	String	ISO-4217 currency code (e.g., US Dollar = "USD").	No
currencySymbol	String	String to use as currency symbol (e.g., '$' for USD).	No
groupingUsed	boolean	If true (default), grouping separators are included in the result.	No
integerOnly	boolean	If true, only the integer portion is parsed. The default is false.	No
locale	String or java.util.Locale	The locale to use instead of the default determined by **FacesContext.getViewRoot( ).getLocale( )**.	No
maxFractionDigits	int	The maximum number of fraction digits to be formatted (in the output).	No
maxIntegerDigits	int	The maximum number of integer digits to be formatted (in the output).	No
minFractionDigits	int	The minimum number of fraction digits to be formatted (in the output).	No
minIntegerDigits	int	The minimum number of integer digits to be formatted (in the output).	No
pattern	String	The symbols forming a number pattern that is defined in **java.text.DecimalFormat**.	No

Attribute	Type	Description	Required
type	String	One of the accepted type values: Valid values are "number", "currency", and "percentage". The default value is "number".	No
binding (1.2 only)	ValueExpression	The **ValueExpression** expression that evaluates to an object that implements **javax.faces.convert.Converter**.	No

Example Usage

```
<h:inputText id="sal" value="#{employee.salary}">
  <f:convertNumber integerOnly="true"/>
</h:inputText>
```

Pattern Formats

A pattern of symbols determines what a formatted number looks like. For example, the locale-sensitive pattern ###,###.### generates the formatted number 123,456.789 if the locale is en_US. See the Java class **java.text.DecimalFormat** for more information about number patterns and symbols.

The converter Tag

Tag name: **<f:converter>**
UIComponent class: **n/a**
Component type: **n/a**

The **converter** tag creates an instance of the class registered with the specified converter ID, which must implement the **javax.faces.convert.Converter** interface, and associates it with the component represented by the closest parent **UIComponent**.

Attributes

Attribute	Type	Description	Required
converterId	String	The ID (shown next) used to register a class implementing the **Converter** interface	Yes (1.1)No (1.2)
binding (1.2 only)	ValueExpression	A **ValueExpression** expression that evaluates to an object that implements **javax.faces.convert.Converter**	No

Example Usage

```
<h:inputText>
  <f:converter converterId="Converter ID"/>
</h:inputText>
```

Converter ID List

- javax.faces.BigDecimal
- javax.faces.BigInteger
- javax.faces.Boolean
- javax.faces.Byte
- javax.faces.Character
- javax.faces.DateTime
- javax.faces.Double
- javax.faces.Float
- javax.faces.Integer
- javax.faces.Long
- javax.faces.Number
- javax.faces.Short

JSF 1.2 TIP   If type and binding are both specified, the type is used to instantiate the class and the binding is used as the target of a "set" operation where the value will be the created **Converter** *instance. This is useful if you want to manage your converter instances manually yet still allow them to be created from code referenced from the JSP page.*

The facet Tag

Tag name: **<f:facet>**
UIComponent class: **n/a**
Component type: **n/a**

The **facet** tag signifies a nested component that has a special relationship to its enclosing tag. For example, stating that the "header" of a table is to be provided by a JSF component. This element adds the component represented by the JSF action in its body as a facet with the specified name to the component represented by the closest JSF component parent action element. This tag only allows one component to be nested within itself. To use multiple components as a facet, create them as children of a simple container component. For example, nest the corresponding HTML library component actions within the body of a **panelGroup** component.

Attributes

Attribute	Type	Description	Required
name	String	Name of the facet to be created	Yes (1.1)No (1.2)

Example Usage

```
<h:dataTable>
  <h:column>
    <f:facet name="header">
      <h:panelGroup>
        <h:outputText value="header name" />
      </h:panelGroup>
```

PART IV

```
    </f:facet>
     <h:outputText value="column value"/>
   </h:column>
</h:dataTable>
```

The loadBundle Tag

Tag name: **<f:loadBundle>**
UIComponent class: **n/a**
Component type: **n/a**

    The **loadBundle** tag is a localization tag that specifies a resource bundle localized for the **locale** of the current view and exposes it as a **Map**. The action creates an instance of the class implementing the **java.util.Map** interface with a **get( )** method that returns the value of the corresponding resource in the specified resource bundle and saves the instance as a variable in the request scope. Localized resources from the bundle can then be accessed through the **Map** with regular JSF EL expressions.

Attributes

Attribute	Type	Description	Required
basename	String	The base name of the resource bundle to be used	Yes (1.1) No (1.2)
var	String	The name of a usable (request-scoped) variable under which the resource bundle will be exposed as a **Map**	Yes

Example Usage

Let's assume there is a **ResourceBundle** answering to the fully qualified Java class name of **com.foo.ResourceBundle** in the Web application's classpath and that the **ResourceBundle** has a key called **UserNameLabel**. A variable named **resources** is also assigned to this resource bundle. The following JSP code loads the bundle into the request scope and then references a value from that bundle.

```
<f:loadBundle
  basename="com.foo.ResourceBundle"
  var="resources"/>
<h:outputText value="#{resources.UserNameLabel}" />
```

    Recall that the scoped name space searching rules described in Chapter 4 will automatically cause the request scope to be searched.

Using Resource Bundles in JSF

Load the resource bundle specified by the **basename** attribute, localized for the locale of the **UIViewRoot** component of the current view, and expose its key-values pairs as a **Map** under the attribute key specified by the **var** attribute. In this way, value binding expressions may be used to conveniently retrieve localized values. If the named bundle is not found, a **JspException** is thrown. Note: This tag must be nested inside the **<f:view>** component/action.

The param Component

Tag name: **<f:param>**
UIComponent class: **javax.faces.component.UIParameter**
Component type: **javax.faces.Parameter**

The **param** component adds a child **UIParameter** component to the **UIComponent** associated with the closest parent **UIComponent**. It can be used to substitute message parameters when used inside an **<h:outputFormat>** or to add query string name-value pairs to a request when used inside of **<h:commandLink>** or **<h:outputLink>**.

Attributes

Attribute	Type	Description	Required
name	String	The base name of the resource bundle to be loaded	No
value	String	The name of a request scope attribute under which the resource bundle will be exposed as a **Map**	Yes
binding	ValueBinding ValueExpression (1.2)	ValueBinding or **ValueExpression** expression to a backing bean property bound to the component instance for the **UIComponent** created by this custom action	No
id	String	Component identifier of the component	No

Example Usage

The following is a simple way to test **f:param** inside a **commandLink**:

```
<h:commandLink >
  <h:outputText value="Click Here" />
  <f:param  name="empid" value="123456" />
</h:commandLink>

<h:outputText value=" Employee Id is: #{param.empid}"  />
```

Usage of **f:param** inside of an **outputFormat** is shown in the following:

```
<h:outputFormat value="Welcome back, {0}" >
  <f:param value="#{Employees.firstName}" />
</h:outputFormat>
```

The phaseListener Tag (1.2 Only)

Tag name: **<f:phaseListener>**
UIComponent class: **n/a**
Component type: **n/a**

The **phaseListener** tag registers a **PhaseListener** instance on the **UIViewRoot** in which this tag is nested.

Attributes

Attribute	Type	Description	Required
type	String	Fully qualified Java class name of a **PhaseListener** to be created and registered.	No
binding	ValueExpression	**ValueExpression** that evaluates to an object that implements **javax.faces.event.PhaseListener**.	No

The selectItem Component

Tag name: **<f:selectItem>**
UIComponent class: **javax.faces.component.UISelectItem**
Component type: **javax.faces.SelectItem**

The **selectItem** component adds a child **UISelectItem** component to the closest parent **UIComponent**.

Attributes

Attribute	Type	Description	Required
binding	ValueBinding or ValueExpression (1.2)	**ValueBinding** or **ValueExpression** expression to a backing bean property bound to the component instance for the **UIComponent** created by this custom action.	No
id	String	Component identifier of the component.	No
itemDescription	String	Description of the item.	No
itemDisabled	String	The boolean flag used to display the item as disabled. The default value is false.	No
itemLabel	String	The displayed label of the item.	No
itemValue	String	The actual (nondisplayed) value of the item.	No
value	String	The value of the component.	No

Example Usage

Several **f:selectItem** components providing select options for an **h:selectOneMenu** are shown in the following.

```
<h:selectOneMenu>
  <f:selectItem itemLabel="one" itemValue="1"/>
  <f:selectItem itemLabel="two" itemValue="2"/>
  <f:selectItem itemLabel="three" itemValue="3"/>
</h:selectOneMenu>
```

The selectItems Component

Tag name: **<f:selectItems>**
UIComponent class: **javax.faces.component.UISelectItems**
Component type: **javax.faces.SelectItems**

The **selectItems** component locates the closest parent **UIComponent**, creates a new **UISelectItems** component, and attaches it as a child of the associated **UIComponent**. The implementation class for this action must meet the requirements shown in the following table.

Attributes

Attribute	Type	Description	Required
binding	ValueBinding ValueExpression (1.2)	**ValueBinding** or **ValueExpression** expression to a backing bean property bound to the component instance for the **UIComponent** created by this custom action.	No
id	String	Component identifier of the component.	No
value	ValueExpression	Value binding expression of source of items. See the following value description.	No

Example Usage

The following is an example with the **f:selectItems** value bound to a **CountriesMap Map**. This will display a list of countries.

```
<h:selectOneMenu
  <f:selectItems value="#{CountriesMap}"/>
</h:selectOneMenu>
```

The Value Attribute Description

The Value Binding expression for the **value** attribute must be one of the following instances:

- An individual **javax.faces.model.SelectItem**
- A Java language array of **javax.faces.model.SelectItem**
- A java.util.Collection of **javax.faces.model.SelectItem**
- A java.util.Map where the keys are converted to Strings and used as labels, and the corresponding values are converted to Strings and used as values for newly created **javax.faces.model.SelectItem** instances. The instances are created in the order determined by the iterator over the keys provided by the **Map**.

The setPropertyActionListener Tag (1.2 Only)

Tag name: <f:setPropertyActionListener>
UIComponent class: **n/a**
Component type: **n/a**

The **setPropertyActionListener** tag registers an **ActionListener** instance on the **UIComponent** associated with the closest parent **UIComponent** custom action. This **actionListener** will cause the value given by the **value** attribute to be set into the **ValueExpression** given by the **target** attribute. This is useful for easily placing objects into managed beans or other objects accessible via EL.

Attributes

Attribute	Type	Description	Required
value	ValueExpression	**ValueExpression** to be stored as the value of the **target** attribute	Yes
target	ValueExpression	**ValueExpression** that is the destination of the **value** attribute	Yes

Example Usage

```
<h:commandButton action="#{backingBean.registerUser}" value="Register">
  <f:setPropertyActionListener
    target="#{sessionScope.User}" value="#{User}"/>
  </h:commandButton>
```

The subview Component

Tag name: **<f:subview>**
UIComponent class: **javax.faces.component.UINamingContainer**
Component type: **javax.faces.NamingContainer**

The **subview** component serves as a container component for all **UIComponents** used on a nested page included via **<jsp:include>** or any custom action that dynamically includes another page from the same Web application, such as JSTL's **<c:import>**. Note: In JSF 1.2, its use is optional around JSP includes. And in both 1.1 and 1.2, it can be used if you want a **NamingContainer** added to the component hierarchy for ID disambiguation.

Attributes

Attribute	Type	Description	Required
binding	ValueBinding ValueExpression (1.2)	**ValueExpression** expression to a backing bean property bound to the component instance for the **UIComponent** created by this custom action	No
id	String	Component identifier of the component	Yes
rendered	boolean	Boolean value determining whether component is rendered or not	No

Example Usage

Locates the closest parent **UIComponent** and creates a new **UINamingContainer** component, afterward attaching it as a child of the associated **UIComponent**. Such a component provides a scope within which child component identifiers must be unique, but allows child components to have the same simple identifier as child components nested in some other naming container. This is useful in the following scenarios:

main.jsp

```
<f:view>
  <c:import url="foo.jsp"/>
  <c:import url="bar.jsp"/>
</f:view>
```

foo.jsp

```
<f:subview id="aaa">
.. components and other content ...
</f:subview>
```

bar.jsp

```
<f:subview id="bbb">
  components and other content ...
</f:subview>
```

In this scenario, **<f:subview>** custom actions in imported pages establish a naming scope for components within those pages. Identifiers for **<f:subview>** custom actions nested in a single **<f:view>** custom action must be unique, but it is difficult for the page author (and impossible for the JSP page compiler) to enforce this restriction.

The following is an example showing a parent JSP page **main.jsp**:

```
<f:view>
  <f:subview id="aaa">
    <c:import url="foo.jsp"/>
  </f:subview>
  <f:subview id="bbb">
    <c:import url="bar.jsp"/>
  </f:subview>
</f:view>
```

Contents of **foo.jsp**:

```
JSF components and other content...
```

Contents of **bar.jsp**

```
JSF components and other content...
```

In this scenario, the **<f:subview>** custom actions are in the including page, rather than in the included page. As in the previous scenario, the **id** values of the two subviews must be unique; but it is much easier to verify using this style. It is also possible to use this approach to include the same page more than once, but maintain unique identifiers:

Contents of **main.jsp**:

```
<f:view>
  <f:subview id="aaa">
    <c:import url="foo.jsp"/>
  </f:subview>
  <f:subview id="bbb">
    <c:import url="foo.jsp"/>
  </f:subview>
</f:view>
```

Contents of **foo.jsp**:

```
JSF components and other content...
```

In all of the preceding examples, note that **foo.jsp** and **bar.jsp** may not contain **<f:view>**.

The validateDoubleRange Tag

Tag name: **<f:validateDoubleRange>**
UIComponent class: **n/a**
Component type: **n/a**

The **validateDoubleRange** tag creates and configures an instance of the **validator** registered with the ID **javax.faces.DoubleRange** and associates this instance with the closest parent **UIComponent**. It's used to validate a component's **double** value within a specified range.

Attributes

Attribute	Type	Description	Required
binding (1.2 only)	ValueExpression	The **ValueExpression** expression to a backing bean property bound to the component instance for the **validator** created by this custom action	No
maximum	double	The maximum value allowed for this component	No
minimum	double	The minimum value allowed for this component	No

Example Usage
The following is an example of **f:validateDoubleRange** used in an **inputText** component.

```
<h:inputText id="price" value="#{basket.price}">
  <f:validateDoubleRange minimum="0.0"/>
</h:inputText>
```

Either of the **maximum** or **minimum** attributes can be specified individually, or they can be specified together, as shown in the preceding example.

Constraints

- Must be nested inside an **EditableValueHolder** custom action whose value is (or is convertible to) a **double**.
- Must specify either the **maximum** attribute, the **minimum** attribute, or both.
- If both limits are specified, the maximum limit must be greater than the minimum limit. If this tag is not nested inside a **UIComponent** custom action, or the **UIComponent** implementation class does not correctly implement **EditableValueHolder**, then a **JspException** is thrown.

The validateLength Tag
Tag name: **<f:validateLength>**
UIComponent class: **n/a**
Component type: **n/a**
    The **validateLength** tag creates and configures an instance of the **validator** registered with the ID **javax.faces.Length** and associates it with the closest parent **UIComponent**. Is used to validate the String length of a component's value's within a specified range.

Attributes

Attribute	Type	Description	Required
binding (1.2 only)	ValueExpression	The **ValueExpression** expression to a backing bean property bound to the component instance for the **validator** created by this custom action	No
maximum	int	The maximum String length allowed for this component's value	No

Attribute	Type	Description	Required
minimum	int	The minimum String length allowed for this component's value	No

Example Usage

```
<h:inputText id="zip" value="#{employee.zipCode}">
  <f:validateLength minimum="5" maximum="9"/>
</h:inputText>
```

Either of the **maximum** or **minimum** attributes can be specified individually, or they can be specified together, as shown in the preceding example.

Constraints

- Must be nested inside an **EditableValueHolder** custom action whose value is a **String**.
- Must specify either the **maximum** attribute, the **minimum** attribute, or both.
- If both limits are specified, the maximum limit must be greater than the minimum limit. If this tag is not nested inside a **UIComponent** custom action, or the **UIComponent** implementation class does not correctly implement **EditableValueHolder**, then a **JspException** is thrown.

The validateLongRange Tag

Tag name: **<f:validateLongRange>**
UIComponent class: **n/a**
Component type: **n/a**

The **validateLongRange** tag creates and configures an instance of the **validator** registered with the ID **javax.faces.LongRange** and associates it with the closest parent **UIComponent**.

Attributes

Attribute	Type	Description	Required
binding (1.2 only)	ValueExpression	The **ValueExpression** expression that evaluates to an object that implements **javax.faces.validator.Validator**	No
maximum	long	The maximum value allowed for this component	No
minimum	long	The minimum value allowed for this component	No

Example Usage

```
<h:inputText id="sal" value="#{employee.salary}">
  <f:validateLongRange minimum="28000" maximum="100000"/>
</h:inputText>
```

Either of the **maximum** or **minimum** attributes can be specified individually, or they can be specified together, as shown in the preceding example.

Constraints

- Must be nested inside an **EditableValueHolder** custom action whose value is a **long**, which is convertible to a **Long**.
- Must specify either the **maximum** attribute, the **minimum** attribute, or both.
- If both limits are specified, the maximum limit must be greater than the minimum limit. If this tag is not nested inside a **UIComponent** custom action, or the **UIComponent** implementation class does not correctly implement **EditableValueHolder**, then a **JspException** is thrown.

The validator Tag

Tag name: <f:validator>
UIComponent class: **n/a**
Component type: **n/a**

The **validator** tag creates and registers a named **Validator** instance on the **UIComponent** associated with the closest parent **UIComponent** custom action.

Attributes

Attribute	Type	Description	Required
binding (1.2 only)	ValueExpression	The **ValueExpression** expression that evaluates to an object that implements **javax.faces.validator.Validator**	No*
validatorId	String	The validator identifier of the **Validator** to be created	Yes (1.1) No (1.2)*

* See constraints.

Example Usage

The following is an example using the **javax.faces.Length** validator.

```
<h:inputText value="#{UserBean.bio}" >
  <f:validator validatorId="javax.faces.Length"/>
</h:inputText>
```

Constraints

- Must be nested inside a **UIComponent** that implements **EditableValueHolder**.
- **validatorId** and/or **binding** must be specified. If this tag is not nested inside a **UIComponent**, or the **UIComponent** implementation class does not correctly implement **EditableValueHolder**, a **JspException** is thrown.

The valueChangeListener Tag

Tag name: <f:valueChangeListener>
UIComponent class: **n/a**
Component type: **n/a**

The **valueChangeListener** tag registers a **ValueChangeListener** instance on the **UIComponent** associated with the closest parent **UIComponent** custom action.

Attributes

Attribute	Type	Description	Required
binding (1.2 only)	ValueExpression	The **ValueExpression** expression that evaluates to an object that implements **javax.faces.event .ValueChangeListener**	No*
type	String	The fully qualified Java class name of a **ValueChangeListener** to be created and registered	Yes (1.1) No (1.2)*

* See constraints.

Example Usage

The following shows an example where a custom **ValueChangeListener** instance (**jsf.MyValChangeListener**) is associated with an **inputText**.

```
<h:inputText id="inputText1">
  <f:valueChangeListener type="jsf.MyValChangeListener"/>
</h:inputText>
```

Constraints

- Must be nested inside a **UIComponent**.
- The corresponding **UIComponent** implementation class must implement **EditableValueHolder**, and therefore define a public **addValueChangeListener()** method that accepts a **ValueChangeListener** parameter.
- The specified listener class must implement **javax.faces.event.ValueChangeListener**.
- **type** and/or **binding** must be specified.

The verbatim Component

Tag name: **<f:verbatim>**
UIComponent class: **javax.faces.component.UIOutput**
Component type: **javax.faces.Output**

The **verbatim** component creates and registers a child **UIOutput** instance on the **UIComponent** associated with the closest parent **UIComponent** custom action which renders nested XML, HTML, or other markup body content.

Attributes

Attribute	Type	Description	Required
escape	boolean	The boolean value indicating whether or not to render special HTML and XML characters ("<", ">", etc.) as character entity codes ("<", ">", respectively). If true, generated markup is escaped in a manner appropriate for the markup language being rendered. The default value is false.	No

Attribute	Type	Description	Required
rendered (1.2 only)	boolean	The flag indicating whether or not this component should be rendered. The default is true.	No

Example Usage

The following is a generic example.

```
<f:verbatim escape="true">
  ...(HTML/XML Markup/Template text)
</f:verbatim>
```

Constraints

- The body may be either markup or JSP content. However, no **UIComponent** custom actions, or custom actions from the JSF core tag library, may be nested inside.

The view Component

Tag name: **<f:view>**
UIComponent class: **javax.faces.component.UIViewRoot**
Component type: **javax.faces.ViewRoot**

The **view** component serves as the container for all JSF core and component custom actions used on a page.

Attributes

Attribute	Type	Description	Required
locale	String or Locale	The name of a locale to use for localizing this page (such as en_uk), or a value binding expression that returns a **Locale** instance	No
renderKitId (1.2 only)	String	The identifier for the render-kit to use for rendering this page	No
beforePhase (1.2 only)	String	The **MethodExpression** expression that points to a method whose signature takes a single **PhaseEvent** parameter	No
afterPhase (1.2 only)	String	The **MethodExpression** expression that points to a method whose signature takes a single **PhaseEvent** parameter	No

Example Usage

The following is an example with custom before and after **PhaseListeners**:

```
<f:view  beforePhaseListener="#{bean.MyBeforePhaseListener}"
  afterPhaseListener="#{bean.MyAfterPhaseListener}">
  ...(Nested template text and custom actions)
</f:view>
```

Constraints

- Any JSP-created response using actions from the JSF core tag library, as well as actions extending **javax.faces.webapp.UIComponentTag or javax.faces.webapp.UIComponentELTag** from other tag libraries, must be nested inside an occurrence of the **<f:view>** action.

- JSP page fragments included via the standard **<%@ include %>** directive need not have their JSF actions embedded in a <f:view> action, because the included template text and custom actions will be processed as part of the outer page as it is compiled, and the <f:view> action on the outer page will meet the nesting requirement.

- For JSF 1.1 only, JSP pages included via <jsp:include> or any custom action that dynamically includes another page from the same Web application, such as JSTL's **<c:import>**, must use an **<f:subview>** (either inside the included page itself, or surrounding the <jsp:include> or custom action that is including the page).

- If the **renderKitId** attribute is present, its value is stored in **UIViewRoot**. If the **renderKitId** attribute is not present, then the default render-kit identifier as returned by **Application.getDefaultRenderKitId()** is stored in **UIViewRoot** if it is not null. Otherwise, the render-kit identifier as specified by the constant **RenderKitFactory. HTML_BASIC_RENDER_KIT** is stored in **UIViewRoot**.

- If the **locale** attribute is present, its value overrides the **Locale** stored in **UIViewRoot**, normally set by the **ViewHandler**, and the **doStartTag()** method must store it by calling **UIViewRoot.setLocale()**.

The Standard HTML Library

A quick reference of the standard HTML library is provided in Table 19-2.

Component/Tag	Description
column	The child container component for a **dataTable** component. The element can be equipped with a **header** and **footer** facet for a column header and footer. Its children are used to display/process the column's data.
commandButton	Renders as an HTML <**input**> element with the **type** attribute set to "submit", "reset", or "image" depending on the value of this action element's type and **image** attribute values, the **name** attribute set to the component's client ID, and the **value** attribute set to the component's value.
commandLink	Renders as an HTML <**a**> element with an **href** attribute containing "#", and an **onclick** attribute.
dataTable	Renders an HTML <**table**> element where **UIColumn** child components are responsible for rendering the table columns. The columns can hold any type of component, including input and command. The **value** attribute value can be of any type, but the primary model type is the **javax.faces.model.DataModel** class. Both the **dataTable** component and its column children components may be equipped with a header and footer facet. The table rows are rendered within a <**tbody**> element with a <**tr**> element for each row and a <**td**> element for each column child. The first row to render and how many rows to render can be specified by the first and rows attributes.

TABLE 19-2   The Standard HTML Library Quick Reference

Component/Tag	Description
form	Renders as an HTML input form. The inner tags of the form receive the data that will be submitted with the form. Displays an HTML <**input**> element with an **action** attribute set to the URL that defines the view containing the form, and a **method** attribute set to "post". When the form is submitted, only components that are children of the submitted form are processed.
graphicImage	Displays an image. The component is rendered as an HTML <**input**> element with the **src** attribute holding the component's value or the **url** attribute, adjusted to a context-relative path.
inputHidden	Renders as an invisible field, which is an HTML <**input**> element with the **type** attribute set to "hidden", a **name** attribute set to the component's client ID, and a **value** attribute set to the component's value.
inputSecret	Renders as an HTML <**input**> element with the **type** attribute set to "password", a **name** attribute set to the component's client ID, and a **value** attribute set to the component's value only if the action's redisplay attribute is set to "true".
inputText	Renders as an HTML <**input**> element with the **type** attribute set to "text", a **name** attribute set to the component's client ID, and a **value** attribute set to the component's value.
inputTextarea	Renders as an input text area for multiple lines of text. Displays an HTML <**textarea**> element with a **name** attribute set to the component's client ID and a body holding the component's value.
message	Displays the first **Faces** message queued for the component and identified by its **for** attribute.
messages	Displays all queued **Faces** messages or only those queued without a component identifier if the **globalOnly** attribute is set to "true".
outputFormat	Can display parameterized and/or localized messages.
outputLabel	Renders as an HTML <**label**> element with a **value** as content. Has an optional **for** attribute that can be set to the client ID for the component identified by the action element's **for** attribute value.
outputLink	Renders as an HTML <**a**> element with an **href** attribute set to the component's value.
outputText	Renders as text within an HTML <**span**> element if any of the HTML attributes or the **id** attribute is set.
panelGrid	Renders an HTML table that serves as a container for other components.
panelGroup	Creates a panel container to group a set of components under one parent. It renders its children within an HTML <**span**> element if any of the HTML attributes or the **id** attribute is set.
selectBooleanCheckbox	Renders as a **boolean** checkbox. Displays an HTML <**input**> element with the **type** attribute set to "checkbox" and a **name** attribute set to the client ID.
selectManyCheckbox	Renders as a set of checkboxes from which the user can select multiple values.
selectManyListbox	Renders as a <**select**> element where multiple items can be selected.
selectManyMenu	Renders as a <**select**> element with a **name** attribute set to the component's client ID, a **multiple** attribute, and a **size** attribute set to "1" as the value.
selectOneListBox	Renders as a <**select**> element with a **name** attribute set to the component's client ID, a **multiple** attribute, and a **size** attribute set to "1" as the value.

TABLE 19-2 The Standard HTML Library Quick Reference (continued)

Component/Tag	Description
selectOneMenu	Renders as a `<select>` element with a **name** attribute set to the component's client ID, a **multiple** attribute, and a size attribute set to "1" as the value.
selectOneRadio	Renders as a set of radio buttons from which the user can select one value.

TABLE 19-2   The Standard HTML Library Quick Reference *(continued)*

A detailed description for the components referenced in Table 19-2 follows.

The column Component

Tag name: **<h:column>**
UIComponent class: **javax.faces.component.UIColumn**, (1.2) **javax.faces.component.html .HtmlColumn**
Component type: **javax.faces.Column**
The **column** component serves as an immediate child of an **<h:dataTable>** component. The element can be equipped with a header and footer facet for a column header and footer. Its children are used to process the column's data.

Attributes

Attribute	Type	Description	Required
binding	Value Binding or ValueExpression (1.2)	The binding reference to a like **UIComponent** instance	No
id	String	The identifier for the component	No
rendered	boolean	The boolean flag that defines whether the component is rendered	No
footerClass (1.2 only)	String	The space-separated list of CSS style class(es) that is applied to any column footer generated for this table	No
headerClass (1.2 only)	String	The space-separated list of CSS style class(es) that is applied to any column header generated for this table	No

Example Usage

Use the "header" facet on a **column** to create the column header. The following example creates a two-column table with the column headers "Firstname" and "Lastname":

```
<h:dataTable>
  <h:column>
```

```
    <f:facet name="header">
      <h:outputText value="Firstname"/>
    </f:facet>
    ...
  </h:column>
  <h:column>
    <f:facet name="header">
      <h:outputText value="Lastname"/>
    </f:facet>
    ...
  </h:column>
</h:dataTable>
```

The child components of each **column** display the data for each row in that column. The **column** does not create child components per row; instead, each child is repeatedly rendered (stamped) once per row. Because of this stamping behavior, only certain types of components are supported as children inside a **column**.

The commandButton Component

Tag name: **<h:commandButton>**
UIComponent class: **javax.faces.component.html.HtmlCommandButton**
Component type: **javax.faces.HtmlCommandButton**

The **commandButton** component is rendered as an HTML **<input>** element with the **type** attribute set to "submit", "reset", or "image" depending on the value of this action element's **type** and **image** attribute values, the **name** attribute set to the component's client ID, and the **value** attribute set to the component's value.

Ungrouped Attributes

Attribute	Type	Description	Required
accesskey	char	The mnemonic character used to establish focus to this component.	No
action	javax.faces .el.MethodBinding	The reference to an action method sent by the command component, or the static outcome of an action.	No
actionListener	javax.faces .el.MethodBinding	The method reference to an action listener.	No
alt	String	The alternate textual description of the element rendered by this component.	No
disabled	boolean	When **true**, renders the component in a disabled state.	No
image	String	The absolute or relative URL of the image to be displayed for this button. If specified, this "input" element will be of type "image".	No

Attribute	Type	Description	Required
immediate	boolean	Determines whether or not data validation should occur when events are generated by this component. When **true**, any action or **ActionListener** should be executed during the Apply Request Values phase instead of the Invoke Application phase.	No
readonly	boolean	The boolean flag that specifies whether the component is read only.	No
rendered	boolean	The boolean flag that defines whether the component is rendered.	No
tabindex	int	Determines the tabbing order position of the component. The value must be an integer between 0 and 32767.	No
type	String	Must be submitted or reset.	No

Core Attributes

Attribute	Type	Description	Required
binding	Value Binding or ValueExpression (1.2)	The binding reference to a like **UIComponent** instance	No
id	String	The identifier for the component	No
value	String	The value of the component	No

Internationalization Attributes

Attribute	Type	Description	Required
dir	String	The reading direction of the generated HTML component: RTL (right to left) or LTR (left to right).	No
lang	String	The applied **lang** attribute to the generated HTML output. For more information on the HTML **lang** attribute, visit **www.w3.org/TR/REC-html40/struct/dirlang.html**.	No

Style Attributes

Attributes for CSS styles that are applied to the generated HTML output of the component are shown next.

style	styleclass

These style attributes accept arguments of type **String** and are not specifically required.

JavaScript Attributes
Attributes for the common JavaScript events are shown next.

onblur	onchange	onclick	ondblclick	onfocus
onkeydown	onkeypress	onkeyup	onmousedown	onmousemove
onmouseout	onmouseover	onmouseup	onselect	

All JavaScript attributes accept arguments of type **String** and none are specifically required.

Example Usage
The following is an example of a button rendered with "Register" text that submits the form and invokes the **action** method specified by "#{Register_Backing.register}".

```
<f:form>
  <h:inputText id="firstName" value="Jake"
    binding="{Register_Backing.firstNameInputText}" />
  <h:commandButton value="Register" action="#{Register_Backing.register}"/>
</f:form>
```

The following is an additional **commandButton** Cancel button that submits the form but without performing any validation.

```
<f:form>
  <h:inputText id="firstName" value="Jake"
    binding="{Register_Backing.firstNameInputText}" />
  <h:commandButton value="Register" action="#{Register_Backing.register}"/>
  <h:commandButton value="Cancel" immediate="true" action="cancel"/>
</f:form>
```

The commandLink Component
Tag name: **<h:commandLink>**
UIComponent class: **javax.faces.component.html.HtmlCommandLink**
Component type: **javax.faces.HtmlCommandLink**

The **commandLink** component renders an HTML hyperlink using an **<a>** anchor element but also executes a form submit when clicked.

Ungrouped Attributes

Attribute	Type	Description	Required
accesskey	char	The mnemonic character used to establish focus to this component.	No
action	javax.faces .el.MethodBinding	The reference to an action method sent by the command component, or the static outcome of an action.	No
actionListener	javax.faces .el.MethodBinding	The method reference to an action listener.	No
charset	String	The character encoding of the resource referred by this hyperlink.	No

Attribute	Type	Description	Required
coords	String	The position and shape of the hotspot on the screen (for use in client-side image maps).	No
hreflang	String	The language code of the resource designated by this hyperlink.	No
immediate	boolean	Determines whether or not data validation should occur when events are generated by this component. When **true**, any action or **ActionListener** should be executed during the Apply Request Values phase instead of the Invoke Application phase.	No
rel	String	The relationship from the current document to the anchor specified by this hyperlink. The value of this attribute is a space-separated list of link types.	No
rendered	boolean	The boolean flag that defines whether this component is rendered.	No
rev	String	The reverse link from the anchor specified by this hyperlink to the current document. The value of this attribute is a space-separated list of link types.	No
shape	String	The shape of the hotspot in client-side image maps. Valid values are **default**, **circle**, **rect**, and **poly**.	No
tabindex	int	The tabbing order position of the component. The value must be an integer between 0 and 32767.	No
target	String	The name of a frame where the resource retrieved via this hyperlink is to be displayed.	No
type	String	The content type of the resource designated by this hyperlink.	No

Core Attributes

Attribute	Type	Description	Required
binding	Value Binding or ValueExpression (1.2)	The binding reference to a like **UIComponent** instance.	No
id	String	The identifier for the component.	No
title	String	The title of the component. This is passed through to the rendered HTML **title** element.	No
value	String	The value of the component.	No

Internationalization Attributes

Attribute	Type	Description	Required
dir	String	The reading direction of the generated HTML component: RTL (right to left) or LTR (left to right).	No
lang	String	The applied **lang** attribute to the generated HTML output. For more information on the HTML **lang** attribute, visit **www.w3.org/TR/REC-html40/struct/dirlang.html**.	No

Style Attributes
Attributes for CSS styles that are applied to the generated HTML output of the component are shown next.

style	styleclass

These style attributes accept arguments of type **String** and are not specifically required.

JavaScript Attributes
Attributes for the common JavaScript events are shown next.

onblur	onchange	onclick	ondblclick	onfocus
onkeydown	onkeypress	onkeyup	onmousedown	onmousemove
onmouseout	onmouseover	onmouseup	onselect	

All JavaScript attributes accept arguments of type **String** and none are specifically required.

Example Usage
The following is a simple **commandLink** example of a button that submits an input field.

```
<h:commandLink action="an action"
    binding="#{backing_newhello.commandLink2}"
    id="commandLink2">
  <h:outputText value="This text will appear as a link"
    binding="#{backing_newhello.outputText1}"
    id="outputText1"/>
</h:commandLink>
```

The preceding creates an input form. The inner tags of the form receive the data that will be submitted with the form. It displays an HTML **<input>** element with an action attribute set to the URL that defines the view containing the form and a method attribute set to "post". When the form is submitted, only components that are children of the submitted form are processed.

The dataTable Component
Tag name: **<h:dataTable>**
UIComponent class: **javax.faces.component.html.HtmlDataTable**
Component type: **javax.faces.HtmlDataTable**
    The **dataTable** component is a tabular container component for other child components that is rendered as an HTML <table> with a number of attributes, such as **border**, **width**,

and so on, which are directly passed to the rendered HTML table. The component's children are rendered in the table cells, with new rows added when the number of columns is reached.

For further information on the attributes that are passed onto the rendered HTML table, visit **www.w3.org/TR/REC-html40/struct/tables.html**.

Ungrouped Attributes

Attribute	Type	Description	Required
bgcolor	String	The background color of the rendered HTML table representing the **dataTable**.	No
border	int	The border size in pixels of the rendered HTML table.	No
cellpadding	int	The **cellpadding** attribute of the rendered HTML table.	No
cellspacing	int	The **cellspacing** attribute of the rendered HTML table.	No
first	int	The first row to display (starting with 0).	No
frame	String	A **frame** that is passed onto the rendered HTML table. This attribute specifies which sides of the frame surrounding the table will be visible. Valid values are **none**, **above**, **below**, **hsides**, **vsides**, **lhs**, **rhs**, **box**, and **border**.	No
rendered	boolean	The boolean attribute that defines whether the component will be rendered.	No
rows	int	Determines how many rows are displayed in the rendered table.	No
rules	String	A **rules** attribute that is passed onto the rendered HTML table. Valid values are **none**, **groups**, **rows**, **cols**, and **all**.	No
summary	String	A **summary** attribute that is passed onto the rendered HTML table.	No
var	String	An iterator variable.	No
width	String	A **width** attribute that is passed onto the rendered HTML table. For pixel width, enter a non-zero integer. For percentage width, append '%' to the value. For example: "80%".	No

Core Attributes

Attribute	Type	Description	Required
binding	Value Binding or ValueExpression (1.2)	The binding reference to a like **UIComponent** instance.	No
id	String	The identifier for the component.	No
title	String	The title of the component. This is passed through to the rendered HTML **title** element.	No
value	String	The value of the component.	No

Style Attributes

Attribute	Type	Description	Required
columnclasses	String	The comma-separated list of CSS classes to be associated with the rendered columns. The classes will be applied in a repeating fashion to all columns in the **panelGrid** component.	No
footerclass	String	The CSS class to be associated with the rendered HTML table footer (bottom row).	No
headerclass	String	The CSS class to be associated with the rendered HTML table header (top row).	No
rowclasses	String	A comma-separated list of CSS classes to be associated with the rendered rows. The classes will be applied in a repeating fashion to all rows in the **panelGrid** component.	No
style	String	Inline style(s) that are applied to the **panelGrid** component.	No
styleclass	String	The CSS style class that is applied to the **panelGrid** component.	No

Internationalization Attributes

Attribute	Type	Description	Required
dir	String	The reading direction of the generated HTML component: RTL (right to left) or LTR (left to right).	No
lang	String	The applied **lang** attribute to the generated HTML output. For more information on the HTML **lang** attribute, visit **www.w3.org/TR/REC-html40/struct/dirlang.html**.	No

JavaScript Attributes

Attributes for the common JavaScript events are shown next.

onclick	ondblclick	onkeydown	onkeypress	onkeyup
onmousedown	onmousemove	onmouseout	onmouseover	onmouseup

All JavaScript attributes accept arguments of type **String** and none are specifically required.

Example Usage

The following is a simple **dataTable** example containing two child **column**s with nested **outputText** components.

```
<h:dataTable >
  <h:column>
    <h:outputText value="outputText1"/>
  </h:column>
  <h:column>
```

```
    <h:outputText value="outputText2"/>
  </h:column>
</h:dataTable>
```

Consider a managed bean **EmpList** of type **java.util.ArrayList** with list items defined in faces-config as **list-entries**. The following **dataTable** example will render the **Emplist** in an HTML table.

```
<h:dataTable  border="1" value="#{EmpList}" var="row">
  <h:column>
    <f:facet name="header">
      <h:outputText value="Emplist"/>
    </f:facet>
    <h:outputText value="#{row}"/>
  </h:column>
</h:dataTable>
```

The following is a more advanced usage example from the Virtual Trainer application in Chapter 9. It displays all of the training events for a particular user in the application.

```
<h:dataTable id="eventsTable" rows="5"
    value="#{Main_Backing.trainingEventsForUser}"
    var="te" rowClasses="list-row-odd,list-row-even"
    width="100%" binding="#{Main_Backing.data}">
  <h:column rendered="#{UserBean.trainer}">
    <f:facet name="header">
      <h:outputText value="User Account"/>
    </f:facet>
    <h:outputText value="#{te.userAcctId}"/>
  </h:column>
  <h:column>
    <f:facet name="header">
      <h:outputText value="Event Name"/>
    </f:facet>
    <h:outputText value="#{te.ename}"/>
  </h:column>
  <h:column>
    <f:facet name="header">
      <h:outputText value="Completion Date"/>
    </f:facet>
    <h:outputText value="#{te.completionDate}">
      <f:convertDateTime pattern="MM-dd-yy"/>
    </h:outputText>
  </h:column>
...
</h:dataTable>
```

The form Component

Tag name: **<h:form>**
UIComponent class: **javax.faces.component.html.HtmlForm**
Component type: **javax.faces.HtmlForm**

The **form** component renders as an input form. The inner tags of the form receive the data that will be submitted with the form. It displays an HTML **<input>** element with an action attribute set to the URL that defines the view containing the form and a method attribute set to "post". When the form is submitted, only components that are children of the submitted form are processed.

Ungrouped Attributes

Attribute	Type	Description	Required
accept	String	The list of content types that a server processing this form will handle correctly.	No
acceptcharset	String	The list of character encodings for input data that are accepted by the server processing this form.	No
enctype	String	The content type used to submit the form to the server. If not specified, the default value is "application/x-www-form-urlencoded".	No
rendered	boolean	The boolean flag that defines whether this component is rendered.	No
target	String	The name of a frame where the response retrieved after the form submit is to be displayed.	No

Core Attributes

Attribute	Type	Description	Required
binding	Value Binding or ValueExpression (1.2)	A binding reference to a like **UIComponent** instance.	No
id	String	The identifier for the component.	No
prependId (1.2 only)	boolean	Boolean value indicating whether or not this form should prepend its **id** to its descendant's **id** during the **clientId** generation process. The default is true.	No
title	String	The title of the component. This is passed through to the rendered HTML **title** element	No
value	String	The value of the component.	No

Internationalization Attributes

Attribute	Type	Description	Required
dir	String	The reading direction of the generated HTML component: RTL (right to left) or LTR (left to right).	No
lang	String	The applied **lang** attribute to the generated HTML output. For more information on the HTML **lang** attribute, visit **www.w3.org/TR/REC-html40/struct/dirlang.html**.	No

Style Attributes
Attributes for CSS styles that are applied to the generated HTML output of the component are shown next.

style	styleclass

These style attributes accept arguments of type **String** and are not specifically required.

JavaScript Attributes
Attributes for the common JavaScript events are shown next.

onclick	ondblclick	onkeydown	onkeypress	onkeyup
onmousedown	onmousemove	onmouseout	onmouseover	onmouseup

All JavaScript attributes accept arguments of type **String** and none are specifically required.

Example Usage

```
<h:form id="formid" >
  ...(form input components)
</h:form>
```

The graphicImage Component

Tag name: **<h:graphicImage>**
UIComponent class: **javax.faces.component.html.HtmlGraphicImage**
Component type: **javax.faces.HtmlGraphicImage**

The **graphicImage** component displays an image. It is rendered as an HTML **<input>** element with the **src** attribute holding the component's **value** or the **URL** attribute, adjusted to a context-relative path. (If the URL is preceded by a slash ("/"), then it uses a context-relative path, otherwise it uses a relative path.)

Ungrouped Attributes

Attribute	Type	Description	Required
alt	String	An alternate textual description of the element rendered by this component.	No
height	String	The override for the height of this image.	No
ismap	boolean	The boolean flag indicating that this image is to be used as a server-side image map. Such an image must be enclosed within a hyperlink ("a").	No
longdesc	String	The URI to a long description of the image represented by this element.	No
rendered	boolean	The boolean flag that defines whether the component is rendered.	No
usemap	String	The name of a client-side image map (an HTML map element) for which this element provides the image.	No

Attribute	Type	Description	Required
url	String	The context-relative URL indicating the location of the image resource.	No
width	String	The override for the width of this image.	No

Core Attributes

Attribute	Type	Description	Required
binding	Value Binding or ValueExpression (1.2)	A binding reference to a like **UIComponent** instance.	No
id	String	The identifier for the component.	No
title	String	The title of the component. This is passed through to the rendered HTML **title** element.	No
value	String	The value of the component.	No

Internationalization Attributes

Attribute	Type	Description	Required
dir	String	The reading direction of the generated HTML component: RTL (right to left) or LTR (left to right).	No
lang	String	The applied **lang** attribute to the generated HTML output. For more information on the HTML **lang** attribute, visit **www.w3.org/TR/REC-html40/struct/dirlang.html**.	No

Style Attributes
Attributes for CSS styles that are applied to the generated HTML output of the component are shown next.

style	styleclass

These style attributes accept arguments of type **String** and are not specifically required.

JavaScript Attributes
Attributes for the common JavaScript events are shown in the following.

onclick	ondblclick	onkeydown	onkeypress	onkeyup
onmousedown	onmousemove	onmouseout	onmouseover	onmouseup

All JavaScript attributes accept arguments of type **String** and none are specifically required.

Example Usage

```
<h:graphicImage  id="graphicImage1" url="/myimage.jpg" height="143" width="143"
  binding="#{backing.graphicImage1}" />
```

The inputHidden Component

Tag name: **<h:inputHidden>**
UIComponent class: **javax.faces.component.html.HtmlInputHidden**
Component type: **javax.faces.HtmlInputHidden**

The **inputHidden** component renders a field that is invisible to the user, which is typically used to pass variables from page to page. Displays an HTML **<input>** element with the **type** attribute set to "hidden", a **name** attribute set to the component's client ID, and a **value** attribute set to the component's value.

Attributes

Attribute	Type	Description	Required
binding	Value Binding or ValueExpression (1.2)	A binding reference to a like **UIComponent** instance.	No
converter	String	Converter instance registered with this component.	No
converterMessage (1.2 only)	String	When present, this overrides the default **Converter** validation message. The message can be a **ValueExpression**.	No
id	String	The identifier for the component.	No
immediate	boolean	When **true**, the component's value must be converted and validated immediately during the Apply Request Values phase rather than waiting until the Process Validations phase.	No
rendered	boolean	The boolean flag that defines whether the component is rendered.	No
required	boolean	The boolean flag specifying whether this component is required to have a value.	No
requiredMessage (1.2 only)	String	When present, this overrides the default **required** validation message. The message can be a **ValueExpression**.	No
validator	String	The EL reference to the validator method.	No
validatorMessage (1.2 only)	String	When present, this overrides the default **Validator** validation message. The message can be a **ValueExpression**.	No

Attribute	Type	Description	Required
value	String	The value of the component.	No
valueChangeListener	String	The EL reference to a method that accepts a **ValueChangeEvent** argument.	No

Example Usage
The following shows a simple usage of **InputHidden**.

```
<h:inputHidden id="inputHidden1" binding="#{backing_bean.inputHidden1}"
   value="A hidden value"/>
```

The inputSecret Component
Tag name: **<h:inputSecret>**
UIComponent class: **javax.faces.component.html.HtmlInputSecret**
Component type: **javax.faces.HtmlInputSecret**

The **inputSecret** component renders as a password input field. It displays an HTML **<input>** element with the **type** attribute set to **password**, a **name** attribute set to the component's client ID, and a **value** attribute set to the component's **value** only if the action's redisplay attribute is set to **true**.

Ungrouped Attributes

Attribute	Type	Description	Required
accesskey	char	The mnemonic character used to establish focus to this component.	No
alt	int	The alternate textual description of the element rendered by this component.	No
converter	String	The full classpath reference to **Converter** to associate with this component.	No
converterMessage (1.2 only)	String	When present, this overrides the default **Converter** validation message. The message can be a **ValueExpression**.	No
disabled	boolean	When **true**, this renders the component in a disabled state.	No
immediate	boolean	When **true**, the component's value must be converted and validated immediately during the Apply Request Values phase rather than waiting until the Process Validations phase.	No
maxlength	int	The integer value specifying the maximum length of the rendered HTML input element.	No
readonly	boolean	When **true**, this renders the component in a read-only state.	No

Attribute	Type	Description	Required
redisplay	boolean	The boolean flag indicating that any existing value in this field should be rendered when the form is created. Because this is a potential security risk, password values are not displayed by default	No
rendered	boolean	The boolean flag that defines whether the component is rendered.	No
required	boolean	The boolean flag specifying whether text area is required to have a value.	No
requiredMessage (1.2 only)	String	When present, this overrides the default **required** validation message. The message can be a **ValueExpression**.	No
size	int	The size (in characters) of the input component.	No
tabindex	int	The tabbing order position of the component. The value must be an integer between 0 and 32767.	No
validator	String	The EL reference to the validator method.	No
validatorMessage (1.2 only)	String	When present, this overrides the default **Validator** validation message. The message can be a **ValueExpression**.	No
valueChangeListener	String	The EL reference to the method that accepts a **ValueChangeEvent** argument.	No

Core Attributes

Attribute	Type	Description	Required
binding	Value Binding or ValueExpression (1.2)	A binding reference to a like **UIComponent** instance.	No
id	String	The identifier for the component.	No
title	String	The title of the component. This is passed through to the rendered HTML **title** element.	No
value	String	The value of the component.	No

Internationalization Attributes

Attribute	Type	Description	Required
dir	String	The reading direction of the generated HTML component: RTL (right to left) or LTR (left to right).	No
lang	String	The applied **lang** attribute to the generated HTML output. For more information on the HTML **lang** attribute, visit **www.w3.org/TR/REC-html40/struct/dirlang.html**.	No

PART IV

Style Attributes

Attributes for CSS styles that are applied to the generated HTML output of the component are shown next.

style	styleclass

These style attributes accept arguments of type **String** and are not specifically required.

JavaScript Attributes

Attributes for the common JavaScript events are shown in the following.

onblur	onchange	onclick	ondblclick	onfocus
onkeydown	onkeypress	onkeyup	onmousedown	onmousemove
onmouseout	onmouseover	onmouseup	onselect	

All JavaScript attributes accept arguments of type **String** and none are specifically required.

Example Usage

An example showing a simple usage of **inputSecret**.

```
<h:inputSecret id="password" value="#{UserBean.password}" />
```

The inputText Component

Tag name: **<h:inputText>**
UIComponent class: **javax.faces.component.html.HtmlInputText**
Component type: **javax.faces.HtmlInputText**

The **inputText** component renders as a user input text field. It displays an HTML **<input>** element with the **type** attribute set to "text", a **name** attribute set to the component's client ID, and a **value** attribute set to the component's value.

Ungrouped Attributes

Attribute	Type	Description	Required
accesskey	char	The mnemonic character used to establish focus to this component.	No
alt	int	The number of columns or width of the rendered text area.	No
converter	String	The full classpath reference to **Converter** to associate with this component.	No
converterMessage (1.2 only)	String	When present, this overrides the default **Converter** validation message. The message can be a **ValueExpression**.	No
disabled	boolean	When **true**, this renders the component in a disabled state.	No

Attribute	Type	Description	Required
immediate	boolean	When **true**, the component's value must be converted and validated immediately during the Apply Request Values phase rather than waiting until the Process Validations phase.	No
maxlength	int	The integer value specifying the maximum length of the rendered HTML input element.	No
readonly	boolean	When **true**, this renders the component in a read-only state.	No
rendered	boolean	The boolean flag that defines whether the component is rendered.	No
required	boolean	The boolean flag specifying whether the text area is required to have a value.	No
requiredMessage (1.2 only)	String	When present, this overrides the default **required** validation message. The message can be a **ValueExpression**.	No
size	int	The size (in characters) of the input component.	No
tabindex	int	The tabbing order position of the component. The value must be an integer between 0 and 32767.	No
validator	String	The EL reference to the validator method.	No
validatorMessage (1.2 only)	String	When present, this overrides the default **Validator** validation message. The message can be a **ValueExpression**.	No
valueChangeListener	String	The EL reference to the method that accepts a **ValueChangeEvent** argument.	No

Core Attributes

Attribute	Type	Description	Required
binding	Value Binding or ValueExpression (1.2)	A binding reference to a like **UIComponent** instance.	No
id	String	The identifier for the component.	No
title	String	The title of the component. This is passed through to the rendered HTML **title** element.	No
value	String	The value of the component.	No

PART IV

Internationalization Attributes

Attribute	Type	Description	Required
dir	String	The reading direction of the generated HTML component: RTL (right to left) or LTR (left to right).	No
lang	String	The applied **lang** attribute to the generated HTML output. For more information on the HTML **lang** attribute, visit **www.w3.org/TR/REC-html40/struct/dirlang.html**.	No

Style Attributes

Attributes for CSS styles that are applied to the generated HTML output of the component are shown next.

style	styleclass

These style attributes accept arguments of type **String** and are not specifically required.

JavaScript Attributes

Attributes for the common JavaScript events are shown next.

onblur	onchange	onclick	ondblclick	onfocus
onkeydown	onkeypress	onkeyup	onmousedown	onmousemove
onmouseout	onmouseover	onmouseup	onselect	

All JavaScript attributes accept arguments of type **String** and none are specifically required.

Example Usage

An example showing the simple usage of **InputText**.

```
<h:inputText id="userid"/>
```

The inputTextarea Component

Tag name: **<h:inputTextarea>**
UIComponent class: **javax.faces.component.html.HtmlInputTextarea**
Component type: **javax.faces.HtmlInputTextarea**

The **inputTextarea** component renders as a user HTML input text area with multiple lines of text. The rendered HTML **<textarea>** element's name attribute is set to the component's client ID and a body holding the component's **value**.

Ungrouped Attributes

Attribute	Type	Description	Required
accesskey	char	The mnemonic character used to establish focus to this component.	No
cols	int	The number of columns or width of the rendered text area.	No
converter	String	The full classpath reference to **Converter** to associate with this component.	No

Attribute	Type	Description	Required
converterMessage (1.2 only)	String	When present, this overrides the default **Converter** validation message. The message can be a **ValueExpression**.	No
disabled	boolean	When **true**, this renders the component in a disabled state.	No
immediate	boolean	When **true**, the component's value must be converted and validated immediately during the Apply Request Values phase rather than waiting until the Process Validations phase.	No
readonly	boolean	When **true**, this renders the component in a read-only state.	No
rendered	boolean	The boolean flag that defines whether the component is rendered.	No
required	boolean	The boolean flag specifying whether text area is required to have a value.	No
requiredMessage (1.2 only)	String	When present, this overrides the default **required** validation message. The message can be a **ValueExpression**.	No
rows	int	The number of rows of the rendered text area.	No
tabindex	int	The tabbing order position of the component. The value must be an integer between 0 and 32767.	No
validator	String	The EL reference to the validator method.	No
validatorMessage (1.2 only)	String	When present, this overrides the default **Validator** validation message. The message can be a **ValueExpression**.	No
valueChangeListener	String	The EL reference to the method that accepts a **ValueChangeEvent** argument.	No

Core Attributes

Attribute	Type	Description	Required
binding	Value Binding or ValueExpression (1.2)	A binding reference to a like **UIComponent** instance.	No
id	String	The identifier for the component.	No
title	String	The title of the component. This is passed through to the rendered HTML **title** element.	No
value	String	The value of the component.	No

Internationalization Attributes

Attribute	Type	Description	Required
dir	String	The reading direction of the generated HTML component: RTL (right to left) or LTR (left to right).	No
lang	String	The applied **lang** attribute to generated HTML output. For more information on the HTML **lang** attribute, visit **www.w3.org/TR/REC-html40/struct/dirlang.html**.	No

Style Attributes

Attributes for CSS styles that are applied to the generated HTML output of the component are shown next.

style	styleclass

These style attributes accept arguments of type **String** and are not specifically required.

JavaScript Attributes

Attributes for the common JavaScript events are shown next.

onblur	onchange	onclick	ondblclick	onfocus
onkeydown	onkeypress	onkeyup	onmousedown	onmousemove
onmouseout	onmouseover	onmouseup	onselect	

All JavaScript attributes accept arguments of type **String** and none are specifically required.

Example Usage

An example showing a simple usage of **InputTextarea**.

```
<h:inputTextarea id="inputTextarea1"
  binding="#{backing_bean.inputTextarea1}"
  value="this is some text in a text area" />
```

The message Component

Tag name: **<h:message>**
UIComponent class: **javax.faces.component.html.HtmlMessage**
Component type: **javax.faces.HtmlMessage**

The **message** component renders a Faces message for the component identified by the **for** attribute. The message properties identified by the **showdetail** and **showsummary** attributes for this message are rendered as text, within an HTML **<span>** element if any of the CSS style attributes apply or the **id** attribute is set. If the **tooltip** attribute is set to **true** and both the summary and the detailed text are rendered, the message summary is rendered as the value of the **<span>** element's **title** attribute.

Ungrouped Attributes

Attribute	Type	Description	Required
for	String	The ID of the UI component with which to be associated.	Yes

Attribute	Type	Description	Required
rendered	boolean	A boolean flag that defines whether the component is rendered.	No
showDetail	boolean	When **true**, this displays the detail portion of message. The default is **false**.	No
showSummary	boolean	When **true**, this displays the summary portion of the message. The default is **true**.	No
tooltip	boolean	A boolean flag indicating whether the detail portion of the message should be displayed as a tooltip.	No

Core Attributes

Attribute	Type	Description	Required
binding	Value Binding or ValueExpression (1.2)	A binding reference to a like **UIComponent** instance.	No
id	String	The identifier for the component.	No
title	String	The title of the component. This is passed through to the rendered HTML **title** element.	No

Style Attributes

Attribute	Type	Description	Required
errorclass	String	The CSS style class to apply to any message with a severity class of "ERROR"	No
errorstyle	String	The CSS style(s) to apply to any message with a severity class of "ERROR"	No
fatalclass	String	The CSS style class to apply to any message with a severity class of "FATAL"	No
fatalstyle	String	The CSS style(s) to apply to any message with a severity class of "FATAL"	No
infoclass	String	The CSS style class to apply to any message with a severity class of "INFO"	No
infostyle	String	The CSS style(s) to apply to any message with a severity class of "INFO"	No
style	String	The CSS style(s) to be applied when this component is rendered	No
styleClass	String	The space-separated list of CSS style class(es) to be applied when this element is rendered	No
warnclass	String	The CSS style class to apply to any message with a severity class of "WARN"	No
warnstyle	String	The CSS style(s) to apply to any message with a severity class of "WARN"	No

Example Usage

The following displays any Faces messages for the **inputTextarea1** field.

```
<h:inputTextarea id="inputTextarea1"  … />
<h:message for="inputTextarea1"/>
```

The messages Component

Tag name: **<h:messages>**
UIComponent class: **javax.faces.component.html.HtmlMessages**
Component type: **javax.faces.HtmlMessages**

The **messages** component renders all queued messages, or only those queued without a component identifier if the **globalOnly** attribute is set to **true**. The message properties identified by the **showDetail** and **showSummary** attributes for this message are rendered as cells in an HTML table if the layout attribute is set to **table** or an HTML list if set to **list**.

Ungrouped Attributes

Attribute	Type	Description	Required
globalOnly	boolean	The boolean flag indicating that only global messages (not associated with any client ID) are to be displayed.	No
layout	String	The type of HTML layout used when rendering error messages. Valid values are **list** (default) or **table**.	No
rendered	boolean	The boolean flag that defines whether the component is rendered.	No
showDetail	boolean	When **true**, this displays the detail portion of the message. The default is **false**.	No
showSummary	boolean	When **true**, this displays the summary portion of the message. The default is **true**.	No
tooltip	boolean	The boolean flag indicating whether the detail portion of the message should be displayed as a tooltip.	No

Core Attributes

Attribute	Type	Description	Required
binding	Value Binding or ValueExpression (1.2)	A binding reference to a like **UIComponent** instance.	No
id	String	The identifier for the component.	No
title	String	The title of the component. This is passed through to the rendered HTML **title** element.	No

Style Attributes

Attribute	Type	Description	Required
errorclass	String	The CSS style class to apply to any message with a severity class of "ERROR"	No
errorstyle	String	The CSS style(s) to apply to any message with a severity class of "ERROR"	No
fatalclass	String	The CSS style class to apply to any message with a severity class of "FATAL"	No
fatalstyle	String	The CSS style(s) to apply to any message with a severity class of "FATAL"	No
infoclass	String	The CSS style class to apply to any message with a severity class of "INFO"	No
infostyle	String	The CSS style(s) to apply to any message with a severity class of "INFO"	No
style	String	The CSS style(s) to be applied when this component is rendered	No
styleClass	String	The space-separated list of CSS style class(es) to be applied when this element is rendered	No
warnclass	String	The CSS style class to apply to any message with a severity class of "WARN"	No
warnstyle	String	The CSS style(s) to apply to any message with a severity class of "WARN"	No

Example Usage

The following example displays global Faces messages with details.

```
<h:messages layout="list" globalOnly="true" showDetail="true"/>
```

The outputFormat Component

Tag name: **<h:outputFormat>**
UIComponent class: **javax.faces.component.html.HtmlOutputFormat**
Component type: **javax.faces.HtmlOutputFormat**

The **outputFormat** component renders parameterized text. Text is rendered within an HTML **<span>** element if any of the CSS style attributes are set or the **id** attribute is set.

Accrues the values of any child **UIParameter** components, converts the list of parameter values to an **Object** array, and calls **MessageFormat.format()**, passing the value of this component as the first argument, and the array of parameter values as the second argument. It then renders the result. If no arguments are provided, it just renders the **value** of the component unmodified.

Attributes

Attribute	Type	Description	Required
binding	Value Binding or ValueExpression (1.2)	A binding reference to a like **UIComponent** instance.	No
converter	String	The full classpath reference to **Converter** to associate with this component.	No
escape	boolean	The boolean flag indicating whether or not to *escape* HTML or XML characters in the value of the component. For example, when **true**, the character "<" is *escaped* to "<". It is **true** by default.	No
id	String	The identifier for the component.	No
rendered	boolean	The boolean attribute that defines whether the component is rendered.	No
style	String	The inline style(s) that is applied to the **panelGrid** component.	No
styleClass	String	The CSS style class that is applied to the **panelGrid** component.	No
title	String	The title of the component. This is passed through to the rendered HTML **title** element.	No
value	String	The value of the component.	No

Example Usage

The following is an example of the formatted output with a parameter.

```
<h:outputFormat  id="outputFormat1" binding="#{backing.outputFormat1}">
  <f:param name="parname" value="parval" />
</h:outputFormat>
```

The outputLabel Component

Tag name: **<h:outputLabel>**
UIComponent class: **javax.faces.component.html.HtmlOutputLabel**
Component type: **javax.faces.HtmlOutputLabel**

The **outputLabel** component renders as a text label using the HTML **<label>** element and can optionally be specified for an input field. The client ID for the associated component is set using the component's **for** attribute value. The generated **<label>** element body is provided by the **h:outputLabel** body and/or its **value** attribute.

Ungrouped Attributes

Attribute	Type	Description	Required
accesskey	char	The mnemonic character used to establish focus to this component.	No
converter	String	The full classpath reference to **Converter** to associate with this component.	No
for	String	The ID of the UI component with which to be associated.	No
rendered	boolean	The boolean attribute that defines whether the component is rendered.	No
tabindex	int	The tabbing order position of the component. The value must be an integer between 0 and 32767.	No

Core Attributes

Attribute	Type	Description	Required
binding	Value Binding or ValueExpression (1.2)	A binding reference to a like **UIComponent** instance.	No
id	String	The identifier for the component.	No
title	String	The title of the component. This is passed through to the rendered HTML **title** element.	No
value	String	The value of the component.	No

Internationalization Attributes

Attribute	Type	Description	Required
dir	String	The reading direction of the generated HTML component: RTL (right to left) or LTR (left to right).	No
lang	String	The applied **lang** attribute to the generated HTML output. For more information on the HTML **lang** attribute, visit **www.w3.org/TR/REC-html40/struct/dirlang.html**.	No

Style Attributes

Attributes for CSS styles that are applied to the generated HTML output of the component are shown next.

style	styleclass

These style attributes accept arguments of type **String** and are not specifically required.

PART IV

JavaScript Attributes
Attributes for the common JavaScript events are shown next.

onblur	onclick	ondblclick	onfocus
onkeydown	onkeypress	onkeyup	onmousedown
onmousemove	onmouseout	onmouseover	onmouseup

All JavaScript attributes accept arguments of type **String** and none are specifically required.

Example Usage
The following is an example of the simple usage of an **outputLabel** associated with an **inputTextarea**.

```
<h:outputLabel for="inputTextarea1" value="Text Input Label" />
<h:inputTextarea id="inputTextarea1" />
```

The outputLink Component
Tag name: **<h:outputLink>**
UIComponent class: **javax.faces.component.html.HtmlOutputLink**
Component type: **javax.faces.HtmlOutputLink**

The **outputLink** component is rendered as an HTML hyperlink, **<a>**, element with an **href** attribute set to the component's value. If the component has **UIParameter** component children, their name and value properties are added as query string parameters to the **href** attribute value, with both the name and value URL encoded. If the component's children are not **UIParameter** components, they are rendered as the content of the **<a>** element, such as the link text or image.

Ungrouped Attributes

Attribute	Type	Description	Required
accesskey	char	The mnemonic character used to establish focus to this component.	No
charset	String	The character encoding of the resource referred by this hyperlink.	No
converter	String	The full classpath reference to **Converter** to associate with this component.	No
coords	String	The position and shape of the hotspot on the screen (for use in client-side image maps).	No
rel	String	The relationship from the current document to the anchor specified by this hyperlink. The value of this attribute is a space-separated list of link types.	No
rendered	boolean	The boolean flag specifying whether the component is rendered.	No
rev	String	A reverse link from the anchor specified by this hyperlink to the current document. The value of this attribute is a space-separated list of link types.	No

Attribute	Type	Description	Required
shape	String	The shape of the hotspot in client-side image maps. Valid values are **default**, **circle**, **rect**, and **poly**.	No
tabindex	int	The tabbing order position of the component. The value must be an integer between 0 and 32767.	No
target	String	The name of the frame where the resource retrieved via this hyperlink is to be displayed.	No
type	String	The content type of the resource designated by this hyperlink.	No

Core Attributes

Attribute	Type	Description	Required
binding	Value Binding or ValueExpression (1.2)	A binding reference to a like **UIComponent** instance.	No
id	String	The identifier for the component.	No
title	String	The title of the component. This is passed through to the rendered HTML **title** element.	No
value	String	The value of the component.	No

Internationalization Attributes

Attribute	Type	Description	Required
dir	String	The reading direction of the generated HTML component: RTL (right to left) or LTR (left to right).	No
lang	String	The applied **lang** attribute to the generated HTML output. For more information on the HTML **lang** attribute, visit **www.w3.org/TR/REC-html40/struct/dirlang.html**.	No
hreflang	String	This attribute is passed onto the rendered HTML hyperlink and is the language code of the resource designated by this hyperlink.	No

Style Attributes
Attributes for CSS styles that are applied to the generated HTML output of the component are shown next.

style	styleclass

These style attributes accept arguments of type **String** and are not specifically required.

JavaScript Attributes
Attributes for the common JavaScript events are shown next.

onblur	onclick	ondblclick	onfocus	onkeydown
onkeypress	onkeyup	onmousedown	onmousemove	onmouseout
onmouseover	onmouseup			

All JavaScript attributes accept arguments of type **String** and none are specifically required.

Example Usage
The following is an example of a simple **outputLink** usage that links to the Google Web site.

```
<h:outputLink value="http://google.com" >
  <f:verbatim >This will appear as a Link to Google.</f:verbatim>
</h:outputLink>
```

The outputText Component
Tag name: **<h:outputText>**
UIComponent class: **javax.faces.component.html.HtmlOutputText**
Component type: **javax.faces.HtmlOutputText**

The **outputText** component renders the component's **value** as text within the page.

Ungrouped Attributes

Attribute	Type	Description	Required
converter	String	The full classpath reference to **Converter** to associate with this component.	No
escape	boolean	The boolean flag indicating whether or not to *escape* HTML or XML characters in the value of the component. For example, when **true**, the character "<" is *escaped* to "<". It is **true** by default.	No
rendered	boolean	The boolean flag specifying whether the component is rendered.	No

Core Attributes

Attribute	Type	Description	Required
binding	Value Binding or ValueExpression (1.2)	A binding reference to a like **UIComponent** instance.	No
id	String	The identifier for the component.	No
title	String	The title of the component. This is passed through to the rendered HTML **title** element.	No
value	String	The value of the component.	No

Style Attributes

Attributes for CSS styles that are applied to the generated HTML output of the component are shown next.

style	styleclass

These style attributes accept arguments of type **String** and are not specifically required.

Internationalization Attributes

Attribute	Type	Description	Required
dir(1.2 only)	String	The reading direction of the generated HTML component: RTL (right to left) or LTR (left to right).	No
lang(1.2 only)	String	The applied **lang** attribute to the generated HTML output. For more information on the HTML **lang** attribute, visit **www.w3.org/TR/REC-html40/ struct/dirlang.html**.	No

Example Usage

The following is an example of a simple usage of **outputText**.

```
<h:outputText value="This is an outputText component" />
```

The panelGrid Component

Tag name: **<h:panelGrid>**
UIComponent class: **javax.faces.component.html.HtmlPanelGrid**
Component type: **javax.faces.HtmlPanelGrid**

The **panelGrid** component is a tabular container for other child components and is rendered as an HTML **<table>** with a number of attributes which are directly passed onto the rendered HTML table, such as border, width, and so on. The component's children are rendered in the table cells, with new rows as the number of columns is reached.

For further information on the attributes that are passed onto the rendered HTML table, visit **www.w3.org/TR/REC-html40/struct/tables.html**.

Ungrouped Attributes

Attribute	Type	Description	Required
bgcolor	String	The background color of the rendered HTML table representing the **panelGrid**.	No
border	int	The border size in pixels of the rendered HTML table.	No
cellpadding	int	The **cellpadding** attribute of the rendered HTML table.	No
cellspacing	int	The **cellspacing** attribute of the rendered HTML table.	No
columns	int	The number of columns to be rendered in the HTML table.	No

Attribute	Type	Description	Required
frame	String	A **frame** that is passed onto the rendered HTML table. This attribute specifies which sides of the frame surrounding the table will be visible. Valid values are **none**, **above**, **below**, **hsides**, **vsides**, **lhs**, **rhs**, **box**, and **border**.	No
rendered	boolean	The boolean attribute that defines whether the component will be rendered.	No
rules	String	A **rules** attribute that is passed onto the rendered HTML table. Valid values are **none**, **groups**, **rows**, **cols**, and **all**.	No
summary	String	A **summary** attribute that is passed onto the rendered HTML table.	No
width	int or String	A **width** attribute that is passed onto the rendered HTML table. For pixel width, enter a non-zero integer. For percentage width, append "%" to the value (e.g., "80%").	No

Core Attributes

Attribute	Type	Description	Required
binding	Value Binding or ValueExpression (1.2)	A binding reference to a like **UIComponent** instance.	No
id	String	The identifier for the component.	No
title	String	The title of the component. This is passed through to the rendered HTML **title** element.	No

Style Attributes

Attribute	Type	Description	Required
columnclasses	String	A comma-separated list of CSS classes to be associated with the rendered columns. The classes will be applied in a repeating fashion to all columns in the **panelGrid** component.	No
footerclass	String	The CSS class to be associated with the rendered HTML table footer (bottom row).	No
headerclass	String	The CSS class to be associated with the rendered HTML table header (top row).	No
rowclasses	String	A comma-separated list of CSS classes to be associated with the rendered rows. The classes will be applied in a repeating fashion to all rows in the **panelGrid** component.	No

Attribute	Type	Description	Required
style	String	Inline style(s) that are applied to the **panelGrid** component.	No
styleClass	String	The CSS style class that is applied to the **panelGrid** component.	No

Internationalization Attributes

Attribute	Type	Description	Required
dir	String	The reading direction of the generated HTML component: RTL (right to left) or LTR (left to right).	No
lang	String	The applied **lang** attribute to generated HTML output. For more information on the HTML **lang** attribute, visit **www.w3.org/TR/REC-html40/struct/dirlang.html**.	No

JavaScript Attributes
Attributes for the common JavaScript events are shown next.

onclick	ondblclick	onkeydown	onkeypress	onkeyup
onmousedown	onmousemove	onmouseout	onmouseover	onmouseup

All JavaScript attributes accept arguments of type **String** and none are specifically required.

Example Usage
A **panelgrid** containing an **outputText** and an **inputText**. The code that follows will render a two-column HTML table with border 2 and a silver background. The contents of the table will contain the rendered UI components.

```
<h:panelGrid border="2" bgcolor="Silver" columns="2" >
  <h:outputText value="Name: "/>
  <h:inputText  value="enter name here" />
</h:panelGrid>
```

The panelGroup Component
Tag name: **<h:panelGroup>**
UIComponent class: **javax.faces.component.html.HtmlPanelGroup**
Component type: **javax.faces.HtmlPanelGroup**

The **panelGroup** component creates a container to group a set of components under one parent. It renders its children, within an HTML **<span>** element, and can be used to conditionally render groups of UI components by employing its **rendered** attribute.

Attributes

Attribute	Type	Description	Required
binding	Value Binding or ValueExpression (1.2)	A binding reference to a like **UIComponent** instance.	No
id	String	The identifier for the component.	No
layout (1.2 only)	String	The type of layout to use when rendering this group. If the value is "block", the renderer produces an HTML "div" element; otherwise, the HTML "span" element is produced.	No
rendered	boolean	The boolean attribute that defines whether the component is rendered.	No
style	String	The inline style for the component.	No
styleClass	String	The referenced style class to be applied to the component.	No

Example Usage

The following example displays some UI components inside a **panelGroup**. It will only render if **Bean.renderOption** is **true**.

```
<h:panelGroup  id="panelGroup1" rendered="#{Bean.renderOption}">
  <f:verbatim>This is <cTypeface:Italic>HTML</i> inside of a panelGroup</f:verbatim>
  <h:selectManyCheckbox id="pizzaToppings" value="#{PizzaBean.toppings}">
    <f:selectItems value="#{PizzaBean.toppingsList}"/>
  </h:selectManyCheckbox>
  ...
</h:panelGroup>
```

The selectBooleanCheckbox Component

Tag name: **<h:selectBooleanCheckbox>**
>   UIComponent class: **javax.faces.component.html.HtmlSelectBooleanCheckbox**
>   Component type: **javax.faces.HtmlSelectBooleanCheckbox**

The **selectBooleanCheckbox** component renders as a single HTML <input> element of **type** "checkbox". The **name** attribute is set to the client ID.

Ungrouped Attributes

Attribute	Type	Description	Required
accesskey	char	A mnemonic character used to establish focus to this button.	No
converter	String	A full classpath reference to **Converter** to associate with this component.	No

Attribute	Type	Description	Required
converterMessage (1.2 only)	String	When present, this overrides the default **Converter** validation message. The message can be a **ValueExpression**.	No
disabled	boolean	When **true**, the component is not usable and is rendered in a disabled state.	No
immediate	boolean	When **true**, the component's value must be converted and validated immediately during the Apply Request Values phase rather than waiting until the Process Validations phase.	No
readonly	boolean	Displays the component as read-only when **true**.	No
rendered	boolean	The boolean attribute that defines whether the component is rendered.	No
required	boolean	When **true**, this will cause a validation error when no value is supplied.	No
requiredMessage (1.2 only)	String	When present, this overrides the default **required** validation message. The message can be a **ValueExpression**.	No
tabindex	int	The tabbing order position of the component. The value must be an integer between 0 and 32767.	No
validator	String	The EL reference to the validator method.	No
validatorMessage (1.2 only)	String	When present, this overrides the default **Validator** validation message. The message can be a **ValueExpression**.	No
valueChangeListener	String	The EL reference to the method that accepts a **ValueChangeEvent** argument.	No

Core Attributes

Attribute	Type	Description	Required
binding	Value Binding or ValueExpression (1.2)	A binding reference to a like **UIComponent** instance.	No
id	String	The identifier for the component.	No
title	String	The title of the component. This is passed through to the rendered HTML **title** element.	No
value	String	The value of the component.	No

Internationalization Attributes

Attribute	Type	Description	Required
dir	String	The reading direction of the generated HTML component: RTL (right to left) or LTR (left to right).	No
lang	String	The applied **lang** attribute to the generated HTML output. For more information on the HTML **lang** attribute, visit **www.w3.org/TR/REC-html40/struct/dirlang.html**.	No

Style Attributes

Attributes for CSS styles that are applied to the generated HTML output of the component are shown next.

style	styleclass

These style attributes accept arguments of type **String** and are not specifically required.

JavaScript Attributes

Attributes for the common JavaScript events are shown in the following.

onblur	onchange	onclick	ondblclick	onfocus
onkeydown	onkeypress	onkeyup	onmousedown	onmousemove
onmouseout	onmouseover	onmouseup	onselect	

All JavaScript attributes accept arguments of type **String** and none are specifically required.

Example Usage

Consider a managed bean (**UserBean**) with a **boolean** property of **smoker**. This can then be value-bound to the **SelectBooleanCheckbox** component, as shown in the following.

```
<h:outputLabel value="Do you smoke?:" for="smokercheck"/>
<h:selectBooleanCheckbox id="smokercheck" value="#{UserBean.smoker}"/>
```

The selectManyCheckbox Component

Tag name: **<h:selectManyCheckbox>**
UIComponent class: **javax.faces.component.html.HtmlSelectManyCheckbox**
Component type: **javax.faces.HtmlSelectManyCheckbox**

The **selectManyCheckbox** component renders as an HTML table with a set of checkboxes. The **<input>** checkboxes are represented by the children components **UISelectItem** and/or **UISelectItems**, and are rendered with a **type** attribute set to "checkbox" and a **name** attribute set to the component's client ID. Each **<input>** checkbox is also nested within a **<label>** element with a **for** attribute set to the component's client ID.

Ungrouped Attributes

Attribute	Type	Description	Required
accesskey	char	The mnemonic character used to establish focus to this button.	No
border	int	The border width in pixels of the generated table around the options list.	No
converter	String	The full classpath reference to **Converter** to associate with this component.	No
converterMessage (1.2 only)	String	When present, this overrides the default **Converter** validation message. The message can be a **ValueExpression**.	No
disabled	boolean	When **true**, the component is not usable and rendered in a disabled state.	No
immediate	boolean	When **true**, the component's value must be converted and validated immediately during the Apply Request Values phase rather than waiting until the Process Validations phase.	No
layout	String	The option list orientation. This can be either **pageDirection** (vertical) or **lineDirection** (horizontal). When not specified, **lineDirection** is the default.	No
readonly	boolean	Displays the component as read-only when **true**.	No
rendered	boolean	The boolean attribute that defines whether the component is rendered.	No
required	boolean	When **true**, this will cause a validation error when no value is supplied.	No
requiredMessage (1.2 only)	String	When present, this overrides the default **required** validation message. The message can be a **ValueExpression**.	No
tabindex	int	The tabbing order position of the component. The value must be an integer between 0 and 32767.	No
validator	String	The EL reference to the validator method.	No
validatorMessage (1.2 only)	String	When present, this overrides the default **Validator** validation message. The message can be a **ValueExpression**.	No
valueChangeListener	String	The EL reference to the method that accepts a **ValueChangeEvent** argument.	No

Core Attributes

Attribute	Type	Description	Required
binding	Value Binding or ValueExpression (1.2)	A binding reference to a like **UIComponent** instance.	No
id	String	The identifier for the component.	No
title	String	The title of the component. This is passed through to the rendered HTML **title** element.	No
value	String	The value of the component.	No

Internationalization Attributes

Attribute	Type	Description	Required
dir	String	The reading direction of the generated HTML component: RTL (right to left) or LTR (left to right).	No
lang	String	The applied **lang** attribute to the generated HTML output. For more information on the HTML **lang** attribute, visit **www.w3.org/TR/REC-html40/struct/dirlang.html**.	No

Style Attributes

Attributes for CSS styles that are applied to the generated HTML output of the component are shown next.

disabledclass	enabledclass	style	styleclass

These style attributes accept arguments of type **String** and are not specifically required.

JavaScript Attributes

Attributes for the common JavaScript events are shown in the following.

onblur	onchange	onclick	ondblclick	onfocus
onkeydown	onkeypress	onkeyup	onmousedown	onmousemove
onmouseout	onmouseover	onmouseup	onselect	

All JavaScript attributes accept arguments of type **String** and none are specifically required.

Example Usage

Consider a managed bean (**PizzaBean**) with a **List** property of **toppingsList**. This can be value-bound to the **SelectManyCheckbox** component, as shown in the following:

```
<h:selectManyCheckbox id="pizzaToppings" value="#{PizzaBean.toppings}">
  <f:selectItems value="#{PizzaBean.toppingsList}"/>
</h:selectManyCheckbox>
```

Next is an example with hard-coded select items:

```
<h:selectManyCheckbox id ="pizzaToppings" value="#{PizzaBean.toppings}">
  <f:selectItem itemLabel="cheese" itemValue="ch"/>
  <f:selectItem itemLabel="pepperoni" itemValue="pep"/>
  <f:selectItem itemLabel="sausage" itemValue="saus"/>
  <f:selectItem itemLabel="mushrooms" itemValue="msh"/>
</h:selectManyCheckbox >
```

The selectManyListbox Component

Tag name: **<h:selectManyListbox>**
UIComponent class: **javax.faces.component.html.HtmlSelectManyListbox**
Component type: **javax.faces.HtmlSelectManyListbox**

The **selectManyListbox** component renders an HTML **<select>** with its **name** attribute set to the component's client ID, its **size** attribute set to the number of **selectItem** children, and its **multiple** attribute set to "multiple". Each menu choice is rendered by either **UISelectItem** and/or **UISelectItems** components, and is rendered as an **<option>** element. If a choice is marked as disabled, the **disabled** attribute is also added to the option element.

Ungrouped Attributes

Attribute	Type	Description	Required
accesskey	char	The mnemonic character used to establish focus to this button.	No
converter	String	The full classpath reference to **Converter** to associate with this component.	No
converterMessage (1.2 only)	String	When present, this overrides the default **Converter** validation message. The message can be a **ValueExpression**.	No
disabled	boolean	When **true**, the component is not usable and rendered in a disabled state.	No
immediate	boolean	When **true**, the component's value must be converted and validated immediately during the Apply Request Values phase rather than waiting until the Process Validations phase.	No
readonly	boolean	Displays the component as read-only when **true**.	No
rendered	boolean	The boolean attribute that defines whether the component is rendered.	No
required	boolean	When **true**, this will cause a validation error when no value is supplied.	No
requiredMessage (1.2 only)	String	When present, this overrides the default **required** validation message. The message can be a **ValueExpression**.	No

PART IV

Attribute	Type	Description	Required
tabindex	int	The tabbing order position of the component. The value must be an integer between 0 and 32767.	No
validator	String	The EL reference to the validator method.	No
validatorMessage (1.2 only)	String	When present, this overrides the default **Validator** validation message. The message can be a **ValueExpression**.	No
valueChangeListener	String	The EL reference to the method that accepts a **ValueChangeEvent** argument.	No

Core Attributes

Attribute	Type	Description	Required
binding	Value Binding or ValueExpression (1.2)	A binding reference to a like **UIComponent** instance.	No
id	String	The identifier for the component.	No
title	String	The title of the component. This is passed through to the rendered HTML **title** element.	No
value	String	The value of the component.	No

Internationalization Attributes

Attribute	Type	Description	Required
dir	String	The reading direction of the generated HTML component: RTL (right to left) or LTR (left to right).	No
lang	String	The applied **lang** attribute to the generated HTML output. For more information on the HTML **lang** attribute, visit **www.w3.org/TR/REC-html40/struct/dirlang.html**.	No

Style Attributes
Attributes for CSS styles that are applied to the generated HTML output of the component are shown next.

disabledclass	enabledclass	style	styleclass

These style attributes accept arguments of type **String** and are not specifically required.

JavaScript Attributes
Attributes for the common JavaScript events are shown next.

onblur	onchange	onclick	ondblclick	onfocus
onkeydown	onkeypress	onkeyup	onmousedown	onmousemove
onmouseout	onmouseover	onmouseup	onselect	

All JavaScript attributes accept arguments of type **String** and none are specifically required.

Example Usage

Consider a managed bean (**PizzaBean**) with a **List** property of **toppingsList**. This can then be value-bound to the **selectManyListbox** component, as in the following:

```
<h:selectManyListbox id="pizzaToppings" value="#{PizzaBean.toppings}">
  <f:selectItems value="#{PizzaBean.toppingsList}"/>
</h:selectManyListbox>
```

An example with hard-coded select items is shown next:

```
<h:selectManyListbox id ="pizzaToppings" value="#{PizzaBean.toppings}">
  <f:selectItem itemLabel="cheese" itemValue="ch"/>
  <f:selectItem itemLabel="pepperoni" itemValue="pep"/>
  <f:selectItem itemLabel="sausage" itemValue="saus"/>
  <f:selectItem itemLabel="mushrooms" itemValue="msh"/>
</h:selectManyListbox >
```

The selectManyMenu Component

Tag name: **<h:selectManyMenu>**
UIComponent class: **javax.faces.component.html.HtmlSelectManyMenu**
Component type: **javax.faces.HtmlSelectManyMenu**

The **selectManyMenu** component renders an HTML **<select>** with its **name** attribute set to the component's client ID, its **size** attribute set with a value of "1", and its **multiple** attribute set to "multiple". Each menu choice is rendered by either **UISelectItem** and/or **UISelectItems** components, and is rendered as an **<option>** element. If a choice is marked as disabled, the **disabled** attribute is also added to the option element.

Ungrouped Attributes

Attribute	Type	Description	Required
accesskey	char	The mnemonic character used to establish focus to this button.	No
converter	String	The full classpath reference to **Converter** to associate with this component.	No
converterMessage (1.2 only)	String	When present, this overrides the default **Converter** validation message. The message can be a **ValueExpression**.	No
disabled	boolean	When **true**, the component is not usable and is rendered in a disabled state.	No
immediate	boolean	When **true**, the component's value must be converted and validated immediately during the Apply Request Values phase rather than waiting until the Process Validations phase.	No

Attribute	Type	Description	Required
readonly	boolean	Displays the component as read-only when **true**.	No
rendered	boolean	A boolean attribute that defines whether the component is rendered.	No
required	boolean	When **true**, this will cause a validation error when no value is supplied.	No
requiredMessage (1.2 only)	String	When present, this overrides the default **required** validation message. The message can be a **ValueExpression**.	No
tabindex	int	The tabbing order position of the component. The value must be an integer between 0 and 32767.	No
validator	String	The EL reference to the validator method.	No
validatorMessage (1.2 only)	String	When present, this overrides the default **Validator** validation message. The message can be a **ValueExpression**.	No
valueChangeListener	String	The EL reference to the method that accepts a **ValueChangeEvent** argument.	No

Core Attributes

Attribute	Type	Description	Required
binding	Value Binding or ValueExpression (1.2)	A binding reference to a like **UIComponent** instance.	No
id	String	The identifier for the component.	No
title	String	The title of the component. This is passed through to the rendered HTML **title** element.	No
value	String	The value of the component.	No

Internationalization Attributes

Attribute	Type	Description	Required
dir	String	The reading direction of the generated HTML component: RTL (right to left) or LTR (left to right).	No
lang	String	The applied **lang** attribute to the generated HTML output. For more information on the HTML **lang** attribute, visit **www.w3.org/TR/REC-html40/struct/dirlang.html**.	No

Style Attributes

Attributes for CSS styles that are applied to the generated HTML output of the component are shown next.

disabledclass	enabledclass	style	styleclass

These style attributes accept arguments of type **String** and are not specifically required.

JavaScript Attributes

Attributes for the common JavaScript events are shown in the following.

onblur	onchange	onclick	ondblclick	onfocus
onkeydown	onkeypress	onkeyup	onmousedown	onmousemove
onmouseout	onmouseover	onmouseup	onselect	

All JavaScript attributes accept arguments of type **String** and none are specifically required.

Example Usage

Consider a managed bean (**PizzaBean**) with a **List** property of **toppingsList**. This can then be value-bound to the **selectManyMenu** component, as in the following:

```
<h:selectManyMenu id="pizzaToppings" value="#{PizzaBean.toppings}">
  <f:selectItems value="#{PizzaBean.toppingsList}"/>
</h:selectManyMenu>
```

An example with hard-coded select items is shown next:

```
<h:selectManyMenu id ="pizzaToppings" value="#{PizzaBean.toppings}">
  <f:selectItem itemLabel="cheese" itemValue="ch"/>
  <f:selectItem itemLabel="pepperoni" itemValue="pep"/>
  <f:selectItem itemLabel="sausage" itemValue="saus"/>
  <f:selectItem itemLabel="mushrooms" itemValue="msh"/>
</h:selectManyMenu >
```

The selectOneListbox Component

Tag name: **<h:selectOneListbox>**
UIComponent class: **javax.faces.component.html.HtmlSelectOneListbox**
Component type: **javax.faces.HtmlSelectOneListbox**

The **selectOneListbox** component renders an HTML **<select>** with its **name** attribute set to the component's client ID, and its **size** attribute set to the number of **<option>** element choices rendered by either **UISelectItem** and/or **UISelectItems** components. If the **size** attribute is specified, it will override the number of **SelectItems** and pass through the size value to the rendered **<select>**. If a choice is marked as disabled, the **disabled** attribute is also added to the option element.

Ungrouped Attributes

Attribute	Type	Description	Required
accesskey	char	The mnemonic character used to establish focus to this button.	No
converter	String	The full classpath reference to **Converter** to associate with this component.	No
converterMessage (1.2 only)	String	When present, this overrides the default **Converter** validation message. The message can be a **ValueExpression**.	No
disabled	boolean	When **true**, the component is not usable and is rendered in a disabled state.	No
immediate	boolean	When **true,** the component's value must be converted and validated immediately during the Apply Request Values phase rather than waiting until the Process Validations phase.	No
readonly	boolean	Displays the component as read-only when **true**.	No
rendered	boolean	The boolean attribute that defines whether the component is rendered.	No
required	boolean	When **true**, this will cause a validation error when no value is supplied.	No
requiredMessage (1.2 only)	String	When present, this overrides the default **required** validation message. The message can be a **ValueExpression**.	No
size	int	Overrides the **size** attribute of the generated HTML **select** that is otherwise set to the number of **SelectItems**.	No
tabindex	int	The tabbing order position of the component. The value must be an integer between 0 and 32767.	No
validator	String	The EL reference to the validator method.	No
validatorMessage (1.2 only)	String	When present, this overrides the default **Validator** validation message. The message can be a **ValueExpression**.	No
valueChangeListener	String	The EL reference to the method that accepts a **ValueChangeEvent** argument.	No

Core Attributes

Attribute	Type	Description	Required
binding	Value Binding or ValueExpression (1.2)	A binding reference to a like **UIComponent** instance.	No
id	String	The identifier for the component.	No

Attribute	Type	Description	Required
title	String	The title of the component. This is passed through to the rendered HTML **title** element.	No
value	String	The value of the component.	No

Internationalization Attributes

Attribute	Type	Description	Required
dir	String	The reading direction of the generated HTML component: RTL (right to left) or LTR (left to right).	No
lang	String	The applied **lang** attribute to the generated HTML output. For more information on the HTML **lang** attribute, visit **www.w3.org/TR/REC-html40/struct/dirlang.html**.	No

Style Attributes

Attributes for CSS styles that are applied to the generated HTML output of the component are shown next.

disabledclass	enabledclass	style	styleclass

These style attributes accept arguments of type **String** and are not specifically required.

JavaScript Attributes

Attributes for the common JavaScript events are shown next.

onblur	onchange	onclick	ondblclick	onfocus
onkeydown	onkeypress	onkeyup	onmousedown	onmousemove
onmouseout	onmouseover	onmouseup	onselect	

All JavaScript attributes accept arguments of type **String** and none are specifically required.

Example Usage

Consider a managed bean **shirt** with a **List** property of **sizeList**. This can then be value-bound to the **SelectOneListBox** component, as shown in the following:

```
<h:selectOneListBox id="size" value="#{shirt.size }">
  <f:selectItems value="#{shirt.sizeList}"/>
</h:selectOneListBox>
```

An example with hard-coded select items is shown next:

```
<h:selectOneListBox id ="size" value="#{shirt.size}">
  <f:selectItem itemLabel="Small" itemValue="s"/>
  <f:selectItem itemLabel="Medium" itemValue="m"/>
  <f:selectItem itemLabel="Large" itemValue="l"/>
  <f:selectItem itemLabel="Extra-Large" itemValue="xl"/>
</h:selectOneListBox >
```

The selectOneMenu Component

Tag name: **<h:selectOneMenu>**
UIComponent class: **javax.faces.component.html.HtmlSelectOneMenu**
Component type: **javax.faces.HtmlSelectOneMenu**

The **selectOneMenu** component renders an HTML **<select>** with its **name** attribute set to the component's client ID and its **size** attribute set with a value of "1". Each menu choice is rendered by either **UISelectItem** and/or **UISelectItems** components and is rendered as an **<option>** element. If a choice is marked as disabled, the **disabled** attribute is also added to the option element.

Ungrouped Attributes

Attribute	Type	Description	Required
accesskey	char	The mnemonic character used to establish focus to this button.	No
converter	String	The full classpath reference to **Converter** to associate with this component.	No
converterMessage (1.2 only)	String	When present, this overrides the default **Converter** validation message. The message can be a **ValueExpression**.	No
disabled	boolean	When **true**, the component is not usable and is rendered in a disabled state.	No
immediate	boolean	When **true**, the component's value must be converted and validated immediately during the Apply Request Values phase rather than waiting until the Process Validations phase.	No
readonly	boolean	Displays the component as read-only when **true**.	No
rendered	boolean	The boolean attribute that defines whether the component is rendered.	No
required	boolean	When **true**, this will cause a validation error when no value is supplied.	No
requiredMessage (1.2 only)	String	When present, this overrides the default **required** validation message. The message can be a **ValueExpression**.	No
tabindex	int	The tabbing order position of the component. The value must be an integer between 0 and 32767.	No
validator	String	The EL reference to the validator method.	No
validatorMessage (1.2 only)	String	When present, this overrides the default **Validator** validation message. The message can be a **ValueExpression**.	No
valueChangeListener	String	The EL reference to the method that accepts a **ValueChangeEvent** argument.	No

Core Attributes

Attribute	Type	Description	Required
binding	Value Binding or ValueExpression (1.2)	A binding reference to a like **UIComponent** instance.	No
id	String	The identifier for the component.	No
title	String	The title of the component. This is passed through to the rendered HTML **title** element.	No
value	String	The value of the component.	No

Internationalization Attributes

Attribute	Type	Description	Required
dir	String	The reading direction of the generated HTML component: RTL (right to left) or LTR (left to right).	No
lang	String	The applied **lang** attribute to the generated HTML output. For more information on the HTML **lang** attribute, visit **www.w3.org/TR/REC-html40/struct/dirlang.html**.	No

Style Attributes

Attributes for CSS styles that are applied to the generated HTML output of the component are shown next.

disabledclass	enabledclass	style	styleclass

These style attributes accept arguments of type **String** and are not specifically required.

JavaScript Attributes

Attributes for the common JavaScript events are shown next.

onblur	onchange	onclick	ondblclick	onfocus
onkeydown	onkeypress	onkeyup	onmousedown	onmousemove
onmouseout	onmouseover	onmouseup	onselect	

All JavaScript attributes accept arguments of type **String** and none are specifically required.

Example Usage

Consider a managed bean **shirt** with a **List** property of **sizeList**. This can then be value-bound to the **SelectOneMenu** component, as shown in the following:

```
<h:selectOneMenu id="size" value="#{shirt.size }">
  <f:selectItems value="#{shirt.sizeList}"/>
</h:selectOneMenu>
```

An example with hard-coded select items is shown next:

```
<h:selectOneMenu id ="size" value="#{shirt.size}">
  <f:selectItem itemLabel="Small" itemValue="s"/>
  <f:selectItem itemLabel="Medium" itemValue="m"/>
```

```
    <f:selectItem itemLabel="Large" itemValue="l"/>
    <f:selectItem itemLabel="Extra-Large" itemValue="xl"/>
</h:selectOneMenu>
```

The selectOneRadio Component

Tag name: **<h:selectOneRadio>**
UIComponent class: **javax.faces.component.html.HtmlSelectOneRadio**
Component type: **javax.faces.HtmlSelectOneRadio**

The **selectOneRadio** component renders as an HTML table with a set of radio buttons from which the user can select. The **<input>** elements are represented by the children components **UISelectItem** and/or **UISelectItems** components, and are rendered with a **type** attribute set to "radio" and a **name** attribute set to the component's client ID. Each **<input>** element is nested also within a **<label>** element with a **for** attribute set to the component's client ID.

Ungrouped Attributes

Attribute	Type	Description	Required
accesskey	char	The mnemonic character used to establish focus to this button.	No
border	int	The border width in pixels of the generated table around the options list.	No
converterMessage (1.2 only)	String	When present, this overrides the default **Converter** validation message. The message can be a **ValueExpression**.	No
converter	String	The full classpath reference to **Converter** to associate with this component.	No
disabled	boolean	When **true**, this component is not usable and is rendered in a disabled state.	No
immediate	boolean	When **true**, this component's value must be converted and validated immediately during the Apply Request Values phase rather than waiting until the Process Validations phase.	No
layout	String	Option list orientation. Can be either **pageDirection** (vertical) or **lineDirection** (horizontal). When not specified, **lineDirection** is the default.	No
readonly	boolean	Displays the component as read-only when **true**.	No
rendered	boolean	The boolean attribute that defines whether the component is rendered.	No
required	boolean	When **true**, this will cause a validation error when no value is supplied.	No

Attribute	Type	Description	Required
requiredMessage (1.2 only)	String	When present, this overrides the default **required** validation message. The message can be a **ValueExpression**.	No
tabindex	int	The tabbing order position of the component. The value must be an integer between 0 and 32767.	No
validator	String	The EL reference to the validator method.	No
validatorMessage (1.2 only)	String	When present, this overrides the default **Validator** validation message. The message can be a **ValueExpression**.	No
valueChangeListener	String	The EL reference to the method that accepts a **ValueChangeEvent** argument.	No

Core Attributes

Attribute	Type	Description	Required
binding	Value Binding or ValueExpression (1.2)	A binding reference to a like **UIComponent** instance.	No
id	String	The identifier for the component.	No
title	String	The title of the component. This is passed through to the rendered HTML **title** element.	No
value	String	The value of the component.	No

Internationalization Attributes

Attribute	Type	Description	Required
dir	String	The reading direction of the generated HTML component: RTL (right to left) or LTR (left to right).	No
lang	String	The applied **lang** attribute to the generated HTML output. For more information on the HTML **lang** attribute, visit **www.w3.org/TR/REC-html40/struct/dirlang.html**.	No

Style Attributes

Attributes for CSS styles that are applied to the generated HTML output of the component are shown next.

disabledclass	enabledclass	style	styleclass

These style attributes accept arguments of type **String** and are not specifically required.

JavaScript Attributes
Attributes for the common JavaScript events are shown next.

onblur	onchange	onclick	ondblclick	onfocus
onkeydown	onkeypress	onkeyup	onmousedown	onmousemove
onmouseout	onmouseover	onmouseup	onselect	

All JavaScript attributes accept arguments of type **String** and none are specifically required.

Example Usage
Consider a managed bean **shirt** with a **List** property of *sizeList*. This can then be value-bound to the **selectOneRadio** component, as shown in the following:

```
<h:selectOneRadio id="size" value="#{shirt.size }">
  <f:selectItems value="#{shirt.sizeList}"/>
</h:selectOneRadio>
```

An example with hard-coded select items is shown next:

```
<h:selectOneRadio id ="size" value="#{shirt.size}">
  <f:selectItem itemLabel="Small" itemValue="s"/>
  <f:selectItem itemLabel="Medium" itemValue="m"/>
  <f:selectItem itemLabel="Large" itemValue="l"/>
  <f:selectItem itemLabel="Extra-Large" itemValue="xl"/>
</h:selectOneRadio>
```

The MyFaces Implementation and Component Library

The beauty of JavaServer Faces lies in the fact that it is a *framework specification*. Being a specification means that there can be many implementations of the specification—each implementation unique in its own right (for example, added features that go beyond the specification, performance enhancements, and so on). Conformance to the JSF specification ensures that each implementation is fully compatible at an API level so that applications can easily be migrated from one implementation to another.

MyFaces is a popular open source implementation of the JavaServer Faces specification that provides a fully API-compliant and Sun Technology Compatible Kit (TCK) certified implementation of the framework along with substantial added functionality. MyFaces' added functionality is principally comprised of a separately packaged library called Tomahawk that includes extensions to the base JSF UI components, a set of custom UI components, a set of custom validators, and support for using the Tiles framework with JSF. Additionally, MyFaces includes a new subproject called Tobago that includes a set of layout-oriented components. MyFaces also includes a repository for experimental development called the Sandbox. Finally, at the time of this book's writing, Oracle donated its ADF Faces component library to the MyFaces project and it is currently going through the Apache incubation process so that it can become a formally Apache-licensed code set.

This chapter covers acquiring, installing, and using MyFaces along with broad coverage of the MyFaces-specific Tomahawk functionality that extends beyond the JavaServer Faces specification.

As a point of interest, while each JavaServer Faces implementation must conform to the specification, each can have many proprietary elements that may prevent applications from being migrated from one implementation to another. MyFaces, however, has been designed so that its proprietary Tomahawk components and extensions can be used on any JSF implementation. For example, you can use the Tomahawk component library with the Sun JavaServer Faces reference implementation.

In summary, MyFaces is comprised of two distinct sets of functionality: the core implementation of the JSF specification and a set of enhanced and custom components known as Tomahawk. These functionalities can be used in tandem or independent of each other—the choice is yours. For example, you may want to use the MyFaces JSF implementation, but may not be interested in the Tomahawk library. Conversely, you may simply want to use the Tomahawk components with another JSF implementation. Of course, you can use them together as well.

Acquiring MyFaces

MyFaces is available free of charge and can be downloaded from the Apache MyFaces site at **http://myfaces.apache.org/**. Because MyFaces is open source, you have a couple of options when downloading the MyFaces software. You can download the software in its binary, precompiled form, or you can download the source code for compiling on your own. For most cases, the binary distribution will suffice. However, if you want to make changes to the MyFaces source code, the source distribution is available.

If you choose to download a binary distribution of MyFaces, you again have a couple of options. You can download a released version of the code, which has been rigorously tested and certified as being of good quality, or you can download a nightly build of the code, which is less stable and not intended for production use. The released versions of MyFaces are broken down into yet another level of options:

- **Main Distribution**   Includes the JSF specification implementation libraries and the MyFaces common code library.

- **Tomahawk Distribution**   Includes the Tomahawk library and the MyFaces common code library.

- **Example Applications Distribution**   Includes a set of example MyFaces applications.

Opting to use a nightly build allows you to have access to the latest enhancements and bug fixes that have been made to the MyFaces codebase ahead of an official release. However, it's important to point out that nightly builds have no guarantee on quality because adding a new feature to MyFaces could potentially break another feature that has been stable for some time.

Similar to downloading a binary distribution of MyFaces, if you choose to download a source distribution, you have a couple of options. You can download the source for an officially released version of MyFaces or you can choose to get the "latest and greatest" version of the MyFaces source code directly from the MyFaces Subversion source control repository. Just as with the binary distribution, choosing to download the latest MyFaces source code can get you the newest enhancements and bug fixes to the software, but it may also be laden with new bugs.

What You Get (Binary)

Since MyFaces is an implementation of the JavaServer Faces Web application framework specification and not a stand-alone application, MyFaces distributions are principally comprised of the MyFaces implementation of the JavaServer Faces API libraries and their associated files, such as Document Type Definitions (DTDs) for XML configuration files and JSP Tag Library Descriptor (TLD) files. Additionally, MyFaces distributions include the Tomahawk API libraries for the MyFaces-specific features. JavaDoc format API documentation is provided as well.

What You Get (Source)

Similar to the binary distribution, the source distribution is comprised of the MyFaces implementation of the JavaServer Faces API libraries and their associated files along with the Tomahawk libraries for the MyFaces-specific features. The major difference, however, is that all of the code for the libraries is in source form. This is particularly useful for projects for which the source code may need to be changed or where you may want access to the source code for debugging an application and so on. As a point of interest, you can browse the MyFaces source code online at **http://svn.apache.org/viewcvs.cgi/myfaces/**.

Using MyFaces

Once you have downloaded your desired MyFaces distribution, this section will assist you in installing and using the MyFaces libraries. As discussed earlier, MyFaces is composed of two sets of functionality—an implementation of the JSF specification and a set of enhanced and custom components known as Tomahawk. The functionality you choose to use will drive the steps you must follow to install and use MyFaces. The remainder of this section is broken down into two areas specific to each piece of functionality.

NOTE *It's very important to point out that MyFaces is undergoing many changes to its distribution packaging. The details in this chapter about acquiring and using the MyFaces implementation are up to date at this book's publishing; however, they may become incorrect once changes are made to the MyFaces distributions. Please check the MyFaces Web site for the latest information on acquiring and using MyFaces.*

Using the MyFaces JSF Implementation

Using the MyFaces JSF implementation is the same as using any other JSF implementation. You simply have to place the appropriate jar files in your Web application's **/WEB-INF/lib** directory (or in a directory that your application server has access to via its classpath). MyFaces has two main jar files that contain the JSF implementation: **myfaces-api.jar** and **myfaces-impl.jar**. Additionally, MyFaces has a **myfaces-common.jar** file that contains common code shared between the JSF implementation and the Tomahawk library. Copy those three jar files to your Web application's **WEB-INF/lib** directory and you're ready to go.

The rest of the process for using the MyFaces JSF implementation—such as configuring your Web application's **web.xml** file, configuring a **faces-config.xml** file, and referencing JSF TLD files from JSPs—is the same as any other JSF implementation and is covered in Chapter 2.

Using the MyFaces Tomahawk Library

Using the MyFaces Tomahawk library is as simple as placing the **tomahawk.jar** and **myfaces-commons.jar** files in your Web application's **/WEB-INF/lib** directory (or in a directory that your application server has access to via its classpath) and configuring the MyFaces Extensions Filter. Note that you can alternatively use the **myfaces-all.jar** file instead of the **tomahawak.jar** file.

Setting Up the MyFaces Extensions Filter

After installing the Tomahawk jar file, the next step in making use of the Tomahawk library is to configure the MyFaces Extensions Filter in your Web application's **web.xml** file. The MyFaces Extensions Filter manages inserting the required support resources (for example, scripts, style sheets, and images) into JSPs for the Tomahawk custom components. Many of the Tomahawk custom components require support resources, and instead of burdening you, the developer, with having to add the support resources to your application (and maintain them), they are stored in the Tomahawk library. The Extensions Filter manages retrieving the resources from the library and automatically inserting them into the necessary JSPs at runtime.

NOTE *Installation of the MyFaces Extensions Filter is only required if you are making use of the Tomahawk custom components. The extended components and Tiles support do not require the filter.*

Following is the Extensions Filter definition that must be inserted into the **web.xml** file:

```
<filter>
  <filter-name>MyFacesExtensionsFilter</filter-name>
  <filter-class>
    org.apache.myfaces.component.html.util.ExtensionsFilter
  </filter-class>
  <init-param>
    <param-name>uploadMaxFileSize</param-name>
    <param-value>10m</param-value>
  </init-param>
  <init-param>
    <param-name>uploadThresholdSize</param-name>
    <param-value>50k</param-value>
  </init-param>
  <init-param>
    <param-name>uploadRepositoryPath</param-name>
    <param-value>/tmp</param-value>
  </init-param>
</filter>
```

The Extensions Filter has three optional initialization parameters that can be set to modify the behavior of the Input File Upload custom component. The following table explains the usage of each of the initialization parameters. Note that the parameters are not required and, if not specified, default values will be applied.

Parameter	Description
uploadMaxFileSize	Specifies the maximum size of a file that can be uploaded. This parameter accepts values with the following formats: 10 – 10 bytes 10k – 10 kilobytes 10m – 10 megabytes 1g – 1 gigabyte
uploadThresholdSize	Specifies the threshold at which files are no longer stored in memory and are instead stored on disk in the directory specified by the **uploadRepositoryPath** parameter. This parameter accepts values with the following formats: 10 – 10 bytes 10k – 10 kilobytes 10m – 10 megabytes 1g – 1 gigabyte
uploadRepositoryPath	Specifies the file path in which uploaded files will be temporarily stored if they exceed the file size threshold specified by the **uploadThresholdSize** parameter.

In addition to adding the MyFaces Extensions Filter to your application's **web.xml** file, you must insert filter mapping definitions that specify which URLs the filter should be applied to. There are two filter mappings that must be defined. The first mapping, shown here, maps the filter to the main JSF servlet.

```
<filter-mapping>
  <filter-name>MyFacesExtensionsFilter</filter-name>
  <servlet-name>Faces Servlet</servlet-name>
</filter-mapping>
```

The names specified by the **<filter-name>** and **<servlet-name>** tags must match exactly with the names defined for the MyFaces Extensions Filter and the JSF servlet, respectively. Note that you can alternatively map the filter to the main JSF servlet using a URL pattern as shown here:

```
<filter-mapping>
  <filter-name>MyFacesExtensionsFilter</filter-name>
  <url-pattern>*.jsf</url-pattern>
</filter-mapping>
```

The second mapping maps the Extensions Filter back to URLs generated by the filter. It is shown here:

```
<filter-mapping>
  <filter-name>MyFacesExtensionsFilter</filter-name>
  <url-pattern>/faces/myFacesExtensionResource/*</url-pattern>
</filter-mapping>
```

When the Extensions Filter inserts resources into JSPs it is actually inserting references to resources (for example, links to style sheets or scripts) that will be served by the Extensions Filter. Those references all begin with **/faces/myFacesExtensionResource/**, thus the need to set up a filter mapping to that path.

Referencing the Tomahawk Components TLD

To make use of the Tomahawk extended and custom components in your JSPs, you must include the following tag library directive:

```
<%@ taglib prefix="t" uri="http://myfaces.apache.org/tomahawk"%>
```

The MyFaces Extended Components

The MyFaces Tomahawk library provides extended functionality to many of the components in the JavaServer Faces Standard HTML Library. The extended functionality includes things such as role-based display/non-display of components, the ability to display only the value of components (instead of rendering the components with a value), and the ability to definitively specify the ID of components. The extended components are just that—an extension of the base components defined by the JSF specification. All of the functionality of the base components is intact and the components are used exactly the same way you would use the base components—you simply have some added functionality to use as well.

The following table lists the components that MyFaces provides extended functionality for.

commandButton	inputSecret	messages	panelGroup	selectManyMenu
commandLink	inputText	outputLabel	selectBooleanCheckbox	selectOneListbox
dataTable	inputTextArea	outputText	selectManyCheckbox	selectOneMenu
graphicImage	message	panelGrid	selectManyListbox	selectOneRadio
inputHidden				

Each of the extended components has a section dedicated to it in this chapter that shows its extended attributes and use. For information on how to use the base functionality of the components, see Chapter 18.

Common Extended Attributes

The majority of the extended components have the same set of extended attributes. Instead of repeating the descriptions of the common attributes in each component's section, they are listed in Table 20-1.

The commandButton Component

Tag name: **<t:commandButton>**
Component class: **org.apache.myfaces.component.html.ext.HtmlCommandButton**
Component type: **org.apache.myfaces.HtmlCommandButton**

Extended Attributes

Attribute	Type	Description	Required
enabledOnUserRole	String	See "Common Extended Attributes" section.	No
forceId	String	See "Common Extended Attributes" section.	No
forceIdIndex	String	See "Common Extended Attributes" section.	No
visibleOnUserRole	String	See "Common Extended Attributes" section.	No

The commandLink Component

Tag name: **<t:commandLink>**
Component class: **org.apache.myfaces.component.html.ext.HtmlCommandLink**
Component type: **org.apache.myfaces.HtmlCommandLink**

Extended Attributes

Attribute	Type	Description	Required
enabledOnUserRole	String	See "Common Extended Attributes" section.	No
forceId	String	See "Common Extended Attributes" section.	No
forceIdIndex	String	See "Common Extended Attributes" section.	No
visibleOnUserRole	String	See "Common Extended Attributes" section.	No

Attribute	Type	Description	Required
displayValueOnly	boolean	Accepts true or false to specify whether only the component's value should be rendered instead of the component and its value. Defaults to false.	No
displayValueOnlyStyle	String	Specifies the CSS style to use when rendering the component's value if the **displayValueOnly** attribute is set to true.	No
displayValueOnlyStyleClass	String	Specifies the CSS style class to use when rendering the component's value if the **displayValueOnly** attribute is set to true.	No
enabledOnUserRole	String	Specifies a comma-delimited list of security roles. The current user must be assigned to at least one in order for this component to be enabled. If the current user is not assigned to one of the roles, the component will be rendered in a disabled state (i.e., grayed out).	No
forceId	boolean	Accepts true or false to specify whether the component ID specified with the **id** attribute should be definitive. A definitive ID will override any ID auto-generated by the JSF implementation and is useful for situations where an explicit non-dynamic ID is required (e.g., in conjunction with CSS or JavaScript code). Defaults to false.	No
forceIdIndex	boolean	Accepts true or false to specify whether an index suffix (e.g., [0]) should be added to the ID specified by the **id** attribute when the component is contained within a list. Defaults to true.	No
visibleOnUserRole	String	Specifies a comma-delimited list of security roles. The current user must be assigned to at least one role in order for this component to be displayed. If the current user is not assigned to one of the roles, the component will not be rendered.	No

TABLE 20-1   The Common Extended Attributes for the Extended Components

The dataTable Component

Tag name: <t:dataTable>
Component class: **org.apache.myfaces.component.html.ext.HtmlDataTable**
Component type: **org.apache.myfaces.HtmlDataTable**

Extended Attributes

Attribute	Type	Description	Required
enabledOnUserRole	String	See "Common Extended Attributes" section.	No
forceId	String	See "Common Extended Attributes" section.	No
forceIdIndex	String	See "Common Extended Attributes" section.	No
forceIdIndexFormula	String	Specifies a value binding expression whose generated values will be used as the IDs for the row components (e.g., "#{currentRow.key}").	No
preserveDataModel	boolean	Accepts true or false to specify whether the data model for the table should be saved and restored between requests. Defaults to false.	No
preserveSort	boolean	Accepts true or false to specify whether the **sortColumn** and **sortAscending** attribute values should be saved and restored between requests. Defaults to true.	No
previousRowDataVar	String	Specifies the name of the JSP variable that will hold a reference to the previous row's data object. Note: The JSP variable will be stored in request scope.	No
renderedIfEmpty	boolean	Accepts true or false to specify whether the table should be rendered if its data model is empty. Defaults to true.	No
rowCountVar	String	Specifies the name of the JSP variable that will hold the row count. Note: The JSP variable will be stored in request scope.	No
rowed	String	Specifies the ID to use for **<tr>** HTML elements that are generated for the table.	No

Attribute	Type	Description	Required
rowIndexVar	String	Specifies the name of the JSP variable that will hold the current row index. Note: The JSP variable will be stored in request scope.	No
rowOnClick	String	Specifies the value for the JavaScript **onclick** event handler for each row of the table.	No
rowOnDblClick	String	Specifies the value for the JavaScript **ondblclick** event handler for each row of the table.	No
rowOnKeyDown	String	Specifies the value for the JavaScript **onkeydown** event handler for each row of the table.	No
rowOnKeyPress	String	Specifies the value for the JavaScript **onkeypress** event handler for each row of the table.	No
rowOnKeyUp	String	Specifies the value for the JavaScript **onkeyup** event handler for each row of the table.	No
rowOnMouseDown	String	Specifies the value for the JavaScript **onmousedown** event handler for each row of the table.	No
rowOnMouseMove	String	Specifies the value for the JavaScript **onmousemove** event handler for each row of the table.	No
rowOnMouseOut	String	Specifies the value for the JavaScript **onmouseout** event handler for each row of the table.	No
rowOnMouseOver	String	Specifies the value for the JavaScript **onmouseover** event handler for each row of the table.	No
rowOnMouseUp	String	Specifies the value for the JavaScript **onmouseup** event handler for each row of the table.	No
rowStyle	String	Specifies the CSS style to use when rendering each row of the table.	No
rowStyleClass	String	Specifies the CSS style class to use when rendering each row of the table.	No
sortAscending	String	Specifies a value binding expression whose generated value specifies the direction in which the table should be sorted.	No
sortColumn	String	Specifies a value binding expression whose generated value specifies the column name the table should be sorted by.	No
visibleOnUserRole	String	See "Common Extended Attributes" section.	No

The graphicImage Component

Tag name: **<t:graphicImage>**
Component class: **org.apache.myfaces.component.html.ext.HtmlGraphicImage**
Component type: **org.apache.myfaces.HtmlGraphicImage**

Extended Attributes

Attribute	Type	Description	Required
align	String	Corresponds one-to-one with the attribute of the same name as the rendered HTML tag.	No
border	String	Corresponds one-to-one with the attribute of the same name as the rendered HTML tag.	No
enabledOnUserRole	String	See "Common Extended Attributes" section.	No
forceId	String	See "Common Extended Attributes" section.	No
forceIdIndex	String	See "Common Extended Attributes" section.	No
hspace	String	Corresponds one-to-one with the attribute of the same name as the rendered HTML tag.	No
visibleOnUserRole	String	See "Common Extended Attributes" section.	No
vspace	String	Corresponds one-to-one with the attribute of the same name as the rendered HTML tag.	No

The inputHidden Component

Tag name: **<t:inputHidden>**
Component class: **org.apache.myfaces.component.html.ext.HtmlInputHidden**
Component type: **org.apache.myfaces.HtmlInputHidden**

Extended Attributes

Attribute	Type	Description	Required
forceId	String	See "Common Extended Attributes" section.	No
forceIdIndex	String	See "Common Extended Attributes" section.	No

The inputSecret Component

Tag name: **<t:inputSecret>**
Component class: **org.apache.myfaces.component.html.ext.HtmlInputSecret**
Component type: **org.apache.myfaces.HtmlInputSecret**

Extended Attributes

Attribute	Type	Description	Required
displayValueOnly	boolean	See "Common Extended Attributes" section.	No
displayValueOnlyStyle	String	See "Common Extended Attributes" section.	No

Attribute	Type	Description	Required
displayValueOnlyStyleClass	String	See "Common Extended Attributes" section.	No
enabledOnUserRole	String	See "Common Extended Attributes" section.	No
forceId	String	See "Common Extended Attributes" section.	No
forceIdIndex	String	See "Common Extended Attributes" section.	No
visibleOnUserRole	String	See "Common Extended Attributes" section.	No

The inputText Component

Tag name: **<t:inputText>**
Component class: **org.apache.myfaces.component.html.ext.HtmlInputText**
Component type: **org.apache.myfaces.HtmlInputText**

Extended Attributes

Attribute	Type	Description	Required
displayValueOnly	boolean	See "Common Extended Attributes" section.	No
displayValueOnlyStyle	String	See "Common Extended Attributes" section.	No
displayValueOnlyStyleClass	String	See "Common Extended Attributes" section.	No
enabledOnUserRole	String	See "Common Extended Attributes" section.	No
forceId	String	See "Common Extended Attributes" section.	No
forceIdIndex	String	See "Common Extended Attributes" section.	No
visibleOnUserRole	String	See "Common Extended Attributes" section.	No

The inputTextarea Component

Tag name: **<t:inputTextarea>**
Component class: **org.apache.myfaces.component.html.ext.HtmlInputTextarea**
Component type: **org.apache.myfaces.HtmlInputTextarea**

Extended Attributes

Attribute	Type	Description	Required
displayValueOnly	boolean	See "Common Extended Attributes" section.	No
displayValueOnlyStyle	String	See "Common Extended Attributes" section.	No
displayValueOnlyStyleClass	String	See "Common Extended Attributes" section.	No
enabledOnUserRole	String	See "Common Extended Attributes" section.	No
forceId	String	See "Common Extended Attributes" section.	No
forceIdIndex	String	See "Common Extended Attributes" section.	No
visibleOnUserRole	String	See "Common Extended Attributes" section.	No

The message Component

Tag name: **<t:message>**
Component class: **org.apache.myfaces.component.html.ext.HtmlMessage**
Component type: **org.apache.myfaces.HtmlInputMessage**

Extended Attributes

Attribute	Type	Description	Required
detailFormat	String	Specifies the **java.text.MessageFormat** format that will be used to render the message detail. The message's detail value will be passed as the first argument ({0}) to the format. If the component associated with this message has a label, the label's value will be passed as the second argument ({1}) to the format. Example format value: "The {1} field has an incorrect value: {0}"	No
enabledOnUserRole	String	See "Common Extended Attributes" section.	No
forceId	String	See "Common Extended Attributes" section.	No
forceIdIndex	String	See "Common Extended Attributes" section.	No

Attribute	Type	Description	Required
replaceIdWithLabel	boolean	Accepts true or false to specify whether the ID of the component associated with the message should be replaced by the component's label. That is, any instance of the component's ID in the message will be replaced with the component's label. Defaults to true.	No
summaryFormat	String	Specifies the **java.text.MessageFormat** format that will be used to render the message summary. The message's summary value will be passed as the first argument ({0}) to the format. If the component associated with this message has a label, the label's value will be passed as the second argument ({1}) to the format. Example format value: "The {1} field has an incorrect value: {0}"	No
visibleOnUserRole	String	See "Common Extended Attributes" section.	No

The messages Component

Tag name: **<t:messages>**
Component class: **org.apache.myfaces.component.html.ext.HtmlMessages**
Component type: **org.apache.myfaces.HtmlMessages**

Extended Attributes

Attribute	Type	Description	Required
detailFormat	String	Specifies the **java.text.MessageFormat** format that will be used to render the message details. Each message's detail value will be passed as the first argument ({0}) to the format. If the component associated with the message has a label, the label's value will be passed as the second argument ({1}) to the format. Example format value: "The {1} field has an incorrect value: {0}"	No
enabledOnUserRole	String	See "Common Extended Attributes" section.	No

Attribute	Type	Description	Required
forceId	String	See "Common Extended Attributes" section.	No
forceIdIndex	String	See "Common Extended Attributes" section.	No
globalSummaryFormat	String	Specifies the **java.text.MessageFormat** format that does the same thing as the **summaryFormat**, but for global messages—that is, messages that are not associated with a component. If a value is not specified for this attribute, the value of the **summaryFormat** attribute will be used if available.	No
replaceIdWithLabel	boolean	Accepts true or false to specify whether the ID of the component associated with each message should be replaced by the component's label. That is, any instance of the component's ID in the message will be replaced with the component's label.

Defaults to true. | No |
| summaryFormat | String | Specifies the **java.text.MessageFormat** format that will be used to render the message summaries. Each message's summary value will be passed as the first argument ({0}) to the format. If the component associated with the message has a label, the label's value will be passed as the second argument ({1}) to the format.

Example format value: "The {1} field has an incorrect value: {0}" | No |
| visibleOnUserRole | String | See "Common Extended Attributes" section. | No |

The outputLabel Component

Tag name: **<t:outputLabel>**
Component class: **org.apache.myfaces.component.html.ext.HtmlOutputLabel**
Component type: **org.apache.myfaces.HtmlOutputLabel**

Extended Attributes

Attribute	Type	Description	Required
enabledOnUserRole	String	See "Common Extended Attributes" section.	No
forceId	String	See "Common Extended Attributes" section.	No
forceIdIndex	String	See "Common Extended Attributes" section.	No
visibleOnUserRole	String	See "Common Extended Attributes" section.	No

The outputText Component

Tag name: **<t:outputText>**
Component class: **org.apache.myfaces.component.html.ext.HtmlOutputText**
Component type: **org.apache.myfaces.HtmlOutputText**

Extended Attributes

Attribute	Type	Description	Required
enabledOnUserRole	String	See "Common Extended Attributes" section.	No
forceId	String	See "Common Extended Attributes" section.	No
forceIdIndex	String	See "Common Extended Attributes" section.	No
visibleOnUserRole	String	See "Common Extended Attributes" section.	No

The panelGrid Component

Tag name: **<t:panelGrid>**
Component class: **org.apache.myfaces.component.html.ext.HtmlPanelGrid**
Component type: **org.apache.myfaces.HtmlPanelGrid**

Extended Attributes

Attribute	Type	Description	Required
displayValueOnly	boolean	See "Common Extended Attributes" section.	No
displayValueOnlyStyle	String	See "Common Extended Attributes" section.	No
displayValueOnlyStyleClass	String	See "Common Extended Attributes" section.	No
enabledOnUserRole	String	See "Common Extended Attributes" section.	No
forceId	String	See "Common Extended Attributes" section.	No
forceIdIndex	String	See "Common Extended Attributes" section.	No
visibleOnUserRole	String	See "Common Extended Attributes" section.	No

The panelGroup Component

Tag name: **<t:panelGroup>**
Component class: **org.apache.myfaces.component.html.ext.HtmlPanelGroup**
Component type: **org.apache.myfaces.HtmlPanelGroup**

Extended Attributes

Attribute	Type	Description	Required
displayValueOnly	boolean	See "Common Extended Attributes" section.	No
displayValueOnlyStyle	String	See "Common Extended Attributes" section.	No
displayValueOnlyStyleClass	String	See "Common Extended Attributes" section.	No
enabledOnUserRole	String	See "Common Extended Attributes" section.	No
forceId	String	See "Common Extended Attributes" section.	No
forceIdIndex	String	See "Common Extended Attributes" section.	No
visibleOnUserRole	String	See "Common Extended Attributes" section.	No

The selectBooleanCheckbox Component

Tag name: **<t:selectBooleanCheckbox>**
Component class: **org.apache.myfaces.component.html.ext.HtmlSelectBooleanCheckbox**
Component type: **org.apache.myfaces.HtmlSelectBooleanCheckbox**

Extended Attributes

Attribute	Type	Description	Required
displayValueOnly	boolean	See "Common Extended Attributes" section.	No
displayValueOnlyStyle	String	See "Common Extended Attributes" section.	No
displayValueOnlyStyleClass	String	See "Common Extended Attributes" section.	No
enabledOnUserRole	String	See "Common Extended Attributes" section.	No
forceId	String	See "Common Extended Attributes" section.	No
forceIdIndex	String	See "Common Extended Attributes" section.	No
visibleOnUserRole	String	See "Common Extended Attributes" section.	No

The selectManyCheckbox Component

Tag name: `<t:selectManyCheckbox>`
Component class: **org.apache.myfaces.component.html.ext.HtmlSelectManyCheckbox**
Component type: **org.apache.myfaces.HtmlSelectManyCheckbox**

Extended Attributes

Attribute	Type	Description	Required
displayValueOnly	boolean	See "Common Extended Attributes" section.	No
displayValueOnlyStyle	String	See "Common Extended Attributes" section.	No
displayValueOnlyStyleClass	String	See "Common Extended Attributes" section.	No
enabledOnUserRole	String	See "Common Extended Attributes" section.	No
forceId	String	See "Common Extended Attributes" section.	No
forceIdIndex	String	See "Common Extended Attributes" section.	No
visibleOnUserRole	String	See "Common Extended Attributes" section.	No

The selectManyListbox Component

Tag name: `<t:selectManyListbox>`
Component class: **org.apache.myfaces.component.html.ext.HtmlSelectManyListbox**
Component type: **org.apache.myfaces.HtmlSelectManyListbox**

Extended Attributes

Attribute	Type	Description	Required
displayValueOnly	boolean	See "Common Extended Attributes" section.	No
displayValueOnlyStyle	String	See "Common Extended Attributes" section.	No
displayValueOnlyStyleClass	String	See "Common Extended Attributes" section.	No
enabledOnUserRole	String	See "Common Extended Attributes" section.	No
forceId	String	See "Common Extended Attributes" section.	No
forceIdIndex	String	See "Common Extended Attributes" section.	No
visibleOnUserRole	String	See "Common Extended Attributes" section.	No

The selectManyMenu Component

Tag name: **<t:selectManyMenu>**
Component class: **org.apache.myfaces.component.html.ext.HtmlSelectManyMenu**
Component type: **org.apache.myfaces.HtmlSelectManyMenu**

Extended Attributes

Attribute	Type	Description	Required
displayValueOnly	boolean	See "Common Extended Attributes" section.	No
displayValueOnlyStyle	String	See "Common Extended Attributes" section.	No
displayValueOnlyStyleClass	String	See "Common Extended Attributes" section.	No
enabledOnUserRole	String	See "Common Extended Attributes" section.	No
forceId	String	See "Common Extended Attributes" section.	No
forceIdIndex	String	See "Common Extended Attributes" section.	No
visibleOnUserRole	String	See "Common Extended Attributes" section.	No

The selectOneListbox Component

Tag name: **<t:selectOneListbox>**
Component class: **org.apache.myfaces.component.html.ext.HtmlSelectOneListbox**
Component type: **org.apache.myfaces.HtmlSelectOneListbox**

Extended Attributes

Attribute	Type	Description	Required
displayValueOnly	boolean	See "Common Extended Attributes" section.	No
displayValueOnlyStyle	String	See "Common Extended Attributes" section.	No
displayValueOnlyStyleClass	String	See "Common Extended Attributes" section.	.No
enabledOnUserRole	String	See "Common Extended Attributes" section.	No
forceId	String	See "Common Extended Attributes" section.	No
forceIdIndex	String	See "Common Extended Attributes" section.	No
visibleOnUserRole	String	See "Common Extended Attributes" section.	No

The selectOneMenu Component

Tag name: **<t:selectOneMenu>**
Component class: **org.apache.myfaces.component.html.ext.HtmlSelectOneMenu**
Component type: **org.apache.myfaces.HtmlSelectOneMenu**

Extended Attributes

Attribute	Type	Description	Required
displayValueOnly	boolean	See "Common Extended Attributes" section.	No
displayValueOnlyStyle	String	See "Common Extended Attributes" section.	No
displayValueOnlyStyleClass	String	See "Common Extended Attributes" section.	No
enabledOnUserRole	String	See "Common Extended Attributes" section.	No
forceId	String	See "Common Extended Attributes" section.	No
forceIdIndex	String	See "Common Extended Attributes" section.	No
visibleOnUserRole	String	See "Common Extended Attributes" section.	No

The selectOneRadio Component

Tag name: **<t:selectOneRadio>**
Component class: **org.apache.myfaces.component.html.ext.HtmlSelectOneRadio**
Component type: **org.apache.myfaces.HtmlSelectOneRadio**

Extended Attributes

Attribute	Type	Description	Required
displayValueOnly	boolean	See "Common Extended Attributes" section.	No
displayValueOnlyStyle	String	See "Common Extended Attributes" section.	No
displayValueOnlyStyleClass	String	See "Common Extended Attributes" section.	No
enabledOnUserRole	String	See "Common Extended Attributes" section.	No
forceId	String	See "Common Extended Attributes" section.	No
forceIdIndex	String	See "Common Extended Attributes" section.	No
visibleOnUserRole	String	See "Common Extended Attributes" section.	No

PART IV

The MyFaces Custom Components

The MyFaces Tomahawk library provides a set of custom components that extend beyond what is provided by the JSF specification. Table 20-2 lists each of the custom components and gives a short description of each component's functionality.

Component	Description
aliasBean	Creates a new bean with a specified value.
aliasBeansScope	Creates a context (scope) for which beans defined with the **aliasBean** component will be available.
buffer	Stores (buffers) a portion of a page's rendered output in a JSP variable.
checkbox	Renders an HTML checkbox control populated with data from a **selectManyCheckbox** component whose layout is set to **spread**.
collapsiblePanel	Creates a panel that can have two states: visible and collapsed.
commandNavigation	Renders a clickable menu item for a menu created using the **panelNavigation** component.
commandNavigation2	Renders a clickable menu item for a menu created using the **panelNavigation2** component.
commandSortHeader	Renders a sortable column header for a **dataTable** component.
dataList	Renders a data table as a list instead of a traditional table. Each row is rendered as an item in the list.
dataScroller	Renders paging mechanism for scrolling through "pages" of data.
div	Renders a set of HTML **<div>** tags around content.
htmlTag	Renders an HTML tag (e.g., ** **, **<p>**, **<h1>**).
inputCalendar	Renders a calendar component that allows users to choose a date from a month view and select different months using a toolbar.
inputDate	Renders a set of fields for entering a date.
inputFileUpload	Renders a file upload control (textfield) that allows users to select a file from their browser and upload its contents to the server.
inputHTML	Renders a Kupu HTML editor.
inputTextHelp	Renders an input text component pre-populated with help text that will either be cleared or selected when the text field receives focus.
jscookMenu	Renders a **JSCookMenu** menu.
jsValueChangeListener	Creates a JavaScript value change listener that works similar to the way JSF value change listeners work.
jsValueSet	Creates a JavaScript variable with the specified name and value.
newspaperTable	Creates a data table that wraps its content into multiple columns instead of having one long column.

TABLE 20-2   The MyFaces Custom Components

Component	Description
panelNavigation	Renders a clickable menu composed of menu items created using the **commandNavigation** component.
panelNavigation2	Renders a clickable menu composed of menu items created using the **commandNavigation2** component.
panelStack	Creates a group of stacked panels where each panel is stacked on top of one another and one panel is visible.
panelTab	Creates an individual tab panel for a tabbed pane defined by the **panelTabbedPane** component.
panelTabbedPane	Creates a tabbed pane consisting of multiple tab panels defined by the **panelTab** component.
popup	Displays a user-defined tool tip (pop-up) when a specified element is moused over.
radio	Renders an HTML radio control populated with data from a **selectOneRadio** component whose layout is set to **spread**.
saveState	Saves arbitrary objects with the same scope as the JSF component tree.
selectOneCountry	Renders a **selectOne** component populated with the list of ISO 3166 countries.
selectOneLanguage	Renders a **selectOne** component populated with the list of ISO 639 languages.
stylesheet	Renders a link to a cascading style sheet or inlines the contents of the specified style sheet.
tree	Renders a tree component that allows users to traverse nodes of data.
tree2	An enhancement to the original tree component.
treeColumn	Makes a **tree** component render as a table with one column (defined by this component) displayed as the tree.
updateActionListener	A JSP tag that serves as a specialized **ActionListener** implementation; useful when dealing with http parameters.

TABLE 20-2   The MyFaces Custom Components *(continued)*

NOTE *Since MyFaces is an open source technology and is constantly in development, there may be some components missing from this list and in the descriptions that follow. To see the current list of Tomahawk components in development, please refer to* **http://myfaces.apache.org/ tomahawk/tlddoc/index.html**.

The remainder of this section discusses each custom component in detail, including a complete description of the component, tables listing each of the component's attributes, and a usage example for the component.

In the tables that describe each component's attributes, pay special attention to the Required column. It simply denotes whether or not the given attribute is required when using the component. If an attribute is required and you do not specify it when using the component, the component will throw a **javax.servlet.jsp.JspException** at runtime. Note that you can declare an error page in your JSP with a **page** directive to capture any **JspException**s that might be thrown, as shown here:

```
<%@ page errorPage="error.jsp" %>
```

If an exception occurs, the page specified by the **errorPage** attribute will be internally redirected to display an error page.

Common Attributes

Many of the custom components have several attributes in common. Instead of repeating the descriptions of the common attributes in each component's section, they are listed in Table 20-3.

Attribute	Type	Description	Required
action	String	Specifies a method binding expression that references a method that will be invoked when the component is selected.	No
actionListener	String	Specifies a method binding expression that references a method that will be invoked with action event notifications when the component is selected.	No
binding	String	Specifies a value binding expression that evaluates to the value for the component.	No
converter	String	Specifies the name of a converter that will be applied to the component's value for either display or input, depending on the type of component. Converters applied to output components will convert the component's value before display. Converters applied to input components will require the value being input to conform to the converter's format.	No
displayValueOnly	boolean	Accepts true or false to specify whether only the component's value should be rendered instead of the component and its value. Defaults to false.	No
displayValueOnlyStyle	String	Specifies the CSS style to use when rendering the component's value if the **displayValueOnly** attribute is set to true.	No
displayValueOnlyStyleClass	String	Specifies the CSS style class to use when rendering the component's value if the **displayValueOnly** attribute is set to true.	No

TABLE 20-3   The Common Attributes for the MyFaces Custom Components

Attribute	Type	Description	Required
enabledOnUserRole	String	Specifies a comma-delimited list of security roles. The current user must be assigned to at least one in order for this component to be enabled. If the current user is not assigned to one of the roles, the component will be rendered in a disabled state (i.e., grayed out).	No
forceId	String	Specifies a definitive component ID that will be assigned to this component. The ID specified will override any ID auto-generated by the JSF implementation and is useful for situations where an explicit non-dynamic ID is required (e.g., in conjunction with CSS or JavaScript code).	No
forceIdIndex	String	Accepts true or false to specify whether an index suffix (e.g., [0]) should be added to the ID specified by the **forceId** attribute when the component is contained within a list. Defaults to true.	No
id	String	Specifies the identifier for the component.	No
immediate	String	Accepts true or false to specify whether the default **ActionListener** should be invoked immediately. That is, should the **ActionListener** be invoked during the Apply Request Values phase of the request processing lifecycle rather than during the Invoke Application phase? Defaults to false.	No
rendered	String	Accepts true or false to specify whether the component should be rendered. Defaults to true.	No
required	String	Accepts true or false to specify whether the component is required to have a value entered or selected. Defaults to false.	No
validator	String	Specifies a method binding expression that references a method that will be invoked during the Process Validations phase of the request processing lifecycle.	No

TABLE 20-3 The Common Attributes for the MyFaces Custom Components *(continued)*

Attribute	Type	Description	Required
value	String	Specifies a value for the component. This can either be a value binding expression that evaluates to a value or a hard-coded value.	No
valueChangeListener	String	Specifies a method binding expression that references a method that will be invoked when the component's value changes.	No
visibleOnUserRole	String	Specifies a comma-delimited list of security roles. The current user must be assigned to at least one role in order for this component to be displayed. If the current user is not assigned to one of the roles, the component will not be rendered.	No

TABLE 20-3 The Common Attributes for the MyFaces Custom Components *(continued)*

The aliasBean Component

Tag name: **<t:aliasBean>**
Component class: **org.apache.myfaces.custom.aliasbean.AliasBean**
Component type: **org.apache.myfaces.AliasBean**

The **aliasBean** component is used to create a new bean with a specified value. The bean's value can be the result of an expression or a hard-coded value.

Attributes

Attribute	Type	Description	Required
alias	String	Specifies the name for the new bean.	No
id	String	See "Common Attributes" section.	No
value	String	See "Common Attributes" section.	No

Example Usage

```
<t:aliasBean alias="#{newBean}" value="#{existingBean}"/>
```

The aliasBeansScope Component

Tag name: **<t:aliasBeansScope>**
Component class: **org.apache.myfaces.custom.aliasbean.AliasBeansScope**
Component type: **org.apache.myfaces.AliasBeansScope**

The **aliasBeansScope** component is used to create a context (scope) for which beans defined with the **aliasBean** component will be available. Beans defined by the **aliasBean** component inside enclosing **aliasBeansScope** component tags will be visible to any other components inside the enclosing tags.

Attributes

Attribute	Type	Description	Required
id	String	See "Common Attributes" section.	No

Example Usage

```
<t:aliasBeansScope>
  <t:aliasBean alias="#{newBean}" value="#{existingBean}"/>
  <t:aliasBean alias="#{newBean2}" value="bean value"/>
</t:aliasBeansScope>
```

The buffer Component

Tag name: **<t:buffer>**
Component class: **org.apache.myfaces.custom.buffer.Buffer**
Component type: **org.apache.myfaces.Buffer**

The **buffer** component is used to store (buffer) a portion of a page's rendered output in a JSP variable. The buffered output can then be later displayed at the desired point.

Attributes

Attribute	Type	Description	Required
into	String	Specifies the name of the JSP variable in which the buffered output will be stored.	Yes

Example Usage

```
<t:buffer into="pageBuffer">
  <h:outputText value="page content"/>
</t:buffer>

<!-- Display buffered content -->
<h:outputText value="#{pageBuffer}" escape="false"/>
```

The checkbox Component

Tag name: **<t:checkbox>**
Component class: **org.apache.myfaces.custom.checkbox.HtmlCheckbox**
Component type: **org.apache.myfaces.HtmlCheckbox**

The **checkbox** component is used to render an HTML checkbox control populated with data from a **selectManyCheckbox** component whose layout is set to **spread**.

Attributes

Attribute	Type	Description	Required
binding	String	See "Common Attributes" section.	No
enabledOnUserRole	String	See "Common Attributes" section.	No
for	String	Specifies the ID of the **selectManyCheckbox** component whose data will be used for this component.	Yes
id	String	See "Common Attributes" section.	No
index	String	Specifies the (0-based) index of the **selectManyCheckbox** component's select item that will be used to populate this component.	Yes
rendered	String	See "Common Attributes" section.	No
visibleOnUserRole	String	See "Common Attributes" section.	No

Example Usage

```
<t:selectManyCheckbox id="colors" layout="spread">
  <f:selectItem itemValue="0" itemLabel="Red"/>
  <f:selectItem itemValue="1" itemLabel="Green"/>
  <f:selectItem itemValue="2" itemLabel="Blue"/>
</t:selectManyCheckBox>

<t:checkbox for="colors" index="0"/>
<t:checkbox for="colors" index="1"/>
```

The collapsiblePanel Component

Tag name: **<t:collapsiblePanel>**
Component class: **org.apache.myfaces.custom.checkbox.HtmlCollapsiblePanel**
Component type: **org.apache.myfaces.HtmlCollapsiblePanel**

The **collapsiblePanel** component is used to create a panel that can have two states: visible and collapsed. In the visible state the panel's contents are shown. In the collapsed state the panel's contents are hidden.

Core Attributes

Attribute	Type	Description	Required
binding	String	See "Common Attributes" section.	No
collapsed	boolean	Accepts true or false to specify whether the panel should be collapsed by default. Defaults to false.	No

Attribute	Type	Description	Required
enabledOnUserRole	String	See "Common Attributes" section.	No
id	String	See "Common Attributes" section.	No
rendered	String	See "Common Attributes" section.	No
value	String	See "Common Attributes" section.	No
visibleOnUserRole	String	See "Common Attributes" section.	No

HTML Attributes

Attributes	Type	Description	Required
dir, lang, style, styleClass, title	String	Each of the HTML attributes corresponds one-to-one with an HTML attribute of the same name as the rendered HTML tag.	No

JavaScript Attributes

Attribute	Type	Description	Required
onclick, ondblclick, onkeydown, onkeypress, onkeyup, onmousedown, onmousemove, onmouseout, onmouseover, onmouseup	String	Each of the JavaScript attributes corresponds one-to-one with a JavaScript attribute of the same name as the rendered HTML tag.	No

Example Usage

```
<t:collapsiblePanel collapsed="#{panelBean.collapsed}" value="Panel Title">
  <h:outputText value="Line 1"/>
  <h:outputText value="Line 2"/>
</t:collapsiblePanel>
```

The commandNavigation Component

Tag name: **<t:commandNavigation>**
Component class: **org.apache.myfaces.custom.navigation.HtmlCommandNavigation**
Component type: **org.apache.myfaces.HtmlCommandNavigation**

The **commandNavigation** component is used to render a clickable menu item for a menu created using the **panelNavigation** component.

NOTE *Although the* **panelNavigation** *component and the associated* **commandNavigation** *component are still included in the Tomahawk library, they have been supplanted by the* **panelNavigation2** *and* **commandNavigation2** *components, respectively.*

Core Attributes

Attribute	Type	Description	Required
action	String	See "Common Attributes" section.	No
actionListener	String	See "Common Attributes" section.	No
binding	String	See "Common Attributes" section.	No
enabledOnUserRole	String	See "Common Attributes" section.	No
id	String	See "Common Attributes" section.	No
immediate	String	See "Common Attributes" section.	No
rendered	String	See "Common Attributes" section.	No
value	String	See "Common Attributes" section.	No
visibleOnUserRole	String	See "Common Attributes" section.	No

HTML Attributes

Attribute	Type	Description	Required
accesskey, charset, coords, dir, hrefLang, lang, rel, rev, shape, style, styleClass, tabindex, target, title, type	String	Each of the HTML attributes corresponds one-to-one with an HTML attribute of the same name as the rendered HTML tag.	No

JavaScript Attributes

Attribute	Type	Description	Required
onblur, onclick, ondblclick, onfocus, onkeydown, onkeypress, onkeyup, onmousedown, onmousemove, onmouseout, onmouseover, onmouseup	String	Each of the JavaScript attributes corresponds one-to-one with a JavaScript attribute of the same name as the rendered HTML tag.	No

Example Usage

```
<t:panelNavigation id="linkMenu">
  <t:commandNavigation action="gotoMenuItem1">
    <h:outputText value="Menu Item 1"/>
  </t:commandNavigation>
  <t:commandNavigation action="gotoMenuItem2">
    <h:outputText value="Menu Item 2"/>
  </t:commandNavigation>
</t:panelNavigation>
```

The commandNavigation2 Component

Tag name: **<t:commandNavigation2>**

Component class: **org.apache.myfaces.custom.navmenu.htmlnavmenu**
.HtmlCommandNavigationItem
Component type: **org.apache.myfaces.HtmlCommandNavigationItem**
The **commandNavigation2** component is used to render a clickable menu item for
a menu created using the **panelNavigation2** component.

Core Attributes

Attribute	Type	Description	Required
action	String	See "Common Attributes" section.	No
actionListener	String	See "Common Attributes" section.	No
binding	String	See "Common Attributes" section.	No
enabledOnUserRole	String	See "Common Attributes" section.	No
id	String	See "Common Attributes" section.	No
immediate	String	See "Common Attributes" section.	No
rendered	String	See "Common Attributes" section.	No
value	String	See "Common Attributes" section.	No
visibleOnUserRole	String	See "Common Attributes" section.	No

HTML Attributes

Attribute	Type	Description	Required
accesskey, charset, coords, dir, hrefLang, lang, rel, rev, shape, style, styleClass, tabindex, target, title, type	String	Each of the HTML attributes corresponds one-to-one with an HTML attribute of the same name as the rendered HTML tag.	No

JavaScript Attributes

Attribute	Type	Description	Required
onblur, onclick, ondblclick, onfocus, onkeydown, onkeypress, onkeyup, onmousedown, onmousemove, onmouseout, onmouseover, onmouseup	String	Each of the JavaScript attributes corresponds one-to-one with a JavaScript attribute of the same name as the rendered HTML tag.	No

Example Usage

```
<t:panelNavigation2 id="linkMenu">
  <t:commandNavigation2 action="gotoMenuItem1">
    <h:outputText value="Menu Item 1"/>
  </t:commandNavigation2>
  <t:commandNavigation2 action="gotoMenuItem2">
    <h:outputText value="Menu Item 2"/>
  </t:commandNavigation2>
</t:panelNavigation2>
```

PART IV

The commandSortHeader Component

Tag name: **<t:commandSortHeader>**
Component class: **org.apache.myfaces.custom.sortheader.HtmlCommandSortHeader**
Component type: **org.apache.myfaces.HtmlCommandSortHeader**

The **commandSortHeader** component is used to render a sortable column header for a **dataTable** component.

Core Attributes

Attribute	Type	Description	Required
action	String	See "Common Attributes" section.	No
actionListener	String	See "Common Attributes" section.	No
arrow	boolean	Accepts true or false to specify whether a sort direction arrow should be rendered beside the column label. Defaults to false.	No
binding	String	See "Common Attributes" section.	No
columnName	String	Specifies a name for this sortable column. The name must be unique among all sortable columns for the table.	Yes
enabledOnUserRole	String	See "Common Attributes" section.	No
id	String	See "Common Attributes" section.	No
immediate	String	See "Common Attributes" section.	No
rendered	String	See "Common Attributes" section.	No
value	String	See "Common Attributes" section.	No
visibleOnUserRole	String	See "Common Attributes" section.	No

HTML Attributes

Attribute	Type	Description	Required
accesskey, charset, coords, dir, hrefLang, lang, rel, rev, shape, style, styleClass, tabindex, target, title, type	String	Each of the HTML attributes corresponds one-to-one with an HTML attribute of the same name as the rendered HTML tag.	No

JavaScript Attributes

Attribute	Type	Description	Required
onblur, onclick, ondblclick, onfocus, onkeydown, onkeypress, onkeyup, onmousedown, onmousemove, onmouseout, onmouseover, onmouseup	String	Each of the JavaScript attributes corresponds one-to-one with a JavaScript attribute of the same name as the rendered HTML tag.	No

Example Usage

```
<t:dataTable value="#{search.results}" var="result">
  <h:column>
    <f:facet name="header">
      <t:commandSortHeader columnName="name" arrow="true">
        <h:outputText value="Name"/>
      </t:commandSortHeader>
    </f:facet>
    <h:outputText value="#{result.name}"/>
  </h:column>
  <h:column>
    <f:facet name="header">
      <h:outputText value="Description"/>
    </f:facet>
    <h:outputText value="#{result.description}"/>
  </h:column>
</t:dataTable>
```

The dataList Component

Tag name: **<t:dataList>**
Component class: **org.apache.myfaces.custom.datalist.HtmlDataList**
Component type: **org.apache.myfaces.HtmlDataList**

The **dataList** component is used to render a data table as a list instead of a traditional table. Each row is rendered as an item in the list.

Core Attributes

Attribute	Type	Description	Required
binding	String	See "Common Attributes" section.	No
enabledOnUserRole	String	See "Common Attributes" section.	No
first	String	Specifies the first row to display. Defaults to 0.	No
forceId	String	See "Common Attributes" section.	No
forceIdIndex	String	See "Common Attributes" section.	No
id	String	See "Common Attributes" section.	No
layout	String	Specifies the layout type for the list. Valid values: "simple" – Each row is rendered normally. "unorderedList" – Each row is rendered as an HTML unordered list. "orderedList" – Each row is rendered as an HTML ordered list.	No
rendered	String	See "Common Attributes" section.	No

Attribute	Type	Description	Required
rowCountVar	String	Specifies the name of the JSP variable that will hold the row count.	No
rowIndexVar	String	Specifies the name of the JSP variable that will hold the row index.	No
rows	String	Specifies the number of rows that will be displayed.	No
value	String	See "Common Attributes" section.	No
var	String	Specifies the name of the JSP variable that will be populated with the current row's object.	Yes
visibleOnUserRole	String	See "Common Attributes" section.	No

HTML Attributes

Attribute	Type	Description	Required
dir, lang, style, styleClass, title	String	Each of the HTML attributes corresponds one-to-one with an HTML attribute of the same name as the rendered HTML tag.	No

JavaScript Attributes

Attribute	Type	Description	Required
onclick, ondblclick, onkeydown, onkeypress, onkeyup, onmousedown, onmousemove, onmouseout, onmouseover, onmouseup	String	Each of the JavaScript attributes corresponds one-to-one with a JavaScript attribute of the same name as the rendered HTML tag.	No

Example Usage

```
<t:dataList type="orderedList" value="#{addressForm.countries}" var="country">
  <h:outputText value="#{country.name}"/>
</t:dataList>
```

The dataScroller Component

Tag name: **<t:dataScroller>**
Component class: **org.apache.myfaces.custom.datascroller.HtmlDataScroller**
Component type: **org.apache.myfaces.HtmlDataScoller**

The **dataScroller** component is used to render a paging mechanism for scrolling through "pages" of data. Note that this component is dependent on the Tomahawk extended version of the **dataTable** component and will not work with the standard JSF implementation of the **dataTable** component.

Core Attributes

Attribute	Type	Description	Required
actionListener	String	See "Common Attributes" section.	No
binding	String	See "Common Attributes" section.	No
displayedRowsCountVar	String	Specifies the name of the JSP variable that will hold the displayed rows count.	No
enabledOnUserRole	String	See "Common Attributes" section.	No
fastStep	Int	Specifies the number of rows to skip with the fast step buttons of the paginator.	No
firstRowIndexVar	String	Specifies the name of the JSP variable that will hold the index of the first row.	No
for	String	Specifies the ID of the component that this component is for.	No
id	String	See "Common Attributes" section.	No
immediate	boolean	See "Common Attributes" section.	No
lastRowIndexVar	String	Specifies the name of the JSP variable that will hold the index of the last row.	No
pageCountVar	String	Specifies the name of the JSP variable that will hold the page count.	No
paginator	boolean	Accepts true or false to specify whether the paginator will be rendered. Defaults to false.	No
paginatorActiveColumnClass	String	Specifies the CSS style class for the paginator's active column.	No
paginatorActiveColumnStyle	String	Specifies the CSS style for the paginator's active column.	No
paginatorColumnClass	String	Specifies the CSS style class for the paginator's columns.	No
paginatorColumnStyle	String	Specifies the CSS style for the paginator's columns.	No
paginatorMaxPages	Int	Specifies the maximum number of pages for the paginator.	No
paginatorTableClass	String	Specifies the CSS style class for the paginator's table.	No

Attribute	Type	Description	Required
paginatorTableStyle	String	Specifies the CSS style for the paginator's table.	No
pageIndexVar	String	Specifies the name of the JSP variable that will hold the index of the current page.	No
rendered	String	See "Common Attributes" section.	No
renderFacetIfSinglePage	boolean	Accepts true or false to specify whether facets should be rendered if all of the data fits in a single page. Defaults to true.	No
rowsCountVar	String	Specifies the name of the JSP variable that will hold the row count.	No
rowIndexVar	String	Specifies the name of the JSP variable that will hold the index of the current row.	No
visibleOnUserRole	String	See "Common Attributes" section.	No

HTML Attributes

Attribute	Type	Description	Required
style, styleClass	String	Each of the HTML attributes corresponds one-to-one with an HTML attribute of the same name as the rendered HTML tag.	No

Example Usage

```
<t:dataTable id="countries"
          value="#{addressForm.countries}"
            var="country"
           rows="10">
  <h:column>
    <f:facet name="header">
      <h:outputText value="Code"/>
    </f:facet>
    <h:outputText value="#{country.code}"/>
  </h:column>
  <h:column>
    <f:facet name="header">
      <h:outputText value="Name"/>
    </f:facet>
    <h:outputText value="#{country.name}"/>
  </h:column>
</t:dataTable>
```

```
<t:dataScroller for="countries"
           fastStep="10"
       pageCountVar="pageCount"
       pageIndexVar="pageIndex"
          paginator="true">
  <f:facet name="first">
    <t:graphicImage url="images/arrow-first.gif"/>
  </f:facet>
  <f:facet name="last">
    <t:graphicImage url="images/arrow-last.gif"/>
  </f:facet>
  <f:facet name="previous">
    <t:graphicImage url="images/arrow-previous.gif"/>
  </f:facet>
  <f:facet name="next">
    <t:graphicImage url="images/arrow-next.gif"/>
  </f:facet>
  <f:facet name="fastforward">
    <t:graphicImage url="images/arrow-ff.gif"/>
  </f:facet>
  <f:facet name="fastrewind">
    <t:graphicImage url="images/arrow-fr.gif"/>
  </f:facet>
</t:dataScroller>
```

The div Component

Tag name: **<t:div>**
Component class: **org.apache.myfaces.custom.div.Div**
Component type: **org.apache.myfaces.Div**
   The **div** component is used to render a set of HTML **<div>** tags around content.

Core Attributes

Attribute	Type	Description	Required
binding	String	See "Common Attributes" section.	No
enabledOnUserRole	String	See "Common Attributes" section.	No
forceId	String	See "Common Attributes" section.	No
forceIdIndex	String	See "Common Attributes" section.	No
id	String	See "Common Attributes" section.	No
rendered	String	See "Common Attributes" section.	No
visibleOnUserRole	String	See "Common Attributes" section.	No

HTML Attributes

Attribute	Type	Description	Required
style, styleClass	String	Each of the HTML attributes corresponds one-to-one with an HTML attribute of the same name as the rendered HTML tag.	No

PART IV

Example Usage

```
<t:div>
  <h:outputText value="content"/>
</t:div>
```

The htmlTag Component

Tag name: **<t:htmlTag>**
Component class: **org.apache.myfaces.custom.htmlTag.HtmlTag**
Component type: **org.apache.myfaces.HtmlTag**

The **htmlTag** component is used to render an HTML tag (e.g., **
, **<p>, **<h1>**). Any HTML tag can be rendered using this tag.

Core Attributes

Attribute	Type	Description	Required
binding	String	See "Common Attributes" section.	No
enabledOnUserRole	String	See "Common Attributes" section.	No
forceId	String	See "Common Attributes" section.	No
forceIdIndex	String	See "Common Attributes" section.	No
id	String	See "Common Attributes" section.	No
rendered	String	See "Common Attributes" section.	No
value	String	Specifies the name of the HTML tag to render.	Yes
visibleOnUserRole	String	See "Common Attributes" section.	No

HTML Attributes

Attribute	Type	Description	Required
style, styleClass	String	Each of the HTML attributes corresponds one-to-one with an HTML attribute of the same name as the rendered HTML tag.	No

Example Usage

```
<!-- renders a <br> tag -->
<t:htmlTag value="br"/>

<!-- renders a <p> tag -->
<t:htmlTag value="p"/>

<!-- renders a <h1> tag -->
<t:htmlTag value="h1"/>
```

The inputCalendar Component

Tag name: **<t:inputCalendar>**
Component class: **org.apache.myfaces.custom.calendar.HtmlInputCalendar**
Component type: **org.apache.myfaces.HtmlInputCalendar**

The **inputCalendar** component is used to render a calendar component that allows users to choose a date from a month view, and select different months using a toolbar.

Core Attributes

Attribute	Type	Description	Required
addResources	boolean	Accepts true or false to specify whether the calendar resources (e.g., images, JavaScript, and CSS) will be automatically added to the JSP using the MyFaces Extensions Filter. Defaults to true.	No
binding	String	See "Common Attributes" section.	No
converter	String	See "Common Attributes" section.	No
currentDayCellClass	String	Specifies the CSS class for the current day cell of the calendar.	No
dayCellClass	String	Specifies the CSS class for each day cell of the calendar.	No
enabledOnUserRole	String	See "Common Attributes" section.	No
forceId	String	See "Common Attributes" section.	No
forceIdIndex	String	See "Common Attributes" section.	No
id	String	See "Common Attributes" section.	No
immediate	String	See "Common Attributes" section.	No
monthYearRowClass	String	Specifies the CSS class for the header row of the calendar showing the month and year.	No
popupButtonString	String	Specifies the label that will be on the button that is used to pop up the calendar.	No
popupDateFormat	String	Specifies the date format used by the pop-up.	No
popupGotoString	String	Specifies the value for the goto label. Defaults to "Go To Current Month."	No
popupSelectDateMessage	String	Specifies the value for the select date label. Defaults to "Select [date] as date." [date] should be in this attribute's value and will be replaced by the current date.	No

Attribute	Type	Description	Required
popupSelectMonthMessage	String	Specifies the value for the select month label. Defaults to "Click to select a month."	No
popupSelectYearMessage	String	Specifies the value for the select year label. Defaults to "Click to select a year."	No
popupScrollLeftMessage	String	Specifies the value for the scroll left label. Defaults to <<.	No
popupScrollRightMessage	String	Specifies the value for the scroll right label. Defaults to >\>.	No
popupTodayString	String	Specifies the value for the today label. Defaults to "Today is."	No
popupWeekString	String	Specifies the value for the week label. Defaults to "Wk."	No
renderAsPopup	boolean	Accepts true or false to specify whether the calendar will be rendered as a pop-up instead of inline. Defaults to false.	No
rendered	String	See "Common Attributes" section.	No
renderPopupButtonAsImage	boolean	Accepts true or false to specify whether the button for popping up the calendar will be rendered as an image instead of an HTML button control. Defaults to false.	No
required	String	See "Common Attributes" section.	No
validator	String	See "Common Attributes" section.	No
value	String	See "Common Attributes" section.	No
valueChangeListener	String	See "Common Attributes" section.	No

Attribute	Type	Description	Required
visibleOnUserRole	String	See "Common Attributes" section.	No
weekRowClass	String	Specifies the CSS class for the header row of the calendar showing the week days.	No

HTML Attributes

Attribute	Type	Description	Required
accesskey, align, alt, dir, disabled, lang, maxlength, readonly, size, style, styleClass, tabindex, title	String	Each of the HTML attributes corresponds one-to-one with an HTML attribute of the same name as the rendered HTML tag.	No

JavaScript Attributes

Attribute	Type	Description	Required
onblur, onchange, onclick, ondblclick, onfocus, onkeydown, onkeypress, onkeyup, onmousedown, onmousemove, onmouseout, onmouseover, onmouseup, onselect	String	Each of the JavaScript attributes corresponds one-to-one with a JavaScript attribute of the same name as the rendered HTML tag.	No

Example Usage

```
<t:inputCalendar value="#{userForm.birthDate}"/>
```

The inputDate Component

Tag name: **<t:inputDate>**
Component class: **org.apache.myfaces.custom.date.HtmlInputDate**
Component type: **org.apache.myfaces.HtmlInputDate**

The **inputDate** component is used to render a set of fields for entering a date. The set of fields rendered for entering the date is based on the type of date specified using the **type** attribute.

Core Attributes

Attribute	Type	Description	Required
binding	String	See "Common Attributes" section.	No
converter	String	See "Common Attributes" section.	No
enabledOnUserRole	String	See "Common Attributes" section.	No
id	String	See "Common Attributes" section.	No

Attribute	Type	Description	Required
immediate	String	See "Common Attributes" section.	No
popupCalendar	boolean	Accepts true or false to specify whether the component's value can be specified using an **inputCalendar** component pop-up. Defaults to false.	No
rendered	String	See "Common Attributes" section.	No
required	String	See "Common Attributes" section.	No
timeZone	String	Specifies the time zone for the date value.	No
type	String	Specifies the type of date that the component will accept. Valid values: "both", "date", "full", "short_time", or "time"	No
validator	String	See "Common Attributes" section.	No
value	String	See "Common Attributes" section.	No
valueChangeListener	String	See "Common Attributes" section.	No
visibleOnUserRole	String	See "Common Attributes" section.	No

HTML Attributes

Attribute	Type	Description	Required
accesskey, align, alt, dir, disabled, lang, maxlength, readonly, size, style, styleClass, tabindex, title	String	Each of the HTML attributes corresponds one-to-one with an HTML attribute of the same name as the rendered HTML tag.	No

JavaScript Attributes

Attribute	Type	Description	Required
onblur, onchange, onclick, ondblclick, onfocus, onkeydown, onkeypress, onkeyup, onmousedown, onmousemove, onmouseout, onmouseover, onmouseup, onselect	String	Each of the JavaScript attributes corresponds one-to-one with a JavaScript attribute of the same name as the rendered HTML tag.	No

Example Usage

```
<t:inputDate id="date" value="#{userForm.birthDate}" type="date"/>
```

The inputFileUpload Component

Tag name: **<t:inputFileUpload>**
Component class: **org.apache.myfaces.custom.fileupload.HtmlInputFileUpload**
Component type: **org.apache.myfaces.HtmlInputFileUpload**

The **inputFileUpload** component is used to render a file upload control (textfield) that allows users to select a file from their browser and upload its contents to the server. Note that the form's encoding type must be set to "multipart/form-data" in order for the file upload functionality to work in the browser. Following is an example of configuring the form's encoding type:

```
<h:form id="uploadForm" name="uploadForm" enctype="multipart/form-data">
...
</h:form>
```

NOTE *Use of the* **inputFileUpload** *component requires that the MyFaces Extensions Filter be set up in your application's* **web.xml** *file. Additionally, you must create a backing bean that contains an* **org.apache.myfaces.custom.fileupload.UploadedFile** *field to store the uploaded files' contents in. The* **UploadedFile** *field must be bound to the* **inputFileUpload** *component using the* **value** *attribute.*

Core Attributes

Attribute	Type	Description	Required
binding	String	See "Common Attributes" section.	No
converter	String	See "Common Attributes" section.	No
enabledOnUserRole	String	See "Common Attributes" section.	No
id	String	See "Common Attributes" section.	No
immediate	String	See "Common Attributes" section.	No
rendered	String	See "Common Attributes" section.	No
required	String	See "Common Attributes" section.	No
validator	String	See "Common Attributes" section.	No
value	String	See "Common Attributes" section.	No
valueChangeListener	String	See "Common Attributes" section.	No
visibleOnUserRole	String	See "Common Attributes" section.	No

HTML Attributes

Attribute	Type	Description	Required
accept, accesskey, align, alt, dir, disabled, lang, maxlength, readonly, size, storage, style, styleClass, tabindex, title	String	Each of the HTML attributes corresponds one-to-one with an HTML attribute of the same name as the rendered HTML tag.	No

PART IV

JavaScript Attributes

Attribute	Type	Description	Required
onblur, onchange, onclick, ondblclick, onfocus, onkeydown, onkeypress, onkeyup, onmousedown, onmousemove, onmouseout, onmouseover, onmouseup, onselect	String	Each of the JavaScript attributes corresponds one-to-one with a JavaScript attribute of the same name as the rendered HTML tag.	No

Example Usage

```
<t:inputFileUpload id="fileUpload" value="uploadForm.file"/>
```

Following is an example backing bean in which to store the uploaded file. Note that the bean must have an **org.apache.myfaces.custom.fileuploadUploadedFile** field to hold the uploaded files' content.

```
import org.apache.myfaces.custom.fileupload.UploadedFile;

public class UploadForm {
  private UploadedFile file;

  public UploadedFile getFile() {
    return file;
  }

  public void setFile(UploadedFile file) {
    this.file = file;
  }
}
```

The inputHTML Component

Tag name: **<t:inputHtml>**
Component class: **org.apache.myfaces.custom.inputHtml.InputHtml**
Component type: **org.apache.myfaces.InputHtml**

The **inputHtml** component is used to render a Kupu HTML editor. Kupu is a very popular JavaScript-based HTML editor library. For more details on Kupu, visit the project Web site at **http://kupu.oscom.org/**.

Core Attributes

Attribute	Type	Description	Required
addKupuLogo	boolean	Accepts true or false to specify whether the Kupu logo will be displayed on the editor's toolbar. Defaults to true.	No

Attribute	Type	Description	Required
allowEditSource	boolean	Accepts true or false to specify whether users will be allowed to edit the source HTML for the document created in the editor. Defaults to true.	No
allowExternalLinks	boolean	Accepts true or false to specify whether users will be allowed to insert external links into the document created in the editor. Defaults to true.	No
binding	String	See "Common Attributes" section.	No
converter	String	See "Common Attributes" section.	No
displayValueOnly	boolean	See "Common Attributes" section.	No
displayValueOnlyStyle	String	See "Common Attributes" section.	No
displayValueOnlyStyleClass	String	See "Common Attributes" section.	No
enabledOnUserRole	String	See "Common Attributes" section.	No
fallback	String	Accepts true or false to specify whether the editor should "fall back" to an HTML textarea control if the rich JavaScript-based editor cannot be rendered. Defaults to false.	No
id	String	See "Common Attributes" section.	No
immediate	String	See "Common Attributes" section.	No
rendered	String	See "Common Attributes" section.	No
required	String	See "Common Attributes" section.	No

Attribute	Type	Description	Required
showAllToolBoxes	boolean	Accepts true or false to specify whether all of the toolboxes will be shown in the editor. Defaults to false.	No
showCleanupExpressionsToolBox	boolean	Accepts true or false to specify whether the Cleanup Expressions toolbox will be shown in the editor. Defaults to false.	No
showDebugToolBox	boolean	Accepts true or false to specify whether the Debug toolbox will be shown in the editor. Defaults to false.	No
showImagesToolBox	boolean	Accepts true or false to specify whether the Images toolbox will be shown in the editor. Defaults to false.	No
showLinksToolBox	boolean	Accepts true or false to specify whether the Links toolbox will be shown in the editor. Defaults to false.	No
showPropertiesToolBox	boolean	Accepts true or false to specify whether the Properties toolbox will be shown in the editor. Defaults to false.	No
showTablesToolBox	boolean	Accepts true or false to specify whether the Tables toolbox will be shown in the editor. Defaults to false.	No
type	String	Specifies the type of HTML document the editor will be creating: either a fragment or a full document. Valid values: "fragment" or "document". Defaults to "fragment".	No

Attribute	Type	Description	Required
validator	String	See "Common Attributes" section.	No
value	String	See "Common Attributes" section.	No
valueChangeListener	String	See "Common Attributes" section.	No
visibleOnUserRole	String	See "Common Attributes" section.	No

HTML Attributes

Attribute	Type	Description	Required
style, styleClass	String	Each of the HTML attributes corresponds one-to-one with an HTML attribute of the same name as the rendered HTML tag.	No

Example Usage

```
<t:inputHtml/>
```

The inputTextHelp Component

Tag name: **<t:inputTextHelp>**
Component class: **org.apache.myfaces.custom.inputTextHelp.HtmlInputTextHelp**
Component type: **org.apache.myfaces.HtmlInputTextHelp**

The **inputTextHelp** component is used to render an input text component pre-populated with help text that will either be cleared or selected when the text field receives focus.

Core Attributes

Attribute	Type	Description	Required
binding	String	See "Common Attributes" section.	No
converter	String	See "Common Attributes" section.	No
displayValueOnly	boolean	See "Common Attributes" section.	No
displayValueOnlyStyle	String	See "Common Attributes" section.	No
displayValueOnlyStyleClass	String	See "Common Attributes" section.	No
forceId	String	See "Common Attributes" section.	No
forceIdIndex	String	See "Common Attributes" section.	No
enabledOnUserRole	String	See "Common Attributes" section.	No
helpText	String	Specifies the help text that will be cleared when the component receives focus.	No

Attribute	Type	Description	Required
id	String	See "Common Attributes" section.	No
immediate	String	See "Common Attributes" section.	No
rendered	String	See "Common Attributes" section.	No
required	String	See "Common Attributes" section.	No
selectText	String	Specifies the help text that will be selected when the component receives focus.	No
validator	String	See "Common Attributes" section.	No
value	String	See "Common Attributes" section.	No
valueChangeListener	String	See "Common Attributes" section.	No
visibleOnUserRole	String	See "Common Attributes" section.	No

HTML Attributes

Attribute	Type	Description	Required
accesskey, align, alt, dir, disabled, lang, maxlength, readonly, size, style, styleClass, tabindex, title	String	Each of the HTML attributes corresponds one-to-one with an HTML attribute of the same name as the rendered HTML tag.	No

JavaScript Attributes

Attribute	Type	Description	Required
onblur, onchange, onclick, ondblclick, onfocus, onkeydown, onkeypress, onkeyup, onmousedown, onmousemove, onmouseout, onmouseover, onmouseup, onselect	String	Each of the JavaScript attributes corresponds one-to-one with a JavaScript attribute of the same name as the rendered HTML tag.	No

Example Usage

```
<!-- Text that will be cleared on focus -->
<t:inputTextHelp helpText="Enter search term"/>

<!-- Text that will be selected on focus -->
<t:inputTextHelp selectText="Enter search term"/>
```

The jscookMenu Component

Tag name: **<t:jscookMenu>**

Component class: **org.apache.myfaces.custom.navmenu.jscookmenu**
.HtmlCommandJSCookMenu
Component type: **org.apache.myfaces.JSCookMenu**

The **jscookMenu** component is used to render a JSCookMenu menu. JSCookMenu is a very popular JavaScript menuing library created by Heng Yuan. For more details on JSCookMenu, visit the project Web site at **http://www.cs.ucla.edu/~heng/JSCookMenu**.

Attributes

Attribute	Type	Description	Required
binding	String	See "Common Attributes" section.	No
enabledOnUserRole	String	See "Common Attributes" section.	No
id	String	See "Common Attributes" section.	No
imageLocation	String	Specifies an alternate location from which to load image resources for the menu. If a value is not specified for this attribute, images will be loaded from the resources directory by the MyFaces Extensions Filter.	No
javascriptLocation	String	Specifies an alternate location from which to load JavaScript resources for the menu. If a value is not specified for this attribute, scripts will be loaded from the resources directory by the MyFaces Extensions Filter.	No
layout	String	Specifies the menu layout that will be used. This value is passed directly to the JSCookMenu library. Valid values: "hbl", "hbr", "hul", "hur", "vbl", "vbr", "vul", "vur".	Yes
rendered	String	See "Common Attributes" section.	No
styleLocation	String	Specifies an alternate location from which to load CSS style sheet resources for the menu. If a value is not specified for this attribute, style sheets will be loaded from the resources directory by the MyFaces Extensions Filter.	No
theme	String	Specifies the menu theme that will be used. This value is passed directly to the JSCookMenu library. Valid values: "ThemeIE", "ThemeMiniBlack", "ThemeOffice", "ThemePanel".	Yes
visibleOnUserRole	String	See "Common Attributes" section.	No

PART IV

Example Usage

```
<t:jscookMenu layout="hbr" theme="ThemeIE">
  <t:navigationMenuItem id="menuItem1"
               itemLabel="Menu Item 1"
                  action="goMenuItem1"/>
  <t:navigationMenuItem id="menuItem2"
               itemLabel="Menu Item 2"
                  action="goMenuItem2"/>
</t:jscookMenu>
```

The jsValueChangeListener Component

Tag name: **<t:jsValueChangeListener>**
Component class: **org.apache.myfaces.custom.jslistener.JsValueChangeListener**
Component type: **org.apache.myfaces.JsValueChangeListener**

The **jsValueChangeListener** component is used to create a JavaScript value change listener that works similar to the way a JSF value change listener works. The JavaScript value change listener is used to capture change events on a component and trigger changes in other components when the events occur. This is useful for keeping two components' values in sync.

Attributes

Attribute	Type	Description	Required
expressionValue	String	Specifies the JavaScript expression that evaluates to the value that will be assigned to the target control. The expression may contain the following keywords: **$srcElem** – Resolves to the source control **$destElem** – Resolves to the destination control	Yes
for	String	Specifies the ID of the target control that should be updated when the component this listener is registered with has its value change.	No
property	String	Specifies the property of the target control that will be updated with the value defined by the **expressionValue** attribute.	No

Example Usage

```
<h:inputText id="email">
  <t:jsValueChangeListener for="emailConfirm"
                    property="value"
              expressionValue="$srcElem.value"/>
</h:inputText>
```

The jsValueSet Component

Tag name: **<t:jsValueSet>**
Component class: **org.apache.myfaces.custom.jsvalueset.HtmlJsValueSet**
Component type: **org.apache.myfaces.HtmlJsValueSet**

The **jsValueSet** component is used to create a JavaScript variable with the specified name and value. This tag is useful for assigning values from JSF beans to JavaScript variables using a value binding expression.

Attributes

Attribute	Type	Description	Required
name	String	Specifies the name of the JavaScript variable that will be created.	Yes
value	String	See "Common Attributes" section.	Yes

Example Usage

```
<t:jsValueSet name="username" value="#{loginForm.username}"/>
```

The newspaperTable Component

Tag name: **<t:newspaperTable>**
Component class: **org.apache.myfaces.custom.newspaper.HtmlNewspaperTable**
Component type: **org.apache.myfaces.HtmlNewspaperTable**

The **newspaperTable** component is used to create a data table that wraps its content into multiple columns instead of having one long column.

Core Attributes

Attribute	Type	Description	Required
binding	String	See "Common Attributes" section.	No
columnClasses	String	Specifies a comma-delimited list of CSS classes to be applied to the columns.	No
first	Int	Specifies the first row to display. Defaults to 0.	No
footerClass	String	Specifies the CSS class for the table footer.	No
headerClass	String	Specifies the CSS class for the table header.	No
id	String	See "Common Attributes" section.	No
newspaperColumns	Int	Specifies the number of columns to wrap content across. Defaults to 1.	No

Attribute	Type	Description	Required
rendered	String	See "Common Attributes" section.	No
rowClasses	String	Specifies a comma-delimited list of CSS classes to be applied to the rows.	No
rows	String	Specifies the number of rows that will be displayed in the table.	No
value	String	See "Common Attributes" section.	No
var	String	Specifies the name of the JSP variable that will be populated with the current row's object.	No

HTML Attributes

Attribute	Type	Description	Required
align, border, bgcolor, cellpadding, cellspacing, datafld, datasrc, dataformatas, dir, frame, lang, rules, style, styleClass, summary, title, width	String	Each of the HTML attributes corresponds one-to-one with an HTML attribute of the same name as the rendered HTML tag.	No

JavaScript Attributes

Attribute	Type	Description	Required
onclick, ondblclick, onkeydown, onkeypress, onkeyup, onmousedown, onmousemove, onmouseout, onmouseover, onmouseup	String	Each of the JavaScript attributes corresponds one-to-one with a JavaScript attribute of the same name as the rendered HTML tag.	No

Example Usage

```
<t:newspaperTable newspaperColumns="3"
                          value="#{addressForm.countries}"
                          var="country">
  <h:column>
    <h:outputText value="#{country.code}"/>
  </h:column>
  <h:column>
    <h:outputText value="#{country.name}"/>
  </h:column>
</t:newspaperTable>
```

The panelNavigation Component

Tag name: **<t:panelNavigation>**

Component class: **org.apache.myfaces.custom.navigation.HtmlPanelNavigation**
Component type: **org.apache.myfaces.HtmlPanelNavigation**

The **panelNavigation** component is used to render a clickable menu composed of menu items created using the **commandNavigation** component.

NOTE *Although the* **panelNavigation** *component and the associated* **commandNavigation** *component are still included in the Tomahawk library, they have been supplanted by the* **panelNavigation2** *and* **commandNavigation2** *components, respectively.*

Core Attributes

Attribute	Type	Description	Required
activeItemClass	String	Specifies the CSS style class for the component's active menu item.	No
activeItemStyle	String	Specifies the CSS style for the component's active menu item.	No
binding	String	See "Common Attributes" section.	No
id	String	See "Common Attributes" section.	No
itemClass	String	Specifies the CSS style class for the component's menu items.	No
itemStyle	String	Specifies the CSS style for the component's menu items.	No
openItemClass	String	Specifies the CSS style class for the component's open menu items.	No
openItemStyle	String	Specifies the CSS style for the component's open menu items.	No
rendered	String	See "Common Attributes" section.	No
separatorClass	String	Specifies the CSS style class for the component's menu separators.	No
separatorStyle	String	Specifies the CSS style for the component's menu separators.	No

HTML Attributes

Attribute	Type	Description	Required
align, border, bgcolor, cellpadding, cellspacing, datafld, datasrc, dataformatas, dir, frame, lang, rules, style, styleClass, summary, title, width	String	Each of the HTML attributes corresponds one-to-one with an HTML attribute of the same name as the rendered HTML tag.	No

JavaScript Attributes

Attribute	Type	Description	Required
onclick, ondblclick, onkeydown, onkeypress, onkeyup, onmousedown, onmousemove, onmouseout, onmouseover, onmouseup	String	Each of the JavaScript attributes corresponds one-to-one with a JavaScript attribute of the same name as the rendered HTML tag.	No

Example Usage

```
<t:panelNavigation id="linkMenu">
  <t:commandNavigation action="gotoMenuItem1">
    <h:outputText value="Menu Item 1"/>
  </t:commandNavigation>
  <t:commandNavigation action="gotoMenuItem2">
    <h:outputText value="Menu Item 2"/>
  </t:commandNavigation>
</t:panelNavigation>
```

The panelNavigation2 Component

Tag name: **<t:panelNavigation2>**
Component class: **org.apache.myfaces.custom.navmenu.htmlnavmenu**
.HtmlPanelNavigationMenu
Component type: **org.apache.myfaces.HtmlPanelNavigationMenu**
    The **panelNavigation2** component is used to render a clickable menu composed of menu items created using the **commandNavigation2** component.

Core Attributes

Attribute	Type	Description	Required
activeItemClass	String	Specifies the CSS style class for the component's active menu item.	No
activeItemStyle	String	Specifies the CSS style for the component's active menu item.	No
binding	String	See "Common Attributes" section.	No
id	String	See "Common Attributes" section.	No
itemClass	String	Specifies the CSS style class for the component's menu items.	No
itemStyle	String	Specifies the CSS style for the component's menu items.	No
openItemClass	String	Specifies the CSS style class for the component's open menu items.	No

Attribute	Type	Description	Required
openItemStyle	String	Specifies the CSS style for the component's open menu items.	No
rendered	String	See "Common Attributes" section.	No
separatorClass	String	Specifies the CSS style class for the component's menu separators.	No
separatorStyle	String	Specifies the CSS style for the component's menu separators.	No

HTML Attributes

Attribute	Type	Description	Required
align, border, bgcolor, cellpadding, cellspacing, datafld, datasrc, dataformatas, dir, frame, lang, rules, style, styleClass, summary, title, width	String	Each of the HTML attributes corresponds one-to-one with an HTML attribute of the same name as the rendered HTML tag.	No

JavaScript Attributes

Attribute	Type	Description	Required
onclick, ondblclick, onkeydown, onkeypress, onkeyup, onmousedown, onmousemove, onmouseout, onmouseover, onmouseup,	String	Each of the JavaScript attributes corresponds one-to-one with a JavaScript attribute of the same name as the rendered HTML tag.	No

Example Usage

```
<t:panelNavigation2 id="linkMenu">
  <t:commandNavigation2 action="gotoMenuItem1">
    <h:outputText value="Menu Item 1"/>
  </t:commandNavigation2>
  <t:commandNavigation2 action="gotoMenuItem2">
    <h:outputText value="Menu Item 2"/>
  </t:commandNavigation2>
</t:panelNavigation2>
```

The panelStack Component

Tag name: **<t:panelStack>**
Component class: **org.apache.myfaces.custom.panelstack.HtmlPanelStack**
Component type: **org.apache.myfaces.HtmlPanelStack**

The **panelStack** component is used to create a group of stacked panels where each panel is stacked on top of one another and one panel is visible.

Attributes

Attribute	Type	Description	Required
id	String	See "Common Attributes" section.	No
selectedPanel	String	Specifies the name of the panel that should be visible (selected).	Yes

Example Usage

```
<t:panelStack id="stack" selectedPanel="#{stackBean.selected}">
  <h:panelGroup id="panel1">
    <h:outputText value="Panel 1"/>
  </h:panelGroup>
  <h:panelGroup id="panel2">
    <h:outputText value="Panel 2"/>
  </h:panelGroup>
</t:panelStack>
```

The panelTab Component

Tag name: **<t:panelTab>**
Component class: **org.apache.myfaces.custom.tabbedpane.HtmlPanelTab**
Component type: **org.apache.myfaces.HtmlPanelTab**

The **panelTab** component is used to create an individual tab panel for a tabbed pane defined by the **panelTabbedPane** component.

Core Attributes

Attribute	Type	Description	Required
binding	String	See "Common Attributes" section.	No
enabledOnUserRole	String	See "Common Attributes" section.	No
id	String	See "Common Attributes" section.	No
label	String	Specifies the value that will be displayed on the panel's tab.	No
rendered	String	See "Common Attributes" section.	No
visibleOnUserRole	String	See "Common Attributes" section.	No

HTML Attributes

Attribute	Type	Description	Required
dir, land, style, styleClass, title	String	Each of the HTML attributes corresponds one-to-one with an HTML attribute of the same name as the rendered HTML tag.	No

JavaScript Attributes

Attribute	Type	Description	Required
onclick, ondblclick, onkeydown, onkeypress, onkeyup, onmousedown, onmousemove, onmouseout, onmouseover, onmouseup	String	Each of the JavaScript attributes corresponds one-to-one with a JavaScript attribute of the same name as the rendered HTML tag.	No

Example Usage

```
<t:panelTabbedPane>
  <t:panelTab id="tab1" label="Tab 1">
    <h:outputText value="Tab 1"/>
  </t:panelTab>
  <t:panelTab id="tab2" label="Tab 2">
    <h:outputText value="Tab 2"/>
  </t:panelTab>
</t:panelTabbedPane>
```

The panelTabbedPane Component

Tag name: **<t:panelTabbedPane>**
Component class: **org.apache.myfaces.custom.tabbedpane.HtmlTabbedPane**
Component type: **org.apache.myfaces.HtmlPanelTabbedPane**

The **panelTabbedPane** component is used to create a tabbed pane consisting of multiple tab panels defined by the **panelTab** component. Each tab panel has its own tab with a label that, when clicked, activates that tab and makes its content visible.

Core Attributes

Attribute	Type	Description	Required
activeSubStyleClass	String	Specifies the CSS style class for the active subtab.	No
activeTabStyleClass	String	Specifies the CSS style class for the active tab.	No
binding	String	See "Common Attributes" section.	No
disabledTabStyleClass	String	Specifies the CSS style class for disabled tabs.	No
enabledOnUserRole	String	See "Common Attributes" section.	No
id	String	See "Common Attributes" section.	No
inactiveSubStyleClass	String	Specifies the CSS style class for the inactive subtabs.	No
inactiveTabStyleClass	String	Specifies the CSS style class for the inactive tabs.	No

Attribute	Type	Description	Required
rendered	String	See "Common Attributes" section.	No
selectedIndex	Int	Specifies the index of the tab that will be selected by default.	No
tabContentStyleClass	String	Specifies the CSS style class for the content area of the active tab.	No
visibleOnUserRole	String	See "Common Attributes" section.	No

HTML Attributes

Attribute	Type	Description	Required
align, border, bgcolor, cellpadding, cellspacing, datafld, datasrc, dataformatas, dir, frame, lang, rules, style, styleClass, summary, title, width	String	Each of the HTML attributes corresponds one-to-one with an HTML attribute of the same name as the rendered HTML tag.	No

JavaScript Attributes

Attribute	Type	Description	Required
onclick, ondblclick, onkeydown, onkeypress, onkeyup, onmousedown, onmousemove, onmouseout, onmouseover, onmouseup	String	Each of the JavaScript attributes corresponds one-to-one with a JavaScript attribute of the same name as the rendered HTML tag.	No

Example Usage

```
<t:panelTabbedPane>
  <t:panelTab id="tab1" label="Tab 1">
    <h:outputText value="Tab 1"/>
  </t:panelTab>
  <t:panelTab id="tab2" label="Tab 2">
    <h:outputText value="Tab 2"/>
  </t:panelTab>
</t:panelTabbedPane>
```

The popup Component

Tag name: **<t:popup>**
Component class: **org.apache.myfaces.custom.popup.HtmlPopup**
Component type: **org.apache.myfaces.HtmlPopup**

The **popup** component is used to display a user-defined tool tip (pop-up) when a specified element is moused over.

Core Attributes

Attribute	Type	Description	Required
binding	String	See "Common Attributes" section.	No
closePopupOnExitingElement	boolean	Accepts true or false to specify whether the pop-up should be closed when the mouse has left the triggering element. Defaults to false.	No
closePopupOnExitingPopup	boolean	Accepts true or false to specify whether the pop-up should be closed when the mouse has left the pop-up itself. Defaults to false.	No
displayAtDistanceX	Int	Specifies the number of horizontal pixels from the event location at which the pop-up should be displayed.	No
displayAtDistanceY	Int	Specifies the number of vertical pixels from the event location at which the pop-up should be displayed.	No
enabledOnUserRole	String	See "Common Attributes" section.	No
id	String	See "Common Attributes" section.	No
rendered	String	See "Common Attributes" section.	No
visibleOnUserRole	String	See "Common Attributes" section.	No

HTML Attributes

Attribute	Type	Description	Required
dir, lang, style, styleClass, title	String	Each of the HTML attributes corresponds one-to-one with an HTML attribute of the same name as the rendered HTML tag.	No

JavaScript Attributes

Attribute	Type	Description	Required
onclick, ondblclick, onkeydown, onkeypress, onkeyup, onmousedown, onmousemove, onmouseout, onmouseover, onmouseup	String	Each of the JavaScript attributes corresponds one-to-one with a JavaScript attribute of the same name as the rendered HTML tag.	No

Example Usage

```
<t:popup>
  <h:outputText value="This text will have the tooltip."/>
  <f:facet name="popup">
    <h:outputText value="This is the content inside the popup"/>
  </f:facet>
</t:popup>
```

The radio Component

Tag name: **<t:radio>**
Component class: **org.apache.myfaces.custom.radio.HtmlRadio**
Component type: **org.apache.myfaces.HtmlRadio**

The **radio** component is used to render an HTML radio control populated with data from a **selectOneRadio** component whose layout is set to **spread**.

Attributes

Attribute	Type	Description	Required
binding	String	See "Common Attributes" section.	No
enabledOnUserRole	String	See "Common Attributes" section.	No
for	String	Specifies the ID of the **selectOneRadio** component whose data will be used for this component.	Yes
id	String	See "Common Attributes" section.	No
index	String	Specifies the (0-based) index of the **selectOneRadio** component's select item that will be used to populate this component.	Yes
rendered	String	See "Common Attributes" section.	No
visibleOnUserRole	String	See "Common Attributes" section.	No

Example Usage

```
<t:selectOneRadio id="colors" layout="spread">
  <f:selectItem itemValue="0" itemLabel="Red"/>
  <f:selectItem itemValue="1" itemLabel="Green"/>
  <f:selectItem itemValue="2" itemLabel="Blue"/>
</t:selectOneRadio>

<t:radio for="colors" index="0"/>
<t:radio for="colors" index="1"/>
```

The saveState Component

Tag name: **<t:saveState>**
Component class: **org.apache.myfaces.custom.savestate.UISaveState**
Component type: **org.apache.myfaces.SaveState**

The **saveState** component is used to save arbitrary objects with the same scope as the JSF component tree. This scope persists objects longer than request scope, but shorter than session scope.

NOTE *Any objects stored using this component must implement the* **java.io.Serializable** *interface.*

Attributes

Attribute	Type	Description	Required
id	String	See "Common Attributes" section.	No
value	String	Specifies the value that should be saved. This can either be an expression that evaluates to a value or a hard-coded value.	Yes

Example Usage

```
<t:saveState id="savedForm" value="#{myForm}"/>
```

The selectOneCountry Component

Tag name: **<t:selectOneCountry>**
Component class: **org.apache.myfaces.custom.selectOneCountry.SelectOneCountry**
Component type: **org.apache.myfaces.SelectOneCountry**

The **selectOneCountry** component is used to render a **selectOne** component populated with the list of ISO 3166 countries.

Core Attributes

Attribute	Type	Description	Required
binding	String	See "Common Attributes" section.	No
converter	String	See "Common Attributes" section.	No
displayValueOnly	boolean	See "Common Attributes" section.	No
displayValueOnlyStyle	String	See "Common Attributes" section.	No
displayValueOnlyStyleClass	String	See "Common Attributes" section.	No
enabledOnUserRole	String	See "Common Attributes" section.	No
forceId	String	See "Common Attributes" section.	No
forceIdIndex	String	See "Common Attributes" section.	No
id	String	See "Common Attributes" section.	No
immediate	String	See "Common Attributes" section.	No
maxLength	Int	Specifies the maximum number of characters of the country name to display.	No
rendered	String	See "Common Attributes" section.	No
required	String	See "Common Attributes" section.	No
validator	String	See "Common Attributes" section.	No
value	String	See "Common Attributes" section.	No
valueChangeListener	String	See "Common Attributes" section.	No
visibleOnUserRole	String	See "Common Attributes" section.	No

PART IV

HTML Attributes

Attribute	Type	Description	Required
cellpadding, cellspacing, datafld, datasrc, dataformatas, dir, disabled, disabledclass, enabledclass, lang, readonly, style, styleClass, tabindex, title	String	Each of the HTML attributes corresponds one-to-one with an HTML attribute of the same name as the rendered HTML tag.	No

JavaScript Attributes

Attribute	Type	Description	Required
onblur, onchange, onclick, ondblclick, onfocus, onkeydown, onkeypress, onkeyup, onmousedown, onmousemove, onmouseout, onmouseover, onmouseup	String	Each of the JavaScript attributes corresponds one-to-one with a JavaScript attribute of the same name as the rendered HTML tag.	No

Example Usage

```
<t:selectOneCountry maxLength="25"/>
```

The selectOneLanguage Component

Tag name: **<t:selectOneLanguage>**
Component class: **org.apache.myfaces.custom.selectOneLanguage.SelectOneLanguage**
Component type: **org.apache.myfaces.SelectOneLanguage**

The **selectOneLanguage** component is used to render a **selectOne** component populated with the list of ISO 639 languages.

Core Attributes

Attribute	Type	Description	Required
binding	String	See "Common Attributes" section.	No
converter	String	See "Common Attributes" section.	No
displayValueOnly	boolean	See "Common Attributes" section.	No
displayValueOnlyStyle	String	See "Common Attributes" section.	No
displayValueOnlyStyle Class	String	See "Common Attributes" section.	No
enabledOnUserRole	String	See "Common Attributes" section.	No
forceId	String	See "Common Attributes" section.	No
forceIdIndex	String	See "Common Attributes" section.	No

Attribute	Type	Description	Required
id	String	See "Common Attributes" section.	No
immediate	String	See "Common Attributes" section.	No
maxLength	Int	Specifies the maximum number of characters of the language name to display.	No
rendered	String	See "Common Attributes" section.	No
required	String	See "Common Attributes" section.	No
validator	String	See "Common Attributes" section.	No
value	String	See "Common Attributes" section.	No
valueChangeListener	String	See "Common Attributes" section.	No
visibleOnUserRole	String	See "Common Attributes" section.	No

HTML Attributes

Attribute	Type	Description	Required
cellpadding, cellspacing, datafld, datasrc, dataformatas, dir, disabled, disabledclass, enabledclass, lang, readonly, style, styleClass, tabindex, title	String	Each of the HTML attributes corresponds one-to-one with an HTML attribute of the same name as the rendered HTML tag.	No

JavaScript Attributes

Attribute	Type	Description	Required
onblur, onchange, onclick, ondblclick, onfocus, onkeydown, onkeypress, onkeyup, onmousedown, onmousemove, onmouseout, onmouseover, onmouseup	String	Each of the JavaScript attributes corresponds one-to-one with a JavaScript attribute of the same name as the rendered HTML tag.	No

Example Usage

```
<t:selectOneLanguage maxLength="25"/>
```

The stylesheet Component

Tag name: **<t:stylesheet>**
Component class: **org.apache.myfaces.custom.stylesheet.Stylesheet**
Component type: **org.apache.myfaces.Stylesheet**

The **stylesheet** component is used to render a link to a cascading style sheet or to inline the contents of the specified style sheet.

Attributes

Attribute	Type	Description	Required
binding	String	See "Common Attributes" section.	No
enabledOnUserRole	String	See "Common Attributes" section.	No
inline	boolean	Accepts true or false to specify whether the style sheet contents should be output inline. Defaults to false.	No
path	String	Specifies the URL to the style sheet. This may be a fully qualified URL to an external resource or a URL to a server-local resource.	Yes
id	String	See "Common Attributes" section.	No
rendered	String	See "Common Attributes" section.	No
visibleOnUserRole	String	See "Common Attributes" section.	No

Example Usage

```
<t:stylesheet path="/css/site.css"/>
```

The tree Component

Tag name: **<t:tree>**
Component class: **org.apache.myfaces.custom.tree.HtmlTree**
Component type: **org.apache.myfaces.HtmlTree**

The **tree** component is used to render a tree component that allows users to traverse nodes of data.

Attributes

Attribute	Type	Description	Required
columnClasses	String	Specifies a comma-delimited list of CSS classes to be applied to the columns.	No
expandRoot	boolean	Accepts true or false to specify whether the root node of the tree should be expanded. Defaults to false.	No
expireListeners	Long	Specifies the number of seconds that the tree will remain registered as a listener before being expired.	No
footerClass	String	Specifies the CSS class for the tree footer.	No

Attribute	Type	Description	Required
headerClass	String	Specifies the CSS class for the tree header.	No
iconChildFirst	String	Specifies the URL for the icon of first child nodes.	No
iconChildLast	String	Specifies the URL for the icon of last child nodes.	No
iconChildMiddle	String	Specifies the URL for the icon of middle child nodes.	No
iconClass	String	Specifies the CSS class for icons.	No
iconLine	String	Specifies the URL for the icon for node lines.	No
iconNodeClose	String	Specifies the URL for the icon for closed nodes.	No
iconNodeCloseFirst	String	Specifies the URL for the icon of first closed nodes.	No
iconNodeCloseLast	String	Specifies the URL for the icon of last closed nodes.	No
iconNodeCloseMiddle	String	Specifies the URL for the icon of middle closed nodes.	No
iconNodeOpen	String	Specifies the URL for the icon for open nodes.	No
iconNodeOpenFirst	String	Specifies the URL for the icon of first open nodes.	No
iconNodeOpenLast	String	Specifies the URL for the icon of last open nodes.	No
iconNodeOpenMiddle	String	Specifies the URL for the icon of middle open nodes.	No
iconNoLine	String	Specifies the URL for the icon for nodes without lines.	No
id	String	See "Common Attributes" section.	No
nodeClass	String	Specifies the CSS class for the nodes.	No
rowClasses	String	Specifies a comma-delimited list of CSS classes to be applied to the rows.	No
selectedNodeClass	String	Specifies the CSS class for the selected node.	No
styleClass	String	Specifies the CSS class for the tree.	No
value	String	See "Common Attributes" section.	No
var	String	Specifies the name of the JSP variable that will be populated with the current node's object.	No

Example Usage

```
<t:tree id="tree" value="#{resultsForm.treeModel}"/>
```

The tree2 Component

Tag name: **<t:tree2>**
Component class: **org.apache.myfaces.custom.tree2.HtmlTree**
Component type: **org.apache.myfaces.HtmlTree2**

The **tree2** component is used to render a tree component that allows users to traverse nodes of data. The **tree2** component is newer than the other **tree** components and more popular.

---

*NOTE   Use of the **tree2** component can require that the MyFaces Extensions Filter be set up in your application's **web.xml** file. This is because the component uses the filter to serve some resources if no alternative is specified. You must also create a backing bean that contains an **org.apache** .**myfaces.custom.tree2.TreeNode** field to store the tree data in. The **TreeNode** field must be bound to the **tree2** component using the **value** attribute. There are two implementations of **TreeNode** available: **TreeNodeBase** and **TreeNodeChecked**. **TreeNodeChecked** inherits **TreeNodeBase** and adds some conveniences for using checkboxes inside the tree.*

Attributes

Attribute	Type	Description	Required
value	String	See "Common Attributes" section.	Yes
var	String	Variable that will be populated with the current node's object.	No
varNodeToggler	String	Variable used for expanding and collapsing nodes. Also possible to set via an **actionListener** an active node.	No
showNav	String	Shows the icons for "plus" and "minus" on the navigation. Default value is true and this attribute is ignored if **clientSideToggle** is true.	No
showLines	String	Shows the connecting lines between the icons. Default value is true.	No
clientSideToggle	String	Uses client-side toggling (with JavaScript) for expand and collapse. Default value is true.	No
showRootNode	String	Identifies if the root node should be displayed. Default value is true.	No
preServeToggle	String	Preserves changes in client-side toggle information between requests. Default value is true.	No
javascriptLocation	String	Specifies an alternative resource for JavaScript. If not set, the default JavaScript will be served by ExtensionsFilter.	No

Attribute	Type	Description	Required
imageLocation	String	Specifies an alternative resource for the images. If not set, the default images are served by ExtensionsFilter.	No
styleLocation	String	Specifies an alternative resource for style sheet. If not set, the default style sheet will be served by ExtensionsFilter.	No
id	String	See "Common Attributes" section.	No
binding	String	See "Common Attributes" section.	No
rendered	String	See "Common Attributes" section.	No

Example Usage

```
<t:tree2 id="tree" value="#{tree.tree}" clientSideToggle="true"
  varNodeToggler="t" var="node">
  <f:facet name="facetName_analysisFolder">
    <h:panelGroup>
      <h:selectBooleanCheckbox value="#{node.checked}" />
      <t:graphicImage value="images/yellow-folder-closed.png" border="0"/>
      <h:outputText value="#{node.description}" styleClass="nodeFolder"/>
    </h:panelGroup>
  </f:facet>
  <f:facet name="facetName_root">
<h:panelGroup>
  <t:graphicImage value="images/yellow-folder-closed.png" border="0"/>
  <h:outputText value="#{node.description}" styleClass="nodeFolder"/>
</h:panelGroup>
</f:facet>
</t:tree2>
```

The following is an example backing bean in which to store the tree data. Note that the bean must have some classes from the **org.apache.myfaces.custom.tree2** package imported.

```
import org.apache.myfaces.custom.tree2.TreeNode;
import org.apache.myfaces.custom.tree2.TreeNodeBase;
import org.apache.myfaces.custom.tree2.TreeNodeChecked;

public class TreeBacking {

  public TreeBacking() {

    tree = new TreeNodeBase("facetName_root","displayName", false);

    tree.getChildren().add(
      new TreeNodeChecked("facetName_analysisFolder", "displayName" ,
    "id", false, true));
}
  }
  private TreeNode tree;
```

PART IV

```
  public TreeNode getTree() {
    return tree;
  }

  public void setFile(TreeNode tree) {
    this.tree = tree;
  }
}
```

The treeColumn Component

Tag name: **<t:treeColumn>**
Component class: **org.apache.myfaces.custom.tree.HtmlTreeColumn**
Component type: **org.apache.myfaces.HtmlTreeColumn**

The **treeColumn** component is used to make a **tree** component render as a table with one column (defined by this component) displayed as the tree. The other columns are normal table columns.

Attributes

Attribute	Type	Description	Required
binding	String	See "Common Attributes" section.	No
id	String	See "Common Attributes" section.	No
rendered	String	See "Common Attributes" section.	No

Example Usage

```
<t:tree id="tableTree" value="#{resultsForm.treeModel}" var="treeItem">
  <t:treeColumn>
    <h:outputText value="#{treeItem.name}"/>
  </t:treeColumn>
  <h:column>
    <h:outputText value="#{treeItem.description}"/>
  </h:column>
</t:tree>
```

The updateActionListener Tag

Tag name: **<t:updateActionListener>**
Component class: **org.apache.myfaces.custom.updateactionlistener.UpdateActionListener**
Component type: **none**

The **updateActionListener** is not a custom component in the sense of the JavaServer Faces specification. It is a specialized **ActionListener** implementation, useful when dealing with http parameters. Instead of adding lots of parameters with the **<f:param>** tag to a

<h:commandLink>, the **UpdateActionListener** is able to push a complete object to another backing bean.

Attributes

Attribute	Type	Description	Required
property	String	Specifies a property that will be updated, when the parent action occurs.	Yes
value	String	Specifies the value that will be assigned to the specified property.	Yes
converter	String	Specifies the name of a registered converter object that will be invoked to convert the value into an appropriate datatype for assigning to the specified property. If not specified, then an appropriate converter will be selected automatically.	No

Example Usage

```
<h:dataTable id="masterTable" value="#{masterBean.data}" var="current" ...>
    ...
    <h:commandLink action="showDetails">
        <h:grapicImage ...>
        <t:updateActionListener value="#{current}"
                    property="#{detailBean.entry}" />
    </h:commandLink>
    ...

</h:dataTable>
```

The MyFaces Custom Validators

The MyFaces Tomahawk library provides a set of custom validators that extend beyond what is provided by the JSF specification. Currently, the majority of the MyFaces custom validators are wrappers for validation routines provided by the Jakarta Commons Validator framework. The MyFaces validators simply proxy validation calls to the underlying Jakarta Commons validation routines for processing. Leveraging the Jakarta Commons code reduces code duplication and provides a familiar set of validation routines to those users who have used those routines in other frameworks, such as Struts. For more information on the Jakarta Commons Validator framework, visit the Jakarta Commons Web site at **http://jakarta .apache.org/ commons/validator/**.

Table 20-4 lists each of the MyFaces custom validators and a short description of each validator's purpose.

The remainder of this section discusses each validator in detail, including a complete description of the validator, a table listing each of the validator's attributes, and a usage example for the validator.

In the tables that describe each validator's attributes, pay special attention to the Required column. It simply denotes whether or not the given attribute is required when using the validator. If an attribute is required and you do not specify it when using the validator, the validator will throw a **javax.servlet.jsp.JspException** at runtime. Note that you can declare an error page in your JSP with a **page** directive to capture any **JspException**s that might be thrown, as shown here:

```
<%@ page errorPage="error.jsp" %>
```

If an exception occurs, the page specified by the **errorPage** attribute will be internally redirected to display an error page.

The validateCreditCard Validator

The **validateCreditCard** validator is used to determine whether or not the value of the enclosing UI component is a valid credit card number. It supports validating that the value is a valid American Express, Discover, MasterCard, or Visa credit card number. Each of these credit card type validations can be individually enabled or disabled using attributes of the **validateCreditCard** validator. By default, **validateCreditCard** validates the UI component value to be any of the supported credit card type numbers. The **none** attribute provides a convenient mechanism for disabling all credit card type number validations.

Validator	Description
validateCreditCard	Determines whether or not the value of the enclosing UI component is a valid credit card number.
validateEmail	Determines whether or not the value of the enclosing UI component is a valid e-mail address.
validateEqual	Determines whether or not the value of the enclosing UI component equals the value of another specified UI component.
validateRegExpr	Determines whether or not the value of the enclosing UI component matches the specified regular expression.

TABLE 20-4   The MyFaces Custom Validators

Attributes

Attribute	Type	Description	Required
amex	boolean	Accepts true or false to specify whether the UI component value should be validated as an American Express credit card number.

Defaults to true. | No |
| discover | boolean | Accepts true or false to specify whether the UI component value should be validated as a Discover credit card number.

Defaults to true. | No |
| mastercard | boolean | Accepts true or false to specify whether the UI component value should be validated as a MasterCard credit card number.

Defaults to true. | No |
| none | boolean | Accepts true or false to specify whether the UI component value should *not* be validated against each of the individual credit card type validations. This attribute provides a convenient mechanism for disabling all of the credit card type validations in one easy place. For example, during testing it may be helpful to set this attribute to true to turn off all credit card type validations instead of having to set each of the individual type attributes to false.

Defaults to false. | No |
| visa | boolean | Accepts true or false to specify whether the UI component value should be validated as a Visa credit card number.

Defaults to true. | No |

Example Usage

The following example illustrates the basic usage of the **validateCreditCard** validator:

```
<h:inputText id="creditCardNumber"
        value="#{paymentForm.creditCardNumber}"
     required="true">
  <t:validateCreditCard/>
</h:inputText>
```

This tag will look up the value of the **inputText** UI component and perform the validation against that value. Because no attributes have been specified for the **validateCreditCard** tag and all of the credit card type attributes default to true when not specified, the value specified will be validated to be a valid number for one of the credit card types.

The validateEmail Validator

The **validateEmail** validator is used to determine whether or not the value of the enclosing UI component is a valid e-mail address. The e-mail address validation is performed by checking the format of the e-mail address. The validation ensures that the address has an "@" symbol as well as other common format characteristics. If the address does not conform to the common format characteristics, it will be deemed invalid.

Example Usage

The following example illustrates the basic usage of the **validateEmail** validator:

```
<h:inputText id="emailAddress"
        value="#{paymentForm.emailAddress}"
        required="true">
  <t:validateEmail/>
</h:inputText>
```

This tag will look up the value of the **inputText** UI component and perform the validation against that value.

An alternative way to use the **validateEmail** validator is to use the standard JSF validator and specify **validateEmail** with the **validatorId** attribute, as shown here:

```
<h:inputText id="emailAddress"
        value="#{paymentForm.emailAddress}"
        required="true">
  <f:validator validatorId="org.apache.myfaces.validator.Email"/>
</h:inputText>
```

The validateEqual Validator

The **validateEqual** validator is used to determine whether or not the value of the enclosing UI component equals the value of another specified UI component. This validator is especially useful for the scenario where it is necessary to validate that a user has input the same value into two separate fields on a form (e.g., password and password confirm).

NOTE *When using the **validateEqual** validator, the component referenced by the **for** attribute must exist in the JSF component tree before the component to which the **validateEqual** validator is being applied. For example, if the **validateEqual** validator is being used to validate if a **passwordConfirm** field value is equal to the value in a **password** field, the **password** field must exist in the JSF component tree before the **passwordConfirm** field in order for the **validateEqual** validator to work.*

Attributes

Attribute	Type	Description	Required
for	String	Specifies the component ID of another component that the component associated to this validator should have its value validated against for equality.	Yes

Example Usage

The following example illustrates the basic usage of the **validateEqual** validator:

```
<h:inputText id="password"
         value="#{paymentForm.password}"
      required="true">
  <t:validateEqual for="passwordConfirm"/>
</h:inputText>
```

This tag will look up the value of the **inputText** UI component and perform the validation against that value.

The validateRegExpr Validator

The **validateRegExpr** validator is used to determine whether or not the value of the enclosing UI component matches the specified regular expression. A *regular expression* is a group of characters that describes a character sequence. This general description, called a *pattern*, can then be used to find matches in other character sequences. Regular expressions can specify wildcard characters, sets of characters, and various quantifiers. Thus, you can specify a regular expression that represents a general form that can match several different specific character sequences.

The syntax and rules that define a regular expression are similar to those used by the Perl programming language. Although no single rule is complicated, there are a large number of them and a complete discussion is beyond the scope of this book. However, a few of the more commonly used constructs are described here.

In general, a regular expression is comprised of normal characters, character classes (sets of characters), wildcard characters, and quantifiers. A normal character is matched as is. Thus, if a pattern consists of "xy", the only input sequence that will match it is "xy". Characters such as newlines and tabs are specified using the standard escape sequences, which begin with a backslash (\). For example, a newline is specified by **\n**. In the language of regular expressions, a normal character is also called a *literal*.

A character class is a set of characters. A character class is specified by putting the characters in the class between brackets. For example, the class **[wxyz]** matches w, x, y, or z. To specify an inverted set, precede the characters with a circumflex (**^**). For example, **[^wxyz]** matches any character except w, x, y, or z. You can specify a range of characters using a hyphen. For example, to specify a character class that will match the digits 1 through 9, use **[1–9]**.

The wildcard character is the dot (.), and it matches any character. Thus, a pattern that consists of "." will match these (and other) input sequences: "A", "a", "x", and so on.

A quantifier determines how many times an expression is matched. The quantifiers are shown here:

+	Match one or more.
*	Match zero or more.
?	Match zero or one.

For example, the pattern **x+** will match **x**, **xx**, and **xxx**, among others.

For more information on regular expressions, visit the comprehensive review of them on the Wikipedia encyclopedia Web site at **http://en.wikipedia.org/wiki/Regular_expression**.

Attributes

Attribute	Type	Description	Required
pattern	String	Specifies the regular expression pattern that will be used to determine the validity of the UI component value.	Yes

Example Usage

The following example illustrates the basic usage of the **validateRegExpr** validator:

```
<h:inputText id="ssNumber"
        value="#{paymentForm.ssNumber}"
      required="true">
  <t:validateRegExpr pattern="^\d{3}-\d{2}-\d{4}$"/>
</h:inputText>
```

This tag will look up the value of the **inputText** UI component and perform the validation against that value. The regular expression specified here with the **pattern** attribute is for matching a Social Security Number (e.g., 333-22-4444). The expression expects the value to have three digits followed by a hyphen followed by two digits followed by a hyphen and finally followed by four digits. If the UI component's value does not match that pattern, the validation will fail.

The MyFaces Support for the Tiles Framework

In addition to the many extended components, custom components, and custom validations provided by the MyFaces Tomahawk library, there is support for using the Tiles framework with JSF. Tiles is a user interface layout framework that was originally developed as an extension to the Struts framework. Tiles has become very popular and its usefulness extends beyond just Struts-based applications. Tiles can be used to simplify and enhance all Java Web applications. This section provides an overview of the Tiles framework followed by step-by-step instructions for using the MyFaces support for Tiles with JSF applications.

Tiles Overview

Tiles expands the concept of code reuse via JSP *includes* by allowing you to define layouts (or templates) and then specify how the layouts are populated with content. To understand the value of Tiles, first consider how the JSP include paradigm works. Each JSP specifies its layout and explicitly populates that layout through includes. Most JSP layouts are identical, sourcing in the same files, in the same places, and then having a section of unique content, which is usually body content. Thus, there is significant duplication. Tiles takes the reverse approach.

With Tiles, you define a master layout JSP that specifies each of the includes that fill in the layout and then you define which content should fill in the layout in an external configuration file. The same layout can be used over and over by simply specifying different filler content for the layout in the configuration file.

For example, consider a typical Web site layout that has a header at the top of the page, a menu on the left, body content in the middle, and a footer on the bottom, as shown in Figure 20-1. If you were to implement this page using only JSP includes, each JSP that has this layout would have to explicitly include the header, menu, and footer sections of the page, and the body content would be in the JSP itself. Essentially, the only unique part of the page is the body content.

Alternatively, if you were to implement this layout with Tiles, you'd create one JSP that includes the header, menu, and footer and then dynamically include the body based on a parameter passed to the layout that indicates which JSP to use for the body content. This Tiles layout could then be reused for as many pages as you'd like and the only thing your content JSPs would have to contain is the body content that goes in the middle of the page. Tiles takes care of wrapping the body content JSP with the layout. As you can see, Tiles significantly enhances JSP development and allows for an even greater amount of reuse than JSP includes offer.

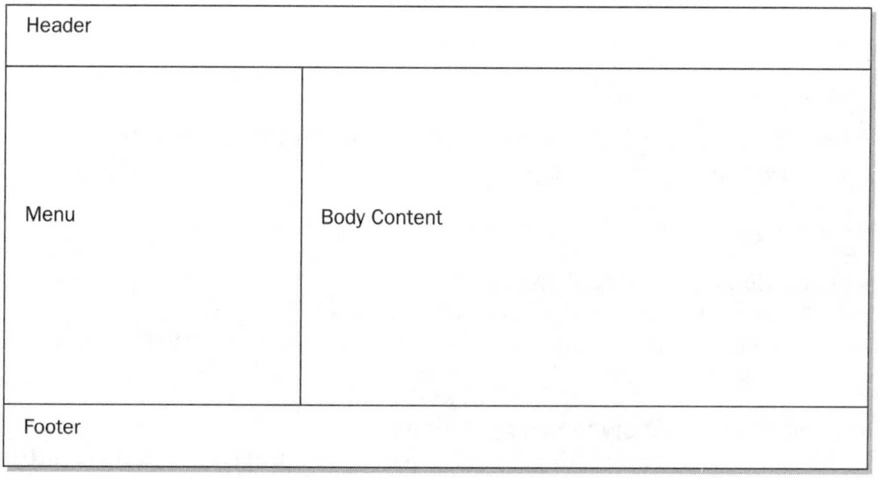

FIGURE 20-1   Typical Web site layout

As described, Tiles allows you to exploit the concept of JSP includes by providing a framework for defining and dynamically populating page layouts. Each page layout is simply a JSP that defines a template frame (or outline) with placeholders for where content should go. At runtime, Tiles replaces the placeholders with their associated content, creating a complete page and unique instance of the layout. To accomplish this, Tiles uses its concepts of *definitions* and *attributes*.

A Tiles definition creates a piece of content that Tiles can insert into a JSP using that definition's name. Each definition consists of a name (or identifier), a layout JSP, and a set of attributes associated to the definition. Once defined, a definition can be included in a page or, as is most often the case, be used as the target of a JSF navigation rule. In both cases, when the definition is encountered, Tiles passes to the layout JSP specified by the definition the set of attributes that were declared for that definition. An attribute value can be the path to a JSP, a literal string, or a list of either.

To facilitate the use of definitions and attributes, Tiles uses an XML configuration file (**tiles-defs.xml**) for storing their definitions. Tiles also provides a JSP tag library for defining definitions and attributes. Additionally, the Tiles Tag Library is used for inserting attributes into JSPs. For an in-depth discussion of the Tiles framework, see the Tiles chapter in *Struts: The Complete Reference* by James Holmes (McGraw-Hill, 2004).

Using the MyFaces Support for Tiles

Now that you've reviewed the benefits of using the Tiles framework and how it works, you are ready to update your application to use Tiles. Here is the list of steps that you will follow to add Tiles to your application:

1. Add Tomahawk library to your application.
2. Download and add the Tiles library to your application.
3. Add Tiles View Handler configuration to the **faces-config.xml** file.
4. Create layout JSPs.
5. Update existing JSPs to work with layouts.
6. Create a **tiles-defs.xml** file.
7. Specify the location of the Tiles configuration file in the **web.xml** file.
8. Repackage and run the updated application.

The following sections walk you through each step of the process in detail.

Add Tomahawk Library to Your Application

Adding the MyFaces Tomahawk library to your Web application is as simple as placing the **tomahawk.jar** and **myfaces-commons.jar** files in your application's **/WEB-INF/lib** directory (or in a directory that your application server has access to via its classpath).

Download and Add Tiles Library to Your Application

As mentioned, the Tiles library is distributed as part of the Struts framework. In order to acquire the Tiles library, you must download a Struts distribution and copy the Tiles library from the distribution to your Web application. Struts has multiple distributions available:

binary, source, and library. You can choose any of these distributions; however, the library distribution is the easiest to work with for this scenario.

NOTE *At the time of this writing, work was underway to separate the Tiles framework from Struts, making it an independent project once again. When that separation is complete, it will only be necessary to download the Tiles distribution to get the Tiles library.*

The Tiles library is contained in the **struts.jar** file that comes packaged with Struts distributions. Simply copy **struts.jar** to your application's **/WEB-INF/lib** directory (or to a directory that your application server has access to via its classpath). Each of the JSPs modified and created to use Tiles must include the following tag library reference:

```
<%@ taglib prefix="tiles" uri="http://struts.apache.org/tags-tiles" %>
```

Add Tiles View Handler Configuration to the faces-config.xml File

In order to integrate Tiles with JSF, the MyFaces custom Tiles View Handler must be used. The Tiles View Handler extends the behavior of the default JSF View Handler by adding in logic to look up Tiles definitions and process accordingly if found. Basically, the Tiles View Handler looks at each view ID passing through and attempts to find a matching Tiles definition inside your Tiles definitions file. If a matching definition is found, the view ID is handled as a Tiles page; otherwise, it is processed normally.

To match view IDs to Tiles definitions, the Tiles View Handler substitutes the view ID's extension with **.tiles** and then looks for a definition in the Tiles definitions file with that name. For example, **/page.jsp** becomes **/page.tiles**. If your application makes use of path mapping instead of extension mapping for JSF pages, **.tiles** will be appended to the path to perform a matching definition lookup. Note that you can modify the extension that the Tiles View Handler uses to match view IDs to Tiles definitions by setting a context parameter in your application's **web.xml** file. Following is an example of doing that.

```
<context-param>
  <param-name>tiles-extension</param-name>
  <param-value>.tilesdef</param-value>
</context-param>
```

The bolded portion of the following snippet is what must be added to your application's **faces-config.xml** file to enable the Tiles View Handler.

```
<faces-config>
  <application>
    <view-handler>
      org.apache.myfaces.application.jsp.JspTilesViewHandlerImpl
    </view-handler>
  </application>
</faces-config>
```

Create Layout JSPs

Now that you have added the necessary libraries to your application and configured the **web.xml** and **faces-config.xml** files, you can create the layout JSPs. To illustrate the basic concepts of Tiles, this section demonstrates how to create one layout based on the structure of the application's existing pages. Following is an example **login.jsp** page that will be used to extract a common template:

```
<%@ taglib prefix="f" uri="http://java.sun.com/jsf/core" %>
<%@ taglib prefix="h" uri="http://java.sun.com/jsf/html" %>

<html>
<head>
<title>Login Page</title>
</head>

<f:view>
<body>

<font size="+1">ABC, Inc. Portal</font><br>
<hr width="100%" noshade="true">

<h:form>
<table>
<tr>
<td align="right">Username:</td>
<td>
<h:inputText id="username"
  value="#{LoginBean.username}" required="true"/>
</td>
</tr>
<tr>
<td align="right">Password:</td>
<td>
<h:inputSecret id="password"
  value="#{LoginBean.password}" required="true"/>
</td>
</tr>
<tr>
<td></td>
<td><h:commandButton value="Login" action="login"/></td>
</tr>
</table>
</h:form>

<hr width="100%" noshade="true">
Copyright &copy; ABC, Inc.

</body>
</f:view>

<html>
```

The body content of the page is shown in bold. This section will be different for each distinct page. The rest of the page, however, will be consistent across several pages, thus allowing it to be abstracted into a general-purpose layout.

There are three JSP files that make up the layout: **mainLayout.jsp**, **header.jsp**, and **footer.jsp**. The **mainLayout.jsp** file is shown here:

```
<%@ taglib prefix="f" uri="http://java.sun.com/jsf/core" %>
<%@ taglib prefix="h" uri="http://java.sun.com/jsf/html" %>
<%@ taglib prefix="tiles" uri="http://struts.apache.org/tags-tiles" %>

<html>
<head>
<title><tiles:getAsString name="title"/></title>
</head>

<f:view>
<body>

<f:subview id="header">
<tiles:insert attribute="header" flush="false"/>
</f:subview>

<f:subview id="body">
<tiles:insert attribute="body" flush="false"/>
</f:subview>

<f:subview id="footer">
<tiles:insert attribute="footer" flush="false"/>
</f:subview>

</body>
</f:view>

</html>
```

This JSP defines the layout's template and is used to source in the other layout JSPs as well as the body content that will be defined by pages utilizing the layout. The body content and other layout JSPs are sourced in with **<tiles:insert>** tags. These tags specify the names of attributes defined in the Tiles configuration file whose values are the names of the JSPs that should be inserted into the JSP at runtime. Observe that each of the **<tiles:insert>** tags is wrapped in **<f:subview>** tags. This is necessary because the Tiles content is dynamically included. Notice also the use of the **<tiles:getAsString>** tag between the **<title>** tags. This tag works similarly to the **<tiles:insert>** tag, but instead of using the specified attribute's value as the name of a page to include, it is used as a literal string. This is useful for defining variables that can be customized by page definitions that extend layout definitions in the Tiles configuration file.

Following are the header and footer layout JSPs.

header.jsp:

```
<font size="+1">ABC, Inc. Portal</font><br>
<hr width="100%" noshade="true">
```

footer.jsp:

```
<hr width="100%" noshade="true">
Copyright &copy; ABC, Inc.
```

As you can see, the header and footer JSPs are quite simple and do not contain much HTML. The content of these JSPs could have been placed directly in the **mainLayout.jsp** file instead of here and content pages would still only have to contain the body content of the page. However, breaking the pages up into smaller chunks allows for more flexibility in how layouts are used. For example, if you wanted all pages to have the standard header and footer, you wouldn't have to worry about changing anything. On the other hand, if you needed some pages to have a custom header and footer and others to use the standard ones, separating the header and footer into discrete chunks would allow you to do that. You would simply define values for the header and footer attributes at the layout level, and each page that wanted a custom header, footer, or both would override the necessary attributes with new values at the page level. This will make more sense after you see the Tiles configuration file, which is discussed shortly.

Update Existing JSPs to Work with Layouts

Once you have created the layout JSPs, the next step is to update your application's original JSPs to contain only the body content of their pages. To do this, you must remove each of the pieces of the original page that were used to craft the common layout. Following is the updated **login.jsp** page containing only body content:

```
<%@ taglib prefix="f" uri="http://java.sun.com/jsf/core" %>
<%@ taglib prefix="h" uri="http://java.sun.com/jsf/html" %>

<h:form>
<table>
<tr>
<td align="right">Username:</td>
<td>
<h:inputText id="username"
  value="#{LoginBean.username}" required="true"/>
</td>
</tr>
<tr>
<td align="right">Password:</td>
<td>
<h:inputSecret id="password"
  value="#{LoginBean.password}" required="true"/>
</td>
</tr>
<tr>
<td></td>
<td><h:commandButton value="Login" action="login"/></td>
</tr>
</table>
</h:form>
```

As you can see, the updated page no longer contains the header or footer portions of the content. At runtime, the layout JSPs will surround the contents of this updated page with the common layout content to create the complete page.

Create a tiles-defs.xml File

As mentioned, there are two ways to declare Tiles layouts: with Tiles tags in a master JSP that gets included into each of the layout JSPs or by declaring them in an XML configuration file. This example uses the configuration file option because it is the most flexible and easy-to-maintain approach. Following is the **tiles-defs.xml** file that declares the layouts. This file should be placed inside your application's **/WEB-INF/** folder.

```xml
<?xml version="1.0"?>

<!DOCTYPE tiles-definitions PUBLIC
  "-//Apache Software Foundation//DTD Tiles Configuration 1.1//EN"
  "http://jakarta.apache.org/struts/dtds/tiles-config_1_1.dtd">

<tiles-definitions>

  <!-- Main Layout -->
  <definition name="main.layout" path="/mainLayout.jsp">
      <put name="title"  value=""/>
      <put name="header" value="/header.jsp"/>
      <put name="body"   value=""/>
      <put name="footer" value="/footer.jsp" />
  </definition>

  <!-- Login Page -->
  <definition name="login.tiles" extends="main.layout">
      <put name="title"  value="Login Page"/>
      <put name="body"   value="/login.jsp"/>
  </definition>

</tiles-definitions>
```

There are two Tiles definitions in this file. The first definition in the file declares a layout named **main.layout**. The **.layout** extension given to the definition's name is used to denote that it is a *layout* definition. This is not a formal naming scheme; however, it is a simple way to distinguish the types of definitions. Generally speaking, layout definitions specify the template for a page and the list of attributes whose values will be used to fill in the template. *Page* definitions extend layout definitions and provide values for the attributes defined in the extended layout. So, essentially, page definitions are instances of a layout with attributes set to the content for a specific page. Remember that in order for the MyFaces Tiles View Handler to identify page definitions, they must have a **.tiles** extension (this extension is configurable).

Notice that the first definition defines four attributes with **put** tags. These attributes will be available for use by the layout JSP specified by the **path** attribute. The layout JSP uses these attributes to supply it with the locations of its content. Additionally, attributes can be used to supply literal strings, as is the case with the **title** attribute. This attribute will be used by **mainLayout.jsp** to enable a dynamic title based on the value set by page definitions that extend the layout definition.

The second definition in the file declares a page definition named **login.tiles**. This definition extends the **main.layout** layout definition and supplies values for the attributes that don't have values in the layout definition. This definition can override any of the attributes in the layout definition if so desired; however, only the **title** and **body** attributes are overridden in this case.

Specify the Location of the Tiles Configuration File in the web.xml File

After creating a **tiles-defs.xml** file for your application, you must update your application's **web.xml** file with a context parameter pointing to the Tiles definitions configuration file, as shown here:

```
<!DOCTYPE web-app PUBLIC
  "-//Sun Microsystems, Inc.//DTD Web Application 2.3//EN"
  "http://java.sun.com/dtd/web-app_2_3.dtd">
<web-app>
  <!-- Tiles Configuration File -->
  <context-param>
    <param-name>tiles-definitions</param-name>
    <param-value>/WEB-INF/tiles-defs.xml</param-value>
  </context-param>
</web-app>
```

The **tiles-definitions** context parameter is used to inform the MyFaces Tiles View Handler of the location of your Tiles definitions configuration file. To use multiple Tiles definitions files, simply delimit them with commas (,) as shown here:

```
<param-value>
  /WEB-INF/tiles-defs.xml,
  /WEB-INF/tiles-defs-2.xml,
  /WEB-INF/tiles-defs-3.xml
</param-value>
```

Repackage and Run the Updated Application

Because no Java code was modified during this process, it's not necessary to recompile your application. However, several files have been added and a few have been modified, so the application needs to be repackaged and redeployed before it is run. Once you have your updated application running, everything should work as it did before. However, now you can add new pages and make global changes to the application with minimal effort.

Appendixes

PART

V

APPENDIX A
Faces Console Quick
Reference

APPENDIX B
Third-Party JSF Component
Libraries

APPENDIX C
Migrating from Struts
to Faces

APPENDIX D
JSF Futures: Apache Shale

Faces Console Quick Reference

A fundamental advantage of using the JavaServer Faces framework for Java Web application development is its declarative nature. Instead of binding components of an application together in code, JavaServer Faces applications use a centralized XML configuration file to declaratively connect components together. Unfortunately, modifying XML configuration files by hand can be tedious and error prone. If you mistakenly leave off a closing bracket for a tag or misspell a tag or attribute name, the XML document becomes invalid; thus, JavaServer Faces is unable to parse the configuration file and does not function properly. Trying to correct errors like these for a typical application, whose configuration file is usually quite long, can be time consuming because of the many details involved. For this reason, the Faces Console GUI tool was created to simplify the creation and maintenance of the JavaServer Faces configuration file. Faces Console provides a simple and intuitive graphical interface with which to edit JavaServer Faces configuration files.

Faces Console has evolved significantly since its initial release and continues to evolve today. Originally, Faces Console supported editing of only Faces configuration files. Since then, Faces Console has been updated to support editing of JSP Tag Library Descriptor (**.tld**) files. Faces Console is written in Java and thus can be run on any platform that supports Java GUI applications (such as Microsoft Windows, Macintosh, GNU/Linux, and so on). In its original release, Faces Console could be run only as a stand-alone application. Subsequently, Faces Console has been updated to support being run as a plug-in in most of the major Java IDEs. Following is the list of IDEs that Faces Console can be used with:

- Borland JBuilder (versions 4.0 and later)
- Eclipse (versions 1.0 and later)
- IBM Rational Application Developer for WebSphere (previously known as WebSphere Studio Application Developer (WSAD)) (versions 4.0.3 and later)
- IntelliJ IDEA (versions 3.0 build 668 and later)
- NetBeans (versions 3.2 and later)
- Oracle JDeveloper (versions 9*i* and later)
- Sun Java Studio (previously known as Forte or Sun ONE Studio) (versions 3.0 and later)

The following sections explain how to acquire, install, and use Faces Console, both as a stand-alone application and as a plug-in inside all the supported IDEs. Because IDEs are continually evolving, some of the instructions for using Faces Console inside the IDEs may change over time. If any of the instructions found in this chapter do not work for you, visit James Holmes' Web site at **www.jamesholmes.com/JavaServerFaces/** for up-to-date instructions.

NOTE *For in-depth coverage on the format of JavaServer Faces configuration files, see Chapter 19. Chapter 19 provides details on each tag and its attributes as well as working examples.*

Supported Configuration Files

As mentioned, the current version of Faces Console supports editing of both JavaServer Faces configuration files and JSP Tag Library Descriptor (**.tld**) files. Both of these are XML-based. In order for Faces Console to distinguish these files from any other type of XML file, they must have a proper XML **<!DOCTYPE>** declaration, or reference a JavaServer Faces schema in the **<faces-config>** tag. The **<!DOCTYPE>** declaration specifies the Document Type Definition (DTD) to which the file must conform, while the schema does the same for JavaServer Faces 1.2 (and later versions) configuration files. Following is a list of the configuration files supported by Faces Console and their corresponding **<!DOCTYPE>** definitions or schema definitions.

The JavaServer Faces 1.2 Configuration File

```
<faces-config xmlns="http://java.sun.com/xml/ns/j2ee"
   xmlns:xsi="http://www.w3.org/2001/XMLSchema-instance"
   xsi:schemaLocation="http://java.sun.com/xml/ns/j2ee http://java.sun.com/xml/ns/
j2ee/web-facesconfig_1_2.xsd"
   version="1.2">
```

The JavaServer Faces 1.1 Configuration File

```
<!DOCTYPE faces-config PUBLIC
   "-//Sun Microsystems, Inc.//DTD JavaServer Faces Config 1.1//EN"
   "http://java.sun.com/dtd/web-facesconfig_1_1.dtd">
```

The JavaServer Faces 1.0 Configuration File

```
<!DOCTYPE faces-config PUBLIC
   "-//Sun Microsystems, Inc.//DTD JavaServer Faces Config 1.0//EN"
   " http://java.sun.com/dtd/web-facesconfig_1_0.dtd">
```

The JSP Tag Library 2.1 File

```
<taglib xmlns="http://java.sun.com/xml/ns/j2ee"
   xmlns:xsi="http://www.w3.org/2001/XMLSchema-instance"
   xsi:schemaLocation="http://java.sun.com/xml/ns/j2ee http://java.sun.com/xml/ns/
j2ee/web-jsptaglibrary_2_1.xsd"
   version="2.1">
```

The JSP Tag Library 1.2 File

```
<!DOCTYPE taglib PUBLIC
  "-//Sun Microsystems, Inc.//DTD JSP Tag Library 1.2//EN"
  "http://java.sun.com/dtd/web-jsptaglibrary_1_2.dtd">
```

The JSP Tag Library 1.1 File

```
<!DOCTYPE taglib PUBLIC
  "-//Sun Microsystems, Inc.//DTD JSP Tag Library 1.1//EN"
  "http://java.sun.com/j2ee/dtds/web-jsptaglibrary_1_1.dtd">
```

NOTE   Your configuration file must contain one of the preceding **<!DOCTYPE>** *or schema declarations; otherwise Faces Console will be unable to load your configuration file.*

Acquiring and Installing Faces Console

Faces Console is free software and can be used both noncommercially and commercially free of charge. However, Faces Console is not open-source software like the MyFaces reference implementation. Faces Console can be acquired from James Holmes' Web site at **www.jamesholmes.com/JavaServerFaces/**.

Faces Console comes packaged as both a Zip file (**.zip**) and a Gzipped Tar file (**.tar.gz**). Select your desired packaging and download the file. Once you have downloaded Faces Console, installing it is straightforward. Because Faces Console is simply packaged in an archive file and not as an executable installation program, all you have to do is unpack the archive file into your desired installation directory. All the files inside the archive file are beneath a version-specific directory (such as **faces-console-1.8**); thus, when you unpack them into your desired directory, they will all be beneath the version-specific directory. For example, if you were to download version 1.8 of Faces Console and unpack its archive to **c:\java**, the Faces Console files would all be located at **c:\java\faces-console-1.8**. That's all you have to do to install Faces Console.

NOTE   Because Faces Console does not use an installer to place any special files into system directories, multiple versions of Faces Console can be installed on the same machine if necessary or desired.

Using Faces Console as a Stand-Alone Application

Most often, Faces Console is used as an IDE plug-in because of the convenience of working seamlessly inside one tool. However, Faces Console can just as easily be run as a stand-alone application. Before running Faces Console as a stand-alone application though, you must set the **JAVA_HOME** environmental variable. Many JDKs set this for you when you install them; however, if it is not set on your machine, you have to set it before you run Faces Console. The **JAVA_HOME** variable must be set to the directory where you have your JDK installed. For example, if you have JDK 1.5.0_01 installed at **c:\java\jdk1.5.0_01**, your **JAVA_HOME** variable should be set to **c:\java\jdk1.5.0_01**.

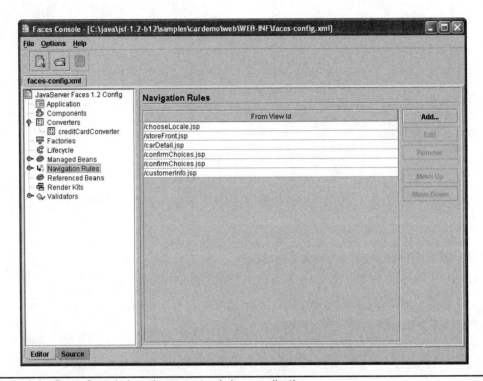

FIGURE A-1   Faces Console in action as a stand-alone application

Once you have set the **JAVA_HOME** environmental variable, you are ready to run Faces Console. Simply navigate to the directory where you installed Faces Console (for example, **c:\java\faces-console-1.8**) and then navigate to the **bin** directory. The **bin** directory contains two files: **console.bat** and **console.sh**. If you are using a Microsoft Windows machine, run **console.bat**. However, if you are using GNU/Linux, Unix, or Macintosh, run **console.sh**.

Once Faces Console is up and running, you can open an existing configuration file or create a new configuration file for editing. Figure A-1 shows Faces Console in action as a stand-alone application. Notice that open files have an Editor and a Source tab at the bottom. The Source tab shows you the source XML for the configuration file. Unlike many of the Faces Console IDE plug-ins, you cannot edit the XML source directly. This, however, may be a new feature in the future.

NOTE   *On GNU/Linux, Unix, and Macintosh, you must set the executable flag on the* **console.sh** *file before it can be executed.*

Using Faces Console Inside Borland JBuilder

Faces Console can be run as a plug-in inside Borland JBuilder versions 4.0 and later. To do so, you first must install the Faces Console JBuilder plug-in. Following is the list of steps for installing the Faces Console JBuilder plug-in:

1. Shut down JBuilder if it is currently running.

2. Navigate to the directory in which you have JBuilder installed (for example, **c:\ Program Files\JBuilder**) and then navigate to the **lib** directory.

3. In another window, navigate to the directory in which you installed Faces Console (say, **c:\java\faces-console-1.8**), and then navigate to the **com.jamesholmes .console.faces** directory and afterward to the **lib** directory.

4. Copy the **xerces.jar** file from the Faces Console **lib** directory (for instance, **c:\java\ faces-console-1.8\lib**) to the JBuilder **lib** directory (perhaps **c:\Program Files\ JBuilder\lib**), *if and only if xerces.jar does not already exist in the JBuilder **lib** directory.*

NOTE   *This step should only be necessary for JBuilder version 4.*

5. Navigate to the **ext** directory (for example, **c:\Program Files\JBuilder\lib\ext**) from the JBuilder **lib** directory.

6. Copy the **faces-console.jar** file from the Faces Console **lib** directory to the JBuilder **ext** directory.

After you have installed the Faces Console JBuilder plug-in, you must restart JBuilder. Once JBuilder is running, to use Faces Console, simply open a valid configuration file supported by Faces Console. Faces Console will be a tab option for the file, as shown in Figure A-2. You can edit the configuration file using Faces Console, or you can edit the file by hand from the Source tab. Changes made in either tab are automatically reflected in the other tab.

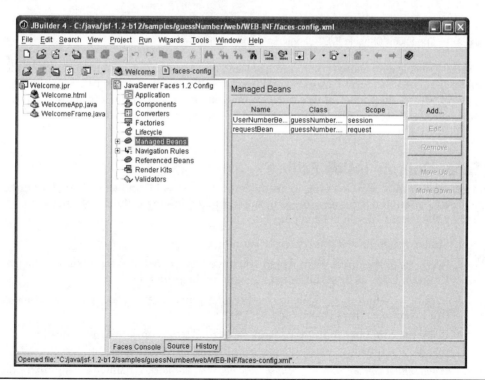

FIGURE A-2   Faces Console inside JBuilder

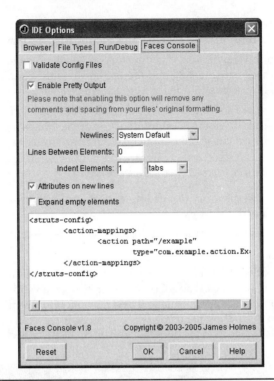

FIGURE A-3   The Faces Console IDE Options dialog box in JBuilder

Faces Console also allows you to modify some of its configuration settings from inside JBuilder. To access the Faces Console configuration settings, select Tools | IDE Options. Figure A-3 shows the Faces Console IDE Options dialog box. For more information on these configuration settings, see the "Configuring the Faces Console Output Options" section later in this chapter.

Using Faces Console Inside Eclipse

Faces Console can be run as a plug-in inside Eclipse versions 1.0 and later. To do so, you first have to install the Faces Console Eclipse plug-in. Following is the list of steps for installing the Faces Console Eclipse plug-in:

1. Shut down Eclipse if it is currently running.

2. Navigate to the directory in which you have Eclipse installed (for example, **c:\ Program Files\eclipse**) and then navigate to the **plugins** directory.

3. In another window, navigate to the directory in which you installed Faces Console (for instance, **c:\java\faces-console-1.8**).

4. Copy the **com.jamesholmes.console.faces** directory from the Faces Console installation directory to the Eclipse **plugins** directory.

5. *If and only if you are running Eclipse versions 3.0m7 or later,* rename the **plugin.xml** file beneath the Eclipse **plugins** directory to **plugin.xml.bak**. Next, rename **plugin-3.0.xml**

to **plugin.xml**. This step is necessary because there are two Faces Console Eclipse plug-ins, one for Eclipse versions 3.0m7 and later and one for earlier versions of Eclipse.

After you have installed the Faces Console Eclipse plug-in, you must restart Eclipse. Once Eclipse is running, to use Faces Console, simply right-click a valid configuration file and select Open With | Faces Console, as shown in Figure A-4.

For Eclipse versions 3.0m7 and later, after you have opened the file, it will load into the Faces Console editor inside of Eclipse, as shown in Figure A-5. You can edit the configuration file using Faces Console or you can edit the file by hand from the Source tab. Changes made in either tab are automatically reflected in the other tab. For versions of Eclipse prior to 3.0m7, the file will load into a separate Faces Console window, as shown in Figure A-6.

NOTE   *The Faces Console Eclipse plug-in requires that your configuration files have specific filenames in order for the plug-in to recognize them. JavaServer Faces configuration files must be named* **faces-config.xml**, *and JSP TLD files only need to have a file extension of* **.tld**.

Faces Console also allows you to modify some of its configuration settings from inside Eclipse. To access the Faces Console configuration settings, select Window | Preferences. Figure A-7 shows the Faces Console Preferences dialog box. For more information on these configuration settings, see the "Configuring the Faces Console Output Options" section later in this chapter.

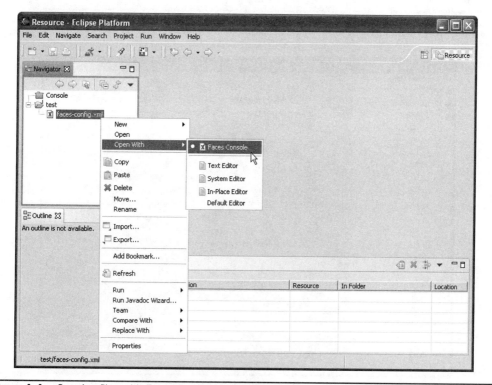

FIGURE A-4   Opening files with Faces Console in Eclipse

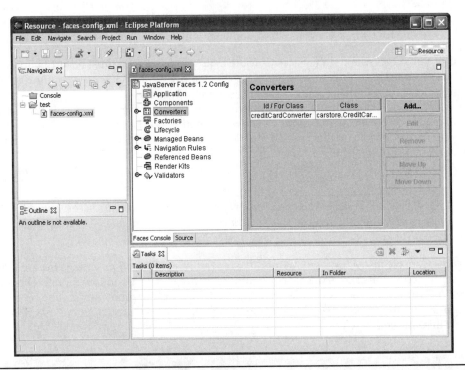

FIGURE A-5   The Faces Console editor inside Eclipse

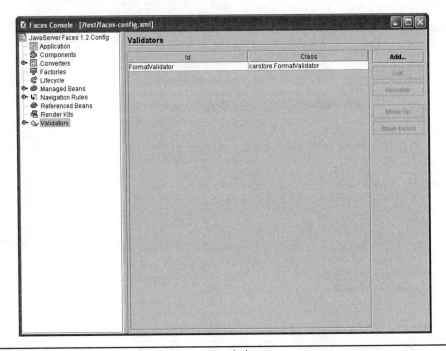

FIGURE A-6   The Faces Console editor in a separate window

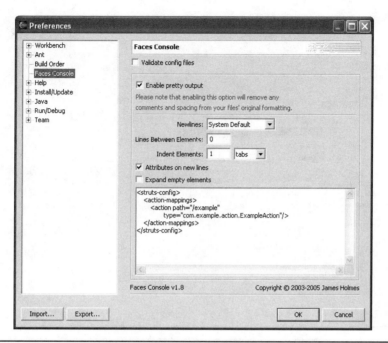

FIGURE A-7   The Faces Console Preferences dialog box in Eclipse

Using Faces Console Inside IBM Rational Application Developer for WebSphere

Faces Console can be run as a plug-in inside IBM Rational Application Developer for WebSphere versions 4.0.3 and later. To do so, you first have to install the Faces Console Eclipse plug-in. Following is the list of steps for installing the Faces Console Rational Application Developer plug-in:

1. Shut down Rational Application Developer if it is currently running.

2. Navigate to the directory in which you have Rational Application Developer installed (say, **c:\Program Files\IBM\WebSphere Studio**) and then navigate to the **eclipse** directory and then to the **plugins** directory.

3. In another window, navigate to the directory in which you installed Faces Console (for instance, **c:\java\faces-console-1.8**).

4. Copy the **com.jamesholmes.console.faces** directory from the Faces Console installation directory to the WSAD **plugins** directory.

After you have installed the Faces Console Rational Application Developer plug-in, you must restart Rational Application Developer.

Once Rational Application Developer is running, to use Faces Console, simply right-click a valid configuration file and select Open With I Faces Console, as shown in Figure A-8.

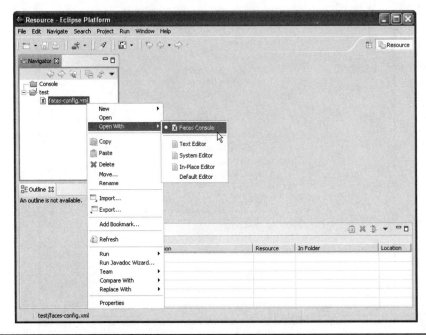

FIGURE A-8 Opening files with Faces Console in Rational Application Developer

After you have opened the file, it will load into a separate Faces Console window, as shown in Figure A-9.

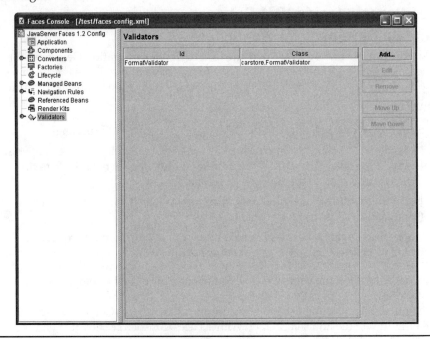

FIGURE A-9 The Faces Console editor in a separate window

NOTE *The Faces Console Rational Application Developer plug-in requires that your configuration files have specific filenames in order for the plug-in to recognize them. Faces configuration files must be named* **faces-config.xml**, *while JSP TLD files only need to have a file extension of* **.tld**.

Faces Console also allows you to modify some of its configuration settings from inside Rational Application Developer. To access the Faces Console configuration settings, select Window | Preferences. Figure A-10 shows the Faces Console Preferences dialog box. For more information on these configuration settings, see the "Configuring the Faces Console Output Options" section later in this chapter.

Using Faces Console Inside IntelliJ IDEA

Faces Console can be run as a plug-in inside JetBrains' IntelliJ IDEA versions 3.0 build 668 and later. To do so, you first have to install the Faces Console IDEA plug-in. Following is the list of steps for installing the Faces Console IntelliJ IDEA plug-in:

1. Shut down IntelliJ IDEA if it is currently running.

2. Navigate to the directory in which you have IntelliJ IDEA installed (for example, **c:\ Program Files\IntelliJ-IDEA-4.0**) and then navigate to the **plugins** directory.

3. In another window, navigate to the directory in which you installed Faces Console (for instance, **c:\java\faces-console-1.8**). Then navigate to the **com.jamesholmes .console.faces** directory and afterward to the **lib** directory.

4. Copy the **faces-console.jar** file from the Faces Console **lib** directory to the IDEA **plugins** directory.

After you have installed the Faces Console IDEA plug-in, you must restart IDEA.

Once IDEA is running, to use Faces Console, simply right-click a valid configuration file and select Edit With Faces Console, as shown in Figure A-11.

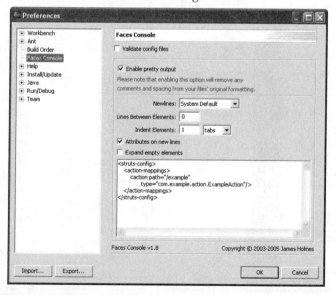

FIGURE A-10   The Faces Console Preferences dialog box in Rational Application Developer

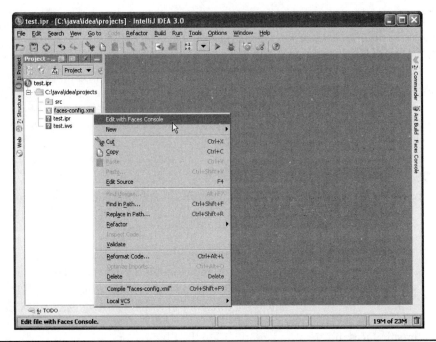

Figure A-11 Opening files with Faces Console in IDEA

After you have opened the file, it will load into the Faces Console editor, as shown in Figure A-12.

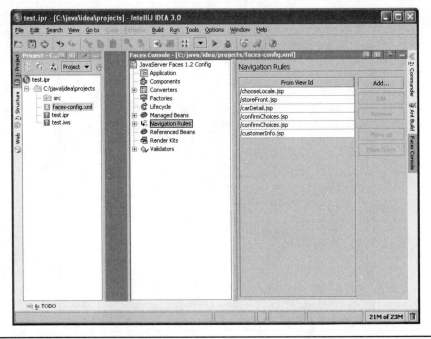

Figure A-12 The Faces Console editor inside IDEA

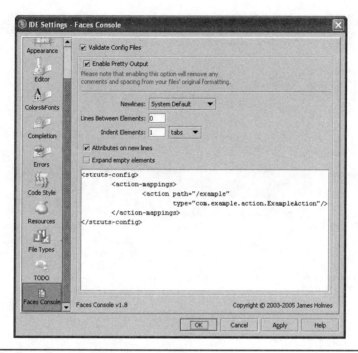

FIGURE A-13   The Faces Console IDE Settings dialog box in IDEA

Faces Console also allows you to modify some of its configuration settings from inside IDEA. To access the Faces Console configuration settings, select Options ⊢ IDE Settings. Figure A-13 shows the Faces Console IDE Settings dialog box. For more information on these configuration settings, see the "Configuring the Faces Console Output Options" section later in this chapter.

Using Faces Console Inside NetBeans and Sun ONE Studio (Forte)

Faces Console can be run as a plug-in inside NetBeans versions 3.2 and later, and inside Sun ONE Studio (Forte) versions 3.0 and later. To do so, you first have to install the Faces Console NetBeans plug-in. Following is the list of steps for installing the Faces Console NetBeans plug-in:

1. Start up NetBeans if it is not currently running.

2. Select Tools | Options. In the Options dialog box, navigate to the Options | IDE Configuration | System | Modules node in the tree on the left and then right-click it and select Add | Module, as shown in Figure A-14.

3. Using the file chooser, navigate to the directory in which you installed Faces Console (for instance, **c:\java\faces-console-1.8**). Then navigate to the **com .jamesholmes.console.faces** directory and afterward to the **lib** directory.

4. Select the **faces-console.jar** file and then click the Install button, as shown in Figure A-15.

PART V

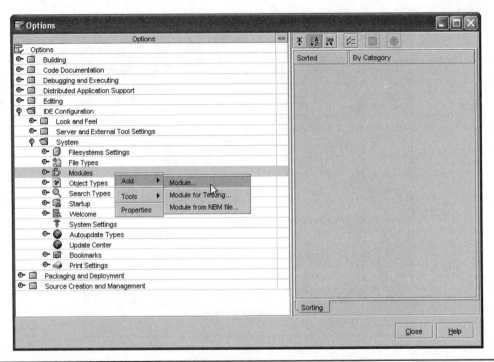

Figure A-14   Invoking the Add Module dialog box

After you have installed the Faces Console NetBeans plug-in, you must restart NetBeans.

Once NetBeans is running, to use Faces Console, simply open a valid configuration file supported by Faces Console. The file will load into the Faces Console editor inside of NetBeans, as shown in Figure A-16.

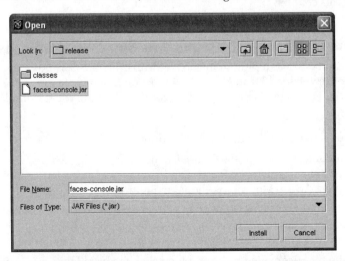

Figure A-15   Selecting the **faces-console.jar** file

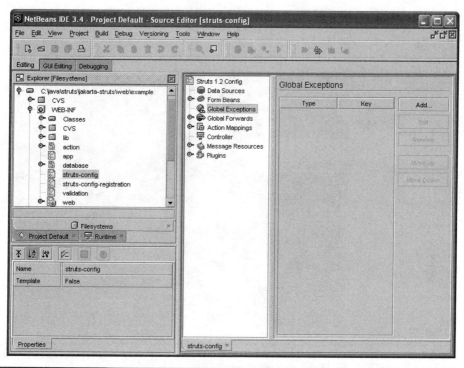

FIGURE A-16   Faces Console inside NetBeans

Using Faces Console Inside Oracle JDeveloper

Faces Console can be run as a plug-in inside Oracle JDeveloper versions 9*i* and later. To do so, you first have to install the Faces Console JDeveloper plug-in. Following is the list of steps for installing the Faces Console JDeveloper plug-in:

1. Shut down JDeveloper if it is currently running.

2. Navigate to the directory in which you have JDeveloper installed (for instance, **c:\ Program Files\JDeveloper**). Next, navigate to the **jdev** directory, followed by the **lib** directory, and then the **ext** directory.

3. In another window, navigate to the directory in which you installed Faces Console (for example, **c:\java\faces-console-1.8**). Afterward, navigate to the **com .jamesholmes.console.faces** directory and then to the **lib** directory.

4. Copy the **faces-console.jar** file from the Faces Console **lib** directory to the JDeveloper **ext** directory.

After you have installed the Faces Console JDeveloper plug-in, you must restart JDeveloper.

Once JDeveloper is running, to use Faces Console, simply right-click a valid configuration file and select Faces Console, as shown in Figure A-17.

After you have opened the file, it will load into the Faces Console editor inside of JDeveloper, as shown in Figure A-18.

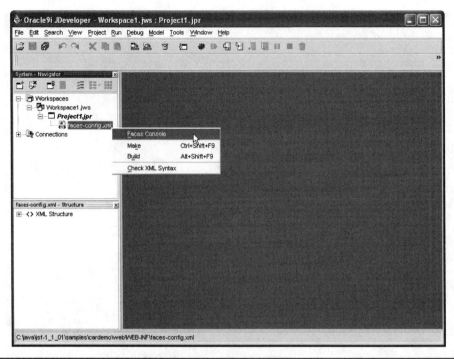

Figure A-17 Opening files with Faces Console in JDeveloper

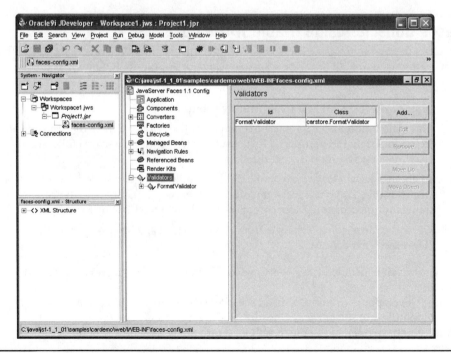

Figure A-18 The Faces Console editor inside JDeveloper

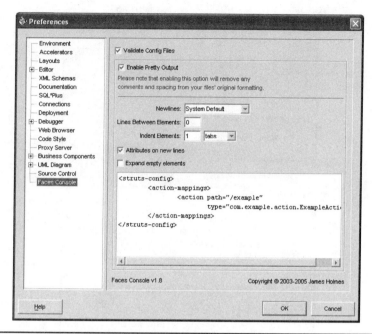

FIGURE A-19 The Faces Console Preferences dialog box in JDeveloper

Faces Console also allows you to modify some of its configuration settings from inside JDeveloper. To access the Faces Console configuration settings, select Tools | Preferences. Figure A-19 shows the Faces Console Preferences dialog box. For more information on these configuration settings, see the next section, "Configuring the Faces Console Output Options."

Configuring the Faces Console Output Options

Faces Console uses an XML parser to read in XML configuration files and then it manipulates the files in memory. Because XML parsers do not retain all of a file's original formatting when the file is parsed, the files are often poorly formatted when they are saved. By default, Faces Console simply retains the in-memory representation of configuration files, which results in poorly formatted XML files. To get around the limitation of XML parsers not retaining complete formatting information, Faces Console has a feature called Pretty Output that allows you to configure the format in which XML files are saved.

The Pretty Output options can be configured in the stand-alone version of Faces Console as well as from inside IDEs that Faces Console plugs into. For information on accessing the Pretty Output options in a supported IDE, see that IDE's section in this chapter. To configure the Pretty Output options in the stand-alone version of Faces Console, select Options | Output. This opens the dialog box shown in Figure A-20 with options for specifying the details of how XML files should be formatted when they are saved.

Following is an explanation of each of the output options:

- **Enable Pretty Output**   Enables and disables the use of Pretty Output options.
- **Newlines**   Specifies the type of newline character to use. System Default is the default and recommended setting. System Default defaults to the newline character

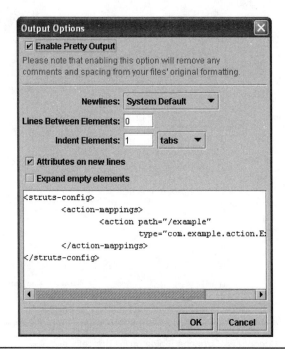

FIGURE A-20 The Output Options dialog box in the Faces Console stand-alone version

for the given system on which the application is running. For example, if run on Windows, System Default uses Windows-style newline characters.

- **Lines Between Elements** Specifies the number of new lines to place in between tags.

- **Indent Elements** Specifies the number and type of indenting to use. Indenting is used for tags and is hierarchical. Each level in the tag hierarchy is a level of indenting.

- **Attributes on New Lines** Specifies whether a tag's attributes should each be placed on a new line or if each should be placed on the same line as the tag.

- **Expand Empty Elements** Specifies whether or not empty tags (that is, tags without nested tags) should be expanded (for example, <tag/> versus <tag></tag>).

- **Bottom pane** Shows an example of how the output will look with the current output options applied. This changes as you change the output options.

NOTE *Enabling Pretty Output removes any XML comments (for instance, <!-- -->) and formatting from your original configuration files.*

Third-Party JSF Component Libraries

O ne of the key goals of JavaServer Faces was to create an API from which the developer community could create a robust set of complementary, third-party component libraries and implementations. Although not actually part of the core JSF libraries, these third-party libraries play an important role in the overall JSF development community by offering exceptional value-add capabilities above and beyond what is available with the base components from the specification. Therefore, this appendix offers a brief overview of this area. It begins by briefly describing two notable third-party libraries: Sun's Extended UI component library and JScape's WebGalileo Faces. It then offers a detailed look at Oracle's ADF Faces component library, which illustrates how a custom Faces UI component library can go above and beyond what is included in the Standard set of components provided in the specification.

Sun's Extended UI Component Library

As shown in Chapter 17, Sun's Studio Creator development environment version 2 bundles their default extended UI component library into the IDE. This UI component library provides richer functionality than what is available with the Standard components. The extended components include an improved table/grid component that supports column sorting, paging, and inline editing support. Other components include a tree, file upload, and a popup calendar.

The extended components are also capable of rendering in an applicationwide appearance known as a *theme*. Four accompanying *themes* are also provided with the components as starter examples.

More information on these components can be found at the Studio Creator Web page at Sun's Web site: **http://developers.sun.com/prodtech/javatools/jscreator/**.

JScape's WebGalileo Faces

Like Sun's extended components, JScape's WebGalileo Faces also provides a rich set of Faces UI components that pick up where the Standard components stop. WebGalileo Faces components consist of fully customizable components such as tree components, tables, date pickers, and so on.

More information on JScape's WebGalileo Faces UI component library can be found at **http://www.jscape.com/webgalileofaces/**.

Oracle's ADF Faces

Oracle's ADF Faces has garnered considerable attention since it was first released in a series of *Early Adopter (EA)* releases from Oracle's Technology Network Web site at **http://otn.oracle.com**. ADF Faces is a robust JSF component library that has its roots in an earlier technology known as UIX, which was a J2EE-based Web technology designed specifically for Oracle's Applications. In fact, one of the key architects of UIX, Adam Winer, was also one of the key JSF JSR Expert Group members. Thus, a lot of the lessons learned from building an industrial-strength J2EE Web framework with UIX have been directly applied to the JSF API.

As JSF became a standard, Oracle's UIX technology was revamped and fully standardized onto the JSF API. This was a fairly simple conversion since the original UIX was already very similar to what became standard for JSF.

The remainder of this appendix is devoted to providing useful information on developing JSF applications with ADF Faces.

Acquiring ADF Faces

ADF Faces can be acquired in two ways. First, it is already bundled with Oracle JDeveloper 10*g* (as mentioned in Chapter 17). Second, it can be downloaded separately from the Apache MyFaces Web site. At the time of this writing, the source code of the ADF Faces component library was in the process of being donated to the Apache MyFaces project. Further information on the ADF Faces contribution to Apache MyFaces can be found at **http://myfaces.apache.org**.

Many tutorials on using Oracle's ADF Faces within JDeveloper 10*g* can be found at the JDeveloper homepage of Oracle's Technology Network Web site at **http://www.oracle.com/technology/products/jdev/**.

ADF Faces Component Reference

The following section serves as a quick component reference for the two main libraries of ADF Faces: ADF Faces Core and ADF Faces HTML.

The ADF Faces Core Library

The ADF Faces Core library represents the real bulk of the ADF Faces components. These components provide the *core* functionality that ADF Faces provides. The ADF Faces Core library is accessible in JSP via a JSP tag library that has a URI of **http://xmlns.oracle.com/adf/faces** with a default prefix of **af**. A quick reference of the ADF Faces Core library is provided in Table B-1.

Component/Tag	Description
attribute	The **attribute** tag is a fixed version of the JSF **<f:attribute>** tag that correctly evaluates **ValueBinding**s bound to the value attribute.
chooseColor	The **chooseColor** component creates a palette for picking colors.
chooseDate	The **chooseDate** component is used in conjunction with a **selectInputDate** to allow the user to quickly select a date value without having to navigate to a secondary window.
column	The **column** component is used as a child of the **Table** component. The **column** component defines the header, footer, and data for a single column in an ADF Faces **table**.
commandButton	The **commandButton** component creates a button representation of a **UIXCommand** component.
commandLink	The **commandLink** component creates a link representation of a **UIXCommand** component.
commandMenuItem	The **commandMenuItem** component creates a menu item representation of a **UIXCommand** component.
convertColor	The **convertColor** tag converts a string to and from **java.awt.Color** objects.
convertDateTime	The **convertDateTime** tag converts a string into **java.util.Date**, and vice versa, based on the pattern and style set.
convertNumber	The **convertNumber** converts a **String** to a **Number**, and vice versa, based on the pattern or the type set.
document	The **document** component creates each of the standard root elements of an HTML page: **<html>**, **<body>**, and **<head>**.
forEach	The **forEach** tag is a replacement for the JSTL **<c:forEach>** tag that works with ADF Faces components.
form	The **form** component creates an HTML **<form>** element.
goButton	The **goButton** component creates a push button that navigates directly to another location instead of delivering an action.
goLink	The **goLink** component renders an HTML link.
goMenuItem	The **goMenuItem** component creates a menu item representation of a **UIXGo**.
importScript	The **importScript** component supports importing the built-in scripts provided by ADF Faces.
inputFile	The **inputFile** component can be used to upload a file. It supports displaying a label, text, and messages.
inputHidden	The **inputHidden** component adds a value that will be submitted with a page, but not displayed to the user.
inputText	The **inputText** component creates a browser input text widget; it may be single-line, a multiline, or a secret password field. It supports displaying a label, text, and messages.
iterator	The **iterator** component is a representation of the **UIXIterator** and is a component that does iteration.

TABLE B-1 The ADF Faces Core Library

Component/Tag	Description
menuBar	The **menuBar** component creates a series of navigation items representing one level in a navigation hierarchy.
menuButtons	The **menuButtons** component creates a series of navigation items representing one level in a navigation hierarchy.
menuChoice	The **menuChoice** component creates a series of navigation items representing one level in a navigation hierarchy.
menuList	The **menuList** component creates a series of navigation items representing one level in a navigation hierarchy.
menuPath	A **menuPath** component is used in hierarchical site layouts to indicate the path back to the root page of the hierarchy with links.
menuTabs	The **menuTabs** component creates a series of navigation items representing one level in a navigation hierarchy.
menuTree	The **MenuTree** is used to display data that is structured in a hierarchical format.
message	The **message** component displays a message on behalf of a component. ADF Faces input components typically support automatically showing their own messages.
messages	The **messages** component is used at the top of an application page to give the user important messaging information.
objectIcon	The **objectIcon** component renders a look-and-feel-specific icon.
objectImage	The **objectImage** component creates an image tag.
objectLegend	The **objectLegend** component adds a legend describing the meaning of an icon.
objectMedia	The **objectMedia** component displays media content—such as audio, video, or image—in a player embedded in the user agent.
objectSeparator	The **objectSeparator** component creates a horizontal separator.
objectSpacer	The **objectSpacer** component occupies a fixed amount of space in a layout.
outputFormatted	The **outputFormatted** component accepts a string in its **value** attribute containing a very limited set of HTML markup and outputs formatted results.
outputLabel	The **outputLabel** component that displays a label for a **form** component.
outputText	The **outputText** component supports styled text.
page	The **page** component is similar to the **panelPage** component except that instead of having **menu1**, **menu2**, **menu3**, and **menuGlobal** facets for adding menu information, the user binds a model object and a stamp to render these areas.
panelBorder	The **panelBorder** component is a layout element which lays out all of its children consecutively in its middle, and supports the following facets: **top**, **bottom**, **left**, **right**, **start**, **end**, **innerTop**, **innerBottom**, **innerRight**, **innerStart**, **innerLeft**, and **innerEnd**.
panelBox	The **panelBox** component is used to place ancillary information on a page, offset by a certain color.
panelButtonBar	The **panelButtonBar** component lays out a set of buttons.
panelForm	The **panelForm** component lays out input form controls, such that their labels and fields line up vertically.

TABLE B-1   The ADF Faces Core Library *(continued)*

Component/Tag	Description
panelGroup	The **panelGroup** component is a layout element that arranges its children in one of a few simple patterns.
panelHeader	The **panelHeader** component places a label and optional icon at the top of a section.
panelHorizontal	The **panelHorizontal** component lays out its children components in a horizontal fashion.
panelLabelAndMessage	The **panelLabelAndMessage** component lays out a label, children, tip, and an associated message.
panelList	The **panelList** component outputs each visible child in a list with a bullet next to it.
panelPage	The **panelPage** component lays out an entire page.
panelPageHeader	The **panelPageHeader** component lays out the top portion of a page.
panelPartialRoot	The **panelPartialRoot** component enables partial-page rendering on pages that cannot use the ADF body or document tag.
panelSideBar	The **panelSideBar** component renders a side navigation bar.
panelTip	The **panelTip** component provides a container for page or section level hints to the user.
poll	The **poll** component polls the server periodically so that any dependent components get a chance to update themselves.
processChoiceBar	The **processChoiceBar** component is a **UIXProcess** component that renders a previous button, a choice bar, and a next button.
processTrain	The **processTrain** component is a **UIXProcess** component that renders a train. A train is a horizontal series of train stations connected by a horizontal line. Each train station is an image and text describing the page in the multipage process.
progressIndicator	The **progressIndicator** component can be used to give users an understanding that there is a background task in progress.
regionDef	The **regionDef** tag allows a common UI to be defined once and reused many times.
resetActionListener	The **resetActionListener** tag is a declarative way to allow an action source to fire a reset event.
resetButton	The **resetButton** component creates a push button that will reset the content of a form.
selectBooleanCheckbox	The **selectBooleanCheckbox** component is a standard browser input checkbox. It supports displaying a prompt, text, and messages.
selectBooleanRadio	The **selectBooleanRadio** component maps to a single browser input radio, grouped with all other **selectBooleanRadio** controls in the same form which share the same **group** attribute. It supports displaying a prompt, text, and messages.
selectInputColor	The **selectInputColor** component creates a text field for entering colors and a button for picking colors from a palette.
selectInputDate	The **selectInputDate** component creates a text field for entering dates and a button for picking dates from a calendar.
selectInputText	The **selectInputText** component is a text field that also supports launching a dialog to assist users in entering a value.

TABLE B-1   The ADF Faces Core Library *(continued)*

Component/Tag	Description
selectItem	The **selectItem** component represents a single item that the user may select from a list, choice, radio, or shuttle ADF control.
selectManyCheckbox	The **selectManyCheckbox** component renders a series of **selectItem** children components (**f:selectItem**, **f:selectItems**, or **af:selectItem**) as checkboxes.
selectManyListbox	The **selectManyListbox** component creates a component that allows the user to select many values from a list of items.
selectManyShuttle	The **selectManyShuttle** component provides a mechanism for selecting multiple values from a list of values by allowing the user to move items between two lists.
selectOneChoice	The **selectOneChoice** component creates a menu-style component, which allows the user to select a single value from a list of items.
selectOneListbox	The **selectOneListbox** component creates a component that allows the user to select a single value from a list of items.
selectOneRadio	The **selectOneRadio** component creates a component that allows the user to select a single value from a set of items displayed as a series of radio buttons.
selectOrderShuttle	The **selectOrderShuttle** component provides a mechanism for selecting multiple values from a list of values by allowing the user to move items between two lists, and reordering that list of values.
selectRangeChoiceBar	The **selectRangeChoiceBar** component is employed to allow the user to select a range of records to display from a larger set of records. It permits the user to move back and forth through these records using a choice of buttons.
setActionListener	The **setActionListener** tag is a declarative way to allow an action source to set a value before navigation.
showDetail	The **showDetail** component provides a means of toggling a group of components between being hidden or shown.
showDetailHeader	The **showDetailHeader** component provides a means of toggling the contents under a header between being disclosed (shown) or undisclosed (hidden).
showDetailItem	The **showDetailItem** component represents a single item with specific contents that can be selected by users to be shown in a **showOne** component.
showOneChoice	The **showOneChoice** component creates, contains, and shows a series of items defined by **showDetailItem** components.
showOnePanel	The **showOnePanel** component creates, contains, and shows a series of items defined by **showDetailItem** components.
showOneRadio	The **showOneRadio** component creates, contains, and shows a series of items defined by **showDetailItem** components.
showOneTab	The **showOneTab** component creates, contains, and shows a series of items defined by **showDetailItem** components.
singleStepButtonBar	The **singleStepButtonBar** component is a **UIXSingleStep** component that renders a Previous button, text describing the current step, the maximum steps, and a Next button.
subform	The **subform** component represents an independently submittable region of a page. The contents of a **subform** will only be validated (or otherwise processed) if a component inside of the **subform** is responsible for submitting the page.

TABLE B-1   The ADF Faces Core Library *(continued)*

Component/Tag	Description
switcher	The **switcher** component dynamically decides which facet component should be rendered.
table	The **table** component is used to display tabular data. it also supports selection (both single and multiple), sorting, record navigation, and detail-disclosure.
tableSelectMany	The **tableSelectMany** is a "selection" facet component that implements multiple-selection.
tableSelectOne	The **tableSelectOne** is a "selection" facet component that implements single-selection.
tree	The **tree** component is used to display data that is structured in a hierarchical format.
treeTable	The **treeTable** component is used to display data that is structured in a hierarchical format.
validateByteLength	The **validateByteLength** tag validates the byte length of strings when encoded.
validateDateTimeRange	The **validateDateTimeRange** tag validates that the date entered is within a given range.
validateRegExp	The **validateRegExp** tag validates expressions using Java regular expression syntax.
validator	The **validator** tag is an implementation of the future JSF 1.2 **<f:validator>** tag that supports a **binding** attribute.

TABLE B-1   The ADF Faces Core Library *(continued)*

The ADF Faces HTML Library

Table B-2 presents the ADF Faces HTML component library along with short descriptions of each component. This library is accessible in JSP via the JSP tag library at the URI of **http://xmlns.oracle.com/adf/faces/html** with a default prefix of **afh**.

Component/Tag	Description
body	The ADF Faces **body** tag renders the HTML body element. In addition to providing support for the standard HTML body functionality, the ADF Faces **body** component enables Partial Page Rendering (PPR) support and assigning of the initial page focus.
cellFormat	The **cellFormat** component is used to format cells in a **rowLayout** component.
frame	The **frame** component is used to specify attributes needed by an HTML frame. It should only be used as a facet on a **frameBorderLayout** component. The content of a frame is defined by using the source attribute. On mobile devices, a list linking to each frame is rendered for a **frameBorderLayout**, and each frame is brought up as a separate page.
frameBorderLayout	The **frameBorderLayout** component can be used to place seven frames at the left, right, top, bottom, inner left, inner right, and center positions.
head	The **head** component for the HTML head element. It includes the document's title and any stylesheets needed by the current look and feel. When used, page authors do not need to use a **styleSheet** component because it will automatically be included.

PART V

TABLE B-2   The ADF Faces HTML Library

Component/Tag	Description
html	The **html** component renders the **\<html\>** element for an HTML page. It automatically generates **locale** and **dir** attributes based on the current locale.
rowLayout	The **rowLayout** components can be used on their own, or to define a row of **tableLayout** components. They can contain any arbitrary content, one per cell, but clients that need formatting beyond just a simple **\<td\>** element must wrap the child nodes in **cellFormat** components.
script	The **script** component supports importing libraries and inline scripts.
styleSheet	The **styleSheet** component generates the stylesheet link reference to a generated ADF Faces stylesheet. This is automatically included for you if you use the ADF Faces **head** component.
tableLayout	A **tableLayout** component is a thin wrapper around the HTML **\<table\>** element. It contains a series of row layout elements.

TABLE B-2   The ADF Faces HTML Library

ADF Faces Key Technologies

The remainder of the chapter is devoted to focusing on the unique features of the ADF Faces component library. Specifically covered in this section are the following:

- ADF Faces Partial Page Rendering (PPR) feature
- The ADF Faces processScope
- The ADF Faces dialog framework
- ADF Faces skinning feature

ADF Faces Partial Page Rendering Feature

The ADF Faces Partial Page Rendering (PPR) technology, which is sometimes referred to as Partial Page Refresh, allows individual portions of an ADF Faces page to be refreshed without having to refresh the entire page, thus improving the end user's experience. Using PPR in ADF Faces applications is very easy because many components are automatically PPR-enabled. Some of these components include **tree**, **treeTable**, **menuTree**, **table**, **showDetail**, and **page**, as well as all of the input/select components (**inputText**, **selectManyCheckBox**, and so on). It's also important to point out that in addition to the ADF Faces components that are PPR-enabled and can initiate a PPR request, any JSF components (outside of ADF Faces) can be redrawn independent of a page refresh as a result of a PPR request.

Of the ADF Faces components that support PPR, all share several common PPR-associated attributes. They are described in Table B-3.

To better understand how to work with PPR in ADF Faces, let's walk through a simple example. Assume that there is an input field (**inputText**) and an output field (**outputText**) on a page and that changing a value in the input field (and tabbing out of the field) causes the value of the output field to change. For this example, the output field will simply display the current value in the input field. In addition to the input and output fields, also assume that there is a Java class (**PprTest**) that is registered as a managed bean (**pprbean**) with **request** scope. This bean will have two properties. The first is **input** (of type **CoreInputText**). The second is **output** (of type **CoreOutputText**). There is also a **currentTime** property (of type

Attribute	Description
autoSubmit	For ADF Faces input components that implement **EditableValueHolder**, such as an input field (**CoreInputText**) or a select menu (**CoreSelectOneChoice**), you can set **autoSubmit** to **true** in order to trigger a form submission containing the component. For example, tabbing out of an input field with **autoSubmit** set to **true** will cause the form to submit. Usually a listener attribute such as **ValueChangeListener** is also set on this component in order to execute logic when the value of the component has changed. (For example, you might update another component's value.)
partialSubmit	For ADF Faces components that implement **ActionSource** such as command buttons, setting the **partialSubmit** attribute to **true** allows for the partial submission of the form. This is often used in conjunction with an **actionListener** method to execute logic when the button is clicked.
partialTriggers	All ADF Faces components that can render support the **partialTriggers** attribute. Setting the **partialTriggers** to one or more (space-separated) ID values of other components on the page triggers a refresh for this component, too. For example, an **outputText** could have its **partialTriggers** attribute set to the ID of an **inputText** and when the value of the **inputText** changes (such as with an **autosubmit**) the linked **outputText** will also be refreshed. Of course, to see a change, the value of the **outputText** must change as a result of the changed **inputText**.

TABLE B-3   Component Attributes Involved in PPR

Date) that will be used to print the current time on the page. Finally, the class will also contain a method that can process a **ValueChangeEvent** for the input field. The following is the source for the class:

```
// import statements omitted

public class PprTest {
  public PprTest() {
  }

  private  Date currentTime = new java.util.Date();
  private CoreInputText input;
  private CoreOutputText output;

  public void handleValueChange(ValueChangeEvent vce) {
    output.setValue(input.getValue());
  }

// Getters and Setters omitted
}
```

As you can see, the **handleValueChange()** method applies the value of the input component to the output component during a **ValueChangeEvent**. (Incidentally, an alternative way to do this would be to set the value of the output component with **vce.getNewValue()**, which simply retrieves the new value from the event instead of the input component. This eliminates the need to bind the input component.)

In the JSP page, both the input field and output field will be bound to their respective bean property counterparts. The input field will also have its **valueChangeListener** attribute set to the method in the managed bean that assigns the value of the input field to the output field. This is shown next:

```
<af:inputText label="Enter Value:"
    valueChangeListener="#{pprbean.handleValueChange}"
    binding="#{pprbean.input}"/>
```

and in the following:

```
<af:outputText binding="#{pprbean.output}"/>
```

Normally, a page would require a button (**commandButton**) to perform a submission to force the value change in the output field. Alternatively, a JavaScript-based automatic form submission could also be enabled without a button by setting the input field's JavaScript attribute **Onchange** to **form.submit()**. However, in both these cases, the entire page would have to be refreshed.

The ADF Faces PPR feature alleviates the need to include a button, or add JavaScript code to autosubmit the form. Instead, ADF Faces PPR can autosubmit the form, but only refresh part of a page simultaneously. To enable PPR in the example, a few changes are needed. First, two additional attributes must be added to the **inputText** tag, as shown next:

```
<af:inputText id="input1" label="Enter Value:"
    valueChangeListener="#{pprbean.handleValueChange}"
    binding="#{pprbean.input}" autoSubmit="true"/>
```

The **autoSubmit** attribute causes the form to partially submit when a value has changed. The **id** attribute is used to identify the input field, as described next.

The second change is to add the **partialTriggers** attribute to the output field, as shown in the following:

```
<af:outputText binding="#{pprbean.output}" partialTriggers="input1"/>
```

Notice that the input field ID is used by the output field and is assigned to the **partialTriggers** attribute. This attribute can also contain multiple space-separated IDs to establish dependencies on multiple fields.

Finally, to demonstrate that only the interdependent fields are being refreshed and not the entire page, you can use another **outputText** field that is value-bound to the **currentTime** property of the managed bean. (Notice the use of the ADF Faces **convertDateTime** to display the current time.)

```
<af:outputText value="#{pprbean.currentTime}" >
  <af:convertDateTime type="time" timeStyle="long"/>
</af:outputText>
```

As shown in Figure B-1, when a user changes a value in the input field and then tabs out of the field, a partial submit occurs and only the dependent output field is updated. However, the output field displaying the current time does not refresh.

The preceding example was used purely to explain the procedures for enabling PPR in ADF Faces applications. This same approach can be applied to the more complex ADF Faces components, such as **table** and **treeTable**, which can use PPR in a similar fashion.

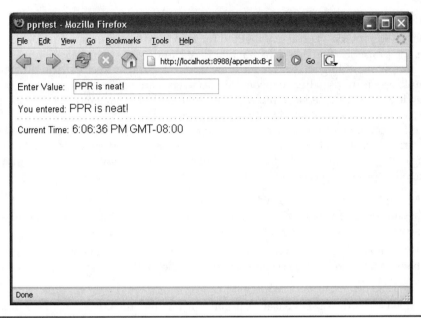

FIGURE B-1   PPR in action: Only the output field is refreshed.

Adding PPR to Non–ADF Faces Components

You may be surprised to find out that in addition to ADF Faces components supporting PPR, it is also possible to enable non-ADF Faces components to support PPR as well. While non-ADF Faces components don't necessarily have the **partialTriggers** attribute, it is possible to programmatically assign a partial trigger (target) programmatically. For example, it is possible to use a standard **h:outputText** to display the value entered in the input field (via PPR) from our previous example instead of an **af:outputText**.

To do this, we could replace the **af:outputText** with an **h:outputText**.

```
<h:outputText id="std_output" binding="#{pprbean.stdOutput}"/>
```

Notice that the new **h:outputText** is also bound to a backing bean property, so this would require adding the property **stdOutput** of type **HtmlOutputText** (along with setters and getters) to the backing bean. Also notice that in order to programmatically assign a partial trigger, the component must have its **id** set.

Next, in the code that handles the **ValueChangeEvent**, we simply add a statement to enable PPR for the standard output field and then set its value based on the input field's value as was done before:

```
public void handleValueChange(ValueChangeEvent vce) {
  // No longer needed  - output.setValue(input.getValue());

  // Add partial target programmatically to stdOutput component
  AdfFacesContext.getCurrentInstance().addPartialTarget(stdOutput);
  stdOutput.setValue(input.getValue());

}
```

PART V

The ADF Faces processScope

To simplify and provide a consistent method for interpage communication, ADF Faces provides the **processScope**. Before JavaServer Faces, interpage communication was often done by simply providing an extra request parameter argument, such as **?rowid=99**. For very simple applications, where noncomplex data-types are needed to be stored between page viewings, this provided a solution. However, it has the problem of being easily hacked because the variables are exposed in the request string.

The other common approach was to use the **HttpSession** to store objects as **session**-scoped variables instead. It involved placing an object onto the **HttpSession**, such as a shopping cart with items. This had the benefit of being able to store complex data-types; however, other problems can arise, like the following:

- Multiple windows, such as when using HTML frames, cause problems with **session**-scoped variables since both pages could be operating on the same **session**-scoped variable.

- Pressing the Back button can cause problems because the page you are navigating back to might rely on a **session**-scoped variable that may have changed in the page you came from.

The ADF Faces **processScope** feature is aimed at eliminating or reducing these problems. In short, the ADF Faces **processScope** provides an additional scope to the existing Faces **applicationScope**, **sessionScope**, and **requestScope** objects. As with the oft-used **sessionScope**, developers are able to store values/objects onto the **processScope** but without the previously mentioned problems. The key difference from the **sessionScope** is that the values stored onto the **processScope** are only visible from the user's current process. This means that if a new window of the same page is displayed and subsequent navigations occur, they will have an independent **processScope** from the original. This automatically forks off another instance of the **processScope**. Even better, if the user then clicks the Back button on the original page, the **processScope** is reset to its original state.

Retrieving and editing an item such as a **Cart** object that has an **ItemCount** property from the **processScope** can be done using the following code in an action method:

```
public String incrementCart_action() {
... (other code)
  // retrieve "Cart" object from processScope
  AdfFacesContext afctx = AdfFacesContext.getCurrentInstance();
  Cart pscart = (Cart) afctx.getProcessScope().get("cart");

  // Update itemcount value in Cart
  int current = pscart.getItemcount();
  current++;

  // Create new instance of Cart and set new itemcount
  Cart newcart = new Cart();
  newcart.setItemcount(current);

  //place new Cart back onto processScope
  afctx.getProcessScope().put("cart", newcart);
...
  return "proceed";
}
```

Using this approach to increment a **Cart** object's **itemcount**, one could create a series of pages that are linked together with a series of action methods (as previously described) that each increment the **Cart**'s **itemcount** and return a String value to enable a navigation to the next page (which also has an increment button and similar action method) and so on. At runtime when following the sequence of pages and clicking the increment buttons, the **Cart**'s **itemcount** would be incremented as expected. The interesting thing about using the **processScope** feature is that if you spawned a new browser window (using CTRL-N), it would effectively spawn a new **Cart** with its own independent **itemcount** which starts at the same point where the parent browser's page was. This is depicted in Figure B-2.

Subsequent clicks on the newly spawned page would refer to its own copy of the **Cart** object and thus maintain a different **itemcount**, as depicted in Figure B-3.

You could test this behavior by clicking the original browser to proceed to **page 5** and increment the **itemcount** to a value of **4**, but then click in the other browser to proceed to **page 4'** to see that its value is now **3** and is independent of the first browser.

You would also find that the browser's Back button returns the **Cart** back to its original state so you could effectively decrement the **Cart**'s **itemcount** by simply clicking the browser's Back button.

Displaying Data from the processScope

To display items stored in the **processScope** in a JSP page, you can use the JSF EL expression: **#{processScope.objectkey}**. To extract the current **itemCount** from the **Cart** object stored in the **processScope**, use the following:

```
<h:outputText    value="#{processScope.cart.itemcount}"/>
```

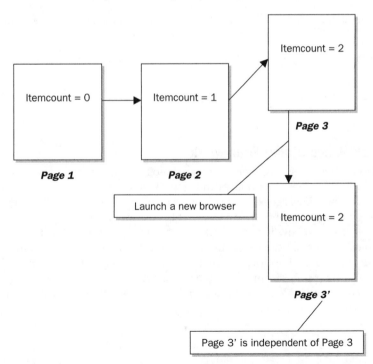

FIGURE B-2   Spawning a new Cart by launching a new browser window

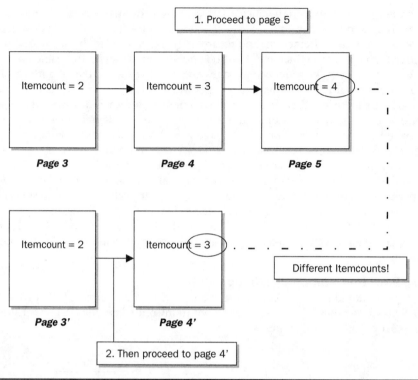

Figure B-3   Separate **itemcount**s based on the original Cart object

Incidentally, both Standard and ADF Faces components can access items stored in the **processScope** because they are equally available via JSF EL. For example, this statement

```
<af:outputText    value="#{processScope.cart.itemcount}"/>
```

would work as well.

Using the ADF Faces Dialog Framework

Web applications often allow the user to invoke dialog windows for a variety of reasons. However, to implement this functionality in a generic sense requires the addition of custom-coded JavaScript. The ADF Faces dialog framework, on the other hand, allows the developer to create popup dialogs without having to resort to custom JavaScript code.

The best way to learn how to use the ADF Faces dialog framework is to start with a simple example. The one used here creates a popup window that displays a message and has a button that closes the window. To create this dialog, you first start with an initial page that serves as a starting point from which the dialog window will be launched (**home.jsp**). An ADF Faces **commandLink** can be added to the page with attribute settings for the launched window, as shown next.

```
<af:commandLink text="About"
  action="dialog:about"
  useWindow="true"
  windowHeight="300" windowWidth="300"/>
```

Notice the **action** attribute which has its value set to a special **dialog:about** value. The "dialog" prefix instructs ADF Faces to treat this navigation as a dialog window launch. The action referred to responds to the following navigation rule in the application's **faces-config.xml** file.

```
<navigation-rule>
  <from-view-id>*</from-view-id>
  <navigation-case>
    <from-outcome>dialog:about</from-outcome>
    <to-view-id>/about.jsp</to-view-id>
  </navigation-case>
</navigation-rule>
```

Next a dialog page, **about.jsp**, must be created. It can contain any content. In this example, it is used as an about page, which shows the application's version information. The single important component on the about page is the button that allows it to close. This is coded as shown next:

```
<af:commandButton text="return">
  <af:returnActionListener/>
</af:commandButton>
```

Notice that this button contains a default **returnActionListener** inside it. This is the default action listener that allows the dialog to simply close the window and return to the page that launched it. At this point, the about dialog window will work as expected, as shown in Figure B-4.

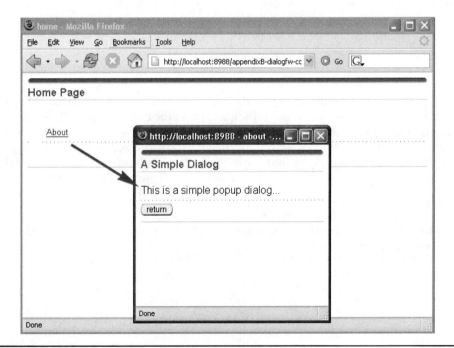

FIGURE B-4   Creating a simple about dialog page in ADF Faces

An obvious enhancement for this dialog would be to make one that accepts an input value and then sends this value back to the launch page. To enable this case, we can build a dialog that allows the user to enter a value into a text field in the dialog and then have it appear in a text field on the main page (**home.jsp**).

As before, we can add another command component to the home page to launch the dialog. This time we'll use a **commandButton**, as shown next:

```
<af:commandButton id="lookup_button" text="Lookup"
   action="dialog:lookup" useWindow="true"
    windowHeight="200"  windowWidth="300"
    returnListener="#{backing_home.handleReturn}"
    partialSubmit="true" />
```

The new button's **action** is set to a dialog navigation case (not shown) that directs the user to a different dialog page (**lookup.jsp**) which accepts a value. The new **Lookup** dialog is shown hovering above the main (**Home**) page in Figure B-5.

We'll continue reviewing the remainder of launch button's attributes shortly, but first let's have a look at the **lookup.jsp** dialog page's most important components:

```
<af:inputText label="Enter value:" id="inputText1" />
<af:commandButton text="return"
   action="#{backing_lookup.returnAction}"/>
```

As you can see, this dialog contains an input field that allows the user to enter a value along with a button that is bound to an action method **returnAction()** in the page's backing bean. The source for this method is as follows:

```
public String returnAction(){
  AdfFacesContext.getCurrentInstance().returnFromDialog(inputText1.getValue()
    , null);
  return null;
}
```

As shown here, this method calls the ADF Faces context method, **returnFromDialog()**, which closes down the dialog and sends back a value in the first argument. In this example, the value of the input text field (**inputText1**) is passed back.

In order for the value sent back from the dialog to be processed, a corresponding **returnListener** must be used. Recall from the button of the launch page where a **handleReturn()** method was referred to in the button's **returnListener** attribute, as shown next:

```
returnListener="#{backing_home.handleReturn}"
```

The **handleReturn()** method is a method in the backing bean of the launch page that processes the incoming value from the dialog. It is shown next:

```
public void handleReturn(ReturnEvent event) {
  if (event.getReturnValue() != null){
    outputText1.setValue(event.getReturnValue());
  }
}
```

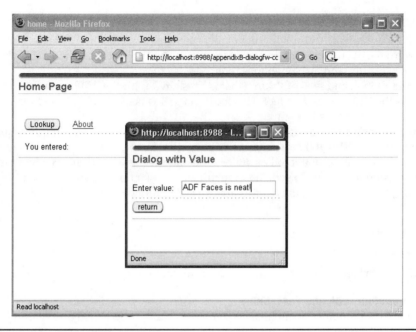

FIGURE B-5   A dialog that accepts an input value

As you can see, it sets the output text field on the launch page to the value returned from the **ReturnEvent**. When the dialog finishes, the original launch page must be refreshed in order to show the new value returned from the dialog. This is done by setting the **partialSubmit** attribute of the original launch button to **true** as well as setting the **partialTriggers** attribute of the text field being updated to the ID of the launch button.

```
<af:outputText id="outputText1" partialTriggers="lookup_button"/>
```

Recalling the PPR discussion, the **partialTriggers** attribute establishes a dependency from the output text field to the launch button and forces a partial refresh to update the output field. Figure B-6 shows the update value of the output text field.

FIGURE B-6   An updated field based on a dialog

ADF Faces Skinning Technology

With ADF Faces *skinning* technology, developers can create applicationwide look and feels, which govern the overall user interface appearance of the application. Other Web technologies have similar features and are sometimes referred to as *themes*.

The default look and feel, or "skin," that is presented with the ADF Faces components is known as the Oracle look and feel. This look and feel was originally created for Oracle applications and is shown in Figure B-7.

To quickly change this look and feel to another built-in look and feel simply requires a quick edit of the **/WEB-INF/adf-faces-config.xml** file. In addition to the built-in **oracle** look and feel, there are also two other built-in look and feels, **simple** and **minimal**, which can then be extended upon. To switch to the **minimal** look and feel, you must edit the **adf-faces-config.xml** and replace the default **oracle** skin-family with **minimal**, as shown next:

```
...
<skin-family>minimal</skin-family>
...
```

Re-running the application presents it in its **minimal** look and feel, as shown in Figure B-8.

Creating a Custom Look and Feel (Skin)

It is possible to build upon the minimal look and feel (skin), shown in Figure B-8, and create a new, custom look and feel. Here is how the process works. First, create a new file, **adf-faces-**

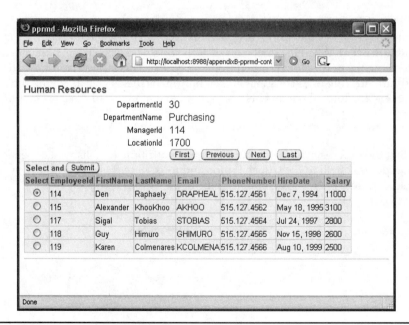

FIGURE B-7 ADF Faces default look and feel

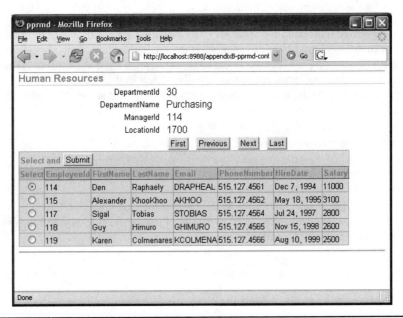

Figure B-8   ADF Faces minimal look and feel

skin.xml, in the **WEB-INF** directory. The contents of this file will define the new **custom** skin. It's shown next. (This skin is named **custom** but could be any name you define.)

```
<?xml version="1.0" encoding="ISO-8859-1"?>
<skins xmlns="http://xmlns.oracle.com/adf/view/faces/skin">
  <skin>
    <id>
      custom.desktop
    </id>
    <family>
      custom
    </family>
    <render-kit-id>
      oracle.adf.desktop
    </render-kit-id>
    <style-sheet-name>
      skins/custom/custom.css
    </style-sheet-name>
  </skin>
</skins>
```

Now that a new **adf-faces-skins.xml** has been created, the **skin-family** defined inside must be referenced in the main **adf-faces-config.xml**, as shown in the following:

```
<skin-family>custom</skin-family>
```

The final step is to place the referenced **custom** files that are in the **skin-family** definition in the **adf-faces-skins.xml** onto the file system so they are accessible at runtime. This involves creating a **skins** subdirectory along with a child **custom** directory under the HTML root. The **custom** directory will contain a style sheet named **custom.css** that will hold all of the styles of the individual elements of the user interface, such as button appearance, foreground font, and so on. Since images are often referred to in the styles, a corresponding **images** directory containing any referred images is usually added in this location.

Taking a closer look at the example **custom.css** file, you will see style entries such as:

```
...
.AFDefaultFontFamily:alias {
  font-family:Tahoma,Arial,Helvetica,Geneva,sans-serif;
}
.AFLinkForeground:alias {color:#003399}
...
```

These entries apply visual attributes to the default font family as well as for the foreground link color. The following is an example of using styles to apply images to the front and back portions of a button:

```
.AFButtonEndIcon:alias {
  content:url(/skins/custom/images/btnEnd.gif); width:7px; height:18px
}
.AFButtonEndIcon:alias:rtl {
  content:url(/skins/custom/images/btnStart.gif); width:7px; height:18px
}
```

To determine which stylable elements can be referred to in the **custom.css** style sheet, check the global styles definition file, **adf-faces-skins-doc.xml**, which is provided by ADF Faces. This file provides a complete set of definitions for the named styles, icons, and components that can be referred to in the **adf-faces-skins.xml** file. It has the following form:

```
<?xml version='1.0' encoding='ISO-8859-1'?>
<skinMetadata xmlns="http://xmlns.oracle.com/adf/faces/view/skin/metadata"
              xmlns:html="http://www.w3.org/TR/REC-html40"
              id="minimal-desktop"
              name="Minimal Skin keys" >
  <globalMetadata>
    <styles>
      <namedStyle id=".AFDefaultFontFamily:alias">
        <description>
          Specifies the default font family list ("font-family" property) for
          the skin.
        </description>
      </namedStyle>
...
(more global style definitions)
...
    </styles>
    <icons>
      <icon id="af|panelBox::dark-header-start-icon">
        <description>

          This icon is rendered at the start of the header region for
          dark panelBoxes.
        </description>
      </icon>
```

```
...
... (more global icon definitions)
...

    </icons>
  </globalMetadata>
  <componentMetadata>
    <component name="af:selectInputDate">
      <icons>
        <icon id="af|selectInputDate::launch-icon">
          <description>
            The button icon which is used to launch the secondary
            date picker dialog.
          </description>
        </icon>
      </icons>
    </component>
  </component>

...
...(more component definitions)
...

  </componentMetadata>
</skinMetadata>
```

The previous code example shows single items from the **globalMetadata** group (**styles** and **icons)** and a single **component** group from the **componentMetadata**.

After the **custom.css** has been edited with new/updated styles for the different UI elements, the custom look and feel will take on a different appearance from the base **minimal** look and feel from which it extends. Figure B-9 shows the new **custom** skin at runtime.

The following list summarizes the steps necessary to create a custom skin.

1. Create a CSS (3.0) style sheet (such as **custom.css**).

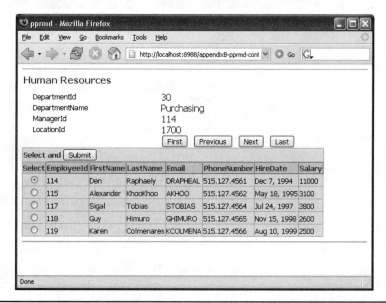

FIGURE B-9   A custom look and feel (skin)

2. Add any referenced external resources in the style sheet, such as a directory of referenced images.

3. Reference style sheet and external resources in a **skin-family** declaration in an **adf-faces-skins.xml** file.

4. Reference the custom **skin-family** in the main **adf-faces-config.xml** file.

Oracle JDeveloper's Visual Design Time Experience for ADF Faces

Oracle JDeveloper 10*g* provides a sleek design time experience for working with ADF Faces. In addition to offering built-in development support for the Standard specification components (core and HTML), JDeveloper also provides integrated, visual development support for ADF Faces. These features include visual rendering of the ADF Faces components in the JSP visual editor, integrated context-sensitive documentation, integration of the components on the Component Palette, and re-entrant wizards allowing quick code generation for composite components (such as tables and select menus), as well as advanced databinding support when building applications using the overall ADF framework.

The ADF Faces design time experience provided by Oracle JDeveloper 10*g* is shown in Figure B-10.

More information on the JSF design time experience can be found in Chapter 17 and by going to the Oracle JDeveloper Web site at **http://www.oracle.com/technology/products/jdev**.

JSFCentral—A Reference for Third-Party Components

Before concluding this appendix, it is necessary to mention an important Web site to consider when searching for third-party components: JSFCentral. This site provides a detailed index of a wide variety of independently developed JSF technologies, including references to various Faces UI component libraries. JSFCentral is located at **http://jsfcentral.com**.

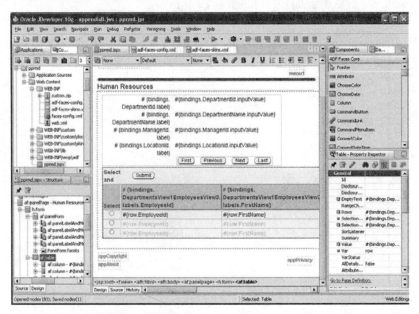

FIGURE B-10   JDeveloper's ADF Faces design time experience

Migrating from Struts to Faces

B y the time the JSF 1.0 Expert Group first began to meet in late 2001, Apache Struts was already the most popular Web application framework. As of this writing, it is probably still the most widely deployed Web application framework, though developers have grown in sophistication over time and have come to crave the power of component-based frameworks such as JavaServer Faces. The Struts community has responded to these cravings and has broken the Struts project into two separate frameworks. **Struts Action** is the classic Struts we all know and (some of us) love. Struts Shale is a layer of extensions on top of JSF and is described in detail in Appendix D. This appendix covers issues relating to Struts Action and JSF. Most importantly, a popular strategy for migrating from Struts to Faces is described.

Similarities and Differences

This appendix assumes familiarity with Struts. For a thorough treatment of Struts, please see James Holmes's *Struts: The Complete Reference* (McGraw-Hill, 2004). To build a firm foundation of understanding, we present a concept map from Struts concepts to Faces concepts (see Table C-1).

Struts Concept	Faces Concept	Struts Description	Faces Description
ActionServlet	FacesServlet	In both cases, this concept is the "front controller" design pattern: every request that can change the state of the application goes through the front controller. The **ActionServlet** in Struts delegates to the **RequestProcessor** to continue processing. There may only be one instance of the **ActionServlet** per Web application.	The FacesServlet in Faces delegates to the lifecycle to continue processing. There can be several lifecycle instances, each with its own custom lifecycle, if necessary.

TABLE C-1   A Concept Map from Struts to Faces

Struts Concept	Faces Concept	Struts Description	Faces Description
RequestProcessor	lifecycle	The **RequestProcessor** examines the URL of the incoming postback request and selects one of the developer-defined **<action>** elements from the **struts-config .xml file**. The **<action>** element corresponds to a developer-provided Action subclass.	The lifecycle puts the incoming request through a number of phases, one of which is called "invoke application," which loosely resembles the responsibility of the **RequestProcessor** in Struts. This phase examines the **UICommand** that represents the button or link that was pressed on the form and extracts its action. The use of the action is described elsewhere in this table.
Action	action **MethodExpression**	Responsible for examining the request, including the data entered into the form by the user, and returning an appropriate **ActionForward** instance that describes where the application should go "next."	Any arbitrary **MethodExpresion**, pointing to a method on any arbitrary managed bean, can act as an action. This method returns a simple String (or Object in JSF 1.2) that is used to look up the "next" view from the navigation-rules in the **faces-config.xml**.
ActionForword (or **ForwardConfig**), **ActionRedirect**	outcome (return value) from the action **MethodExpression**	The runtime representation of the **<forward>** element in the **struts-config.xml**. Simply denotes the page where the application should go "next," along with some information about how this transition should be done: via Servlet redirect or not.	The outcome is plugged into the navigation-rules element and the "next" view is derived.
ActionMapping	UICommand component	Used by the **RequestProcesser** to locate the appropriate **ActionForward** instance.	A **UICommand** is a component that represents a button or a link in the page. It has an action attribute that is a **MethodExpression**. The action is described elsewhere in this table.

TABLE C-1   A Concept Map from Struts to Faces *(continued)*

Struts Concept	Faces Concept	Struts Description	Faces Description
ActionMessage, ActionMessages, ActionErrors	FacesMessage	Returned by the **ActionForm** in response to calling its **validate( )** method. Represents a validation message for display in the page.	**FacesMessage** instances are added to the **FacesContext** during the process validations phase. They are extracted from the **FacesContext** for display to the user during the Render Response phase.
ActionForm, also known as **Form Bean**	The target of any **ValueExpression** in the page, such as **<h:inputText value="#{bean .name" />**.	A developer subclasses **ActionForm** and provides JavaBeans properties corresponding to the values in the page that can be filled in by the user. These properties are populated with the values from the form.	Any value in the page can be read from, and submitted to, a **ValueExpression**. Contrast with Struts where all the values in the page must go into the single **ActionForm** for this page.
ActionFormBean	"backing-bean" concept	A runtime representation of the **<form-bean>** element in the **struts-config.xml**	The JSF backing-bean concept allows a JavaBean to vend **UIComponent** instances that match form fields.
DynaActionForm	"backing-bean" concept	A subclass of **ActionForm** that obviates the need to hard-code JavaBeans properties for each value in the form.	See **ActionFormBean**.

TABLE C-1   A Concept Map from Struts to Faces *(continued)*

Development Style

Before continuing with a description of one migration strategy of moving from Struts to Faces, it is useful to discuss the development style of Struts in comparison to other frameworks, including JSF. The terminology in this discussion is commonly used and was captured nicely by JSF Expert Group member and Facelets originator Jacob Hookom in his blog. One way to classify Web application frameworks is by the way they assign responsibilities. In this scheme, frameworks fall into three classifications:

- Traditional Action Frameworks
- Hybrid Component/Action Frameworks
- True Component Frameworks

These frameworks are summarized in Table C-2.

Frameworks	Description	Examples
Traditional Action	Developer writes an Action in Java code tailored to the needs of each request. Generally, you end up with a 1:1 mapping between Views and Actions.	Struts, WebWork, Plain JSP/ Servlet
Hybrid Component/Action	Developer still needs custom Action for each kind of request, but **UIComponent** frameworks are present.	Tapestry, Wicket, Rife
True Component	Action is totally decoupled from the per-request type Java code.	JSF, Echo2

TABLE C-2   Classifying Web Frameworks

The benefits of component-based frameworks are evident in the entire content of this book and need not be discussed further here. One oft-noted shortcoming present in Struts but not in Faces is the need to subclass the **Action** and/or **ActionForm** in Struts. Less common but no less troublesome is the subclassing of **RequestProcessor**. Requiring subclassing for even the most basic uses of the framework leads to systems that are fragile and can be difficult to maintain. This is because changing the base class can often break subclasses, and special care must be taken to avoid this problem.

Migration Strategy: The Struts-Faces Integration Library

The recommended strategy from Craig McClanahan on moving from Struts to Faces is to continue to use Struts for enhancements to existing development, and to use Faces when performing new development. That said, there is a middle-of the road story, the Struts Faces Integration Library. Available for download from **http://struts.apache.org/**, this library allows you to use the simple rendering behavior of JSF components in a Struts application, while keeping Struts for the data integration and controller behavior. This section lists the steps you must take to migrate your pure Struts application to using Struts-Faces. It is only intended to be an introduction to the Struts-Faces library. Complete documentation can be found at the Struts site listed earlier.

This discussion assumes you have a working Struts application and want to migrate the usages of the Struts HTML tag library within that application to use JSF components instead. An application using the Struts-Faces library is both a Struts application and a Faces application. Therefore, the standard configuration steps for a Faces application must be followed.

Before diving in we must share one word of anecdotal caution. We've heard from several people who have tried to use this library that it was difficult to get it working as advertised. These people just decided to rewrite the UI layer in JSF and keep the model tier as stable as possible. However, we've been assured that many of these problems have been fixed with the latest version of the library.

Satisfying Compile-Time and Runtime Dependencies

If using a container that does not contain a JSF implementation, make sure to include JSF and its required jars in **WEB-INF/lib**. For Sun's JSF implementation, this is **jsf-api.jar** and

jsf-impl.jar. Sun's JSF implementation also requires **commons-beanutils.jar, commons-collections.jar, commons-logging.jar**, and **commons-digester.jar**. If you plan to use JSTL (and in most cases you will have to do so) the **jstl.jar** and **standard.jar** must also be included. Finally, incorporate the **struts-faces.jar** in **WEB-INF/lib**.

Note that all required taglibs that you must use in a **Struts-Faces** application are bundled in the preceding jars. Therefore, it is not necessary to take any action to place TLD files in any specific place in the system. In fact, you don't need TLD files at all if they are all inside the jars.

Declaring the FacesServlet

As shown in Chapter 2, you need to declare the **FacesServlet** in your web.xml:

```
<servlet>
  <servlet-name>FacesServlet</servlet-name>
  <servlet-class>javax.faces.webapp.FacesServlet</servlet-class>
  <load-on-startup>1</load-on-startup>
</servlet>
```

Note the **<load-on-startup>** element. This is important in order to ensure that the **FacesServlet** is loaded before the Struts **ActionServlet**, which must have a **load-on-startup** value of 2 or higher.

Mapping the FacesServlet

Again, as in Chapter 2, you must map the **FacesServlet** to the prefix or extension mapping of your choice. It is acceptable to use both kinds of mappings:

```
<servlet-mapping>
  <servlet-name>FacesServlet</servlet-name>
  <url-pattern>/faces/*</url-pattern>
  <url-pattern>*.jsf<url-pattern>
</servlet-mapping>
```

Replacing the Standard Struts Request Processor

Modify your application's **struts-config.xml** file to include the appropriate custom **RequestProcessor** implementation. If your application uses tiles, include the following markup:

```
<controller>
  <set-property property="processorClass"
   value="org.apache.struts.faces.application.FacesTilesRequestProcessor"/>
</controller>
```

Otherwise include the markup shown next:

```
<controller>
  <set-property property="processorClass"
   value="org.apache.struts.faces.application.FacesRequestProcessor"/>
</controller>
```

The two different **RequestProcessor** implementations extend **TilesRequestProcessor** and **RequestProcessor**, respectively, but are otherwise identical.

Migrating the JSP Pages

For each JSP page in your Struts application, migrate them to use JSF components instead of the Struts HTML tag library. For example, in Struts you might have the following:

```
<html:radio property="instrument" value="TRUMPET"/>Trumpet
<html:radio property="instrument" value="CLARINET"/>Clarinet
<html:radio property="instrument" value="SAXOPHONE"/>Saxophone
```

Whereas, in JSF you would have

```
<h:selectOneRadio id="instrument" value="#{bean.instruments}"
                  layout="pageDirection" />
```

where #{bean.instruments} is a method expression that points to a value that is a list of **javax.faces.model.SelectItem** instances. This migration may be done in a page by page fashion; it doesn't all have to be done at once. For example, you could migrate just the "store front" page at first, and leave the rest for later.

A vital part of migrating a page is converting the use of a subset of the tags in the Struts HTML tag library that are not present in Faces. Such tags are provided in the **tags-faces** tag library, included in the Struts-Faces distribution. This tag library is declared in your application in place of the **tags-html** tag library. For example, using pure Struts you would have

```
<%@ taglib uri="http://struts.apache.org/tags-html" prefix="html" %>
```

However, using the Struts-Faces library you would have the following:

```
<%@ taglib prefix="s" uri="http://struts.apache.org/tags-faces" %>
```

The required taglibs are shown in Table C-3.

Note that the **tags-logic** and **tags-bean** libraries have been replaced with the **jstl/core** library. It is recommended to use JSTL wherever possible to replace a Struts tag library.

Taglib URI in Struts	Conventional Prefix	Taglib URI in Faces	Conventional Prefix
http://struts.apache.org/tags-logic	logic	http://java.sun.com/jsp/jstl/core	c
http://struts.apache.org/tags-tiles	tiles	No direct analog in Faces, though you can use Tiles in Faces as is.	tiles
ttp://struts.apache.org/tags-bean	bean	http://java.sun.com/jsp/jstl/core	c
http://struts.apache.org/tags-html	html	http://java.sun.com/jsf/html	h

TABLE C-3 Struts and Faces JSP Tag Libraries

JSF 1.2 Tip *While the recommendation to use JSTL still stands for JSF 1.1 and 1.2, some caveats are necessary for JSF 1.1. In JSF 1.1, c:forEach and c:if did not work properly with JSF. Unfortunately, neither do their Struts taglib counterparts. These problems have been fixed in JSF 1.2.*

Not all tags in the Struts tag libraries have analogs in their Faces counterparts. Most importantly is the case of the **tags-html** library. For these cases, the Struts Faces distribution provides the **tags-faces** tag library. The URI for this tag library is **http://struts.apache.org/ tags-faces** and the common prefix is **s**. Use the following rule when answering the question: What taglib should I use when I'm trying to migrate from **tags-html** to JSF?

Tip *Look first in the **tags-faces** tag library for a corresponding tag to the one in **tags-html** or **jsf/ html**. If there is no tag in **tags-faces** in either of the **tags-html** or **jsf/html** libraries, then just use the tag in **jsf/html**.*

Most importantly, always use the **s:form** tag instead of the **h:form** one. The **s:form** is the key to enabling many of the Struts features and omitting it will essentially break your application.

Another special case is the **html:cancel** tag. Usages of this tag must be replaced by **h:commandButton** with the **id** attribute set to "cancel". This special **id** enables Struts to recognize this as a cancel button.

Modifying the Action Forwards

Because both Struts and Faces depend on the front controller design pattern, any action forwards in your **struts-config.xml** that name a migrated JSP page as the path must be made to go through the Faces front controller. For example, if you mapped the **FacesServlet** to the **url-pattern** of "/faces/*", you would add the following prefix to the action rule:

```
<forward name="editEvent" path="/faces/editPath.jsp" />
```

If the **FacesServlet** was mapped with a **url-pattern** of "*.jsf", you would change the extension as follows:

```
<forward name="editEvent" path="/editPath.jsf" />
```

These steps should be enough to get you started on migrating from Struts to JSF. Don't be afraid to experiment until you get the results you desire.

JSF Futures: Apache Shale

A s shown in the previous chapters in the book, JSF is a complete Web Application Framework suitable for building the front end of production-quality enterprise applications. However, the initial design requirements did not call for JSF to be a complete Web Application Framework. The technical benefit of JSF was intended to come from the component model, the event model, and the request processing lifecycle. For JSF to succeed in the marketplace, it had to be fully functional as a stand-alone Web Application Framework. The challenge for the JSF Expert Group was to meet the core requirements and include as much Web Application Framework functionality as could be cleanly specified and implemented in the 1.0 time frame, while leaving the door open for innovation and future development on top of the core JSF API. As of this writing, there are two major frameworks built on top of JSF: JBoss Seam and Apache Struts-Shale. The latter is the subject of this appendix.

As mentioned in Chapter 1, Craig McClanahan is the inventor of Struts and a key contributor to the development of the JSF 1.0 specification. All while working on JSF, Craig did not forget his Apache roots, and when the 1.1 version of the specification was completed, Craig launched a new project at Apache intended to be the successor to Struts. Ultimately, the new development was being done by the Struts community on both Shale and "Struts Classic" in parallel. Struts-Shale, or simply Shale, was a clean break from the design of Struts. The most fundamental difference between Shale and Struts Classic is that the former builds on the services provided by JSF. There is a firm historical precedent for this practice: Apache Shale and JBoss Seam are two popular frameworks that have, to date, taken advantage of JSF this way.

We first provide a brief historical background for Shale, and then address some early adoption and migration concerns, before jumping into how to get the code and run the sample application. Afterward, we close with a brief survey of the main components of the Shale project.

Shale, the Java Community Process, and Innovation

The Java Community Process has proven itself as a successful governing body for the Java Platform. However, its effectiveness as an incubator for innovation has been called into question as the open-source development model has gained more acceptance in the corporate world. The main reason is speed. JCP standards must be developed carefully, with extreme regard for the longevity and backwards compatibility of the Java Platform, as determined by its large corporate stakeholders such as Oracle, IBM, Bea, Borland, and

Macromedia. JCP standards also must make a clean separation between interface and implementation to allow for the platform vendors to integrate the standards into their products in a way that best benefits them and their shareholders. Open-source projects, on the other hand, are not shackled by such burdens and can feel free to break backwards compatibility, bypass the need to separate interface and implementation as well as many other required practices of corporate software development. Of course, many open-source projects do maintain these best practices, and indeed several JCP specs, including JSF, have high-quality open-source implementations. This gives open source an advantage in delivering a working solution, though the way the solution works may change very quickly between versions. This tension between the agendas of corporate and open-source software will be a major influence on how the JCP evolves, and thankfully, everyone stands to gain.

The Shale project is intended to be a proving ground for ideas that may one day end up in a JCP specification, such as JSF 2.0 or some yet-to-be-devised technology. But presently, these concepts are implemented in Shale as a collection of loosely coupled features from which developers can pick and choose to use in their applications. For example, one could choose to employ the Shale validation feature which is simply an adapter layer allowing one to use the popular Jakarta Commons Validator framework inside a JSF application. If you want quick, easy, powerful, flexible client-side validation from JSF, this is the way to go. Another independently useful feature is Shale remoting. This is a set of JSF extensions that are useful for AJAX applications. They are a generalization of the AJAX concepts presented in Chapter 11, and include some other handy ideas well suited to AJAX. Table D-1 summarizes the main features of Shale.

Feature	Description	Covered in this Appendix
ViewController	Abstracts the backing bean concept enforced in Sun Java Studio Creator into a generically usable form. Namely, this enforces a 1:1 relationship between a JSF View and a single backing bean, as well as providing page lifecycle events defined as methods on that bean.	Yes
Dialog Manager	Builds on the concepts of the Faces navigation system to allow grouping a collection of views together so they form a coherent entity and share state and transitions.	Yes
Application Manager	Similar to ViewController in that it supplements the JSF lifecycle, but different in that it is implemented as a filter that operates before and after the JSF lifecycle for *all* requests, not just those specific to a certain view.	Yes
Validation	Allows using Jakarta Commons Validator in a JSF application.	Yes

TABLE D-1   Top-Level Features of Shale

Feature	Description	Covered in this Appendix
Remoting	A generalization of the AJAX patterns described in Chapter 11, along with additional AJAX-related features.	Yes
JNDI Integration	A **VariableResolver** that allows accessing JNDI via EL Expressions.	No. See the online Shale documentation.
Spring Integration	Allows Spring to vend managed beans to a Shale application.	No. See Chapter 12 for more on JSF/Spring integration.
Tiles Integration	Allows the use of stand-alone Tiles in a Shale application.	No. Facelets is functionally equivalent to this feature. See Chapter 13 for more information.
Clay	A non-JSP view description technology.	No. Facelets is functionally equivalent to this feature. See Chapter 13 for more information.
Test Framework	Enables unit-testing of JSF Applications.	No
Tiger Extensions	Allows using Java SE 5 annotations to create JSF managed beans and register JSF components, converters, validators, and renderers.	No

TABLE D-1   Top-Level Features of Shale *(continued)*

Migration Concerns: Should I Depend on Shale?

As of this writing, Shale has had its 1.0 release and a follow-up bug-fix release. A wary IT developer may still safely classify Shale as "cutting edge." As yet, it hasn't proven itself in the market. It is important to keep in mind that every Shale application is a JSF application and will run in any JSF-compliant container. Just because Shale is new doesn't mean one shouldn't feel safe in developing production applications on top of it. The JSF technology on which it is built is pretty well established, so even if Shale doesn't take off the way Struts did, your investment will still be safe because of the connection with JSF. Please consult **http://shale.apache.org/api-stability.html** for a guide to the stability of each of the Shale features.

Getting and Running Shale

This section will cover where to get Shale and how to deploy and run the sample application on the Java EE SDK. The latest release of Shale can be downloaded from **http://struts.apache.org/struts-shale/**. The distribution consists of several war, tar, and Zip files. To get started, just download the **shale-usecases.war**. This war file, and the **shale-blank.war**, include all the many dependencies necessary to run Shale. To deploy the application, enter the command **.\asadmin deploy --user admin --password adminadmin shale-usecases.war**, where the user and password arguments are correct for your installation.

PART V

If you are using a container other than the Java EE SDK, please follow the instructions for deploying a war on that container.

The usecases sample application contains usecases for most of the major features of Shale, but for starters, we'll cover the "Log On Dialog" usecase. This will introduce two of the major features of Shale: **Dialog Manager** and **Application Manager**. These and other features will be covered in more detail at the end of this appendix.

Once you deploy the **shale-usecases** Web application, visit **http://localhost:port/shale-usecases/** and you'll be presented with a page containing a number of links to the various usecase examples. Click **Log On Dialog**, then click the **Create New User Profile** link. This will take you to the first page of a wizard-style interface where you can create a new user. If you've ever installed software on Windows, you know what a wizard is. The page will look something like Figure D-1.

Note the familiar Next, Previous, Finish, and Cancel buttons, with the Previous button grayed out. A wizard interface is the simplest example of the usage of a Shale dialog. In Shale terms, a dialog is just a collection of pages that are related to some common processing task. The Shale Log On Dialog Use Case allows a user to create a new ID in the system and enter some profile information into it. The first page lets you to enter a username and password for the profile you would like to create. This page features Next and Previous buttons, where the Previous button is grayed out because we are on the first page. Pressing Next takes you to a page where you can enter in your full name and e-mail address. While on this page, you have the option of pressing Next, Previous, Finish, or Cancel. Pressing Finish takes you back to the main page. Pressing Next takes you to a page where you can edit the categories of messages you would like to receive. Pressing Previous has the obvious effect of taking you back to the previous page. Finally, pressing Cancel on any of the pages will cancel the current action without applying any values.

The Dialog Manager

This whole interaction is well suited to modeling with a UML 2 State Diagram, as shown in Figure D-2. Don't worry if you're not familiar with UML 2 State Diagrams; all will be explained next.

The most basic way to understand a Shale dialog is as a set of pages where one of the pages is marked as the "start" page, and another is marked as the "end." There are zero or more intermediary pages between the start and end, and the flow between all of these is governed by the Shale Dialog Manager. At first glance, this doesn't seem be any more useful than the existing JSF navigation system described in Chapter 5. The benefit of the Shale Dialog Manager comes mainly from reuse. It's possible to take a Shale dialog and treat it as a "black box" that can be called by more than one dialog subroutine, or from nondialog pages. In addition, the Dialog Manager introduces a special session-scoped variable, called "dialog," that is used to store state information related to the current dialog.

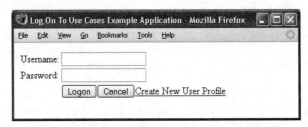

FIGURE D-1   logon.jsp in the Shale Log On Dialog Use Case

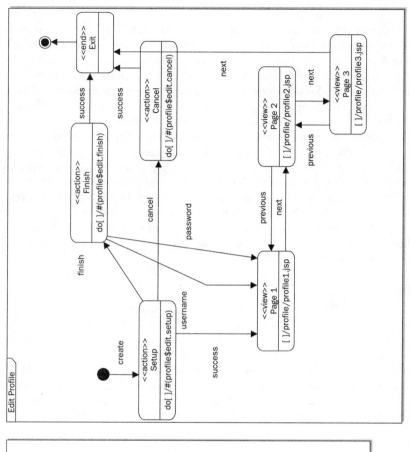

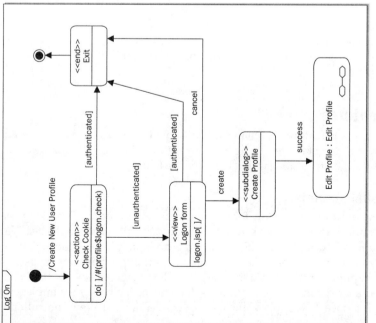

FIGURE D-2   The State Diagram of the Shale Log On Dialog Use Case

The first thing to note about Figure D-2 is that there are two state diagrams. This is because Shale supports the notion of sub-dialogs; the Log On Dialog Use Case happens to be modeled using one outer dialog and one sub-dialog. Dialogs and sub-dialogs are implemented in Shale using a stack data structure. When a user enters into a dialog in a Shale application, the runtime actually pushes the dialog onto a stack. If a sub-dialog is entered within that dialog, it too is pushed on the stack, and popped when the dialog exits. The benefit of using sub-dialogs is cleaner encapsulation and reusability. For example, you can reuse a dialog as a sub-dialog wherever it makes sense to do so. Returning to Figure D-2, the outer dialog is entered via the Create New User Profile link. The system checks for the existence of a cookie from a previous login, and if present, the login dialog exits. If the cookie does not exist, the user is directed to the Logon Form page. If the user successfully logs in, we proceed to the exit state. If not, we allow the user to create a profile, at which point we enter into the sub-dialog on the right of Figure D-2. The start state for the sub-dialog is Setup, which transitions to the cancel state, the finish state, or the first page of the wizard depending on the return from the #{profile$edit. setup} **MethodExpression**. Once we reach page 1, it's a simple wizard with Next, Previous, Cancel and Finish buttons as described earlier.

The Application Manager

The usage of the Application Manager feature in **shale-usecases.war** is limited to a security-like role: the feature is used to disallow direct access to JSP pages within the application without passing through the proper JSF Servlet. Now, it is true that this can also be accomplished with standard Servlet security features as described in Chapter 15. One value offered by the Application Manager over the Servlet security features is the use of a complete regular expression package for operating on the URLs of incoming requests. Regardless of the limited use of the Application Manager feature in the **shale-usecases.war**, the core benefit of the feature is its ability to supplement the standard JSF request processing lifecycle (as described in Chapter 3) to allow pre- and post-processing of all JSF requests. The Application Manager can be used to gather application-wide resources—for example, database connections—that need to be initialized for all JSF pages. Another possible use is to take action on an incoming request based on the IP address or hostname of the originating client. This could be used, for example, to block access from clients originating in a certain country. The Application Manager will be covered in more detail next.

A Guide to Shale Features

This section is a guide to the features of Shale listed in Table D-1. After reading this section, you should know enough to get started using Shale in your application. The name of each feature is followed by the distribution jar that contains the feature.

ViewController (shale-core.jar)

The purpose of **ViewController** is to allow for the automatic creation of a JSF backing bean for each page in the application. Thus, let's now review the concepts of managed beans and backing beans introduced in Chapter 4. A JSF managed bean is simply a JavaBean that is used to store model data in a JSF application. For example, one might have a managed bean to represent a shopping cart. A "backing bean" is a JSF managed bean that has been associated with a specific page in the application. Backing beans in Shale must implement the **ViewController** interface. If you follow the naming conventions of **ViewController** when declaring your backing beans in your **faces-config.xml** file, you can be assured that they will be created and placed into request scope when the corresponding **view** is requested by the user. This is more "eager" than the lazy instantiation naturally provided by managed beans. In the case of regular managed beans, the instantiation happens when an EL expression containing a reference to the **managed-bean-name** is encountered. With **ViewController**, the instantiation happens when the **view** is requested. Figure D-3 illustrates this relationship.

In addition to the auto-creation of managed beans, **ViewController** also provides a way for your backing bean to be notified of the various events in the JSF lifecycle as described in Table D-2. The following methods of the **ViewController** interface will be called on your backing bean at the specified times in the JSF lifecycle.

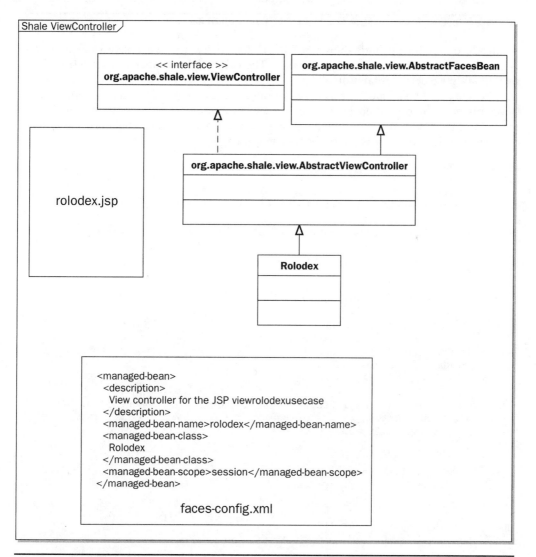

FIGURE D-3 **ViewController** and backing beans

ViewController Method Name	Description
init( )	Called before the request processing lifecycle for this view is executed.
preprocess( )	If the request is a postback, this method is called after the view has been restored in the *Restore View* phase but before any further processing.
prerender( )	Called before the *Render Response* phase for this request.
destroy( )	Called after the request processing lifecycle for this request has executed.

TABLE D-2   Request Processing Lifecycle Methods on **ViewController**

In addition to the methods shown in Table D-2, a Boolean **postback** JavaBeans property is initialized before the **init( )** method is called. The value of this property is set to **true** if the request is a postback, and **false** otherwise.

Users of Sun's Java Studio Creator will recognize this arrangement. Creator enforces this development technique where every page has a corresponding backing bean automatically created for it, and Creator also provides similar lifecycle notifications. The following is an example of a Shale backing bean for the register.jsp page.

```
package com.jsfcompref.trainer.backing;

import org.apache.shale.view.ViewController;
// Other import statements omitted

public class Register implements ViewController {

  private JSFUtil myJSFUtil = new JSFUtil();
  private HtmlInputText firstName;
  private HtmlInputText lastName;
  private HtmlSelectOneRadio gender;
  private HtmlInputText dob;
  private HtmlInputText email;
  private HtmlSelectOneMenu serviceLevel;
  private HtmlInputText userid;
  private HtmlInputSecret password;
  private HtmlInputSecret passwordCheck;

  public void validateEmail(FacesContext context, UIComponent toValidate,
    Object value) throws ValidatorException {
    // method body omitted, see Chapter 9.
  }

  public void validatePassword(FacesContext context, UIComponent toValidate,
    // method body omitted, see Chapter 9.
  }

  public String registerUser() {
    // method body omitted, see Chapter 9.
  }

  // Methods from ViewController
```

```
  private boolean postback = false;
  // This will be called by the Shale runtime if the request is a
  // postback.  This will be called before the init() method is
  // called.
  public void setPostback(boolean postback) {
    this.postback = postback;
  }

  public boolean isPostback() {
    return postback;
  }

  // Called before the request processing lifecycle for this view is
  // executed.
  public void init() {
    // If accessing a database, this is where you would set up any
    // per-request connections needed.
  }

  public void preprocess() {
    // Shale must call this method only if isPostback() is true.
    assert(isPostback());
    // Take any action on the restored view before the apply request
    // values phase starts.
  }

  public void prerender() {
    // Shale will call this method before the view is rendered.
  }

  public void destroy() {
    // Here is where you might put code that needs to, perhaps, log
    // a notification that a new user was created or when releasing a
    // database connection.
  }

// Getters and setters omitted.
}
```

For convenience, the **AbstractViewController** class provides no-op implementations of the preceding methods and a working JavaBeans property for the **postback** property. Also, there is an experimental Shale feature that allows you to simply annotate a backing bean to indicate that it is a **ViewController**. Please see the Shale documentation for more on this and other so-called "Tiger" features.

As with any JSF managed bean, it must be declared in the **faces-config.xml** file. The important thing with Shale is naming the managed bean so that it gets picked up by the Shale runtime when the corresponding view is encountered. Because the earlier **Register** backing bean is for the page **register.jsp**, the backing bean name is **register**, as shown in the following:

```
<managed-bean>
  <managed-bean-name>register</managed-bean-name>
  <managed-bean-class>com.jsfcompref.backing.Register</managed-bean-class>
  <managed-bean-scope>request</managed-bean-scope>
</managed-bean>
```

viewId	managed-bean-name
/admin/console.jsp	admin$console
/parameter/list.jsf	_parameter$list
1stPage.jsp	_1stPage

TABLE D-3   Some Example **viewId** to **managed-bean-name** Mappings

It is vitally important that the **managed-bean-scope** be set to request. Failure to do this will result in inconsistent results. The rules for naming your backing bean are as follows.

Shale will take the **viewId** and strip off any leading "/" and extension. It will then convert any remaining "/" characters into "$" characters. This is useful to allow the creation of Shale **ViewController** instances when you have JSP pages that are nested within directories. If the resulting name results in a JSF-implicit object name, prefix it with "_". If the resulting name starts with a number, also prefix it with "_". See Table D-3 for examples.

Dialog Manager (shale-core.jar)

The Dialog Manager enhances the navigation features of JSF to provide a way to group a set of pages together along with a common data object shared among them. The shared state and data is the main benefit of the dialog feature. A secondary benefit is the ability to treat a dialog as a black-box subroutine that can be reused without fear of side effects. A dialog is described in the **WEB-INF/dialog-config.xml** file. The **dialog-config.xml** file from the Log On Use Case is shown next. This dialog is represented graphically in Figure D-2.

```xml
<!DOCTYPE dialogs PUBLIC
  "-//Apache Software Foundation//DTD Shale Dialog Configuration 1.0//EN"
  "http://struts.apache.org/dtds/shale-dialog-config_1_0.dtd">
<dialogs>
  <!-- Log On / Create Profile Dialog -->
  <dialog       name="Log On"
          start="Check Cookie">
    <action       name="Check Cookie"
          method="#{profile$logon.check}">
      <transition  outcome="authenticated"
          target="Exit"/>
      <transition  outcome="unauthenticated"
          target="Logon Form"/>
    </action>
    <view       name="Logon Form"
          viewId="/profile/logon.jsp">
      <transition  outcome="authenticated"
          target="Exit"/>
      <transition  outcome="create"
          target="Create Profile"/>
      <transition  outcome="cancel"
          target="Exit"/>
    </view>
    <subdialog       name="Create Profile"
          dialogName="Edit Profile">
      <transition  outcome="success"
```

```
                      target="Exit"/>
     </subdialog>
     <end          name="Exit"
                    viewId="/usecases.jsp"/>
   </dialog>
     <!-- Edit Profile Dialog -->
   <dialog         name="Edit Profile"
                   start="Setup">
   <!-- Global transition definitions -->
     <transition      outcome="cancel"
                    target="Cancel"/>
     <transition      outcome="finish"
                    target="Finish"/>
     <action          name="Setup"
                    method="#{profile$edit.setup}">
       <transition   outcome="success"
                    target="Page 1"/>
     </action>
     <view           name="Page 1"
             viewId="/profile/profile1.jsp">
       <transition   outcome="next"
                    target="Page 2"/>
     </view>
     <view           name="Page 2"
                viewId="/profile/profile2.jsp">
       <transition   outcome="next"
                    target="Page 3"/>
       <transition   outcome="previous"
                    target="Page 1"/>
     </view>
     <view           name="Page 3"
                viewId="/profile/profile3.jsp">
       <transition   outcome="next"
                    target="Exit"/>
       <transition   outcome="previous"
                    target="Page 2"/>
     </view>
     <action          name="Cancel"
                method="#{profile$edit.cancel}">
       <transition    outcome="success"
                    target="Exit"/>
     </action>
     <action          name="Finish"
                method="#{profile$edit.finish}">
       <transition    outcome="password"
                    target="Page 1"/>
       <transition    outcome="success"
                    target="Exit"/>
       <transition    outcome="username"
                    target="Page 1"/>
     </action>
     <end          name="Exit"
                    viewId="/usecases.jsp"/>
   </dialog>
</dialogs>
```

All of the dialogs in your application are grouped in a **<dialogs>** element. Within this element, you may have zero or more **<dialog>** elements. Within the **<dialog>** element there are five kinds of top-level nodes: **<action>**, **<view>**, **<subdialog>**, **<end>**, and **<transition>**. Returning to Figure D-2, note that there are four different kinds of nodes in the state diagram, as shown by the UML **<<prototype>>** declarations on the nodes. These correspond to the **<action>**, **<view>**, **<subdialog>**, and **<end>** elements. The edges in the diagram correspond to the **<transition>** element.

Notice the **<dialog>** element has **name** and **start** attributes. The application signals entry into the dialog by returning a special value from its **action** method. For details on action methods, please see Chapter 5. Briefly, an action method is any method that takes no arguments and returns a String. Action methods are called in response to buttons or links on the page being clicked. To enter a dialog named "Log On" for example, return the string "dialog:Log On" (without the quotes) from your action method. This will cause the dialog manager to enter into the state listed in the value of the **start** attribute, and push a dialog onto the dialog stack. How to use the stack will be described later in this section. Once the application is within the scope of a dialog, the special "dialog" prefix must be omitted from other action methods within the dialog.

Each of the elements is represented in Java code as implementations of interfaces in the **org.apache.shale.dialog** package, as described next.

- **ActionState (<action> element)**   Entering into this state will cause the action method referenced by the **method** attribute to be executed. The return from that method should match one of the **outcome** attributes of the **transition** elements nested within. When a match is found, the state given by the value of the **target** attribute is entered.

- **ViewState (<view> element)**   Entering into this state will cause the view referenced by the **viewId** attribute to be rendered. The return from the action method of that view must match one of the **outcome** attributes of the **transition** elements. When a match is found, the state given by the value of the **target** attribute is entered.

- **SubdialogState (<subdialog> element)**   Entering into this state will cause the start state of the dialog referenced by the **dialog** attribute to be entered. It also causes a new dialog to be pushed onto the dialog stack. The sub-dialog exits when the **end** state is reached and that state returns an outcome that matches the **outcome** element of the **transition** element inside of the **<subdialog>** element. At this point, the system transitions to the state named by the **target** attribute of the **transition** element inside of the **<subdialog>** element.

- **EndState (<end> element)**   Entering into this state will cause the system to navigate to the viewId given by the **viewId** attribute, and pop the current dialog off the dialog stack.

As mentioned previously, the dialog is essentially a state machine implementation in JSF. As such, it is necessary to access the current state of the state machine programmatically. This is accomplished by looking in the session scope variable of type **org.apache.shale.dialog .Status** called **dialog**. This variable is stored and maintained by the dialog implementation and can be accessed by the user using the EL or programmatically by calling

```
FacesContext.getCurrentInstance().getExternalContext().
    getSessionMap().get("dialog").
```

Method on Status Interface	Description
setData(Object data)	Set an arbitrary object that contains the state information associated with this dialog. Note that this can be accessed via the EL using the expression **#{dialog.data}**.
getData( )	Returns the data object set by a previous call to **setData( )** (or also set via the EL).
getDialogName( )	Returns the name of the current dialog, if any.
getStateName( )	Returns the name of the current state, if any.
peek( )	Returns a **Status.Position** for the currently executing state. Not generally called by user code.
pop( )	Pops off the current **Status.Position** and returns the previously executing one. Not generally called by user code.
push(Status.Position position)	Pushes a new **Status.Position** onto the stack, and makes it the currently executing state. Not generally called by user code.
transition(String stateName)	Transitions to the specified state in the currently executing dialog. Not generally called by user code.

TABLE D-4   The Dialog **Status** Interface

If your managed bean extends the **AbstractViewController** class, you can also call **getBean("dialog")** to get the dialog implementation.

This **Status** interface is the main programmatic access point to the Dialog Manager feature. The methods of Status are shown in Table D-4.

Application Manager (shale-core.jar)

The Application Manager supplements the features of the **ViewController** to provide per-application lifecycle notifications. You can take action on a "preprocess" event before the JSF lifecycle is even reached. Some examples of things you might want to do during the "preprocess" event include the following:

- Intercept the request and prevent the JSF lifecycle from being reached—for example, you could restrict access to certain parts of the site in this way, or you could restrict access from certain IP addresses
- Initialize any per-request resources

As expected, there is also a "postprocess" event that tends to be useful for releasing resources aquired during "preprocess."

To use this feature, you must include a special Servlet filter and listener in your **web.xml** as shown next.

```
<filter>
  <filter-name>shale</filter-name>
  <filter-class>
    org.apache.shale.faces.ShaleApplicationFilter
  </filter-class>
</filter>
```

```
<!-- any intervening XML omitted -->
<filter-mapping>
  <filter-name>shale</filter-name>
  <url-pattern>/*</url-pattern>
</filter-mapping>

<listener>
  <listener-class>
    org.apache.commons.chain.web.ChainListener
  </listener-class>
</listener>
```

The Application Manager feature is really nothing more than an application of the Apache **Commons Chain** project (**http://jakarta.apache.org/commons/chain/**). This project provides a Web-friendly implementation of the "Chain of Responsibility" design pattern. Detailed instructions for using Commons Chain are beyond the scope of this text. We will cover only what is required to use this feature in Shale. The main abstraction to understand is the **Command** interface. This interface has one method, **execute( )**, that takes a **Context** argument and returns a Boolean that indicates whether or not the next link in the chain should be consulted. In Shale, this **Context** argument is actually an instance of **ShaleWebContext** and implements **java.util.Map**. In Commons Chain, **Command** implementations are grouped into a named "catalog." The Servlet Filter declared in the earlier XML looks for a Commons Chain "catalog" named "shale." If you define such a catalog in your **WEB-INF/chain-config.xml**, any **Command** declarations therein will be executed. The following is an abbreviated version of the **chain-config.xml** file from **shale-usecases.war**.

```
<catalogs>
  <!-- Define preprocessing command chain for Shale to execute -->
  <catalog                name="shale">
    <chain                name="preprocess">
      <!-- Disallow direct access to JSP and JSFP resources -->
      <command className=
        "org.apache.shale.application.ContextRelativePathFilter"
includes="\S*\.xml,\S*\.faces,\S*\.html,\S*\.gif,\S*\.jpg,/index\.jsp"
                          excludes="\S*\.jsp,\S*\.jspf"/>
    </chain>
  </catalog>
</catalogs>
```

The **<catalogs>** element contains all of the commons chain catalogs for the application. Within the **<catalog>** element, you must have one or more **<chain>** elements. Shale knows about two chains, "preprocess" and "postprocess." Any commands declared in the "preprocess" chain will be executed before the JSF request processing lifecycle is executed. Likewise, any commands in the "postprocess" chain (not shown earlier) will be called after the JSF request processing lifecycle.

Shale provides three concrete **Command** implementations suitable for use in your application. They are described in Table D-5. Each one has its own configurable attributes and behaviors as described on the Shale Web site.

Name	Description
ContextRelativePathFilter	Allows using Regular Expressions to take action on the context-relative portion of the request URI. The main advantage of this is the Regular Expression feature, which far surpasses the capabilities of the URI matching allowed in a web.xml.
RemoteAddrFilter	Like **ContextRelativePathFilter**, but matches against the remote address obtained from the **getRemoteAddr( )** method of the incoming **ServletRequest**.
RemoteHostFilter	Like **ContextRelativePathFilter**, but matches against the remote address obtained from the **getRemoteHost( )** method of the incoming **ServletRequest**.

TABLE D-5 **Command** Implementations Provided by Shale

Validation (shale-core.jar)

The Jakarta Commons Validator project (**http://jakarta.apache.org/commons/validator/**) is a mature, popular, and feature-rich validation framework. It offers client- and server-side validation of popular data-types such as credit card numbers, ISBN numbers, e-mail addresses, and dates. Shale provides three JSP custom tags that allow you to use the full capabilities of Commons Validator inside of JSF applications. Let's start by converting the **register.jsp** from the sample application in Chapter 9 in order to use Shale Validation.

```
<h:form onsubmit="return validateForm(this);">
<h:messages globalOnly="true" infoClass="RegError"/>
<h:panelGrid width="70%" columns="3" border="0">
  <h:outputLabel value="First Name:"/>
  <h:inputText id="fname" binding="#{Register_Backing.firstName}">
    <s:commonsValidator type="required"
      message="I need your first name!"
      server="true" client="true" />
  </h:inputText>
  <h:message for="fname" errorClass="ValidateError"/>
  <h:outputLabel value="Last Name:"/>
  <h:inputText id="lname" binding="#{Register_Backing.lastName}">
    <s:commonsValidator type="required"
      message="I need your last name!"
      server="true" client="true" />
  </h:inputText>
  <h:message for="lname" errorClass="ValidateError"/>
  <h:outputLabel value="Date of Birth:(mm-dd-yy)"/>
  <h:inputText id="dob"
      binding="#{Register_Backing.dob}" >
    <f:convertDateTime pattern="mm-dd-yy"/>
    <s:commonsValidator type="date" datePatternStrict="mm-dd-yy"
      server="true" client="true" />
  </h:inputText>
```

```
<h:message for="dob" errorClass="ValidateError"/>
<h:outputLabel value="Email:"/>
<h:inputText id="email"
    binding="#{Register_Backing.email}"
    validator="#{Register_Backing.validateEmail}">
  <s:commonsValidator type="required"
     message="Must provide an email address."
     server="true" client="true" />
  <s:commonsValidator type="email"
     message="Email address must be valid."
     server="true" client="true" />
</h:inputText>
<h:message for="email" errorClass="ValidateError"/>
<h:outputLabel value="Userid:"/>
<h:inputText id="userid"
    binding="#{Register_Backing.userid}">
  <s:commonsValidator type="minlength"
         message="Userid must be at least 6 characters long"
         client="true" server="true" minlength="6" />
  <s:commonsValidator type="mask"
         message="Userid must consist of letters and numbers
                  but no special characters or spaces"
         client="true" server="true" >
    <s:validatorVar name="mask" value="[a-zA-Z0-9].*"/>
  </s:commonsValidator>
</h:inputText>
<h:message for="userid" errorClass="ValidateError"/>
<h:outputLabel value="Password:"/>
<h:inputSecret required="true" id="password"
    binding="#{Register_Backing.password}"
    validator="#{Register_Backing.validatePassword}"/>
<!-- this was left to use the standard JSF validator -->
<h:message for="password" errorClass="ValidateError"/>
<h:outputLabel value="Retype Password:"/>
<h:inputSecret required="true" id="password2"
    binding="#{Register_Backing.passwordCheck}"/>
<!-- this was left to use the standard JSF validator -->
<h:message for="password2" errorClass="ValidateError"/>
<f:verbatim> </f:verbatim>
<h:commandButton value="Register"
    action="#{Register_Backing.registerUser}"/>
<h:commandButton value="Cancel" action="cancel"
    immediate="true" />
</h:panelGrid>
<s:validatorScript functionName="validateForm"/>
</h:form>
```

In the preceding JSP code, the parts that relate to Shale Validation have been printed in boldface type. Shale Validation is exposed to the page author via the three JSP custom tags used earlier and described in Table D-6.

The **<s:commonsValidator>** tag has a type attribute that indicates which of the Commons Validators to use. There are three different types of validators at work in the preceding JSP code: **required**, **minlength**, and **mask**. The default allowable values for the type attribute are given in Table D-7. All of them work in both client- and server-side mode.

Tag Name	Description
s:commonsValidator	Exposes a commons validator, identified by type, for use by the page author. This will cause a standard JSF **Validator** instance to be created and added to the component, inside which this tag is nested. The **Validator** instance will call through to the corresponding Commons Validator.
s:validatorVar	Name/value pairs for configuring the validator. Must be nested inside of **s:commonsValidator**.
s:validatorScript	Generates the JavaScript that performs client-side validation for validators that request it. This script is callable from any JavaScript event handler, but most commonly it is called from the **h:form**'s onsubmit. This tag should occur just before the closing **</h:form>** tag.

TABLE D-6   Shale Validator Tags

The set of supported types may be expanded by providing an additional **validator-rules.xml** file. For information on how to do this, please consult the Shale documentation, referenced in the later **Resources** section.

Remoting (shale-remoting.jar)

As shown in Chapter 11, one of the ways to leverage JSF in an AJAX application is by using a **PhaseListener** to act on incoming AJAX requests and serve up the JavaScript file to the client, while also taking action on the component tree. If access to the component tree is not needed when processing AJAX requests, but access to such things as managed beans and other non-view artifacts *is* necessary, the Remoting feature of Shale is useful.

Type	Description
required	A value is required for this field.
minlength	The length of the value of the field must be at least N characters.
maxlength	The length of the value of the field must be less than N characters.
byte	Value must be convertible to a corresponding primitive type.
short	Value must be convertible to a corresponding primitive type.
integer	Value must be convertible to a corresponding primitive type.
float	Value must be convertible to a corresponding primitive type.
date	Value must be convertible to a date.
intRange	Value must be between two specified extremes.
floatRange	Value must be between two specified extremes.
creditCard	Value must be a semantically correct credit card number. Note that this does not actually perform any account verification.
email	Value must be a semantically correct Internet e-mail address. Note that this does not actually perform any SMTP verification.

TABLE D-7   Types of Commons Validator Validators Supported in Shale by Default

To configure Shale remoting, simply drop the **shale-remoting.jar** file into the **WEB-INF/lib** directory of your Web application. This jar includes a **PhaseListener** declaration in its **META-INF/faces-config.xml** file, which causes the **PhaseListener** to be automatically added to the JSF application on startup. Let us examine Shale remoting by considering two use cases the feature was designed to handle: accessing static resources, and invoking a method binding.

Accessing Static Resources

In order to make the job of the page authors as easy as possible, it is generally a good idea to minimize the amount of configuration they need to do to use your component. For example, if the implementation of your component includes JavaScript script files and CSS style sheets, the easiest thing is for the page author to not even know these dependencies exist. In Chapter 11, this magic was achieved by having a **PhaseListener** look at the incoming request and discern the name of a Java resource which was then requested via **ClassLoader .getResourceAsStream()** and sent back to the client. The JSF component whose implementation included the JavaScript or CSS style sheet would then render markup to cause these elements to be requested by the browser, as in the **encodeEnd()** method of the **SpellCheckTextArea** in Chapter 11.

```
public void encodeEnd(FacesContext context) throws IOException {
  getStandardTextareaRenderer(context).encodeEnd(context, this);
  ExternalContext extContext = context.getExternalContext();
  ResponseWriter writer = context.getResponseWriter();
  // Render the main script, only once per page
  if (!extContext.getRequestMap().containsKey("ajaxflag.ajaxScript")) {
    extContext.getRequestMap().put("ajaxflag.ajaxScript", Boolean.TRUE);
    writer.startElement("script", this);
    writer.writeAttribute("type", "text/JavaScript", null);
    writer.writeAttribute("src", SpellcheckPhaseListener.RENDER_SCRIPT_VIEW_ID,
                          null);
    writer.endElement("script");
  // Remainder omitted.
  }
```

Then, the **SpellCheckPhaseListener** would render the script in response to the request made by the browser when it encounters the **<script>** element rendered previously.

```
public void afterPhase(PhaseEvent event) {
  // If this is the restoreView phase and the viewId is
  // the script view id...
  if (-1 != event.getFacesContext().getViewRoot().
      getViewId().indexOf(RENDER_SCRIPT_VIEW_ID)) {
    // render the script
    writeScript(event);
    event.getFacesContext().responseComplete();
  }
}
```

Shale remoting generalizes this approach so the preceding **encodEnd()** excerpt can be rewritten as follows.

```
import org.apache.shale.remoting.XhtmlHelper;
import org.apache.shale.remoting.Mechanism;

public void encodeEnd(FacesContext context) throws IOException {
```

```
getStandardTextareaRenderer(context).encodeEnd(context, this);
ResponseWriter writer = context.getResponseWriter();
// Render the main script, only once per page
XhtmlHelper helper = new XhtmlHelper();
helper.linkJavaScript(context, this, writer,
  Mechanism.CLASS_RESOURCE, "com/jsfcompref/scripts/ajax.js");
// Remainder omitted.
}
```

Shale does the work of generating the **<script>** element, as well as ensuring that it is only rendered once per page. There is no sense in rendering the same **<script>** element twice in one page, since the script is already loaded and the second request will be pointless. This code uses the Shale remoting **XhtmlHelper** class, which provides several useful methods for including JavaScript and CSS files in the rendered output of your components. Let's examine the arguments to the **linkJavaScript()** method in Table D-8.

The **Mechanism.CLASS_RESOURCE** constant prevents downloading .class files because this would be a security risk. For the usecase of accessing static resources from the Web application, instead of from the classpath, use the **Mechanism.WEBAPP_RESOURCE** constant instead.

Name	Description
context	The **FacesContext** for this request. In most cases, this will already be passed as a parameter to the method in which you're calling **linkJavaScript()**.
this	The **UIComponent** that is rendering this **<script>** element as a part of its rendering. Because the previous code excerpt is from the **encodeEnd()** method of the **SpellCheckTextArea** component, the **this** pointer is the **UIComponent** instance itself.
writer	The **ResponseWriter** for this request. If you are rendering a component, you probably already have this anyway. If not, you can always get it from the **FacesContext**.
Mechanism.CLASS_RESOURCE	Tells Shale what kind of resource loading to use to find the resource. This mechanism instructs Shale to look in the runtime classpath for the resource. Other mechanisms will be covered in the following.
"com/jsfcompref/scripts/ajax.js"	This is the name of the file within your component jar that you want to be served up in response to the request. Actually, it need not be in the jar; it only must be on the runtime classpath. However, including it in the component jar is the most common case.
"text/JavaScript"	This argument was not shown in the preceding code because it is optional. If not specified, it defaults to "text/JavaScript". If specified, this is what gets rendered as the value of the "type" attribute of the **<script>** tag.

TABLE D-8 Arguments to **linkJavascript()**

PART V

In addition to the **linkJavaScript()** method, there is also a **linkStylesheet()** method, with similar arguments intended for loading a CSS style sheet.

Invoking a MethodExpression

The server-side requirements of many AJAX applications can be met simply by easily invoking a **MethodExpression** (known as **MethodBinding** in JSF 1.1). Shale provides this feature with the **mapResourceId()** method of **XhtmlHelper** combined with the **Mechanism.DYNAMIC_RESOURCE** constant. The **SpellCheckTextArea** component in Chapter 11 uses its **decode()** method to return an XML document to the browser containing the suggestions for the current word. Another way to do this would be to implement this feature on a request-scoped managed bean which could be accessed via the EL. Of course, doing so would break the cohesiveness of the **SpellCheckTextArea** component because then there would be another configuration step to perform (declaring the managed bean properly). Even so, the user would not see this step because the managed-bean declaration could be included in the **META-INF/faces-config.xml** file in the jar housing the **SpellCheckTextArea** component. Let's cover at a high level what must be done to this component to convert it to leveraging Shale remoting.

For discussion purposes, let's say we have a managed bean with the following declaration in **META-INF/faces-config.xml**.

```
<managed-bean>
  <managed-bean-name>jsfcompref_suggester</managed-bean-name>
  <managed-bean-class>
    com.jsfcompref.trainer.components.SpellCheckTextAreaHelper
  </managed-bean-class>
  <managed-bean-scope>request</managed-bean-scope>
</managed-bean>
```

And that the class for the bean is packaged into the component jar. Let's say this bean has a method that returns the suggestions:

```
public void getSuggestions() {
  String suggestions[];
  FacesContext context = FacesContext.getCurrentInstance();
  Map requestParamMap = context.getExternalContext().
    getRequestParameterMap();
  String word = requestParamMap.get("wordToCheck");
  try {
      suggestions = (String [])
    getWordServer().invoke(context, new Object [] { word });
  } catch (Exception e) {
      System.out.println("Exception: " + e.getMessage());
  }
  if (null == result) {
      return;
  }

  HttpServletResponse response = (HttpServletResponse)
  context.getExternalContext().getResponse();

  // set the header information for the response
  response.setContentType("text/xml");
```

```
    response.setHeader("Cache-Control", "no-cache");

    try {
        ResponseWriter writer = Util.getResponseWriter(context);
        writer.startElement("message", this);
        writer.startElement("suggestions", null);
        for (int i = 0; i < result.length; i++) {
    writer.startElement("word", this);
    writer.writeText(result[i], null);
    writer.endElement("word");
        }
        writer.endElement("suggestions");
        writer.startElement("currentWord", this);
        writer.writeText(value, null);
        writer.endElement("currentWord");
        writer.startElement("clientId", this);
        writer.writeText(clientId, null);
        writer.endElement("clientId");
        writer.endElement("message");
    } catch (IOException e) {
        // log message
    }
    context.responseComplete();
}
```

The **SpellCheckTextArea** component would then include the following in its **encodeEnd()**.

```
String callback = helper.mapResourceId(context,
    Mechanism.DYNAMIC_CALLBACK, "/jsfcompref_suggester/getSuggestions");
writer.startElement("script", this);
writer.writeAttribute("type", "text/javascript", null);
writer.write("var " + this.getClientId() + "_suggestions = " +
            + "\"" + callback + "\";");
writer.endElement("script");
```

This code causes the URI of the MethodBinding that invokes the **getSuggestions()** method to be stored in a globally scoped JavaScript variable on the browser. Assuming the **id** of the **<jcr:spellCheckTextArea>** is "textarea", this would cause the following JavaScript to be rendered as:

```
var textarea_suggestions = "<SHALE_SPECIFIC_PREFIX>/jsfcompref/getSuggestions";
```

The **<SHALE_SPECIFIC_PREFIX>** is something generated by Shale and cannot be counted on to be any specific value at runtime. With the **textarea_suggestions** variable in hand, our AJAX JavaScript can now issue a simple GET request over XmlHttpRequest. The URI for that request is simply the **textarea_suggestions** variable with the query string containing the **wordToCheck** appended to it. This code will look something like the following:

```
var request = getXMLHttpRequest();
request.open("GET", textarea_suggestions + "?wordToCheck=" + word);
request.onreadystatechange = processAjaxResponse;
request.send();
```

Note that this is considerably easier than using a POST method as the first argument to **request.open()**, because we don't need any post data.

Conclusion and Resources

This appendix is only an introduction to Shale, and the technology itself is rapidly evolving. Please consider reading the documentation at **http://struts.apache.org/struts-shale/** for additional information.

Index

A

accessibility, 399–402
action events, 150–152
action methods, 83
ActionListener, 153–155, 340
ADF Faces, 97, 98, 784
    Core library, 784–789
    dialog framework, 796–799
    HTML library, 789–790
    Oracle JDeveloper's visual design time experience
      for, 804
    Partial Page Rendering (PPR), 790–793
    processScope, 794–796
    skinning technology, 800–804
AJAX (Asynchronous JavaScript and XMLHttpRequest)
    architecture, 288–290
    debugging, 318–319
    DirectorySearch example, 292–297
    DirectorySearch JSF component, 299–303
    high-level elements of an AJAX system in JSF, 297–299
    issuing an XML HTTP request, 290–291
    overview, 287–288
    SpellCheck JSF component, 303–317
    tips, 318–319
    using XMLHttpRequest with HTML, 291–292
    XMLHttpRequest reference, 319–320
alternate view description technology, 359–360
authentication, 403
    basic, 405–406
    certificate, 410–412
    container-managed, 404–405
    form-based, 406–410
    See also JAAS; security
authorization, 403
    container-managed, 412
    and phase listeners, 421–422
    and servlet filters, 416–421
    See also JAAS; security
automated testing. *See* testing

B

backing beans, 75–78
    used by Virtual Trainer, 176–177
BEA Workshop Studio, 492–497
Borland JBuilder, using Faces Console inside of, 768–770

C

Cactus, 453–455
character encoding, 395–397
ChartData, 259
Common Gateway Interface (CGI), 4–5
compiling applications, 32–33
component libraries
    JScape's WebGalileo Faces, 784
    JSFCentral, 804
    Sun's extended UI component library, 783
    See also ADF Faces; standard JSF component library

component-based Web development, 94–96
components, defined, 93
components.jar package example, 280–285
composition, 368–369
configuration file, 531–532
    action-listener element, 541–542
    application element, 542–543
    application-factory element, 543
    attribute element, 543–546
    attribute-class element, 546–547
    attribute-name element, 547
    base-name element, 547–548
    component element, 548–549
    component-class element, 549–550
    component-family element, 550
    component-type element, 551
    converter element, 551–552
    converter-class element, 552–553
    converter-for-class element, 553
    converter-id element, 554
    default-locale element, 554–555
    default-render-kit-id element, 555–556
    default-value element, 556–557
    editing with Faces Console, 611–612
    elements, 534–541
    el-resolver element, 557–558
    extension elements, 608–609
    faces-config element, 558–559
    faces-context-factory element, 559–560
    facet element, 560–561
    facet-name element, 561–562
    factory element, 562
    from-action element, 563
    from-outcome element, 563–564
    from-view-id element, 564
    key element, 564–565
    key-class element, 565–566
    lifecycle element, 566–567
    lifecycle-factory element, 567–568
    list-entries element, 568–569
    locale-config element, 569–570
    managed-bean element, 570–571
    managed-bean-class element, 571
    managed-bean-name element, 572
    managed-bean-scope element, 572–573
    managed-property element, 573–574
    map-entries element, 574–576
    map-entry element, 576–577
    message-bundle element, 577
    metadata elements, 609–611
    navigation-case element, 578
    navigation-handler element, 578–579
    navigation-rule element, 579–580
    null-value element, 580–582
    phase-listener element, 582
    placing navigation rules outside of faces-config.xml, 91
    processing, 533–534
    property element, 583–584

property-class element, 584–585
property-name element, 585–586
property-resolver element, 586–587
redirect element, 587
referenced-bean element, 587–588
referenced-bean-class element, 588–589
referenced-bean-name element, 589
renderer element, 593–594
renderer-class element, 594
renderer-type element, 595
render-kit element, 589–590
render-kit-class element, 590–591
render-kit-factory element, 591–592
render-kit-id element, 592–593
resource-bundle element, 595–596
state-manager element, 596–597
suggested-value element, 597–598
supported-locale element, 598–599
to-view-id element, 599–600
validator element, 600–601
validator-class element, 601
validator-id element, 601–602
value element, 602–604
value-class element, 604–606
var element, 606
variable-resolver element, 606–607
view-handler element, 607–608
converters, 111–112, 326
associating with a UIComponent instance,
120–125
custom, 126–130
DateTimeConverter, 119
examples, 112–113
explicit, 121–124, 126
Faces converter system, 117–130
implicit, 120–121, 126
lifetime of, 125–126
NumberConverter, 119–120
in the request processing lifecycle, 114–117
standard converters, 118

D

data security, 403
container-managed, 412–414
See also security
dataTable component, 203
selecting and editing a single row from, 197–198
updating row data, 202–203
using a custom scroller component with, 195–197
data-tier sorting, 210–212
debugging
with Eclipse, 473–475
logging using Jakarta Commons Logging, 469–472
logging using java.util.logging, 467–469
with NetBeans, 475–478
with Oracle JDeveloper, 478–480
with PhaseListener, 472–473
without a source-level debugger, 467
decoration, for custom ViewHandler, 364–367

development environment
setting up your JSF development environment, 30–32
See also IDEs (Integrated Development Environments)
device independence, 401

E

eager initialization, 367
Eclipse
debugging with, 473–475
using Faces Console inside of, 770–773
EditableValueHolder, 99
ELResolver (JSF 1.2), 330–339
event model
action events, 150–152
creating custom events and listeners, 166
custom action and value change listeners, 153–155
event listener and event classes, 147–148
how events work, 146–147
overview, 145–146
phase events, 163
processing events, 148–149
using a PhaseListener to observe the Faces lifecycle,
163–166
using a value change event to auto-fill fields, 156–163
value change events, 152–153
Exadel Studio Pro, 521–529
explicit converters, 121–124, 126
Expression Language (EL), 65
changes between JSF 1.1 and 1.2, 65–67
expression operators, 70
implicit objects, 69
method expressions, 70–72
setting managed properties using, 62–63
Unified EL concepts, 67
value expressions, 67–70

F

Facelets, 368
architecture, 380–381
compared to JSP, 369–370
composition, 368–369
tag libraries, 370–374
templating, 368–369, 374–380
and ViewHandler, 381–384
Faces Console
acquiring and installing, 767
compatible IDEs, 765
configuring output options, 781–782
editing configuration files with, 611–612
as a stand-alone application, 767–768
supported configuration files, 766–767
using inside Borland JBuilder, 768–770
using inside Eclipse, 770–773
using inside IBM Rational Application Developer for
WebSphere, 773–775
using inside IntelliJ IDEA, 775–777
using inside NetBeans and Sun ONE Studio (Forte),
777–779
using inside Oracle JDeveloper, 779–781

Faces converter system, 117–130
  See also converters
Faces validation system, 130–137
faces-config.xml, how JSF runtime loads, 279
FacesMessage class
  FacesMessage-related methods on FacesContext, 137–139
  rendering, 140–143
  standard Message keys, 141, 142
  when and how instances are created and added to
    FacesContext, 139–140
factories, 351–352
  ApplicationFactory, 357–358
  FacesContextFactory, 355–356
  LifecycleFactory, 356
  registering, 352–353
  RenderKitFactory, 353–355

━━━ **H** ━━━

HtmlInputDateRenderer, 246–252

━━━ **I** ━━━

IBM Rational Application Developer for WebSphere, using Faces
  Console inside of, 773–775
IBM Rational Web Developer, 513–521
IDEs (Integrated Development Environments)
  key strengths, 483
  See also BEA Workshop Studio; development environment;
    Exadel Studio Pro; IBM Rational Web Developer; Oracle
    JDeveloper; Sun Java Studio Creator
immediate attribute, and the request processing lifecycle, 49–51
implicit converters, 120–121, 126
InputDate component, 244–245
  HtmlInputDateRenderer, 246–252
  WML variation, 253–256
IntelliJ IDEA, using Faces Console inside of, 775–777
internationalization
  for custom components, 398
  and localization, 393–398
internationalizing, Virtual Trainer application, 225–227
Inversion of Control (IoC), 53

━━━ **J** ━━━

JAAS, 436–444
Jakarta Cactus, 453–455
Jakarta Commons Logging, 469–472
Jakarta Struts. *See* Struts
JAR files, packaging JSF components into, 278–280
Java Authentication and Authorization Service. *See* JAAS
Java Community Process, 3, 813–814
Java Servlet API, 5
JavaServer Faces
  application architecture, 10–11
  for corporate and systems developers, 9–10
  design goals, 7–9
  development of, 7
  history of, 4–7
  overview, 3–4
JavaServer Faces 1.2
  modifying components to use method expressions, 276–278
  updating components for, 274–276

JavaServer Pages (JSP), 5–6
  compared to Facelets, 369–370
  and UI components, 105–110
  used by Virtual Trainer, 176–177
java.util.logging, 467–469
JDK Logging, 471
JMeter, 458–463
  profiling, 463–467
JSFCentral, 97, 99, 804
JSFReg sample application, 15–16
  application files, 17
  assembling, 17–18
  building a registration system in Virtual Trainer, 186–190
  compiling, 32–33
  configuration files, 18–20
  JSP pages, 20–30
  packaging, 33
  setting up your JSF development environment, 30–32
JUnit, 449–453

━━━ **L** ━━━

label element, 402
lazy initialization, 367
listeners
  custom, 166
  See also phase listeners
localization, 387
  benefits, 387–389
  example, 389–393
  and internationalization, 393–398
Log4J, 470–471
logging
  JDK Logging, 471
  Log4J, 470–471
  MyFaces logging classes, 472
  Sun JSF logging classes, 471
  using Jakarta Commons Logging, 469–472
  using java.util.logging, 467–469

━━━ **M** ━━━

managed beans, 24–26
  accessing programmatically, 72–75
  as backing beans for JSF pages, 75–78
  declaring lists and maps directly as, 61
  defined, 53–54
  elements needed for a basic managed bean declaration, 55
  elements required for managed bean properties, 56
  example, 54
  initializing properties, 54–60
  interdependence, 61–62
  list properties, 57–58
  map properties, 59–60
  scopes, 63–64
  setting managed properties using EL, 62–63
markup, 400–401
metadata, the future of JSF component metadata, 285–286
method binding, updating HtmlHelloInput UI component to
  use, 270–274
method expressions, modifying JSF 1.2 components to use,
  276–278

Model-View-Controller design pattern, 80–81
MyFaces, 96–97, 475, 683
    acquiring, 684–685
    aliasBean component, 706
    aliasBeansScope component, 706–707
    buffer component, 707
    checkbox component, 707–708
    collapsiblePanel component, 708–709
    commandButton component, 688
    commandLink component, 688
    commandNavigation component, 709–710
    commandNavigation2 component, 710–711
    commandSortHeader component, 712–713
    custom components, 702–704
    custom components common attributes, 704–706
    custom validators, 749–754
    dataList component, 713–714
    dataScroller component, 714–717
    dataTable component, 690–691
    div component, 717–718
    extended component common attributes, 689
    extended components, 687–688
    Extensions Filter, 685–687
    graphicImage component, 692
    htmlTag component, 718
    inputCalendar component, 718–721
    inputDate component, 721–722
    inputFileUpload component, 723–724
    inputHidden component, 692
    inputHTML component, 724–727
    inputSecret component, 692–693
    inputText component, 693
    inputTextarea component, 693–694
    inputTextHelp component, 727–728
    jscookMenu component, 728–730
    JSF implementation, 685
    jsValueChangeListener component, 730
    jsValueSet component, 731
    logging classes, 472
    message component, 694–695
    messages component, 695–696
    newspaperTable component, 731–732
    outputLabel component, 696–697
    outputText component, 697
    panelGrid component, 697
    panelGroup component, 698
    panelNavigation component, 732–734
    panelNavigation2 component, 734–735
    panelStack component, 735–736
    panelTab component, 736–737
    panelTabbedPane component, 737–738
    popup component, 738–740
    radio component, 740
    saveState component, 740–741
    selectBooleanCheckbox component, 698
    selectManyCheckbox component, 699
    selectManyListbox component, 699
    selectManyMenu component, 700
    selectOneCountry component, 741–742
    selectOneLanguage component, 742–743
    selectOneListbox component, 700
    selectOneMenu component, 701
    selectOneRadio component, 701
    stylesheet component, 743–744
    and the Tiles framework, 754–762
    Tomahawk component tag library directive, 687
    Tomahawk library, 685
    tree component, 744–746
    tree2 component, 746–748
    treeColumn component, 748
    updateActionListener tag, 748–749

N

natural language, 401
Navigation Model, 13–14, 79
    action methods, 83
    Model-View-Controller design pattern, 80–81
    navigation rules, 83–89
    NavigationHandler, 81–83
    overview, 80–83
    placing navigation rules outside of faces-config.xml, 91
    redirects, 90–91
    wildcards, 89–90
navigation rules, 83–89
    placing outside of faces-config.xml, 91
NavigationHandler, 339–340
NetBeans
    debugging with, 475–478
    Profiler, 463–467
    using Faces Console inside of, 777–779
non-UI custom components, 321–324
    ActionListener, 340
    converters and validators, 326
    ELResolver (JSF 1.2), 330–339
    factories, 351–358
    NavigationHandler, 339–340
    phase listeners, 324–326
    PropertyResolver, 327–330
    RenderKit, 343–351
    StateManager, 341–343
    VariableResolver, 327–330
    ViewHandler, 326–327

O

Oracle JDeveloper, 497–513
    debugging with, 478–480
    using Faces Console inside of, 779–781
    visual design time experience for ADF Faces, 804

P

packaging applications, 33
persistence technology, 216–225
phase listeners, 51, 324–326
    and authorization, 421–422
    observing the Faces lifecycle in action, 163–166
profiling, 463–467
    See also testing
PropertyResolver, 327–330

R

realm, 405–406
redirects, 90–91

Reference Implementation (RI), downloading, 31–32
Remember Me feature, 422–423
    lifecycle and state management, 423–427
    properties, 431
    RememberMeLoginComponent, 423–431
    RememberMeLoginTag, 432–434
    RememberMePhaseListener, 434–436
    rendering behavior, 427–431
renderers
    dynamically changing at runtime, 256–257
    registering, 255–256
RenderKit, 343–351
    and ViewHandler, 362
render-kits, registering, 255–256
request processing lifecycle, 8, 12–13
    automatic server-side view management and
        synchronization, 37
    compared to other web technologies, 36–37
    key concepts of, 51–52
    overview, 35–36
    phase listeners, 51
    phases, 38–45
    processing validations and conversions immediately, 50–51
    stepping through lifecycle phases of JSFReg application,
        45–48
    using the immediate attribute, 49–51
ResourceBundles, 387–393
    exposing to JSF, 397
    See also localization
roles, 412

S

security
    application-managed, 415–422
    authentication, 403
    authorization, 403
    container-managed, 404–415
    data security, 403
    JAAS, 436–444
    Remember Me feature, 422–436
    and Virtual Trainer application, 414–416
servlet filters, and authorization, 416–421
Shale
    Application Manager, 818, 825–827
    deploying, 815–818
    Dialog Manager, 816–818, 822–825
    features, 814–815
    invoking a MethodExpression, 832–834
    migration concerns, 815
    remoting, 829–830
    static resources, 830–832
    Validation, 827–829
    ViewController, 818–822
slider component, 264–270
sorting
    data-tier, 210–212
    Web-tier, 212–216
standard core library
    actionListener tag, 616–617
    convertDateTime tag, 617–619
    converter tag, 620–621

    convertNumber tag, 619–620
    core library quick reference, 614–616
    facet tag, 621–622
    loadBundle tag, 622
    param component, 622–623
    phaseListener tag, 623
    selectItem component, 624
    selectItems component, 624–625
    setPropertyActionListener tag, 625–626
    subview component, 626–627
    validateDoubleRange tag, 627–628
    validateLength tag, 628–629
    validateLongRange tag, 629–630
    validator tag, 630
    valueChangeListener tag, 630–631
    verbatim component, 631–632
    view component, 632–633
standard HTML library
    column component, 635–636
    commandButton component, 636–638
    commandLink component, 638–640
    dataTable component, 640–643
    form component, 643–645
    graphicImage component, 645–646
    inputHidden component, 647–648
    inputSecret component, 648–650
    inputText component, 650–652
    inputTextarea component, 652–654
    message component, 654–656
    messages component, 656–657
    outputFormat component, 657–658
    outputLabel component, 658–660
    outputLink component, 660–662
    outputText component, 662–663
    panelGrid component, 663–665
    panelGroup component, 665–666
    quick reference, 633–635
    selectBooleanCheckbox component, 666–668
    selectManyCheckbox component, 668–671
    selectManyListbox component, 671–673
    selectManyMenu component, 673–675
    selectOneListbox component, 675–677
    selectOneMenu component, 678–680
    selectOneRadio component, 680–682
standard JSF component library
    acquiring and installing, 614
    terminology, 613–614
StateManager, 341–343
    and ViewHandler, 362, 363
Struts, 6–7
    comparison to JSF, 805–807
    development style, 807–808
    migrating to Faces, 808–811
stylesheets, 400–401
Sun Java Studio Creator, 485–492
Sun ONE Studio (Forte), using Faces Console inside of, 777–779
SVG bar chart, rendering, 260–264

T

Tapestry, 96, 374, 383
templating, 368–369, 374–377
    tags, 377–380

terminology, 613–614
testing
    Cactus, 453–455
    HTMLUnit, 456–457
    integration, 448
    JMeter, 458–463
    JUnit, 449–453
    profiling, 463–467
    stress, 448
    system, 448
    terminology, 446–447
    test-driven development, 448–449
    tools, 449–467
    unit, 447–448
text equivalents, to nontextual content, 400
Tiles framework, MyFaces support for, 754–762
TLD files, how JSP runtime loads, 279–280
Tomcat, installing, 32

U

UI components
    architecture, 99–105
    behavioral interfaces, 99
    binding in JSP, 109–110
    conditionally rendering, 201–202
    defined, 93–94, 230
    goal of, 96–99
    and JSP, 105–110
    moving parts, 103–105, 230–232
    state management of, 103
    tree, 101–103
    See also UI components, custom
UI components, custom, 229
    accepting form input, 239–241
    components.jar package example, 280–285
    custom chart component, 258–264
    dynamically changing renderers at runtime, 256–257
    Hello World example, 232–241
    InputDate component with multiple renderers, 244–256
    internationalization, 398
    JSF stock quote component, 242–244
    modifying JSF 1.2 components to use method expressions, 276–278
    packaging into self-contained JAR files, 278–280
    rendering an SVG bar chart, 260–264
    updating components for JSF 1.2, 274–276
    updating HtmlHelloInput UI component to use method binding, 270–274
    using JavaScript in a custom JSF component, 264–270
    when to build a custom UI component, 230
    See also non-UI custom components; UI components
UIViewRoot, and its locale property, 139
user interface components. *See* UI components

V

validators, 111–112, 326
    associating with a UIComponent instance, 133–135
    custom, 136–137
    DoubleRangeValidator, 132

examples, 112–113
    Faces validation system, 130–137
    LengthValidator, 132
    lifetime of, 135–136
    LongRangeValidator, 131–132
    in the request processing lifecycle, 114–117
    "required" facility, 132–133
    standard validators, 131
value change events, 152–153
    example, 156–163
ValueChangeListener, 153–155
ValueHolder, 99
VariableResolver, 327–330
view description technology, 359–360
ViewHandler, 326–327, 360, 361
    building and installing a custom ViewHandler, 362–368
    and Facelets, 381–384
    relationship with RenderKit and view construction, 360–362
    relationship with StateManager, 362, 363
Virtual Trainer application, 484
    architecture, 175–178
    basic page layout and formatting, 179–180
    browse and edit pages, 190–195
    building the registration system, 186–190
    creating a new training event workout plan, 172
    creating a simple authentication system, 181–185
    creating training events, 204–209
    custom scroller component, 195–197
    data-tier sorting, 210–212
    deleting a training event, 203–204
    drilling down to an edit form, 198–203
    internationalizing, 225–227
    JSF data model components, 177–178
    logging in as an online trainer and updating comments, 174
    logging out, 185–186
    navigational page flow, 177
    overview, 169–170
    persisting data, 216–225
    registering and logging into, 170–171
    requirements, 175
    and security, 414–416
    selecting and editing a single row from a dataTable, 197–198
    selecting and updating training events, 172–174
    sortable columns, 209–216
    using JAAS in, 436–444
    Web-tier sorting, 212–216

W

Web-tier sorting, 212–216
wildcards, 89–90

X

XML DTDs, 532–533
XML schemas, 533
XMLHttpRequest reference, 319–320
    See also AJAX (Asynchronous JavaScript and XMLHttpRequest)